THE ROUTLEDGE HISTORY
OF WITCHCRAFT

The Routledge History of Witchcraft is a comprehensive and interdisciplinary study of the belief in witches from antiquity to the present day, providing both an introduction to the subject of witchcraft and an overview of the on-going debates.

This extensive collection covers the entire breadth of the history of witchcraft, from the witches of Ancient Greece and medieval demonology through to the victims of the witch hunts, and onwards to children's books, horror films, and modern pagans. Drawing on the knowledge and expertise of an international team of authors, the book examines differing concepts of witchcraft that still exist in society and explains their historical, literary, religious, and anthropological origin and development, including the reflections and adaptions of this belief in art and popular culture. The volume is divided into four parts, beginning with Antiquity and the Middle Ages in Part One, Early Modern witch hunts in Part Two, modern concepts of witchcraft in Part Three, and ending with an examination of witchcraft and the arts in Part Four. Each chapter offers a glimpse of a different version of the witch, introducing the reader to the diversity of witches that have existed in different contexts throughout history.

Exploring a wealth of texts and case studies and offering a broad geographical scope for examining this fascinating subject, *The Routledge History of Witchcraft* is essential reading for students and academics interested in the history of witchcraft.

Johannes Dillinger is Professor of Early Modern History at Oxford Brookes University. He has published widely on witchcraft and magic, political crime, and constitutional history. His previous publications include *Hexen und Magie* (2018) and *Magical Treasure Hunting in Europe and North America* (2012).

THE ROUTLEDGE HISTORIES

The Routledge Histories is a series of landmark books surveying some of the most important topics and themes in history today. Edited and written by an international team of world-renowned experts, they are the works against which all future books on their subjects will be judged.

THE ROUTLEDGE HISTORY OF GLOBAL WAR AND SOCIETY
Edited by Matthew S. Muehlbauer and David J. Ulbrich

THE ROUTLEDGE HISTORY OF TWENTIETH-CENTURY
UNITED STATES
Edited by Jerald R. Podair and Darren Dochuk

THE ROUTLEDGE HISTORY OF WORLD PEACE SINCE 1750
Edited by Christian Philip Peterson, William M. Knoblauch and Michael Loadenthal

THE ROUTLEDGE HISTORY OF MEDIEVAL MAGIC
Edited by Sophie Page and Catherine Rider

THE ROUTLEDGE HISTORY OF MONARCHY
Edited by Elena Woodacre, Lucinda H.S. Dean, Chris Jones,
Russell E. Martin and Zita Eva Rohr

THE ROUTLEDGE HISTORY OF EMOTIONS IN EUROPE, 1100–1700
Edited by Andrew Lynch and Susan Broomhall

THE ROUTLEDGE HISTORY OF HUMAN RIGHTS
Edited by Jean H. Quataert and Lora Wildenthal

THE ROUTLEDGE HISTORY OF WOMEN IN EARLY MODERN EUROPE
Edited by Amanda L. Capern

THE ROUTLEDGE HISTORY OF WITCHCRAFT
Edited by Johannes Dillinger

For more information about this series, please visit: www.routledge.com/Routledge-Histories/book-series/RHISTS

THE ROUTLEDGE HISTORY OF WITCHCRAFT

Edited by
Johannes Dillinger

LONDON AND NEW YORK

First published 2020
by Routledge
2 Park Square, Milton Park, Abingdon, Oxon OX14 4RN

605 Third Avenue, New York, NY 10017

First issued in paperback 2021

Routledge is an imprint of the Taylor & Francis Group, an informa business

Publisher's Note
The publisher has gone to great lengths to ensure the quality of this reprint but points out that some imperfections in the original copies may be apparent.

British Library Cataloguing-in-Publication Data
A catalogue record for this book is available from the British Library

Library of Congress Cataloging-in-Publication Data
A catalog record for this book has been requested

ISBN 13: 978-1-03-208261-5 (pbk)
ISBN 13: 978-1-138-78220-4 (hbk)

Typeset in New Baskerville
by Apex CoVantage, LLC

CONTENTS

7   Germany – "the mother of the witches"   94
JOHANNES DILLINGER

8   Witch hunts in the low countries (1450–1685)   113
DRIES VANYSACKER

9   Witch hunts in France   125
MARYSE SIMON

10   Witch hunting in Spain: the sixteenth and seventeenth centuries   134
LU ANN HOMZA

11   Witch hunts in Britain   145
JAMES SHARPE

12   Witchcraft in Scandinavia   160
PER SÖRLIN

13   Witch hunts in Eastern Central Europe   171
PETR KREUZ

14   Witch hunts in Eastern Europe   188
PETR KREUZ

15   The Salem witch hunt   198
ROBERT W. THURSTON

16   Witchcraft and the early modern media   208
ABAIGÉAL WARFIELD

17   Witchcraft and gender   219
RAISA MARIA TOIVO

18   Child-witches   233
NICOLE J. BETTLÉ

19   Witchcraft in everyday life   244
EDWARD BEVER

20   The interrelationship of magic and witchcraft   257
KATHRYN EDWARDS

CONTENTS

List of figures   vi
List of tables   i
Editor's preface

PART 1
Witches in antiquity and in the Middle Ages

1 **Witches in Greece and Rome**
   GIORGOS ANDRIKOPOULOS

2 **Witchcraft, magic and demonology in the Bible, ancient Judaism
   and earliest Christianity**   1⁹
   MARCO FRENSCHKOWSKI

3 **Demons and witchcraft in the early Church**   36
   NAOMI JANOWITZ

4 **Witchcraft and demonology in the Middle Ages**   46
   MICHAEL D. BAILEY

5 **The rise of the witchcraft doctrine**   61
   MARTINE OSTORERO

PART 2
The early modern witch hunts: regions and issues   79

6 **Witchcraft and witch hunting in late medieval and early
   modern Italy**   81
   MATTEO DUNI

CONTENTS

PART 3
Modern concepts of witches   277

21 Child eaters and other problems of democracy: witchcraft and the
    American frontier   279
    ADAM JORTNER

22 Witchcraft accusations in nineteenth- and twentieth-century Europe   289
    OWEN DAVIES

23 Shifting figures of the witch in colonial and postcolonial Africa   299
    PETER GESCHIERE

24 Wicca   317
    LINDA J. JENCSON

25 Disciples of Hell: the history of Satanism   332
    PER FAXNELD

PART 4
Witches and the arts   349

26 Witchcraft and early modern art (1450–1550)   351
    SIGRID SCHADE

27 The witch figure in nineteenth- and twentieth-century literature   370
    JUSTYNA SZACHOWICZ-SEMPRUCH

28 Where have all the witches gone? The disappearing witch and
    children's literature   382
    JOHN STEPHENS

29 Witchcraft in film   392
    DAVID NASH

    Index   403

FIGURES

26.1 Ms Fr 12476 fol.105v Two witches from "Le Champion des Dames" by Martin le Franc (1410–61) 1451 (vellum) (b/w photo), French School, (fifteenth century)/Bibliotheque Nationale, Paris, France/ Bridgeman Images   354

26.2 Two witches cooking up a hailstorm, illustration of malefic sorcery in Ulrich Molitor, "Von den bosen weibern, die man nennet die hexen" (De laniis et phitonicis mulieribus), Ulm, Johann Zainer 1490/91. INTERFOTO / Alamy Stock Photo   357

26.3 Hans Schäuffelein, Crimes of malefic sorcery, woodcut, in Ulrich Tengler "Der neü Layenspiegel", ed. b. Christoph Tengler, Augsburg 1511. Wikimedia: https://commons.wikimedia.org/ wiki/File:Sorcery_and_witch_craze.jpg   358

26.4 Witch riding backwards on a goat, c.1505 (Burin engraving), Dürer or Duerer, Albrecht (1471–1528)/Private Collection/ Photo © Luisa Ricciarini/Bridgeman Images   360

26.5 Hans Baldung Grien, Group of witches preparing for the ride to the Sabbath, chiaroscuro woodcut 1510 (Schade, Schadenzauber, Abb. 18, S. 54) INTERFOTO / Alamy Stock Photo   362

26.6 Hans Baldung Grien, Three witches (New years' greetings), pen drawing on tinted paper, heightened with white, 1514, Wien Albertina, (Schade, Schadenzauber, Abb. 51, S. 112) Art Heritage / Alamy Stock Photo   364

26.7 Lucas Cranach the Elder, *Melancholy*, oil on panel 1532, Museum Unterlinden, Colmar Peter Horree / Alamy Stock Photo   366

TABLES

7.1   Parts of Germany most affected by the witch hunts   94
8.1   Total number of witches executed in the Southern Netherlands
        (1450–1685)   114
8.2   Ratio of executed witches and population in several regions in the
        Netherlands (1450–1682)   117

EDITOR'S PREFACE

What exactly we mean when we say 'witch' depends a lot on the situation and on our point of view. The witches in literature are quite unlike the witches anthropologists hear about. Both have fairly little in common with the witches of the Bible. Even in history, we find a bewildering number of witches. The witches of Antiquity are not the witches of the early modern period. It is problematic to compare the witches of the past to the modern witches of today. And yet, most people would claim that they know what a witch is. We have all known the witch for a long time. We encountered her when we were still very young, in fairy tales and children's books.

All the authors who contributed to this volume know very well that it is impossible to do justice to all of the different witches that inhabit Western culture and helped to shape it. The witch hunts of history have had the most drastic social consequences of all kinds of witch beliefs. Therefore, most of the texts in this volume focus on the history of the witch trials. However, we tried to do more than that and to offer at least brief glimpses of very different witches. All of the authors of this volume tried to present the witches they know best. As experts in their fields, they offer the readers short texts that summarize what they think is essential about witches, witchcraft and the wider context of magic they are an integral part of. Thus, the readers will encounter a wide variety of texts. They represent a large variety of concepts of witchcraft as well as a number of different approaches to the subject. This book wants to introduce its audience to the diversity of witchcraft studies.

No text in this volume is supposed to be the 'final word' about its topic. On the contrary, each text could or should be one of the 'first words' the audience reads about the subject. The authors invite the readers to build upon the information they find here and to keep studying the various forms of witchcraft and witch beliefs. After decades of research, we have learnt so much about witches that many works published before Midelfort's 1972 seminal study about the witch hunts in Southwestern Germany are hardly useable anymore. On the basis of this 'new' witchcraft research, we see how much there is still to learn. If this volume encourages further research into witches and witchcraft it has reached its aim.

Any number of difficulties have bedevilled the genesis of the volume. The contributors helped the editor to overcome them with angelic patience. The editor would like to thank Dr Fiona Mann, Ciaran Jones and especially Dr Marianne Dillinger, who helped him with the tedious work of checking references and bibliographical data.

Oxford, July 2019
Johannes Dillinger

PART 1

WITCHES IN ANTIQUITY AND IN THE MIDDLE AGES

1

WITCHES IN GREECE
AND ROME

Giorgos Andrikopoulos

This chapter discusses some subjects pertaining to the larger topic of magic or witch-craft in Greco-Roman antiquity. Since "magic" and "witchcraft" do not correspond to separate concepts in ancient thought, I will use them interchangeably, in the same manner as the terms for their practitioners, who will be called "sorcerers", "magicians" or, in the case of women, "witches". The subjects to be discussed are harmful forms of magic and their practitioners; the representation of witches in literature and some insights to be gained from this about ancient concepts of gender; and the legal status of magic in the Greek world and the Roman Empire.

Although it is customary for one to define their terms before proceeding into a discussion, the reader will, hopefully, be relieved to know that I will not attempt to give a definition of what the ancients understood as "magic" nor, for lack of space, will I attempt to give an overview of the endless discussions this topic has generated so far. Attempting today to give a definition of magic that would have been valid for most people in antiquity is an exercise in futility, since even then, apparently, there was hardly a consensus. Apuleius, defending himself in court against accusations of witchcraft, says that anyone in his day can be accused of being a sorcerer, if they do something slightly differing from religious custom, like praying silently or inscribing a wish on a statue's thigh;[1] he practically admits that he is a *magus*, but not the kind which common people mean by the term. Magicians have had a reputation for impiety since their introduction into the literary record in the Greek world in the sixth to fifth centuries BC, but in a letter attributed to Apollonius of Tyana (first century AD), he attacks an opponent by saying that magicians (*magoi*) are the ones who are wise in divine matters, while his opponent is not a *magos* but a disbeliever in the gods (*atheos*).[2] What is treated as magic or as related to it in this study are practices and stereotypes that were treated as such, for whatever reason, in antiquity.

Harmful magic

Two major categories of harmful magic can be discerned in Greco-Roman antiquity. One is concerned with the production and administration of potions, called *phar-maka* in Greek and *uenena* in Latin. The type of potion most usually encountered is the love potion, the Greek *philtron* and Latin *amatorium*, but lethal poisons fall within that category as well. The term applied to this practice is *pharmakeia* and *ueneficium* in Greek and Latin respectively. These terms, however, came to be applied to magic-working as a whole, as in our sources we find other types of witchcraft being associated with the individuals involved in this process.

The second category, on which we possess much more detailed information, thanks to the abundance of curse tablets, the Greek Magical Papyri and frequent references in a variety of literary sources, is what is called "binding magic". This is a subset of what was termed *goēteia* (sorcery), the magic that worked through *epōidai* or *carmina*, i.e. incantations. The term "binding magic" derives from the description of such spells by the Greek term *katadesis* or *katadesmos* ("binding down"), which is known in Latin as a *defixio* ("holding down in place"). The "binding" designation of those spells refers to the practitioner's (the *defigens*) intent to restrain some kind of activity or, in a few cases, any kind of activity of their victim (the *defixus* or *defixa*), usually until the spell's intended goal has been achieved. It should be noted that there is little if anything in execution to differentiate Latin from Greek *defixiones*; the Roman practice seems to be wholly derivative from the Greek.

Types of binding spells

Binding spells, which will be referred to henceforth as *katadesmoi* or *defixiones*, have been classified by Audollent[3] according to their intended goals. This is a classification that has not been majorly revised since then. a) Judicial *defixiones* are aimed against adversaries or witnesses in a court case, with the goal of impairing their ability to speak or testify efficiently. b) "Agonistic" *defixiones* target athletes, most often charioteers and their horses, in order to cause them to fail at a specific event. c) *Defixiones* against thieves and slanderers aim at recovery of stolen objects and retribution against those who inflicted harm on the *defigens* in the first place. d) Erotic *defixiones* are targeted against a man or woman in order to cause sexual desire or love towards the *defigens*; although this might seem an odd subject for a curse, one should keep in mind that erotic passion was considered a form of madness or a disease in antiquity, therefore the regular formula of a curse was apt to bring this affliction about to the victim. e) Faraone[4] has identified that several of what were considered up to then judicial *defixiones* must have had a different goal; those were in fact *defixiones* against professional rivals, most often tavern keepers and prostitutes, targeting their businesses, and are known as commercial *defixiones*.

Technology

The physical remains of binding rituals as well as spell recipes found in the Greek Magical Papyri allow us, to an extent, to reconstruct the process and theorize about the manner in which *defixiones* were supposed to achieve their goal. By far the most common of physical remains is the curse tablet, which itself can be called a *katadesmos* or *defixio*; occasionally one can find lead figurines, and some curse tablets make reference to dead animals, such as cats, that were part of the ritual and deposited alongside the tablet. The extant tablets themselves are mostly lead, but this appears to be more due to the durability of the material rather than a special ritual purpose it served from the very beginning; the magical papyri prescribe that for some spells papyrus of the highest quality be used, while literary sources mention tablets made of wax as well.[5]

The tablets are inscribed with text denoting the purpose of the ritual or even the actual words that were probably spoken by the *defigens* during the ritual. There seems to be great variation in execution, but the types of formulae utilized are not too numerous.[6] One common formula is to write down simply the names of the victims, in which case one can only guess at the purpose of the *defixio* today. Most often, the tablet will provide a verb denoting what is done to the victims, with meanings like "to bind down (*katadeō*)", "to register (*katagraphō, apographō*)" or "to dedicate (*anatithēmi, anieroō*) or their Latin equivalents (to bind: *ligare, adligare*; to dedicate: *dedicare, demandare*). In several instances, some chthonic deity or deities, like Hermes "He-Who-Holds-Down" (*Hermēs Katokhos*), Persephone, Demeter or Hecate, is noted as the one to which the victim is bound or dedicated, and the purpose of the *defixio* is given. Another common formula is what has been known since Audollent as the *similia similibus* formula, i.e. "to do like by like". In these instances, the *defigens* will point at some aspect of the ritual wishing for a similar effect upon the victim; an example of this can be found in a *defixio*[7] mentioning a cat's corpse being deposited along with it, wherein the *defigens* asks that the victims be as ineffective in court as the dead animal, that they be as unable to defend themselves as the cat's mother was to defend her young and finally that they be immobilized and twisted as the cat now is.

A constant feature of *defixiones* is the nature of the places where they have been deposited. Graveyards, wells, sanctuaries of chthonic deities like Demeter and Persephone – all of these and the like denote a desire, on the part of the *defigens*, to come into contact with the powers of the Underworld, to which they turn for assistance.[8] Tombstones were particularly preferred, because the dead were seen either as messengers to the chthonic gods, or as agents carrying out the will of the sorcerer. Furthermore, not just any grave was sought out, but those of people who had died unnaturally, those who had died by violence (*biaiothanatoi*) or before their time (*ahōroi*) or "without being complete" (*atelestoi*), referring possibly to the uninitiated or unmarried. The restless dead were seen as apt to carry out the sorcerer's wishes, possibly out of spite and envy towards the living or, in case *atelestoi*, refers to the uninitiated in the mysteries, who were easy targets since they did not enjoy the protection of the gods in their death.[9]

It is possible that this movement towards the netherworld is an instance of the theme of reversal of mainstream practice, as Graf has pointed out, that seems to characterize magical ritual: words can be seen written backwards in some tablets, persons are specified by the name of their mother rather than their father, as is normal practice in a Greek city or in Rome, and similarly, in the instance of seeking out the powers below, the sorcerer is moving downwards instead of upwards, towards the celestial gods, whom the city honors in its public rituals.[10] As Johnston has argued, however, it is unlikely that this reversal is a deliberate subversion of mainstream ritual on the sorcerer's part, given that one magical formula for bringing the wrath of a deity upon an adversary is to slander them to the deity in question, as having made a mockery of their proper rites.[11]

Still, we are probably far from having the whole picture about the performance of a binding ritual in every instance. Artifacts such as wax figurines mentioned by Plato as being used in *katadesmoi* are unlikely to survive, while literary depictions of witchcraft can mention ritual actions that would not be traceable through the physical remains of a *defixio,* or indeed where no curse tablet would be deposited at all. Such are for example, the binding ritual performed by Simaetha,[12] where no curse tablet is mentioned, or the instructions for a spell given to a lovelorn youth in an elegy by Tibullus, wherein he has to recite a magical charm three times and spit three times after.[13] It is in fact hard to imagine that there was no ritual or further utterances involved in the deposition of some of the oldest *katadesmoi,* which consist of nothing but lists of names.

Practitioners of magic

People whom the Greeks would call sorcerers appear for the first time in literature in a fragment attributed to Heraclitus (sixth century BC), wherein a divine punishment is proscribed for night "wanderers, magicians (*magoi*), lēnai, bacchants and initiates" on account of their impiety.[14]

In the fifth century BC, the Hippocratic author of *On the Sacred Disease* attacks magicians (*magoi*), purifiers (*kathartai*), mendicant priests (*agurtai*) and charlatans (*alazones*) on account of their impiety in attributing epilepsy to the will of the gods and for their claims that they can persuade the gods to heal it through purifications and incantations, as well as for their other outlandish claims, like being able to control the weather and the seasons as well as bring down the moon and darken the sun.[15]

One finds again mention of that class of people as "mendicant priests" and "seers" in Plato's Republic, wherein Adeimantos mentions that these individuals approach wealthy citizens claiming that they have gained the ability through sacrifice and incantation to propitiate the gods and that they can perform binding rituals (*katadesis*) or send a ghost (an act known as *epagōgē*) to harm the enemies of anyone willing to pay.[16]

What we can see from these earliest instances, where mention of magic practitioners is made, is that these individuals are not simply sorcerers who perform binding spells but also religious specialists who claim to be able to perform all kinds of services by communicating with the gods, for the appropriate fee. There is in fact no evidence to show that there were, in the Greco-Roman world, people who specialized only in *defixiones* and the like; there are several words used to refer to these religious specialists, and although those might have at some point denoted individuals specializing in different forms of witchcraft, the terms seem to be used interchangeably.[17]

Those religious specialists made a living apparently by providing their services to the wealthy, if we are to believe Plato. The *defixiones,* however, show that their clientele must have included people from all walks of life, including the lowest. Particularly telling are the commercial *defixiones* from Athens. Since some of those target tavern establishments and prostitutes associated with them,[18] it stands to reason that those *defixiones* must have been commissioned by some rival establishment owner. Erotic binding magic seems to have been a constant and banal feature in the lives of prostitutes and courtesans, who are frequently depicted as adept at it, in their attempt to seduce and keep their clients or to steal them from professional rivals. It is worth keeping in mind that the disdain of the intellectual elite towards magic and its practitioners, exemplified by the opinions of Plato and the author of *On the Sacred Disease,* was probably not mainstream. Magic-working seems to have been widespread in the Greco-Roman world and its professional practitioners must have not been hard to find, although, as we will see later, they could run afoul of the law, especially in Rome of the Imperial Period.

Witches in Greek and Latin literature

It is sometimes stated that love magic is seen in the ancient world and its literature as the exclusive domain of female practitioners as well as the clients thereof, and there is some speculation as to the reasons for this in connection with ancient gender politics. The claim that women are shown to practice love magic to the exclusion of men in literature has already been shown by Dickie[19] to be inaccurate; while there are more instances and mentions of women engaging in love magic than men, the sample is too small and the ratio of women to men practitioners not really that high, so as to allow for any sort of bias to be identified, based on numbers alone. Then again, there is much to be said about the power of literary portrayals of female magic-workers or per uses of love magic in comparison to those of men. Picking a few examples, on the one hand, one comes across poignant depictions of the terrifying magical display of Medea's fury and jealousy in Euripides or a cabal of grotesque witches performing a gruesome human sacrifice in Horace, while on the other hand, one comes upon a ribald frame story in Lucian about how a young man paid some sorcerer a lot of money to make a married woman have sex with him, when he could have had her for less, had he paid her directly. Such portrayals do not carry the same emotional weight, and this could be the reason why portrayals of witches engaging in love magic in ancient literature are more memorable than those of male magicians engaging in the same sort of activity.

Care should also be taken when attempting to attribute universal motives to writers about literary portrayals of witches as engaging in love magic. This is not the place to argue whether Circe was seen as a witch by Homer's contemporaries, but I believe that Ogden has demonstrated at least that her portrayal in the Odyssey served as an archetype for portrayals of witches in literature thereafter.[20] The Witch is thus already, by the Classical Era, a traditional literary trope of some versatility and antiquity. It is safer, in principle, for each story containing a portrayal of female magic-working to be examined on its own merits.

Witches, courtesans and gender roles

This is not to suggest in the least that portrayals of female magic-working do not reflect male concerns about the social status of women in Greco-Roman antiquity. A primary concern does become evident from several portrayals of female magic-working, namely that witchcraft is seen as a catalyst for the reversal of traditional gender roles: Heracles declares himself emasculated (*thēlus heuremai*: "I am found to be female!") in the *Trachiniae* as he dies suffering and weeping "like a young girl (*hōste parthenos*)" from the effects of a poison (mistaken for a love potion) administered by his wife,[21] Deianeira, who has already performed heroic suicide like a man by plunging a sword through her side.[22] Plutarch warns women against the use of love potions, because they render men inert; Circe's witchcraft, he adds, turned men into animals useless to her as mates, while Odysseus, who remained unaffected, was most loved by her.[23] Juvenal tells of how women in his day take up manly past-times, such as jurisprudence, sports and swordplay, all the while dominating their husbands with magical incantations.[24] Folia, a member of Canidia's cabal, is described as possessing "a man's sex drive (*masculae libidinis*)".[25] It is fairly evident from such examples that men in Greece and Rome were concerned about becoming victims of female witchcraft, which is viewed as a means of reversing patriarchal gender roles.

This could be because, as it has been suggested, binding magic of the erotic kind was in actuality primarily practiced by men, as evidenced by extant curse tablets. However, there is no reason to accept this,[26] given that not only is the sample too small, but the ratio of men to women is neither tellingly high nor impossible to attribute to other causes. Faraone's[27] distinction between erotic binding magic as being the domain of males and what he calls *philia* magic (namely the use of love potions by wives on their husbands) as being the domain of women is also, in my view, hardly tenable, in light of several mentions in our sources of men using love potions to outright seduce women. The writers of the magical papyri do not seem to work under any such assumptions, either; the instructions make evident that erotic spells can be used by either men or women to seduce persons of either gender. It does not emerge from our sources that erotic binding magic was conceptualized as the domain of any particular gender.

There is, however, a pattern to be discerned when attitudes of female characters in literature towards magic-working are examined. One will find that respectable women, like Deianeira and Dido,[28] turn to magic only reluctantly and in desperation. On the other hand, women who are either wanton, like those in Juvenal's sixth Satire, or who are courtesans and prostitutes by profession, such as Simaetha or Canidia, show no such scruples when they turn to witchcraft. A humorous episode in Xenophon's *Memorabilia* illustrates that love magic was an almost mundane part of the job of a courtesan:[29] Socrates, in a discussion with the courtesan Theodote, playfully complains that he is very busy, as his girl friends pester him day and night because he has to teach them all about love potions (*philtra*) and incantations (*epōidai*). Theodote retorts in surprise, "Do you know of those things too, Socrates?", to which he jokingly replies that it would have been impossible for him to have kept his disciples close to him otherwise. This exchange is based on the understanding or at least common perception that courtesans employed erotic binding magic (*epōidai*) as well as love potions to acquire and keep their clientele and that they learned those techniques from some more experienced courtesan, which is what Socrates pretends to be in this instance.[30]

While witches are credited in fiction with marvelous magical powers allowing them to pluck the moon from the sky, control seasons and the natural flow of rivers and perform necromantic rituals to raise the dead,[31] we rarely see them do anything other than employ their witchcraft for erotic purposes, either for themselves or their clients. Given that a very large portion of women in literature who specialize in erotic magic are, at the very least, implied to be courtesans, due to the circumstances of their lives,[32] one could conclude that erotic magic was not thought of as the exclusive domain of courtesans, but the women who practiced it most likely were courtesans. This could provide some context as to the reluctance of respectable women in fiction to turn to witchcraft, as they would not wish to be associated with a practice often attributed to courtesans and prostitutes. Women of this class are, as is to be expected, often depicted as and considered lecherous; however, the "male sex drive" attributed to the witch Folia is more telling. If the sexuality of courtesans and prostitutes was indeed seen as a grey area and they were considered to behave like men, owing both to their sexual freedom and their aggressive pursuit of sexual partners, one could tentatively explain the fear of gender role reversal through magic by this syllogism: respectable women who turn to magic act like prostitutes, thus becoming sexually aggressive, end up dominating their husbands.

Erichtho

The portrayal of the Thessalian witch Erichtho[33] in Lucan's epic about the Roman civil war is in some manner both following the literary topos of the Roman witch to its extremes and simultaneously averting it. It is noticeable that professional witches in Latin literature are physically portrayed as monstrous hags and engage in vile activities such as grave-robbing, while their magic-working is often described in gruesome detail. Canidia, who among others keeps vipers in her unkempt hair, starves a boy to death to make a love potion out of his liver;[34] Meroe opens a victim's throat with a sword, removes his beating heart through the wound and replaces it with a sponge.[35] It is plausible that this "gothic" element, as Ogden has called it, displayed in the portrayal of Roman witches is a native development, since nothing of the sort is found in Classical or Hellenistic literature. Furthermore, it may well be that this development owes more to Roman predilection for the violent and gruesome spectacles of the arena than to anything else.[36]

At any rate, in a similar vein, Lucan gives, in lurid detail, a description of Erichtho's decrepit and pale as a shade activities: she lives in deserted tombs; she harvests body parts for necromancy from the dead, tearing the bodies limb to limb in her rage, plucking eyes from their sockets, grasping bones from the maws of wolves, cutting ropes, from which dead men hang, with her teeth; she poisons the air with her breath; she tears newborns from their mothers' womb to place on sacrificial altars and creates ghosts for necromantic purposes; the gods themselves fear her, and grant her whatever she asks, lest she asks them a second time. The list goes on, but I believe the point is clear; this is the most over-the-top description of a witch's activities, but mostly in tune with the trope, as found elsewhere in Latin literature. What is surprising is the absence of any reference to erotic magic-working among Erichtho's activities or interests; indeed, Erichtho's magic-working is wholly devoted to necromancy, raising the dead and controlling nature and the gods. One could claim that the reason for this is that love magic is irrelevant to the scene at hand, the focus of which is Sextus Pompey's necromantic consultation of the Thessalian witch about the outcome of the civil war. This is a possibility, in which case this whole scene could be an attack on the character of Sextus Pompey, a man indirectly implicated with necromancy in the Gabienus anecdote found in Pliny. Erichtho, however, is noted not to have interest in other living human beings, as she even lives among the dead. She is portrayed, in a way, as a force of nature, and is maybe intended by Lucan as a metaphor for the evils and decay brought to the Roman Empire by the civil war; the multiple references to her bringing death to people who were owed a longer life by fate, to youths and infants, and the culmination of the scene, wherein she performs a necromantic ritual on the body of a dead soldier, could point in that direction.[37] If this is the case, we have in Erichtho the clearest portrayal of the witch as a symbol of anti-social evil, an attribute that would follow the trope into medieval times and to our day.

Magic and the law in the Greek world

The evidence for legislation concerning magical practices in the Greek world is scant, as no complete legal corpus from any of the Greek cities survives. What little can be pieced together about the legal status of practitioners of magic in the Greek world comes, on the one hand, from a few passing mentions of trials of certain women conducted in fourth-century Athens and, on the other hand, from the so-named *Dirae Teiorum*,[38] a fifth-century legal inscription from Teos prescribing laws as well as curses that should be recited annually by magistrates against certain groups inimical to the community. The question we should be attempting to answer, based on the ancient testimonies, is if there were special laws concerning actions considered magical and if magic as a whole was prescribed as an illegal activity. The focus will necessarily be classical Athens.

The case of Theoris and Athenian law

The most cited of those trials is the case of a woman called Theoris, hailing from the island of Lemnos, whose trial took place in Athens not long before 338 BC. The first mention of Theoris is found in the speech *Against Aristogeiton*,[39] attributed to Demosthenes. The speaker reminds the court of Athenian citizens that they had recently condemned Theoris, whom he calls "a witch (*pharmakis*)", and her entire family to death on account of her "potions and incantations (*pharmaka kai tas epōidas*)". After her death, those had come into possession of Aristogeiton's brother, Eunomos, through his relation to Theoris' maid, and thereafter the disreputable couple made a living by pretending to cure ailments and epileptic fits by means of those same potions. The mention of Eunomos' connection to "the wretched Theoris" in the context of the speech is meant to discredit him as a witness in the case at hand. For this reason, this fleeting mention does not elucidate the charges against Theoris or the exact crimes for which she was put to death.[40]

The case of Theoris' trial and execution is briefly mentioned in two other later sources, but at first sight, those accounts seem to obfuscate the matter more than elucidate it. On the one hand, the Hellenistic historian Philochoros relates that Theoris was a seer (*mantis*) who was tried and executed for impiety (*asebeia*).[41] On the other hand, Plutarch in his biography of Demosthenes relates that Theoris was a priestess (*hiereia*) who was accused by Demosthenes himself and condemned to death for "teaching slaves how to deceive" and for other unspecified machinations.[42]

The first question which arises is what Theoris' profession was. She is called a "witch" by Demosthenes, a "seer" by Philochoros and a "priestess" by Plutarch. As has been pointed out by other commentators, Plutarch is probably confusing Theoris' case with that of Ninos, a priestess who was executed after having been charged with *asebeia* in the 350–40s.[43] The designations of "witch" and "seer", however, are not at odds for describing the same individual. What is meant here is a certain class of religious specialists and purifiers who could engage in fortune telling as well as in the production of *pharmaka*. This is what Eunomos is described, in disparaging terms, as having turned to after taking hold of Theoris' magical apparatus.

The question of the nature of Theoris' crime and consequently the law under which she was prosecuted is a more complex one. Demosthenes, as we saw, says that the Athenians condemned her on account of her "potions and incantations". Now, we know that magical potions (*pharmaka*) as a whole were not illegal to manufacture or even use and administer in Athens, and the distinction between "good" and "bad" potions was valid. This is demonstrated by the fact that in cases of accidental murder by poisoning of their husbands, it was possible for women to claim that they had intended to administer a love potion rather than a deadly poison.[44] Cases of murder by poison were regular murder cases, such as the one addressed by Antiphon's speech *On the Stepmother*, and no special law was in place to turn them into what we might think of as "witch trials", simply because the means of murder could have been considered magical. Murder of Athenian citizens by poison could very well have been the crime of which Theoris was accused. The sentence of death for such a crime is consistent with Athenian law, but the execution of her entire family as well, if Demosthenes is accurate, poses some problems. There is a possible parallel for this in a law from Teos, from the aforementioned *Dirae Teiorum*, wherein it is prescribed that anyone who manufactures "deadly potions (*pharmaka dēlētēria*)" will be put to death along with their entire family. This, however, seems exceedingly harsh by Athenian standards and there is no guarantee that a law from Teos would have had an exact parallel in Athens. It is possible however, that, whatever Theoris was convicted of, her family was involved in the same crime and that they were tried and convicted separately.

Demosthenes, however mentions incantations along with potions as the reason Theoris was put to death. If poison is considered a magical means that harms directly, incantations, *epōidai* and *katadesmoi* are meant to harm indirectly through the agency of the powers of the Underworld. There are certain reasons, though, to believe that this kind of witchcraft did not fall under the provisions of any Athenian law. The exchange of Menon and Socrates in Plato's dialogue, *Meno*, is sometimes cited to show that Athens had no legislation against witchcraft.[45] Menon, dumbfounded by Socrates' arguments, jokingly says that it seems as if Socrates has "drugged, enchanted and completely bewitched" him so that he is unable to respond, despite being a proficient speaker on the matter at hand, describing, one could note, the symptoms one would expect of a judicial *katadesmos*. He then advises Socrates never to go abroad, because if he had acted so as a stranger in any other city, he would have been apprehended as a sorcerer (*goēs*). What is more telling, however, are the harsh punishments Plato prescribes in his ideal republic for sorcerers, the seemingly abundant religious specialists in his day, who are hired by the wealthy to inflict curses upon their enemies or to avert the wrath of the gods, by means of magic.[46] Plato prescribes the punishments that should have existed for sorcerers in his opinion, because they probably did not exist in Athens.[47] It is plausible that Demosthenes' mention of the incantations along with potions in relation to Theoris' crimes is meant as a rhetorical flourish to underline the low character of the woman and further discredit the witness, Eunomos, who allegedly inherited her practice.

Several scholars, on the other hand, accept Philochoros' account on the matter, namely that the charge Theoris faced was that of *asebeia*.[48]

Now, *asebeia*, or impiety, was a serious charge involving not believing or honoring the deities of the city and bringing religious innovations into the state religion. This was essentially the charge faced by Socrates, and as seen at least from his case, if not others, the penalty was death. There is evidence that a person of Theoris' profession could face the charge of *asebeia*. This comes in the form of one of Aesop's fables,[49] in which a "woman magician (*gunē magos*)" is charged with and condemned for *asebeia*, because she professed to be able to placate the wrath of the gods. While a fable of Aesop is not the best place to go to in order to seek understanding of the Athenian legal process, this particular one has been shown to originate most probably from late fourth-century Athens. On account of its contemporaneity with Theoris' case and the fact that a fable referring to real world processes should make some sense in order to get its moral across, we could tentatively accept that it reflects a legal reality faced by people of Theoris' profession. These people are the sorcerers, purifiers, mendicant priests and charlatans, against whom the Hippocratic author of the tract *On the Sacred Disease* delivers a tirade, because they profess to be able to heal epilepsy by placating those gods, who allegedly inflicted it upon the epileptic in the first place. That Theoris was this kind of religious specialist is implied, as already seen, by the fact that Eunomos, who took up her potions and incantations after her death, professed to heal epilepsy. What all this means is that the charge of *asebeia* could be levied against those religious specialists under the right conditions, but not that magic was banned as a whole under that same law, so as for them to be under constant threat by it.[50] As to whether Theoris was prosecuted for *asebeia*, it is not possible to say, but if she were, Demosthenes using the phrase "potions and incantations" to refer to that charge seems bizarre.

Based on the scarce evidence examined earlier we can conclude the following about the legal status of magic in classical Athens: a) There was no law against magical practice as a whole. b) Certain magical practices, namely the administering of deadly poisons, were tried under other laws, i.e. murder by poison was considered a murder case. c) People of that class of professional seers, purifiers and charlatans mentioned by both Plato and the Hippocratic author of *On the Sacred Disease* were likely to be prosecuted under the charge of *asebeia* at least for attempting to placate the gods outside the confines and rituals of state religion. This is not to say that the law concerning *asebeia* was a law against magic; it just happened that magicians could be seen as a class of people likely to violate its clauses. d) There was probably no law against the use of magical incantations as a whole, the depositing of *katadesmoi* and magical curses.

Magic and the law in Rome

Servius, Virgil's late fourth-century commentator, attempts to explain Queen Dido's reluctance in the Aeneid to turn to the magical arts in order to bring her lover, Aeneas, back to her, by relating that the Romans, despite having adopted many foreign religious rites, had always condemned "the rites of magic (*magica sacra*)".[51] Servius' remark is elucidated by a similar statement made by Apuleius in his defense speech against accusations of witchcraft, where he claims that magic had been outlawed in Rome since the time of the Twelve Tables legislation (fifth century BC), because of what he humorously calls "the unbelievable practice of seducing crops away".[52] What Apuleius is referring to here is one of two antique laws, evidently found in the Twelve Tables and known to us through quotations and passages of much later writers, who tended to interpret them as ancient Roman laws against magic.

The Twelve Tables

The law[53] Apuleius refers to in the aforementioned passage seems to have addressed the practice of stealing crops from another field and transferring them to one's own, by means of "some magical arts", as Servius comments elsewhere in Virgil's work, where reference to that practice is made. In the original quotations from the Twelve Tables, it seems that these "magical arts" were thought of as incantations, but Virgil and Pliny connect those practices to the use of *uenena* as well. It is, however, conceivable, given that the law seems to have comprised two clauses, that one dealt with the removal of crops through incantations and the other through the use of *uenena*.[54] Whether the punishment for violation of this law was a fine or the death penalty is unclear as well; in Pliny's probably fictionalized account of a trial taking place in 191 BC,[55] the punishment awaiting the accused is evidently paying a fine,[56] while Augustine claims that according to Cicero the penalty was death. At any rate, as far as we can tell, what is at stake here is violation of property, not the means by which it is accomplished; this is a law against a form of theft, not against magic *per se*.

The case of the second law[57] from the Twelve Tables, thought to have dealt with malicious incantations (*carmina*) by authors of the Imperial Era, illustrates the problems one is faced with when attempting to reconstruct the wording and intent of lost legislation through later quotations and interpretations of it. It is unclear whether the law in question is one law comprised of two clauses or whether we are dealing with two separate laws altogether. At any rate, the Twelve Tables contained provisions against those who would sing or even compose a malicious *carmen*. The question then becomes whether by the term *carmen* we are to understand a magical incantation, as Pliny does, or whether, following Cicero,[58] we are to understand this law as one against mockery and lampooning through malicious songs, namely what was otherwise later known as *conuicium*. It should be pointed out, however, that while a magical curse and a lampooning song are two very distinct things for us, this need not have been the case for the Romans of the fifth century BC. English usage is not always too meticulous about differentiating "cursing" from "verbal abuse", and for that matter neither is Latin; the literal translation of the phrase *male dictis figere*, most often translated as "to verbally abuse", is to "hold someone in place with evil words". This is often what a *defixio* is thought to accomplish, a word ultimately derived from the verb used in this instance, namely *figere*. It is conceivable, then, that we are dealing with one law seeking to regulate malicious speech, with, possibly, magical cursing and mockery being distinct expressions of the same category, one we could describe as "malediction".[59] The punishment for the composition and singing of those malicious *carmina* was death according to Cicero, who maintained this was a law against lampooning. This does seem at first exceedingly harsh, given that the Twelve Tables prescribe mere fines for bodily injuries. However, if we are to consider that a malicious song insulting the dignity of a person or *gens* could be disseminated and remembered for a long time after its composition, it is conceivable that, at a time when Rome was held in a tenuous class equilibrium between patricians and plebeians, this was a law concerned with, among others, maintaining public order in a volatile political environment.[60]

The Lex Cornelia de sicariis et ueneficiis

According to Roman legislative practice, older laws tended to be augmented in time with newer clauses that seemed relevant to the general type of cases treated under them. This is what probably gave the illusion of continuity to authors of the Imperial Era, when a definite legal framework against harmful magical activities was in place, so as to claim that Roman law had always prohibited magic working. The law in question was passed in 81 BC under Sulla and was known as the *Lex Cornelia de sicariis et ueneficiis*. This is the law that seems to have dealt with cases of witchcraft in the Imperial Period, be that *defixiones*, *uenena* or whatever could be construed as such and used with harmful intent. The original text of the law is not extant, and again one has to rely on quotations from Cicero and late imperial legislation, as found in the *Sententiae Pauli*, the *Digesta* and the Justinian and Theodosian *codices*.

Originally,[61] the law appears to have dealt with intentional homicide or intent to cause the death of another through non-readily detectable means and guile.[62] One of the known clauses concerned those who carry a weapon with the intent to commit murder (*sicarii*), a second clause was about those who cause the death of another by knowingly participating in miscarriage of justice and a third clause dealt with *uenena*, potions, outlawing the process of concocting, selling, buying possessing and administering them.[63] The potions in question are specified as being of the kind used to kill a person, i.e. poisons.[64] The ancient commentators on jurisprudence insist that when one speaks of *uenenum*, one has to specify whether it is harmful (*malum*) or benevolent (*bonum*), as the word *uenenum* could refer to either category, in the same manner as the Greek *pharmakon*.[65] Through the process of reinterpretation of the law, however, the *Lex Cornelia* came to treat cases where potions could lead to accidental death of the recipient, such as love potions (*amatorium*), abortifacients or fertility potions.[66] Eventually the manufacture and usage of all those types of *uenena* was made into a punishable act, as it set a bad precedent, even if no malicious intent was established in administering them.[67] The penalty for violation of the clauses pertaining to *ueneficium* in the Imperial Period was exile and confiscation of property or death if the perpetrators' actions led to death of another. Around the time of Diocletian, probably, high class high-class citizens were sentenced to exile, while lower-class citizens (*humiliores*) must have been sentenced to death, by being thrown to the beasts in the arena.[68]

As the notion of *ueneficium* came to encompass magical practice as a whole, whether or not there were *uenena* involved, the *Lex Cornelia* became the law dealing with other instances of witchcraft or aberrant ritual acts. These clauses are not very numerous in the legislation of the pre-Christian period. There are, however, some clear references in the *Sententiae Pauli* prohibiting the practice of *defixio*, human sacrifice and blood offerings, desecration of temples and the very knowledge of the magical arts on pain of death; those who have knowledge of witchcraft are to be crucified or thrown to the beasts, while actual sorcerers are to be burnt alive.[69] The reference to such practices as "impious or nocturnal rituals (*sacra impia nocturnaue*)" in the same clause as the desecration of temples shows that the *Lex Cornelia* was, even by that time, operating under some religious considerations, namely witchcraft being in opposition to proper conduct towards the gods. It is only under the Christian emperors, however, that a fully theological justification is added to the universal prohibition of witchcraft and all forms of divination, even those ancient and well-respected practices of *augurium* and *haruspicium*: "let those who disturb the minds of men by invocation of demons be punished by all sorts of punishment". In the eyes of the Christian commentator, sorcerers and diviners, who are by now called *malefici*, i.e. "evil-doers", work through the agency of demons, the enemies of the divine order, and thus deserve every available punishment.[70] This seems to have been the conclusion to a developing trend which identified witchcraft and divination outside of official channels with religious deviance and sedition, which posed threats to the monarchical institution of the Empire. A probably fictitious speech composed by Cassius Dio and attributed to Agrippa as a piece of political advice towards Augustus elucidates such concerns of the third century AD:

> those people (i.e. religious deviants) bring in new deities and persuade many to follow foreign customs, out of which conspiracies, seditions and dissident groups arise, things very harmful to a monarchy. Do not allow therefore anyone to disbelieve in the gods *nor allow any sorcerer* (*goes*) *to exist*. Divination is necessary and you have to approve of haruspices and augurs, whom people can consult. Magic workers (*mageutai*) on the other hand should not exist at all. For such individuals instigate many, by imparting some truths, but mostly falsehoods, to act in a seditious manner.[71]

The Augustan Edict of 11 AD

Brief mention should at the very least be made of the Augustan edict of 11 AD, which prohibited a particular subject of divination, namely attempting to enquire into the future of another to determine their time of death.[72] When the object of divination, most often through astrology, was the emperor, this was construed as high treason, treated under the *Lex Iulia Maiestatis*. The importance of this piece of legislation for the political life during the Principate becomes clear when one examines the accounts of numerous treason trials found in Tacitus. The first of those, concerning the conspiracy of Libo Drusus in 16 AD,[73] and the one which initiated the wave of treason trials under Tiberius, already contained accusations of "magical rituals (*magorum sacra*)" and the consultation of astrologers about the future of the imperial position. Another celebrated case, that of the mysterious death of Tiberius' heir, Germanicus, in 19 AD, also contained charges of *defixiones* and *ueneficium*.[74] Those were offenses treated under the *Lex Cornelia*, but the trial was obviously one of treason, since those were perpetrated against a member of the imperial family. About a dozen similar cases are known from Tacitus and Dio Cassius, from the reigns of Tiberius, Claudius, Nero and Septimius Severus, wherein accusations of treason are trumped up with charges of witchcraft or divination targeting the emperor. It is probably that long-existing political milieu Cassius Dio has in mind when he has Agrippa advise Augustus on how to treat sorcerers and unsanctioned diviners, where accusations of witchcraft bolster accusations of treason against members of the senatorial elite, making magic an important and dangerous aspect of Roman political life in the Imperial Period.

Notes

1 Apuleius, *Apologia* 12.7.
2 Apollonius, *Epist*, 17.
3 Auguste Audollent, *Defixionum Tabellae Quotquot Innotuerunt: Tam in Graecis Orientis Quam in Totius Occidentis* (Paris: A. Fontemoing, 1904), XC.
4 Christopher A. Faraone, "The Agonistic Context of Early Greek Binding Spells," in *Magika Hiera*, ed. Christopher Faraone and Dirk Obbink (New York, Oxford: Oxford University Press, 1991), 3–32.
5 Fritz Graf, *Magic in the Ancient World*, trans. Franklin Philip (Cambridge, MA, London: Harvard University Press, 1997), 133.
6 See Ibid., Faraone, "Agonistic Context," 5–7.
7 *DTAud*, 111–112.
8 Graf, *Magic in the Ancient World*, 127.
9 Sarah Iles Johnston, *Restless Dead: Encounters Between the Living and the Dead in Ancient Greece* (Berkeley, Los Angeles, London: University of California Press, 1999), 78 and n.127 for discussion on the meaning of *atelestoi*.
10 Graf, *Magic in the Ancient World*, 127, 128, 132.
11 Sarah Iles Johnston, "Sacrifice in the Greek Magical Papyri," in *Magic and Ritual in the Ancient World*, ed. Paul Mirecki and Alvin Meyer (Leiden, Boston, Köln: Brill, 2002), 347–349.
12 Theocritus, *Idylls*, 2.
13 Tibullus, 1.2, 55–56.
14 DK 22 B 14.
15 *De morbo sacro* 1.10, 1.27–31.
16 364b5–c5.
17 Matthew W. Dickie, *Magic and Magicians in the Greco-Roman World* (London, New York: Routledge, 2001), 76.
18 *DTAud* 70–75. See Dickie, *Magic and Magicians*, 85–87.
19 Matthew W. Dickie, "Who Practiced Love-Magic in Classical Antiquity and in the Late Roman World?" *CQ* 50.2 (2000): 563–583.
20 Daniel Ogden, *Night's Black Agents: Witches, Wizards and the Dead in the Ancient World* (London, New York: Hambledon Continuum, 2008), 21–27.
21 *Trach*, 1070–1075.
22 Ibid., 920–931. See also Kimberly B. Stratton, *Naming the Witch: Magic Ideology and Stereotype in the Ancient World* (New York: Columbia University Press, 2007), 56–57.
23 *Moralia*, 139a.
24 *Sat*. 6.610–615.
25 *Epod*. 5.41–42.
26 Dickie, "Who Practised Love-Magic."
27 Advanced in Christopher A. Faraone, *Ancient Greek Love Magic* (Cambridge, MA, London: Harvard University Press, 1999).
28 *Trach*. 581–582. Verg. *Aen*. 492–493.
29 3.11.16–17.
30 See Faraone, *Love Magic*, 2.
31 See for example Tibullus, 1.2.45–49.
32 This hypothesis has been advanced by Dickie in *Magic and Magicians*.
33 *De Bello Ciuili* 6. 507–830.
34 Hor. *Epod*. 5.
35 Apuleius *Met*. 1.13.
36 Ogden, *Night's Black Agents*, 75–76.
37 See Stratton, *Naming the Witch*, 91.

38 Daniel Ogden, *Magic Witchcraft and Ghosts in the Greek and Roman Worlds: A Sourcebook* (Oxford: Oxford University Press, 2002), 275.
39 25.79–80.
40 Derek Collins, "Theoris of Lemnos and the Criminalization of Magic in Fourth-Century Athens," *CQ* 51.2 (2001), 493.
41 Philochorus apud Harpokration, s.v.
42 Plut. *Dem.* 14.4.
43 Collins, "Theoris," 490.
44 Aristot, *Magna Moralia*, 16; cf. Collins, "Theoris," 488.
45 *Meno*, 80b.
46 *Laws*, 10.909b.
47 Collins, "Theoris," 483.
48 See Dickie, *Magic and Magicians*, 50.
49 https://fablesofaesop.com/perry-index, 56.
50 Cf. Dickie, *Magic and Magicians*, 54.
51 Servius ad *Aen.* 4.493.
52 Apuleius, *Apologia* 47.3.
53 The law is reconstructed through: Verg. *Ecl.* 8.95–99; Aug. *de civ. Dei* 8.19; Plin. *Nat.Hist.* 28.17.
54 James B. Rives, "Magic in the XII Tables Revisited," *CQ* 52 (2002): 276.
55 Plin. *Nat.Hist.* 18.41–43.
56 Richard A. Bauman, "Criminal Prosecution by the Aediles," *Latomus* 33 (1974); Rives, "Magic in the XII Tables," 277.
57 The law is reconstructed through: Plin. *Nat.Hist.* 28.18; Cic. *Rep.* 4.12 = Aug. *de civ. Dei* 2.9.
58 Cic. *Tusc. Disp.* 4.4.
59 Cf. George L. Hendrickson, "Verbal Injury, Magic or Erotic Comus?" *CP* 20 (1925): 293; Rives, "Magic in the XII Tables," 285.
60 Eduard Fraenkel, "Anzeige zu Beckman, E. Zauberei und Recht in Roms Frühzeit," *Gnomon* 1 (1925): 198–199; Rives, "Magic in the XII Tables," 288; Arnaldo Momigliano, review of *Freedom of Speech in the Roman Republic*, by L. Robinson, *JRS* 32 (1942): 122.
61 For reconstruction of the law see Jean L. Ferrary, "Lex Cornelia de sicariis et veneficiis," *Athenaeum* 79 (1991): 417–434; Jean L. Ferrary, "Lex Cornelia de sicariis et veneficiis," in *Roman Statutes*, 2 vols, ed. Michael H. Crawford (London: Institute of Classical Studies, 1996), vol. 2. 749–753.
62 Graf, *Magic in the Ancient World*, 46; James B. Rives, "Magic in Roman Law: The Reconstruction of a Crime," *Classical Antiquity* 22 (2003): 318.
63 Cic. *Pro Cluentio* 54.148.
64 *Dig.* 48.8.3; Paulus, *Sent.* 5.23.1.
65 *Dig.* 48.8.3.2.
66 Paulus, *Sent.* 5.23.14.
67 *Dig.* 48.8.3.3.
68 *Dig.* 48.8.3.5; Rives, "Magic in Roman Law," 332.
69 Paulus *Sent.* 5.23.15–18.
70 *CTh.* 9.16.3–4.
71 Dio Cass. 52.36.
72 Dio Cass. 56.25.5.
73 Tac. *Ann.* 2.27–31.
74 Tac. *Ann.* 2.69; Dio Cass. 57.18.9.

Bibliography (selection)

Collins, Derek, "Theoris of Lemnos and the Criminalization of Magic in Fourth-Century Athens." *CQ* 51:2 (2001): 477–493.
Dickie, Matthew W., *Magic and Magicians in the Greco-Roman World.* London, New York: Routledge, 2001.

Faraone, Christopher A., *Ancient Greek Love Magic.* Cambridge, MA, London: Harvard University Press, 1999.

Graf, Fritz, *Magic in the Ancient World.* Translated by Franklin Philip. Cambridge, MA, London: Harvard University Press, 1997.

Johnston, Sarah Iles, *Restless Dead: Encounters Between the Living and the Dead in Ancient Greece.* Berkeley, Los Angeles, London: University of California Press, 1999.

Ogden, Daniel, *Night's Black Agents: Witches, Wizards and the Dead in the Ancient World.* London, New York: Hambledon Continuum, 2008.

2

WITCHCRAFT, MAGIC AND DEMONOLOGY IN THE BIBLE, ANCIENT JUDAISM AND EARLIEST CHRISTIANITY

Marco Frenschkowski

Biblical traditions about magic and witchcraft, and later European Christianity: some preliminary considerations

It is still a wide-spread idea that late medieval and early modern witchcraft persecutions and witch imaginations are a product of Christian abhorrence of female sexuality, of male clerical dominance and theological teachings suspicious of folk tradition, and that these are rooted in Biblical, Jewish and ancient Christian concepts. This once popular view is clearly deeply erroneous, and not even just an oversimplification. Late antique and medieval images of magic and witchcraft are influenced more by Greek and even more by Latin pagan literature than by any Biblical examples and texts. Magic is also an important aspect of early Christianity (Biblical texts e.g. were widely used as amulets), though it has often been criticized by theological writers.[1] But this "Christian magic" as such is not simply identical to medieval and early modern images of magic. Ideas about magic have changed to a large degree, and recent definitions of magic also differ widely and yield quite different histories of discourses on magic when applied to sources from antiquity. Many basic observations do not agree with older stereotypes both in theological literature and in literature critical of Christianity, and the emergence of magic in antiquity as a field of specialized cultural studies in the last decades has significantly changed commonly accepted ideas about its place both in the Christian mainstream (the "Church") and in its minority forms (as gnostic groups). Female witchcraft, for instance, surprisingly is mentioned only rarely in early Christian narrative texts, though male sorcerers are quite common. Women in such stories usually are victims of witchcraft, not perpetrators. A popular and naïve believe in demons is still often seen as part of a common antique "weltbild", shared and indeed intensified by Christians. Once again, things become much more complicated when the full range of sources is allowed to speak. Jewish views differ substantially from Christian ones, and there are even Christian as well as Jewish sources that use terms like "magician" (magos) in surprisingly positive contexts (Mt 2). Ideas of magic and witchcraft in Christian history have changed much, and not only for theological reasons. The New Testament as a collection of foundational Christian writings only rarely deals in magic as such, though Jesus himself was accused by his opponents as someone in league with Beelzebul.

All of these aspects are to be placed into a framework of late antique discourses. Ideas like a formal contract or pact with demons or the devil only much later become part of imaginations on magic. The idea of a witch-cult, a kind of demonic anti-religion with meetings and witches' Sabbaths, also does not yet exist in Christian antiquity, though in Greek and Latin literature witches sometimes work together to effect mischief. A boundary distinction magic–religion (even when put into different terminology as prayer vs. spell), also though definitely pre-Christian, takes new forms and a new prevalence in the Church. On the other side, in some ancient cultures, such as in the Egyptian one, it is almost non-existent or meaningless. Observations from later Christian societies also must not be projected onto late antique social realities and belief systems.

In a preliminary step, facing the different phenomena of what we might call magic in ancient Judaism and Christianity, we can fundamentally distinguish: 1. magical practices that would have been clearly identified as such by ancient practitioners; 2. practices that would have been criticized in theological literature as connected with magic, divination or even idolatry, though they were part of folk religious practice, and we do not clearly see whether practitioners themselves might have accepted a description as magic or witchcraft; and 3. practices that in a modern view, informed e.g. by ethnology or comparative studies of religion, can be qualified as magic in a rather wider sense but which were not seen as problematical by Church authors or rabbis.[2] A special case are slurs targeted against Christianity as connected to evil-doing magic in pagan writers (cf. already Celsus in Origen, Against Celsus 1, 6 a.o., and see still Augustine, On the Harmony of the Gospels 1:9, 14; 10, 15; 11, 17), connected to suspicions about Christianity as a kind of secret cult. In any case, we use magic and witchcraft here as wide interpretative terms hinting at a variety of motifs, not corresponding to a clear-cut segment of culture (or religion), and often (though not always) used as a delegitimizing label on non-standard, private or subversive forms of religion. Both are often related to concepts and rituals of gaining power over supernatural beings. Already in antiquity they are as much a matter of narrative imagination and stories as of actual rituals, and they clearly exist on all social levels.

Old Testament/Hebrew Bible magic

When we ask from the point of view of later reception history, we will have to start with a single verse from Pentateuchal religious law, which had a massive impact on later witch images. Exodus 22:18 says "You shall not permit a sorceress to live", in a context separating Israelite religion from paganism. The verse perhaps originally has in view a divining trance medium serving non-Jewish gods, or some form of popular magic. Already the Septuagint, the Greek version of the Old Testament, substitutes the quite conspicuous singular feminine of the Hebrew for a masculine plural, without doubt to give the verse a more general meaning. The Babylonian Talmud (Sanhedrin 67a) generalizes the statement, but also explains the feminine form from an alleged factual majority of female witches. General prohibitions of magic are not rare in Jewish Biblical tradition (Dtn 18:10–12; Lev 19:26; cf. Mi 5: 11; Is 47:8–15; Jer 27:9s.; Nah 3:4 and also Ex 20:7 = Dtn 5:11 etc.), in Mal 3:5 as part of a list of evildoers, etc., though it is quite unclear what exactly might have been defined

20

as illegitimate magic. In any case the reference frame of such prohibitions in ancient Israel always is the fight against idolatry and other gods in the name of Yahweh as the national God of Israel. Necromantic divination is strictly forbidden, though it has been believed to be quite efficient ("the witch of Endor" 1 Sam 28). Saul, who had lost his divine protection, desperately looks for supernatural guidance and visits a *ba'alat 'ōḇ*, a wise woman who possesses a dug-out pit used for sacrifices to chthonic numina (what in Greek is called a bothros) and is able to invoke the spirits of the dead (similar to the necromantic scene in Odyssey 11). She brings up from Sheol the spirit of the prophet Samuel, who confirms to King Saul his impending doom.

Later Christian writers discuss whether Samuel himself had truly appeared to Saul, or whether this may have been just a demonic illusion (cf. Eustathius of Antioch, On the ventriloquist against Origen). Texts such as 2 Kgs 21:5s. allude to other illegitimate practices. Of particular interest is Hes 13:17–23, where the male prophet polemizes against female diviners, who successfully manipulate lives with magical knots and scarfs (German "Nestelknüpfen"). "And say, Thus saith the Lord GOD; Woe to the women that sew pillows to all armholes, and make kerchiefs upon the head of every stature to hunt souls! Will ye hunt the souls of my people, and will ye save the souls alive that come unto you?" (Ez 13:18 King James version, which sounds to us slightly archaic, as such a text may have sounded in NT times). The gender constellation of male charismatic prophet vs. female (technical) diviner able to manipulate lives is of vital interest for discourses on "magic". The slowly emerging monotheism of ancient Judaism became a lead factor repelling and repressing many forms of popular religion and magic. But the image we receive from canonized scriptures is certainly biased, and archaeology can only to some degree complete our knowledge, as only certain aspects of magic have left material traces.[3] The story about achieving cattle ringstraked, speckled and spotted by magically imbued water in Gen 30 can be seen as a classical case of Frazerian sympathetic magic, as can be the apotropaic snake on a pole (Num 21:4–7) later allegedly destroyed by Hezekiah (2 Kgs 18:4). Another story cycle related to both ancient and modern concepts of magic is Ex 7:1–8:15, which can be read as a magical contest narrative (a genre mainly known from late Egyptian and demotic literature). Moses waving his wand and parting the sea becomes an archetypical image of both "man of God" and magician: in pagan sources he is often interpreted as a sorcerer (Pliny mai., Natural history 30:11; Apuleius, Apology 90; also in some magical papyri). Already the Jewish novel writer Artapanos (2nd century BCE) has a story about Moses whispering the secret name of God to Pharaoh, making him tremble and fall unconscious, but later revivifying him by the same means (frg. 3 Holladay from Eusebius, Preparation of the Gospel 9:27, 24s.). Harmful spells may be in view Job 3:8, where sorcerers curse the day and wake up the Livjatan, a primeval dragon symbolizing chaotic forces.

Some rituals in modern research have been interpreted as magic, though they were not qualified so in ancient Judaism: the ordeal of the bitter water (Num 5:11–31), the purification ritual of the red heifer (Num 19), or the eliminatory rites (Lev 13s. 16). Amulets were part of everyday life as in all ancient societies (Jer 3:18–23). The miraculous powers of the "men of God" Elijah and Elisha are strictly seen as a gift of God and never as acquired by magical means. But a narrative as 1 Kgs 18:41–45 can easily be mistaken for some kind of rain-magic. Elijah's strange posture (head between his knees) becomes stereotypical for Jewish mysticism. Ḥanina ben Dosa, a famous 1st-century BCE healer and rainmaker, also imitates it (Talmud Bavli Berakhot 34b), as do medieval mystics. According to Talmud Bavli Sanhedrin 113a Ḥanina has at his disposal the "keys of rain", as did Elijah. Prophetic symbolism and anticipations of divine action may have some affinity to magical rites (1 Kgs 22:11; Jer 51:59–64), and God, in an extremely audacious metaphor, can even be compared to a snake charmer (Ps 58:6). Military magic may be a background of both Jer 19:1–13 (a charm against enemies, using an Egyptian pattern; cf. Ps 2:9) and 2 Kgs 2:8.14. A more far-reaching theory has been expressed by the Norwegian OT scholar Sigmund Mowinckel (1884–1965). He interprets the pōˁalê ʾāwen "workers of iniquity" (some 16 times in Psalms) as evil sorcerers using the divine name for harmful charms. This theory about sorcery, aimed at in individual psalms of lament, has not generally become accepted, but it has demonstrated the impact of magic in ancient Israel and it has reminded scholarship of the vital importance of witchcraft fears in oriental societies, also well documented for instance in Assyrian and Babylonian sources. The "theocentric" theory that in Israel magical performance was always directly connected with God[4] can hardly be upheld, however. The relation between magical practices and divine intervention was never systematized.

Demons and the rise of the devil

As all oriental (and indeed all ancient) religions, Israel had a complex and multi-faceted demonology that is probably only partly reflected in the texts that became later canonical literature in Judaism and Christianity. Some of its figures can be interpreted as being derived from a common Meditearranean substratum, whereas other mythological entities as Lilith and Asmodaeus/Ashmedai have a background in particular Near Eastern religions (Babylonian and Persian in these two cases). A number of very different Hebrew terms denote what later becomes metamorphized into Christian demonology. Šēdîm (Dtn 32:17 and Ps 106:37, where they are said to receive sacrifices) in post-Biblical times turns into a general term for demons as malevolent and dangerous spirits. As the related Akkadian šēdu is a positive term for certain spirits, the Hebrew word may represent a deliberate reversal of terminology. "The hairy ones" (śeˁîrîm Lev 17:7; Is. 13:21; 34:14; 2 Chron 11:15 a.o.) are satyr-like beings (reminiscent of later goat-demons). The name became unintelligible to later readers and was only rarely used in Rabbinic Judaism. According to Jes 34:14 they can be found in ruins and eerie places, together with animals and the spirit Lilith (transformed into a central mythological figure in late antique Jewish demonology). Other, more general demonological terms are ruʾaḥ raʾa "evil spirit" (1 Sam 19:8), also the "destroyer" (Ex 12:23), the "destroying angel" (1 Chron 21:15), the "evil angels" (Ps 78:49) and others. Interestingly, these spirits remain part of the divine cosmos and can be used by Yahweh for certain errands. The Hebrew Bible does not yet have any clear dichotomy "angels"–"demons" as later became central for Christian mythology (and to some degree also developed in late pagan contexts, as for Porphyry). Particularly telling is the story of Micha ben Jimla (1 Kgs 22), where God himself sends a lying spirit to cause the doom of King Ahab (cf. Zeus sending a deceiving dream to Agamemnon, Ilias 2, 1ss.), though of course the manoeuvre is revealed by the prophet Micha to the king, and thus becomes a kind of paradoxical intervention.

Pagan deities can be demonized, as the West Semitic deity Resheph (god of heat and the plague) (Dtn 32:24; Hab 3:5; Ps 78:48), or Baal Zebub "Lord of flies" in Ecron (2 Kgs 1, 2.3 etc.), who is a caricature of the Canaanite Baal Zebul "Lord of glory" (though there is also a Greek God "Zeus averter of flies", Pausanias 5:14, 1), a name that in the New Testament becomes a major synonym of the devil as prince of evil spirits (Mk 3:22; Mt 12:24; Lk. 11:15 etc.).

Demonology only slowly becomes part of an organized system of otherworldly beings. Lilith, mentioned above (translated as lamia in the vulgate), is a central fig-ure in Aramaic magical bowls from Mesopotamia (4th–7th century CE), and in early medieval Jewish folklore became Adam's first wife, created before Eve, but unwilling to serve Adam (the story is first mentioned in the geonic "Alphabet of Ben Sira", though it may be older). As a demon with a woman's face, long hair and wings, she is feared as a child murderer (imperilling women in childbirth), and many amulets are used against her in apotropaic magic. A man sleeping alone in a house has to be careful not to be seized by her seductive power (Talmud Bavli Shabbat 15b). Another demonic figure is Azazel (Lev 16:8.10.26), to whom a goat (the "scapegoat") is driven into the desert as an eliminatory ritual. In later writings, such as 1 Hen 10:8, he turns into a major demonic figure, having originally been one of the "watchers" sent to earth, then mingling with human women and siring giants which are destroyed in the deluge. In the 1st century CE Apocalypse of Abraham, Azazel is a devil, as for the Christian theologian Origen (Against Celsus 6:43).

Asmodaeus (Greek Asmodaíos, Hebrew Ashmedai) is a demon from the book of Tobit, much spoken of also in later Jewish literature. His name is connected to Iranian aēšma-daēva, a demon of wrath. But in the Book of Tobit his function is dif-ferent: he moves in the dangerous sphere of marriage and sexuality. The wedding bed, the bathroom, the cemetery, desert places are always prone to demonic influ-ences and may necessitate protective magic. The worlds of the dead and of demons are also likely to intersect easily. Generally speaking, it is an act of taboo breaking that opens the human sphere to demonic influences and invasions, but "dangerous" times such as birth, marriage and death may also need ritual protection against par-ticular demons. Both the plague (Hab 3:5) and death (Jes 28:15; Job 18:13 etc.), and also other calamities, can be mythologized into quasi-personal demonic figures.

Another such figure of late antique Judaism is Beliar (from Beliyaʿal "worthless-ness", with common interchange of l and r, a name often used of evil powers in Qumran literature and in the perhaps 1st-century BCE "Testament of 12 Patriarchs"). Paul uses this name (2 Cor 6:15), as do later Latin sources (mostly spelled Belial) for the devil as a figure clearly defined in Christian theology. A difference between Jewish and Christian demonology is indeed the increased concentration on such a devil figure as an adversary of God in Christianity (though dualism is strictly avoided: in Apc 12 it is Michael, not God, fighting the "old serpent"). The rabbinic tradition has much to say about both internal forces shaping human conduct and external demonic forces threatening health and welfare, but it does not concentrate its theo-ries of evil on a devil figure (though such figures are far from unknown), and demon-ology only rarely exculpates human weakness.

Belief in evil spirits and demons is universal: belief in the devil is not. It is par-ticularly important not to use the complete repertoire of ideas about the devil as if they had existed already in antiquity, but to give careful attention to the exact constellation of demonological concepts at a given time and place. In Old Testament studies, the theory has gained some plausibility that, on a deeper level, the devil figure came into being by disincorporating or separating evil from the image of Yahweh, thus creating an autonomous figure of evil. Locus classicus (1 Chron 21:1) is where Satan as a tempter takes a role filled by God himself in the literary pretext (2 Sam 24:1). In sources like Iob 1s. and Sach 3:1s., Satan is part of the heavenly court and thus also part of a monarchical metaphorical world, accusing mankind in the face of God as judge of the world (cf. Apc 12:10). Hebrew *Śāṭān* means adversary or prosecutor and perhaps also slanderer (Num. 22: 22. 32). Not yet in Iob but in 1 Chron, the word is used anarthrous as a personal name. The emerging devil figure takes over traces from the destroying angel (Ex 12) or the desert demon Azazel, and also from personifications of chaos as Tiamat, Livjatan and others. He receives already in Judaism many names: Belial, Satan, Beelzebul, Mastema, Semjaza, Samael and in Greek Diabolos "slanderer, accuser" (> Old Saxon diuval, English devil). He tempts men both with evil thoughts and as an embodiment of destructive forces. Texts like the Greek "Testament of Solomon" (Jewish, but read and copied by Christians, 4th century CE?) describe in much detail demonic figures. No magical incantations are given, however, though a rich Jewish tradition of conjuring angelic entities arises not much later (Sefer haRazim and other writings, known from medieval manuscripts).

In Christian stories, the devil also causes heresy. Stories about human beings possessed by demons are known in ancient Judaism, but are not very common, though they become more prominent in late antique sources. Josephus gives an elaborate and rather technical exorcism story (Jewish Antiquities 8:46–49), differing markedly from the exorcisms performed by Jesus, which do not use magical plants or spells. The term commonly used for demons exorcised by Jesus is "unclean spirits" (which by enallage adiectivi means spirits causing uncleanness). Once exorcised, demons walk "arid places" and, finding no rest, may return to their previous home (Luke 11:24–26).

The perhaps most important element in Christian demonology, however, was the identification of the pagan gods with demons (already 1 Cor 10:21, but cf. also 8:4). All paganism now became some kind of devil-worship, and magic and divination became by-paths of paganism. This idea is much more prominent in the ancient church than might be said about an approach that sees other gods as simply non-existent.

Jesus interprets his exorcisms and healing miracles as overcoming the devil, anticipating the expected Kingdom of God (Lk 10:18; 11:14–26 par.). The devil is accompanied by a host of evil angels (Mt 25:41; 2 Cor 12:7 etc.). The central metaphor for the devil's realm is not so much a monarchy as a military unit, an invading army causing disease and death (Mk 3:22–30; cf. the demon name "legion" Mk 5:9). This military aspect of demons "invading" God's world stays important also for medieval demonology: good and evil are never just static possibilities of human behaviour, but humans are in league with either God or the devil, both fighting for men's souls. For Paul, the devil is "God of the aeon" (2 Cor 4:4), for the Gospel of John "ruler of this world" (12:31; 14:30; 16:11). Imperial world power (Mt 4:1–11 par.) and the Roman state (Apc 13:17s. a.o.) can be spheres of devilish influence, and heretic teachers (2 Cor 11:15) and Jews rejecting the gospel (Joh 8:44; Apc 2:9; 3:9) can be regarded as being possessed by the devil. Older texts such as Mark or the genuine epistles of Paul often used the Hebrew word Satan(as), whereas later texts prefer the

Greek diabolos. Many taboo names for the devil go back already to early Christian literature (the "old snake", the "black one", the "fiend", the "evil one", the "one who brings ruin" on men, etc.). Snake and dragon symbolism (much reinforced in Apc 12s. etc.) is derived from the pre-Christian identification of the snake in Gen 3 with the devil (Wisdom of Solomon 2:24; 1st century BCE). In NT times, the devil has not yet any similarity with Pan-like animal figures, though he can be imagined in animal shape (dragon). In early Christianity, he is more a source of temptation and terror, not so much a monarch of hell as in later medieval imagination. The name Lucifer ("bringer of light") combines the symbolism of Venus with a mythology of a demonic entity thrown from heaven as a result of its pride and ambition (Is 14:12, where the vulgate has "Lucifer").

This mythology of Satan thrown from heaven (also Lk 10:18) in later Christianity allows for an integration of Satan and demons into a concept of all creatures created good by God. Another such common trait is the conviction that Satan can mask himself as an angel of light (2 Cor 11:14). In Rabbinic Judaism, the devil tempts with evil inclinations; he accuses man before God and destroys life (Babylonian Talmud Baba Bathra 16a). Satan (often called also Samael, Samiel or Sammuel, from "sami" "blind") and the "evil inclination" can sometimes also be identified as death (e.g. Targum Ps.-Jonathan on Gen 3:6). Stories are repeatedly told about tests of the pious by veiled demonic visitants. In Christian imagination, the devil is a more clear-cut figure, fallen through pride, expulsed from Heaven and bent on destroying men by temptation (cf. e.g. Augustine, The City of God, Book 11). He cannot be redeemed (Synod of Constantinople 543 CE against Origen, On First Principles 3:6). Gregory of Nyssa, in the 4th century, believed in the existence of male and female demons and supported the idea that demons procreated with other demons and with human women. Other scholars supported the idea that they could not procreate and that the number of demons was constant. The idea, well-known from medieval and Renaissance sources, that both angels and devils form special hierarchies opposed to each other is only slowly emerging in late antiquity.

Magic in ancient Judaism

Some ambivalence about magic permeates ancient Judaism as well as early Christianity. Delegitimizing discourses and an unbroken practice of magic go almost hand in hand. Magical dealings with drugs and poisons (pharmakeía) as well as "unholy mysteries" are expressions of pagan religion (Wisdom of Solomon 12:4), whereas Egyptian "juggleries of the magical art" do not help against God-send plagues (17:7). Magic and faith can be seen as direct opponents (18:13). Second Maccabees 12:40 polemizes against amulets, well known from excavations in Palestine. Many other passages in Jewish literature attack magic, though it is often quite unclear which practices exactly are in view (e.g. Testament of Judah 23; Ps.-Philo, Biblical Antiquities 34. 64; Ascension of Isaiah 2:5; Sibylline Oracles 3:218–34 a.o.). A basic observation is a linking of magic, divination and idolatry that we meet in Christian literature as well. On the other side, Graeco-Jewish texts like the 1st-century BCE Prayer for vengeance, found at Rheneia, or the Prayer of Jacob (PGM XXIIb:1–26) cannot be distinguished from spells, and Rabbinic literature is full of evidence for magical practices.[5] Even taboo-breaking rituals using urine and menstrual blood are not unknown (Josephus, Jewish War 7:180–185, cf.

Apollonius Rhodius, Argonautics 3:845–866). Revulsion and disgust are important elements in many magical rituals, expressing a break from "normality" by sheer will power; at least, this interpretation is given by modern practitioners of similar rituals.

Magic destined to harm is known e.g. from 3rd-century BCE Hellenistic Maresha (Tell Sandaḥanna), where 16 small statuettes in human form bound in chains of lead, iron or bronze have been found that certainly have a magic intention (but also demons can be "bound" or "sealed"). In Caesarea Maritima, leaden curse tablets (defixions) are known from the Roman period, some meant to harm competing charioteers in sport events. For court magicians, Greek *magos* is used in Greek versions of Dan 2:2. 10 LXX; 1:20; 2:2. 10. 27; 4:4 Ps.-Theodotion, translating Hebrew 'aśāf. Novelistic tales about magic, demons, angels abound, as in the early Hellenistic-Jewish (or late Persian) tale of Tobit, where folk medicine also has an important part, or in the later Graeco-Jewish novel about the sorcerors Jannes and Jambres, all of which were also read by Christians.

In Second Temple Jewish literature, magic can be explained as an evil art revealed by demons. In the Enoch tradition (1 Enoch 6–36, 3rd–2nd century BCE), the Sons of God, appointed as "watchers" over mankind, start consorting with human women (begetting "giants") and teach them weaponry, idolatry, divination, astrology, hate-inducing charms, cosmetics and other questionable arts, and also magic (as the art of using roots). They are deprived of their power and imprisoned in hidden places in the earth, and their offspring with human women are killed in the deluge (or are somehow connected to demons), but the evil arts they have revealed stay with humanity. Evil spirits are children of angels and women (1 Enoch 15:8); later Rabbinic stories can e.g. speak about demons coming from male sperm ejaculated outside a female body (and thus "useless"). Demons in such cases are uncontrolled, unrestrained powers that eventually will do damage to men. In a more general sense, their mission is to induce humans to sin, and particularly to be idolatrous. Such stories were known to the Church also (the Epistle of Jude in the NT cites 1 Enoch, and Tertullian, Clement of Alexandria and Lactance share the "watchers mythology"), though their impact on later Christians was rather limited, and theologians preferred other explanations for evil. The story line of Gen 6:1–4 was transferred to purely human actants, as by Augustine. Still, the idea magic is some kind of knowledge gleaned from demons (and thus of dubious value) also became a Christian stereotype.

In the later but still pre-Christian Testament of Ruben (5:5s.), the women themselves initiate the contact with the "watchers": this emphasizes female guilt and makes magic more of a "female art". The witch as a figure is well known in ancient Judaism. Talmudic tradition even tells about an execution of 80 witches instigated by Shimon be Shetach, a 1st-century BCE religious leader, in Ashkelon, a pagan city at the Mediterranean coast (Talmud Yerushalmi Hagiga 2, 2, 77d, and some parallel passages), in the time of Alexandra Salome (who ruled 76–67 BCE). These witches, living in a cave, had harmed their neighbours with maleficent magic. But as this tradition is rather late, and such an event is not known from any non-Jewish source, it is highly probable that the story is somehow symbolic and connected to polytheistic ritual at the Aphrodite Urania temple of Ashkelon (witches as priestesses of Ashtoreth). The Mishna (ca. 200 CE) even says: "The more possessions the more care; the more women the more witchcraft; the more bondwomen the more lewdness" (Avot 2:7 transl. Danby). The Talmud asserts a connection of women–witchcraft (Bavli Erubin

64b). Of course, being a minority religion with only limited political power, no witch persecutions on a grand scale have been possible within ancient (and medieval) Judaism. But the mentality of persecution could have developed in Judaism as well as in Christianity. Rabbi Shimon ben Yochay (later pseudepigraphic author of the cabbalistic Zohar) is reported to have said that even the best of women is full of witchcraft (Talmud Yerushalmi Qiddushin 4, 66c), and when two women sit at a crossroads facing each other surely they are involved in witchcraft (Talmud Bavli Pesachim 111a). The obvious misogyny and fear of witchcraft of such passages, however, is not shared by other Jewish writings, such as Josephus, wisdom literature, the Qumran texts or other Rabbinic sources. Obviously such texts do not describe social reality as such, but illustrate aspects of patriarchal imaginations of the female as the dangerous other, taking up motifs from folk magic.

Jews in pagan texts are often imagined as sorcerers (Pliny, Natural history 30:11; Juvenal satires 3:13; 6:542–547; Pompeius Trogus 36:2, 8–11; Strabon 16:2; Lucian, Tragodopodagra 173s.; cf. also the Qumran text 4QOrNab), as are other ethnic groups from an outsider perspective.[6] Christian physicians still use Jewish magic (as the charm against the gout in Alexander Trallianus, Therapeutics 12 Puschmann 2:583). Moses also for pagan writers is the magician par excellence. The Council of Elvira (Spain, early 3rd century) even forbids Christian landowners to ask Jewish magicians for magical blessings of their crops and fields, so this may have been a common practice (can. Eliberat. 49). Talmud Babli Taanith 24b tells a story about King Shapur II testing (by advice of his mother) whether Jews can be used as rain charmers. Stories about Jewish sorcerers are a common element in Christian narratives and historiography as well.

Josephus, our most important source for 1st-century CE Judaism, quite rationalistic in his attitude, never uses "magic" to explain disasters and gives scant attention to prohibitions of magic (Jewish Antiquities 4:279). He uses words like *goes* ("sorcerer, charlatan") in his defamation of prophetic and pseudo-messianic figures, however (Jewish War 2:261. 264; 4:85; 5:317; Jewish Antiquities 20:97. 161. 167. 188; vita 40). During the Jewish war, in which he initially took part as a Jewish general, he saved two Jewish nobles from an accusation of using magic in favour of the Roman side (vita 113. 149–153). We find a more ambivalent attitude towards magic in the Jewish religious philosopher Philo of Alexandria, a contemporary of Jesus. Magic is an art connected to the forces of nature, illuminating its hidden aspects. It is rooted in researching nature, meditation and initiation. As such, magic is a royal art, practiced e.g. by the Persian kings initiated into its mysteries. On the other side, there is a vile evil-doing art practiced by slaves, women and itinerant quacks, dealing in purifications, spells and charms, changing love to hate and hate to love, and often resulting in disaster. Sorcerers are to be executed immediately. Obviously for Philo, both sides of magic have little in common and have to be strictly distinguished.[7]

The main symbolic figure of Jewish magic is King Solomon. Already Josephus (Jewish Antiquities 8: 45–40) tells about a Jewish exorcist Eleazar using a magical ring and spells allegedly written by Solomon. The exemplary sage (cf. 1 Kgs 5:9–15 or the Book of Wisdom, particularly 7:17–21) in the magical tradition is turned into a magical king. His questionable character (tolerating idolatry and possessing a large harem) may even have helped in this development, but most of all his famous wisdom allowed for ascribing to him all kind of occult and demonological knowledge.

Already Origen, in Commentary on Matthew 26:63, knows books attributed to Solomon containing spells and invocations of demons. The "Testament of Solomon" (4th century, but with older traditions) is no grimoire, but a kind of demonological handbook framed by a narrative on Solomon. Its main interest is medical: certain demons cause certain diseases, and it is useful to know these connections.

The Dead Sea scrolls, usually ascribed to an Essene community, additionally contain many Biblical and Para-Biblical texts as well as examples of exorcisms, brontologia, physiognomic texts, oaths and others (4Q186; 4Q561; 4Q318 u.a.). In 4Q510–511 are apotropaic songs of a "wise man" against evil spirits, 5Q14 ritual curses; 4Q560 may be a magical protection of a pregnant woman, etc. These were obviously not seen as illegitimate magic. They also have a strong interest in angelology and demonology. The prohibition of magic in Hebrew Bible texts of course was well known (11Q19 col. LX, 16–21). The most important sources for Jewish magic in late antiquity are apotropaic magical bowls, inscribed on the inside (more rarely also on the outside) and put into the corners of the house and below thresholds as places symbolic of inside–outside borderlines. Many hundreds such bowls from the area of Northern Iraq, Eastern Syria and Western Iran have been published (though only a few from controlled archaeological diggings) and can be dated mostly to the 4th–8th century; even more are unpublished. Written in different Aramaic dialects (later also in Arabic) by Jews, Mandaeans and perhaps Manichaeans, i.e. religious minorities, they seem to have been bought also by Christians and Zoroastrians.[8] Highly syncretist, they combine Hebrew Bible, later Jewish and clearly pagan invocations and apotropaic prayers. Jewish curse texts are also not rare. Such specimens of practical magic will have served personal coping with strokes of fate, disease, bad luck, theft and other invasions of the private sphere, and with what was perceived as maleficent witchcraft.

Only a few remarks are possible here on Rabbinical Judaism with its immense corpora of collected haggadic and halachic tradition. It has become increasingly clear in recent years that this corpus still cannot be identified with the totality of late antique Judaism, however, but with only some of its major elements.[9] In a manner comparable to the Church fathers, the Rabbis struggle to some degree against both popular and professional magic, whereas some of their own practices in a wider sense clearly can be interpreted as magic as well. A special mythology is derived from the arcane nature of the divine name, the knowledge of which is seen as the most desirable magical mystery (cf. already 1 Enoch 69: 14; Jubilees 36: 7; Mishna Taanith 3: 8). The miracle-working rabbi is not just a healer: his curse can be fatal. A particular stratum of stories is woven around some 1st-century BCE–1st century CE figures, often called "Galilean charismatics". They work by miraculous powers of prayer, both for healing and rain making, and may be of some importance as comparative data to understand the historical Jesus. Ḥanina ben Dosa, Ḥoni the Circle-drawer, Abba Hilkijah and others must have been well-known names in 1st-century Palestine (Ḥoni is also mentioned by Josephus), living in a popular sphere where magic and religion, prayer and inherent healing power cannot be clearly separated. These are not "sorcerers", but have been described as "men of deed" (miracle men). Comparable to Jesus, they lived in personal poverty and were popular primarily as healers, but also known for a special relation to God describable in a son–father imagery. A strange trait also important in early Christianity is their immunity against snake and scorpion bites (cf. Mk 16:17s.; Lk 10:19; Acts 28:1–6).

Rabbinic Judaism tries hard to minimize the place of magical practices, e.g. by forbidding to use Thora verses in healing rituals (Mishna Sanhedrin 10:1; cf. 6:6; 7:7.10). The gemara to these passages argues with much detail against diviners, necromancers, ventriloquists and similar popular professions. The most elaborate discussion of questions of limitation and definition of magic in Rabbinic literature is to be found in Talmud Babli Sanhedrin 65a–66a. 67a–68a, where it is also distinguished from show illusionism posing as magic. A judge has to have a solid knowledge of magic to be able to judge respective cases. We can even reconstruct from different sources a full Jewish Book of magic, the late antique Sefer haRazim "Book of mysteries";[10] it is difficult to date the text more clearly, as it existed in quite different versions. Magic here often has obviously ill intent: spells and practices are given to send bad dreams, overthrow a wall or make a ship capsize, though apotropaic magic is much more common, protecting e.g. a woman in childbirth. In a few cases, evocation formulas even use pagan names of deities such as Helios, Hermes or Aphrodite. The magician may have seen these as minor supernatural beings not competing with monotheism. The compiler of the spell book may even not have regarded his compilations as transgressing the boundaries of traditional religions, as his spells may have been used against "witchcraft".

Magic in earliest Christianity

As many other religious foundational figures (Mani, Muhammad and others), Jesus as a healer and exorcist was accused of magic by his contemporaries. He was said to be possessed (Mk 3:20–30 par.; Joh 8:48; cf. Lk 7:33 par. about John the Baptist) or even in league with the devil (Lk 11:14–23 par. from the Sayings Source Q). Jesus interestingly takes this suspicion up with arguments against it: if the devil himself were active in his exorcisms, the realm of evil could not endure, as it would be divided against itself. The devil's realm in Jesus' exorcisms is envisaged as a structured unity, more of a military army than a kingdom, like locusts invading a country. Healing miracles using saliva (Mk 7:31–37; 8:22–26; Joh 9:1–12) or transferring health by laying on of hands (Mk 1:31; 5:24–34 a.o.; cf. Philostratus v. Apoll. 3:39; 4:45; Sueton, Vespasian 7; Tacitus, Histories 4:81 a.o.) will have reminded ancient spectators of magic. Even more, Jesus' short Aramaic command words in a Greek-speaking world might have been misunderstood as magical spells. Such similarities to magic already in the gospels are pushed back, as when Matthew leaves out the saliva in the healing stories. And already Mark, the oldest gospel, emphasizes that Jesus' command words (Mk 5:41 Talitha kum; 7:34 Ephatha) can be translated and so are no Voces magicae.

The Greek gospel obviously wants to put some distance between Jesus and the image of the magus. Onomata barbarica, strange-sounding formulas in exorcisms and healing miracles are otherwise quite common (cf. Lucian, Philopseudes 9:31; 34, 15; Alexander Abon. 13; and as Christian texts see e.g. Jerome, Life of Hilarion 18; Acta Philippi 132).[11] The pericope about Pharisees and scribes asking Jesus for a sign from heaven (Mk 8:11–13 par.; Lk 11:16. 29–32 par. from Q) also has to be understood in the context of distinguishing Jesus from magic. Signs on earth (miracles) are ambivalent: they may be demon work. A sign in heaven, where demons cannot reach, would be unambiguous. The tradition knows different answers of Jesus (which may go back to different occasions): the flat denial of the request, or the "sign of Jonah" (preaching; later understood as hinting at the resurrection). Such passages try to put some distance between Jesus and popular magicians that we know well from Greek, Jewish and Egyptian sources. He was far from alone in this: even success-ful physicians now and then had to struggle against suspicions of being magicians, as we hear even about the quite rationalist Galen. The exorcisms and healing miracles of Jesus have to be understood in the reference frame of his preaching about the coming Kingdom of God (Lk 11:20). He does not use spells, stones, plants or other magical means, and gives no attention to special times or circumstances (contrast Josephus, Jewish War 7:180–185). Jesus was indeed no magician, but from an out-sider perspective could be mistaken for a wizard. The precise meaning of faith in this context is not easy to see ("your faith has saved you", in the sense of "has healed you", Mk 5:34, and parallel passages; cf. Mk 5:36 "just believe" and the words on having faith like a grain of mustard seed). Faith in these tales and sayings is not just belief in the miracle-working power of the healer, but it also does not have the soteriological precision it has in Paul's letters. Jesus clearly wants to state miracles depend not just on a magical *dynamis* ("power", Mk 5:30) of the healer but also on something else. The gospels on the other side can use terminology known from loosening spells for therapeutic events (Mk 7:35; Lk 13:16; cf. Busch 41–44). But there is no wider recep-tion of any technical terminology of magic in the gospels. Jesus successfully cursing a fig-tree (Mk 11:12–14. 20–25) certainly is meant to prove somehow the power of faith. The well-known word of faith "moving mountains" (Mk 11:22–24; Mt 21:21–22; cf. 1 Cor 13:2) has some affinity to imaginations of power as stated in magical texts.

The healing story Mk 5:23–34 (healing from touching Jesus' clothes) at least comes close to a kind of magical automatism. The trust of the bleeding woman in the magical power of the miracle-worker (*dynamis* v. 30) is changed into something more personal by Jesus forcing her to a direct encounter. Peter Busch has made the basic ambivalences of many religious phenomena visible by confronting "magical" and "non-magical" interpretations of may passages.[12] In some cases, the affinities are obvious: the temptation of Jesus (Lk 4:1–13; Mt 4:1–11 from Q) has reminded readers of the "flying magician" as known from the later Simon Magus legend (Acta Petri Vercell. 7–29; Pseudo-clementine recognitions 2–3; homilies 3:16–19 and many other texts).

Interpreting Jesus as a sorcerer was particularly attractive for both pagans and Jews (e.g. Talmud Babli Sanhedrin 43a), as it allowed miraculous happenings around Jesus to be accepted without conceding any soteriological interpretation. Christian authors like Justin (First Apology 30:1; Dialogue with Trypho 69:7; 108:2), Origen (Against Celsus 1:6. 38), Tertullian (Apology 21:17) Athenagoras (On the incarna-tion) and many others had to defend Jesus against this accusation. In pagan circles, such an image of Jesus might otherwise be the outcome of a fascination with the miracle worker, and could easily go together with stereotypes such as having learned magic in Egypt. Scholars like Morton Smith (1915–1991) have tried to understand the Jesus tradition as deeply involved in magical ideas and practices. This has not convinced the majority of experts, though there certainly are similarities e.g. between the gospels and the Life of Apollonius of Tyana (Philostrat, early 3rd century). The names of Jesus and even of the apostles could be used as "power words" by non-Chris-tian exorcists (Mk 9:38s.; Acts 19:13s.), as we know also from magical papyri (PGM IV, 1230s. 3020s.; XII, 190. 390; XXIIb, 18; CXXIII, 50), perhaps from Jewish tradition.

This reminds us of late antique Jewish magical bowls using names of miracle workers like Chanina ben Dosa and Joshua ben Perachja.

Paul never shows any deeper concern about magic; explicit allusions such as perhaps Gal 5:29 are rare. He is convinced, however, of Christ's eschatological victory over all astral and demonic forces and powers of destiny (1 Cor 15:25; Phil 2:11; cf. also post-Pauline passages as Col 2:15; Eph 1:20s. etc.). The excommunication and "deliverance unto Satan" (1 Cor 5:3–5) has some affinities to curse rituals (cf. 1 Tim 1:20 and as Jewish models cf. Dtn 27:11–26; 1QS II 4–18 a.o.). Cursing as causing miraculous events is well known in the New Testament, and even Jesus is known to have used curses, though not against human beings (Mk 11:12–14. 20–25; cf. Acts 13: 9–11 and contrast Lk 9:52–56 with important textual variants). Many other practices may have some affinity to syncretist magic, e.g. the veneration of angels and the elements (stoicheia) in Colossae (Col 2:18–20). Lists of supernatural charisms (1 Cor 12:4–11; Rom 12:4–8; Ps.-Mk 16:17s.) can be read as an antithesis to lists of the supernatural effects of magical rituals. (Even lists of famous sorcerers, well known in pagan literature, can be reproduced by Christian writers: cf. Tertullian, On the soul 57:1; Arnobius, Against the nations 1:52 with Pliny, Natural History 30:2–11; Apuleius, Apology 90).

We get a much more vivid, detailed and even humorous depiction of the gospel in confrontation with popular magic, divination and other pagan practices from the Acts of the Apostles. Besides the Simon Magus episode (8:4–25) we may think of stories about Paul cursing the professional magician Barjesus Elymas (13:4–12; perhaps a Nabataean, cf. Arab 'alīm "having (secret) knowledge"), or Paul being exposed and almost stalked by a woman possessed by a snake spirit (*pneuma python*) and speaking as a kind of ventriloquist (Acts 16:16–18), or we may think of legends telling about the healing effect of the shadow of Peter and the handkerchiefs or aprons that had touched Paul's skin and were carried away to the sick, so that their diseases left them (Acts 5:15; 19:12). A Jewish guild of exorcists seems to have used the fancy name of "seven sons of Skeuas" (19:13–17), who is said to have been a high priest, but must be a fictitious figure (lat. Scaeva); the name may have been an advertising gimmick, or the group used the stereotype about Jews as magicians (cf. the "Hebrew exorcism" PGM IV:3007–3027).[13] Glossolalia, described in Acts 2 and 1Cor 14, has sometimes been compared to magical spells, but this is not convincing. It has no "magical effect", though it can be interpreted as an Angelic tongue (1 Cor 13:2, similar to magical words interpreted as the gods' language).[14] The miraculous opening of a door (Acts 12:7) is also a common motif in tales of magic (Philostratus, Life of Apollonius 8:5; Jamblichus, Life of Pythagoras 217; Arnobius, Against the nations 1:43; PGM XIII:327. 1065; IV:447; XII:161 etc.), though of course in Acts it is an angel who does the miracle. A small episode of wide influence is the famous burning of magical books by Christians in Ephesus (19:19), who in their former pagan days had spent 50,000 silver denarii on these books. This financial value seems high, but we hear often about the large amounts of money magicians and exorcists charged their customers (cf. e.g. Tacitus, Annals 16:31; Lucian, Philopseudes 16). This episode became a main legitimation of later censures against magical literature (e.g. Zacharias Scholasticus, Life of Severinus of Antioch 63. 65. 69s.). The author of Acts playfully alludes to the famous Ephesia Grammata, though these are not books, but actually a special magical formula well known in antiquity, connecting Ephesus with magic.

"Make no potions, keep away from magical books", says the late-Hellenistic Jew-ish-Greek didactic poet Ps.-Phokylides 149 (tr. P. W. van der Horst). The combination of poison-making and sorcery is common in both Jewish and Christian literature (cf. Testamentum Ruben 4:9; Sibylline Oracles 1:96; Ascension of Isaiah 2:5; Philon, de spec. leg. 3:92–103; Didache 2:2; Barn. 20:1; Acts of Paul 4:35 and many other passages). For Christians, the burning of magical books will have been a liberating experience, a getting free from the supremacy of fate and demonic powers. The possession of magical books in Roman jurisprudence is first clearly prohibited in the late 3rd century CE, in a context with severe threats against magic (Ps.-Paulus, Sentences 5:29 (23), 17s.), though this can only to a very small degree have been actual legal practice. The magical papyri show no fear of persecution by the state. Fear of witchcraft in a more general sense is well documented for Roman imperial society, however. An inscriptional oracle of Apollon e.g. dated 165 CE speaks about the apotropaic powers of the Ephesine Artemis, which is declared as overcoming the workings of evil sorcerous art using magical dolls with malefic intent.[15] The NT on the other side does not speak about wide-spread sorcery fears (though we may cf. Apc 18:23 where pharmakeia is "witchcraft"). But the scenario mission vs. magic proves "magic" to have been a competitive factor in the mutual rivalry between religions, an aspect of primary importance for early Christian missionary history.

This scenario, only hinted at in canonical Acts, is much elaborated on in the apocryphal Acts of the Apostles and pseudo-Clementine literature ("Recognitions", "Homilies"), Christian religious novels (2nd–5th century CE) telling the life and death of the apostles. Apostles preaching the gospel and magicians looking for cus-tomers in these narratives relate to the same clientele, and legitimizing miracles compete on a quite basic level. The problem of how to distinguish between divine miracles and magic is present, but not discussed in much depth. The Christian mir-acle very simply is more effective than any work of magic. Popular subjects such as love magic or invocations against serpents are mentioned a number of times, and the Acts of Andrew and Matthew 1 even know a "zombification potion" used by blood-drinking cannibals turning men into will-less slaves. It is unclear whether such fairy tale-like motifs were actually believed in: the entertainment aspect of these reli-gious novels must not be underrated. Divination using the corpse of a child killed by Simon Magus is put into effect not by the soul of the boy but by a demon: pagan inter-pretation of magical practice is changed into a Christian reference frame (ps.-clem-entine Recognitions 2:13–15; 3:44s.; homilies 2:25–30). The attempt by Simon Magus to fly through magic, thwarted by Peter praying and causing Simon's downfall, is perhaps the most famous legend on magic in Christian history. It became the basic iconographic representation of the competition between magic and the Christian mission. The interpretation of Simon Magus as a magician trying to fly has also been read as a caricature on Paul's claim to have visited Paradise in the Third Heaven during an ecstatic experience, perhaps even corporeally (2 Cor 12:1–5), though this seems unlikely. He later becomes a central figure in ideas about the history of magic (as in Ireland as the teacher of the Druid magician Mog Ruith).

Ideas about malefic magic and love magic may be echoed in passages such as Gal 5:20; Apc 9:21; 18:23; 21:8, but rituals of "forcing the Gods", defixions (curse tablets, a wide-spread practice) and similar arts are never in view, as divinatory practices like physiognomics (known in Qumran) and astrology o do not occur (but astral symbolism is frequent). We never get a detailed description of magical rituals, as in many ancient epics and novels. Apc in its catalogues of vices assigns sorcery to demonic evil (9:21; 18:23; 21:8; 22:15). Some aspects of Apc have nevertheless a (perhaps antithetical) affinity to revelatory magic, stressing e.g. the quickness of Jesus' parousia (Apc 2:16; 3:11; 22:7.12.20), which has been interpreted as a counter phenomenon to the very typical impatience in magical spells ("now, now; quick, quick" PGM III:123s.; IV:1245. 1593. 1924. 2037 cf. I:89s.; IV:236s.; VI:14; VII:248s. 329/31). The Pastor Hermae (mand. 11), a 2nd-century writing from Rome, strongly criticizes "prophets", the behaviour of which has similarity to a professional diviner, speaking in private for payment, not freely in the congregation. The worlds of magic, divination and Christian charismatics can clearly converge. An attitude of derision and strong opposition about magic is also not rare in pagan writings: Lucian, a contemporary of Hermas, makes fun of a sorcerer promising to make other men give to his customers everything they might desire (Demonax 23). Augustine wants to try experimentally the supernatural powers of a mandrake, and complains about the high price he has to pay for the root (Against Faustus 22:56). Amulets and talismans have been in common Christian use, though often criticized by theological writers. Arnobius, writing in the early 4th century, takes it as a matter of course that Christians bought apotropaic small tablets (laminae) produced by Marsians and Psyllians (Against the nations 2:32), and John Chrysostom complains about the wide-spread use of little crosses born as amulets (Homilies in Matthew 54:4). Texts such as the Our Father, Psalm 90 and John 1:1–18 are well-documented as amulets, as are the beginnings of the gospels. The extremely small papyrus P 78 (P. Oxyrhynchus XXXIV 2684) has the text of Jude probably as an amulet, etc. Early sacramental piety calls the Eucharist a "medicine bringing immortality" (Ignatius, Letter to the Ephesians 20:2), or simply "medicine" (Acts of Thomas 135), perhaps using a fairy tale motif. Other ritual acts can attract magical symbolism as well, such as the laying on of hands in curing diseases which can be accompanied by anointing with oil (cf. Mk. 6:13, not taken over by Matthew and Luke who may have found the ritual problematic, and perhaps saw oil only as medicine as in Luke 10:34; see also James 5:14).

Minority groups such as Christian gnostics could easily be suspected of practising magic, and this became a central reproach in haeresiological literature. But non-Christian authors also saw an affinity between gnostic esotericism, ascent mysticism and magical rituals destined to convey revelation experiences. Plotin, in his tract against the gnostics (Enneads II, 9), enumerates practices as invocations of heavenly entities, spells imitating animal shouts (well known from Graeco-Egyptian magic) and exorcisms, and he is aware of the inner relation between experiences of powerlessness in real life and fantasies of omnipotence, supernatural knowledge and transcending the human condition. A feeling of superiority connects magic (cf. PGM XXXIV) and gnosticism. A fine observer such as Origen takes it for granted that parts of gnostic symbolism and ritual language are directly derived from magic (Against Celsus 6:31s. 38; 7:40, where he speaks about Ophites). The accusation of magic is also used against gnostics by Basilides, Karpocrates and particularly Marcus Magus, a Valentinian. Marcus (according to Irenaus, Against the heresies 1:13, 1–16, 2; Hippolytus, Refutation 6:39, 1–54, 2 and others) used illusionist techniques in the Eucharist sacrament to counterfeit a change of water to wine. He also was said to use love magic and a familiar spirit (a parhedros).[16]

As Jesus was accused of magic, so his followers quite regularly during persecutions both in the Roman and in the Sasanian (Persian) empire were suspected of using sorcery, e.g. to avoid a lawsuit (Acts of Perpetua and Felicitas 16; Lactance, Divine Institutes 5:3, 19; Ps.-clementine recognitions 1:58, 1; Origen, Against Celsus 7:69 and very often). The apocryphal Acts of Thecla 15 (part of the larger Acts of Paul, a late 2nd-century Christian novel) know about allegations against Paul having "bewitched" Thekla with his words. It is essentially the same kind of suspicion which up to recent times has been used by majority religions against competing new religious movements (with labels such as "Satanism", "brain washing", "mesmerism"). Tertullian defends Christianity against a general suspicion of witchcraft (ad. uxor. 2, 4, 5), an accusation still used by Iulian Apostata (Socrates, Church history 3:13, 11, 12).

Mt 2 is the only NT text that speaks about magicians from the East (magoi apo anatolon) in a surprisingly positive sense. The number and names of these wise men drawn to the new-born messiah varies in the old church; Justin (Dialogue with Trypho 44:3) interprets them as coming from Arabia. They represent the messianic hope as something also known to non-Jewish humanity. The term magoi here may simply mean astrologers: Babylonia was famed for its astrological expertise, and "Chaldeans" had come to mean simply astrologers (e.g. Diodor. Sicul. 2:30, 4s.). According to Pseudo-Aristotle, a Syrian magos travelling in Athens predicted to Socrates his violent death (Diogen. Laert. 2:45), and a connection between Iranian magicians star lore and divination for certain nations is already known to Herodotus (7:37, 2s.). It may be no coincidence, however, that magoi – originally Median priests, and later adherents of Zoroastrianism – are visiting the messianic child, people who have strongly developed messianic hopes. In this case, the pre-Matthean Jewish-Christian legend in Mt 2 may choose "magoi" as representatives of non-Jewish messianic hopes with some deliberation, and indeed quite appropriately. The ancient church with Mt 2 in view found it difficult to completely disclaim astrology, though it generally discredited divination. Writers like Tertullian (Against idolatry 9:5) or John Chrysostom (Sermons in Matthew 6:1) argue against people using Mt 2 to legitimize astrology, and Augustine (in his younger days an adherent of astrology) also speaks out against those who, quoting Mt 2, would try to defend astrology's essential fatalism (Sermon 20:3s.). More common is the idea that magic and divination have been bereft of their power by the birth of Christ. Ignatius, Letter to the Ephesians 19:3 (ca. 110 CE), even can say that all magic was vanquished and all bondage of evil comes to naught by the messianic birth and its accompanying star of Bethlehem (cf. Ignatius, Letter to Polycarp 5:1). Origen (Against Celsus 1:60) says a century later, the magicians from the East had started their voyage because they realized their magic had lost all power. This assurance of having overcome magic was lost in later theology, and aspects of witchcraft fears became common ground to Christians and non-Christians. "There is indeed nobody who does not fear to be spell-bound by imprecations", Pliny the Elder had written (Natural history 28:19; cf. Apuleius, Metamorphoses 2:20).

The ancient church in successive steps took over images of magic and witchcraft that had developed in Greek and Roman literature, and it participated also in the increasing criminalization of magic in late antique legal discourses and 4th-century court proceedings. This heritage came to be of vital importance for medieval and early modern images and theories of witchcraft, much more than e.g. Germanic, Celtic or Slavic polytheist pagan ideas.

Notes

1 Brice C. Jones, *New Testament Texts on Greek Amulets From Late Antiquity* (London: Bloomsburg T&T Clark, 2016).
2 Marco Frenschkowski, *Magie im Antiken Christentum. Eine Studie zur Alten Kirche und ihrem Umfeld* (Stuttgart: Hiersemann, 2016), 243.
3 Andrew T. Wilburg, *Materia Magica: The Archaeology of Magic in Roman Egypt, Cyprus, and Spain* (Ann Arbor: University of Michigan Press, 2012).
4 Rüdiger Schmitt, *Magie im Alten Testament* (Münster: Ugarit-Verlag, 2004), 395.
5 Pieter Willem van der Horst/J.H.H. Newman, *Early Jewish Prayers in Greek* (Berlin: de Gruyter, 2008), 135–143, 215–246.
6 Frenschkowski, *Magie*, 49–54, 171–174.
7 Frenschkowski, *Magie*, 175–177.
8 Gideon Bohak, *Ancient Jewish Magic: A History* (Cambridge: Cambridge University Press, 2008).
9 Cf. Bohak; Daniel Sperber, "Some Rabbinic Themes in Magical Papyri," *Journal for the Study of Judaism in the Persian, Hellenistic and Roman Period* 16 (1985): 93–103; Guiseppe Veltri, *Magie und Halakha* (Tübingen: Mohr, 1997).
10 *Sefer ha-Razim I und II – Das Buch der Geheimnisse I und II*, edited by Bill Rebiger/Peter Schäfer (Tübingen: Mohr Siebeck, 2012).
11 Marco Frenschkowski, "Zauberworte. Linguistische und sprachpsychologische Beobachtungen zur spätantiken griechischen und römischen Magie," *Annali di Storia dell' Esegesi* 24.2 (2007): 323–366.
12 Peter Busch, *Magie in neutestamentlicher Zeit* (Göttingen: Vandenhoeck & Ruprecht, 2006), 98–103.
13 Frenschkowski, *Magie*, 171–174.
14 Frenschkowski, "Zauberworte," 354–360.
15 James R. Harrison, "Artemis Triumphs over a Sorcerer's Evil Art," *New Documents Illustrating Early Christianity* 10 (2012): 37–47.
16 For more details on gnosis and magic cf. Frenschkowski, *Magie*, 259–272.

Bibliography (selection)

Bohak, Gideon, *Ancient Jewish Magic: A History*. Cambridge: Cambridge University Press, 2008.
Busch, Peter, *Magie in neutestamentlicher Zeit*. Göttingen: Vandenhoeck & Ruprecht, 2006.
Frenschkowski, Marco, "Zauberworte. Linguistische und sprachpsychologische Beobachtungen zur spätantiken griechischen und römischen Magie." *Annali di Storia dell' Esegesi* 24:2 (2007): 323–366.
Frenschkowski, Marco, *Magie im antiken Christentum. Eine Studie zur Alten Kirche und ihrem Umfeld*. Stuttgart: Hiersemann, 2016.
Klutz, Todd (ed.), *Magic in the Biblical World: From the Rod of Aaron to the Ring of Salomon*. London: T&T Clark, 2003.
Luck, Georges, "The Survival of Ancient Magic in the Early Church." *MHNH. Revista Internacional de Investigación sobre Magia y Astrología Antiguas* 3 (2003): 29–54.
Noege, Scott et al. (eds.), *Prayer, Magic, and the Stars in the Ancient and Late Antique World*. University Park, PA: Pennsylvania State University Press, 2003.
Schmitt, Rüdiger, *Magie im Alten Testament*. Münster: Ugarit-Verlag, 2004.

3

DEMONS AND WITCHCRAFT IN THE EARLY CHURCH[1]

Naomi Janowitz

Introduction

No uniquely Christian theory of daimons existed in the ancient world.[2] Since "Christianity was a development of pagan monotheism," pagan articulations of the roles of daimons were taken up and used by Christians as needed.[3] Stretching back to the pre-Socratics, a daimon was a jigsaw piece that had to fit in with other pieces to make a complete cosmology (one type of eternal, non-human power among many). In the pre-Christian world, "daimon" was interchangeable with "god" or, more commonly,[4] with lower-level divine figures that mediated between humans and the higher gods."[5] Their two-sided nature as trouble-makers and helpful guides made them problematic for humans. Cultic activity kept them in check, meeting most of their needs for recognition and sustenance. Arthur Darby Nock's comment about deities was true of daimons as well: "paganism had plenty of deities who were to be feared if you did not take the right steps to appease them, but paganism knew the right steps to take." More specifically, demons, as Augustine outlined, are "affronted at dishonor done to them, placated by gifts, pleased by being honored, delighted by various rituals and angered if any point of ritual is omitted" (CG 8.16). They depended on the smoke and blood from animal sacrifices to remain in the air closest to the earth, their bodies imagined as mixtures of fire and air.[6]

Despite the strategic claims made by ancients and moderns, daimons did not represent an inherent challenge to monotheism (just as angels do not).[7] As part of the rise of the creator god from Plato on, a sort of "creeping monotheism" demanded new demons. In Fraser's recent study of Neo-Platonic demon discourse, the inherent growth of a stricter sense of monotheism explains the negative shift towards demons and embodiment in general. The seemingly inevitable push towards monotheism also resulted in the first clear statements about creatio ex nihilo. Where that doctrine emerges, demons are likely to find themselves implicated in discussions of evil.[8]

Demons played small but central roles in daily life, whether in abstract theology or in attempts to negotiate the ups and downs of human existence. These figures jostled with other late antique characters such as good and bad (fallen) angels, archangels, principalities, and rulers of the world. Personality traits could be swapped around among these figures as well as with malevolent and helpful humans. Peter Brown noted a tendency in Christian literature to describe "the somewhat faceless daemones of pagan beliefs" with specific terms that might have been used for sorcerers in an earlier age.[9]

Like the corpse in a murder mystery, daimons functioned in ancient narratives as trip-wires for plot development. Early Christian authors made good use of these figures to add intrigue to their writing, sometimes a shadowy figure and sometimes a very abstract claim about ontology and cosmology. These characters permit a fine delineation of etiquette about divine/human interactions by focusing attention on distinct flavors of mixed human/divine motivation and agency. Possession by a daimon changes the status of the person, who becomes a sort of amalgam of the daimon/spirit and the human body, and controlling them demanded very specific techniques to suit the job.

According to one line of modern analysis, as the history of early Christianity unfolded in the 2nd–6th centuries, ambivalently good and bad "daimons" are rethought as generally evil "demons." But Christianization of daimons, like that of the Roman Empire, was never a simple theological conversion from good to bad. Tracing the vicissitudes of daimons/demons demands a broad view. Since "daimon" is not a substantive category but instead a relational one with mobile boundaries, if there is any stability to the mobile boundaries, it was a freelance type of superhuman agency that helped delineate other types of agency by contrast.[10] In general, demons helped demarcate the possibilities of human/divine engagement on an ad hoc basis, possibilities that needed to be clarified so that humans put employ them.

Making any sense of reshuffled daimons/demons leads us to keep several themes in mind as we review specific examples of early Christian demon discourse. First is the increasing alliance of Christians with or over institutions of political control. Daimons changed because Christians did, or perhaps better put, because Christianity itself turned out to be protean. With a Christian emperor leading an army, demons were most likely to be working for other earthly authorities. Second is the now-familiar rise of the Holy Man as a demon-specialist.[11] The Holy Man rose to prominence domesticating daimons. The focus on his special power reverses the Gospel image of Jesus disseminating power over demons. Though some Christian authorities claimed divine-right over daimons, they did not always have the earthly power to corner the market on right for demon management. And third, the association of inappropriate ideas about daimons with inadequate theology, or with heresy. Within the context of a larger reclassification of embodied divinity (how the deity manifests in the world), the fluid meaning of daimons was increasingly fixed by association with bad angels. Sloppy ideas about demons were also under attack since they were a means of disqualifying alternate "heretical" theologies (overly vague or too-dualistic sounding monotheism).

Demon discourse, 2nd–6th century

Demons were more than simple pests because they worked for the arch-enemy Satan, a favorite theme from Jewish texts as well. When Paul outlines "salvation (soteria)," he means salvation from the world, not in the world. A demon could thwart his timely arrival in Thessalonika, one small sign of their power. How actively Christ's followers should try to burn down the world, or whether it was better to leave it to the deity's forces, was debatable.[12] For Paul, the Eucharist had power against death and demons, a point that would be debated at length in later formulations of central Christian rites (Eucharist, baptism).[13] Satan (dragon) controls the Roman Empire, along with other nations, for the author of Revelation (Rev 12:10), while the Gospel of John calls Satan "the prince of the world (John 18:36)."

The Synoptic Gospels present Jesus as a daimon-expelling exorcist. In the Gospel of Mark, daimons recognize Jesus as another extra-ordinary being. Demons clarify for the reader the connection between Jesus and the deity. As Fraser explains, "it is the ritualist's identification with the High God that legitimates his control over daimonic and infernal agencies" (Fraser 2009, 148).[14] Luke recounts Jesus giving his disciples authority over daimons and then sending them out both proclaim the "kingdom of God" and heal (Luke 9).

While the Gospel portrayal of daimons cast a long shadow, later theological treatises, lives of saints, and stories told for entertainment used daimons as finely articulated character actors who played roles based on easy recognition.[15] For 2nd-century Christian authors, demons continued to persecute Christians individually and as a social group. Martyrdom of Christians by daimon-controlled functionaries of the Roman Empire demonstrated the power of the forces of evil against which the martyr was thought to triumph.[16] The conviction of the martyr was a vivid demonstration of what it meant to be a Christian, and any temptation to deny Christ would align the individual with evil forces in a sort of "demonization" of the human. Christians encountered this evidence sometimes in person but more often as a memorial.[17]

For Ignatius, bishop of Antioch (approx. 50–117 C.E.), the lines are sharply drawn for every Christian, who must uncompromisingly line up with Jesus against the powers of evil temporarily holding sway over the world. Satan and his daimons acted through the Roman Empire, evidence of the extent of their tentacles and the size of their power. True Christians must oppose any and all representatives of Rome with a fatal opposition that led inevitably to martyrdom.

Ignatius is Pauline in his stance against the mundane world and the government and emphasizes these points in his letters. Any attempt to make a deal with "the Prince of the world" was a betrayal of the deity, so Christians should avoid anything that looks like collaboration or involving themselves in Roman bureaucracy (*Ep. to Romans* ch. 3). Working within Roman institutions was "corruption" since, for the Christian, "when he is hated by the world, he is beloved of God" (*Ep. to Romans* ch. 3). Ignatius acted out his intense rhetoric about "the dreadful torment of the devil" with his death as a martyr on route to Rome, signifying a different type of victory over demons than simply exorcism. Given the level of demonic domination of the world, special precautions were needed. Baptismal water itself must be exorcised in order to be effective (Ignatius *Ep. to Ephesians* 18).

Christian cultic demon rites warded them off demons instead, though once again following quite closely non-Christian demon discourse that, despite Christian rhetoric, was facing new demons as well. Platonic interpreters re-worked their views about daimons as they re-evaluated traditional religious practices such as sacrifice.[18] Ancient authors could calibrate just how questionable a religious practice was by its connection with now completely suspect daimons. Demon fondness for the smoke animal sacrifices, which once had been thought to control them, became yet one more nail in the coffin of animal sacrifice.

For Justin Martyr (100–160 C.E.), the power of the evil angels was nearly overwhelming. They were led by the mighty Satan in a battle larger and more threatening than any previously known on earth. The evil minions already had control over much of the human world in their daily existence and did not show any signs of easy retreat; even if they were correct, the Christians were the minority and wielded little earthly power. In order for them to win, the world as it was known would have to radically change. The devil and his minions knew what the deity was planning for them, the consequences if they lost, so would fight until the battle ended the human world. The continued existence of the world hinged on the war with demons; if it had not been necessary to give sinners the opportunity to convert, the deity would have long since brought the sorry existence of the world to an end.

Following earlier Jewish critiques, Justin labeled the gods of nations as "demons," to which he added his own ideas that Jews were also led astray by demons.[19] Justin's history of demons extended far into the past, including one of the most famous demon examples from the ancient world, Socrates. Incorporating Socrates' daimon was a way of appending the recent history of Christianity to a long pre-history that included the entire world and not simply the history of the Jews. In the prolonged battle of human history, daimons were a permanent fixture and hidden agents.

Before Christians had their own armies, Christians could fight demons on a case-by-case basis not only via martyrdom, as he did, but also following Ignatius and others, by means of the central Christian rites. Justin offers the formula "in the name of Jesus Christ, crucified under Pontius Pilate" to drive out demons (1Apol 61, 2Apol6, Dial 30, 76, 85).

As the number of Christians grew and persecution died out, demons lost their institutional role as aides de camp to the Romans persecutors. Their roles were limited to personal, not political attacks on individual Christians as demons lost their institutional and military credentials. Now internal Christian theological fault-lines were implicated in demon debates. A "heretic" might be both too impressed with demons, thereby impugning the deity's goodness, and yet not be willing to die as a martyr. Ironically, even though acknowledging demon power was a traditional stance, it could also earn a theologian censure as a "know it all (gnostic)." These theologians erred in the intensity they attributed to evil power and were marginalized for a New-Testament literalism that no longer made sense in a world where Christians and their deity were gaining very this-worldly power.

With Tertullian (160–220 C.E.), we see a more confident face for Christian demon discourse, reflective of the move by many Christians from the periphery to the center of society. Daimons are on the run, subjected to Christian control as the tables are turned and the daimons themselves act possessed. They are forced to confess the superiority of Christianity (Apol c xxiii). Just like other parts of the natural world (iron, herbs), the demons are forces created by God and thereby limited (De Spec).

Origen (184–253 C.E.) takes the optimistic stance that all daimons will be saved. The deity created two types of rational creatures, humans and angels (First Principles 1:4–8, 2.9–10, 3.2), and fallen angels are the source of the problems of the world. While many readers might wish for a clearer explanation of the enigmatic "fall" of the angels, the point for Origen is that mapping the mysterious fall is matched by much clearer instructions for exactly how Christians reverse the process (contra Celsum I, 31).

A less apocalyptic and more personal reading of daimon-conflict is found in numerous texts about monks, including Athanasius' 4th-century *Life of Saint Anthony*.[20] For this desert father, "at the heart of his identity was struggle, resistance, and combat with the forces of evil that surrounded the ancient person." The monk was pitted against an army of daimons to test and forge his character as they "brutally attack Anthony visually, vocally, and physically, leaving him near dead." According to David Brakke, the monk is the successor to the martyr in the battle against the demons.[21]

Following tropes from Paul and the Gospels, the monks and the demons are caught in a duet of competition. In these battles, however, techniques focus on the will of the monk and the will of the demon. Demons often tempt scholars towards psychological interpretations.[22] These demons send visions of women and black boys to distract and mislead monks in stories that seem to demand psychoanalytic interpretations.[23] A reverse reading is also possible: the demon stories show how the unconscious is constructed as Christians examine what it is permissible and not permissible to think about.[24] A formulaic application of Freudian ideas about the unconscious works, since it is a rediscovery of its own genealogy. Perhaps most interesting is the extent to which these modern classifications do not work; that is, the story of demons is imagined to take place not within the human mind but between the will of the monk and the will of the demon so the product is an understanding of the elite human will and not the unconscious.

A monk engaged with his demon was like an Olympic athlete: the vast majority of people could only watch in awe. This extreme-sport level of struggle was the mark of a superior soul who had undergone the extensive training that set him apart. Top athletes did not have a corner on all competition, and many other people engaged in some way in this struggle depending on their social standing, their finances, and their imaginations. These stories tell us more about the theories used by those engaged in the fight than in what they fought. We do not find surprising revelations about demons. Instead, we are much more likely to find out shocking, disturbing, or simply new ideas about demon-wrangling technique.[25]

Far from the desert of Egypt, in Turkey the Cappadocian church fathers Gregory of Nazianzus (330–390 C.E.) and Basil (330–379 C.E.) offer a fine-tuned window onto demons, carefully outlined by Morwenna Ludlow. For both these writers, demons are a way of thinking about what Ludlow calls "personal behavior" and not the status of Jesus or the level of evil-infestation in the world. Gregory and Basil's general agreement breaks down on the very fine question of the extent to which demons will be agents of the deity's wrath, yet another version of trying of think through the problem of evil.[26]

The demons continue to occupy a "liminal" space, so they are still posed between good and evil. Here Ludlow attempts to refine the history of demons drawn by Dale Martin. He contrasts a Greek philosophical view of only-good demons with a popular image of ambivalent demons that the elites ultimately surrender to, even as Christians make the demons into entirely evil fallen angels. But demons are, as Ludlow notes, parasitic, taking on the character of their host, and no single reading of hierarchy or ontology exists.[27] Do daimons belong on only one hierarchy (can higher up be bad or must higher up imply better?) and on another of will (can a higher being opt to be evil?). And then, to confuse matters, how do these two scales interact? Such is the dilemma of relational categories. Since, Jeopardy-style, the answer the monks are working with is free will (and its central place in any theology of good vs. evil, of Christian vs. non-Christian, correct Christian vs. heretic), the question is: What are demons?

Augustine analyzes and rejects some parts of the common demon discourse, making him seem almost modern in his sensibilities.[28] Most importantly, the question of which entities have real existences has been redrawn.[29] The dividing line between corporeal and incorporeal now puts everything important on the completely non-corporeal side of the equation. Augustine tinkers with the cosmological hierarchy: demons are not higher than humans any more than animals that run faster than humans are. Evil has no substance, so he stresses terms for them such as phantasmata (fantastic illusions). Demons can provide evidence only for some questions and can only operate in limited spheres. Since they have only a certain kind of "flesh," they can only interact with human "flesh" in like manner. Souls are incorporeal, too, so this is the central coin of the realm. To say that demons do not exist would be to say that souls do not either, a heretical thought. But we only encounter souls in very specific ways, and so too with demons. They cloud the mind, so a particularly clear mind is needed. A demon is not simply a thought, even though thoughts and demons share the same stage, that is, the mind (as does the soul as well).

Demons have profound impacts on the world, which is why, when the humans use their free choice to fill their minds with the deity and not-demons thoughts, the glory of the deity is all the greater. Augustine's mother does not show up at his bedside every time he is unhappy, and her level of devotion was high. He might imagine that he sees her, but all such channels of communication are easy to distort, both how demons inhabit human and how humans open themselves to other presences. Every piece of evidence must be thoroughly examined since every mind may be suffering from demon-distortion and unable to break free from that cycle.

The power of the devil lurks inside every human due to Original Sin. An act of "scrutiny" is part of the process of being catechized and exorcised, since that is part of the process of removing the devil and his minions out of human beings and filling that space instead by the Holy Spirit. A fine-tuned demon is needed to represent the fine-tuned theology of Original Sin, one that holds up to scrutiny even as exorcism remains one vital part of becoming a child of God.

Demons continue to pose all sorts of questions that permit unfolding Christian answers after Augustine. Illness could be put at the door of demons or humors, or at both. A 6th-century text recounts the incurable demon-possession of emperor Justin II. Sufferers of continuing possession found themselves living in Christian "hospitals" for extended periods of their lives. Demons had moved in for good.[30]

Contextualizing early Christian demon discourse

In the ancient worldview familiar from Ancient Near Eastern texts and sometimes referred to as "locative," daimons were out of place in human habitations.[31] They belonged at the edges of the map and become problematic when they invade the parts of the social world organized by the gods for humans. Intricate techniques were needed to return them to their native "homes," techniques elaborated with in, for example, Temple cults. Possession by a daimon changes the status of the person, who becomes a sort of amalgam of the daimon/spirit and the human body. When daimons inhabit a human body, the body becomes a site of uncleanliness. The possessed person is not charged with any specific sinful action or state of being. This uncleanliness is completely divorced from human intentionality, though some people were thought to be especially susceptible.

With the emergence of the utopian worldview in the last centuries B.C.E., which did not replace so much as supplement the locative view, human were now the invaders into the realm of the daimon.[32] As Kyle Fraser outlines, in the extensive debates about daimons carried on by Plutarch and Apuleius, "to the extent that embodiment was perceived as 'imprisonment,' the daimones appeared in a rather sinister light."[33] No final escape was possible from daimons without escaping the world completely. Humans were trapped in the sub-lunar world of bodies, a world that inherently belonged to the daimons. The utopian worldview, in which daimons are in place and human out of place, only makes sense as a critique of the locative and cannot stand on its own. Even when they have taken over the earth, demons were not of the earth, nor can they live on earth happily when the "saved Savior" and his followers return to their original home.

Christian demon discourse unfolded in relation to these two worldviews and their many layered combinations. As the role of Christians in relation to the state changed, daimons lost some of their political roles since Satan no longer ruled the world (though this theology was available for resuscitation any time needed). Whenever an authority figure thought a Christian strayed from the correct path, the language of daimons is ready at hand. Christians are never safe from the personal attacks of daimons, whose tool chest remains just as elaborate as when they were in league with earthly authorities, even if the scale of the battle is smaller. Some texts, such as the Life of Anthony discussed earlier, champion a specific Holy Man, but the breadth of textual evidence and the archeological evidence demonstrate that many others had their hands busy with demons. While we can draw a line from Ignatius to Augustine, that line does not cover all the evidence. A demon-suffering person might have turned to a healer trained in humor-based bodily practices, a local female herbalist who might be a family member, or an amulet-maker thought to be skilled in his trade. Flexibility, human creativity, and above all new techniques were needed for demon combat, and in all these categories the Christians shared ideas with their neighbors.

Notes

1 In contrast to the frequent references to daimons, and despite the immense importance of witches in 15–18th-century Europe, references to witches are rare in early Christian literature, and this chapter focuses on daimons. See Kimberly Stratton, *Naming the Witch: Magic, Ideology, and Stereotype in the Ancient World* (New York: Columbia University, 2007).

2 The transliteration "daimon" is used since it has broader connotations than demon. For a review of the term, see Greg J. Riley, "Demons," in *Anchor Dictionary of the Bible*, ed. David Noel Freedman (New York: Doubleday, 1992) and Riley, "Demon," in *Dictionary of Deities and Demons*, ed. Karel van der Toorn (Leiden: Brill, 1995).

3 Kyle Fraser, "The Contested Boundaries of 'Magic' and 'Religion' in Late Pagan Monotheism," *Magic, Ritual, and Witchcraft* 4 (2009): 131–151, 136. See also Michael Frede, "Monotheism and Pagan Philosophy in Later Antiquity," in *Pagan Monotheism in Late Antiquity*, ed. Polymnia Athanassiadi and Michael Frede (Oxford: Clarendon Press, 1999) and Heidi Marx-Wolf, "A Strange Consensus: Daemonological Discourse in Origen, Porphyry, and Iamblichus," in *The Rhetoric of Power in Late Antiquity: Religion and Politics in Byzantium*,

Europe and the Early Islamic World, ed. Robert M. Frakes, Elizabeth DePalma Digester and Justin Stephens (London: Taurus, 2010), 219–239 for the close connection to non-Christian thought.

4 Empedocles, for example, thought daimons were fallen gods on their way back to being good, sent into a temporary exile until they expiated their sins of bloodshed. So too for Homer daimons were a particular type of god.

5 Plato's most influential statement, the claim that daimons transmit the will of the higher gods to the world below the moon, was not necessarily his most central (Symposium). In the Timaeus, a daimon is a soul given to a person, which dwells in the top of the body and pulls the person up (90a2-b1).

6 Arthur Nock, *Conversion: The Old and the New in Religion from Alexander the Great to Augustine of Hippo* (London: Oxford University Press, 1933), 104–105; Gregory Smith, "How Thin Is a Demon?" *Journal of Early Christian Studies* 16 (2008): 479–512. To avoid over-psychologizing them, a modern analogy might include the well-disguised mice in *Hitchhiker's Guide to the Galaxy* or perhaps, as a physical analogy, squirrels in the modern cityscape: the source of fantasies about nature for some and the carriers of disease for others, partially tamable but still erratic, the focus of legislation and with some tension between abstract theory and actual encounters. While city officials may have special obligations with regards to legislation, social standing does not determine any specific response to encountering a specific squirrel eyeing one's lunch.

7 This did not stop polemical attacks that incorrect beliefs about daimons impugned claims about monotheisms.

8 David Sedley, *Creationism and its Critics in Antiquity* (Berkeley: University of California, 2007); Kyle Fraser, "The Contested Boundaries of 'Magic' and 'Religion' in Late Pagan Monotheism," *Magic, Ritual, and Witchcraft* 4 (2009), 131–151. The origin of evil becomes a major theological concern since speculation about it can lead to what is often called "dualism," the belief that evil was aboriginal and outside the power of the deity and constituted a real threat.

9 Peter Brown, *Religion and Society in the Age of St. Augustine* (New York: Harper and Row, 1972), 137.

10 The goal here is to build on Smith's very general point that they serve as "classificatory markers which signal what is strong and weak, controlled and exaggerated in a given society at a given moment – see Jonathan Z. Smith, "Towards Interpreting Demonic Powers in Hellenistic and Roman Antiquity," in *Aufstieg und Niedergang der römischen Welt*, ed. Wolfgang Hasse (Berline:Walter de Gruyter, 1978), 254–394.

11 Peter Brown, "The Rise and Function of the Holy Man in Late Antiquity," *Journal of Roman Studies* 61 (1971): 80–101.

12 Morton Smith, "Salvation in the Gospels, Paul, and the Magical Papyri," *Helios* 13 (1986): 63–74. Should one actively try to become a living sacrifice (Romans 12) or wait to be sacrificed?

13 A few examples of these debates are included below. For an overview see Henry A. Kelly, *The Devil at Baptism: Ritual, Theology, and Drama* (Ithaca: Cornell University Press, 1985).

14 Geert van Oyen, "Demons and Exorcisms in the Gospel of Mark," in *Demons and the Devil in Ancient and Medieval Christianity*, ed. Nienke Vos and Willemien Otten (Leiden: Brill, 2011), 99–116; Fraser, "Contested," 148.

15 Theater often served as a source of imagery for outlining social roles – see Ruth Webb, *Demons and Dancers: Performance in Late Antiquity* (Cambridge, MA: Harvard University Press, 2008).

16 Martyrdom is discussed here only in terms of its connection to demons. The general bibliography on this is immense, including the recent work of Candida Moss, *The Myth of Persecution* (New York: HarperCollins, 2013).

17 Elizabeth Castelli, *Martyrdom and Memory: Early Christian Culture Making* (New York: Columbia University Press, 2004).

18 Fraser, "Contested."

19 The "bad religion" of non-Christians was outlined using traditional Greco-Roman terms such as "superstitio" and "desdemonia" (see James Rives, "Human Sacrifice Among Pagans

and Christians," *Journal of Roman Studies* 85 (1995)." Reed details Justin's use of demons to argue against both Jews and pagans (Reed 2004).

20 Athanasius lived 296–373 C.E. His *Life of Anthony* (251–356 C.E.) was probably written around 360.

21 David Brakke, *Demons and the Making of the Monk: Spiritual Combat in Early Christianity* (Cambridge, MA: Harvard University Press, 2006), 23, 28, 240–241.

22 Cam Grey's careful psychological interpretation of late antique demons is revealing (Cam Grey, "Demoniacs, Dissent, and Disempowerment in the Late Roman West: Some Case Studies from the Hagiographical Literature," *Journal of Early Christian Studies* 13 (2005): 39–69); however, it is also striking that only demons, and not gods, warrant this analysis (permitting people to utter anti-social comments, for example). The point here is simply that it is not evenly applied to divine beings, except in theories such as Freud's.

23 See Brakke's careful study: Brakke, *Demons.* Psychoanalytic analysis is also popular in the study of witchcraft trials and recently of evil in general (Daniel Frankfurter, *Evil Incarnate: Rumors of Demonic Conspiracy and Ritual Abuse in History* (Princeton, NJ: Princeton University Press, 2006)) though in the latter case the evil that needs to be repressed is people who believe in evil.

24 Lyndal Roper encourages seeing the repression not simply as the imposition of control, but instead as an active part of the formation of sexual identity (Lyndal Roper, *Oedipus and the Devil: Witchcraft, Sexuality, and Religion in Early Modern Europe* (London, New York: Routledge, 1994)).

25 Much as an exterminator might tell a customer to get used to living with bees since the means used to get rid of them was often more toxic than the bees themselves.

26 Morwenna Ludlow, "Demons, Evil and Liminality in Cappadocian Theology," *Journal of Early Christian Studies* 20 (2012): 179–211, 184.

27 Ludlow, "Demons," 189; Dale Martin, *Inventing Superstition: From the Hippocratics to the Christians* (Cambridge, MA, London: Harvard University Press, 2004).

28 The "nexus" between demons and humans is "purely psychological," writes Peter Brown, *Augustine of Hippo: A Biography* (Berkeley: University of California Press, 1969), 311. For Augustine's ideas about exorcism as only including symbolic demons and not real ones, see Kelly, *Devil*, 113.

29 That is to say, Augustine is drawing upon a different set of non-Christian thinkers for whom evil had no real existence.

30 Peregrine Horden, "Responses to Possession and Insanity in the Earlier Byzantine World," *The Social History of Medicine* 6 (1993): 177–194, 191–192.

31 Outlined by Martin Nilsson, "The New Conception of the Universe in Late Greek Paganism," *Eranos* 44 (1946): 20–27 and refined by numerous subsequent scholars. (Richard Gordon, "Cosmology, Astrology, and Magic: Discourse, Schemes, Power, and Literacy," in *Panthée: Religious Transformation in the Graeco-Roman Empire*, ed. L. Bricault and C. Bonnet (Leiden: Brill, 2013), 92) emphasizes, contra Nilsson, that placing the earth at the center of the cosmos lead not to one new cosmology but many. This is an important corrective since new ideas were added without negating the earlier views supported by ancient textual traditions.

32 This view was not a Christian development, though scholars of early Christianity who emphasize the Christian contribution often in turn stress unique Jewish contributions (Guy Stroumsa, *The End of Sacrifice: Religious Transformations in Late Antiquity* (Chicago: University of Chicago Press, 2009)). Scholars of Neo-Platonism have recently made strong arguments for the pivotal role of Neo-Platonic philosophers.

33 The shift was taken for granted by Peter Brown's claim that "violence was articulated in terms of the daimonic" (P. Brown, "The Rise and Function of the Holy Man in Late Antiquity," *Journal of Roman Studies* 61 (1971): 89).

Bibliography (selection)

Brakke, David, *Demons and the Making of the Monk: Spiritual Combat in Early Christianity.* Cambridge, MA: Harvard University Press, 2006.

Fraser, Kyle, "The Contested Boundaries of 'Magic' and 'Religion' in Late Pagan Monotheism." *Magic, Ritual, and Witchcraft* 4 (2009): 131–151.

Grey, Cam, "Demoniacs, Dissent, and Disempowerment in the Late Roman West: Some Case Studies From the Hagiographical Literature." *Journal of Early Christian Studies* 13 (2005): 39–69.

Ludlow, Morwenna, "Demons, Evil and Liminality in Cappadocian Theology." *Journal of Early Christian Studies* 20 (2012): 179–211.

Martin, Dale, *Inventing Superstition: From the Hippocratics to the Christians.* London: Harvard University Press, 2004.

Smith, Gregory, "How Thin Is a Demon?" *Journal of Early Christian Studies* 16 (2008): 479–512.

Stratton, Kimberly, *Naming the Witch: Magic, Ideology, and Stereotype in the Ancient World.* New York: Columbia University, 2007.

Webb, Ruth, *Demons and Dancers: Performance in Late Antiquity.* Cambridge, MA: Harvard University Press, 2008.

4

WITCHCRAFT AND DEMONOLOGY IN THE MIDDLE AGES

Michael D. Bailey

Throughout the Middle Ages, Christian authorities linked most forms of magic to the demonic. Reliance on demons defined magic for many clerical thinkers and served to differentiate it from legitimate religious rites of prayer, blessing, or the deployment of sacramental power.[1] The fully developed idea of diabolical, conspiratorial witchcraft that framed most of the major European witch trials, however, only emerged in the fifteenth century. This "collective concept" (*Kollektivbegriff*) has often been presented in terms of a fairly precise set of stereotypes. Gerhard Schormann, for example, identified four key elements of witchcraft: a pact with the devil, sexual congress with demons (often to seal that pact), harmful magic (performed at the behest of the devil), and the gathering of groups of witches at sabbaths. Of these, he identified the sabbath as the "most consequential," since it created a basis for one witch to accuse many others in the course of a trial, and he determined that only cases involving all four elements should be labeled as "witch trials," while other cases involving harmful magic should be designated as "sorcery" (*Hexerei* vs. *Zauberei*).[2] Jeffrey Russell went further and designated eight characteristics of European witchcraft beyond just the practice of harmful magic, including infanticide, cannibalism, and the desecration of the cross and Eucharist, all of which were thought to occur primarily at the witches' sabbath.[3]

More recent scholarship has complicated such rigid categorizations, showing, for example, how multiple stereotypes of witchcraft developed in the late-medieval period, differing from one another in important ways.[4] Some experts now go so far as to argue, in direct opposition to scholars like Russell and Schormann, that the only essential feature of European witchcraft should be harmful magic alone, thereby allowing for more direct comparison to forms of magical practice that have been designated as witchcraft in non-Christian societies around the globe.[5] Such an approach might also more accurately reflect the primary concern of the great majority of the European populace when dealing with witches, since most people seem to have focused far more on harm wrought through magic than on issues of diabolism, which was mainly an elite legal and theological concern.[6] Despite such cautionary notes, however, most scholars would still agree that within the context of Western European history, witchcraft has generally been defined by two basic characteristics: the practice of harmful magic (*maleficium*) and some kind of essential connection that many people, especially those in power, believed to exist between the witch and the devil.[7] The phenomenon of witchcraft cannot be understood completely, in this context, if these two elements are separated. Moreover, although the idea of full-blown sabbaths and sexually consummated pacts between witches and demons developed mainly in the fifteenth century and thereafter, connections between the performance of harmful magic (*maleficium*) and demonology extend much deeper into the medieval past.[8] This chapter will explore how those connections developed across the medieval centuries, as an essential basis for understanding how various components of the collective concept of witchcraft functioned during the witch hunts of the early modern period.

Early medieval developments

The Christian demonization of magic, to use Valerie Flint's apt phrase, began in the very earliest days of the new faith.[9] Much pre-Christian magic relied on the gods and spirits of pagan pantheons, which Christian leaders understood to be demons. In the middle of the first century, the apostle Paul communicated this to the Christian community in Corinth when he wrote, "what pagans sacrifice, they sacrifice to demons and not to God. I do not want you to be partners with demons."[10] Several centuries later, the church father Augustine of Hippo declared that all magical and superstitious arts were "constituted through a certain pestiferous association of human beings and demons as if by a pact of faithless and deceitful friendship."[11] In his *City of God*, he stated that "all the wonders of magicians . . . are done through the teachings and works of demons."[12] Even astrological divination, viewed by many as a science, was based not on "the art of observing and examining horoscopes, which does not exist," but on "the secret inspiration of spirits that are in no way good."[13] Later still, in the early seventh century, the archbishop Isidore of Seville included a section on magicians (*De magis*) in his encyclopedic *Etymologies*. Here, he reiterated the idea that all of the magic arts derived "from the instruction of evil angels."[14] He also specified a class of magician who performed only harmful magic, whom he labeled as witches (*malefici*): "There are magicians who are commonly called 'witches' on account of the magnitude of their crimes. They agitate the elements, disturb the minds of men, and kill just by the violence of their spells, without any use of poison."[15]

By linking magic so completely to entanglement with demonic spirits, Christianity created the grounds for a sweeping moral condemnation of all kinds of magical practices, whether they were intended to be harmful or beneficial, although as Isidore shows, intellectual authorities often maintained a separate category of specifically harmful magic or witchcraft. Similarly, most of the law codes issued by Christian rulers in the early medieval period tended to preserve a distinction between magic used specifically for harmful ends and other kinds of magical rites. Such differentiation was typical of classical legal codes, and is found preserved under Christian auspices in the imperial Theodosian Code of 438. In its section *De maleficis et mathematicis*, which could be translated as "on witches and astrologers," it condemned those who used magical practices to cause harm, but not those who used them to provide "remedies" against bewitchments.[16] In its "interpretation" of this statute, however, the code went on to link the performance of magic, especially harmful magic, explicitly to demons, stating that "witches or enchanters or storm-raisers or those who disturb the minds of men through the invocation of demons should be punished with every kind of punishment."[17] Furthermore, it specified that any diviners who invoked demons in the course of their practices should be put to death, even though presumably their prognostications about the future were not directly harmful.[18] Lastly, it stipulated that anyone who "offers nocturnal sacrifices to demons or invokes demons with incantations, should be put to death."[19] Here too there was no indication that specifically harmful or criminal behavior had to ensue. Rather, we find a strict Christian declaration that involvement with demons is grounds for capital punishment in its own right, although presumably these harsh statues would have been read in light of this section of the code's overall concentration on the harmful practices of *maleficium*.[20]

The Germanic peoples who came to power in Western Europe as the Roman Empire declined had their own ideas of witchcraft, and these blended and in some instances clashed with classical and Christian conceptions in the early medieval law codes that these new rulers produced. In the Burgundian Code, for example, if a man found his wife engaging in witchcraft (*maleficium*), this was one of three permissible grounds for divorce (the other two being if she committed adultery or was caught violating graves).[21] Here we have a clear indication that practices of witchcraft were often associated with women, although by no means exclusively so. In many other cases in Germanic law, the use of language, which inevitably employed the masculine forms of nouns and pronouns when referring to generic examples of proscribed practices, leaves the gender of the practitioners in doubt.

Another aspect of Germanic law that points to a gendering of witchcraft as more a female than a male act is the clear evidence that certain words translatable as "witch" were being used as a means to denigrate women, against which the law tried to offer some protection. For example, in a neat inversion of the Burgundian Code's stipulation that a man could divorce his wife if she practiced witchcraft, the seventh-century Edict of Rothair, which was the first written codification of Lombard law, allowed a woman to leave her husband is he falsely accused her of being a witch (*striga*).[22] A subsequent edict makes clear that calling a woman a *striga* in this context was not so much a specific legal charge as a form of general insult, much like calling a respectable woman a whore or harlot.[23] The Lombard laws also prohibited a man from killing another man's female servant or slave "as if she were a witch . . . because it is in no way to be believed by Christian minds that it is possible that a woman can eat a living man from within."[24] Here it appears that the ruling elites within Lombard society, who in other contexts clearly accepted Christian ideas of harmful demonic "witchcraft" designated by terms like *maleficium,* also opposed and sought to suppress certain popular conceptions of what a witch might be. The particular terminology used in this case referred to a woman who was considered to be "a *striga,* which the people call *masca.*"[25]

Such tensions continue to be evident in the later laws of the Franks. A Carolingian capitulary from 785 condemned to death anyone who believed that either a woman or a man could be a witch (*striga*) "after the manner of the pagans."[26] Frankish law clearly accepted and condemned the Christian understanding of witchcraft, however. The general capitulary of 802 ordered that all counts and other royal administrators should diligently pursue all "witches [*maleficos*] and performers of incantations and auguries" and bring them to justice, along with other categories of criminals such as thieves, murderers, and adulterers.[27] More than a decade earlier, the general admonition (*admonitio generalis*) of 789 instructed all priests that they should in some way police their parishioners (no methods were stipulated) so that they would not risk becoming "sorcerers, witches, enchanters or enchantresses."[28] Further on, here explicitly drawing on the biblical prohibition of magical practices in Deuteronomy 18:10–12, it ordered that all "sorcerers, enchanters, storm-raisers, or makers of magical ligatures" were to be either corrected from their sinful ways or else condemned.[29] The passage from Deuteronomy made clear that all such practices were "abhorrent to the Lord," and it specifically mentioned divination by consulting spirits, which Christian authorities would have read to mean invocation of demons. The *admonitio* alluded to such grounds for condemning magic, and it also condemned remnants of pagan rites such as people worshipping at certain trees, stones, or springs, which Christian authorities would have understood as demonic. Notably, however, it did not raise the issue of demons explicitly in its prohibitions. Again we see secular laws tending to focus more on "witchcraft" in terms of harmful magic, although the shadow of the demonic and the absolute moral condemnation it entails hovers over all these codes.

Canon law and scholastic demonology

Not surprisingly, church law stressed the demonic elements of magic in general and witchcraft in particular far more than secular law codes. Like secular law, however, early canon law included a good deal of skepticism about popular ideas related to the supposed power and practices of magicians and witches. Undoubtedly the most famous statute in canon law regarding witchcraft is the canon *Episcopi*, thought by medieval authorities to have originated at the early fourth-century council of Ancyra but in fact first recorded in the early tenth-century legal collection of Regino of Prüm. The canon began by ordering bishops to "labor with all their strength to eradicate the pernicious art of sorcery and witchcraft [*sortilegam et maleficam artem*], invented by the devil, entirely from their districts." Following this brief and straightforward injunction, the canon changed tone and issued a long condemnation of

> "certain wicked women, turned aside after Satan, seduced by the illusions and phantasms of demons, [who] believe and profess that in the hours of the night they ride upon certain beasts with Diana, the goddess of the pagans, and an innumerable multitude of women."

In the medieval understanding, the figure of Diana was, of course, a demon merely posing as a pagan deity, and this description became fundamental to later notions of the night-flight of witches to demonic sabbaths. The canon, however, presented this nocturnal journey as entirely illusory, a demonic deception that took place only in spirit, and it derided anyone who would be "so foolish and stupid" as to believe that it occurred in reality.[30]

The canon almost certainly originated as two separate documents. The first addressed the performance of diabolical witchcraft (*maleficium*), taken to be a very real threat against which bishops should "labor with all their strength," and which the text explicitly associated with either men or women. The second dealt only with women who falsely believed that they gathered at night in a large company headed by a demon. These women were not labeled by any term that might be translated as "witch," nor were they ever described as performing any kind of harmful magic, but in medieval readings of this document that distinction was washed away. What remained was the canon's clear statement that certain popular beliefs now associated with witchcraft were not real. Later theorists of witchcraft returned to this problem again and again, either finding ways to argue around the canon and maintain that events supposedly taking place at a witches' sabbath could be physically real despite its authoritative declaration, or asserting that the reality of a sabbath made no difference because simply to imagine oneself to be in the presence of demons and to swear fidelity to them was a horrible crime for any Christian.[31]

Almost exactly one hundred years after the canon *Episcopi's* first appearance in Regino of Prüm's collection, the canonist Burchard of Worms included it in his *Decretum*, composed in the early eleventh century. He highlighted the canon's condemnation of false beliefs associated with witchcraft by specifying a penalty: anyone who "believed these vanities" that women actually traveled with demons physically in the night should do penance for two years.[32] Particularly in Book 19 of his collection, often circulated separately and known as *Corrector sive medicus* (*The Corrector, or the Physician*), he addressed a wide range of what he considered to be magical and superstitious practices. Sometimes he condemned the practice itself, such as when people would collect "medicinal herbs with evil incantations."[33] Just as often, however, he castigated belief in the real efficacy of various practices, such as the idea that "enchanters" could raise storms or that certain women could move men either to love or hatred by "witchcraft and incantations" (*maleficia et incantationes*).[34] In addition to the canon *Episcopi*, Burchard also included a statute that condemned women who believed that they went out secretly at night in physical form in order to kill other Christians and devour their flesh.[35]

The most fundamental canon law collection, which remained authoritative within the Catholic Church for the rest of the medieval period and well beyond, was the *Concordia discordantium canonum* (*Concordance of Discordant Canons*), again commonly called the *Decretum* and generally attributed to the twelfth-century Bolognese legal scholar Gratian.[36] For all its authoritative weight, however, Gratian's collection added relatively little new material to discussions of witchcraft. Citing Augustine, he linked all the "magic arts" to demons, including astrology, divination, and sorcery (*sortilegium*).[37] He also addressed a long section to the issue of how "the tricks of demons are not real but only imaginary."[38] While *Causa* 26 of the *Decretum* dealt with magic generally, *Causa* 33 focused on the case of a "man impeded by witchcraft" who was unable to perform sexually with his wife.[39] The main legal issues at stake were whether the man could be cured, by what means, and whether divorce was possible if no effective cure could be found. Such questions had been debated by legal experts for some time. An important text on this matter, the canon *Si per sortiarias*, had been circulating since the time of the Carolingian archbishop Hincmar of Reims in the ninth century.[40] Throughout the high medieval period (roughly 1000–1300), church law would continue to reiterate mostly well-established proscriptions on witchcraft and against demonic magic more generally. For major conceptual advances in this period, we need to turn to the realm of theology and demonology.

As canon law was being codified (and secular Roman law was being rediscovered, on which more to come) at cathedral schools and universities in the eleventh and twelfth centuries, the general intellectual revival promoted by those institutions created a market for a major influx of ancient and Arabic texts, and ancient texts transmitted through or with Arabic commentaries, into Western Europe. Among these were many that dealt in whole or in part with magic.[41] They presented learned discussions of astrology, astral magic, and also magic explicitly based on the invocation of spiritual entities, which Christian authorities understood to be demons. Here was a form of demonic magic that was far removed from the perceived foolish practices of uneducated rustics or deluded women. It was a refined and learned art with an impressive intellectual pedigree that had to be taken seriously. Many clergymen became intrigued or even infatuated with this new knowledge, experimenting with it in their school days and sometimes further into their careers as well.[42] Some were no doubt drawn to the risqué nature of what they saw as dark and illicit practices. Others, however, sought to rehabilitate at least some aspects of this knowledge, positing a category of natural magic that they maintained was uninfected by the corrupting influence of demons. Such questions forced scholastic theologians to think about the nature of demonic power and its relation to magical rites in increasingly rigorous ways, and to draw far-reaching and influential conclusions.

William of Auvergne was one of the most important figures in the development of scholastic demonology.[43] He was a theologian and then served as bishop of Paris from 1228 until his death in 1249. He appears to have been the first to use "natural magic" (*magia naturalis*) as a defensible and legitimate category.[44] He did not reject the possibility of demonic magic, however, and he discussed the extent of demonic power and its operation in many areas of the magic arts at some length in later works.[45] For example, in one oft-cited passage, he explained how demons could appear to impregnate women even though these spiritual creatures were incapable of natural reproduction. Using its ability to move matter at great speed, a demon could first appear to a man as a succubus, abscond with his semen, and then in the form of incubus use it when mimicking sex with a woman.[46] Another of William's influential ideas was his postulation that pacts formed the basis of both sacramental operations and demonic invocations.[47] He also discussed the actions of "witches" (*malefici*) and explicitly attributed the efficacy of their harmful magic to demons.[48] It is important to note here that when William used the terms *maleficus* or *maleficium*, he probably meant to imply educated (and male) practitioners performing more complex forms of ritual demonic magic, not the simple spells or poisons typically associated with a village witch. When discussing the famous biblical injunction in Exodus 22:18, rendered in the medieval Vulgate as "maleficos non patieris vivere" and in the English of the King James Bible as "thou shalt not suffer a witch to live," he defined *malefici* as "magicians or enchanters" who performed idolatrous rites that called upon demons.[49] But of course the ambiguity between harmful magic of any kind and a more specific category of witchcraft was already inherent in the Latin terminology.

Even more than William of Auvergne, Thomas Aquinas, perhaps the greatest scholastic theologian of the thirteenth century, kept his discussions of magic at an abstract and theoretical level, not stooping to particular cases. It is well known that he had essentially nothing to say about witches of the sort who would later become the focus of the witch trials.[50] He addressed the abilities of demons and the reliance of most forms of magic on demonic power in many works, however, notably his *Summa contra gentiles* and his masterpiece *Summa theologiae*.[51] These became the basis of almost all subsequent theological and demonological analysis of magical operations.

The anxious fourteenth century

While canon lawyers and theologians debated the nature and consequences of demonic magic in university settings in the twelfth and thirteenth centuries, actual magical practices remained widespread across Europe, just as they had been throughout the earlier medieval period. People relied on rites that might be labeled "magical" (whether they themselves primarily thought of their actions in this way is more debatable) to heal illness and injury, to protect themselves from harm, to divine the future, and for numerous other purposes.[52] The belief that people could harm as well as heal through magic was common, and those who fell under suspicion of performing harmful magic could face terrible consequences. In 1075, citizens of Cologne threw a suspected witch from the city wall. In 1128, citizens of Ghent had a supposed "enchantress" disemboweled. Both of these were instances of mob justice, not court sentences.[53] As we have seen, early medieval law codes certainly allowed for strict penalties, up to and including the death sentence for the performance of harmful magic, but they also expressed some skepticism about certain popular ideas of what might constitute "witchcraft." For many centuries church law tended to be even more permissive, often assigning penances rather than punishments, and even at its most severe generally opting to exile convicted magical malefactors rather than execute them. Even the seemingly immutable biblical command "maleficos non patieris vivere" was usually interpreted only as an injunction to separate *malefici* from faithful Christians, thus removing them from the sphere of those "truly" alive.[54] Certainly insofar as surviving records allow us to discern, no medieval court system, ecclesiastical or secular, prosecuted witchcraft with any great ferocity throughout most of the Middle Ages. This, however, began to change in the fourteenth century.

If Thomas Aquinas, writing in the mid-thirteenth century, provided the intellectual framework for most subsequent opposition to demonic magic (as well as reaffirming the ancient Christian position that most magic was in fact demonic), then Pope John XXII, reigning from 1316 until 1334, provided the legal foundations for most subsequent prosecutions, at least by ecclesiastical courts, as well as prompting clerical authorities to pursue legal action against suspected demonic magicians more vigorously than ever before. Driven by concern about demonic magic being practiced within his own court and by his political enemies elsewhere, John personally instigated a number of investigations in Avignon, where the papacy then resided, and in other courts across France and Italy.[55] In 1320, he also convened a special commission of theologians and canon lawyers to consider exactly what kind of crimes were entailed in demonic invocation, and specifically whether such demonic magic automatically amounted to heresy.[56] This was a complicated question because at least in theory heresy had to involve incorrect beliefs, not just improper or illicit actions.[57] Clerical necromancers (that is, learned magicians engaged in demonic invocations) regularly claimed that they did not hold any false beliefs about the demons they summoned, nor did they worship them. Instead, they believed that they commanded these evil spirits, ultimately exercising an authority that Christ had conferred upon his apostles, and by extension to all faithful Christians, in the Gospels.[58] The issue of legitimate exorcism therefore became central to many discussions of demonic magic. Again Aquinas provided the most influential statement. Christians could properly adjure demons only by "compulsion," never by "supplication." Furthermore, even if the method of compulsion was used, "it is not, however, licit to adjure them for the purpose of learning something from them, or of obtaining something through them, for this would involve having some kind of fellowship with them."[59]

The issue of an implied "fellowship," and of a pact at least tacitly entered into, lay at the heart of what might make demonic invocation an automatic heresy. John's commission moved through a number of tangled points in its considerations, but ultimately it concluded that the very action of invoking a demon always entailed heretical error, and so demonic magic was automatically subject to ecclesiastical jurisdiction. In that same year, 1320, John ordered papal inquisitors in Carcassonne and Toulouse to investigate anyone accused of having "invoked demons in order to perpetrate some kind of witchcraft [*maleficium*]."[60] Then in 1326 the pope issued the sweeping decree *Super illius specula*, which proclaimed any Christian who engaged in demonic invocation to be automatically excommunicated.[61] Curiously, this proclamation was not immediately encoded into canon law. Some scholars even suggest that its attribution to John may not be genuine, although the concerns and even the language of the decree reflect John's approach to these issues.[62] It gained real prominence only 50 years later, when the theologian and inquisitor Nicolas Eymerich cited it as one of the principal justifications for inquisitorial jurisdiction over "magicians and magical superstitions" in his *Directorium inquisitorum*.[63]

Even before Eymerich, however, Pope John was influencing inquisitorial action. One of the inquisitors whom he would have ordered to begin stepping up investigations of demonic magic in 1320 was Bernard Gui, then operating in Toulouse. Within just a few years, Gui was to write one of the first great medieval inquisitor's handbooks, *Practica inquisitionis*. Although he appears never to have tried a case involving demonic magic himself, he made sure to cover the procedures for doing so in his handbook.[64] His most extensive treatment dealt with clergymen engaging in demonic invocations and described complex rites of learned magic in language very similar to John's decrees, for example a rite involving wax images over which certain conjurations were performed, along with rites involving "blood taken from some part of his [the magician's] own body and mixed with the blood of a toad, and with oblation given to the demons invoked in the place of sacrifice," all in order to "procure such and such *maleficia*."[65] Significantly, however, Gui described much simpler forms of magic as well, such as "curing disease by conjurations or verbal spells" (*per conjuria seu carmina verborum*), gathering herbs, as well as divination, rites used to identify thieves, and love magic.[66] These are all practices that would later be associated with witches in the course of major trials. Gui does not describe anything like diabolical sabbaths, but he does indicate that people engaging in these more common kinds of magic were also invoking demons, showing them reverence or worship, and possibly offering sacrifices to them.[67]

Half a century later, Nicolau Eymerich's *Directorium* would become even more influential on subsequent inquisitorial practice than Gui's *Practica*.[68] To an even greater extent that Gui, he confined himself to discussions of learned ritual magic featuring elaborate ceremonies that could without much effort be interpreted as showing reverence or worship to a demonic spirit. Eymerich, for example, described rites involving prayers and singing, inscribing symbols and characters on various surfaces, burning candles or incense, and directly sacrificing birds or other animals to the demons being invoked.[69] He presented these actions as patently and automatically heretical. As already noted, he included John XXII's *Super illius specula* as one of the primary grounds for inquisitorial jurisdiction over cases of demonic invocation, and he himself concluded that

> "to invoke is considered an act of adoration, and is counted and placed among the acts of adoration, [. . .] therefore if a demon is invoked by a Christian, even if it does not appear that any other act of adoration has been offered to the demon, that savors of manifest heresy and such people must be considered heretics."[70]

While Eymerich did not include any descriptions of simpler forms of magical practice such as might be performed by ordinary people without a clergyman's ritual training and access to Latin texts, there can be no doubt that he meant the basic legal and theological principles he elucidated to apply to the sort of women (and to a lesser extent men) who would become the main victims of witch trials. He also quoted the canon *Episcopi* in this section of his *Directorium*, and he stated without hesitation that the women it described "are perfidious and faithless and deviate from the right way" and therefore "they must be considered heretics."[71] This was true even though he had to admit that he could find no overt evidence of demon-worship in their practices, very much unlike what he had found in the elaborate rites of elite necromancers. He was prepared to acknowledge about the women described in the canon *Episcopi* that "it is not certain that they offer sacrifices to the demons they invoke." But this did not matter. By his own logic, any act of *maleficium* relied on demonic power, and to call on a demon for such purposes, intentionally or not, constituted a form of adoration and so entailed heresy. With this equation firmly in place, inquisitors could now confidently condemn anyone suspected of performing any kind of harmful magic as being in league with demons and ultimately a servant of Satan. From this point, the progression toward the idea of the witches' sabbath and large-scale witch hunts, while still far from inevitable, becomes much easier to perceive.[72]

Secular law in the later Middle Ages

While demonology and inquisitorial procedure developed rapidly in the thirteenth and fourteenth centuries, secular law remained fairly static in regard to demonic magic and the crime of witchcraft, perpetuating but not elaborating much on earlier prohibitions.[73] For example, one of the most comprehensive secular legal codes of this period, Castile's *Las siete partidas*, composed in the thirteenth century and enacted in the fourteenth, made little mention of witchcraft aside from repeating the longstanding position that bewitchment that incurably impeded sexual function in marriage could be grounds for divorce.[74] It included only somewhat more extensive treatment of learned forms of magic, including necromancy and divination by means of astrology. Practitioners of such arts relied on demons, it concluded, and so should be put to death.[75] Interestingly, although it addressed these forms of magic as explicitly demonic, and therefore worthy of inherent condemnation, it also maintained the distinction typical of many earlier secular legal codes between harmful magic and magic used for positive purposes. To that end, it stated that those people who were found to

> "practice enchantments or anything else with good intentions, as, for instance, to cast out devils from the bodies of men; or to dissolve the spell cast over husband and wife so that they are unable to perform their marital duties; or to turn aside a cloud from which hail or a fog is descending, that it may not injure crops; or to kill locusts or insects which destroy grain or vines; or for any other beneficial purpose similar to these, cannot be punished, but we decree they shall be rewarded for it."[76]

Presumably Castilian authorities did not think that such beneficial forms of magic would be demonic, although that flew in the face of centuries of church teaching.

Undoubtedly, however, the most important contribution made by secular law during the high medieval period to the later witch trials was a matter not of legal understandings of magic but of methods of prosecution. The monumental consequences of the recovery of Roman civil law in the twelfth and thirteenth centuries and especially the gradual replacement of earlier accusatorial procedure with inquisitorial methods in most medieval courts is well established, in particular in terms of facilitating the prosecution of magical crimes.[77] Most importantly, under the new procedure the responsibility for investigating suspected crimes and issuing indictments fell on the magistrates of the court, not individual accusers, who no longer faced the threat of legal retribution if their accusations could not be substantiated by sufficient evidence, as was often the case in secretive crimes such as witchcraft. The courts, for their part, did not need direct evidence of a major crime to launch an inquest, because they could proceed simply on the basis of a suspect's bad reputation (*infamia*), which was exactly the sort of stigma that would cling to a person suspected by her neighbors of performing harmful magic. Convictions still required direct evidence or the "queen of proofs," confession. For that, in very serious cases courts could now resort to torture. While church courts did as much as secular ones to develop inquisitorial procedure generally, secular law took the lead in the revival of torture as a legal method to extract confessions.[78] The first known jurisdiction to employ torture in this way in the medieval West was the Italian commune of Verona in 1228. By contrast, Pope Innocent IV did not explicitly sanction the torture of heretics until the decretal *Ad extirpanda*, issued in 1252.[79] From that point, both secular and ecclesiastical courts developed this method of "inquiry" with gusto.

Prior to the first real witch hunts of the fifteenth century, a number of clearly political trials took place in the fourteenth century that featured elements of harmful magic, conspiracy, and torture.[80] The most famous of these were the trials of the Knights Templar in France beginning in 1307. While charges of demonic magic were not a major part of these trials, they certainly saw officials of the French king Philip IV employing coercion and torture to extract spectacular confessions of conspiratorial guilt from some of the knights.[81] In 1308, Philip also brought charges of demonic magic against Bishop Guichard of Troyes in connection with the sudden death of Philip's queen, Jeanne de Navarre, a few years earlier.[82] Then in 1314 charges of trying to kill the king himself were lodged against the royal chamberlain Enguerran of Marigny, and in 1316 Mahaut of Artois was accused of using magic to rekindle the affections of a new king, Philip V, for her daughter, Queen Jeanne of Burgundy. She was also rumored to have poisoned Philip's older brother Louis X to maneuver her son-in-law onto the throne in the first place. Finally, in 1331, King Philip VI wrote to Pope John XXII, who as we have seen had his own concerns about diabolical magical conspiracies, regarding magicians at court whom he suspected of plotting against him. The pope ordered the bishop of Paris to launch an investigation.[83] Similar cases, though never in quite so intense a sequence, occurred at other courts throughout the fourteenth century.

None of these cases could be called witch trials in any strict sense. Nevertheless, they represent the refinement of certain procedures, namely inquest and torture, and the ramping-up of certain concerns, namely about the use of harmful demonic magic in plots aimed at subverting proper Christian society, that would come to characterize the witch hunts at their height. In these ways, developments in the secular world, and not just among theologians and inquisitors, laid an important foundation for what was to come.

Conclusion

Learned magic, necromantic ritual, and political intrigue may seem quite far from the worlds of the (mostly) simple peasant women accused of witchcraft in the fifteenth century and thereafter, but they were all arenas in which concerns about harmful magic coalesced with those about demonic presence and power in the world, culminating in the ready acceptance, at least by many authorities, of an automatic and inevitable relationship between the practitioner of *maleficium* – the witch – and the devil. This development was not, itself, inevitable. Areas of skepticism and hesitation existed in both law and demonology for many centuries. Eventually, however, most of these were overcome, at least enough so that larger and larger trials could ensue. Moreover, as even simple magical rites came to be regarded as forms of demonic invocation, and as invocation came to be regarded as automatically constituting heresy, horrific stereotypes of cultic activities and conspiratorial plotting that had long featured in medieval ecclesiastical thinking about other kinds of heretics began to be applied to witches as well. Secret nocturnal assemblies, rampant orgies, formal abnegations of faith, and desecrations of the cross or the Eucharist all began to appear in charges against witches and especially in the emerging concept of the witches' sabbath.[84]

Witchcraft can be defined in many ways. Even when limited to the context of pre-modern Western Europe, an overly strict definition can hamper real historical understanding, as much as it might also provide valuable analytical precision in some cases. Certainly to try to make witchcraft into an absolutely precise scholarly category would obscure the fact that the very terms that meant or came to mean "witch" in various European languages have often had imprecise meanings and have changed their connotations over time. Nevertheless, for the period in which the category of "witch" became the focus of greatest concern and elicited the most terrible consequences in European history, its two most essential features were the performance of harmful magic linked to some kind of perceived relationship with demons and the devil. It was during the Middle Ages that those connections were slowly but firmly established.

Notes

1 Richard Kieckhefer, "The Specific Rationality of Medieval Magic," *American Historical Review* 99 (1994): 813–836.

2 Gerhard Schormann, *Hexenprozesse in Deutschland*, 3rd ed. (Göttingen: Vandenhoeck & Ruprecht, 1996), 23.

3 Jeffrey B. Russell, *A History of Witchcraft: Sorcerers, Heretics and Pagans* (London: Thames & Hudson, 1980), 55.

4 Richard Kieckhefer, "Mythologies of Witchcraft in the Fifteenth Century," *Magic, Ritual, and Witchcraft* 1 (2006): 79–108.

5 Wolfgang Behringer, *Witches and Witch Hunts: A Global History* (Cambridge: Polity, 2004), 3.

6 Richard Kieckhefer, *European Witch Trials: Their Foundations in Popular and Learned Culture, 1300–1500* (Berkeley: University of California Press, 1976).

7 Brian P. Levack, *The Witch Hunt in Early Modern Europe*, 3rd ed. (London: Pearson Longman, 2006), 4–10.

8 For simplicity's sake, I will generally use the word "witchcraft" to translate *maleficium* and "witch" to translate *maleficus* or other terms such as *striga* or *lamia* whenever they are used, with the recognition that these words carried different connotations in different periods.

9 Valerie Flint, "The Demonisation of Magic and Sorcery in Late Antiquity: Christian Redefinitions of Pagan Religions," in *Witchcraft and Magic in Europe: Ancient Greece and Rome*, ed. Bengt Ankarloo and Stuart Clark (Philadelphia: University of Pennsylvania Press, 1999), 277–348.

10 1 Corinthians 10:20.

11 Augustine, *De doctrina Christiana* 2.23.36, ed. Joseph Martin, Corpus Christianorum Series Latina 32 (Turnhout: Brepols, 1962).

12 Augustine, *De civitate dei* 8.19, ed. Bernard Dombart and Alphonse Kalb, Corpus Christianorum Series Latina 47–48 (Turnhout: Brepols, 1962): "At omnia miracula magorum, quos recte sentit esse damnandos, doctrinis fiunt et operibus daemonum."

13 Augustine, *De civitate dei* 5.7: "His omnibus consideratis non inmerito creditur, cum astrologi mirabiliter multa uera respondent, occulto instinctu fieri spirituum non bonorum."

14 Isidore, *Etymologiarum sive originum libri XX* 8.9.3, ed. W. M. Lindsay, 2 vols. (1911; reprint Oxford: Clarendon, 1971).

15 Isidore, *Etymologies* 8.9.9: "Magi sunt, qui vulgo malefici ob facinorum magnitudinem nuncupantur. Hi et elementa concutiunt, turbant mentes hominum, ac sine ullo veneni haustu violentia tantum carminis interimunt."

16 *Theodosiani libri XVI cum Constitutionibus Sirmondianis et Leges et novella ad Theodosianum pertinentes* 9.16.3, ed. Theodor Mommsen and Paul M. Meyer, 2 vols. (Berlin: Wiedemann, 1905): "Nullis vero criminationibus implicanda sunt remedia humanis quaesita corporibus aut in agrestibus locis."

17 *Theodosiani libri XVI* 9.16.3: "Interpretatio: Malefici vel incantatores vel immissores tempestatum vel hi, qui per invocationem daemonum mentes hominum turbant, omni poenarum genere puniantur."

18 *Theodosiani libri XVI* 9.16.4.

19 *Theodosiani libri XVI* 9.16.7: "Quicumque nocturna sacrificia daemonum celebraverit vel incantationibus daemones invocaverit, capite puniatur."

20 For further analysis, see Derek Collins, *Magic in the Ancient Greek World* (Oxford: Blackwell, 2008), 162–164.

21 Katherine Fischer Drew, *The Burgundian Code* (Philadelphia: University of Pennsylvania Press, 1959), 45.

22 Katherine Fischer Drew, *The Lombard Laws* (Philadelphia: University of Pennsylvania Press, 1973), 90.

23 Ibid., 90.

24 Ibid., 126–127. I have modified the translation slightly.

25 Drew, *Lombard Laws*, 126.

26 Alfred Boretius, ed., *Capitularia regnum Francorum*, Monumenta Germaniae Historica Leges 2 (Hanover: Hahn, 1883), 68.

27 Ibid., 96.

28 Ibid., 55: "cauculearii, malefici, incantatores vel incantatrices."

29 Boretius, *Capitularia regnum Francorum*, 59: "cauculatores nec incantatores nec tempestarii nec obligatores."

30 Joseph Hansen, ed., *Quellen und Untersuchungen zur Geschichte des Hexenwahns und der Hexenverfolgung im Mittelalter* (1901; reprint Hildesheim: Georg Olms, 1963), 38–39. The canon was reissued in several later collections, and finally in Gratian's *Decretum* C. 26 q. 5 c. 12.

31 Werner Tschacher, "Der Flug duch die Luft zwischen Illusionstheorie und Realitätsbeweis: Studien zum sog. Kanon Episcopi und zum Hexenflug," *Zeitschrift der Savigny-Stiftung für Rechtsgeschichte* 116, Kan. Abt. 85 (1999): 225–276; Martine Ostorero, *Le diable au sabbat: Littérature démonologique et sorcellerie (1440–1460)*, Micrologus' Library 38 (Florence: SISMEL, 2011), 580–617.

32 Burchard, *Decretorum libri vingti* 19.5.90, in *Patrologiae cursus completus series latina*, ed. J.-P. Migne, vol. 140 (Paris: Garnier, 1880), cols. 960–964.

33 Burchard, *Decretum* 19.5.65, col. 961.

34 Burchard, *Decretum* 19.5.68–69, cols. 961–962.

35 Burchard, *Decretum* 19.5.170, col. 973.

36 On its textual history and the possibility of multiple authors, see Anders Winroth, *The Making of Gratian's Decretum* (Cambridge: Cambridge University Press, 2000).

37 Gratian, *Decretum* C. 26 q. 2 c.6.

38 Gratian, *Decretum* C. 26 q. 5 c. 14.

39 Gratian, *Decretum* C. 33: "Quidam uir maleficiis inpeditus uxori suae debitum reddere non poterat."

40 Gratian, *Decretum* C. 33 q. 1 c. 4. See Catherine Rider, *Magic and Impotence in the Middle Ages* (Oxford: Oxford University Press, 2006), 39–42, 56–60.

41 Richard Kieckhefer, *Magic in the Middle Ages* (Cambridge: Cambridge University Press, 1989), 116–119; Jean-Patrice Boudet, *Entre science et* nigromance*: Astrologie, divination et magie dans l'Occident médiéval (XIIe-XIVe siècle)*, Histoire ancienne et médiévale 83 (Paris: Publications de la Sorbonne, 2006), 35–36.

42 Kieckhefer, *Magic*, 151–156.

43 Thomas B. de Mayo, *The Demonology of William of Auvergne: By Fire and Sword* (Lewiston, NY: Mellen Press, 2007), makes this point, but is not fully reliable. See still Lynn Thorndike, *A History of Magic and Experimental Science*, 8 vols. (New York: Macmillan and Columbia University Press, 1923–58), 2:338–371.

44 William, *De legibus* 24, in William of Auvergne, *Opera omnia* (Venice, 1591), 67; Boudet, *Entre science et* nigromance, 128.

45 William, *De universo* 2.3.22, in *Opera omnia*, 998–1000.

46 William, *De universo* 2.3.35, 1009.

47 William, *De legibus* 27, 1009; Alain Boureau, *Satan the Heretic: The Birth of Demonology in the Medieval West*, trans. Teresa Lavender Fagan (Chicago: University of Chicago Press, 2006), 64–65.

48 William, *De legibus* 27, 88–89.

49 William, *De legibus* 4, 33: "prout malefici intelliguntur magi et incantatores."

50 Charles Edward Hopkin, "The Share of Thomas Aquinas in the Growth of the Witchcraft Delusion" (originally Ph.D. diss., University of Pennsylvania, 1940; subsequently published New York: AMS Press, 1982).

51 Most systematically treated in Thomas Linsenmann, *Die Magie bei Thomas von Aquin*, Veröffentlichungen des Grabmann-Institutes 44 (Berlin: Akademie Verlag, 2000).

52 See Kieckhefer, *Magic*, 56–94; Karen Jolly, "Medieval Magic: Definitions, Beliefs, Practices," in *Witchcraft and Magic in Europe: The Middle Ages*, ed. Bengt Ankarloo and Stuart Clark (Philadelphia: University of Pennsylvania Press, 2002), 1–71.

53 Kieckhefer, *Magic*, 188.

54 Edward Peters, "The Medieval Church and State on Superstition, Magic and Witchcraft," in *Witchcraft and Magic in Europe: The Middle Ages*, ed. Bengt Ankarloo and Stuart Clark (Philadelphia: University of Pennsylvania Press, 2002), 173–245, at 209.

55 A number of his pronouncements are collected in Hansen, *Quellen*, 2–8.

56 Boureau, *Satan the Heretic*, 14–15, 43–67; Isabel Iribarren, "From Black Magic to Heresy: A Doctrinal Leap in the Pontificate of John XXII," *Church History* 76 (2007): 32–60; documentation in Alain Boureau, *Le pape et les sorciers: Une consultation de Jean XXII sur la magie en 1320 (Manuscrit B.A.V. Borghese 348)*, Sources et documents d'histoire de Moyen Âge 6 (Rome: École Française de Rome, 2004).

57 In point of fact, though, see Richard Kieckhefer, "Witchcraft, Necromancy and Sorcery as Heresy," in *Chasse aux sorcières et démonologie: Entre discours et pratiques (XIVe–XVIIe siècles)*, ed. Martine Ostorero, Georg Modestin, and Kathrin Utz Tremp, Micrologus' Library 36 (Florence: SISMEL, 2010), 133–153.

58 Matt. 10:1, Mark 3:15, Luke 9:1.

59 Aquinas, *Summa theologiae* 2.2.90.2.

60 Hansen, *Quellen*, 4–5.

61 Ibid., 5–6.

62 For the case against attributing *Super illius specula* to John, see Patrick Nold, "Thomas Braunceston O.M./O.P," in *Kirchenblild und Spiritualität: Dominikanische Beiträge zur Ekklesiologie und zum kirchlichen Leben in Mittelalter, Festschrift für Ulrich Horst O.P.*, ed. Thomas Prügl and Marianne Schlosser (Paderborn: Schöningh, 2007), 179–195; pro see Boureau, *Satan the Heretic*, 12–14; fuller discussion in Michael D. Bailey, *Fearful Spirits, Reasoned Follies: The Boundaries of Superstition in Late Medieval Europe* (Ithaca, NY: Cornell University Press, 2013), 79–80.

63 Eymerich, *Directorium inquisitorum* 2.43.9, ed. F. Peña (Rome, 1587), p. 341.

64 Gui, *Practica inquisitionis heretice pravitatis* 3.40–43, 5.6.1–2, ed. Celestin Douais (Paris: Alphonse Picard, 1886), 150–159, 292–293. On Gui not trying such cases himself, see Henry Charles Lea, *A History of the Inquisition of the Middle Ages*, 3 vols. (New York: Harper, 1887), 2:454.

65 Gui, *Practica* 3.40, p. 153.

66 Gui, *Practica* 5.6.2, p. 292.

67 Gui, *Practica* 5.7.12, p. 301.

68 Lea, *History of the Inquisition*, 2:174; Edward Peters, *Inquisition* (Berkeley: University of California Press, 1989), 60.

69 Eymerich, *Directorium* 2.43.2, p. 338.

70 Eymerich, *Directorium* 2.43.14, p. 344.

71 Eymerich, *Directorium* 2.43.8, p. 341.

72 More fully charted in Michael D. Bailey, "From Sorcery to Witchcraft: Clerical Conceptions of Magic in the Later Middle Ages," *Speculum* 76 (2001): 960–990.

73 Kieckhefer, *Magic*, 179.

74 *Las Siete Partidas* 4.8.6–7, trans. Samuel Parsons Scott, ed. Robert J. Burns, S.J., 5 vols. (Philadelphia: University of Pennsylvania Press, 2001), 4:916.

75 *Las Siete Partidas* 7.23, 5:1431–32.

76 *Las Siete Partidas* 7.23.3, 5:1432.

77 For a general summary, see Edward Peters, *Torture*, rev. ed. (Philadelphia: University of Pennsylvania Press, 1996), 40–44; regarding witch trials, see Levack, *Witch Hunt* (as n. 7 above), 75–80.

78 Peters, *Torture*, 49.

79 Ibid., 65.

80 William R. Jones, "Political Uses of Sorcery in Medieval Europe," *The Historian* 34 (1972): 670–687; Kieckhefer, *Witch Trials* (as n. 6 above), 10–15; Peters, "Medieval Church and State" (as n. 54 above), 218–222.

81 Malcolm Barber, *The Trial of the Templars*, 2nd ed. (Cambridge: Cambridge University Press, 2006).

82 Alain Provost, "On the Margins of the Templars' Trials: The Case of Bishop Guichard of Troyes," in *The Debate on the Trial of the Templars (1307–1314)*, ed. Jochen Burgtorf, Paul F. Crawford, and Helen J. Nicholson (Farnham, UK: Ashgate, 2010), 117–127.

83 Hansen, *Quellen*, 7–8.

84 Magisterially treated by Kathrin Utz Tremp, *Von der Häresie zur Hexerei: "Wirkliche" und imaginäre Sekten im Spätmittelalter*, Monumenta Germaniae Historica Schriften 59 (Hannover: Hahnsche Buchhandlung, 2008).

Bibliography (selection)

Ankarloo, Bengt and Stuart Clark (eds.), *Witchcraft and Magic in Europe: The Middle Ages.* Philadelphia, PA: University of Pennsylvania Press, 2002.

Bailey, Michael D., *Fearful Spirits, Reasoned Follies: The Boundaries of Superstition in Late Medieval Europe.* Ithaca, NY: Cornell University Press, 2013.

Boudet, Jean-Patrice, *Entre science et nigromance: Astrologie, divination et magie dans l'Occident médiéval (XIIe–XIVe siècle)*, Histoire ancienne et médiévale 83. Paris: Publications de la Sorbonne, 2006.

Kieckhefer, Richard, *Magic in the Middle Ages.* Cambridge: Cambridge University Press, 1989.

Ostorero, Martine, *Le diable au sabbat: Littérature démonologique et sorcellerie (1440–1460)*, Florence: SISMEL, 2011.

Utz Tremp, Kathrin, *Von der Häresie zur Hexerei: "Wirkliche" und imaginäre Sekten im Spätmittelalter*, Monumenta Germaniae Historica Schriften 59. Hannover: Hahnsche Buchhandlung, 2008.

5

THE RISE OF THE
WITCHCRAFT DOCTRINE

Martine Ostorero
(translation: Mireille Pasquer)

Around 1400, it is commonly accepted that individuals accomplish forms of magic, with the help of the devil, be it through invocation or pactising with him. In the first decades of the fifteenth century, this acceptance facilitates the forging of a terrifying idea: that certain individuals, while accomplishing magic, are also in a sect of sorcerers and witches. They meet in secret to adore the devil and sabotage Christian society. Their meetings result in the death of people and the destruction of harvests. Formulated in this way, this belief is the basis for the Witchcraft Doctrine. It will enable the dramatic witch hunts of the fifteenth to seventeenth centuries.

An array of documents of different natures sheds light on the emergence of this new conviction, which is to become the witches' Sabbath. Chronicles, pamphlets, court proceedings, legislation, religious literature and literary works were all meant to inform the population of the dangers of the witches' Sabbath, by depicting it as a loathsome crime. In the second half of the fifteenth century, the time comes for the elaboration of more ample treaties on demonology. These treaties aim at understanding the real practice of harmful magic by sorcerers and the extent of the powers and actions of demons within this context of witchcraft. They are the guidelines that will be used to determine the guilt of presumed witches.

The witches' Sabbath and the gravity of the
witches' crimes (1440–1460)

Beginning in the 1430s, several written works appear, in different contexts, whose objectives are to describe the witches' Sabbath. The authors designate and give shape to a new belief: some men and women form clandestine sects whose members renounce the Christian faith and swear loyalty to the devil and demons. Their allegiance is sealed by a pact; when the devil and the demons call them, the members of the sect meet in isolated places, often by flying through the air. In these places, they worship the devil and set out to accomplish his destructive craft on people, animals and harvests. They are also suspected of engaging in sexual activity with the devil, of killing small children, of eating their flesh and of making ointments and maleficent potions with it. The existence of these sects constitutes a grave menace to society. It is therefore necessary to inform the authorities and the populace and to prepare to fight off this terrible danger.

There are four new principal elements that characterize these practices of harmful magic:

1   The collective dimension: sect or secret society.
2   The bond of absolute fidelity, which ties the witch to the devil: apostasy or demon worship.
3   Act against nature: cannibalism, infanticide and deviant sexual acts.
4   The magic transport of witches through the air.[1]

For the first time, some texts describe and define with precision the imaginary concept of the witches' Sabbath. Within a decade, this concept will have taken root in a territorial space centered in the arc of the Western Alps and the region of Lyon. In the first half of the fifteenth century, regions such as the Pyrenees and Italy are also influenced by the idea of the witches' Sabbath. The belief will spread then rapidly into other regions of Western Europe and will become part of the societal mind for several centuries.

The theologians, inquisitors and magistrates who write these texts are deeply convinced of the reality of the witches' Sabbath and demonic sects. Through their writings, they forge and elaborate upon this concept. In fact, they seek to go against a more skeptic train of thought, which questions the reality of the acts committed by witches, seeing more the likelihood that individuals are victims of deceit, delusion, mental illness or melancholy (within the tradition of the Canon *Episcopi*). The "fanatics" of the Sabbath push for repression and although they are a quantitative minority in the first half of the fifteenth century, their influence strengthens considerably in certain localities and states, such as the Western Alps, Western Switzerland, Savoy, Burgundy and the North and South of France. Their influence stretches also to certain cultural milieus such as the Dominican and Franciscan inquisition and the Council of Basel.

There are six primary written works that testify to the emergence of this new conception of witchcraft.[2] Hans Fründ, a chronicler from Lucern, relates the first witch hunt in Valais, Switzerland, in 1428–1436. Johannes Nider, Dominican and professor at the University of Vienna, takes a look at the question in his book, *Formicarius* (written between 1436 and 1438). The Grand-Judge ("juge-mage", i.e. chief magistrate) of Briançon (Dauphiné), Claude Tholosan, denounces the gravity of the witches' crimes, as he presides over more than a hundred witch trials. Meanwhile, on the other side of the Alps, an anonymous pamphlet appears, entitled *Errores Gazariorum* (*Errors of the Gazarii*). It describes in detail the ritual of the witches' Sabbath and is supported by strong judiciary actions. An enigmatic treaty, entitled the *Vauderye de Lyonois*, testifies to the difficulties faced by the Dominicans of Lyon as they try to institute witch hunts in that part of the French Kingdom. Finally, Martin le Franc, provost of Lausanne and secretary to the Duke of Savoy, Amadeus VIII (the anti-pope Felix V), composes a long poem entitled *Le Champion des Dames* (*The Defender of Ladies*), in response to the quarrel over *Le Roman de la Rose*. This poem is one of the earliest texts of French humanism describing the witches' Sabbath, which Martin Le Franc associates primarily with women.

Unveiling the interest which lies in these first texts requires a detailed presentation of their content, their contexts of time and place and how they were diffused or distributed.

Around 1430, Hans Fründ, chronicler from Lucern, describes in German a witch hunt led in Valais, in 1428.[3] According to him, more than 200 witch burnings occurred in a mere year and a half. The confessions of the accused are stupefying. A new sect of sorcerers, numbering more than 700 members, congregate in clandestine "schools". They meet with the "evil spirit", who indoctrinates them against the Christian faith and coerces them into abandoning God to practice with him. In exchange, he promises them wealth and power. He shows these "heretics" how to ride through the air and how to steal from the cellars of those who have the best wine. The devil also teaches them how to transform themselves into wolves and how to become invisible using certain herbs. This enables them to perpetrate harmful magic against people, animals and harvests. Hans Fründ also tells of how these witches and sorcerers might have killed their own children to feast on them during the gatherings of their "society" (*Gesellschaft*). These clandestine societies would be at the forefront of overturning Christian society, ready to impose their own power and laws. According to Hans Fründ, the number of practitioners of harmful magic had greatly increased during the last nine years and they were one step away from electing their own king! The Lucernois states precisely: in his opinion, witchcraft constitutes a major danger.

We now know that Hans Fründ had invented nothing, though he might have exaggerated some points; a vast witch hunt was held between 1428 and 1436 (at least). The witch hunt is the impulse of the secular courts in Episcopal Valais as well as the ecclesiastic courts in Lower Valais, led by the duke of Savoy. A large part of what is found in Hans Fründ's chronicle can be related directly to the confessions of the accused, whose trials were duly noted and conserved. Hans Fründ holds his information first hand: it was certainly related to him by the members of the Silenen family, who were witnesses or actors in the different judicial proceedings led against the witches in Valais.

In the fifth part of the *Formicarius* (*The Anthill*), written between 1436 and 1438, the Dominican Johannes Nider, describes events similar to those recounted by Hans Fründ; however, they take place in the diocese of Lausanne and on land owned by the city of Bern.[4] Because Johannes Nider was prior in the convent of Basel between 1429 and 1434 and was in charge of leading religious reforms, he probably had easy access to a part of these events. He was a Dominican Observant and eminent professor of theology at the University of Vienna. In his view, harmful magic and the cannibalistic sects of witches constitute the best material needed to dispense a moral education in the light of societal reform. The *Formicarius* is first of all a pastoral work.

Two informers relate the events he details in his book. The first, an inquisitor from Autun, tells of how, around 1437, witches had eaten their newborn babes during a secret meeting. The second informer, a secular judge of the High-Simmental named Pierre, describes how the witches used newborn cadavers to prepare evil potions or transform themselves into animals. This ritual of initiation gives the witches instant knowledge of the secrets of their sect, as long as they had renounced to God and pledged allegiance to the devil. Also according to Pierre and related by Nider are the harmful enchantments cast by the sorcerers Scavius, Hoppo and Scaedeli. These were known to cause sterility, disease, hail and death. Their practices illustrate a popular concept of witchcraft that Nider is quick to demonize. Although he presents several elements that constitute the witches' Sabbath, he does not describe them fully, nor does he give a complete description of the rituals of the Sabbath. However, in these years of transition, Nider is unable to present a complete description of it.

The Dominican is not yet ready to believe everything he is told, because he knows that the devil can easily deceive women. In Book 2 of the *Formicarius*, which deals with dreams and visions, Nider relates the case of an old woman who believes she can fly and yet remains seated at her kneading-trough. For him, she is only dreaming and in a sort of trance. Night flight, then, is not a plausible part of the Sabbath and constitutes a popular belief that he openly mocks. Although skeptical about the night flight, Nider is persuaded of the existence of groups of witches that commit infanticide, eat human flesh and gather around an "evil spirit" in a sort of Sabbath.

During these same years, three works of a similar nature to those described earlier propose a systematic description of the rituals of the witches' Sabbath. The objective of these brief treatises is to denounce the wrongdoings of witches by underlining the gravity of their crimes. Two of these works circulate under the cover of anonymity. The authors of the *Errores Gazariorum* and *Vauderye de Lyonois* are probably close to the inquisitors' sphere in the Val d'Aoste for the first, and Lyon for the second. We will come back to this later. Claude Tholosan writes the third work. He is a lawyer and Grand Judge of Briançon (Dauphiné), at the service of the King of France. His work, *Ut magorum et maleficiorum errores . . .* (*So that the errors of the Magicians and Sorcerers . . .*), written around 1436, is the fruit of his ten years of practice as a judge.[5] He had presided over a hundred witch trials (mostly in the Haut-Dauphiné). As he relates in the first part of the work, the accused belong to a demonical sect whose rituals and practices he describes precisely. He gives details about the ceremony of renunciation (apostasy) and the homages to the devil, which are followed by sexual orgies and cannibalistic banquets. Tholosan also describes the evil spells, their composition and their effects. For example, witches are capable of making men insane and women barren. Although he considers night flight a diabolical illusion, he believes that the Sabbath and the activities of the sect are quite real and perceives them as terrible crimes. That is why he justifies repressive action against the sect. In the second part of the work, the Grand Judge also consults other jurists, namely the southern lawyer Jourdain Brice, whom he cites in his book. Finally, Tholosan concludes his book with an important legal remark, which aims at assimilating witch crimes with homicide and most importantly, with the crime of *lèse-majesté*.[6] In this manner, the Grand Judge seeks to certify the supremacy of Princely Law over Church Law. Contrary to the *Errores Gazariorum* and the *Vauderye de Lyonois*, Tholosan's work was not diffused outside the Dauphiné; it was only conserved in the *Quintus liber fachureriorum*, the fifth book of the Treasury in which Tholosan records the witch trials' proceedings. However, the early onset and amplitude of the witch hunts held in the region of Dauphiné (1424–1445) certainly echoes far into neighboring communities, and this contributes to the spread of the idea of the witches' Sabbath.

Because of the extent of Grand-Judge Tholosan's work and the weight of his actions, most of the repression in Dauphiné is attributed to him. But it is important to remember the active presence of the Mendicant Friars, who work closely with secular judges and who re-ignite pastoral reform in the fourteenth–fifteenth centuries. Indeed, it is after the visit of the Dominican Predicator, Vincent Ferrier, from Cataluña, that the witch hunts start. It is the continuation of a century of crusades against the Waldensian heretics. Tholosan makes no mention of the actual role of the Franciscan inquisitors. This is certainly a means of affirming the importance of Princely justice and of controlling the courts. In this way, the inquisitors could not act alone against the witches. So, actually, it is Princely justice that is at the forefront of the struggles against witches. This might be the ransom paid for the Integration of Dauphiné (then located in the Empire) into the Kingdom of France. At this period, this kingdom felt that it was more Christian than others, holding the divine power. This can explain Tholosan's role as champion of royal absolutism.[7]

There is yet another text, entitled *Errores Gazariorum* (1436–1438), which relates closely to Judge Tholosan's vision of demonical witchcraft.[8] In it, we learn that the devil, when he has succeeded in enlisting a new member in his sect, requires his allegiance. He/she must recruit new members, keep the existence of the sect secret, and defend the members of it. The new members must kill small children and bring them to the Sabbath; they must sterilize men and women through the use of maleficent potions. After this oath taking, new members must worship the devil by kissing his rear end and by promising to give him a part of their body at their death. Once this ritual of homage is complete, the whole sect celebrates the arrival of the new member. There are different foods to eat, mostly small children who have been roasted or boiled. Then there is dancing and when the devil turns out the light and cries *Mestlet, mestlet*, the sexual orgy begins, without regard to blood ties or gender. The members of the sect also prepare powders and ointments, using the fatty tissue of children, snakes, toads, spiders, lizards and other ingredients. This enables them to provoke, with the help of the devil, multiple spells to kill men and animals and destroy harvests.

This text is written as a sort of a manual: a succession of articles (*item*), each one describing a particular aspect of the witches' sect, narrated in question and answer style. The anonymous author of this text relies on the witch trials that were held in the Val d'Aosta (Northern Italy), in the Duchy of Savoy: we find a mention of the trial of Jeannette Cauda (*Johanneta Cauda*), who was burned at the stake in Chambave, August 11, 1428. The *Errores* could have been written by the Franciscan Ponce Feugeyron (or someone close to him), who was a pontifical inquisitor. Its purpose was to act against the witches and demon worshippers present in the Val d'Aosta. This particular region starts its witch hunts in 1428, at least. Then, more important witch hunts are held in the 1430s, 1440s and 1460s, mostly led by Franciscan inquisitors.[9]

Two manuscripts of *Errores* are kept with texts produced by the Council of Basel, which supports the hypothesis that Ponce Feugeyron was the author of the short treaty. It is known that he was present at the Council at different times between 1433 and 1437. The Council of Basel is a perfect place for the distribution and diffusion of literature concerning the witches' Sabbath.[10] One of the manuscripts of this text circulated in the diocese of Lausanne and was completed with informations relative to the trials held in the region of Vevey. One mention can be directly related to the confessions of the young Aymonet Maugetaz of Epesses, recorded in 1438, by the Dominican inquisitor Ulric de Torrenté. Between 1451 and 1457, a third manuscript (Rome, Biblioteca Apostolica Vaticana, Pal. Lat. 1381, f. 190r–192r) was copied by German lawyer Mathias Widmann von Kemnath (died in 1476).[11] He was court chaplain, mathematician and astrologer for the Palatin Prince, Frederik the First, the Victorious (Friederich I., der Siegreiche,

1425–1476). This is how the Valdotan treaty spreads into the Germanic Empire. It is then translated into German by Widmann, which he inserts into his work, "Chronik Friederich der Siegreichen".

The *Errores Gazarorium* presents a number of similarities with another pamphlet produced in the same context and known under the name of the *Vauderye de Lyonois en brief*.[12] The *Vauderye* is written in Latin, at an unknown date, by an unknown author, and details precisely a diabolic sect known as the Waldenses (*Valdesia*). It describes their organization and criminal activities. The members of this sect, called "Faicturiers or Faicturières", supposedly congregate at night in the "Synagogue", also called the "Fait", the "Martinet", or the "Sabbath" as mentioned in a manuscript of Trier, (Stadtbibliothek, Ms. 613). Assembled around the devil depicted in a monstrous and abominable way, the apostates give him homage, profane Christian rites and engage in festivities of a dubious nature, such as sexual orgies.

In revealing the activities of this secret society, the *Vauderye de Lyonois en brief* does little to prove its theoretical existence, but does much to heighten the "enormity" (*enormitas*) of the crimes, possibly to better punish its hypothetical members.[13] In fact, there is a direct correlation between the crimes attributed to the witches' sect and a certain judicial activity in the region of Lyon. Recent research, supported by the discovery of new writings, allows for the substantiation that this treaty belongs to the Dominican inquisition in Lyon. It can also be stated that it was composed at the late end of the 1430s. Indeed, during the 1430s, the prior of the Dominican convent of Lyon, Thomas Girbelli, and Jean Tacot, inquisitor of the same convent, labor to install the structure and conditions necessary to begin a regional witch hunt. However, they faced opposition, notably from the Archbishop of Lyon and the Consulate of the city. Thomas Girbelli and Jean Tacot would have written the treaty in response to their antagonists, as well as to solicit political and financial support from the King and the Pope. This is clearly explained in a recently uncovered continuation of the treaty.[14]

The story of the "vauderie de Lyon" is that of the failure of witch hunts in that region of France. Yet, it still remains as a largely distributed text by the network of Observant Dominicans. Actually, there are three copies of the manuscript remaining.[15] In particular, the treaty was diffused in the region of Burgundy, where the case of the *Vauderie d'Arras* (c. 1460) gave it its name. Then, the treaty reached the city of Trève (Trier), at the gates of the Empire (c. 1470).

The widespread persecutions reaches Martin Le Franc, sometime in 1440: he describes trials led in the Dauphiné (mostly in Vallouise, known by him as the *Valpute*) and in the Piedmont (*mons d'Esture*, probably Stura di Demonte). He is the first to present the persecutions in a literary, humanistic work: *Le Champion des Dames* (*The Defender of Ladies*), which he composes between 1440 and 1442.[16] Martin Le Franc is secretary to the anti-pope Felix V (Duke Amadeus VIII of Savoy) during the Council of Basel and will be provost to the Lausanne Chapter as early as 1443. The poem he writes constitutes an ongoing dialogue between the Defender, *Franc Vouloir*, and his different adversaries. It concerns the reputation of women, in a typical literary court quarrel that arises at the time of Jean de Meun. In the poem, the Detractor of women defends the existence of "old witches", "vaudoises" (Waldenses) and "Faicturières", "who fly through the air like birds", to congregate with the devil and engage in the worst debaucheries: infant cannibalism, sexual orgies, evil spells and the metamorphosis of the devil. The Defender refutes these superstitious tales and discredits magic flight. The ensuing dialogue gives a good idea of the divergent mentalities and sensibilities that coexists in that particular period.

Martin Le Franc gives voice to the ideas of his time through the characters of his poem and integrates into it the representations of traditional knowledge, discussions on heresy, magic and demonology as well as the popular beliefs concerning witchcraft and its practice. The Defender of the poem suggests that rather than burning witches, the Church must act upon the education of women. By educating them, they can be made aware of their weaknesses and shortcomings. His critiques also aim at shaking the papal Court, which he deems unconcerned about sending more pastors to rural regions. In the context of the Christian reform programs of the time, Martin Le Franc's diatribe against the clergy constitutes a burning topic at the Council of Basel.

Written between Basel and the State of Savoy, the *Champion des Dames* is progressively distributed, mostly in the State of Burgundy. The work is dedicated to Philippe le Bon, though the latter does not give it the eulogy the poet was hoping for. One of the copies was made in 1451 in Arras and is adorned with miniature illustrations depicting two women, one on a broom and the other on a stick.

These first six texts all offer a similar view of the witches' Sabbath, labeled "the Lausanne paradigm" by Richard Kieckhefer.[17] Other testimonies, however, offer some variations, influenced by the cultural universe of the classic literary *strige* or vampire witch (*strix, strega*) as well as regional folklore. Such is the case of the testimonies originating from the Italian peninsula and Umbria (the "Umbrian paradigm", according to Kieckhefer) and professed in the sermons of Bernardino of Siena (1427 and 1447).[18] The Franciscan Observant denounces the old soothsayers who believe that they can "run with Herodiade" (*in curso cum Herodia*) and who metamorphose into cats or "striges" (*strix, lamia*), to drink the blood of children. Italian authors, basing themselves on sporadic regional witch trials, describe the witches as a combination of infanticide "striges" and "Good Ladies", who fly with the Bountiful Lady (*Abundia*) or the goddess Diana. These witches do not meet in a "synagogue", as found in the Alps, but rather take part in the "game" (*ludus*) of Diana. The devil has no place in this "game" and is only a character that deceives women. Lastly, incantations and spells are perceived as being the work of old women. This alternative witch mythology spreads beyond the Alps and mix occasionally with the concept of the witches' Sabbath. Beyond that, some regions, such as the Holy Roman Empire, are at first unreceptive and limits themselves to a simpler view of sorcery: the casting of evil spells.

Legislation

Secular authorities were not insensitive to the current mutations of thought. They perceived the interest in persecuting witches as a means of insuring theirs as the high-justice as well as confirming their sovereignty or majesty. Thus, the political dimension of the repression is a high stake. Lay authorities can be potentially active in the arena of repression as long as maleficent crimes endanger people or property without, however, containing the "flavor of heresy". However, there are great regional contrasts in the repression because the perception of the gravity of crimes of witchcraft is not the same everywhere.

In Cataluña, the Statutes of Aneu (County of Pallars, on the border with the County of Foix and the Valley of Aran) are revised in 1424 in light of what is considered the "enormity" of the crimes perpetrated against "God and the Valley" using harmful magic. They prescribe capital punishment by fire for those judged guilty of "going at night with *bruixes*" (witches) to meet the "Goat of Biterne" (probably a demonical entity), of worshipping him rather than God, of killing newborn babes, of provoking disease and of using poisons.[19] Even though trace documents do confirm the existence of judicial repression as early as 1420, the effects of these regulations are hard to measure because of the absence of complete trial proceedings. Principally, secular courts lead the repression, although stimulated by the intense pastoral activities of the Dominicans Vincent Ferrier and Pere Cerdà. However the inquisition intervenes in the procedures mostly to incite caution and moderation. It remains skeptical about the collective dimension of the crimes as well as the Sabbath.

The principal protagonist of the early changes in perception of witch crimes is Nicolas Eymerich, inquisitor in the territories of Cataluña, Aragon, Valencia and Mallorca during the years of 1356 to 1391. His two treatises bear witness to his vision, describing how magic and enchantments are to be assimilated to heresy. They also support the intensity with which he inquires into heresy during his years as inquisitor.[20] The most famous Catalan preacher, Vincent Ferrier (1356–1419), continued in the same vein. His sermons denounce blasphemy, the invocation of demons and soothsaying as well as any popular superstitions. He crisscrosses Western Europe and his fire and brimstone sermons echo all the way into Italy, Dauphiné, Savoy and Western Switzerland.

It is quite possible that Vincent Ferrier's visit into the Alpine Valleys leads to the decreeing of severe regulations against spell casters and witches. It is the case in episcopal Valais in 1428. The Patriots of Valais (the Diet) become the leaders of the repression of witches, evincing the inquisitors and episcopal justice. In 1430 and 1434, other communities, such as Mörel and Rarogne, follow the Patriots' example.[21]

It is during that time that the Duke of Savoy Amadeus VIII issues an edict of his great legislative work, the *Statuta Sabaudie* (Statutes of Savoy, 1430). His ambition is to reform and reorganize his state, which extends over the Alps from the Mediterranean Sea to the shores of Lake Geneva. The first article of his decree order targets the sorcerers, magicians and demon worshippers. As he qualifies acts of sorcery and magic as heretic crimes, he extends into the judicial competence of ecclesiastical courts in that domain. Amadeus VIII feels so strongly about the dangers of witchcraft that he enjoins both the secular and the ecclesiastical justice of his duchy to initiate the pursuit and judgment of heresy and witchcraft. His strategy is political, judicial and financial. In taking the position as defender of divine and human majesty, he consolidates and defines demonic sorcery as a heresy of State.[22]

From the moment that sorcery is rethought as heresy, secular princes seek to maintain control over the punishment of these crimes through offensive repression. Acting thus, they legitimize and affirm their sovereign power. This is precisely what the judge Tholosan achieved for the Prince of the Kingdom of France.

The papacy is slower to react than the secular princes. Papal bulls remain sober and moderate, with the exception of Alexander V, in 1409. This contrasts sharply with the proactive attitude of John XXII, in the preceding century. The bulls make neither allusion to the Sabbath, nor mention the witch's flight through the air; nor do they treat the devil as a dominant figure. This is the case for Eugenius IV (1437–1445), Nicolas V (1451), Calixtus III (1457), Pius II (1459) and Innocent VIII (1484). Nicolas V, though, does authorize the pursuit of witches, without qualifying them as heretics, which permits the inquisition to expand its field of action into sorcery and magical practices. The crimes tend to be qualified as *lèse-majesté* or enormous scandal against the Christian faith.[23]

Understand, convince and justify: the demonological treaties (1450–1470)

From the 1440s, texts about witchcraft not only attempt to describe the Sabbath and the atrocities committed by sorcerers and witches but aim also at understanding the reality of the interactions between demons and witches, as well as their consequences. The texts' objectives are to give the courts an acceptable framework in which to apply the witchcraft doctrine, both legally and theologically. The tracts on demonology, as autonomous works, gain ground as early as the 1450s. The theorists of demonology are mostly intellectuals: theologians, inquisitors, even lawyers or doctors. They seek to integrate the new belief of the witches' Sabbath into traditional Christian demonology. It is about understanding the existence and nature of demons as well as the extent of their powers over humans and the environment. The treaties written by these demonologists are works of synthesis as well as rupture: a concentration of demonological knowledge, magic, witchcraft and possession confronted with the confessions of accused witches.[24]

Close to 30 texts are written before the appearance of the *Malleus maleficarum* (*Hammer of Witches*), written by Heinrich Kramer (Institoris, 1486). The renown of this last text is largely due to the growing use of the printing press and tends to overshadow earlier works, which are interesting for historians but are little known. However, the questions posited by the German Dominican do reflect the thoughts of these earlier works. Besides, the titles of these texts often include the word "hammer" (*malleus*) or "whip" (*flagellum*), indicating the aims of the author; but they can also be more soberly entitled "treaties" or *opusculum* (brief works), or "sermons" or "questions", which bear witness to the intellectual designs behind them.

The tracking down of these fifteenth-century writings owe a lot to the anthology of texts compiled by Joseph Hansen in 1901, entitled *Quellen und Untersuchungen zur Geschichte des Hexenwahns und der Hexenverfolgungen im Mittelalter*. This work is essentially the base for scientific research for these fifteenth-century texts. Yet it is still necessary to prolong the study of manuscripts and written works to deepen the knowledge of who the authors were and the contexts in which the treatises were written. Thus, more complete critical editions should be published. In the last century, other works, coming from the Italian peninsula in particular, have enriched the anthology.[25]

Generally, these texts attempt to evaluate the possibility and by extension the reality of the witches' Sabbath and the acts committed by their protagonists. Christian faith does not permit the authors to doubt the existence of the devil and his maleficent actions, leading them to ask these questions: How can witches cause tempests, disease and sexual impotence? Can they transform others or transform themselves into animals? Are they physically transported to their Sabbaths and are these real events? How can demons, as pure spirits, assume a physical body? How can sorcerers accomplish their vital functions (*operae vitae*), such as eating, speaking and being incubus or succubus? Why does God permit these misfortunes and terrible destructive actions to take place?

To answer all of these questions, the authors employ an argumentation which attempts to be rational. They use the tools of scholastic reasoning and logic. They support their arguments with biblical texts as well as those written by the Church Fathers, such as Augustine and Gregory the Great. They cite theologians, namely Thomas Aquinas, and rely on hagiographic accounts and *exempla*. These practical tracts are the fruit of the late scholasticism, slightly bastardized and twisted to the taste of certain thinkers, but they are not written by perverted or deranged consciences. Demonology must be considered a true science, and demonologists endeavor to describe the place and purpose of demons in the world and in nature.

These treatises also translate the interrogations and divergent thoughts of the demonologists. Contradictory positions can be defended: for example, it is possible for an author to state that the devil does accompany the witches to their Sabbath, while another will defend the idea that demons make the witches dream that they are going to the Sabbath. All is a matter of belief and opinion. This enables certain skepticism to remain regarding the reality of evil spells and Sabbaths. This skepticism can already be found in the earliest reactions to more fanatical positions.

The texts are most often produced in the eaves of judicial courts, as a desire to encourage witch hunting and give it a normative framework, or as a necessity to justify repressive periods. For many authors, the proof of the reality of witchcraft resides in the confessions of the accused, most often obtained through torture or the menace of torture. Treaties and trials fed off of each other in a reciprocal manner.

Jean Vinet, Nicolas Jacquier and Pierre Mamoris

Three treaties are particularly revealing about the fabrication of the witchcraft doctrine: the *Tractatus contra invocatores demonum (Treatise Against Demon Invokers)*, by Jean Vinet (c. 1450–1452), the *Flagellum hereticorum fascinariorum (Scourge of Heretical Enchanters)*, by Nicolas Jacquier (1458), and the *Flagellum maleficorum (Scourge of Those Who Commit Evil Deeds)*, by Pierre Mamoris (before 1462). They are among the first texts that speak of the witchcraft doctrine in terms of Christian demonology and are all written by French authors. The Dominican Jean Vinet completes his studies in theology in Paris and teaches Pierre Lombard's *Sentences* until he is named inquisitor in Carcassonne. Nicolas Jacquier, also a Dominican inquisitor, is attached to the convent in Dijon, then Lille, all the while traveling extensively to the East and North of France, generally between Lyon and the State of Burgundy. Pierre Mamoris, a secular clerk originally from Limoges, is canon in Saintes as well as professor of theology at the University of Poitiers. Let us take a closer look at these three texts, as they are emblematic of the particular ideas on witchcraft of the middle of the fifteenth century.[26]

First off, what intrigues Jean Vinet is the manner in which demons are able to fabricate a body that is manifest to man and capable of acting physically upon the world. He also questions the magic powers that can be obtained by practicing with the devil, which he firmly condemns. And, anxious about liberating man from the grip of demons, he demonstrates the effectiveness of the sacrament of exorcism. However, the actual question of the "criminals of idolatry and allies to the demons", as he calls the sorcerers and witches, is quite diluted in his tract and is not the object of a complete consideration.

Jean Vinet gathers most of his answers from Thomas Aquinas. He selects within the writings of the Angelic Doctor what he needs to demonstrate his point. He accentuates the physical manifestation of demons *in corporibus assumptis* (feigned, artificial or virtual bodies), a notion that makes demonic witchcraft more credible. Demons, with their "virtual" body, can appear to man in a sensible, visible and verbal way. In consequence, demonic apparitions are not visions produced by the imagination or through dreams in sleep (inside), but as realities (outside) to man. The stake is high because he is attempting to demonstrate the actual, physically palpable presence of demons outside the witches' Sabbath. He thinks that the witches' Sabbath is totally possible: demons can meet with humans and unite with them (sexually or through allegiance). Demons can transport people from one place to another (flight to the Sabbath), and demons will help sorcerers cast evil spells.[27] The French Dominican has clearly learned the Thomist lesson on demonic pacts: magical arts are not possible without allegiance with demons. Vinet's explanations are a refreshing re-write of what Thomas Aquinas had written two centuries earlier his position is not one of a witch hunter, but rather a scholar who seeks the limit between what is possible or impossible, and acceptable or unacceptable. However, the passage of time had greatly modified the currents of thought on witchcraft and these changes had enabled the manifest repression of witches.

Vinet's contemporary, Nicolas Jacquier, goes much further in his tract, *Flagellum hereticorum fascinariorum* (1428). Convinced of the reality of the Sabbath, he virulently denounces the "new sects of heretic enchanters". In his view, the witches' Sabbath is a demonic anti-church to which its participants adhere willingly and consciously. It is a demonic "cult" which includes sacrilegious rites and concentrates the entire horror of witch crimes.

Similar to Jean Vinet, Jacquier never ceases to spotlight the demonic body, perceptible to human senses. As a leitmotif, he uses Thomas Aquinas' works to remind his readers of the real and corporeal presence of demons at the Sabbath. Jacquier uses this argument of sensory perception to convince his detractors. Based on the physical experience man can have of the demon body, this latter become indubitable: the devil can really manifest himself physically because human beings can, through their external senses, touch, hear, see and even smell his fetid odors. This repertory of senses helps to establish objective proof of the reality of the Sabbath and the physical presence of the devil in an "artificial body" (*corpus assumptum*). In Jacquier's opinion, sexual intercourse between demons and men or women is the manifest proof of their existence, and it is also for this reason that the revelers of the Sabbath returned from the synagogue affirming their "complete exhaustion due to the extremely violent pleasures" felt with the demons.[28]

Nicolas Jacquier is probably the demonologist who worked the most assiduously on proving what can be called diabolic realism. That is to say, the postulation that, not only are the devil and demons real, but that physical interaction between humans and demons is possible. The Dominican inquisitor is considered an extreme demonologist because he so firmly believes in the existence of demons: for him, the devil is a creature that belongs to a material reality and his actions have concrete and perceptible effects.

In this light, the "synagogue of the devil", which aims at destroying Christianity, constitutes a grave danger. It is of the upmost importance to demonstrate that these sorcerers and witches are not only heretics but also the "worst of the heretics", thus justifying the violence of the repression against them. The inquisitor Jacquier supports a severe hardening of judicial procedures to ensure that the accused have no hope of grace or pardon. They must be condemned to death, in their first charge. The *Flagellum* is a true plea in favor of capital punishment and organized witch hunts.

The Dominican has a double mission: to convince others of the existence of sects of witches and to convince them of the necessity of uniting against these sects. And he also says this: those that do not help fight against the sects become allies to them and their demons. This position sends him to the ranks of fanatics fighting against demonic sorcery in the fifteenth century. His project of eradicating demonic witchcraft is at the heart of his defense for Christian orthodoxy and is parallel to his lifelong battle against the Hussites, of which he writes two tracts.[29] The whole of his work is enveloped in his preoccupations as a Dominican Observant.

The third treaty, coming from a different perspective, makes its author, Pierre Mamoris, slightly more sympathetic. His work, *Flagellum maleficorum* (written around 1462), gives a large range of spells and magical practices witnessed in Poitou and in the Kingdom of Bourges in the middle of the fifteenth century. According to Mamoris, these practices have multiplied since the Hundred Years War. Gathering testimonies from his peers, as well as his own experiences, he offers a sort of ethnographic harvest, with which he opens his treatise. He announces that he wants to "discover the truth" as well as persuade himself: Are the magical arts derived from demons or nature? Is the Sabbath real or is it a demonic delusion? To be persuasive, he compares and contrasts different doctrines and knowledge. He searches for the position to adopt and does not hesitate to speak of his doubts. Pierre Mamoris' point of view changes from the beginning to the end of his treaty, finally resting upon the conviction that the misdeeds of sorcerers and witches are extremely serious. He is particularly marked by a certain trial which made a lot of noise at the time: the conviction of Guillaume Adeline in 1453 in Evreux.[30]

Overall, Pierre Mamoris underlines the great ability demons have of deceiving humans. However, unlike Vinet and Jacquier, Mamoris relies on Bonaventure rather than Thomas Aquinas to support the illusory character of demonic manifestations. According to the theologian from Poitiers, the demon is more of a conjurer who has intimate knowledge of nature's secrets and manipulates this knowledge to deceive men. Pierre Mamoris points out that there is nothing supernatural or miraculous about this; works of the devil are limited to a framework of nature and can be explained by natural laws, such as the optical illusion.

Pierre Mamoris, professor of theology at the University of Poitiers, was an open-minded person and his desire to understand led him to confront different experiences, vaster than those researched by the Dominican inquisitors Vinet and Jacquier.

The Vauderie d'Arras

The *Vauderie d'Arras* can be considered as the judicial implementation of Nicolas Jacquier's ideas. It is the first great witch hunt which was led in France, in the State of Burgundy, as early as 1459, a year after the publication of Jacquier's treaty. The first of the accused, about a dozen, were condemned to the pyre, before the intervention of the Royal Counselors, who ended the hunt and overturn the sentences handed down against the "vaudois" (Waldenses) of Arras. Although the procedural paperwork was destroyed after the rehabilitation ceremony in 1491, the chronicles of Jacques Du Clerq permit the reconstitution of the facts of the Vauderie d'Arras. As demonstrated by Franck Mercier, this witch hunt was the competitive theatre between two sovereignty: the Kingdom of France and the State of Burgundy, which will finally be unable to perpetuate its reign.[31]

It is quite possible that Jacquier's pamphlet in favor of capital punishment influenced the debate. As an example, there is a judicial memo, the *Recollectio . . . Valdensium ydolatrarum*, produced at the time of the Vauderie d'Arras, that aims at legitimizing the persecutions of the "vaudois-sorciers" of Arras. The anonymous author, who might be Jacques du Bois (judge of Arras), might have used Jacquier's *Flagellum* for support, because the memo contains some of the same general reflections, especially concerning the flight of the witches to the Sabbath and the need for capital punishment against demonic witches.

It is in this context that Jean Tinctor, canon of Tournai, raised at the University of Cologne, takes up his pen to justify the repression and writes a *Sermo contra sectam Valdensium* (*Sermon against the Waldensian sect*) (1460). A few years later, he will produce a more complete version in French, entitled *Traité du crime de Vauderie* (*Tract against the crimes of Vauderie*), which was probably destined for the Court of Burgundy and a larger secular public.[32] Jean Tinctor's demonology explores the limits of the devil's power: it is unable to transcend the laws of nature, incapable of creating matter or life and always subjugated by the divine power. Although he remains convinced of the reality of the crimes committed by the sorcerers, he considers that demonic dreams can be instilled upon man to test his morals and his faith. Tinctor is one of the first to conciliate two ideas, which until that time had seemed contradictory: if the accused confesses in believing the demonic illusion, he is therefore responsible for the consequences that follow the hypothetical acts. Then it is important to examine closely the conscience of the accused and their individual responsibilities. The judges should exercise caution and should investigate more in depth for possible material proof of the Sabbath.

The Sabbath between demonic illusion and reality

The question of the reality of the witches' Sabbath is at the crossroads of two paths: the first one is related to the old canon *Episcopi* (eleventh century, Regino of Prüm), and considers that women are victims of demonic delusions. The canon *Episcopi* has been the foundation for most of the treaties on demonology in the fifteenth century. It has served as a pretext for the authors to debate the multitude of stakes surrounding the phenomena. Authors such as Jean Vinet, Nicolas Jacquier and Pierre Mamoris searched for proof of night flight and consequently, for the witches' Sabbath. Others, such as Juan Torquemada, or, the Italian Franciscan Observance, remained loyal to his idea that it was just an illusion, without completely forgiving those who believed in it.[33] From the Milanese Dominican, Girolamo Visconti,[34] to Jean Tinctor, and later still, Heinrich Kramer (Institoris), there finally seems to be a resolution concerning both ideas: either witches are able to fly through the air with the help of demons, or they merely have the illusion of flight in a dreamlike state, always inspired by the devil. In either case, the accused must be condemned.

The other path is related to certain developments in scholastic demonology. It considers the transport of humans by demons as a reality, as well as the latter's ability to take on bodies that are perceived as real by human senses. This trick of demonologists thus creates a fault in the system, enabling the witches' Sabbath to become a real possibility.

The junction of these two paths adds complexity to the ideas circulating about the Sabbath because they enable diverse solutions on how the relationship between men and demons can be perceived. On one hand, the realist theory (a voluntary allegiance to the devil), and on the other, the illusionist theory in which dreams and imagination are troubled by demons. It is important, however, not to consider the division between the realist theory and the illusionist theory as a distinction between guilty or innocent. The fact of simply considering the Sabbath as a demonic illusion does not exclude it from penal action, even moderately. One can be punished for a dream or a belief when one considers as real what is actually an illusion, as when a witch believes she has been to the Sabbath, when she has only been deluded by a demon. Guided by the argumentation of the jurists, the criminal intention is more important than the crime itself. Holding a thesis regarding the reality of the Sabbath is not at all necessary in the actual repression of demonic witchcraft. This thesis is in fact a "limit case" in Christian demonology that reaches its peak in the middle of the fifteenth century. Paradoxically, the debate between the theories of reality and illusion of the Sabbath is falsified by the fact that neither theory disculpates the accused. Although it is a false debate, its importance covers the entire fifteenth century and much has been written about it.

What is exciting about the treatise on demonology is that questions relative to demons are no longer intellectual speculations, but become questions with great implications, be they social, political or cultural, because they deal with repression: the witch hunts. With the Sabbath, scholarly demonology becomes a pressing social problem in the fifteenth century.

Notes

1 Norman Cohn, *Europe's Inner Demons: The Demonization of Christians in Medieval Christendom* (Chicago: The University of Chicago Press, 1975); Brian P. Levack, *The Witch Hunt in Early Modern Europe* (London, New York: Longman, 1987); Michael D. Bailey, «The Medieval Concept of the Witches' Sabbath», *Exemplaria. A Journal of Theory in Medieval and Renaissance Studies* 8 (1996): 419–439; Martine Ostorero, « Witchcraft », in *The Routledge History of Medieval Magic*, eds. Sophie Page and Catherine Rider (London and New York: Routledge, 2019), Chapter 34, 502–522.

2 Editions, French translations and commentaries in *L'Imaginaire du sabbat. Edition critique des textes les plus anciens (1430c.–1440c.)*, ed. Martine Ostorero, Agostino Paravicini Bagliani and Kathrin Utz Tremp, with Catherine Chène, *Cahiers Lausannois d'Histoire Médiévale*, 26

(Lausanne: Université de Lausanne, 1999). Franck Mercier et Martine Ostorero, *L'énigme de la Vauderie de Lyon. Enquête sur l'Essor des Chasses aux Sorcières entre France et Empire (1430–1480)* (Micrologus' Library 72) (Florence: SISMEL-Edizioni del Galluzzo, 2015). Joseph Hansen, *Quellen und Untersuchungen zur Geschichte des Hexenwahns und der Hexenverfolgung im Mittelalter* (Bonn, 1901). English translation in Michael D. Bailey, *Origins of the Witches' Sabbath* (Magic in History Sourcebooks), (University Park, PA: Pennsylvania State University Press, in press). Former English translation (from the extracts of Hansen, *Quellen*) in *The Witchcraft Sourcebook*, ed. Brian P. Levack (New York: Routledge, 2004) and in *Witch Beliefs and Witch Trials in the Middle Ages: Documents and Readings*, ed. P.G. Maxwell-Stuart (London: Continuum, 2011).

3 Ostorero, *L'Imaginaire du sabbat*, 23–98. Another manuscript of this report (Strasbourg, Bibliothèque nationale et universitaire, 2.935), very close to the first, has been edited by Georg Modestin, «'Von den hexen, so in Wallis verbrant wurdent'. Eine wieder entdeckte Handschrift mit dem Bericht des Chronisten Hans Fründ über eine Hexenverfolgung im Wallis (1428)», *Vallesia* 60 (2005): 399–409.

4 Catherine Chène, dans *L'Imaginaire du sabbat*, 99–265. Michael D. Bailey, *Battling Demons. Witchcraft, Heresy and Reform in the Late Middle Ages* (University Park, PA: Pennsylvania State University Press, 2003). Werner Tschacher, *Der* Formicarius *des Johann Nider von 1437/1438. Studien zu den Anfängen der europäischen Hexenverfolgungen im Spätmittelalter* (Aachen: Shaker, 2000).

5 Ostorero, *L'Imaginaire du sabbat*, 361–438. On Tholosan and the witch hunts in Dauphiné, see Pierrette Paravy, *De la chrétienté romaine à la Réforme en Dauphiné*, Livre III (Rome: Ecole française de Rome, 1993).

6 Jacques Chiffoleau, «*Sur le crime de majesté médiéval*», in *Genèse de l'État moderne en Méditerranée. Approches historique et anthropologique des pratiques et des représentations* (Rome: Ecole française de Rome, 1993), 183–213.

7 Mercier, Ostorero, *L'énigme de la Vauderie de Lyon*, 305–341.

8 Ostorero, *L'Imaginaire du sabbat*, 266–353.

9 Silvia Bertolin and Ezio E. Gerbore, *La stregoneria nella Valle d'Aosta medievale* (Quart: Musemeci Editore, 2003). Silvia Bertolin, *Processi per fede e sortilegi nella valle d'Aosta del Quattrocento* (Aosta: Académie Saint-Anselme d'Aoste, 2012). Martine Ostorero, «Itinéraire d'un Inquisiteur gâté: Ponce Feugeyron, les Juifs et le sabbat des Sorciers,» *Médiévales* 43 (automne 2002): 103–118.

10 Michael D. Bailey and Edward Peters, «A Sabbath of Demonologists: Basel, 1431–1440,» *The Historian* 65.6 (December 2003): 1375–1395. Stephan Sudmann, «Hexen – Ketzer – Kirchenreform. Debatten des Basler Konzils im Vergleich,» in *Chasses aux sorcières et démonologie. Entre discours et pratiques*, ed. Martine Ostorero, Georg Modestin and Kathrin Utz Tremp (Micrologus' Library, 36) (Florence: SISMEL – Edizioni del Galluzzo, 2010), 169–197.

11 Martine Ostorero, «Un manuscrit palatin des *Errores gazariorum*,» in *Inquisition et sorcellerie en Suisse romande. Le registre Ac 29 des Archives cantonales vaudoises (1438–1528)*, ed. Martine Ostorero and Kathrin Utz Tremp, with Georg Modestin (CLHM 41) (Lausanne: Université de Lausanne, 2007), 493–504.

12 Mercier, Ostorero, *L'énigme de la Vauderie de Lyon*. Franck Mercier, «La vauderie de Lyon a-t-elle eu lieu? Un essai de recontextualisation (Lyon, vers 1430–1440?),» in *Chasses aux sorcières et démonologie*, 27–44.

13 Julien Théry, «*Atrocitas/enormitas*. Esquisse pour une histoire de la catégorie d' 'énormité' ou 'crime énorme' du Moyen Âge à l'époque moderne», *Clio@themis, Revue électronique d'histoire du droit* 4 (2011): 1–48.

14 Edited in Mercier, Ostorero, *L'énigme de la Vauderie de Lyon*, 395–406.

15 Paris, Bibliothèque nationale de France, Moreau 779, fol. 264r–266r; Paris, Bibliothèque nationale de France, Ms. Lat. 3446, fol. 58r–62r; Trier, Stadtbibliothek, 613 (1552 4°), fol. 50v–53v. Edition and French translation in Mercier, Ostorero, *L'énigme de la Vauderie de Lyon*.

16 Chène, *L'imaginaire du sabbat*, 439–508. Martin Le Franc, *Le Champion des Dames*, ed. Robert Deschaux, IV, (Les Classiques Français du Moyen Age, 130) (Paris: Honoré Champion, 1999), 113–146.

17 Richard Kieckhefer, «The first Wave of Trials for Diabolical Witchcraft,» in *The Oxford Handbook of Witchcraft in Early Modern Europe and Colonial America*, ed. Brian P. Levack (Oxford: Oxford University Press, 2013), 159–178; Id., «Mythologies of Witchcraft in the Fifteenth Century,» *Magic, Ritual, and Witchcraft* (Summer 2006): 79–107.

18 Marina Montesano, '*Supra acqua et supra ad vento'. Superstizioni, maleficia e incantamenta nei predicatori francescani osservanti (Italia, sec. XV)* (Istituto storico italiano per il medio evo, Nuovi studi storici, 46) (Roma, 1999). Ead., «Le rôle de la culture classique dans la définition des *maleficia*. Une démonologie alternative?», in *Penser avec les démons. Démonologues et démonologies (XIIIe–XVIIe siècles)*, ed. Julien Véronèse and Martine Ostorero (Micrologus' Library 71) (Florence: Sismel-Edizioni del Galluzzo, 2015), 277–292. Franco Mormando, *The Preacher's Demons. Bernardino of Siena and the Social Underworld of Early Renaissance Italy* (Chicago, London: University of Chicago Press, 1999).

19 Pau Castell i Granados, «*Sortilegas, divinatrices* et *fetilleres*. Les origines de la sorcellerie en Catalogne», *Cahiers de Recherches Médiévales et Humanistes* 22 (2011): 217–241. Id., *Orígens i evolució de la cacera de bruixes a Catalunya (segles XV–XVI)* (Barcelona: Unpublished Ph.D., 2013); Id., «"Wine vat Witches suffocate Children": The Mythical Components of the Iberian Witch,» *eHumanista. Journal of Iberian Studies* 26 (2014), www.ehumanista.ucsb.edu.

20 Julien Véronèse, «Le *Contra astrologos imperitos atque nigromanticos* (1395–1396) de Nicolas Eymerich (O.P.): Contexte de Rédaction, Classification des Arts Magiques et Divinatoires, édition critique partielle,» in Ostorero, et al., *Chasses aux sorcières et démonologie*, 271–329; Id., «Nigromancie et hérésie: le *De jurisdictione inquisitorum in et contra christianos demones invocantes* (1359) de Nicolas Eymerich (O.P.),» in Véronèse, *Penser avec les démons*, 5–56; Pau Castell Granados, «The Inquisitor's Demons. Nicolau Eymeric's *Directorium Inquisitorum*», in *The Science of Demons: Early Modern Authors Facing the Devil*, ed Jan Machielsen (London: Routledge, in press).

21 Chantal Ammann-Doubliez, «La première chasse aux sorciers en Valais,» in Ostorero, *L'imaginaire du sabbat*, 63–98; Ead., «Les chasses aux sorciers vues sous un angle politique: pouvoirs et persécutions dans le diocèse de Sion au XVᵉ siècle,» in Ostorero, et al., *Chasses aux sorcières et démonologie*, 5–13.

22 On the concept of «heresy of State,» see Jacques Chiffoleau, «L'hérésie de Jeanne. Note sur les qualifications dans le procès de Rouen», in *Jeanne d'Arc. Histoire et mythes*, ed. Jean-Patrice Boudet et Xavier Hélary (Paris: Presses universitaires de Rennes, 2014), 13–55, p. 17 and note 13; Id., « Sur le crime de majesté médiéval », in *Genèse de l'État moderne en Méditerranée* (Rome: Ecole française de Rome, 1993) (Collection de l'EFR, 168), p. 207–211; Julien Théry, « Une Hérésie d'État. Philippe le Bel, le Procès des « Perfides Templiers » et la Pontificalisation de la Royauté Française », *Médiévales* 60 (printemps 2011): 157–186; Mercier, Ostorero, *L'énigme de la Vauderie de Lyon*, 322–325; Martine Ostorero, «Amédée VIII et la Répression de la Sorcellerie Démoniaque: une Hérésie d'Etat?,» in *La loi du Prince. La raccolta normativa sabauda di Amedeo VIII (1430) I, Les* Statuts de Savoie *d'Amédée VIII de 1430. Une œuvre législative majeure/ Gli Statuti sabaudi di Amedeo VIII del 1430. Un'opera legislatia di rilievo*, ed. Mathieu Caesar and Franco Morenzoni, (Biblioteca storica subalpina, 228/1) (Torino : Deputazione subalpina di storia patria, 2019), 317–356.

23 Martine Ostorero, «Des papes face à la sorcellerie démoniaque (première moitié du XVᵉ s.): une dilatation du champ de l'hérésie?», in *Aux marges de l'hérésie. Inventions, formes et usages polémiques de l'accusation d'hérésie au Moyen Age*, ed. Franck Mercier and Isabelle Rosé, Rennes: Presses universitaires de Rennes, 2017, 153–184; Hansen, *Quellen*, 16–24.

24 Stuart Clark, *Thinking with Demons: The Idea of Witchcraft in Early Modern Europe* (Oxford: Oxford University Press, 1997). Walter Stephens, *Demon Lovers. Witchcraft, Sex and the Crisis of Belief* (Chicago, London: The University of Chicago Press, 2002). Martine Ostorero, *Le Diable au sabbat. Littérature Démonologique et Sorcellerie (1440–1460)* (Micrologus' Library, 38) (Florence: SISMEL – Edizioni del Galluzzo, 2011).

25 Hansen, *Quellen*. Some English translations (from the extracts of Hansen, *Quellen*) in *The Witchcraft Sourcebook*, ed. Brian P. Levack (New York: Routledge, 2004) and in Maxwell-Stuart, *Witch Beliefs*. Concerning other texts, for instance the sermons of Bernardino da Siena and other members of the Franciscan Observance, cf. supra note 16 (Montesano and Mormando); Fabio Troncarelli, «*Grata et iocunda est aequalitas*. Mariano Sozzini tra Medioevo

ed Umanesimo», in *La città dei segreti. Magia, astrologia e cultura esoterica a Roma (XV–XVIII)*, a cura di Fabio Troncarelli (Milano, 1985), 55–69; Id. e M.P. Saci, «Il *De potestate spirituum* di Guglielmo Becchi,» in *Stregoneria e streghe nell'Europa moderna. Convegno internazionale di studi (Pisa, 24–26 marzo 1994)*, ed. Giovanna Bosco and Patrizia Castelli (Pisa: Biblioteca Universitaria, 1996), 87–98; Alessia Belli, Astrid Estuardo Flaction, *Les striges en Italie du Nord. Édition critique et commentaire des traités de démonologie et sorcellerie de Girolamo Visconti* (Milan, c. 1460) et de *Bernard Rategno* (Côme, c. 1510), (Micrologus Library 97) (Florence: SISMEL – Edizioni del Galluzzo, 2019).

26 For a detailed analysis of these texts, see Ostorero, *Le Diable au sabbat*. Extracts in Hansen, *Quellen*, 124–212.

27 Walter Stephens, «Marsile Ficin, les démonologues 'orthodoxes' et le dilemme des corps», in Ostorero, et al., *Chasses aux sorcières et démonologie*, 407–425.

28 Martine Ostorero, «Meeting the Devil, Facing the Invisible. Sensory Perception and Emotions in Fifteenth-Century Swiss-French Record», in *Living in a Magical World: Inner Lives, 1300–1900*, ed. S. Page, M. Gaskill and al., (Basingstoke: Palgrave Macmillan) (Historical Studies in Witchcraft and Magic), in press; Ead., «Promoter of the Sabbat and Diabolical Realism: Nicolas Jacquier's Flagellum hereticorum fascinariorum», in *The Science of Demons: Early Modern Thinkers Facing the Devil*, ed. Jan Machielsen (London: Routledge, in press).

29 Olivier Marin, ed., *Les traités anti-hussites du dominicain Nicolas Jacquier († 1472). Une histoire du concile de Bâle et de sa postérité* (Collection des Études augustiniennes: Moyen-Âge et Temps modernes, 49), (Paris: Inst. d'Études Augustiniennes, 2012).

30 Martine Ostorero, « Un prédicateur au cachot. Guillaume Adeline et le sabbat », *Médiévales* 44 (printemps 2003): 73–96.

31 Franck Mercier, *La Vauderie d'Arras. Une chasse aux sorcières à l'Automne du Moyen Age* (Rennes: Presses Universitaires de Rennes, 2006).

32 Franck Mercier, «'Des choses qui surmontent la puissance des anges'. La défense de la toute-puissance divine dans le *Traité du crime de vauderie* de Jean Tinctor,» in *Penser avec les démons*, 121–144. Jean Tinctor, *Invectives contre la secte de vauderie*, éd. Emile Van Balberghe et Frédéric Duval (Tournai: Archives du Chapitre cathédral, 1999).

33 Ostorero, *Le diable au sabbat*, 567–720. Franck Mercier, «Un imaginaire efficace? Le Sabbath et le vol magique des sorcières au XVᶜ siècle», *Médiévales* 42 (printemps 2002): 162–167. Werner Tschacher, «Der Flug durch die Luft zwischen Illusionstheorie und Realitätsbeweis. Studien zum sog. Kanon Episcopi und zum Hexenflug», *Zeitschrift der Savigny Stiftung für Rechtsgeschichte*, Bd. 116, Kan. Abt. 85 (1999): 225–276. Matthew Champion, «Crushing the Canon: Nicolas Jacquier' Response to the Canon *Episcopi* in the *Flagellum haereticorum fascinariorum*,» *Magic, Ritual, and Witchcraft* 6.2 (Winter 2011): 183–211; Stephens, *Demon Lovers*, sp. chap. 5.

34 Astrid Estuardo Flaction, «Girolamo Visconti, un témoin du débat sur la réalité de la sorcellerie au XVᶜ siècle en Italie du Nord», in Ostorero, et al., *Chasses aux Sorcières et Démonologie*, 389–406; Belli, Estuardo Flaction, *Les striges en Italie du Nord*.

Bibliography (selection)

Bailey, Michael D., *Battling Demons: Witchcraft, Heresy and Reform in the Late Middle Ages*. University Park: Pennsylvania State University Press, 2003.

Bailey, Michael D., *Origins of the Witches' Sabbath*, Magic in History Sourcebooks. University Park: Pennsylvania State University Press, in press.

Mercier, Franck, La Vauderie d'Arras. Une chasse aux sorcières à l'Automne du Moyen Age. Rennes: Presses Universitaires de Rennes, 2006.

Mercier, Franck and Martine Ostorero, *L'énigme de la Vauderie de Lyon. Enquête sur l'Essor des Chasses aux Sorcières entre France et Empire (1430–1480)*. Florence: SISMEL-Edizioni del Galluzzo, 2015.

Ostorero, Martine, *Le diable au sabbat. Littérature démonologique et sorcellerie (1440–1460)*, Micrologus' Library, 38, Florence: SISMEL – Edizioni del Galluzzo, 2011.

Ostorer, Martine et al. (eds.), *L'Imaginaire du sabbat. Edition critique des textes les plus anciens (1430c.–1440c.)*, Cahiers Lausannois d'Histoire Médiévale, 26. Lausanne: Université de Lausanne, 1999.

PART 2

THE EARLY MODERN WITCH HUNTS

Regions and issues

WITCHCRAFT AND WITCH HUNTING IN LATE MEDIEVAL AND EARLY MODERN ITALY

Matteo Duni

My chapter will examine witch beliefs and witch hunting from the late fourteenth to the early eighteenth centuries in the territories that are at present part of Italy, but which belonged to many different states before these were unified when the Kingdom of Italy was formed (1861). It will also include some Italian-speaking areas which now belong to Switzerland. Such political fragmentation had important consequences on the prosecution of witchcraft, which was carried out in very different institutional and legal frameworks, as well as on the geographical distribution of the trials, which was extremely uneven, and finally on the relevant archival documentation, which was dispersed and often lost.

Witch beliefs displayed a remarkable variety, in all likelihood stemming from profound original differences in social and cultural contexts. Since the overwhelming majority of the population spoke only in the many native dialects used in the different areas of the Peninsula, the very terminology used to denote a witch was far from uniform. The term could vary from the Northern and Central Italian *strega* to the Southern Italian *magara* and *masciara*, but included also *iana* and *ianara* (both probably deriving from the name of the pagan goddess Diana), and more local variants still.[1] The term *strega* also existed in the male version (*stregone*), and both could interchangeably refer to either agents of the specific set of deeds attributed to night-flying witches (pact with the devil, participation in the Sabbat, and so on), or to the practitioners of generic maleficent, as well as benevolent, magic. Agents of the first type were persecuted harshly, but only in some parts of Italy and for a relatively short time – at least as far as church courts, such as the Inquisition, were concerned. Those of the second type, by contrast, were the object of a sustained attention from tribunals throughout the entire period but were dealt with in fairly lenient terms, especially by the Inquisition. Studying the history of witchcraft and witch hunts in Italy therefore requires the adoption of multiple analytical models, capable of taking into account the extreme diversity of the political and legal backgrounds, as well as of describing and interpreting the folkloric varieties of the witchcraft paradigm. In this chapter, I will first assess the dimensions of the witch hunt both in terms of its geography and of the number of people tried and executed. I will use the term witch hunt to refer specifically to the persecutions of men and women accused of being members of the sect of the witches and of having made a pact with the devil. At the same time, I will also look at the prosecution of all types of magic and of "superstitions", meaning the wide area of practices based on a mixture of folkloric beliefs, magical techniques, and church rituals. Due attention will be devoted to the repressive apparatus and its changing goals and structures. Then I will explore the types of magical operations, the gender of the agents who performed them, and the different versions of the "mythology of witchcraft" found in various parts of Italy.[2] In the conclusion, I will attempt an overall interpretation of the phenomenon.

The dimensions of the witch hunt: times, places, numbers

We can safely assume four things to be true with regard to the Italian witch hunt: it began early, took place almost exclusively north of the present-day region of Tuscany, only rarely reached the mass dimensions it had in northern Europe, and was mostly the work of church courts. This last point requires some explanation. The Inquisition shared with secular justice the responsibility of trying heretics, as magicians and witches were considered to be, because heresy was a crime which both church and state courts could prosecute (a crime of "mixed jurisdiction", as jurists called it), and also because criminal law mandated that harm provoked by witchcraft be punished by the civil magistrate. In practice, however, secular and ecclesiastical judges hunted witches with variable levels of commitment: while inquisitors were responsible for the great majority of trials overall, and were more active in the first phase of the witch hunt (c. 1420s–1520s), secular judges – appointed by the rulers or governments of the different Italian states – took the lead from the early seventeenth century, especially in terms of the number of death sentences. Inquisitors were appointed by the authorities of the Catholic organizations they came from, namely the Dominican and the Franciscan orders, up until 1542. From that year, following the reorganization of the Catholic Church's repressive apparatus, they were appointed by the Holy Office of the Inquisition, as the central institution for the prosecution of heresy in the Italian Peninsula was called. This did not apply to Sicily and Sardinia, however, as the two islands came under the authority of the Spanish Inquisition from the early 1490s.

As far as chronology goes, scholars unanimously consider the trials and eventual execution (in 1385 and 1390) of two Milanese women, Sibilia Zanni and Pierina de' Bugatis, as the earliest cases of capital punishment meted out to persons who had confessed to a series of activities closely resembling those eventually subsumed under the "cumulative concept" of witchcraft.[3] At the other extreme, the executions of two men, a nobleman who had tried to kill his wife casting a malevolent spell and his accomplice, decreed in Turin by a secular court in 1723, were probably the last capital sentences for magical practices.[4]

While the burnings of Sibilia and Pierina were isolated cases at the close of the fourteenth century, from the third decade of the fifteenth century several trials ending with the death penalty testify to the growing concern of authorities for the diffusion of the new heresy. Three clusters of trials, ranging from 1419–20 to 1434–37, ended with the execution of six people, all in the northern region of Valle d'Aosta and at the hand of inquisitors.[5] In Rome, as well as in Perugia and Todi (both towns in Umbria, a central region), a few women were executed between the 1420s and the 1440s in trials which show how effective the anti-witchcraft sermons delivered by the famous Franciscan preacher Bernardino of Siena were in inducing secular judges to mete out harsh sentences. The first large-scale hunt seems to have taken place in the Valle d'Aosta during 1445–49, with nine people tried and seven burned at the stake by papal inquisitors, but the pace of the prosecutions remained otherwise slow in the first half of the century, with a total of twenty-four witches executed. The tempo quickened noticeably in the second half, reaching a first peak in the 1480s – with about forty people put to death in that decade – and showing a marked concentration in the Alpine areas which was to remain a constant feature throughout the Italian witch hunts.[6]

The extremely uneven state of sources makes any estimate very tentative at best, but in all likelihood the first three decades of the sixteenth century were the bloodiest of the entire witch hunting era, claiming the lives of no fewer than two hundred women and men. In the 1510s, the Alpine valleys between Lombardy and Trentino were the epicenter of particularly harsh hunts, such as those in the territory of Como (between thirty and sixty executions in 1513–14, but some accounts relate as many as three hundred) and those in the Valcamonica (between sixty-two and eighty in 1518–19) – all at the hands of inquisitors. The latter were likewise responsible for brutal campaigns in the 1520s, beginning in Lombardy, in the rural district of Varese (Venegono Superiore, seven executions in 1520) and in the mountainous Valtellina (forty trials and seven executions, 1523).[7] This wave of persecution extended south of the Po River, to Mirandola in the region of Emilia, where the southernmost mass witch hunt in the Peninsula took place in 1522–23 (sixty trials and ten executions).[8] Scholars have speculated that witch hunting may have reached such high levels in this period due to the impact of the Italian wars, the almost uninterrupted series of conflicts from 1494 to 1530. While the disrupting effects of prolonged warfare possibly contributed to worsen the witch hunt in some cases, they do not seem to have been its major cause, since trials and executions had reached significant numbers years before the wars and, in any case, did not increase noticeably in some of the areas most affected by the fighting (from Tuscany to Lazio and Campania). The single most influential precipitating factor is more likely to have been the high level of religious zeal of Dominican inquisitors. Forming a vast and well-connected network, they mobilized to fight the witches as both judges and demonologists, exchanging information that helped them write several tracts on the topic as well as guide their endeavors in an apparently coordinated series of witch hunting campaigns closely following one another.[9]

The spread of ideas and movements inspired by the Protestant Reformation in the Peninsula prompted the institution of the Holy Office of the Inquisition in 1542 and the subsequent refocusing of the inquisitors' action on Protestant "heretics", perceived as being a much greater threat to the Catholic Church than witches.[10] An evident consequence of this major shift was the sudden drop in the numbers of capital sentences for witchcraft, which go from circa twenty-five in the 1520s to thirteen in the 1530s, to eight in the 1540s, totaling no more than twelve during 1551–1570 and thirteen in the following decade.[11]

When the danger posed by doctrinal dissent in the Peninsula began to subside, witches were again sent to the stake in substantial numbers from the 1580s, although these prosecutions followed rather different patterns. On the one hand, starting in the last decades of the century, the Holy Office developed cautiously skeptical guidelines, detailed in a key document known as the "Instruction on trial procedure in cases of witchcraft, enchantments and harmful spells". These highlighted the often illusory nature of witchcraft and called for greater care and restraint in its prosecution.[12] On the other hand, a centralized system of supervision of the local branches of the Inquisition made major panics isolated events, rather than parts of a concerted effort, and the work of distinctive figures operating in peculiar circumstances. This was certainly the case with the 1583 witch hunt in the Mesolcina, an Italian-speaking valley in the Swiss canton of Grisons (Graubünden) but under the spiritual jurisdiction of the archbishop of Milan, at the time Cardinal Carlo Borromeo, who launched a harsh campaign ending with over ninety trials and seven women burned alive despite objections from the Holy Office. He eventually delegated the authority to hunt witches to a local arch-priest, Giovan Pietro Stoppani, who went on to try hundreds of people in the valleys between the dioceses of Como and Milan, burning at the stake no fewer than sixty-three (and possibly as many as one hundred) during 1589–97, but this time apparently without opposition from Rome.[13] The exploits of Stoppani, likely the most successful witch hunter in early modern Italy, show that by this time large-scale hunts were led mostly by judges not part of the inquisitorial network supervised by the Holy Office. A case in point is the town of Triora, an outpost of the republic of Genoa located in the Ligurian Alps, where a witch-panic fueled by the local vicar of the Inquisition led to a heavy intervention of the Genoese government and to the trial of over thirty women, five of whom were killed by brutal torture at the hands of a secular judge in 1588. From the beginning of the seventeenth century, state authorities began taking a leading role in the witch hunt. The Holy Office concentrated increasingly on trials for sorcery and "superstitions" and, from this respect, the last decades of the 1500s and the first half of the 1600s seem to have been overall the period of most intense activity. Papal decrees such as Sixtus V's constitution *Immensa Aeterni Dei* (1588), by extending the jurisdiction of the Inquisition to include "simple" spells that did not smack of manifest heresy, spurred local branches to a much more careful control of a wider range of magical practices. The Inquisition of Modena, for example, dealt with eighty-eight magicians and sorceresses during 1581–1600, that is, more than the total number of cases (eighty) for the period 1495–1580.[14] Surviving documents from the Inquisition of Venice for 1580–92 and 1615–30, from the Inquisition of Aquileia-Concordia (in the region of Friuli) for 1596–1610 and 1641–55, and between 1590 and 1650, show a marked increase in the number of prosecutions for sorcery, magic, and witchcraft.[15]

Despite the fact that inquisitors were trying sorcerers and magicians in unprecedented numbers, they were meting out very few death sentences, in keeping with the new policy of the Holy Office, which in practice promoted a much more lenient treatment of diabolical witches while never formally downgrading their crime to the status of a minor offense. In fact, all major witch hunts in this period seem to have been conducted by secular courts, and to have taken place mostly in the Italian-speaking areas of Swiss cantons, or in the valleys of Trentino and of Alto Adige (southern Tyrol) under the authority of prince-bishops of the Holy Roman Empire. In the Val Leventina, not far from Lugano, the secular judges of the canton of Uri tried almost three hundred people, of which ninety-three were sentenced to death, in a series of hunts stretching from 1610 to 1687.[16] Likewise in the Val di Non (1611–15), in the Val di Fassa (1627–31), and at Nogaredo (1646–47), all part of the Trentino, local magistrates executed ten, six, and eight witches respectively, without any intervention from inquisitors. Witch hunts also took a heavy toll in the Duchy of Piedmont, where the courts of local feudal lords in the areas of Asti (1612) and Monferrato (1631–32) were responsible for circa twenty-five deaths.

The complete withdrawal of the Inquisition from witch hunting seems to have characterized the eighteenth century. Trials for magic and superstitions did not decline very rapidly, however, as their numbers actually peaked in some areas, such as in Modena during 1690–1720, and in Siena, where the years between 1716 and 1750 actually set an all-time record.[17] Secular courts increasingly claimed exclusive rights to prosecute black magic when state interests appeared to be at stake. Between 1709 and 1717, a few trials in Turin ended in the death sentence for one man and two women accused of the attempted murder of Duke Victor Amadeus II of Savoy by means of a voodoo-style statuette.[18] Even in Venice, state justice was becoming more jealous of its prerogatives and would interfere with the jurisdiction of the church, as shown in a very late series of trials at Budrio (in the Friuli, 1745) in which the Venetian government overrode the Inquisition, acquitting the culprits and downgrading witchcraft accusations to a case of slandering in 1753.[19] Thus, the centralizing tendencies of state administration, strengthened by the growing skepticism of the intellectual elites, were leading to a de facto decriminalization of witchcraft all over the Italian peninsula around the middle of the 1700s.

The final toll of the witch hunts – to be taken with caution due to the problematic state of sources – varies between a minimum of 418 executions estimated by Andrea Del Col, to an approximate maximum of 2,500 proposed by Wolfgang Behringer.[20] Behringer's estimate seems excessive, since it would imply that the actual number of executions was almost four times that of known executions, which I calculate between 650 and 750 – figures I regard to be closer to the truth.[21] Conjectural counts of the total number of trials for magic and witchcraft range between 22,000 and 33,000.[22] As far as the chronological distribution goes, we can notice that, after a low point between the 1550s and the 1570s, numbers of executions went up sharply during 1580 through 1600 (roughly fifty per decade) but fell even more markedly in the first ten years of the seventeenth century (only two). They rebounded vigorously in the 1610s with over fifty executions, and remained at high levels during the following three decades (between twenty-six and thirty-eight each, the majority from the Leventina hunts). From the 1650s onward, however, the total per decade dropped to very low figures, never again reaching double digits. It appears, therefore, that as far as the number of death sentences is concerned, from the late sixteenth century the witch hunt in Italy roughly echoed the same rhythm it had followed in the heart of Europe (Germany, France), with a very intense period between 1580 and 1630 followed by a slow decline. Interestingly, the activity of the Spanish Inquisition in Sicily also seems to have been wholly aligned with this pattern. While death penalty was an extremely unlikely outcome for a witchcraft trial (we know of only fourteen over the entire era), proceedings against magicians and witches were numerous, circa one thousand, and they peaked during 1590–1655, with over two hundred trials in some of these decades. Trials decreased rather sharply in the second half of the seventeenth century and more drastically from the beginning of the eighteenth, with the last public auto-da-fè (proclamation of the verdict) of two women condemned for witchcraft taking place in Palermo in 1744.[23]

As far as the geography of the hunt goes, a clear-cut distinction separates Alpine territories and those in proximity of the Alps from the rest. Close to 500 executions, or about 70% of the total, took place in the mountainous areas in the northern part of the Peninsula, including Swiss and south-Tyrolian hunts, while another 145 (or circa 20%) occurred in urban centers or in rural and hilly districts located in the North. This means that only 10% of the death sentences (about seventy) were carried out south of the present-day region of Emilia Romagna, with a minimal fraction in the Kingdom of Naples and in Sicily. Witch hunting was thus a stable feature in the life of Alpine communities and occurred with relative frequency in the cities and towns of the Po River valley, but it never established solid roots in the social and religious landscape of the remaining two-thirds of the Peninsula.

Witches and witchcraft: identities and practices

Identities

The proportion of women to men among the victims of the hunt can be evaluated with a minimum of accuracy only in a handful of cases, those of tribunals whose trial series have been preserved and have been systematically studied. In Modena, of the 166 people tried or denounced for all types of magic and witchcraft over the period 1495–1600, 124, or 75% of the total, were women.[24] In Venice, women represent circa 70% of the individuals tried during 1550–1650 (490 over a total of 714).[25] In Siena, research covering a longer series of records shows that while for the period 1580–1650 the percentage of women was identical to that of Venice (71%), it dropped to an average of 45% over the next seventy years (1651–1721) for unknown reasons.[26] Figures for the Spanish Inquisition's activity in Sicily over an even longer time span show percentages comparable to this latter, but inverted rankings: men made up circa 47% (461 over 974), and women 53% (513) of the people condemned between 1543 and 1782.[27] As far as age and marital status of the women tried are concerned, the conclusions we can draw from systematic research indicate that Italian witches were not particularly old, as actually the number of women still in their fertile years was roughly equivalent to that of post-menopausal women.[28] Furthermore, widows or spinsters did not exceed married women by a wide margin, or at all – in fact, these latter could be more numerous, as in Sicily.

Such general considerations, however, are based on a very limited availability of data. Until more detailed, in-depth research is carried out on a wider set of tribunals, it is more meaningful to look for patterns suggested by the specific conditions in which magic and witchcraft were practiced. A closer analysis of these series of trials reveals that the gender distribution of witches seems to have been influenced by a combination of geographical and sociological factors, which in turn determined what witches did, or were believed to be doing.

Women made up the clear majority of those accused of having gone to the Sabbat and made a pact with the devil in the agricultural and mountainous lands of Northern Italy. For example, thirty-one women and nine men were tried in the witch hunts of the Valle d'Aosta (from 1420 to 1544), some of the earliest in Europe. Considering the broader set of known cases, it would seem that the "average" witch hunt – at least in terms of the witches' gender – was similar to that of Sondrio and

Valtellina (in 1523), with twenty-nine women and eleven men tried (thus 70% and 30% of the total).

Surviving records therefore provide a clear sense of the prevalence of women among witches conforming to the "cumulative concept", but they are much less eloquent about their social status. While in some witch hunts – especially those conducted in sparsely populated areas – the women tried were of a lowly condition, it appears that whenever urban centers of some importance were involved, witches were on average lower-middle class (i.e. belonging to the artisans' and shopkeepers' group), and it was not rare to see members of prominent families among those accused. In 1523 at Sondrio, for example, three women out of the four burned at the stake came from middle class or upper-middle class backgrounds – as did two men out of three (they were merchants or notaries).[29] But all the nine people burned by the inquisitor of Piedmont in the villages of Rifreddo and Gambasca (1495) were poor women, just as were the seven sent to the stake in Venegono Superiore by the inquisitor of Lombardy in 1520. In the trials carried out in the Valle d'Aosta (circa 1420–1540), the women accused were also marginal in their communities, not necessarily because they were poor, but because they were regarded as outsiders due to personal traits such as aggressive character, scandalous sexual behavior, or simply because they came from a different locality.[30]

Leaving behind the mountains and the countryside, Italian cities saw the activities of a different type of witch. The night-flying, devil-worshipping enemy of Christianity was almost completely replaced by the less terrifying figure of the enchantress, constantly intent on countering illness through magical healing or on bewitching the body and soul of men at the behest of a mostly (but not exclusively) female clientele. However, the enchantress had to share the stage with considerable numbers of male wizards and sorcerers, who typically presided over more sophisticated kinds of practices, such as the conjuration of demons or treasure hunting. Gender divisions were not rigid, but were certainly marked and could be absolute in some cases. In Siena, for example, women represented an astonishing 99% of those accused of *maleficium* (harmful magic), as well as the overwhelming majority of healers.[31] Furthermore, in urban centers such as Venice, Rome, Modena and Siena, prostitutes made up a significant proportion of those who practiced love magic, both for their own goals (to guarantee their customers' affection) and for other women who wanted to secure a spouse or to fix marital problems.[32] Like prostitutes and courtesans, it was also usual for enchantresses to form clusters in which older women would instruct the younger in the exercise of the forbidden arts.[33] Support from such networks of friends and accomplices often enabled sorceresses and their male counterparts to minimize the consequences of prosecution.[34]

Contrary to the situation in Siena, healing was regularly performed by male agents in Venice and in Modena, especially by clergy.[35] This last point highlights an important element all cities had in common: most men practicing magic belonged to the clergy. In Venice, ninety-nine out of 224 men tried by the Inquisition (or 45%) were clerics, as were twelve out of the twenty-seven men accused in Modena in the last two decades of the sixteenth century.[36] Trials of the Spanish Inquisition in Sicily show similar figures, as 160 out of 461 men tried (35%) were clerics.

Available studies, therefore, show that it is problematic to single out some traits as being "typical" of Italian witches. While confirming that women were generally

the majority of those accused, they indicate that both their age and their social status could vary depending on a number of factors, not differently than in the rest of
Europe.[37] Furthermore, they reveal that men were usually a sizable minority, sometimes nearing half of the total of those tried, and that more often than not they were
ecclesiastics.

Practices

The apparently surprising, marked presence of clerics can be explained in light of
the type of magic men typically performed: necromancy, or ritual magic, based on
complex procedures described in books, thus requiring some degree of literacy, a
characteristic more commonly found among clergy than in the general population.
This was the case of common practices such as the search for hidden treasures: books
of necromancy detailed the procedures necessary to dispose of the demons who
were believed to guard them.[38] However, the primary motive for the prevalence of
clerics was that the majority of the faithful considered the Catholic Church as a locus
of supernatural power which could be resorted to for a variety of objectives, most
often at cross-purposes with official doctrine. The vast majority of magical practices
included elements borrowed from church rituals. Indeed, some of the most common
types of love magic were known as "orazioni", or prayers, whose format and language
they mimicked. One example is that of the "orazione di San Daniele", a love spell
resorted to by the Modenese sorceress Costanza "Barbetta". It required that thir-
ty-three candles be lit on an equal number of days, the same as the supposed age of
Christ at the time of his Passion.[39] The "prayer" then went on to invoke the name of
the person whose love the spell was meant to spark "by the passion of Christ, by the
blows, by the nails", listing the mysteries of the Passion as if it were an orthodox litany.
Since enchantresses such as Costanza tapped into Catholic liturgy, it was only natural
that ecclesiastics, who performed it professionally, would have an even more powerful aura as magicians.[40] Furthermore, due to their mostly rudimentary training and
education, clergy often failed to distinguish between the licit and the illicit in their
manipulation of the sacred, and routinely took part in magico-religious operations.

It would be impossible (and pointless) to analyze the innumerable variations of
such practices found in most surviving trial series. What is worth stressing here is that
they shed light on the climate of regular interaction between different agents, which
characterized the practice of magic in Italian cities. Regardless of their social background and specialization, enchantresses and wizards exchanged magical lore and
even collaborated to produce certain spells. Thus, boundaries between high magic,
codified in books, and low magic, mostly transmitted orally, could be permeable.[41]
The Modenese Bernardina Stadera, a procuress tried for sorcery in 1499, would
use in her spells mysterious signs she had copied from books of necromancy after
borrowing them from some Servite friars. She also kept a demonic spirit in a glass
sphere, another item typically found in the arsenal of more sophisticated magicians,
in order to obtain predictions on future events.[42]

Communication between different practitioners, and cross-fertilization between
their respective cultural worlds, are perhaps nowhere more evident than in the area
of healing magic. Widely resorted to especially by lower-class patients, for whom
official physicians were both culturally distant and expensive, healers could draw on

a variety of sources. Their cures typically consisted of remedies based on the natural properties of plants, animal parts, and minerals, accompanied by rituals supposed to enhance the effectiveness of the process. Magical and religious elements were mixed so intimately that one of the most common forms of healing, performed by lay and clerical healers alike, was to make the sign of the cross ("segnare") over the afflicted part of the body.[43]

Mythologies of witchcraft

Italian judges conducted some of the earliest witchcraft trials, providing important evidence of a wide variety of beliefs which theologians progressively reduced into the mold of the diabolical witch. While the richness of this documentation has attracted considerable attention, the complexity of the witchcraft construct and its multiple local variants still pose a serious challenge to any attempts at synthesis.

In a particularly significant cluster of early cases from Todi and Perugia between 1428 and 1455, a few women confessed to flying at night, entering people's homes in the shape of cats, and killing babies by sucking their blood. Such vampire-witches operated individually, while their collective gathering at the walnut tree of Benevento was not very significant. Richard Kieckhefer classifies these trials as one basic form of witchcraft mythology, reminiscent of the *striges* from classical antiquity, in which the devil was confined to a minor role. Kieckhefer also highlights another type of "Sabbath narrative", whose core feature was a nocturnal meeting, referred to in Latin as *ludus* (in Italian *gioco*, game) or as *cursus* (in the vernacular *corso*, course or ride): a sort of pleasant banquet presided over not by the devil, but by a benevolent female figure, known as *Domina ludi/cursus* (lady of the game/course). This second version is found in a sizable series of trials in the Po River valley area, where apparently many people still recognized the *Domina* as a sort of deity of abundance and fertility as late as the first half of the sixteenth century. A peculiar feature in some of these accounts is the swoon, a sort of trance which women and men would fall into before they experienced the *ludus* and the meeting with the *Domina*.[44] Such an element suggests a comparison between this paradigm and the mythology of the *benandanti*, the atypical witches from the north-eastern region of Friuli made famous by Ginzburg's pioneering book, *The Night Battles*. Male *benandanti*, all "born with the caul" (that is, still wrapped in the amniotic sac), confessed to falling into a sleep so deep they could not be woken up, and going "in spirit" to collectively fight witches. Their battles, which would take place during the nights of the so-called Ember days, were crucial: the victory of the *benandanti* would bring plentiful crops, whereas that of the witches spelled famine.[45] Female *benandanti* would see and talk to the souls of the dead, receiving information about the living and relating it back to their fellow villagers. The belief in a female figure with supernatural powers who could communicate with the dead led Ginzburg to connect the *benandanti* with the cult of the fertility goddesses mentioned earlier. This sort of double-sided north Italian witchcraft construct thus had a wide diffusion as well as significant features in common with the Umbrian paradigm, such as the marginal role of the devil. Furthermore, cases such as that of Orsolina "la Rossa" (Modena, 1539) show that elements from the Umbrian model of the "vampire witch" could coexist with elements stemming from the "fertility goddess'" strand, and suggest that different mythologies of witchcraft could overlap.[46] At the same time, they confirm Martine Ostorero's thesis that in the Italian peninsula the stereotypical witches' Sabbat had been grafted onto a folkloric substratum stronger, and more markedly different from demonological theories, than in Northern Europe.[47] This is particularly evident in the case of the Sicilian *donne di fora* ("the ladies from outside"), supernatural creatures best described as "fairies", which testifies to a folkloric belief-complex largely alien to witchcraft mythology. Between the sixteenth and the seventeenth century the Spanish Inquisition, active in Sicily during the early modern era, tried eighty people (90% women), who told of going "in spirit" to meetings as far away as Naples, where the female leader of the *donne* (sometimes referred to as "the queen") presided over a splendid banquet, and instructed attendees in the use of medicinal herbs.[48] The human participants (often also referred to, confusingly, as *donne di fora*) then received the power to heal the sick and cure the bewitched. Repression was moderate and did not seem to produce long-term results, since Sicilians continued to believe in both spiritual and human *donne di fora* well into the twentieth century.[49]

Conclusions

The witch hunt in Italy was a limited phenomenon, both chronologically and geographically, although it reached high levels in some periods and in specific areas. It was intense and relatively widespread in its early phase (1480s–1520s), but it declined, as far as death sentences are concerned, already from the end of the sixteenth century. Mass prosecutions continued, in some Alpine territories, until the middle of the seventeenth century, mostly at the hands of secular authorities. However, they remained peripheral events and never affected the central and southern regions of the Peninsula to a significant extent.

The main reasons for this are probably to be found in the overall attitude of the Catholic Church towards magic and witchcraft, as well as in the setup of the Inquisition and its transformations. Italian church leaders were apparently slow in accepting the new witchcraft construct in the course of the fifteenth century. They mostly hung on to the traditional positions enshrined in Scholastic theology and canon law, and thus continued to regard the demonic feats of supposed night-flying witches as little more than delusions. The major exception to this situation was represented by members of the Mendicant orders, Franciscan and especially Dominican friars, who were the protagonists of the first wave of the witch hunt.

After a lull in the central decades of the sixteenth century caused by the outbreak of the Protestant Reformation, which monopolized the attention of church authorities, inquisitors returned to the prosecution of magic and witchcraft in a much changed scenario during the Catholic Reformation (or Counter Reformation). Following the Council of Trent (concluded in 1563), the new policy of the church emphasized the need of reforming the religious beliefs and practices of the Italian people. While this goal certainly required the uprooting of magic, it was pursued neither by discouraging belief in it nor by treating harshly those who used it, but by redirecting their demand of supernatural protection towards church-sponsored alternatives. Upgraded Catholic rituals, the sacramentals (which included exorcism), administered by appropriately trained clergy, were to replace magical remedies to illness and misfortune. While any abuse of holy words or rites by wizards and sorceresses was punished, the practice of magic in itself was not automatically regarded as evidence of membership in the witches' sect.[50] Trials for "superstitions", as magical techniques were often held by inquisitors, were one of the tools used by the church to reaffirm its leadership in Italian society, and reached impressive numbers, but they usually ended with mild sentences and seldom escalated into large witch hunts.[51] These were left mostly to the initiative of local secular courts, or occasionally of church judges (though not inquisitors), and did not disappear very soon. Indeed, the Holy Office, while adopting early a moderate stance in the repression of witchcraft, did nothing to encourage Italian governments and rulers to implement similar policies, and only rarely intervened to restrain the excesses of the worst witch-panics.

Notes

1 Marina Montesano, *Caccia alle streghe* (Rome: Salerno, 2012), 15–16.
2 I refer to the terminology proposed by Richard Kieckhefer, "Mythologies of Witchcraft in the Fifteenth Century," *Magic, Ritual, and Witchcraft* 1 (2006): 79–108.
3 The two women were tried by the inquisitor of Milan: Luisa Muraro, *La Signora del Gioco: caccia alle streghe interpretata dalle sue vittime* (Milan: La Tartaruga, 2006). We know of several trials by secular courts against practitioners of demonic magic (both male and female) in Firenze and Perugia, which ended with the death penalty in the course of the fourteenth and in the early fifteenth century: see Dinora Corsi, *Diaboliche, maledette e disperate* (Florence: Firenze University Press, 2013). I have included these death sentences (five) in my total count of the victims of the witch hunt.
4 Andrea Del Col, *L'Inquisizione in Italia* (Milan: Mondadori, 2006), 708–709; Sabina Loriga, "A Secret to Kill a King: Magic and Protection in Piedmont in the Early 18th Century," in *History From Crime*, ed. Edward Muir and Guido Ruggiero (Baltimore: Johns Hopkins University Press, 1994), 88–109.
5 *La stregoneria nella Valle d'Aosta medievale*, ed. Silvia Bertolin and Ezio Gerbore (Quart: Musumeci, 2003); Del Col, *L'Inquisizione*, 195–197.
6 Tamar Herzig, "Witchcraft Prosecutions in Italy," in *The Oxford Handbook of Witchcraft in Early Modern Europe and Colonial America*, ed. Brian Levack (Oxford: Oxford University Press, 2013), 249–267, 250–252.
7 On Venegono Superiore see Anna Marcaccioli Castiglioni, *Streghe e roghi nel Ducato di Milano* (Milano: Telema, 1999). On the Valtellina see Matteo Duni, "Un manuale inedito per cacciatori di streghe: il *Formularium pro exequendo Inquisitionis* officio di Modesto Scrofeo (c. 1523)", Archivio Storico Italiano, 2013, 339–358.
8 Albano Biondi, "Introduzione" in Gianfrancesco Pico, *Strega, o degli inganni dei demoni* (Venezia: Marsilio, 1989), 9–41.
9 Tamar Herzig, "Bridging North and South: Inquisitorial Networks and Witchcraft Theory on the Eve of the Reformation", *Journal of Early Modern History*, 12, 2008, 361–382; Michael Tavuzzi, *Renaissance Inquisitors* (Leiden: Brill, 2007).
10 Giovanni Romeo, *Inquisitori, esorcisti e streghe nell'Italia della Controriforma* (Florence: Sansoni, 1990); Adriano Prosperi, *Tribunali della coscienza* (Turin: Einaudi, 1996), 368–430; Guido Dall'Olio, "Inquisition, Roman", in *Encyclopedia of Witchcraft*, ed. Richard Golden (Santa Barbara: ABC-Clio, 2006) (hereafter *EW*), vol. II, 557–560; Thomas F. Mayer, *The Roman Inquisition* (Philadelphia: University of Pennsylvania Press, 2013), 9–37.
11 Del Col, *L'Inquisizione*, 210–211. It is worth noting that from the 1470s until the 1530s, the number of executions per decade had never been lower than twelve, thus making the drop from the 1530s to the 1570s all the more evident.
12 John Tedeschi, "Inquisitorial Law and the Witch", in *Early Modern European Witchcraft*, ed. Bengt Ankarloo, Gustav Henningsen (Oxford: Clarendon Press, 1990), 83–118; Rainer Decker, *Witchcraft and the Papacy* (Charlottesville: Virginia PU, 2008); Oscar Di Simplicio, "Instructio," in *Dizionario storico dell'Inquisizione*, eds. Adriano Prosperi, Vincenzo Lavenia, John Tedeschi, 4 vols. (Pisa: Edizioni della Normale, 2010), hereafter DSI, II, 845–847.

13 Giovanni Romeo, "Inquisitori domenicani e streghe," in *Praedicatores, Inquisitores*, III, ed. Carlo Longo (Rome: Istituto Storico Domenicano, 2008), 309–344, 324–325.

14 Matteo Duni, *Under the Devil's Spell. Witches, Sorcerers, and the Inquisition in Renaissance Italy* (Florence: Syracuse University, 2007), 34. Figures are drawn, with minor modifications, from *I processi del tribunale dell'Inquisizione di Modena. Inventario generale analitico, 1489–1784*, ed. Giuseppe Trenti (Modena: Aedes Muratoriana, 2003), 49–54, and include investigations not leading to formal trials. Such marked increase was certainly due also to the raising of Modena to the status of main inquisitorial tribunal from that of vicariate, so that over forty cases were brought before the inquisitor in the year 1600 alone.

15 Ruth Martin, *Witchcraft and the Inquisition in Venice, 1550–1650* (Oxford: Blackwell, 1989), 214–218; Del Col, *L'Inquisizione*, 774–776. Records for Venice are anyway incomplete (no trials surviving between 1595 and 1615).

16 The Val Leventina is now in the Canton Ticino but was then part of the Canton of Uri (and of the archdiocese of Milan *in spiritualibus*).

17 Oscar Di Simplicio, "Sienese New State", in *EW*, III, 1034–1036.

18 Loriga, "A Secret".

19 Fabiana Veronese, "La giurisdizione sulla stregoneria e sui reati diabolici nella Repubblica di Venezia (XVIII secolo)", *Società e storia*, 36 (2013), n. 139, 81–111.

20 Del Col, *L'Inquisizione*, 195–197, 210–211, 779–781; Wolfgang Behringer, *Witches and Witch hunts* (Cambridge: Polity Press, 2004), 78–79, 150, 154–155.

21 My count is based on the surveys in Del Col, *L'Inquisizione*, and in Andrea Del Col, "L'attività dell'Inquisizione nell'Italia moderna," in *Caccia alle streghe in Italia tra XIV e XVII secolo* (Bolzano: Praxis, 2007), 361–396; on Vincenzo Lavenia, "Stregoneria, Italia," in *DSI*, vol. III, 2010, 1521–30, and on Herzig, "Witchcraft," 249–267.

22 Del Col, "L'attività", 392–393, also proposes a range between 60,000 and 100,000 as the grand total of all accusations and dossiers (including those which were not made into formal trials).

23 Maria Messana, *Inquisitori, negromanti e streghe nella Sicilia moderna* (Palermo: Sellerio, 2007), 382–383, 400, 290, 298.

24 Duni, *Devil's Spell*, 71.

25 Martin, *Witchcraft*, 226–227.

26 Oscar Di Simplicio, "Sui processi di stregoneria in Italia," in *Caccia alle streghe*, 315–360, 344–345.

27 Messana, *Inquisitori*, 298–302.

28 Martin, *Witchcraft*, 228–229; Di Simplicio, *Autunno della stregoneria. Maleficio e magia nell'Italia moderna* (Bologna: Il Mulino, 2005), 102–105; Messana, *Inquisitori*, 521–523. In the early modern era, the age of menopause was circa forty. In general, it is not frequent to find clear indications of a defendant's age in trial documents.

29 Valerio Giorgetta, *L'inquisitore fra Modesto Scrofeo e i processi per stregoneria a Sondrio (1523). Cronaca di una caccia*, Sondrio, Società Storica Valtellinese, 2016.

30 Bertolin and Gerbore, *Stregoneria*, 267–271 on Rifreddo see Grado G. Merlo, *Streghe* (Bologna: Il Mulino, 2006); on Venegono Superiore see Anna Marcaccioli Castiglioni, *Streghe e roghi nel Ducato di Milano* (Milano: Telema, 1999).

31 Di Simplicio "Processi," 345–346; Oscar Di Simplicio, *Inquisizione stregoneria medicina* (Monteriggioni: Il Leccio, 2000) 211–213; Martin, *Witchcraft*, 226.

32 Martin, *Witchcraft*, 226–227; Jonathan Seitz, *Witchcraft and Inquisition in Early Modern Venice* (Cambridge: Cambridge University Press, 2011), 59–61; Duni, *Devil's Spell*, 71–72; Di Simplicio, *Autunno*, 106–108.

33 Richard Kieckhefer, "Magic and Its Hazards in the Late Medieval West," in *The Oxford Handbook of Witchcraft*, 13–31, 20.

34 Several examples in Guido Ruggiero, *Binding Passions: Tales of Magic, Marriage and Power at the End of the Renaissance*, (New York: Oxford University Press, 1993), 130–174.

35 Martin, *Witchcraft*, 139–141; Duni, *Devil's Spell*, 66–69.

36 Martin, *Witchcraft*, 226; Messana, *Inquisitori*, 405.

37 Alison Rowlands, "Witchcraft and Gender in Early Modern Europe," in *The Oxford Handbook of Witchcraft*, 449–467.

38 Johannes Dillinger, *Magical Treasure Hunting in Europe and North America* (Basingstoke: Palgrave Macmillan, 2012), 153–174.

39 Duni, *Devil's Spell*, 52.

40 David Gentilcore, *From Bishop to Witch: The System of the Sacred in Early Modern Terra d'Otranto* (Manchester: Manchester University Press, 1992), 94–127.

41 Written sources of magic, however, did not all belong to the more sophisticated tradition of ritualistic, astral magic (such as the originally Arabic *Picatrix*), but often consisted in compilations of recipes and experiments for a variety of purposes, from household management, to craftsmanship, to practical jokes, some of which had a marked magical character. On this genre of texts see Richard Kieckehefer, *Magic in the Middle Ages* (Cambridge: Cambridge University Press, 1989).

42 Duni, *Devil's Spell*, 80–83. Similar contacts between agents of differing social and cultural background in Venetian magic in Martin, *Witchcraft*, 96–99.

43 Ruggiero, *Binding*, 149–156, 163–166; David Gentilcore, *Healers and Healing in Early Modern Italy* (Manchester: Manchester University Press, 1998), 1–28, 156–176, especially on the concept of "medical pluralism", or the coexistence of multiple systems explaining both causation of diseases and rationale of their cures.

44 Kieckhefer, "Mythologies". Carlo Ginzburg, *The Night Battles* (Baltimore: Johns Hopkins University Press, 1983), 16, 49–51, 185; Maurizio Bertolotti, "The Ox's Bones and the Ox's Hide", in *Microhistory and the Lost People of Europe*, ed. Edward Muir, Guido Ruggiero (Baltimore: Johns Hopkins University Press, 1991), 41–70.

45 These were four "festivities which had survived from an ancient agricultural calendar cycle and which were eventually incorporated in the Christian calendar", Ginzburg, *The Night Battles*, 22.

46 Matteo Duni, "'What about Some Good Wether?' Witches and Werewolves in Sixteenth-Century Italy", in *Werewolf Histories*, ed. Willem de Blécourt (Basingstoke: Palgrave Macmillan, 2015), 121–141.

47 Martine Ostorero, *Le diable au sabbat: Littérature démonologique et sorcellerie (1440–1460)* (Florence: SISMEL, 2011), 681–700.

48 Gustav Henningsen, "The Ladies from Outside. An Archaic Pattern of the Witches' Sabbath," in *Early Modern European Witchcraft*, 191–215; figures are drawn from Messana, *Inquisitori*, 550–569, which provides the most complete (if not always convincing) analysis of this belief-complex available.

49 Henningsen, "Ladies," 212–215; Elsa Guggino, *La magia in Sicilia* (Palermo: Sellerio, 1978), 125–128; Elsa Guggino, "Nota," *Archivio antropologico mediterraneo* I (1998): 35–44.

50 Euan Cameron, *Enchanted Europe: Superstition, Reason,& Religion, 1250–1750* (Oxford: Oxford University Press, 2010).

51 Romeo, "Inquisitori domenicani."

Bibliography (selection)

Corsi, Dinora, *Diaboliche, maledette e disperate*. Florence: Firenze University Press, 2013.

Decker, Rainer, *Witchcraft and the Papacy*. Charlottesville: Virginia University Press, 2008.

Duni, Matteo, *Under the Devil's Spell: Witches, Sorcerers, and the Inquisition in Renaissance Italy*. Florence: Syracuse University, 2007.

Ginzburg, Carlo, *The Night Battles: Witchcraft and Agrarian Cults in the Sixteenth and Seventeenth Centuries*. Baltimore: Johns Hopkins University Press, 1983.

Romeo, Giovanni, *Inquisitori, esorcisti e streghe nell'Italia della Controriforma*. Firenze: Sansoni, 1990.

Seitz, Jonathan, *Witchcraft and Inquisition in Early Modern Venice*. Cambridge: Cambridge University Press, 2011.

Di Simplicio, Oscar, *Autunno della stregoneria. Maleficio e magia nell'Italia moderna*. Bologna: Il Mulino, 2005.

7

GERMANY – "THE MOTHER OF THE WITCHES"

Johannes Dillinger

About half of all the women and men ever executed for witchcraft were German. Friedrich Spee, the great German opponent of the witch hunts, was right when he called Germany "the mother of so many the witches".[1] Almost 25,000 people were executed for witchcraft in the German lands. Why about 50% of all the executions for witchcraft took place in Germany even though only about 20% of the total population of early modern Europe lived there is the basic question this chapter tries to answer.[2] An analysis of the catastrophic German witch hunts might help us to understand the basic patterns of witchcraft persecutions in general.

The first German witch trials took place late in the 15th century. The witch hunts spread slowly from the Southwest to the North and to the East. Two major waves of witch hunting affected large parts of the county, the first around 1590, the other around 1630.

Demonology and society

Did the German states witness more witch hunts because the influence of the demonological witchcraft doctrine was particularly strong there? It is certainly true that the witchcraft doctrine reached Germany comparatively early and was quick to adapt to the German legal environment. When the persecutions started in Switzerland in the early 15th century, Switzerland was still officially a part of the Holy Roman

Table 7.1 Parts of Germany most affected by the witch hunts

Region	Phase of most intensive witch hunting	Number of executions
Hessia	1600–1605, 1650–1680	1,200
East Main Area-Franconia	1590–1630	3,600
Northern Germany	1570–1630, 1660–1675	3,200
East Germany	1590–1630, 1650–1680	1,100
Southwest Germany	1570–1590, 1610–1630	4,200
Moselle-Rhine Area	1580–1600, 1625–1630	4,600

Empire. Early demonologists like Fründ, Nider and Molitor were German or from German-speaking Switzerland and commented on German and Swiss trials. Heinrich Kramer (Institoris), the author of the notorious *Malleus Maleficarum* (The Witches' Hammer, 1486), came from the Imperial Free City of Schlettstadt (Sélestat, today in France) and spent most of his life in the Empire. He spoke a German dialect that made it easiest for him to communicate with German authorities. At Kramer's request, the papal bull 'Summis desiderantes' (1484) granted him the privilege to investigate against witches in "Germania superior", an ill-defined term that is probably best understood as today's South Germany and the Eastern Alpine region. Kramer's first more or less successful attempt to galvanize local authorities into hunting witches took place in the German Imperial City of Ravensburg. He claimed later on to have brought 48 witches to 'justice' in in the German Southwest. Most of the contemporary examples of witchcraft Kramer quoted in his Malleus Maleficarum came from the German lands.[3] What is more, the Malleus appears to have been written with a German audience in mind. When Kramer gave concrete advice to secular judges in the third part of the Malleus, he seemed to assume that these judges had little formal training but some considerable leeway in making their own decisions, especially decisions concerning the use of torture. Many European regions left judges practically to their own devices in the late 15th century. However, Kramer seemed to suggest an almost arbitrary power of the judges that might best be seen as a reflection of de facto break down of criminal justice in the late medieval German states.[4] Kramer evidently developed his new witchcraft doctrine with Germany in mind. Thus, it was particularly easy for German authorities to relate to Kramer's teachings. There is some evidence for the Malleus' direct influence on local witch hunts in Germany.[5]

During the main phase of witch hunting between the middle of the 16th and the middle of the 17th century, however, there was only one other German among the most important advocates of the witch hunts: Peter Binsfeld, suffragan bishop of Trier. At the request of the prince elector of Trier, he wrote 'De confessionibus maleficorum et sagarum' (1589) in which he not only defended denunciations of witches by their alleged accomplices as reliable but summarized the entire witchcraft doctrine brilliantly.[6]

Some of the most prolific opponents of the witch hunts also wrote their works with Germany in mind. We have already mentioned the Jesuit Spee, who published his seminal work *Cautio Criminalis* in 1631 in direct response to the second major wave of witch hunts that had hit large parts of Germany in the late 1620s. Spee dedicated his work to the German princes. He criticized them for allowing irresponsible and ill-trained judges to use torture arbitrarily. Spee kept hinting at a secret that he did not dare to write down but that he would reveal if any prince agreed to meet him face to face. Spee's secret was undoubtedly that witches did not exist. Outside of the specific German context – a great number of princes who were all at least in theory totally in charge of criminal justice – Spee's argument would have made little sense.[7] Another critical author was a direct 'product' of the German judicial system. Christian Thomasius published two vehement attacks on demonology in 1701 and 1712. Thomasius was one of many law professors who wrote expert opinions for German courts. Imperial law requested local judges to seek the advice of legal experts. The basis for Thomasius' anti-demonology was a trial against a child witch he had had to examine in 1694.[8]

The evidence concerning demonology seems inconclusive: Germany clearly played a major role in early demonological tracts. However, some of the most outspoken opponents of the witch hunts were German, too. It might be more profitable to find out how important demonology really was in concrete German witch hunts. We need to discuss the German witchcraft imagination as documented in the trial records.

Here, the evidence seems to be overwhelming and unambiguous: The witchcraft imagination we find in German trial records was clearly influenced by demonological concepts. The pact with the devil, sexual intercourse with a demon lover, the so-called sabbath and the witches' flight figured very prominently in most parts of Germany. It would be too simple to assume that judges with some demonological knowledge simply forced the defendants to confess what they expected to hear, including details about diabolism that were essentially alien to the accused. Sermons and confessions that were often read out publicly before the executions quickly taught peasants and townspeople the basics of demonology. They adapted the witchcraft doctrine to their own needs and experiences. During the 16th century, a 'popular demonology' came into existence in Germany: The witchcraft doctrine began to mingle with the popular belief in malevolent magic and in a host of spirit beings. As early as 1536 in Saxon trials, a benevolent household spirit in the form of a dragon that was deeply rooted in East German folk belief literally morphed into the devil as a demonic lover. Witchcraft quickly and effectively marginalized other magical thoughts: Strange nightly noises on a mountain top that local tradition had had explained as a ghost battle soon featured in witch trials, where they were presented as evidence for a witches' sabbath. Rituals of popular Catholicism that 'punished' the statue of a saint for sending rain and hail were abolished when witch trials began to punish the witches for weather magic.[9]

The places where the witches supposedly met for their sabbaths could be regarded as metaphors for the immediacy of the witches' menace. Of course, a number of witch trials stated that the witches danced on some lonely and far away mountain. The witches of Rostock, for example, claimed that they flew almost 300 km to the Blocksberg, a mountain that most of them clearly had never seen.[10] In many other trials, however, the witches were said to come together in the immediate vicinity of their villages. An example might be the Hoxberg mountain in the Saar region that was the direct neighbour of a number of villages: The sabbath was supposed to take place about a two hour walk from half a dozen settlements, on a mountain top that was plainly visible for miles around.[11] As if to mock the witch hunters, the witches of Pfullendorf and Laiz in Southwest Germany were said to dance on gallows hill. In Rottenburg, hundreds of witches celebrated the sabbath in the garden of the sheriff's castle. Even witches who had already been arrested managed to join the dances that took place in the castles of the Swabian Hohenzollern, the Catholic cousins of the ruling house of Brandenburg that would rise to the throne of the Second German Empire.[12] Obviously, the witches were not afraid of the princes and officials who were in charge of the witch trials, and they did not fear the grim symbols of criminal justice displayed on gallows hill. The insolence of the witches went even further than that. In Osnabrück, the witches' feast took place on a public square in the city where the usual fairs were held.[13] In Tübingen, the witches were supposed to dance on the market place. In Freiburg im Breisgau, they assembled right outside one of the main city gates, apparently in plain view of the guards who were supposed to man the gates. In Horb, one of the centres of the persecutions in Swabia, the witches met in the hospital, one of Horb's biggest buildings, right in the middle of the town. In one of the earliest German witch hunts, the one conducted by Kramer himself in Ravensburg in 1484, the witches met for a sabbath-like gathering right outside the town wall, only a couple of paces from Ravensburg's main church.[14] These sabbath imaginations drove home alarming messages: The witches did not seem to fear the authorities in the least. They had conquered spaces of everyday life – not only the hilltop you saw every day, but also the market place, the city gate – for their gatherings. This meant that your everyday perception of these places was erroneous or at least did not reveal the entire truth. What seemed to be mundane parts of life, reliable and 'safe', had long been infiltrated by the witches. You could not trust the authorities, you could not trust your own senses. The witches were everywhere.

The witches of the German witch hunts were first and foremost weather magicians. Of course, witches killed and maimed; they brought death and disease to the peasant household, targeting the family as well as the livestock. Still, German witch hunters were most interested in weather magic. The witches supposedly threatened the harvest with rain, hail and frost. Time and again, the only point of the witches' sabbath seemed to have been to give the witches the opportunity to engage in weather magic collectively. In very many cases, a thunderstorm or a frost that threatened a region or a village with crop failure provoked a witch hunt. The connection between witch hunting and the Little Ice Age is obvious. Of course, all of Europe suffered from climate change. However, in Germany, where witches were mostly regarded as weather magicians, it was desperately simple to blame witches for long spells of cold and rain. Centres of the persecutions in Germany were Franconia, the Moselle-Rhine region and some areas in the Southwest. All of these places were wine growing regions. This was no coincidence: The vineyards were of course especially vulnerable to inclement weather. Other regions with more robust economies or a favourable micro-climate experienced fewer witch trials, e.g. the shores of Lake Constance, which were famous for their high temperatures, and the town of Schwäbisch-Hall, which depended on the most stable salt trade, witnessed comparatively few witch hunts.[15]

As the German witchcraft imagination focused on weather magic, witches used their power mainly to do harm, not to further their own interests. As a rule, they did not profit from their magic. A hailstorm that destroyed the crops devastated the witch's own fields as well. The witches did what they did because the demons told them so. Thus, it was never possible to defend oneself against witchcraft accusations simply by pointing out that one's own family suffered from the consequences of crop failure just like everybody else. Witch belief destroyed even the basic communal solidarity that was founded on a shared experience of misery. Weather magic harmed the entire village or even the entire region. Thus, the witch could not be one person's enemy and some other person's friend. She was always everybody's enemy. Nobody could ever side with the witch or even think for a moment that her aggression might in any way be justifiable.

The witches not only conquered large parts of folk belief and everyday culture but also were quick to claim space in the social sphere, too. German witches did not have any specific social profile. Apart from the fact that the vast majority were female – about 80%, even though there were any number of regional differences – little can be said about the social characteristics of the culprits. They came from all age groups and all walks of life. It is certainly true that in some parts of Germany witchcraft accusations started on the margins of society. It could take them months or years to make inroads into the middle class and the upper middle class if they managed to do that at all.[16] In other areas, however, it was taken for granted from the beginning of the witch hunts that there were witches in all strata of society and especially in the upper class. One of the first witch trials of Günzburg in 1530 targeted a woman whose father and grandfather were not only members of the town council but also clearly belonged to its ruling faction.[17] The intensive witch hunts in parts of the Moselle area were based on the conviction that the most aggressive and the most influential witches belonged to the highest echelons of urban society. Germany might be the only country that executed a significant number of Catholic priests for witchcraft.[18]

The 'Evil People Paradigm' might be the best way to describe the genesis of rumours of witchcraft in Germany. On the basis of popular demonology, accusations of witchcraft were a way to express any kind of deep distrust and severe hostility. As a rule, accusations of witchcraft had a background of long-standing tensions within a local community or within a family. In the trial records of the German witch hunts we find time and again the same kind of reasoning: Persons with a bad reputation, persons who were known as overtly aggressive, were accused of witchcraft. They were obviously evil, thus it was likely that they were in league with the devil. Of course, in any kind of protracted conflict, the personal opponent could begin to appear like a truly evil person. In the background of a great number of German witch trials we find real criminal activity; arsonists, for example, were often accused of witchcraft, too. However, we also find banal but bitter family quarrels, conflicts between neighbours or between tenants who had to share the same house in an early modern town. A trial from Coburg seriously presented the fact that the defendant was in the habit of clearing the table before her guests had finished eating as damning evidence in a witch trial. Even corruption and petty political feuds could lead to accusations of witchcraft. Easily the most prominent witch of 16th-century Germany was Dr Diederich Flade, executed in 1589. Flade was not only an exceedingly affluent man and one of the leading officials of Trier but also a judge who had already sent several witches to the stake. Nevertheless, suspicions of witchcraft against him were so widespread and well known that children followed him in the street shouting 'wizard, wizard'. Flade was a careerist who had supported the prince archbishop of Trier in a conflict with the communal authorities. He was a notorious usurer and he took bribes. One might call this connection between seemingly mundane conflicts and accusations of witchcraft an early modern variant of the banality of evil. It is rather telling that in some regions of early modern Germany, the term 'evil people' was used as an equivalent of 'witches'.[19] Thus, large parts of the German population not only used witch trials to deal with general experiences of severe crises like crop failure. Witch hunts were a means to deal with personal crises, experiences of conflict and social tension, too.

The empire and the principalities

Economic hardship caused by crop failure was clearly one of the engines that drove the witch hunts in Germany. However, when we look more closely at the number of victims, it becomes obvious that the Little Ice Age and the agrarian crisis connected with it provided merely the background for much more complicated developments. Wine growing regions were likely to witness large numbers of witch hunts. However, within these regions there were most significant differences. Generally speaking, the intensity of witch hunting in Germany could differ greatly even between territories that were direct neighbours. The comparatively small county of Hohenberg in the Southwest sent about 440 witches to the stake. That equalled an execution rate of 76%. The neighbouring duchy of Württemberg executed only about one third of the accused, a grand total of about 180 persons. The total population of Württemberg was roughly 430,000, that of Hohenberg 15,000. The margraviate of Baden-Durlach executed fewer than ten persons as witches. The sister territory Baden-Baden, ruled by a different branch of the same dynasty, burned more than 270. Other twin territories like Mecklenburg-Güstrow and Mecklenburg-Schwerin exhibited a similar pattern. In the tiny territory of the Protestant Imperial City of Reutlingen more than 50 people were sent to the stake. Seventy kilometers away, in the huge territory of the Protestant Imperial City of Ulm, only about ten persons were executed for witchcraft. The prince electorate of Trier witnessed, like many other territories, two major waves of witch hunting: The first in the 1580s and 1590s, the other in the 1620s. The prince electorate of Trier executed about 700 witches; the execution rate was almost 90%. Both waves failed to reach Trier's neighbour, the Palatinate. The Palatinate remained entirely free of witch trials.[20]

Why did the witch hunts in principalities that were direct neighbours and faced comparable socioeconomic conditions still differ so greatly? It pays to have a closer look at the concrete administrative conditions of these principalities. The Holy Roman Empire of the German Nation was a federation of – depending on your way of counting – hundreds or even thousands of states. There were essentially three types of states: Hereditary monarchies, elective monarchies and republics. The hereditary monarchies were of course governed by aristocratic families. The elective monarchies were ecclesiastical lands ruled by the (elected) princes of the Catholic church: prince abbots, prince bishops and prince archbishops. The political territory a bishop ruled like a prince, his 'Hochstift' (in the case of an archbishop 'Erzstift'; plural: Hochstifte or Erzstifte), must not be confused with the spiritual territory or diocese he governed, his 'Bistum' or 'Erzbistum'. A drastic example is the bishop of Konstanz: His Bistum or diocese reached from the source of the Rhine in the Alps to the Swabian lands North of Stuttgart. His Hochstift, however, was a comparatively small territory on the Northeast shore of Lake Constance. The Hochstift was not simply a piece of land the bishop or the bishopric owned like a private person might own land: The Hochstift was the territory in which a bishop, archbishop or abbot exercised all the rights a secular prince would have in his princedom. The criminal courts of the Hochstift were secular courts as they belonged to secular territories, even though a Catholic ecclesiastic ruled these territories. The courts of the Hochstifte used secular, not canon law. They were no ecclesiastical courts; they were staffed by laypersons. Obviously, they were in no way connected to or even subjected to the Inquisition.[21] The failure to distinguish between the Hochstift and the Bistum and to understand the nature of the criminal courts of the Hochstifte has led to much confusion. It is – together with the long-term effects of Bismarck's Kulturkampf and Nazi propaganda – one of the reasons why the German collective memory has a marked tendency to exaggerate the Catholic church's involvement in the witch hunts.[22]

The third type of state in the Old Empire were quasi-republican city states. These Imperial or Free Cities acknowledged only the emperor himself as their overlord. The town council or a committee formed by the council was at the same time the executive and the legislative body of the town. Members of the town council also served as the judges or the jury of the town's courts. The councils elected the burgomasters as representatives of the town and as the heads of the communal executive. The councils selected their own members themselves by co-optation. As a rule, only members of the old merchant elite, the patricians and leaders of the guilds had access to the town councils. Some of the most populous and wealthiest German cities were Imperial Cities (e.g. Cologne, Augsburg, Nuremberg, Hamburg). Some of the Imperial Cities (e.g. Rottweil, Ulm) controlled large territories outside of the city walls: They were themselves territorial lords that ruled the neighbouring countryside. However, Imperial Cities were not necessarily big or affluent communities. Especially in the German Southwest, there were a number of tiny and rather poor Imperial Cities (e.g. Giengen, Isny, Weil der Stadt) that in terms of their population, cultural significance or economic strength were dwarfed by many of the towns that were under the overlordship of a prince (e.g. Dresden, Mainz, Munich, Stuttgart). The towns that recognized a secular or ecclesiastical prince as their territorial lord had to involve some official(s) of that prince in many of their administrative or jurisdictional activities. Depending on the privileges of the individual town, this involvement could take on any form from authoritarian control that practically prevented the communal institutions from making any important decisions themselves to a loosely defined participation in the selection of local office holders. Again, the political power and privileges of the town had nothing to do with its size. Most German towns had well under 5,000 inhabitants. Only a few could boast a population of more than 30,000. A domineering metropolis like Rome, Paris or London did not exist. The emperor resided in Prague or Vienna, but the Empire as such did not have a capital.[23]

When we talk about late medieval and early modern German territories we can use the term 'state' only in the broadest sense. Many German territories failed to establish a clearly defined citizenry, largely undisputed borders, recognized public authority and state laws as well as some kind of diplomatic representation. When the Final Recess of 1803 did away with the old territorial order of the Empire three years before the Empire itself officially ceased to exist, many of the German territories were 'failed states'.

The 1532 imperial criminal code of Emperor Charles V (usually referred to as the Carolina) presented a legal framework for handling various offences, including magical crimes. The Carolina treated magic rather leniently and ignored the demonological doctrine. The imperial law did not even mention demonic pacts or the sabbath. The Carolina listed a catalogue of permissible evidence in trials against sorcerers that ascribed secondary importance to common rumours. Only harmful magic was explicitly made a capital offense. Judges were to use discretion in punishing all other kinds of magic. As many judges had no formal training, the Carolina explicitly required them to seek the advice of learned jurists. Especially if a judge considered the use of torture, the Carolina required him to ask for expert advice first. Thus, the Carolina certainly did not encourage witch hunts. If the minimum standards of the Carolina had been adhered to, Germany would never have become the heartland of the witch hunts.[24]

However, as far as criminal law was concerned, the Empire respected the sovereignty of the German principalities. Under pressure from the aristocracy and the Free Cities, Charles V had included the so-called salvatory clause in the Carolina: The legislators of princedoms and Free Cities could choose whether to accept the norms of the Carolina in their lands or to replace them with their own laws. While the Carolina ignored demonology, it did not discredit demonological arguments. The dukedom of Württemberg made demonic pacts alone a punishable offense in 1567. In 1572, the prince elector of Saxony passed a law that made pacts a capital crime. Such laws invited the use of torture, as they placed great emphasis on an element of the demonological stereotype the courts could not possible prove by eyewitness accounts or material evidence. The federal nature of the Holy Roman Empire that allowed any German territorial state to have its own witchcraft laws existed well before the main phase of the witch hunts began in the 1560s. It still existed and continued to exist after the end of the German witch trials in the second half of the 18th century. Thus, it is to a certain degree misleading to talk about 'German' witch hunts. It would be more appropriate to talk about 'Bavarian', 'Saxonian', etc. witch hunts instead. Insofar, it makes a lot of sense that most monographs about witch trials in Germany are regional studies.[25]

The federal nature of the Holy Roman Empire strengthened the individual principalities, but it was far from rendering its central institutions entirely passive. There were various appellate courts under Habsburg tutelage that made the German legal system even more complicated. Strictly speaking, appeals were not admissible in criminal cases. The possibility existed, however, to address procedural complaints about any trial to the courts of appeals. The highest courts of the Empire were the Imperial Chamber Court (Reichskammergericht) and the Imperial Aulic Court (Reichshofrat). At times, both competed with each other. Suspects who were sufficiently knowledgeable and well-off so that they could draw the imperial judges' attention to their cases at least slowed their trials down. The Empire's appellate courts exercised a beneficial influence on the witch hunts comparable to that of the parlement of Paris or the High Court of Flanders. The Imperial Chamber Court based all its verdicts strictly on the Carolina. The highly qualified judges of the Imperial Chamber Court set (and often raised) the tone of any legal discussion in which they became involved. Their often harsh criticism of miscarriages of justice in witch trials helped to end some regional persecutions. Thus, the central institutions of the Empire were weak in theory, but they should not be underestimated in practice.[26]

The same holds true for the Empire's highest authority, the emperor himself. Direct appeals to the emperor could slow down witch hunts. The most prominent example is that of the county of Hohenems. Complaints against the gross injustice of the Hohenems witch trials were sent to the emperor. Leopold I demanded a thorough investigation. He subjected the count's authority to that of his most powerful neighbour, the prince abbot of Kempten, who was to serve as an imperial commissioner. The emperor managed to put some very real political 'muscle' behind the Empire's authority by harnessing Kempten's considerable power. In the course of an investigation that unearthed serious miscarriages of justice, the prince abbot eventually wrenched the lordships of Schellenberg and Vaduz from count Hohenems. With the emperor's backing, the Liechtenstein dynasty took possession of these territories, which they have kept as an independent monarchy until the present day.[27]

To sum up: The central institutions of the Empire were certainly not the driving force behind the persecutions. Rather, they curtailed the persecutions by enforcing basic legal standards.

One essential element of the German witch hunts must not be overlooked: In all German criminal courts, the use of torture was perfectly legal. Imperial law officially recognized torture as a means to provide a confession. However, it was meant as the very last resort of the judge: Only if the judge was practically sure that the defendant was guilty could he order him to be tortured in order to achieve a confession. A verdict without a formal confession was highly problematic. The imperial law had wanted judges to use torture in that way only. Unfortunately, many lay judges based the whole legal procedure on torture and were all too ready to use it. This holds especially true in witch trials, where it was always very difficult to find any reliable witnesses or material evidence. Torture became the rule rather than the exception. Even in principalities that officially recognized the standards of the Carolina, lay judges were often left to their own devices and simply ignored the law.[28]

Organizing witch hunts

Who was responsible for Germany's great witch hunts? The names of a small group of prince abbots and prince bishops come to mind. Their respective territories, situated in a great region that today belongs to southern Hessen, northern Bavaria and eastern Baden-Württemberg witnessed some of the worst witch hunts ever. Balthasar von Dernbach (prince abbot of Fulda), Johann Gottfried von Aschhausen (prince bishop of Bamberg and Würzburg), Johann Georg Fuchs von Dornheim (prince bishop of Bamberg, Aschhausen's successor), Julius Echter von Mespelbrunn (prince bishop of Würzburg), Philipp Adolf von Ehrenberg (prince bishop of Würzburg, Echter's nephew and successor) and Johann Christoph von Westerstetten (prince provost of Ellwangen, later prince bishop of Eichstätt). All of these so-called witch-bishops considered themselves the spearheads of Tridentine reform in Germany. For them, the fight against witches was clearly part of an apocalyptic battle against evil and for the purity of the church. In the case of Echter, recent research was able to prove that he was far less pro-active than formerly assumed. Echter apparently tried to exercise a modicum of control over the witch hunts in order to prevent even more miscarriages of justice.[29]

The basic problem was organization, not the stance taken by individuals. Even a very determined prince bishop from the German province whose ideas about true Catholicism would have alienated the Vatican was certainly not enough to start a witch hunt. The basic problem was that the prince bishops either set up special courts for witches or suffered them to come into existence. These institutions were either completely new or they constituted a thorough restructuring of existing agencies. What really mattered was that a small special court or a committee of administrators was able to exercise practically unlimited control over the witch trials. Such witch-finder institutions were small and of comparatively simple structure. Their purpose was not so much the thorough investigation of rumours of witchcraft but rather the persecution of witches as such. The princes let these witch-finder administrations acquire special powers that placed them outside the ordinary legal system and beyond the control of other government agencies. Thus freed of any administrative restraints, the institutions became independent bureaucracies honed for efficiency. They 'processed' a great number of suspects in a very short time. It was typical of these witch hunter administrations that they ignored due process and relied heavily on denunciations and the use of torture. As these administrations owed at least in theory their power to a prince, we could call the persecutions they instigated persecutions 'from above'.[30]

A number of German princes appointed special witch commissioners whose sole function was to organize witch hunts. Some princes made such appointments with the ultimate goal of reducing the number of trials and eventually letting them die out. The witch commissioner Dr Leonhard Neusesser, who virtually ended the witch hunt in the Habsburg territories in modern-day Bavaria, is a case in point.[31] However, most princes apparently employed witch commissioners with special powers to promote witch hunts. For example, the prince elector of Cologne authorized Dr Heinrich von Schultheiß to superintend the witch trials in Westphalia. Dr Wolfgang Kolb worked as a witch-finder for the prince bishop of Eichstätt, the count of Oettingen-Wallerstein and the duke of Bavaria, who gave him the title of 'Rat von Haus aus' (councillor with special commission).[32] Even some towns granted additional powers to clerks who were supposed to investigate rumours of witchcraft. In the Imperial Free City of Esslingen, the town council empowered the attorney Daniel Hauff to prepare all charges against witches. Hauff used his assignment to rise to the position of town councillor. Hermann Cothmann, the notorious 'witch burgomaster' of Lemgo in Westphalia, began his career which would eventually lead him to the very top of the town's hierarchy as Lemgo's 'director of criminal trials against sorcerers and witches'.[33]

Witch-finder institutions were originally meant to bridge the administrative shortcomings of numerous German states. As these special administrations realized the prince's jurisdiction dramatically in all his lands, their witch hunts contributed directly to the process of state formation. However, their 'success' and indeed their usefulness was short-lived. Mounting death tolls began to damage the very fabric of society and state. The increasing power of the witch-finder agencies was viewed with suspicion. Above all, catastrophic witch hunts invited criticism from the relatives of the condemned and from neighbouring states.[34]

Various German principalities witnessed severe witch persecutions 'from below', initiated and organized by so-called subjects without or even against the will of their lord. Peasants and people from small towns made their voices heard during the witch hunts and often even managed to usurp parts of the legal administration. Thus, people without any legal training whatsoever influenced criminal procedures critically. Some of these grassroots witch hunts were among the most ferocious persecutions ever. Some rural communities seemed to be on the verge of committing suicide via witch trials.

Witch hunts 'from below' took various forms. In the Rhine-Moselle-Saar region, communal self-government was traditionally strong. Peasant communities elected village committees to redress local grievances. As a rule, the basis of their power was an ad hoc village covenant that acknowledged the committee as acting on behalf of the whole community. The respective lord had at best nominal control over these institutions. A committee might, for example, reform the local tax system or act as the legal representatives of the village in court. However, a village might also elect a committee for the sole purpose of witch hunting. Such witch hunting committees established their own investigative organization. They actively collected evidence, heard witnesses and contacted official courts to learn about denunciations. They might force their services as prison guards on the prince's officials. Some committees even employed their own scribes and lawyers. Jurists from the nearby towns quickly learned that it was very lucrative business to work for communal witch hunting committees. Committees brought charges against witchcraft suspects collectively. Of course, the activities of the witch hunting committees were costly. Some members of the committees earned a substantial additional income. As a rule, the accused or their relatives had to pay not only the expenses for the trial proper but also for the (strictly speaking extra-legal) investigations of the committee. The committees even invented imaginative schemes to cover the often considerable costs of their activities. Some advocated that well-to-do suspects should pay the expenses for poorer trial victims, others thought it appropriate to have suspects pay for investigations against themselves no matter whether they were proven guilty or not. It was often part and parcel of the village covenant on which the committee's work was based that the local community itself declared that it would cover all the costs caused by witch hunting. Some villages introduced a witch tax to finance the committees.[35]

The local and regional courts of the princes and their law enforcement officers found it difficult or indeed impossible not to cooperate with the committees, let alone to reject charges brought by them. An official from the Moselle area boastfully compared the members of the witch hunting committee to a pack of hounds he used when he wanted to go hunting.[36] In truth, these dogs pulled the hunter into the hunting ground and were ready to bite him if he did not follow them quickly enough. With the authority of the community behind them and officeholders of the prince mostly willing to accept them as partners, communal witch hunting committees enjoyed a uniquely strong position. It was next to impossible for individual witchcraft suspects to protest against the activities of the committees.

Village committees were part of the communal self-government apparatus in a number of West German principalities. In other regions, town councils and traditional peasant assemblies initiated and organized witch hunts. In many German small towns, the town council was partly identical with the town's criminal court. As a rule, the judges of these small town courts had very little or absolutely no legal training. Still, many princes left the town courts to their own devices. The middling sort and even peasants from the neighbouring countryside found it often quite easy to influence such lay courts. In the Black Forrest-Neckar River region, town councils dominated by the middle class organized exceptionally severe persecutions. The town councils of Rottenburg and Horb, for example, were under the influence of petty winegrowers. Both towns witnessed about 200 witch trials. The Hohenzollern princes who hesitated to burn witches had to face very angry representatives of villagers that demanded more severe witch hunts in no uncertain terms. In 1602 in the county of Wertheim, the village population tried to force their somewhat reluctant lord into witch hunting. Villagers carried around a wooden staff, and everybody willing to support the witch hunt was supposed to cut a notch into it. Thus, communities not only made their decisions collectively, they also demonstrated to outsiders (and would-be opponents) how determined they were. The Wertheim government became very nervous when it learned about this witch hunting organization. Traditionally, peasant rebels had used the ritual of cutting notches in a staff to recruit supporters and to organize themselves. The notorious persecutions in the ecclesiastical territory of Marchtal were in fact the persecutions of the village of Alleshausen, an isolated settlement that had contrived to shake off the Marchtal prince abbot's control. In 1745, members of Alleshausen's local elite even managed to gain influence over Marchtal's central court. They ignored expert opinions from learned jurists until they got opinions that suited their witch hunting zeal. The result was a persecution in the 1750s, one of Germany's last great witch hunts.[37] Time and again, reluctant authorities had to face so-called common people who demanded witch hunts aggressively. Witchcraft hysterias like that of Preetz near Kiel in 1665/66 or that of Annaberg in Saxony in 1712–1714 are cases in point.[38]

A variant of communal witch hunting were the persecutions in the German dwarf states. Here, the German gentry or petty nobles ('ritterschaftlicher Adel', especially in northern and eastern Germany) or the prince abbots of minor ecclesiastical lands who were nominally in charge of their miniscule lordships had to cooperate with the population. These miniature states had hardly any legal administration to speak of but could still pass death sentences. As persecutions here had an aristocratic figurehead or even a noble witch hunter as one of the driving forces, they were not strictly communal in character. However, they were still based on local, very small and rather simple legal apparatuses that required close cooperation with the peasant population and worked without outside control. If a community in a dwarf state demanded witch hunts, it would have been political suicide for the petty lord not to comply with these wishes. Vis à vis a community that was determined to rid itself of the witches, the lords of petty states were in the same or even a weaker position as the local officeholders of bigger territorial states. They had hardly any other option than to 'flee forward'. At times, accepting communal demands for witch hunts could be part of a local ruler's populist policy designed to consolidate his structurally weak or newly imposed lordship. A good example might be the witch hunts in the dwarf territories of the monasteries of St Maximin near Trier and Fraulautern in the Saar region. Both the prince abbot of St Maximin and the prince abbess of Fraulautern fought for the independence of their tiny principalities against vastly superior neighbours, the prince archbishop of Trier and the duke of Lorraine, who questioned their authority. Alienating the powerful witch hunting committees of their so-called subjects who burned hundreds in St Maximin and dozens in Fraulautern was hardly an option for the 'authorities' of the dwarf territories.[39]

Princely governments and their officials in the communities proved incapable of controlling the communal agents of persecution. Of course, this does not mean that they welcomed their activities. Even if many local officials were obliged to cooperate with communal witch hunters, no government supported them willingly. Some witch hunting organizations openly ignored direct orders of the princely administration. Even if they did not, communal witch hunting groups questioned per se the authority of the emerging state apparatus. They claimed that they could handle a central element of law enforcement – investigation and accusation – more efficiently than the prince's officeholders. More importantly, the very existence of local witch hunting organizations as a form of criminal justice outside the state apparatus questioned the authority of the state itself. Explicitly or implicitly, the grassroots witch hunts suggested that criminal justice did not belong exclusively to the sovereign.

Authority over the criminal courts was a hallmark of lordship in the emerging states of early modern Germany. All princes and the councils of autonomous towns either strove to achieve this authority or, after successfully monopolizing it, tried to defend it against any encroachment.

The witch hunting agencies of subjects can be regarded as aggressive forms of communalism. The witch hunts show the negative side of communalism. Communalism was a form of voluntary local organization based on periodic meetings of householders resident in the community, and on their right to define local norms and to appoint non-professional office holders. Some historians have gone so far as to call communalism a precondition of republicanism in Europe. Villages and small towns turned witch hunting into an expression of autonomy. It was, in a way, an outward sign that demonstrated their independence from the princely state's hierarchical institutions. The communalistic structure is especially obvious in cases of witch hunting committees and their attempts to finance persecutions. They established their own quasi-legal rules and aimed at creating their own administrative apparatus, including a nascent system of taxation. The reason for the eventual failure of all witch hunting committees was that they never fully achieved that aim. As various members of committees competed for money, they never managed to set up their own fully functional financial administration. The communalist set-up of these organizations prevented them from forming larger structures with better access to sources of revenue. After some years, the local structure of witch hunting broke down due to a lack of finances. The village committees could not compete with the state apparatus.[40]

Grassroots witch hunts organized by the councils of small towns proved to be less prone to financial difficulties than the witch hunting committees of villages in the western territories of the Empire. However, they faced other problems. In contrast to the witch-finder committees, the town councils had of course not been founded for the sole purpose of witch hunting. They had a variety of tasks to master and they needed to integrate conflicting interests. Even if they managed to unite on the issue of witch hunting and to defy outside influence, especially that of the prince, for some time, they were incapable of doing so for more than a few years. Towns and town councils were as a rule too complex in themselves to favour radicalism of any kind. A radical faction that demanded intensive witch hunts was unlikely to hold sway for very long.[41]

What did the witch hunting institutions of the princes and the grassroots witch hunting organizations of the communities have in common? Both had a simple structure that allowed the witch trials to progress swiftly from initial accusation to execution. The reason for this procedural similarity was that both systems lacked internal controls or 'checks and balances'. Intense witch hunting depended on the ability to proceed summarily against witches. States that subjected their criminal courts to administrative control were less prone to witch hunting. The more complicated and critical the legal system, the longer the way to the stake, the less likely it became that the accused actually had to go there. The further removed the controlling agency was from the local milieu in which the suspicion of witchcraft had arisen, the less likely it was to find the suspect guilty. Central high courts that had the power, or indeed the regular duty, to supervise local criminal courts tended to slow down the witch hunts or to quash them altogether.

Some of the larger and better organized German principalities boasted powerful central institutions that were capable of controlling witch hunts. A good example was the duchy of Württemberg. After 1572, the local criminal courts of Württemberg had to report every criminal trial to a central governmental institution, the Oberrat (superior council). The Oberrat superintended all criminal procedures, including the decision whether and when to apply torture. The Oberrat not only was dominated by trained lawyers but also cooperated closely with the law faculty of Tübingen University. Electoral Saxony more or less followed the Württemberg pattern. There, the High Court of Leipzig controlled the progress of witch trials. Brandenburg-Prussia adopted a similar judicial structure. In all of these territories, only about one-third of all accused witches suffered capital punishment. The Palatinate had a similar organizational structure. Here, however, the government agencies were influenced by the sceptical views of Hermann Witekind. Thus, the Palatinate did not execute any witches at all.[42]

If there were no central controlling agencies, open discussions within the court system were a good way to keep witch hunting at a low level. Germany's largest cities and towns experienced remarkably few witch trials. Cologne witnessed the execution of fewer than forty witches, Augsburg sixteen, Hamburg fourteen. Frankfurt and Nuremberg seem not to have executed any witches at all. All of these cities had more than 30,000 inhabitants around 1600, i.e. they were among the biggest cities in the Empire. The main reason why big cities witnessed comparatively few witch trials is that their political elites were simply not part of the communicative circles of the lower strata of urban society. In order to preserve their political power, the well-established council elites of big cities kept themselves informed about rumours in the town but, for the same reason, were sceptical of such popular gossip. The city councils themselves, at least in the larger cities, were relatively complicated political structures. They were often divided into competing factions and staffed by self-assured members of powerful families or guilds. The very structure of those councils made it unlikely that they would arrive at rash or radical decisions. The discussions and critical appraisals that characterized the legal administration of a well-ordered principality existed *in nuce* in the councils of big towns.[43]

Small witch-finder organizations authorized by a prince and communal witch hunting groups bypassed or replaced more complex systems of administration. Only states the legal administration of which was weak to begin with allowed the rise of such witch hunting institutions. This might be the reason why we find the most aggressive variants of both, witch hunting from above and witch hunting from below, in ecclesiastical territories. As elective monarchies, ecclesiastical territories lacked a ruling dynasty. The heads of state, bishops and abbots, usually elected at a mature age, enjoyed relatively short terms in office. Coming from the nobility, many of them had the interest of their aristocratic relatives, not that of the Hochstift as such, in mind. Thus, the policies of ecclesiastical territories were prone to frequent and drastic changes. It was rather unlikely that the cathedral chapter would choose two bishops in a row from the same aristocratic family. (The only real exception here is of course a massive one: The archbishopric of Cologne was for centuries under the control of the Wittelsbachs.) Thus, many prince bishops were not too interested in thorough administrative reforms that would take time and effort or in creating stable governmental structures in their Hochstift. There was little incentive for that. On the contrary, there was, after all, always the very real possibility that the younger son of a competing dynasty would be the next bishop and thus 'inherit' a stronger administration that he could exploit for the benefit of his own family. Thus, many ecclesiastical territories were de facto 'failed states'. Such deficits in state formation invited witch hunts, both 'from above' – as a kind of administrative mistake born out of weakness and a lack of experience – and 'from below' – as the near-total failure of governmental structures in the countryside and their replacement by communal forces.

Ending witch hunts

Even in the comparatively well-organized German principalities, witch hunts could become a controversial political issue. The debate about witch hunts that took place early in the seventeenth century in the duchy of Bavaria is a good example. The severe witch hunts of the 1580s had provoked the formation of two opposing parties at the duke's court. The Zelanti or zealots advocated tough laws against witchcraft and demanded more witch trials. The Zelanti came from a background of well-to-do but provincial families that still fought for a secure foothold in the upper strata of the duke's administration. On the other side stood the Politici, the advocates of *raison d'état*. They were a faction of influential and well-established office holders with an urban background who were very reluctant to allow witch hunts. Whenever the Zelanti managed to goad the ducal administration into another wave of persecutions in the Bavarian province, the Politici opposed them vehemently. They demanded expert opinions and threatened the local witch hunters with dire consequences should they not observe due process. In 1612, Bavaria passed one of the most severe laws against witchcraft in German history. The Zelanti seemed to have won the day. However, their opponents managed to stop the publication of the mandate. The law was watered down and finally rendered inconsequential. One year later, the Politici had a witch hunter executed for miscarriage of justice. The Zelanti faction never recovered from that blow.[44]

Conflicts about witch hunts could play a major role in German community politics. In the Imperial Free City of Reutlingen, witch hunting had become an integral part of the struggle for political power between the 1590s and the 1660s. Whenever the ruling clique of the town council retired, the would-be successors fought among each other. Some of them sought the support of the public by calling for decisive action against the witches. Populist demands for 'tougher' criminal justice were certain to meet with a favourable response from the general public. Thus, Reutlingen temporarily deviated from the urban pattern. As soon as the new power elite of the city council had established its position, witch hunting ceased. The new leaders sometimes even made a positive effort to end the prosecutions they had helped to initiate.[45]

The end of the witch hunts in Germany came in the great reform period after the Thirty Years' War. Most principalities came under the control of complex and flexible governmental apparatuses controlled by responsible professionals. The dead ends of the state building process, overtly simple legal administrations that had given too much power to special administrations or communal agencies, disappeared. The decline of witch hunting was not only a result of this process. In some principalities, the witch hunts drove this process, albeit in a negative way: Excessive witch hunts, especially those 'from below', justified decisive measures of the central government against local autonomy. In Electoral Trier, prince archbishop Karl Kaspar von der Leyen simply banned witch trials in 1652 as part of a reform program designed to increase the government's authority. A few years later in Electoral Mainz, prince archbishop Johann Philipp von Schönborn de facto ended the witch trials for the same reason.[46] The Württemberg government sent armed forces to end the last serious outbreak of witch hunting orchestrated by a rural town. In Brandenburg and annexed Pomerania, King Friedrich Wilhelm I overcame local resistance against his rule during the last prosecutions in the early eighteenth century. As if to express their newfound authority, some monarchs reserved the ultimate verdict in all witch trials for themselves. Friedrich Wilhelm I of Prussia and Empress Maria Theresa did so in 1714 and 1766 respectively. This ultimate complication of the trials ended witch hunting effectively. As witch hunters could not afford to ignore the will of the monarch any more, they would have had to run the gauntlet through a long line of legal appraisals till they finally reached the monarch personally. Even though the German states still did not deny the existence of witches, actual witch trials became a merely theoretical option.[47]

It seems to be possible now to answer the question why Germany was "the mother of the witches". Why did the German lands witness so many witch trials?

German folk culture adopted the demonological concept of witchcraft early and thoroughly. During the 16th century, the demonological witchcraft doctrine mingled with folk belief. A popular demonology came into existence that the so-called common people, the majority of peasants and townspeople, began to use in order to interpret everyday experiences. In the second half of the 16th century, the belief in witches, in the full demonological sense, had taken deep roots in everyday culture. Witchcraft had become a 'passepartout' explanation for evil, be it confrontations with personal adversaries or experiences of misfortune like crop failure.

The Holy Roman Empire of the German Nation consisted of a large number of more or less independent principalities. Most of them had their own criminal courts. Many of these courts were staffed by lay judges. In many small towns, the members of the town council were judges of the town's criminal court even if they had never studied law. Torture was a 'normal' element of the legal system that could be used in all criminal cases. Thus, there were hundreds of criminal courts run by judges who had no or little legal training but could still use torture. A comparatively high number of witch trials was an almost inevitable result. However, in a large number of German states, matters were even worse. Many of the German territories were badly organized – especially the ecclesiastical states of prince bishops and prince abbots. Some of the princes of these weak territories allowed very small special administrations to come into existence that had the sole purpose of eradicating witchcraft. Such witch hunting institutions – be it princely special courts outside of the regular legal system or be it witch hunting committees of peasant villages – could claim hundreds of victims in a couple of years. The professionalization of the judiciary and the rise of a sophisticated state administration that allowed the government to supervise the local courts critically ended the witch hunts. The witch hunts ended when professional judges and sophisticated legal administrations that included a system of governmental controls began to replace the old courts. When such legal and administrative reforms had taken place in a number of the more important German principalities, witch trials lost any semblance of legitimacy. Even governments of poorly organized principalities did not dare to offer their subjects witch trials as a way to react to crisis anymore.

Today, numerous German towns have erected monuments in memory of the victims of the witch hunts. For better or worse, the witches or at least some types of witches are again part of everyday life in Germany. They feature in children's entertainment, in folklore and in kitsch for tourists. No Swabian carnival parade is complete without mummers wearing witch masks. The Brocken (Blocksberg), the most famous meeting place of the German witches, attracts numerous tourists. For a while, German feminists found car stickers with a woman on a broom amusing. German consumers seem to like tea and liquor sold under the label 'herbalist witch' ('Kräuterhexe'). The witches have not left their mother. It is unlikely that they ever will.

Notes

1 Friedrich Spee, *Cautio Criminalis* (Rinteln: 1631), ed. Joachim Ritter (Munich: DTV, 1982), 102.

2 Johannes Dillinger, *Hexen und Magie* (Frankfurt: Campus, 2018), 87–90.

3 Wolfgang Behringer and Günter Jerouschek, "Das unheilvollste Buch der Weltliteratur? Zur Entstehungs- und Wirkungsgeschichte des Malleus Maleficarum und zu den Anfängen der Hexenverfolgung," in *Heinrich Kramer (Institoris) Der Hexenhammer*, ed. Wolfgang Behringer and Günter Jerouschek (Munich: DTV, 2000), 9–100.

4 Sönke Lorenz, *Aktenversendung und Hexenprozeß* (3 vols., Frankfurt: Lang, 1982/83), 47–54.

5 Johannes Dillinger, *"Evil People." A Comparative Study of Witch Hunts in Swabian Austria and the Electorate of Trier* (Charlottesville: Virginia University Press, 2009), 44, 68.

6 Ibid., 37, 58–62, 70–72, 152–154.

7 *Friedrich Spee*, ed. Michael Schiffer (Cologne: Erzbischöfliche Diözesan- und Dombibliothek, 2008); Johannes Dillinger, "Adam Tanner und Friedrich Spee. Zwei Gegner der Hexenverfolgung aus dem Jesuitenorden," *Spee Jahrbuch*, 6 (2000): 31–58.

8 Markus Meumann, "Die Geister, die ich rief – oder wie aus 'Geisterphilosophie' 'Aufklärung' werden kann. Eine diskursgeschichtliche Rekontextualisierung von Christian Thomasius' De crimine magiae," in *Aufklärung und Esoterik: Wege in die Moderne*, ed. Renko Geffarth (Berlin: De Gruyter, 2013), 645–680; Johannes Dillinger, *Kinder im Hexenprozess. Magie und Kindheit in der Frühen Neuzeit* (Stuttgart: Steiner, 2013), 201–211.

9 Manfred Wilde, *Die Zauberei- und Hexenprozesse in Kursachsen* (Cologne: Böhlau, 2003), 113–114; see also Johannes Dillinger, "Money From the Spirit World," in *Money in the German-Speaking Lands*, ed. Mary Lindeman (Oxford: Berghan, 2017), 10–26; Dillinger, *Evil*, 57, 66–67.

10 Andreas Müller, "Elaborated Concepts of Witchcraft? Applying the 'Elaborated Concept of Witchcraft' in a Comparative Study on the Witchcraft Trials of Rostock (1584) and Hainburg (1617–18)," *e-Rhizome* 1 (2019): 1–22, 11.

11 Johannes Dillinger, "The Political Aspects of the German Witch Hunts," *Magic, Ritual, and Witchcraft* 3 (2008): 62–81, 62–63.

12 Tiroler Landesarchiv Innsbruck, Hs. 2402, 363, 442, 542–543; Dillinger, *Kinder*, 197; Johann Schupp, *Denkwürdigkeiten der Stadt Pfullendorf* (Karlsruhe: Badenia, 1967), 266; Johannes Dillinger, "Kinderhexenprozesse in den hohenzollerischen Herrschaften," *Zeitschrift für Hohenzollerische Geschichte*, 55.56 (2019/20), in print.

13 Nicolas Rügge, *Die Hexenverfolgung in der Stadt Osnabrück* (Osnabrück: Selbstverlag, 2015), 114, 120.

14 Johannes Dillinger, "Hexenverfolgungen in der Grafschaft Hohenberg," in *Zum Feuer verdammt*, ed. Johannes Dillinger, Thomas Fritz, and Wolfgang Mährle (Stuttgart: Steiner, 1998), S. 1–161, 55; Dillinger, *Evil*, 83–84; Sully Roecken and Carolina Brauckmann, *Margaretha Jedefrau* (Freiburg i.B.: Kore, 1989), 227–228; Andeas Schmauder, "Frühe

Hexenverfolgung in Ravensburg: Rahmenbedingungen, Chronologie und das Netz-werk der Personen," in: *Frühe Hexenverfolgung in Ravensburg und am Bodensee*, ed. Andreas Schmauder (Konstanz: UVK, 2017), 29–64, 30–31, 44–46.

15 Wolfgang Behringer, "Weather, Hunger and Fear. The Origins of the European Witch Persecution in Climate, Society and Mentality," *German History* 13 (1995): 1–27; Dillinger, *Hexen*, 76–79, 88–89.

16 E.g. Edward Bever, "The Crisis of Confidence in Witchcraft and the Crisis of Authority," in *Early Modern Europe: From Crisis to Stability*, ed. Philip Benedict (Cranbury: University of Delaware Press, 2005), 139–167.

17 Stadtarchiv Günzburg, 5.115, see also Dillinger, *Evil*, 43, 84–95.

18 Harald Schwillus, *Kleriker im Hexenprozeß* (Würzburg: Echter, 1992).

19 Dillinger, *Evil*, 79–97; Dillinger, *Hexen*, 127–135; Dillinger, *Money*, 18–19.

20 Dillinger, *Evil*, 205–211; Dillinger, *Hexen*, 88–90; Dillinger, "Political," 73–74; *Wider alle Hexerei und Teufelswerk. Die europäische Hexenverfolgung und ihre Auswirkungen auf Südwest-deutschland*, ed. Sönke Lorenz and Michael Schmidt (Ostfildern: Thorbecke, 2004).

21 Gerhard Köbler, *Historisches Lexikon der deutschen Länder*, 8th ed. (Munich: Beckh, 2019).

22 Felix Wiedemann, *Rassenmutter und Rebellin. Hexenbilder in Romantik, völkischer Bewegung, Neuheidentum und Feminismus* (Würzburg: Königshausen & Neumann, 2007), 40–50, 117–184.

23 Peter Bühner, *Die Freien und Reichsstädte des Heiligen Römischen Reiches* (Petersberg: Imhof, 2018).

24 Marianne Sauter, *Hexenprozess und Folter. Die strafrechtliche Spruchpraxis der Juristenfakultät Tübingen im 17. und beginnenden 18. Jahrhundert* (Bielefeld: Regionalgeschichte, 2010), 35–52.

25 Sönke Lorenz, "Der Hexenprozeß," in *Wider alle Hexerei und Teufelswerk. Die europäische Hex-enverfolgung und ihre Auswirkungen auf Südwestdeutschland*, ed. Sönke Lorenz and Jürgen Schmidt (Ostfildern: Thorbecke, 2004), 131–154; Michael Ströhmer, *Von Hexen, Ratsherren und Juristen. Die Rezeption der Peinlichen Halsgerichtsordnung Kaiser Karls V. in den frühen Hex-enprozessen der Hansestadt Lemgo* (Paderborn: Bonifatius, 2003).

26 Peter Oestmann, *Hexenprozesse am Reichskammergericht* (Cologne: Böhlau, 1997); Britta Gehm, *Die Hexenverfolgung im Hochstift Bamberg und das Eingreifen des Reichshofrates zu ihrer Beendigung* (Hildesheim: Olms, 2000); Dillinger, "Political," 62–63.

27 Manfred Tschaikner, "'Der Teufel und die Hexen müssen aus dem Land ...' Frühneu-zeitliche Hexenverfolgungen in Liechtenstein," *Jahrbuch des Historischen Vereins für das Fürstentum Liechtenstein* 96 (1998): 1–197.

28 Sauter, *Hexenprozess*, 32–61, 73–75.

29 Dillinger, *Hexen*, 95–96; Andreas Flurschütz da Cruz, *Hexenbrenner, Seelenretter: Fürstbischof Julius Echter von Mespelbrunn (1573–1617) und die Hexenverfolgung im Hochstift Würzburg* (Bielefeld: Regionalgeschichte, 2017).

30 Dillinger, *Hexen*, 95–98; Dillinger, "Political," 66–68.

31 Dillinger, *Evil*, 172–173.

32 Wolfgang Behringer, *Hexenverfolgung in Bayern*, 3rd ed. (Munich: Oldenbourg, 1997), 238–241, 314–317; Tanja Gawlich, "Der Hexenkommissar Heinrich von Schultheiß und die Hexenverfolgungen im Herzogtum Westfalen," in *Das kurkölnische Herzogtum Westfalen von den Anfängen der kölnischen Herrschaft im südlichen Westfalen bis zur Säkularisation 1803*, ed. Harm Klueting (Münster: Aschendorff, 2009), 279–320.

33 Günter Jerouschek, *Die Hexen und ihr Prozeß: Die Hexenverfolgung in der Reichsstadt Esslin-gen* (Esslingen: Stadtarchiv, 1992); Nicolas Rügge, "Cothmann, Hermann," in *Lexikon zur Geschichte der Hexenverfolgung*. www.historicum.net/no_cache/persistent/artikel/1587/ (accessed 07 July 2019).

34 E.g. Gehm, *Hexenverfolgung*, 201–265; Dillinger, *Evil*, 149–151.

35 Walter Rummel, *Bauern, Herren und Hexen* (Göttingen: Vandenhoeck und Ruprecht, 1991); Dillinger, *Evil*, 126–142.

36 Walter Rummel, "'Exorbitantien und Ungerechtigten.' Skandalerfahrung und ordnungs-politische Motive im Abbruch der kurtrierischen und sponheimischen Hexenprozesse 1653/1660," in *Das Ende der Hexenverfolgung*, ed. Dieter Bauer and Sönke Lorenz (Stuttgart: Steiner, 1995), 37–53, 46.

111

37 Dillinger, "Political," 69; Dillinger, *Kinderhexenprozesse*, in print.
38 Dagmar Unverhau, "'Wahr, das sie eine Hexe sey . . .' Zauberfälle zwischen Hexerei und Aberglauben aus dem Gebiet des Klosters Preetz (1643–1735)," *Schleswig-Holstein* 3 (1981): 8–12; Gabor Rychlak, *Hexenfieber im Erzgebirge: die Annaberger Krankheit*, (PhD Thesis, Mainz, 2009).
39 Eva Labouvie, "'Gott zur Ehr, den Unschuldigen zu Trost und Rettung . . .' Hexenverfolgungen im Saarraum und in den angrenzenden Gebieten," in *Hexenglaube und Hexenprozesse im Raum Rhein- Mosel- Saar*, ed. Gunther Franz and Franz Irsigler (Trier: Paulinus, 1995), 389–403; Dillinger, "Political," 70; Dillinger, *Evil*, 127–129.
40 Dillinger, "Political," 71–73; Dillinger, *Evil*, 139–142.
41 Dillinger, *Evil*, 109–148.
42 Dillinger, "Political," 77–79; Jürgen Michael Schmidt, "Die Kurpfalz," in *Wider alle Hexerei und Teufelswerk: Die europäische Hexenverfolgung und ihre Auswirkungen auf Südwestdeutschland*, ed. Sönke Lorenz and Jürgen Schmidt (Ostfildern: Thorbecke, 2004), 237–252, especially 239–242; Sauter, *Hexenprozess*, 105–114.
43 Johannes Dillinger, "Hexenverfolgungen in Städten," *Methoden und Konzepte der historischen Hexenforschung*, ed. Gunther Franz and Franz Irsigler (Trier: Paulinus, 1998), 129–165.
44 Behringer, *Hexenverfolgung*, 241–320.
45 Thomas Fritz, "Hexenverfolgungen in der Reichsstadt Reutlingen," in *Zum Feuer verdammt*, ed. Johannes Dillinger, Thomas Fritz, and Wolfgang Mährle (Stuttgart: Steiner, 1998), 63–327.
46 Dillinger, *Evil*, 183–188, Herbert Pohl, *Zauberglaube und Hexenangst im Kurfürstentum Mainz* (Steiner: Stuttgart, 1998), 32–39.
47 Wolfgang Behringer, *Witches and Witch Hunts: A Global History* (Cambridge: Polity, 2004), 187, 191; Brian P. Levack, "The Decline and End of Witchcraft Prosecutions," in *Witchcraft and Magic in Europe: The Eighteenth and Nineteenth Centuries*, ed. Bengt Ankarloo and Stuart Clark (London: Athlone, 1999), 7–33; Dillinger, "Political," 80–81.

Bibliography (selection)

Behringer, Wolfgang, *Hexenverfolgung in Bayern*, 3rd ed. Munich: Oldenbourg, 1997.
Dillinger, Johannes, "The Political Aspects of the German Witch Hunts." *Magic, Ritual, and Witchcraft* 3 (2008): 62–81.
Dillinger, Johannes, *"Evil People." A Comparative Study of Witch Hunts in Swabian Austria and the Electorate of Trier*. Charlottesville: Virginia University Press, 2009.
Dillinger, Johannes, *Hexen und Magie*. Frankfurt: Campus, 2018.
Franz, Gunther and Franz Irsigler (eds.), *Hexenglaube und Hexenprozesse im Raum Rhein- Mosel- Saar*. Trier: Paulinus, 1995.
Lorenz, Sönke and Michael Schmidt (eds.), *Wider alle Hexerei und Teufelswerk. Die europäische Hexenverfolgung und ihre Auswirkungen auf Südwestdeutschland*. Ostfildern: Thorbecke, 2004.
Oestmann, Peter, *Hexenprozesse am Reichskammergericht*. Cologne: Böhlau, 1997.
Sauter, Marianne, *Hexenprozess und Folter. Die strafrechtliche Spruchpraxis der Juristenfakultät Tübingen im 17. und beginnenden 18. Jahrhundert*. Bielefeld: Regionalgeschichte, 2010.
Schmauder, Andreas (ed.), *Frühe Hexenverfolgung in Ravensburg und am Bodensee*. Konstanz: UVK, 2017.
Wilde, Manfred, *Die Zauberei- und Hexenprozesse in Kursachsen*. Cologne: Böhlau, 2003.

8

WITCH HUNTS IN THE LOW COUNTRIES (1450–1685)

Dries Vanysacker

The historiography of witchcraft has, to the present, depicted the Southern Netherlands (present-day Belgium, without the territories of the Prince-Bishopric of Liège, the Duchy of Bouillon and the Principality of Stavelot-Malmedy) as a region of terrible, organized witch hunts, mainly by the Spanish Habsburg rulers during the sixteenth and seventeenth centuries. At the same time it puts these so-called Spanish Netherlands in total contrast with its northern neighbour, the Northern Netherlands (present-day Netherlands), where mass witchcraft trials were very rare. Archival evidence and the number of people executed as witches seem, at first sight, to confirm this theory. However, we have to discern a clear internal difference – chronologically as well as in terms of the intensity of the prosecutions – between the Flemish-speaking part and the French- and German-speaking parts within present-day Belgium. The witch hunts in the territory of the Prince-Bishopric of Liège – which belonged from 1500 until 1789 to the Lower Rhenish-Westphalian Circle (Niederrheinisch-Westfälischer Reichskreis) and included most of present Belgian provinces of Liège and Limburg – and the Duchy of Bouillon and the Principality of Stavelot-Malmedy will be studied separately.

Times and areas of the most intensive witch hunting and the approximate number of victims

Like most European regions, the Low Countries experienced their real witch hunts during the sixteenth and seventeenth centuries. At that time, the territory of the *Southern Netherlands* covered some major regions such as Flanders, Artois, Brabant, Maastricht, Malines, Gelre, Roermond, Namur, Luxembourg, Limburg-Overmaas, Hainault, Lille, Orchies and Douai, Tournai and Cambray. Recent research has shown that at least 1,150–1,250 witches were executed in the Southern Netherlands during the period 1450–1685. This number considerably exceeds the 160 witches executed in the Northern Netherlands.

However, this absolute figure should be nuanced. Within the Southern Netherlands, a distinction has to be made between the prosecutions north of the linguistic frontier, on the one hand, and the prosecutions south of the linguistic frontier, on the other hand. While the first serious hunts took place in Artois, Lille-Orchies and

Table 8.1 Total number of witches executed in the Southern Netherlands (1450–1685)

North of the linguistic frontier (Dutch-speaking)	South of the linguistic frontier (French-speaking)	South of the linguistic frontier (French- and German-speaking)
County of Flanders: 202	County of Artois, Cambrésis, Lille-Orchies, Tournai: 47	Duchy of Luxembourg: 358 (Dupont-Bouchat) between 2000 and 3000 (R. Voltmer)
Duchy of Brabant: 57	County of Hainault: 200–300	
Limburg: 9	Duchy of Brabant: 67	
Roermond: 46	County of Namur: 164	
in all: 314	in all: minimum 478– maximum 578	in all: 358 (Dupont-Bouchat) in all: between 2000 and 3000 (R. Voltmer)

Cambrésis, Namur and Luxembourg, during the first half of the sixteenth century, they were closely followed by those in Hainault, in the county of Flanders (including a first prosecution phase around 1530–1540). In the Flemish-speaking part of the Duchy of Brabant, the first big trials were yet to come.[1]

In this early phase, one can hardly overestimate the impact of the famous trial that took place in 1459 against the Waldensians in Arras. Fifteen people, who admitted to having taken part in obscene sabbats and paying homage to a black goat, were burned at the stake.[2] The ever-increasing sorcery trials within the French-speaking regions south of the linguistic frontier were described in a similar way. Archival evidence contains the words "sorcerie" (sorcery) and "vauderie" (Waldensian heresy) as inextricable synonyms. At Nivelles, a woman was banned in 1459 on suspicion of being a "vaudoise ou sorcière". Moreover, the crime of sorcery was increasingly mixed with fifteenth-century demonology. The pact with the Devil and his adoration by a sect had become standard. The short-term consequences of the trials at Arras launched large-scale inquiries at Tournai, Douai and Cambray about potential witches. Several episcopal inquisitors became aware of the fact that they had to do with a new phenomenon and published treatises on this new maleficent sect. One of them, Jean Tinctor, had his tract against the Waldensians translated from French into Latin in Bruges. Preachers influenced the common flock by using demonological interpretations of sorcery, thereby articulating the cumulative concept of witchcraft and making everyone believe that witches belonged to an organized sect that serves the Devil. It is striking to historians, such as Monballyu, Vanysacker, de Waardt, de Blécourt, Gijswijt-Hofstra and Frijhoff, to see that this belief or interpretation of the crime of sorcery made no headway in the Flemish- (Dutch-) speaking part north of the linguistic frontier, nor in the Northern Netherlands.[3] In the county of Flanders, sorcery was still punished only in combination with poisoning. After 1520, the county of Flanders intensified its prosecutions of sorcery. It took until 1532 to burn the first witches at the stake on suspicion "of having given themselves to the enemy of Hell" (Bruges). The Flemish-speaking part of the Duchy of Brabant avoided witch hunting for a long time. The custom of buying off prosecutions from the officers of justice generally prevented trials. After a period of relative calm (1510–1570), during which time witches seemed to have been replaced by Protestant heretics, new prosecutions based on cumulative witchcraft started.

North of the linguistic frontier, the actual witch hunt only began in 1589. In the Duchy of Brabant, there was the witch year of Lier (1589), with the execution of Cathelyne van den Bulcke and the trials against women and girls in Breda and Hertogenbosch. The county of Flanders began its witch hunt with the burning at the stake of Lievine Morreeuws in Furnes. In Brabant, Peelland and Maastricht, the witch craze seems to be confined to around 1612, with forty-two executions. The year 1595 was particularly bloody: from June until September 1595, the Flemish-speaking part of Brabant executed twenty-nine women and three men. In the county of Flanders, the first peak lasted until 1628, with at least 161 executions. Westhoek – Furnes, Nieuport, Diksmuide, Sint-Winoksbergen, Dunkirk, Hondschote, Broekburg, Cassel and Ieper – was especially prone to witches. Cities like Bruges (in 1595) and Ghent (in 1601) also had "witch years". The region of Roermond, in the Southern Netherlands, had its witch craze in 1613: forty executions, followed in 1622 with yet another three. In the Duchy of Limburg and Overmaas, Eysden noted seven executions between 1609 and 1613, and Valkenburg had two in 1620.

There was another prosecution peak north of the linguistic frontier around the years 1630–1646. In Bruges and Mechelen, there were four executions in 1634–1635 and three and four executions in 1642 respectively. The most striking characteristic of the witchcraft prosecutions in the County of Flanders is the fact that it did not end until late in the seventeenth century. In Nieuwpoort, there were still four prosecutions between 1650 and 1652; in Olsene, there were two in 1661; in Heestert, three between 1659 and 1667; and in Belsele, the last witch was burned in 1684. In all, there were at least twenty-three executions after 1650.

As far as the Flemish-speaking regions of the Southern Netherlands are concerned, the essential difference with the Northern Netherlands is clearly time related (much later) and not so much the intensity of the prosecutions (314 versus 160 executions).

The situation south of the linguistic frontier was totally different: the prosecutions were much more violent.[4] After an early initial phase, most of the regions had a second peak in witch hunting from 1570 to 1630. In some places, cities continued their witch hunts deep into the seventeenth century, as was certainly the case for Artois and Cambrésis. Nevertheless, Namur and Luxembourg – with respectively 270 trials and 144 executions between 1509 and 1646 and 547 trials with at least 358 persons executed between 1560 and 1683 – were among the most ardent witch hunters in the Southern Netherlands. According to Voltmer – although she only recently produced real evidence – there could have been possibly 2,500–4,000 trials with at least 2,000–3,000 persons executed in Luxembourg. Leaving aside the discussion between Dupont-Bouchat and Voltmer, archival evidence points out that the jurisdictions of Bitburg, Arlon, Grevenmacher, Luxembourg and Remich – all German-speaking – were especially zealous. The proximity of the Diocese of Trier of Archbishop Johann VII von Schöneburg, who ordered around 350 executions between 1581 and 1591, and the direct influence of the demonological tracts of the latter's suffragan bishop, Peter Binsfeld (1545–1598), together with the typical jurisprudential method of "Hexenausschüsse" or "Monopoles" – travelling experts gathering all possible information on witch crimes within villages – surely influenced the attitude of Namur and Luxembourg towards the crime of witchcraft.

In the northern provinces of the Low Countries, the *Northern Netherlands* (present-day Netherlands), trials for witchcraft were rare, with very few mass persecutions. As de Waardt has noted, some areas, like the province of Friesland, remained completely free of witchcraft trials, while in other regions prosecutions began relatively late. As already mentioned, around 160 persons were executed between 1450 and 1608. Despite a considerable lack of archival evidence, the Northern Netherlands seems to have experienced their highest level of witch hunts within the third quarter of the sixteenth century. Nevertheless, the province of Groningen already witnessed its first wave of trials in 1547, when twenty women and one man were executed. In the 1550s, the region between the Rhine and the Meuse Rivers was affected. In the mid-1560s, especially in 1564, the western province of Holland experienced its heaviest persecutions. The last execution on Dutch soil took place in 1608 in the town of Gorcum (province of Holland), after a woman confessed to having made a pact with the Devil and bewitching several people.[5]

As Seibert has indicated, in the territory of the *Prince-Bishopric of Liège* the jurisdictional system under the rulers Ernest (1581–1612) and Ferdinand (1612–1650) of Bavaria, adopted since the beginning of the early modern times, has strongly influenced the attitude towards the crime of witchcraft.[6] A centrally controlled system, whereby the High Courts of Liège and Hasselt (for the Duchy of Looz) had full power, did not allow excesses like the neighbouring prince-bishoprics of Trier and Cologne. Besides, the crime of witchcraft fell under the faculty of the civil tribunals. Only a few exceptional cases, in which clergy were concerned, were handled before ecclesiastical courts. A strange combination of an inciting "Mandement" against sorcerers and wanderers by Ernest in 1605 and a decision by the same prince-bishop in 1608 that accusers in witch trials had to pay the financial costs influenced a premature ending of prosecutions.[7] The fact that his successor, Ferdinand, was not personally involved in the witch hunts in Liège, contrary to his Electorate of Cologne and the aldermen of Liège – members of the "Chiroux" party were faithful to the prince-bishop – also decelerated the number of witch trials in Liège. A lack of archival material – which was destroyed during the Second World War – makes it difficult to give figures. One can imagine that Liège had some persecutions during the years 1580–1590. According to Seibert, the territory counted at least fifty executions during the period 1620–1635, while the persecutions certainly continued into the second part of the seventeenth century.

The *Principality of Stavelot-Malmedy*, a territory of around 600 square kilometres, led by the prince-abbot of the Abbey of Stavelot and the city of Malmedy, experienced its own witchcraft prosecutions during the early modern period. The most known case was the trial of the monk Jean Del Vaulx de Stavelot (1592–1597), who was eventually decapitated in 1597, whichwas brought before an ecclesiastical court.[8] In 1607, six executions followed before the High Court of Liège. Other regions and towns had their own witches burnt at the stake: Chevron, eight between 1604 and 1607; Rahier, forty-four in 1621; Malmedy and Waimes, fifty between 1630 and 1633 – in 1679–1780, Waimes once again experienced a new wave of witchcraft.[9]

Finally, in the autonomous *Duchy of Bouillon*, at least sixteen witches – fifteen of them women – were strangled and burnt at the stake between 1576 and 1685. Sugny was by far the most zealous/intense place, with a lot of investigations and pursuits.[10]

Socioeconomic conditions of witch hunting

Mono-causality has to be avoided in explaining and studying such a complex phenomenon as witchcraft and the history of witch trials, even within a territory. Several elements play a role, and a key element is the socioeconomic situation. As de Waardt has pointed out, in the densely urbanized and highly developed coastal provinces within the Northern and Southern Netherlands, popular fear of witchcraft was largely decided by economic conditions: while war and economic distress attracted it, relative security of subsistence removed much of it.[11] It was not a coincidence that with the economic boom of Holland after 1585 – after the economic focus of north-western Europe shifted to Amsterdam – most of the witch trials in the Northern Netherlands disappeared, whereas the waves of witch trials in the Dutch-speaking part of the Southern Netherlands were just getting underway. Recent research by Aerts and Vanysacker on the ratio between the total population of the different regions and the numbers of executed witches within the Southern Netherlands points in the same direction.[12] The figures in Table 8.2 show that one had one chance in 6.250 or 9.375 to be executed as a witch in the Northern Netherlands compared to one chance in 1.354 or 1.843 in the Southern Netherlands. Within the last region, one sees that the chances to be burned as a witch were very high in the French- or German-speaking parts, especially in Luxembourg, even without Voltmer's figures. In their explanatory theory, the authors added to the economic conjuncture the influence of urbanization and the different attitude towards state and Church intervention within witchcraft matters. In that sense, one could argue that more urbanized and jurisdictionally better structured regions, such as the Northern Netherlands and the Dutch-speaking part of the Southern Netherlands, had fewer witchcraft prosecutions and victims than the more rural French- and German-speaking regions of the Southern Netherlands. Nevertheless, several contradictory examples of extremely heavy "witch years" in Holland, Brabant and Flanders teach historians to be careful in their theories.

In the Netherlands, witchcraft was not by any means an exclusively rural phenomenon. As mentioned, witchcraft started in Arras and spread to many large and small

Table 8.2 Ratio of executed witches and population in several regions in the Netherlands (1450–1682)

Region	Executed witches	Population	Ratio
Southern Netherlands	1,150–1.250	1,557,000–2,119,000	1.354/1.246–1.843/1.695
*Brabant	124	300,000–488,000	2.420–3.930
-Dutch speaking	57	265,000–443,000	4.670–7.770
-French speaking	67	35,000–45,000	520–670
*Hainault	200–300	200,000–250,000	670–1.250
*Namur	164	52,000–60,000	320–370
*Luxembourg	358 (Dupont-Bouchat)	55,000–83,000	155–231 (Dupont-Bouchat)
	2,000–3,000 (Voltmer)	55,000–83,000	19–41 (Voltmer)
*Flanders	202	650,000–750,000	3.220–3.710
Northern Netherlands	160	1,000,000–1,500,000	6.250–9.375

cities: Bruges, Malines, Ghent, Louvain, Antwerp, Breda, Roermond, Lille, Douai, Valenciennes, Nivelles, Bastogne, Durbuy and Bouillon.

The region that is present-day Belgium and the Netherlands reflected the general result that 80% of the witches executed in Europe during the early modern period were female. In Flanders, exactly 80% (162 of 202) of those executed were women. In the Flemish-speaking part of Brabant, this figure rose to 94%. In Hainault, the executed persons were exclusively female, while in Namur their share reached 92%. Only the regions of Luxembourg (75%) and Cambray and Artois (64%) show a somewhat different picture, possibly due to a relative scarcity of sources. Only in the eastern provinces of the Northern Netherlands were roughly half of the accused male. Most of them were considered werewolves, the enemy within, but few were executed.

Local communities, the state and the Church, and the concepts of witchcraft in demonology and popular culture in the Low Countries

With the exception of some isolated cases, Monballyu has observed in numerous studies that, within the territory of the Southern Netherlands, trials in which the pact between a "cumulative" witch and the Devil was the focal point were all held before local secular benches of aldermen or feudal courts; they were not held before episcopal courts or central bodies, like the Council of Flanders or the Council of Brabant. Witchcraft trials followed normal criminal procedures, but the judges, influenced by demonology, accepted a combination of facts, especially the "punctum diabolicum" (the Devil's spot or mark), as indications of guilt. This permitted arrests, torture and even condemnations. Death by fire, the typical punishment for witchcraft, necessarily had to be preceded by the suspect's voluntary confession, twenty-four hours after his torture.[13]

The same procedure was followed in the Northern Netherlands, with the caveat that, together with economic prosperity, secular authorities broadly shared an Erasmian tolerance. According to de Waardt, this explains why the judicial search for witches ended much sooner in the Dutch Republic than elsewhere. In Holland and Zeeland, it became virtually impossible to torture people suspected of witchcraft after the High Council overturned a verdict in 1593. Together with the advice of professors of medicine and philosophy from Leiden University and the tract of Johann Weyer (1515/16–1588), *De Praestigiis Daemonum* (1563), the High Council spread the new jurisprudence regarding witchcraft over the other provinces of the Northern Netherlands.[14]

Recent research has shown that, despite excellent historical research in the nineteenth and twentieth centuries, many false conceptions survived concerning the role of the state and its central administrations within the witch hunt in the Southern Netherlands. Especially the theory that the central government decrees of July 20, 1592, and November 8, 1595, stimulated the witch hunt has become out of date. First of all, those decrees did not speak of cumulative witchcraft, and secondly, they reacted against excesses used by local benches of aldermen at witch trials. As in the Northern Netherlands, the recommendations and juridical prescriptions by the central bodies in the Southern Netherlands, like the provincial Councils and the Private Council, strained the witch hunts rather than initiating them.[15]

The impact of the Church(es) on witchcraft prosecutions differed greatly between the Northern and Southern Netherlands. In both regions, it is a very difficult topic to discuss. The Dutch Republic was nominally Reformed, but secular authorities usually declined the Calvinist ministers' appeals to remodel society, by force if necessary. For instance, when Amsterdam's Reformed ministers demanded that the magistrates should suppress heresy and magic in 1597, the latter answered by stating that it had no desire to replace the Spanish Inquisition with Calvinist intolerance.[16] In this context, one can also place the recent theory by Hoorens to consider Weyer's *De praestigiis daemonum* as a systematic attack on witch theories and witch trials, not only with the aim to defend the witches but also, and perhaps even more, as an instrument to criticize the Catholic Church.[17]

According to Dupont-Bouchat and Thijs, secular and ecclesiastical institutions in the Southern Netherlands had been co-operating to combat witchcraft for centuries. Both authors believe that this fact is an element of a top-down model of social disciplining by both secular and ecclesiastical authorities of the lower class.[18] The implementation of these theories on the field required Roelants and Vanysacker to take a more critical standpoint.[19]

It is a fact that as soon as a person accused of being a witch was discovered by the ecclesiastical court, he or she was transmitted to a secular judge. Moreover, these transmissions did not just supplement ecclesiastical judicial activities. There was in fact an explicit demand for co-operation. Bishop Sonnius of Antwerp stated explicitly that the extirpation of the evil within the whole territory was a task of the state. In 1576, he urged the magistrates "ut hoc malum e tota republica extirpant". At the third provincial council, Archbishop Matthias Hovius (1542–1620) stressed the necessity of co-operation between the two orders in order to combat against magicians and medicine-men. In return, in August 1608, Albert and Isabel promulgated a decree that supported and legitimated the execution of the statutes of this council. This co-operation also proceeded at a lower level (i.e. the level of the provincial secular institutions and their episcopal counterparts). After an administrative re-division in 1559, the bishoprics were part of the same territory. The ecclesiastical authorities also had a consulting function for the secular institutions.

Illustrative of the fact that the secular and ecclesiastical courts approached the witch problem in the same way were several trials of monastic sisters in or around the territory of the Southern Netherlands during the years 1608–1619 (the Abbey of the Brigittines at Lille; the South Brabantine Abbey of Cistercian sisters at Valduc; the Abbey of Cistercian sisters at Beaupré in Grimminge, near to Grammont; the Cistercian Abbey Notre-Dame-du-Verger in Oisy-le-Verger). This does not, however, mean that co-operation between the secular and the ecclesiastical courts was excellent.

Several letters from Bishop Laevinus Torrentius (1525–1594) of Antwerp reveal an obvious mistrust about the secular approach of the crime of witchcraft. Although Torrentius considered "magica vanitas et perfidia" as the highest possible insult to the divine majesty, the bishop wanted the alleged witches to have a fair trial. In a letter to his friend, Frans van Thienen, who had informed him about a witch trial in Breda, he advised him to attend the hearing. He feared that the secular authority would act too severely under the imitation of theologians, jurists and even of the suffragan bishop of Trier, Peter Binsfeld. According to Torrentius, a fair trial consisted of the following elements. First of all, it was up to the competent episcopal judge to decide whether or not the defendant was actually guilty of witchcraft, and to arrive at this decision he relied on a confession that was obtained "libere et sine tormentis". Only then was the witch handed over to the secular magistrates. He also warned Van Thienen to pay attention to whether or not the judges were competent, unbiased or even unscrupulous and devoid of all speculation. Their judgement needed to be a "sanum judicium", and their punishment should be unexaggerated. In January 1590, Torrentius advised the priest of the Saint-Gommarus parish in Lier to attend the trial of an alleged witch. One month later, he asked the same clergyman to be merciful on behalf of a very young girl that had been accused of such a despicable crime. An example could have been made of her as a warning to other women who conspired with the devil. This shows that the bishop believed in the reality of witchcraft, but at the same time he remained sceptical. The unexplainable deeds of magicians and potion minglers were simply explained as allowed by God. The bishop read several demonological works and was thus aware of the developments in literature, but he maintained his sceptical attitude. He even corresponded with Del Rio, but it is not known whether they exchanged ideas about witchcraft. Torrentius' attitude was obviously inspired by the Augustinian tradition. He went to university and was a well-educated man, a humanist poet and in correspondence with the great minds of his time, such as Justus Lipsius (1547–1606). This more critical attitude also characterizes Lindanus. It is striking that both bishops had good contacts with Rome, where the Vatican had a moderate attitude towards witchcraft and magic, having resided there for a few years.

In general, the higher a clergyman climbed the ecclesiastical ladder, the more down-to-earth his views on magic and superstition became. However, this does not mean that they denied the existence of witches. Their belief in these malicious (wo)men as accomplices of the Devil were not a matter of conviction: Satan and his henchmen were as much a part of the Catholic doctrine as were Jesus and his apostles. Whoever denied the existence of witches, denied the existence of the Devil. This was pure heresy. Satan's existence was only exceptionally denied, by Cornelius Loos (c.1540/46–1596) for instance. Furthermore, even the greatest critics at the time of the European witch craze confirmed in their views that witches were a reality. Loos was therefore severely sanctioned by the ecclesiastical authorities for denying the existence of witches, even though his point of view was only marginal in comparison to other views that opposed the witch craze. The opposition of the witch craze in itself was a marginal phenomenon.

The lower the clergymen were on the ecclesiastical ladder, the more likely they were to be involved in the popular belief system. It seems likely that the possibility of uniting these seemingly opposite spheres – superstition and Catholicism – in the mind of one man is related to one's level of literacy. Most bishops and popes (the high clergymen) belonged to more wealthy classes and were educated at universities. The lower clergymen, on the contrary, had to be associated with the common people and were very close to being illiterate themselves. The rites and sacraments of the Church were as incomprehensible and supernatural as the arts of a magician or fortune-teller for both the priest and his parishioners. Moreover, the local clergy acted in a way that fuelled popular belief. Parish priests, nuns and monks disenchanted animals and humans, pointed out witches, testified during trials and occasionally ended up at the stake themselves. Of course, there were exceptions: those who were clearly opposed

to superstition. The Council of Trent understood that the lack of intellectual education and the spread of superstition were linked. The ecclesiastical pyramid consisted
of a series of chains: the bishops between the highest and the lower clergy, and the
parish clergy between the bishops and the parishioners. If the popes intended to
teach their parishioners the true Catholic faith, their priests themselves needed to
be educated so they could properly catechize the faithful. This Counter-Reformatory
shift from repression to education manifested during the 1640s. Briggs remarks that,
starting from this period, a much more strict and consistent style of belief and conduct will dominate.

Both secular and ecclesiastical authorities fought against practices of magic, but
there were significant differences in their approaches. Religious courts prosecuted
superstition and heresy, while their secular pendants prosecuted witchcraft. Both
authorities relied on different literature to justify their decisions. Aldermen and
feudal lords relied on demonological books. These manuals were not appropriate
for the type of magical practices that were tried before episcopal judges. From this
demonological point of view, secular courts usually operated in a severe and cruel
fashion. Their intent was to punish or even exterminate socially deviant behaviour.
The ecclesiastical authorities, on the other hand, aimed to convert their followers
and even tried to do so until the convicted person's last day in prison. The Church
tried to correct religiously deviant behaviour. The policy followed by the episcopal
courts was generally a generous one. They were not very interested in crimes related
to superstition. Apparently, they were aware of the popular worldview, and they tried
to discourage these kinds of practices; but this was not a priority. However, when
evaluating the activities of episcopal courts, one has to remember that the principle
ecclesia "abhorret a sanguine" meant that episcopal judges were not competent for
conflicts concerning witches. Therefore, one cannot easily conclude that ecclesiastical courts had a moderate approach towards witchcraft. Although, this is very likely
if one considers the opinions in the Counter-Reformatory episcopal circles and the
ecclesiastical-judicial policy on superstition. Within the Southern Netherlands, and
certainly north of the linguistic frontier, there were no such 'witch-bishops' like those
who reigned in some of the German electorates or bishoprics.

In historiography, the impact of the *Malleus Maleficarum* (1486) in the territory
of present-day Belgium and the Netherlands on the prosecuting authorities also has
been wrongly stressed. It was rather the *Disquisitiones Magicae libri sex* (1599–1600)
of the Jesuit Martín Delrio that made the theories of the *Malleus* known a century
later. A striking example of its influence was found by Monballyu in a letter from the
educated aldermen of Bruges, dated 1596, to their "ignorant" colleagues at Court-
rai.[20] As this letter states, the aldermen of Bruges – often humanists, as Vanysacker
has pointed out – were acquainted not only with the *Malleus* or with the 'primitive'
demonology of their fellow townsman Joos de Damhouder (1507–1581), but also
with the later demonological tracts of Paolo Grillando, Jean Bodin, Nicolas Rémy
and Del Rio. The presence of a learned witchcraft concept in Bruges can also be
derived from the questions asked by the aldermen during torture sessions, and from
the formulations of verdicts by the magistrates.[21] Together with sermons (e.g. by the
Jesuit Jan David, 1546–1613) and printed folios in the vernacular, these verdicts, read
out publicly in the city before an execution, spread some concepts of the learned
demonology to all levels of populace.[22]

Notes

1 Dries Vanysacker, "Netherlands, Southern," in *Encyclopedia of Witchcraft. The Western Tradition*, ed. Richard M. Golden (Santa Barbara: ABC-CLIO, 2006), 813–817; Idem, "Het aandeel van de Zuidelijke Nederlanden in de Europese heksenvervolging (1450–1685). Een status quaestionis," *Trajecta* 9 (2000): 329–349.

2 Franck Mercier, *La Vauderie d'Arras. Une chasse aux sorcières à l'automne du Moyen Âge* (Rennes: Presses Universitaires, 2006).

3 Jos Monballyu, "De houding van de rechters tegenover hekserij in de Zuidelijke Nederlanden tijdens de 15de tot 17de eeuw," in *La sorcellerie dans les Pays-Bas sous l'ancien régime. De hekserij in de Nederlanden onder het Ancien Régime*, ed. Marie-Sylvie Dupont-Bouchat (Kortrijk-Heule: UGA, 1987), 11–34; Idem, "Die Hexenprozesse in der Grafschaft Flandern (1495–1692). Chronologie, Soziographie, Geographie und Verfahren," in *Hexenprozesse und Gerichtspraxis*, ed. Herbert Eiden and Rita Voltmer (Trier: Edition Spee Verlag, 2002), 279–314; Vanysacker, "Het aandeel van de Zuidelijke Nederlanden," 329–349; Willem de Blécourt and Hans de Waardt, "Das Vordringen der Zaubereiverfolgungen in die Niederlande, Rhein, Maas und Schelde entlang," in *Ketzer, Zauberer, Hexen: die Anfänge der Europäischen Hexenverfolgungen*, ed. Andreas Blauert (Frankfurt am Main: Suhrkamp, 1990), 182–216; Willem de Blécourt, *Termen van toverij: De veranderende betekenis van toverij in Noordoost-Nederland tussen de 16de en 20ste eeuw* (Nijmegen: SUN, 1990); Marijke Gijswijt-Hofstra, "The European witchcraft debate and the Dutch variant," *Social History* 15 (1990): 181–194; *Witchcraft in the Netherlands from the Fourteenth to the Twentieth Century*, ed. Marijke Gijswijt-Hofstra and Willem Frijhoff (Rotterdam: Universitaire Pers, 1991).

4 Émile Brouette, «La sorcellerie dans le comté de Namur au début de l'époque moderne (1509–1646),» *Annales de la Société archéologique de Namur* 47 (1954): 359–420; Jacques Beckman, «Une épidémie de sorcellerie à Noville-les-Bois au début du 17ᵉ siècle,» *Annales de la Société archéologique de Namur* 54 (1968): 425–469; Pierre Corsini, *La répression de la sorcellerie dans le comté de Namur (1550–1620)* (Louvain-la-Neuve: UCL, 2007); Marie Challe, *La répression de la sorcellerie dans la partie belge du Hainaut (1559–1640)* (Louvain-la-Neuve: UCL, 2004); Théophile Louïse, *De la sorcellerie et de la justice criminelle à Valenciennes (XVIe et XVIIe siècles)* (Valenciennes: Typ. de E. Prignet, 1861); Arnold van Gennep, *Le folklore de la Flandre et du Hainaut français (Département du Nord)*, vol. II: *Sources, Arbres et Saints patrons. Magie et Médecine populaire. Littérature et Jeux populaires* (Paris: G.P. Maisonneuve, 1936), 581–582; Robert Muchembled, *Sorcières: justice et société aux 16e et 17e siècles* (Paris: Editions Imago, 1987), 210; Marie-Sylvie Dupont-Bouchat, «La répression de la sorcellerie dans le duché de Luxembourg aux XVIe et XVIIe siècles. Une analyse des structures de pouvoir et de leur fonctionnement dans le cadre de la chasse aux sorcières,» in *Prophètes et sorciers dans les Pays-Bas, 16e–18e siècle*, ed. Marie-Sylvie Dupont-Bouchat, Willem Frijhoff, and Robert Muchembled (Paris: Hachette, 1978), 41–154; Rita Voltmer, «. . . ce tant exécrable et détestable crime de sortilège': Der 'Bürgerkrieg' gegen Hexen und Hexenmeister im Herzogtum Luxemburg, 16. Und 17. Jahrhundert,» *Hémecht. Revue d'Histoire Luxembourgeoise. Zeitschrift für Luxemburger Geschichte* 56 (2004): 57–92.

5 Hans de Waardt, "Netherlands, Northern," in *Encyclopedia of Witchcraft. The Western Tradition*, ed. Richard M. Golden (Santa Barbara: ABC-CLIO, 2006), 810–813; idem, *Toverij en samenleving: Holland 1500–1800* (Den Haag: Stichting Hollandse Historische Reeks, 1991); idem, "Verlöschen und Entfachen der Scheiterhaufen. Holland und Brabant in den 1590er Jahren," in *Hexenprozesse und Gerichtspraxis*, ed. Herbert Eiden and Rita Voltmer (Trier: Edition Spee Verlag, 2002), 315–329; idem, "Staat, Kirche und lokale Kultur: Die Zaubereiverfolgungen im Burgundischen Kreis," in *Hexenforschung aus österreichischen Ländern*, ed. Heide Dienst (Vienna-Berlin: Lit Verlag, 2009), 17–34.

6 Ulrich Seibert, "Gerichtsverfassung und Gerichtspraxis im Fürstbistum Lüttich. Rahmenbedingungen und Verlauf der Hexenverfolgungen unter Ernst und Ferdinand von Bayern (1581–1650)," in *Hexenprozesse und Gerichtspraxis*, ed. Herbert Eiden and Rita Voltmer (Trier: Edition Spee Verlag, 2002), 253–277.

7 Jean-Pierre Delville, «Entre fanatisme et tolérance: les mandements d'Ernest de Bavière, évêque de Liège, contre la sorcellerie (1598–1608),» *Bulletin de la Société d'Art et d'Histoire du Diocèse de Liège* 69 (2011): 181–190.

8 Jean Fraikin, "Eine Seite in der Geschichte der Hexerei in den Ardennen und in Mosel-raum. Die Affäre um Jean del Vaulx, Mönch in Stablo (1592–1797)," in *Hexenglaube und Hexenprozesse im Raum Rhein-Mosel-Saar*, ed. Gunther Franz and Franz Irsigler (Trier: Edition Spee Verlag, 1994), 417–432.

9 Jules Fréson, «Procès de sorcellerie,» *Annales de l'Institut Archéologique du Luxembourg* 39 (1904): 29–86; François Toussaint, «Un procès de sorcellerie à Waimes en 1679–1680,» *Folklore Stavelot-Malmedy Saint-Vith* 32 (1968): 129–183; Edgard Renard, «Procès de sorcellerie au Pays de Stavelot-Malmedy (1679–1680),» *La Vie wallonne* 34 (1960): 223–244.

10 Pierre Bodard, «La répression de la sorcellerie dans le duché de Bouillon aux XVIe et XVIIe siècles,» in *Mémorial Alfred Bertrang, Institut archéologique du Luxembourg* (Arlon: Institut archéologique du Luxembourg, 1964), 31–42; idem, *Histoire de la cour souveraine du Duché de Bouillon sous les La Tour d'Auvergne* (Brussel: Librairie Encyclopédique, 1967), 200; Michel Jean François Ozeray, «Cause célèbre. Les sorcières de Sugny, 1657,» *Annales de l'Institut archéologique du Luxembourg* 5 (1867–69): 211–217.

11 de Waardt, "Netherlands, Northern," 810–813; idem, "Verlöschen und Entfachen der Scheiterhaufen. Holland und Brabant in den 1590er Jahren," in *Hexenprozesse und Gerichts-spraxis*, ed. Herbert Eiden and Rita Voltmer (Trier: Edition Spee Verlag, 2002), 315–329.

12 Erik Aerts and Dries Vanysacker, "Hekserijbestraffing met twee snelheden. Peilen naar geografische verschillen in de Zuidelijke Nederlanden," in *Inter amicos. Liber amicorum Monique Van Melkebeek*, ed. Michiel Decaluwé, Véronique Lambert, and Dirk Heirbaut (Brussels: Koninklijke Vlaamse Academie van België voor Wetenschappen en Kunsten, 2011), 317–343.

13 See, among others, contributions by Monballyu in note 3.

14 de Waardt, "Netherlands, Northern," 812.

15 Vanysacker, "Netherlands, Southern," 817.

16 de Waardt, "Netherlands, Northern," 812.

17 Vera Hoorens, "Why Did Johann Weyer Write De Praestigiis Daemonum? How Anti-Catholicism Inspired the Landmark Plea for the Witches," *BMGN – Low Countries Historical Review* 129 (2014): 3–24.

18 Marie-Sylvie Dupont-Bouchat, «La répression des croyances et des comportements populaires dans les Pays-Bas: l'Église face aux superstitions (xvi^c–xviii^c s.),» *Standen en Landen* 86 (1987): 117–143; Alfons K. L. Thijs, «Toverij in contrareformatorisch Antwerpen,» in *Liber Amicorum Jozef Van Haver aangeboden naar aanleiding van zijn vijfenzestigste verjaardag*, ed. A. Roeck, J. Theuwissen, and S. Top (Brussels: Koninklijke Belgische Commissie voor Volkskunde, 1991), 391–400.

19 Nienke Roelants and Dries Vanysacker, "«Tightrope Walkers on the Border Between Religion and Magic». A Study of the Attitudes of Catholic Clerics North of the Linguistic Frontier within the Southern Netherlands Towards Superstition and the Crime of Witchcraft (1550–1650)," *Revue d'histoire ecclésiastique* 100 (2005): 754–796.

20 Jos Monballyu, "Toverij en Hekserij te Kortrijk en te Brugge in het jaar 1596," *Volkskunde* 81 (1980): 183–195.

21 Dries Vanysacker, *Hekserij in Brugge. De magische leefwereld van een stadsbevolking, 16de–17de eeuw* (Brugge: Genootschap voor Geschiedenis, 1988); idem, "The Impact of Humanists on Witchcraft Prosecutions in 16th and 17th-century Bruges," *Humanistica Lovaniensia. Journal of Neo-Latin Studies* 50 (2001): 393–434.

22 Dries Vanysacker, "Un point de vue de juriste, de théologien ou plutôt de jésuite au service de la Contre-Réforme? L'attitude de Martín Antonio Delrío (1551–1608) et Joannes David (1546–1613) envers la sorcellerie et le mal parmi nous," in *The Quintessence of Lives: Intellectual Biographies in the Low Countries presented to Jan Roegiers*, ed. Dries Vanysacker, Pierre Delsaerdt, Jean-Pierre Delville, and Hedwig Schwall (Turnhout: Brepols, 2010), 63–81; idem, «Een Antwerps vlugschrift uit 1589 over Duitse heksenprocessen en weerwolf Peter Stump: van duivelse trawanten en de beestachtige duivel in persoon,» *Bijdragen tot de Geschiedenis* 85 (2002): 131–150.

Bibliography (selection)

Aerts, Erik and Vanysacker, Dries, "Hekserijbestraffing met twee snelheden. Peilen naar geografische verschillen in de Zuidelijke Nederlanden." In *Inter amicos. Liber amicorum Monique Van Melkebeek*, edited by Michiel Decaluwé, Véronique Lambert, and Dirk Heirbaut, 317–343. Brussels: Koninklijke Vlaamse Academie van België voor Wetenschappen en Kunsten, 2011.

Blécourt, Willem de, *Termen van toverij: De veranderende betekenis van toverij in Noordoost-Nederland tussen de 16de en 20ste eeuw*. Nijmegen: SUN, 1990.

Dupont-Bouchat, Marie-Sylvie (ed.), *La sorcellerie dans les Pays-Bas sous l'ancien régime. De hekserij in de Nederlanden onder het Ancien Régime*. Kortrijk-Heule: UGA, 1987.

Gijswijt-Hofstra, Marijke and Willem Frijhoff (eds.), *Witchcraft in the Netherlands From the Fourteenth to the Twentieth Century*. Rotterdam: Universitaire Pers, 1991.

Vanysacker, Dries, "Het aandeel van de Zuidelijke Nederlanden in de Europese heksenvervolging (1450–1685). Een Status Quaestionis." *Trajecta* 9 (2000): 329–349.

9

WITCH HUNTS IN FRANCE

Maryse Simon

France is an important country in terms of witch hunting not only because it is a very vast and populated country but also because the witch hunts fuelled a powerful debate among the elites and a large number of trials in local courts, and also because they have specificities. If Joan of Arc is sometimes considered as one of the first witches burnt in 1431, the real witch craze was operating later, between 1570 and 1670. The official end of witch persecution took place with the promulgation of an Ordinance in 1682 by Louis XIV.[1]

The question of the number of victims accused of being witches is difficult because it refers to the question of the definition of France. At the time of the witch hunting, the realm of France did not include all the territories on its margins, even if these territories were sometimes strongly related to the kingdom of France. The great witch hunt century (1570–1670) resulted in only a few hundred executions.[2] If we consider only the realm of France, the persecution of witches was not very harsh, with a low number of executions. It is very difficult to estimate the exact number of victims because the local archives are lacking dramatically in many places.

But a sign of the intensity of the witch persecution is given by the most famous sovereign court of the realm, the "*Parlement de Paris*". France had a much-elaborated judicial system during the early modern period that enhanced the activity of the Parlement of Paris, whose area of action, called "*ressort*", covered roughly half the country.[3] Besides the Parlement of Paris, smaller regional Parlements supervised the witch persecution in Rouen, Rennes, Bordeaux, Pau, Toulouse, Aix-en-Provence, Grenoble and Dijon. The role of the Parlement was to supervise all legal procedures, including the criminal causes. The inquisitorial procedure was in use and ruled by the Ordinance of Villers-Cotterets from 1539 until the end of the witch hunting period when, in 1670, Colbert released a new criminal code.

Even if the witchcraft accusations were not extensively detailed in the process under the Parlement, these indications are important because they are usually the only documents available on the cases. The actual proceedings of the local trials and before the high court were not kept, but the accused had to stand in person before the Parlement. So every prisoner entering the Parisian jail at the Conciergerie located in the *Palais de Justice* in the heart of the "*île de la Cité*" should be registered in the "*registre des écrous*", the record of the prisoner's arrival. This very brief paragraph mentioned the crime and the jurisdiction whence the prisoner came. Another paragraph was added when the prisoner was able to leave the jailhouse that mentioned the final decision of the court of justice – called the "*chambre de la Tournelle*" and composed of councillors – the sentence, established by an "*arrêt du parlement*", and the date of its promulgation. The full text of this "*arrêt*", transcribed in very thick and heavy books, usually gives more information about the case, which is precious to historians.

The local courts conducted the trials by collecting witnesses and interrogating the accused. In the case of an accusation of witchcraft, usually called "*sortilège*" in the trials, the local courts had to ask the highest court of justice for permission to torture the suspected witches with the "*question extraordinaire*" after 1624, and the culprit could always send his case up on appeal before the relevant Parlement. Luckily, the archives of the Parlement de Paris are rather complete, and they have been studied by Alfred Soman.[4] The judicial court reveals 1481 accusations of witchcraft for the entire period covered by the archival material, with cases dating from the beginning of the 15th century to the end of the 17th century. This number does not represent all accusations, as many culprits did not know their right to appeal their case, or could not exercise this right because the local courts did not want or could not afford to pay the expense of going to the appeal court. It also does not include all the lynchings which stayed out of the law. But it is an indication of a quite low persecution of witchcraft with legal procedures and extrajudicial executions.

For the other Parlements, only 650 trials are available to be studied: 380 for Rouen between 1564 and 1660, 160 for Dijon and around 100 for Aix-en-Provence. The other archives have been destroyed or are currently unavailable. Concerning the general distribution of the trials, the accusations were not numerous before 1575, but increased suddenly, reaching a level that was stable until about 1620. After that period, only a few cases appeared, although some local witch crazes counterbalanced this decrease. These panics took place in the Champagne-Ardennes and Basque regions, where Pierre de Lancre boasted about executing hundreds of witches; however, he only put 12 culprits to death for certain, with only perhaps 80 in total. The judge in Bordeaux left an interesting demonological book about his experience called *Tableau de l'inconstance des mauvais anges et démons*. The Parlements usually followed the Paris trend, except for in Rouen, where the Norman judges wanted to show more severity than their Parisian peers. The Parlement of Paris was proud to play the role of the prestigious court which embodied the spirit of the educated elite, demonstrating rationality and a strict observance of the law and punishing procedural abuses committed by lesser courts.

The Parlement already in 1491 had rehabilitated the accused from the *Vauderie* of Arras, a famous witch craze that took place in 1459 in northern France, where local abuses had been committed. Despite the fact that this city belonged to Burgundy, Arras was subject to the Parisian appellate system. The Parlement of Paris' clemency is evident in the low level of confirmed death penalty sentences issued by local courts: 40% of the accused were condemned to death by lower justices, but only a quarter of these were actually executed, with the others usually banished or simply released instead. This clemency was animated by the will to restrain abuses but also by the real difficulties of presenting proof other than allegations, as evidence and direct witnesses did not operate as proof in the case of witchcraft. The prestigious court of justice wanted to control any accusations that could have been a simple way to get rid of a neighbour in case of disagreement. And the Parlement did send reprimands to local courts when they failed in their mission, calling the local judges to Paris to explain their cases, especially when illegal swimming tests had been performed. So the result was a decrease in the number of appeal procedures after 1620. The message from the head of the system passed down to the inferior courts. A perfect example illustrated this control: in 1641, three officials of the local court at Bragelonne were found guilty for the murder of a suspected witch and were hanged in the place de Grève in Paris at the exact place where witches were usually executed. The echo of this affair was relayed in the entire *ressort*.

The important role of the Parlements diminished the role of the Church, especially with the absence of national Inquisition and local inquisitorial tribunals after the middle of the 16th century. The Parlement of Paris had a role in religious values even if its councillors had different faiths: the court was always Catholic but showed a quite moderate Gallican position towards papacy and the French Church. The role of the University of Paris should not be neglected, because the scholastic theologians and philosophers had condemned the practice of magic since the Middle Ages. At the turn of the 15th century, in 1398, the practice of ritual magic was declared heretical by the faculty of theology and detailed in 28 articles; four years later, Jean Gerson published his treatise concerning misconceptions about magical arts, *De erroribus circa artem magicam*, which was used as a reference to condemn witchcraft.[5] Calling demons to serve malevolent human beings was a deep fear in the 13th century, even if the magicians tried to justify their rituals by arguing they were not violating Catholic doctrine with their divination. But it was considered erroneous and sometimes blasphemous. The first trial for witchcraft took place at the Parlement de Paris just after the pronouncement of the 28 articles. There was no word about proper witchcraft or practices to harm people or worship the Devil, only theological justifications. Nevertheless, it provided arguments for sentencing the practices associated with *maleficia* or pacts with the Devil and inspired many references in the *Malleus Maleficarum*. It was also used in many demonological treatises of the 16th century, especially in Johann Weyer's *De Praestigiis Daemonum*, where this condemnation of ritual magic is discussed in his final chapter. Jean Bodin reprinted these 28 Latin articles right after his French preface of the *De la Démonomanie des sorciers*, "On the Demon-mania of witches", published in 1580.

French specificity in witchcraft persecution lies not in number but in gender: male witches represented around half of the cases in the Parlements of Paris and Dijon and 75% in Normandy, while only 30% in Aix en Provence. The area within the Parlement of Paris saw a strong distinction between territories: in the west, 70% of the accused were men, but only 30% in the northeast. Even if there were shepherds among these men who were traditionally associated with magic for healing their herds or flocks, this is not sufficient to explain such an extraordinary proportion of male witches. Some priests have also been accused of being witches too, which is another specificity of France, but the number of such cases cannot justify the figures. The lack of archival material and specific studies leaves this situation mainly unexplained. The priests involved in witchcraft cases were described as magicians or cunning folk "devins", and some of them were associated with demonic possession affairs which usually affected convents (in 1611 at Aix, in 1634 at Loudin and in 1643 in Louviers).

127

An early and intense persecution took place in Dauphiné in the 15th century, as an extension of the severe alpine persecution. Preachers combined with ecclesiastical authorities and secular local courts led to more than 300 condemnations between 1420 and 1460, revealing *maleficium* (harmful magic) and diabolic elements. This alpine province saw one of the earliest major witch hunts in Europe documented in archival material such as the *Quintus liber Fachurierorum*, the fifth book of sorcerers, a thick register of more than 1,000 pages of compiled cases from 1424 to 1445. In other sources, 350 witches were accused of witchcraft up to 1511.[6] Most of them were old women (two-third of the 287 suspected witches between 1425 and 1460, and nearly 90% of the accused from the early 16th century). The sentences were severe: in the diocese of Grenoble, 24 out of 29 were sentenced to death, 13 of 16 in the diocese of Gap and three of seven in the diocese of Vienne. In some documented cases, the population and especially the neighbours took a great part in the arrest of the witches, contributing with money and help. Among the accused, there were a minority of wealthy witches (more than 100 florins of estate). The family of the accused witches received permission to have the executions made in secret to protect the honour of the family. Some of these witchcraft cases were conducted by a layman, Claude Tholosan, who claimed to have supervised more than a hundred cases, and who wrote a brief treatise on witchcraft, in which he pins the blame on foreigners who brought this plague to the high mountain valleys. Dauphiné, like Savoy, experienced large numbers of witchcraft trials before the Protestant Reformation but extremely few in the later 16th and 17th centuries. The links between medieval heresy and early witchcraft can be seen here, even if Claude Tholosan did not express it explicitly in order to leave the secular courts sentence the crime of witchcraft.

The Basque country included territories on both sides of the Pyrénées, but research into the persecution of witchcraft in the French part is limited because most archives unfortunately have been lost, unlike in the Spanish part of the country. The situation in Navarre has not been well studied yet. In this land of Inquisition, 410 cases of witchcraft have been counted between 1538 and 1798 as falling under the accusation of *supersticiosos*, which included cunning folk, learned magic and witchcraft. The well-known Great Basque Witch Panic took place on the French side, called *Pays de Labourd*, in 1608. Some nobles, including Tristan de Gamboa d'Alzate, and urban authorities made reciprocal accusations of witchcraft, fighting for local power. Noblemen put the case in the hands of their king, Henri IV, because they were so alarmed that witches had invaded the whole country during the past few years. So, two councillors of the Parlement of Bordeaux, the relevant sovereign judicial court, were sent by royal decree to investigate the case. Pierre de Lancre and Jean d'Espaignet, a president of the Parlement, arrived to interrogate via torture and pronounce the death penalty. They ended their mission before the end of 1609. Because all the original archives were lost, the number of executions is not known: however, eight witches and three priests were burned, prisoners and sent to Bordeaux, where their trials lasted for years. The bishop of Bayonne informed the Spanish bishop of Pamplona of the cases, and the Inquisitor Salazar mentioned in 1612 that more than 80 witches were finally burned during this expedition.[7] The panic was so intense when the French judges arrived that children were kept locked in churches at night to prevent them from being brought to Sabbath. Tristan de Gamboa d'Alzate was the principal instigator of the witch craze and sent many suspected witches behind bars on his sole authority and collaborated closely with the judges to condemn them. This hysterical episode spread firstly to Spanish villages on the northern side, where the Inquisition imprisoned suspected witches. The second inquisitor of the tribunal came to the French tribunal to get copies of the trials. The accused finally confessed, and the panic then exploded, fuelled by active preachers. An *auto da fe* held in Logrono gathered 30,000 people to see the burning stake. The witch craze follows the same pattern: it starts with children and adolescents dreaming of Sabbath, and then denounces participants once they have been led to confess under torture. In March 1611, no less than 1,946 people confessed or were suspected of witchcraft, which led the Inquisitor General from the Holy Office to declare amnesty for those who gave themselves up at an early stage. Almost 1,400 of them were boys and girls. Salazar could not find any proof of witchcraft after a long investigation, and all current cases were suspended. The calm was restored as suddenly as the panic emerged. The Basque panic is a perfect example of uncontrolled, runaway events that ultimately embarrassed the authorities who tried to correct their errors.

The Burgundy persecution against witches started in 1571, as in other French provinces, and the Parlement of Dijon – which was created in 1537 and almost surrounded by the *ressort* of the Parlement of Paris – showed clemency. A couple of witchcraft trials occurred every year until the 1650s. The local judges sentenced the culprits to death, but the Parlement did not confirm this sentence. Between 1582 and 1650, only 17 people out of 200 accused were executed. In 1635, the Parlement took automatic control over Burgundian local tribunals, and the next year none of the 36 prisoners were executed. A witch craze took place in 1644 when a severe hailstorm and late frost ruined wine and harvests. A local witch finder pretended to identify the witches by looking into their eyes. He launched a panic that ended with over 100 accusations that turned into three confirmed dealth penalties out of the 15 cases judged locally. This situation provoked a considerable discontent amongst the population, who decided to take the law into their own hands and used the swimming test to find witches. More than nine cases of lynching, sometimes involving several summary executions with the help of local officials, were reported. The Parlement tried to condemn those who defied the law, but only a few were actually sentenced, including one man who was sent to the galley for life because he participated in the lynching of at least 13 witches. Many were sentenced to death in absentia because they escaped. This peculiar situation shows the popular exasperation towards the scepticism and clemency expressed by the Parlement. It also shows the lack of power for imposing control on the population. This is confirmed by the last episode in Burgundy, that of possession in Auxonne: the Ursuline nuns, like their neighbours in Franche-Comté, were afflicted by demonic possession for many years in the 1660s. The Parlement modified the four death penalty sentences by banishing two individuals and releasing two. In addition, the accusation against one of the nuns, Barbe Buvée, placed the royal intendant of Burgundy in a delicate position with regard to the Dijon Parlement, such that the cases ended up in the hands of the Parlement of Paris, which subsequently buried them in the process.

In Languedoc, the Parlement de Toulouse played a very important role in French witch persecution as the second oldest (created in 1443) and largest appellate court. Like that of Paris, the tendency was to reduce punishment for the crime of witchcraft. The activity of this Parlement started with an emblematic case: a woman accused of being a witch was sentenced with perjured evidence and died under extremely harsh torture without having confessed to any crime. Eight other witches were accused during the same period: three were burned at Millau in 1444, two died before the sentence and three were accused of killing babies and attending Sabbath. The Parlement of Toulouse showed clemency before its Parisian fellow court. In the 1490s, the Parlement did not succeed in stopping six executions in Vivarais or around Nîmes. After a long period of total calm, the Parlement was asked to send commissioners to Bigorre to investigate witchcraft accusations. But the court dismissed the case, calling the accusation "errors and illusions". In 1562, during the first French War of Religion, the attitude changed, with the condemnation of at least three witches. But this unusual severity did not last, since the following 30 women accused had reduced sentences. During the peak period of witch persecution, it is hard to quantify the intensity because most of the sources are lacking until such time as the local judgements had to be brought to the higher court in Toulouse. Hence, the later series of trials is well studied.[8] In two years between 1643 and 1645, 641 witches were accused, 92% of whom were female. The Parlement managed to reduce the number of executions to 50 or 60, and to arrest some active witch finders who operated in several regions and were condemned to death or to the galleys. Two-thirds of the accused were released and 100 were only banished for one to five years. This witch craze inspired a chapbook titled *Wondrous History of the Witches Sabbath*, printed in 1645, which related the story of a mythical witch finder who allegedly identified 3,000 witches, including his wife. The last episode took place in Bigorre, but this time in 1680. The province of Languedoc saw only a few episodes, aside from the exceptional one of 1643–1645.

The northern province of Normandy is famous for the trial of Joan of Arc in its capital, Rouen, and for its exceptional severity towards male witches. The number of accusations and executions are pretty low in the vast province of Normandy, but the Parlement of Rouen saw almost 400 accusations and about 100 executions of witches, 75% of the which defendants were men, between the 1540s and the end of the 17th century.[9] Men also constituted the two-thirds of those executed. The disproportion between male and female witches increased over time, mainly after 1600, to reach the extreme point of the quasi-absence of female accusations in the late 1640s. The stereotype was a shepherd with a complete display of traditional witchcraft, such as toad venom or stolen Eucharists. Another type of witch was also unusually common in Normandy: between 1598 and 1647, not less than 14 priests were punished for witchcraft, with seven burned, six banished and one sent to the galleys. A third model was the blacksmith who harmed and healed horses. If gender is exceptional in Normandy, the chronology is like everywhere else in France: between 1585 and 1610, an average of five trials and one execution per year. There was no panic, no witch finders and no illegal practices such as swimming tests. Even the last wave of possession in convents did not touch the region severely. The only singularity is the persistence of trials after the official Ordinance of 1682. Some shepherds were accused in 1694, in 1703 and even later.

If we consider the present-day borders of France, many regions were outside the frontiers during the witch hunts: Navarre, Savoy, Franche-Comté, Alsace, Lorraine and Spanish Netherlands. The links between these territories and the Kingdom of France are more or less strong, according to the influence and the actual relationship with the French realm. The persecution of witchcraft is therefore very different in terms of insensitivity and pattern.

In Franche-Comté, where the judicial system, with its own Parlement, was not specifically tough against witchcraft at the beginning, persecution was harsh, with more than 800 trials conducted, mainly between 1600 and 1660. In this region, ruled by the Spanish Habsburgs until 1674 when Louis XIV annexed it, the first trials that appeared in the 1430s already showed elements that would become classic, such as flying broomsticks and roasted babies. An ordinance in 1604 imposed capital punishment for witchcraft and enabled a high percentage of death penalty verdicts: 84% for local courts, but this figure is corrected by the appellate court clemency, which reduced it to 53% at the end.[10] The region includes an important witch hunter, Henri Boguet,[11] a judge and a demonologist, who was particularly preoccupied with lycanthropy. This peculiar manifestation of the Devil's power was already known in the region in the 1520s and underlined by Johann Weyer. Even if fewer than ten trials actually implicated male and female werewolves, these affairs attracted attention from the entirety of Europe.[12]

On the German border, Alsace is a region which came progressively under French authority after 1648. Before that, the region was a scattering of many different entities: a large part of southern Alsace and the northern district of Haguenau – located in northern Alsace – belonged to the Habsburgs, while the prince-bishop of Strasbourg owned a large part of the centre. In addition, Alsace included ten imperial free cities, like Strasbourg, which owned rural villages as well as numerous independent ecclesiastical or noble fiefs. Despite this complete dissemination of authorities, the persecution of witchcraft was active almost everywhere and sometimes with severity. The author of the *Malleus Maleficarum*, Heinrich Kramer, who was born in Sélestat, described witchcraft cases in the 1470s and 1480s. The archival material still needs to be studied, but more than 1,000 witches were executed between 1570 and the 1630s. The towns and villages in the wine-growing piedmont were particularly severe, but the worst executions took place in two Jesuit towns, Sélestat and Molsheim, where respectively 90 and more than 100 witches were trialled in 13 years or five years – the witchcraft cases were recorded there in a special book called *Blutebuch*, the blood-book. The end of the Thirty Year's War ceased persecution in many territories, too, but not in the those not controlled by the new French authority. Even after the official end of the criminalization of witchcraft, there were some trials conducted, especially in Bergheim.

The southwestern part of the Ardennes belonged of France during the period and was a part of the *ressort* of the Parlement of Paris and subject to the archbishop of Rheims. This area was characterized by many unofficial lynchings of witches, with an estimated 300 people who were drowned or burned.[13] This is the result of the imposition of Parlement's attitude, of the Parlement judged too restrained by the local authorities.

The duchy of Lorraine was independent at the time of the witch hunting, but the dukes owed homage to the king of France for half of Bar, while they owed feudal allegiance to the Holy Roman Empire for most of their lands. The French invasion and occupation of Lorraine in the early 1630s saw the end of the very severe witch hunts that affected the duchy. It was one of the worst persecutions against witchcraft of Europe with almost 2,000 trials and more than 1,400 executions from the 1470s to the 1630s.[14] One of the reasons for this very severe persecution was the famous public prosecutor Nicolas Rémy, who published an important demonological manual titled the *Daemonolatriae* in 1595. In his experience as the head of the highest court in Lorraine, he claimed he conducted 800 or even 900 trials himself in 15 years of labour This number is far from being attested in the archives; only 12 cases have been clearly identified as his.[15] But his influence was determinant in the entire jurisdiction and even beyond the limits of the duchy.[16]

Outside the limits of the realm of France, the New France experienced very few cases of witchcraft. This recently and minimally populated colony saw a couple of late accusations that brought attention to the court.[17] In 1658, a man cast a spell on the marriage of his former fiancée by the "nouement d'aiguillette", tying a knot in a string to cause male impotence. The suspected witch was finally banished and got married later on. The second case concerned another missed marriage: a man is accused of causing the demonic possession of the woman who rejected him. She was exorcised and he was executed. The third case accused a man of harming people, including the woman who refused his advances. He was found guilty, but the appellate court, the Sovereign Council in Quebec, overturned his conviction. The situation was completely different from the one in New England, where 61 trials led to 36 executions. In New France, the unusual gender ratio made clear the accusations against single men who had been disappointed in their attempts to marry.

The French elite considered the crime of witchcraft and its persecution with different opinions. The context of the Wars of Religion and Catholic Reform modified the perception of the Devil's actions on earth. They still considered that the Devil had the power to harm people and the world, but the elite started to relegate belief in witchcraft into the category of popular superstitions, especially after the scandals of the possession affairs, which put forward zealous witch hunters who managed to sentence to death many accused and even to lynch suspected witches. Scepticism and judicial caution arose until the royal intervention that officially ended the witch hunting. The Ordinance promulgated in 1682 mentioned the now so-called magic, la prétendue magie, which does not deserve death penalty.

Notes

1 Robert Muchembled, *Le Temps des Supplices: de l'Obéissance sous les Rois Absolus, XVe–XVIIIe Siècles* (Paris: Armand Colin, 1992).

2 Robin Briggs, *Communities of Belief: Cultural and Social Tension in Early Modern France* (Oxford: Clarendon Press, 1989).

3 Robert Mandrou, *Magistrats et Sorciers en France au XVIIe Siècle* (Paris: Plon, 1969).

4 Alfred Soman, *Sorcellerie et Justice Criminelle: le Parlement de Paris (16e–18e siècles)* (Basingstoke: Ashgate Publishing, 1992).

5 Brian P. Levack, ed., *The Witchcraft Sourcebook* (New York, London: Routledge, 2004).

6 Pierrette Paravy, *De la Chrétienté romaine à la Réforme en Dauphiné: Evêques, Fidèles et Déviants (vers 1340–vers 1530)*, 2 vols (Rome: Ecole Française de Rome, 1993).

7 Gustav Henningsen, *The Witches' Advocate: Basque Witchcraft and the Spanish Inquisition* (Reno: University of Nevada Press, 1980); and *The Salazar Documents: Alonso de Salazar Frias and Others on the Basque Witch Persecution (1609–1614)* (Leiden, Boston: Brill, 2004).

8 Jacques Vidal, "Le Parlement de Toulouse et la répression de la sorcellerie au milieu du XVIIe siècle," in *Hommages à Gerard Boulvert* (Nice: Université de Nice, 1987), 511–527.

9 William Monter, "Toads and Eucharists: The Male Witches of Normandy, 1564–1660," *French Historical Studies* 20 (1997): 563–595.

10 Brigitte Rochelandet, *Sorcières, Diables et Bûchers en Franche-Comté aux XVIe et XVIIe siècles* (Besançon, Editions du Cêtre, 1997, p. 66).

11 Henri Boguet, *An Examen of Witches*, ed. Montague Summers (London: Rodker, 1929).
12 Caroline Oates, "Metamorphosis and Lycanthropy in Franche-Comté 1521–1643," in *Fragments for a History of the Human Body*, vol. 1, ed. Michel Feher (New York: Zone, 1989), 305–363.
13 Soman, *Sorcellerie*.
14 William Monter, *A Bewitched Duchy, Lorraine and Its Dukes 1477–1736* (Genève: Droz, 2007).
15 Robin Briggs, *Witches and Neighbours: The Social and cultural Context of European Witchcraft* (Oxford: Blackwell Publishers, 2002).
16 Maryse Simon and Antoine Follain, eds., *Sorcellerie Savante et Mentalités Populaires* (Strasbourg: Presses Universitaires de Strasbourg, 2013).
17 Jonathan Pearl, "Witchcraft in New France in the Seventeenth Century: The Social Aspect," *Historical Reflections* 4 (1977): 191–205.

Bibliography (selection)

Briggs, Robin, *Communities of Belief: Cultural and Social Tension in Early Modern France*. Oxford: Clarendon Press, 1989.
Mandrou, Robert, *Magistrats et Sorciers en France au XVIIe Siècle*. Paris: Plon, 1969.
Rochelandet, Brigitte, *Sorcières, Diables et Bûchers en Franche-Comté aux XVIe et XVIIe siècles*. Besançon, Editions du Cêtre, 1997.
Simon, Maryse and Antoine Follain (eds.), *Sorcellerie Savante et Mentalités Populaires*. Strasbourg: Presses Universitaires de Strasbourg, 2013.
Soman, Alfred, *Sorcellerie et Justice Criminelle: le Parlement de Paris, 16e–18e siècles*. Basingstoke: Ashgate Publishing, 1992.

10

WITCH HUNTING IN SPAIN

The sixteenth and seventeenth centuries

Lu Ann Homza

When compared to research on northern Europe, the study of witch hunting in Spain has a rather more limited history: investigations of it are fewer; the vocabulary and concepts that govern it have arisen from work conducted on witchcraft in the Basque country. The emphases within the scholarship have practical and intellectual causes. Obviously, research can only go so far when sources are missing or were never generated from the start.[1] Weighty nineteenth-century academics – such as Marcelino Menéndez Pelayo and Henry Charles Lea – stressed that Basque territories were the classic lands of Spanish witches and highlighted Spanish Inquisition records as the proper medium for studying them.[2] Beginning in 1933, the prolific and persuasive Julio Caro Baroja edited primary sources, offered typologies, and relayed case histories, many grounded on inquisition materials, in his studies of Spanish and especially Basque witchcraft.[3] Significantly, all three men – Menéndez Pelayo, Lea, and Caro Baroja – highlighted a Basque episode of witch hunting that occurred between December 1608 and 1614, which had a heroic sequence of events. At the end of 1608, a serving girl returned from France to her native town of Zugarramurdi, in the Navarrese Pyrenees.[4] She insisted she could identify witches and went on to name members of her village. The Spanish Inquisition took over the investigation, which rapidly grew wider; its inquisitors conducted an *auto de fe* in Logroño in November 1610, in which six persons were sentenced to death at the stake; five who had died in prison were burned in effigy, and eighteen more penanced. Eventually, the tribunal was forced to send its personnel into the field to quell the mass denunciations of witch suspects, which reached into the thousands. The last inquisitor to sally forth, named Alonso Salazar y Frías, spent more than seven months in 1611 listening to confessions and examining witnesses. By the time he returned to the Logroño tribunal in January 1612, Salazar had turned into a "witches' advocate" who ultimately refuted his inquisitorial colleagues and persuaded the Royal General Council of the Inquisition (the *Suprema*) to issue reforms in 1614 on witchcraft prosecutions.[5]

Salazar's actions were not only well known in his own epoch, but have also been emphasized in every survey of European witch hunting in the early modern period. His case has affected the study of Spanish witchcraft in profound ways, even though the episode in which he was involved was anomalous.[6] Because scholars have been accustomed to expect consistency in the Spanish Inquisition, they have presumed inquisitors' skepticism toward witchcraft on the basis of Salazar's example and the Suprema's endorsement of his point of view.[7] (In other words, out of the three inquisitors in the Logroño tribunal, Salazar was the one who counted.) Binary constructions have a long reach in Spanish history, and researchers became accustomed to dividing Spaniards into hard-and-fast camps of incredulous and credulous onlookers where witches were concerned: a dichotomy that, again, was personified in Salazar's conflict with his colleagues.[8] In keeping with the prestige of the Salazar episode – which pointed to modernity within the Inquisition, rather than the reverse – students have tried to find other Salazar-like figures in their investigations.[9] They often have applied the vocabulary and concepts that seemed to be present in the 1609–14 witch hunt to Spanish witchcraft as a whole, while continuing to prefer inquisition materials as the basis for research.

Yet twentieth-century studies have also proven two somewhat clashing facts: first, that Spanish inquisitors never viewed witchcraft as a high priority for prosecution anywhere on the mainland; second, that inquisitors and secular justices in Navarre, Aragón, and Catalonia were more interested in the crime than their counterparts in Castile. Authorities in Pamplona and Logroño became embroiled in witch hunting in 1525, 1539–40, 1575–76, and 1595. The witch they pursued was vivid: she, and less frequently he, venerated the Devil, attended sabbats, raised storms, killed infants, damaged livestock, and robbed graves. Because such witches only rarely appeared by name – *brujas* or *xorguinas* – in inquisition trial summaries for the southern part of the country, scholars have hypothesized that there was a geographic demarcation between the "classic" witches of the North, and sorcerers in Castile, Andalusia, and Valencia, who shared a Mediterranean culture of love magic and treasure-hunting. The same partition has been ventured for urban versus rural practices, with love magic occurring in cities, *maleficia* in the countryside.[10] Though such distinctions may make sense when the sources can be turned into quantitative data, attention to the trials, rather than the trial summaries, also illustrates the presence of the classic witch in places beyond northern Spain.[11]

The point of this chapter is to relay what is currently known about Spanish witch hunting, while avoiding overly blunt classifications. For the sake of clarity, the term "witch hunting" ought to mean the prosecution of persons who were suspected of worshipping the Devil and performing harmful magic, called *maleficia*. The difficulty for Spain is that ecclesiastical, inquisitorial, and secular authorities between 1500 and 1700 viewed witchcraft and sorcery through the same conceptual lens (see pp. 137–138 below), and inquisitors and the episcopate used the overarching label *supersticiones* to encompass a wide range of offenses. Given that the legal vocabulary frequently did not distinguish one kind of superstition from another; that individuals could be tried for more than one offense at a time; and that most records of the Spanish Inquisition no longer exist before 1540, historians' attempts to enumerate the numbers of Spanish witches in any given moment always result in figures that turn out to be more or less provisional.[12]

Conditionality aside, studies of Granada in the sixteenth century have found that out of some 3033 trials conducted by the Inquisition from 1550 to 1590, only twenty-four – less than 1 percent – involved "superstition." During the thirteen visitations that Granada's inquisitors conducted in their district in the sixteenth century, when they indicted 1465 persons for heresy, only eighty-one, or less than 6 percent, were for superstition. The crime was prosecuted more frequently in Málaga, ranging from 9 to 13 percent of indictments in the second half of the sixteenth century. The frequency of trials for superstition rose in the seventeenth century, climbing to slightly more than 10 percent of the 3572 prosecutions for which we have data; investigators tie this rise to the dissemination of the Tridentine decrees. Across the board, women made up 65 percent of the indicted.[13] As for the activities of Granada's witches, they engaged in spells, love magic, poisoning, sex with demons, and explicit demonic pacts. A leading investigator declines to separate rural and urban magical practices because the city of Granada sustained many accusations of *maleficia*.[14]

In contrast, Cuenca, in New Castile, has been studied in a descriptive rather than quantitative way. The first appearance of a suspected witch before the Inquisition tribunal occurred in 1515, with the first witch hunt starting in 1519, after the deaths of multiple children.[15] Cuenca's inquisitors prosecuted a mixture of classical witchcraft and sorcery. The district's witch hunts of 1519, 1526, 1555, and 1567 featured witches who flew into houses through chimneys and closed windows, killed children with *maleficia*, rejected their baptismal vows, attended sabbats, and venerated the Devil.[16]

For northern Spain, we have more data, though again it is disputable.[17] In Navarre, a recent investigator found that the viceroy's court indicted fifty-six suspects in 1525; forty-six between 1539 and 1570; and thirty-seven between 1575 and 1595. The Inquisition tribunal in turn purportedly handled fifty-three witchcraft cases between 1539 and 1570, and seventy between 1575 and 1595; in its most famous case, which began in Zugarramurdi in 1609, its inquisitors heard the confessions of more than 1,585 suspects.[18] Witches in Navarre could engage in the most extreme and complete inversion of Christianity anywhere on the Spanish mainland. In the accusations of 1609–1610, they participated in Black Masses in which the Eucharist and Lord's Prayer were reversed; beyond the usual *maleficia*, they also practiced cannibalism and actively recruited child-witches into their entourage. Meanwhile, insights into Aragonese witch hunting come from a combination of inquisition trials, inquisition trial summaries, episcopal trials when they exist, and documentation that either relays or mentions secular prosecutions.[19] For the region of Huesca, for example, researchers have surveyed twenty-five inquisition summaries for superstition and witchcraft and found that eighteen of the individuals tried were male, some of those men were French, and several were prosecuted multiple times, which probably ought to raise the question of the effectiveness of the Inquisition's sentences.[20] Here, witches were essentially necromancers. For other parts of Aragón, suspects again were often French, while others were clerics.[21] There were *saludadores*, men reputed to be adept at curing, some of whom succeeded in gaining episcopal licenses for their work. Muslims who had converted to Christianity were often cited for diabolical invocations or for teaching the spells to others. Belief in the evil eye was widespread; other *maleficia* included halting a woman's lactation. Night terrors – in which witches flew into houses via closed doors or through chimneys, cast sleeping spells on the inhabitants, and then wounded them – were common.[22] Some of the strongest evidence for the urban/rural divide in types of witchcraft comes from Zaragoza.[23] Recent research has concluded that the worst witch hunt in Spanish mainland history occurred in Catalonia in the seventeenth century; the first wave lasted from 1618 to 1622, with two more occurring in 1626–27 and 1643.[24] Historians have suggested that hundreds of

Catalan women were executed for this crime in what amounted to local rather than centralized prosecutions. The only agents promoting witch hunting in these cases were secular justices attached to baronial tribunals, who were allowed to act with complete impunity by their local lords. They were helped along the way by witch-finders.[25] Suggestively, Catalan witches engaged in identical activities as their Navarrese counterparts: they too killed children, created hail, renounced God, the Virgin Mary, and the Saints, and flew to the devil's gathering, where they kissed his anus and had sexual relations with him.[26] It should be noted that for secular justice in both Aragón and Catalonia, trial records are often missing because judges and towns were not bound to create them. Instead, towns could agree that witches posed an exceptional threat, disavow their own town privileges, and treat suspects according to summary justice by hanging or exile.[27]

Given the legal and emotional energy that went into witch hunting, it makes sense that it was a sporadic exercise, and such holds true for mainland Spain from 1500–1650. It is fair to say that the attention of Spanish inquisitors ebbed and flowed over the early modern period where witches were concerned. When secular justices became transfixed by witchcraft cases, inquisitors tended to follow their lead, though sometimes, as in Catalonia in the seventeenth century, inquisitorial attention could be missing altogether. Episcopal cases from this time period have been studied to a much lesser degree, so extrapolations about such sources are risky: still, in areas where witchcraft had a substantial history and presence, such as Pamplona, bishops seem to have been attentive, at least when they were in residence.

When it comes to large, theoretical causes for witch hunting, historians of early modern Spain have rarely accepted the older, now usually discredited axiom that European intellectuals promoted witch hunting in order to amass power, and did so via the dissemination of elite concepts about the Devil.[28] Spanish elites wrote treatises on witchcraft and superstition in both Latin and the vernacular, across both the sixteenth and seventeenth centuries, and their works tended either toward the encyclopedic (Martin del Río) or the pastoral (Pedro Ciruelo).[29] While it is sometimes possible to trace the popularity and potential influence of these works – either through the quantity of print runs or the works' presence in the libraries of learned men – no historian would be so naïve as to draw a straight line from written treatises to oral accusations.[30] Instead, we prefer to think of the interactions between elite and popular as more dialogical in their communications, even in a courtroom setting. Rather than seeing the accused as helpless victims parroting back what their interrogators wanted to hear, we prefer to imagine that more intricate and subtle interactions were possible, in which both parties took away cues and information about concepts, rhetoric, and acceptable discourse.[31] Luckily, the language of the courts in the sixteenth and seventeenth centuries was most often Spanish in any jurisdiction, which helps contemporary scholars feel relatively confident that trial testimony has some trustworthy connection to the statements offered by witnesses and the accused. At the same time, when Spanish-language trial records from northern Spain feature deponents who spoke only Basque, there is an additional layer of mediation because that witness testimony was translated in the field, as witnesses deposed.

Conceptually, scholars agree that early modern Spanish elites were particularly receptive to the Augustinian notion of an implicit or explicit demonic pact which underlay all magic and witchcraft. It was known via Scripture that the Devil – Spanish

elites did not distinguish between the Devil and demons – actively sought the destruction of human souls and always worked as the father of lies.[32] Witches who explicitly
sought pacts with the Devil were engaging in treason against God, because such diabolical relationships broke a Christian's baptismal vows. At the same time, individuals
who performed ceremonies that had no natural or divine reason for success were
also implicitly asking the Devil to assist them; given the Devil's character, he might
invade the process even without an invitation. Thus, the most innocent-looking rituals or ceremonies could involve the Devil unless there were clear expectations for
the rituals to succeed on the basis of divine or natural law.[33] From a clerical point of
view, witches, love magic, and spells to detect hidden treasure were all linked to the
Devil and to enmity with God, and "the literature attacking the agents of *maleficium*
thus blended imperceptibly into a more general campaign."[34]

It also seems clear that Spanish elites paid special attention to the crucial canon
law text called the *Canon episcopi*, which was included in the *Decretum*, the twelfth-
century collection of canon law compiled by the Italian monk, Gratian. Though
the *Canon episcopi* dates from only the ninth century, Gratian and his peers believed
the text came from the age of the Church Fathers and was composed at the Council of Ancyra in 314; this mistaken belief in the *Canon*'s antiquity helped to give it
weight with medieval and early modern intellectuals. The *Canon episcopi* reported
that certain women thought they could fly through the air with the goddess Diana,
but noted that such females were mistaken, and probably deluded by the Devil himself. By raising the question of night flight – also known as transvection – and linking
it to women and the Devil, the *Canon episcopi* provided a touchstone for identifying
witches: they flew. Because there were episodes in the New Testament in which Jesus
and Paul ascended into the air, no early modern Catholic theologian would have
denied the possibility of transvection altogether; instead, the *Canon episcopi* allowed
women who flew to be deceived. Early modern Spaniards could extrapolate from the
Canon episcopi to raise questions about witches' delusions in general, or they could
pin the question of fantasy onto flight alone. Throughout the sixteenth and seventeenth centuries, Inquisition authorities asked their officers in the field to try and
prove whether witches had actually accomplished what they had confessed, whether
those admissions concerned harmful magic, flight, or Devil-worship.[35] Sometimes,
Spanish elites extended the possibility of mistakes beyond the witches themselves, by
raising the prospect that the authors of Europe's most notorious treatise on witchcraft, the *Malleus maleficarum*, had been misled in their conclusions. In a 1537 instruction from the *Suprema*, it was noted that the *Malleus's* material was extremely subtle
and complex, to the point that even experts could be misled by what they heard.[36]

Even if European intellectuals did not purposefully create the phenomenon of
witch hunting to gain authority, the fact remains that the heresy of witchcraft required
definitions of orthodoxy, and then laws, to make it into an indictable offense. As
St. Paul noted in Romans, one must know what the law is before one can be prosecuted for breaking it. For heresies which arose in the twelfth century, such as
Waldensianism and Catharism, medieval theologians and popes eventually defined
sufficiently the doctrines and practices of the Catholic Church for religious and royal
hierarchies to act against the offenders.[37] When it came to Spanish witches in the
sixteenth and seventeenth centuries, there already was a large body of authoritative
literature which spelled out the forms and characteristics of demonic homage and

deemed all of it heretical. But witches were presumed to do more than worship the devil, for they allegedly practiced *maleficia* to destroy crops, livestock, adult enemies, and children.[38] When witchcraft resulted in bodily harm and the ruination of real or movable property, the crime pertained to secular courts. But it also belonged to bishops' courts if the episcopate chose to try to exercise its ancient pastoral rights. Patristic Christian literature, particularly in the East, charged bishops to care for their flocks' souls; that charge was reiterated in the Council of Trent's decrees in the middle of the sixteenth century. Thus, bishops had reasons to notice witchcraft and superstition in their dioceses, as did priests in their parishes. In the end, three court systems in early modern Spain – the secular, the episcopal, and the inquisitorial – had cause to pursue maleficent witchcraft.

There is no question that these justice systems clashed. From the *Archivo Histórico Nacional* in Madrid, the central repository for most Spanish inquisition sources, there is ample evidence that inquisitors disagreed with secular judges and bishops over jurisdiction.[39] Inquisitors were highly attentive to their privileges.[40] They were convinced that charges of heresy should outweigh charges of *maleficia* and hence affect the proper sequence of trials. The 1526 inquisition congregation in Granada was unanimous that suspected witches should be tried first by the Inquisition, perform first the penances ordered by the Inquisition, and only afterwards be released to secular authorities to make amends for the "deaths, damages, and other crimes they have committed."[41] Not surprisingly, the Inquisition's sensitivity did not stop other courts from attempting to become involved in witchcraft prosecution. For example, the bishop's court in Pamplona investigated clerics who traveled the diocese as healers, wives whose husbands alleged they were demonically possessed, and parish priests who refused to conjure clouds.[42] Secular magistrates as well as inquisitors interrogated witnesses arising from the witchcraft allegations in Navarre in 1609–11.[43] While Catalan witchcraft was prosecuted only by secular courts in the seventeenth century, when it reached a fever pitch in 1619–20, King Philip IV asked the region's nine bishops to consider whether the Inquisition alone should take charge of the prosecutions.[44] In Huesca, bishops were not involved in witch hunting, but secular and inquisitorial authorities routinely clashed over it, as every intrusion by inquisitors appeared to be a threat to traditional liberties.[45]

Throughout the early modern period, inquisitors were convinced of their expertise: they asserted that they not only had better legal processes, but superior investigative skills and far better prisons than their secular or ecclesiastical counterparts. Given such claims, it is difficult to know how to interpret the Inquisition's inconsistent actions toward witch suspects across time. For example, inquisitors in the tribunals of Logroño and Zaragoza used the Suprema's authority to remove cases from secular courts and to pardon witches when there was evidence of over-zealous prosecutions and forced confessions. But inquisitors in the same tribunals also declined to interfere with secular cases even when they should have known from past experience that witch suspects could have been confessing falsely out of torture. Some scholars have attempted to explain the discrepancy by noting that Spanish inquisitors were prohibited from confiscating a suspected witch's property; consequently, those officials had a reason for refusing to prosecute, since there would be no financial benefit coming their way after the trial.[46] At the same time, it would be farfetched to read inquisitors' insistence on their superior skills and procedures as simply defensive rhetoric, when we know they could act to have cases transferred. We seem to have two interpretative options before us: to allow for a wider context behind inquisitors' decisions, involving personalities, circumstances, opinions on privilege, and the Suprema's own willingness to tell its tribunals what to do; or to classify inquisitors, bishops, and secular judges as fundamentally engaged in the same disciplinary enterprise, and to discount the signs of more-or-less benevolence that the records often reveal.[47]

There is no doubt that where centralized authority was fragmented, Spanish witch hunts moved apace: contrary to an older, now discredited paradigm, we now know that witch hunting in early modern Europe happened primarily in the interstitial boundaries of territories, whether such borders were defined in terms of religion or geography. Navarre, Aragón, and Catalonia shared a frontier with France; in terms of space, the Navarrese and Aragonese inquisitorial districts extended far beyond the convenient reach of their respective inquisition tribunals. Catalonia was divided into *comarcas* ruled by local seigneurs, while Granada was only conquered in 1492. Furthermore, the timing of the most virulent witch hunting in Spain – from approximately 1575 to 1630 – coincides with rampant plague and what has been called the "Little Ice Age." The latter was known in Catalonia as the "age of floods." Putting aside functionalist explanations about the environment, it seems clear that fertility, writ large, was a constant factor in Spanish territories when it came to "classic" witchcraft: there are too many dead animals, ruined crops, and murdered infants in the sources from Navarre, Aragón, Catalonia, Cuenca, and Granada to suggest otherwise.[48] Provocatively, there also seems to be a strong link between slander and witchcraft charges in Zaragoza, Navarre, and perhaps in Castile itself, much as historians have discovered for Germany.[49]

There is no doubt that central authorities could be driven into witch hunting through popular pressure. Early modern Spain's justifiable renown for orthodoxy, discipline, and bureaucracy did not inhibit its officials from listening empathetically to popular complaints. In Cuenca in 1519, the parents of dead children made the accusations and were taken seriously by inquisitors; throughout Navarre in the sixteenth century, owners of damaged property and parents of injured offspring went to secular, episcopal, and inquisitorial officials to complain, and obtained significant results. Neighbors in Catalonia, aided by witch-finders, incited secular prosecutions. Within the trials, we can sometimes find clues about the village conflicts that produced such accusations. Debt was a factor for one Navarrese accuser.[50] Child witnesses could be bribed or forcibly inebriated into naming suspects: when they accused their own family members, their statements appeared that much more persuasive because they were so outrageous that they must have been true.[51] No one has yet compiled the longitudinal evidence that would allow us to say confidently that women over a certain age, or widows, or the poor suffered disproportionately from accusations. But an equally compelling question would be how villagers lived with each other after a witch hunting episode such as the one in Elgorriaga, Navarre, in 1611, or Arrayoz, Navarre, in 1613, when perhaps a dozen women were imprisoned and tortured for days on the initiative of local justices, and released only after they had falsely confessed.[52] Shifting our attention to deep readings of extant trials, no matter which court oversaw them, will allow us to capture these episodes in greater detail and thereby amplify our understanding of Spanish witch hunting.

Notes

1 For example, the witch trials conducted by the Logroño tribunal of the Inquisition from 1609 to 1610 were destroyed by Napoleon's troops in the Spanish War of Independence; secular trials against witches in Catalonia and Aragón have left little documentation; episcopal and secular trials for witchcraft in the city of Zaragoza are few and far between. See notes below.

2 Ménendez Pelayo, *Historia de los heterodoxos españoles*, 2nd ed. (Madrid: CSIC, 1963), 374–392; Charles Lea, *History of the Inquisition in Spain*, 4 vols. (New York: American Scholar Publications, Inc., 1966), 217–246.

3 Caro Baroja, *Vidas mágicas e Inquisición*, 2 vols. (Madrid: Tauris, 1967); *Inquisición, brujería, y criptojudaismo* (Barcelona: Editorial Ariel, 1970); *Brujería vasca, Obras completes vascas de Julio Caro Baroja*, vol. 5 (San Sebastián: Editorial Txertoa, 1975); and *The World of the Witches* (Chicago: The University of Chicago Press, 1964, 1965, 1968). William Monter, "Witchcraft in Iberia," in *The Oxford Handbook of Witchcraft in Early Modern Europe and Colonial America*, ed. Brian P. Levack (Oxford: Oxford University Press, 2013): 269–270, agrees that Spain has a peculiar position in witchcraft historiography and ties it to Caro Baroja's singular influence. I find that Caro Baroja's preferences are traceable to earlier historians, which is not to discount his extensive work with primary sources and in the field.

4 Because María Zimeldegui had been in France, the Labourd region was experiencing its own witch hunt under the guidance of Pierre de Lancre, and Spanish inquisitors would complain about the incursion into Navarre of French witches; numerous historians have claimed that the Zugarramurdi episode was galvanized by French influence. As anyone can see from Navarrese documents, that region required no French incentives to create a witch hunt. See Florencio Idoate, *La brujería en Navarra y sus documentos* (Pamplona: Institución *Principe de Viana*, CSIC, 1972).

5 Gustav Henningsen, *The Witches' Advocate: Basque Witchcraft and the Spanish Inquisition (1609–1614)* (Reno, NV: University of Nevada Press, 1980), 185–186, 191 on the *auto de fe*.

6 As examples, see Brian Levack, *The Witch Hunt in Early Modern Europe*, 2nd ed. (London, New York: Longman, 1995), 223; Robin Briggs, *Witches and Neighbors: The Social and Cultural Context of European Witchcraft* (New York: Viking Penguin, 1996), 35–36, 335–336. For a more recent example of the Basque focus, see Joseph Pérez, *Historia de la brujería en España* (Madrid: Espasa, 2010), in which pp. 205–235 are devoted purely to the Logroño *auto de fe* of November 1610.

7 For a forceful endorsement of the Inquisition's skepticism vis-à-vis witchcraft, see Iñaki Reguera, *La inquisición Española en el País Vasco El tribunal de Calahorra, 1514–1570* (Donostia: Txertoa, 1984), 205. Also see William Monter, *Frontiers of Heresy* (Cambridge: Cambridge University Press, 1991), 262; Idem, "Witchcraft in Iberia," 268; and Jesús Usunáriz Garayoa, "La caza de brujas en la Navarra moderna (siglos XVI-XVII)," in *Akelarre: la caza de brujas en el Pirineo (Siglos XIII-XIX) Homenaje al professor Gustav Henningsen, Revista Internacional de los Estudios Vascos [RIEV]* Cuadernos 9 (Donostia Eusko Ikaskuntza=Sociedad de Estudios Vascos D.L., 2012), 343. Though the *Suprema* often urged caution on its officials during witchcraft investigations from 1521 onward, ultimately that skeptical voice was not inevitably present. Scholars have tended to overlook instances in which the Suprema actively supported inquisitors' actions against witches, including 1609–1610, when Salazar and his colleagues were in agreement as to how to proceed and the Suprema backed them up with explicit encouragement.

8 Henningsen, *The Witches' Advocate*, 390; Idem, *The Salazar Documents* (Leiden: Brill, 2004), 82–83, 94–95.

9 Doris Moreno Martínez, "La discrecionalidad de un inquisidor: Francisco de Vacas, ¿el primer abogado de brujas?" in *Akelarre: la caza de brujas en el Pirineo (Siglos XIII-XIX)*, 202–214; Anastasio Rojo Vega, "Testamento, inventario, y biblioteca del Inquisidor Francisco Vaca, abogado de brujas," *EHumanistica* 26 (2014): 196–209.

10 Monter, "Witchcraft in Iberia," 270, 273–274. María Tausiet, *Urban Magic in Early Modern Spain: Abracadabra Omnipotens* (Hampshire: Palgrave MacMillan, 2014) illustrates differences between urban and rural witchcraft around the Aragonese capital of Zaragoza.

11 As the reader will see, Devil-worshipping witches who committed *maleficia* were found in Granada and Cuenca, as well as in northern Spain. They were present in Córdoba – see

Rafael Gracia Boix, *Colección de documentos para la historia de la inquisicón de Córdoba* (Córdoba: Publicaciones del Monte de Piedad y Caja de Ahorros, 1982) – as well as the Canary Islands. Francisco Fajardo Spinola, *Hechicería y brujería en Canarias en la Edad Moderna* (Las Palmas: Ediciones del Cabildo Insular de Gran Canaria, 1991).

12 As an example, see Usunáriz Garayoa, "La caza de brujas," 310–317; or Rafael Martín Soto, *Magia e inquisición en el antiguo reino de Granada (siglos XVI-XVIII)* (Málaga: Editorial Arguval, 2000), 94–97, and especially 94 n. 30.

13 Martín Soto, *Magia e inquisición*, 93–98, 101–102, 105.

14 Ibid., 235.

15 Heliodoro Cordente Martínez, *Brujería y hechicería en el obispado de Cuenca* (Cuenca: Diputacíon Provincial, 1990), 20–27. Cordente's work focuses on Inquisition sources, as does the older treatment by Sebastián Cirac Estopañan, *Los procesos de hechicerías en la Inquisición de Castilla la Nueva (tribunals de Toledo y Cuenca)* (Madrid: CSIC, 1942). Cirac Estopañan's investigations found classical witches in multiple Inquisition sources: see pp. 188–199, 200–201.

16 Cordente Martinez, *Brujería y hechicería*, 20–27, 45–67.

17 Leading scholars on Navarre and Aragón do not agree on numbers of trials conducted by inquisitors. Episcopal cases in both Navarre and Aragón, and secular cases for Navarre in particular, remain understudied. Secular prosecutions against witches in Aragón were conducted according to a type of summary justice which left almost no written documentation (see p. 137). Certain *relaciones de causas* reveal the formal charge and punishment administered to culprits, as well as the indicted persons' sex and age, but little more; others are significantly detailed. To see the range of documentation that can speak to witchcraft in this time and place, see Idoate, *La brujería en Navarra*. To see *relaciones* that are full of particulars, see the Appendices in Gari Lacruz, *Brujería e inquisición en el alto Aragón* (Zaragoza: Diputación General de Aragón, 1991).

18 Garayoa, "La caza de brujas," 316–317; he is indebted to Idoate, *Las brujería en Navarra*, as well as to Henningsen, *The Witches' Advocate*; Mikel Zabala, *Brujería y inquisición en Bizkaia, siglos XVI y XVII* (Bilbao: Ekain, 2000), 50–54, 65–70, 81–88, finds that the tribunal at Logroño prosecuted fifty-one persons in Vizcaya for witchcraft in the late 1530s, twenty-three witches in the 1550s, and oversaw another episode in 1616–17.

19 Tausiet has found six episcopal cases from Zaragoza, dated between 1561 and 1605; six trials belonging to the inquisition tribunal in the same city, dated between 1509 and 1648; at least 121 more inquisition cases documented in the *relaciones de causas*; eleven secular cases, and additional references in the *Green Book of Aragón*. *Urban Magic*, 23, 173–174, nn. 39–41.

20 Garí Lacruz, *Brujería y inquisición en el alto Aragón*, 25, 51, 60–61, 219–221.

21 Tausiet, *Urban Magic*, 53–57.

22 María Tausiet, *Ponzoña en los ojos: brujería y superstición en Aragón en el siglo XVI* (Madrid: Turner, 2004), 325–340, 262, 302–320, 349–358.

23 Tausiet, *Urban Magic*, 36 n. 21; and chapter 5.

24 Agustí Alcoberro, *El segle de les bruixes (segle xvii)* (Barcelona: Barcanova, 1992), 30–33; see as well his "Cacera de bruixes, justicia local I Inquisició a Catalunya, 1487–1643: alguns criteris metodològics," *Pedralbes* 28 (2008): 485–504. The first modern examination of Catalonian witch hunting was Antoni Pladevall i Font, *Persecucio de bruixes a les Comarques de Vic a principis del segle xvii* (Barcelona: Subirana, 1974).

25 Pladevall i Font, *Persecucio de bruixes*, 32.

26 Ibid., 40–41, 44, 48–51.

27 The announcements of the *desaforamiento* were often in Latin. For their importance and their phrasing, see Tausiet, *Ponzoña en los ojos*, 202, 221–222, 233.

28 Norman Cohn, *Europe's Inner Demons* (New York: Basic Books, 1975); Robert Ian Moore, *The Formation of a Persecuting Society* (Oxford: B. Blackwell, 1987).

29 On Rio, see Peter G. Maxwell-Stuart, *Martín del Rio: Investigations into Magic* (Manchester: Manchester University Press, 2000); On Ciruelo, see Homza, *Religious Authority in the Spanish Renaissance* (Baltimore: Johns Hopkins University Press, 2000), chap. 6. For new work on Martín de Castañega, see Iñaki Bázan Díaz, "El tratado de Martín de Castañega como

remedio contra la superstición y la brujería en la diócesis de Calahorra y La Calzada," *EHumanista* 26 (2014): 18–53.

30 As Stuart Clark notes, the opposite dynamic is more often true, whereby witchcraft treatises were written after witchcraft episodes, as a reflective response, or a wish to justify an attack. "Bruíjeria e imagición histórica. Nuevas interpretaciones," in *El Diablo en la Edad Moderna*, ed. James Amelang and María Tausiet (Madrid: Marcial Pons, 2004), 33.

31 Carlo Ginzburg, *Clues, Myths, and the Historical Method* (Baltimore: Johns Hopkins University Press, 1989), 141–149; Homza, "How to Harass an Inquisitor-General: The Polyphonic Law of Francisco Ortíz," in *A Renaissance of Conflicts*, ed. John A. Marino and Thomas Kuehn (Toronto: University of Toronto Press, 2004), 297–334.

32 1 Peter 5:8.

33 On the implicit demonic pact, see Augustine, *De civitate Dei, Opera Corpus christianorum*, Latin Series 47, Part 14:1 (Turnholti: Brepols, 1955), Book 7, chap. 35; Book 8, chap. 19; Book 10, chaps. 8–9. Also see Aquinas, *Summa contra Gentiles* (Notre Dame, IN: University of Notre Dame Press, 1975), Book 3, part 2, chap. 105, pp. 94–97. Jean Gerson, the highly influential chancellor of the University of Paris (d. 1429), also promulgated the implicit demonic pact in his writings.

34 Stuart Clark, *Thinking with Demons: The Idea of Witchcraft in Early Modern Europe* (Oxford: Oxford University Press, 1997), 463.

35 For example, AHN, Secc. Inqu., Libro 319, f. 270r, 1521; ibid., Libro 320, ff. 51v-52, 1528; ibid., Libro 322, f. 146r, 1537. For such instructions to the Logroño tribunal after the Zugarramurdi cases began, see AHN, Secc. Inqu., Libro 332, ff. 231v-323r (11 March 1609); f. 251 v (21 July 1609); ff. 252v-253r (24 July 1609).

36 AHN, Secc. Inqu., Libro 322, ff. 216v-217r.

37 To see this dynamic in practice throughout Western European history, Alan Charles Kors and Edward Peters, *Witchcraft in Europe, 1100–1700: A Documentary History* (Philadelphia: University of Pennsylvania Press, 1972).

38 Sorcerers too could be construed as performing *maleficia* via the poisoning of enemies or rendering men sexually impotent.

39 AHN, Libro 319, f. 219v, 1526; Libro 320, f. 369r-v, 1530; ibid., f. 388v, 1531; Libro 323, ff. 226v-227r; Libro 327, 1r, 1576.

40 For example, Tausiet, *Ponzoña en los ojos*, 123.

41 A quote from future Inquisitor-General Fernando de Valdés; see Homza, *The Spanish Inquisition*, 157.

42 For these episcopal cases, *Archivo Diocesano de Pamplona* [ADP], Secr. Sojo C/107 – N 20, 1598; Secr. Garro. C/207-N. 1; Secr. Trevino C/415-N. 17, 1606.

43 My sources disagree with the conclusions of Jesús Usunáriz, who asserts that the only legal protagonist in the Zugarramurdi case was the Inquisition, "La caza de brujas," 336. See AGN 100654, 1610; AGN 330569, 1612, with testimony collected in 1611; and finally, AGN 100796, 1611. Historians have not realized that multiple successful lawsuits were launched against the accusers of witches in the Zugarramurdi episode.

44 For the remarkable jurisdictional complications in 1619–20 among the Inquisition, the bishops, Catalunya's General Court, and baronial justice, see Albertí Alcoberro, "The Catalan Church and the Witch Hunt: The Royal Survey of 1621," *eHumanista* 26 (2014): 153–169. On more customary patterns in Catalonia's witch hunting, Alcoberro, *El segle de les bruixes*, 55–56.

45 Garí Lacruz, *Brujería y inquisición en el alto Aragón*, 26–27.

46 Monter and Tausiet weight this factor heavily; Monter, *Frontiers of Heresy*, 262; Tausiet, *Ponzoña en los ojos*, 121.

47 Tausiet, *Ponzoña en los ojo*, 245–248, also finds the inconsistency present in the episcopal court. Nevertheless, there was a long-standing record of episcopal opposition to the Spanish Inquisition's methods: *Il vangelo e la spada. L'inquisizione di Castiglia e i suoi critici (1460–1598)* (Rome: Edizione di Storia e Letteratura, 2003).

48 Tausiet, *Ponzoña en los ojos*, argues strongly that witchcraft of all types should be attributed to conflicts of all sorts within communities and families: 253–257, 369–464. In *Urban Magic*, she writes "the myth of witchcraft represent[ed] an attempt to provide an explanation or

language that would both channel and alleviate all kinds of tension, as well as providing a way of interpreting misfortune in its broadest sense," 158.

49 Alison Rowlands, *Witchcraft Narratives in Germany (Rothenburg, 1561–1652)* (Manchester: Manchester University Press, 2003). Though Tausiet, *Urban Magic*, 159, asserts that the slander of calling someone a witch was an actual diminution of conflict, I have found the opposite to be true for Navarre, where lawsuits for slander over witchcraft were routine and resulted in severe penalties. That tradition of suing over slander helped confessed witches find justice in 1611–13. There are also appeals over "injuries" [*injurias*] in the Royal Chancellery in Valladolid which relate to witchcraft accusations.

50 AGN, Proceso 72902 (Arrayoz 1613), f. 14r.

51 In AGN, Proceso 069260, a 5-year-old testifies against his grandmother; for accusations of witchcraft from drunkenness, AGN 330569, f. 15r.

52 AGN, Procesos 100796 and 72902, respectively.

Bibliography (selection)

Alcoberro, Albertí, "The Catalan Church and the Witch Hunt: The Royal Survey of 1621." *EHumanista* 26 (2014): 153–169.

Henningsen, Gustav, *The Salazar Documents*. Leiden: Brill, 2004.

Homza, Lu Ann, *Religious Authority in the Spanish Renaissance*. Baltimore: Johns Hopkins University Press, 2000.

Homza, Lu Ann, "How to Harass an Inquisitor-General: The Polyphonic Law of Francisco Ortíz." In *A Renaissance of Conflicts*, edited by John A. Marino and Thomas Kuehn, 297–334. Toronto: University of Toronto Press, 2004.

Martínez, Heliodoro Cordente, *Brujería y hechicería en el obispado de Cuenca*. Cuenca: Diputacíon Provincial, 1990.

Pérez, Joseph, *Historia de la brujería en España*. Madrid: Espasa, 2010.

Soto, Rafael Martín, *Magia e inquisición en el antiguo reino de Granada siglos XVI-XVIII*. Málaga: Editorial Arguval, 2000.

Spinola, Francisco Fajardo, *Hechicería y brujería en Canarias en la Edad Moderna*. Las Palmas: Ediciones del Cabildo Insular de Gran Canaria, 1991.

Tausiet, María, *Ponzoña en los ojos: brujería y superstición en Aragón en el siglo XVI*. Madrid: Turner, 2004.

Tausiet, María, *Urban Magic in Early Modern Spain: Abracadabra Omnipotens*. Hampshire: Palgrave MacMillan, 2014.

Zabala, Mikel, *Brujería y inquisición en Bizkaia, siglos XVI y XVII*. Bilbao: Ekain, 2000.

11

WITCH HUNTS IN BRITAIN

James Sharpe

During the early modern period, 'Britain' incorporated a number of discrete political entities, and witchcraft and witch hunting in those various entities demonstrated marked differences. The most developed of these political units was England, a large, sophisticated, and by 1700 relatively economically advanced realm with maybe 5 million inhabitants. By 1541, Wales, linguistically and culturally distinct from England, had been incorporated into the English and political system, generally speaking with the assent of the Welsh local elites. To the north lay Scotland, a separate kingdom with a population of maybe 1 million in 1700. Scotland had a troubled relationship with England during the Middle Ages, but the accession to the English crown by James VI of Scotland in 1603 lessened the potential for overt conflict, while in 1707 the Act of Union joined the two realms into a political entity known as Britain. Despite this formal political integration into the new British state, Scotland maintained its own legal, religious, and educational systems. And if we move beyond Britain proper to other parts of that archipelago which is termed the British Isles, we find Ireland, a separate kingdom in which, even after the shattering events of the mid-seventeenth century, was largely inhabited by a Gaelic-speaking population that maintained an uneasy relationship with the English who ruled them and the Scottish Presbyterians who settled in Ulster. It is, however, mainly with England and Scotland that this chapter will be concerned.

England and Scotland experienced different levels of witch hunting. In England, on a fairly generous estimate, perhaps 500 witches were executed.[1] For Scotland, the total of executions was approximately 2,000, meaning that, proportionate to population, a Scot was roughly twelve times more likely to be executed for witchcraft than an inhabitant of England.[2] A major key to understanding this divergence between the two kingdoms lay in their respective judicial systems. In England, witchcraft Acts of 1533 (repealed in 1547), 1563, and 1604 had defined witchcraft as a felony. Although occasional felonies might be tried at county quarter sessions, or at borough courts with rights of gaol delivery, most felonies, criminal offences potentially incurring the death penalty following conviction, were tried at the assizes. These were courts held twice yearly in each English county, and were presided over by trained and experienced judges sent out from Westminster, judges who were, moreover, prohibited from conducting assizes in counties where they owned their main estates.

Additionally, although used in cases of treason, torture was not a part of normal criminal trial process under English common law. Hence two of the main factors contributing to the amplification of witch-panics in many parts of Europe, unqualified judges immersed in local witch hunting cultures and the over-enthusiastic use of torture, were largely absent from England. This was not the case in Scotland.[3] Some witch trials were conducted by the central judicial authorities in Edinburgh, and some by circuit judges, equivalent to the English assize judges. But the majority were tried locally, on commissions issued by the Scottish privy council. These commissions, usually granted in response to local fears of witchcraft, delegated the investigation and trial of supposed witches to local lairds (gentry), ministers, lawyers, and other notables. Such men, driven by the fear of witches in their communities and by the aggressive Calvinism of the Scottish Reformation, were usually anxious to obtain convictions. In so doing, they frequently bypassed normal legal procedure. In particular, they might resort to unauthorised torture (as in England, torture was not a normal part of criminal investigation under Scottish law), the more general maltreatment of suspects, and such practices as pricking suspects in hopes of detecting a witch's mark.

A second major difference lay in the experiences of the Reformation in England and Scotland. The current interpretation is that the English Reformation was very much imposed 'from above', adopting what was essentially a Calvinist theology in the 1559 settlement but retaining the pre-Reformation hierarchy of archbishops, bishops, and archdeacons, and the pre-Reformation structure of ecclesiastical courts. This resulted in a relatively high level of control by the church authorities, and a desire to steer between the spiritual dangers of Catholicism and the excesses of over-enthusiastic Puritanism. The essential caution towards such matters in the upper reaches of the Church of England's hierarchy was shown when the church had to deal with a number of high-profile demonic possession cases, normally involving related witchcraft accusations, around 1600.[4] The key figure here was Richard Bancroft, bishop of London and from 1604 archbishop of Canterbury, who was clearly sceptical about such matters. It is also noteworthy that after Bancroft's erstwhile chaplain and propagandist, Samuel Harsnett, became archbishop of York in 1633, presentment of sorcerers at the Yorkshire church courts virtually ceased.[5] Such clergymen as would have welcomed a more active persecution of witches were kept firmly under control. The situation in Scotland was different. There the Reformation proceeded at a faster pace and with a greater urgency. Old hierarchies and institutional structures were done away with, and those parish clergy who supported the Reformation laboured avidly for the spiritual regeneration of the kingdom. More surely than in England, witches rapidly became established as enemies of godliness who needed to be weeded out.[6] As early as 1568–9, during a period of civil warfare, the reforming churchman John Erskine of Dun led a witch hunt in Angus and Mearns which was clearly connected with the push to achieve the godly society and which drew in forty accused.[7] Scotland was clearly one of those regions where, as Stuart Clark has put it, it is possible to locate witchcraft 'at the very heart of the reforming process'.[8]

This did not, of course, mean that English clergymen were uniformly unconcerned about witchcraft. In the late sixteenth and early seventeenth centuries, a number of English clergymen of a more or less Puritan cast of mind wrote demonological tracts. Perhaps the most important of these authors was William Perkins, a major Protestant theologian whose *Discovery of Witchcraft*, possibly originating as a series of sermons, was published posthumously in 1608. Other contributors to this corpus of demonological works were Henry Holland, George Gifford, and Richard Bernard.[9] Although Scotland boasted the only European monarch to write a demonological tract, the northern kingdom did not produce a corpus of demonological writing on the English scale. Moreover, despite some late examples, Scotland did not produce anything like the stream of pamphlet accounts of witch trials which constitute a major source for historians of English witchcraft between the first of such publications, in 1566, and the last conviction of an English witch, in 1712.[10] Both major demonological works and trial pamphlets ceased to be printed in the 1630s, indicating how witchcraft was dropping out of public discourse in that decade, but the renewal of witch hunting in England in the 1640s heralded the publication of both trial pamphlets and more substantial works. Such publications were to continue after the Restoration of the Stuart monarchy in 1660, with, in particular, weighty volumes being produced arguing for or against the reality of witchcraft. Although speculation about witchcraft was to continue, the last major debate between English authors came in 1718, when Francis Hutchinson, a Church of England cleric who was subsequently to hold a bishopric in Ireland, published his *Historical Essay concerning Witchcraft*.[11]

The history of witchcraft in England, and, by implication, of Europe more generally, was revolutionised by a book published in 1970, Alan Macfarlane's *Witchcraft in Tudor and Stuart England: A Regional and Comparative Study*. The region was the county of Essex, for which archival sources record a uniquely high number of witchcraft references, and the comparative framework was provided by anthropology. Macfarlane's analysis emphasised that most accusations came 'from below', from villagers accusing their neighbours of witchcraft, and that their central concern was *maleficium*, the doing of harm to people, farm animals, or goods by witches. The sources consulted threw up a recurrent model of tensions lying behind accusations, with richer villagers habitually accusing poorer ones of witchcraft after an altercation revolving around the richer villagers' refusal to provide their poorer neighbours with money, food, or work when they came begging to their doorstep.[12] This 'charity refused' model blended well with the established model of socio-economic change in late sixteenth- and seventeenth-century England. Under the pressure of a rising population, village society, perhaps more rapidly in lowland England than in the north or west, was becoming more stratified, with a body of prosperous yeomen farmers doing well out of rising grain prices and the lower real value of the wages they paid those who worked for them, and, conversely, a growing body of the poor. Among the poor or relatively poor themselves, moreover, hard times and increased competition for resources encouraged the sort of neighbourly tensions which so often underpinned a witchcraft accusation. Macfarlane's findings were reinforced the year after the publication of his book when the erstwhile supervisor of his doctoral research, Keith Thomas, published his magisterial *Religion and the Decline of Magic*, which adumbrated an interpretation of early modern English witchcraft fundamentally similar to Macfarlane's.[13]

These two works between them marked a major paradigm shift in how witchcraft was understood as an historical phenomenon, and which was to prove dominant for a quarter of a century. It was gradually realised, however, that despite the originality and strength of the insights that Macfarlane and Thomas, in their slightly different ways, offered, there were some matters which needed further investigation. Firstly, although the need to analyse the background to accusations was accepted as vital, research into other parts of England found that the 'charity refused' model was not universally dominant.[14] Staying with issues of socio-economic change, it remains unclear why Essex should have experienced so many more witchcraft accusations than Kent, Surrey, or Middlesex, all of them south-eastern counties for which the population and survival of relevant records was equivalent to Essex, and which were experiencing the same sort of social and economic pressures. The growth of women's history and the establishment of gender as an important tool of historical analysis encouraged a feeling that they had paid insufficient attention to gender issues. And their use of anthropological insights, while deepening the understanding of the tensions and troubled social relationships underlying witchcraft accusations, did not help explain change over time: neither of the two books are at their strongest when attempting to explain why witchcraft accusations began in England, and why they ended. Moreover, there was growing disquiet with their insistence, echoing pioneering studies of witchcraft in England, that English witchcraft was essentially non-demonic, with little evidence of the demonic pact or the witches' sabbat, being essentially a matter of interpersonal disputes turning on *maleficium*, making it different from 'continental' witchcraft. Especially after historians working on witchcraft in continental territories began to follow the lead given by Macfarlane and Thomas and examine witchcraft on a village level, it became clear that English witchcraft was founded on a set of variables which was present throughout Europe, but which varied in its emphases in different areas.

Witchcraft accusations in Scotland were likewise rooted in neighbourly tensions but, as we have suggested, the Scottish judicial system and the Scottish kirk facilitated the amplification of these accusations into large-scale hunts. There is a general consensus that Scotland experienced five major panics.[15] The first occurred in 1590–1, and included the North Berwick trials in which James VI took a personal interest. Documentation for this period is imperfect, but maybe a hundred people were tried in these two years. Scattered accusations continued throughout the 1590s, and a major wave of witch hunting came in 1597, with 111 accusations that year. There was renewed witch hunting in 1628–30, with 249 accused, 175 of them in 1629 alone. This outbreak has so far been little studied, but is currently interpreted as an aspect of a broader attempt to impose tighter law and order and godly discipline on the Scots. The next big hunt came in 1649–50, with 367 accused in the former year and 188 in the latter. The key element here was surely the need to establish order, and godly discipline, after the disruption of civil warfare and the political shock occasioned by the execution of Charles I in January 1649. English occupation of Scotland during the 1650s helped keep witchcraft accusations low, but renewed political tensions after the Restoration of 1660 led to Scotland's last great witch hunt, with perhaps 210 persons accused of witchcraft in 1661 and 402, the largest in any single year in Scotland, in 1662. Concentration on these big outbreaks should not obscure the fact that witchcraft trials were endemic in Scotland, and that several years witnessed fifty or more prosecutions. The hunts were at their most severe in the Lothians, Fife, and the East Borders, the first two areas in particular being zones where the kirk had achieved a considerable impact. The highlands, largely outside the control of the courts and the kirk, suffered fewer trials, although witchcraft was certainly part of that region's folklore. In 1662, however, the highlands contributed significantly to the overall total of trials, evidence perhaps of the belated penetration of the influence of the Scottish state and the kirk. Throughout these large-scale panics, the social profile of the accused remained the same: people, and especially women, from the middling or lower ranks of rural society.

The great Scottish hunt of 1661–2 was one of the most violent in European history. The context for this mass hunt was surely provided by the politics of the immediate post-Restoration period, when the reimposition of the old order heightened religious tensions, witchcraft accusations being a possible by-product of these. There is also a suspicion that the massive diminution in witch trials caused by the English occupation of Scotland in the 1650s may have created a backlog of suspicions which exploded once trials began in 1661. The immediate origins of the 1661–2 hunt, however, lay in a petition to the Scottish parliament from a landowner, the earl of Haddington, who requested a commission to allow him to try the witches who, he claimed, were rife on his estates, and were causing trouble for his more godly tenants. His petition remarked that:

> 'That upon several malefices committed of late within and about my lands of Samuleson there being several persons suspect of the abominable sin of witchcraft apprehended and searched, the marks of witches were found on them in the ordinary way. Several of them have made confession and have delated sundry others within the said bounds and have acknowledged paction with the devil'.[16]

The language of this passage is interesting. The suspected witches had committed 'malefices', acts of concrete harm, but as was usual with Scottish accusations, witchcraft was clearly identified as an 'abominable sin' and the pact with the devil assumed a central importance. The earl also identified the way in which confessing witches accused ('delated') other people of witchcraft, creating that spreading of accusations which was a feature of all large witch hunts. And there was the searching of suspects for the witch's mark, which, we are told, was frequently found 'in the ordinary way'. This presumably refers to the practice of pricking witches, which was a well-documented feature of the 1661–2 hunt. John Kincaid of Tranent, East Lothian, was an expert in this field, and was responsible for finding the witch's mark – hence helping establish the guilt of suspects in a large if indeterminate number of instances. Gradually, however, central authority, alarmed by the extent and virulence of the craze, and concerned with the numerous distortions of judicial process, assumed control. In April 1662, the Scots privy council issued a proclamation asserting the need for due legal process in witch trials, and demonstrated its resolution by imprisoning John Kinkaid and another witch-pricker, John Dick. This was to be the last major witch hunt in Scotland.

As we have noted, one of the peculiarities of the history of witchcraft in Scotland was the involvement of a monarch, James VI (from 1603 James I of England), both as a proponent of witch hunting and as an author of a work of demonology. The exact nature of James's involvement has, however, been the subject of considerable debate.[17] He is mainly associated with the North Berwick trials of 1590–1, where confessing witches claimed to have attempted to sink the ship carrying home the king and his bride, Anne of Denmark, from marriage celebrations in Copenhagen. James was an active proponent of divine right monarchy, and that Satan's agents were willing to machinate against the Lord's anointed fitted very neatly into his view of politics. Detailed research on the situation at the time of the North Berwick trials, however, suggests that they were only one example of a number of witch trials occurring in Scotland at that time, these being mainly driven by the kirk. Thus James did not initiate the large-scale witch hunting of the 1590s, but became involved in one incident in which royal authority was threatened, although his presence at the North Berwick trials must surely have helped legitimise witch hunting. Similarly, there is disagreement about the date of the composition of his treatise, his *Daemonologie*, published in 1597. It seems likely that it was composed in 1591, in the immediate aftermath of the North Berwick trials, and that his decision to publish the work (a short and entirely conventional Protestant interpretation of witchcraft) in 1597 was prompted by renewed fears of witches threatening the crown as an aspect of the major hunts of that year. But after his accession to the English throne, whatever the level of his involvement in the witchcraft statute of 1604, James adopted a more sceptical stance over witchcraft, evidently adopting the position that he could demonstrate his expertise in the subject as clearly in exposing cases of fraud or misconception as in revealing nests of malefic witches.

Getting large-scale hunts off the ground was difficult in England. The famous Lancashire trials of 1612 marked the largest trials experienced in England up to that point, with ten people executed at Lancaster and another, in a related trial, at York, but even this celebrated affair was very minor compared to the large-scale Scottish outbreaks.[18] Tellingly, when a large-scale hunt seemed to be looming in the same county in 1633, central authority, alerted to the problem by an assize judge, intervened rapidly to close things down. England did, however, experience one large-scale hunt. This began in the spring of 1645 and petered out by the summer of 1647.[19] Fragmented and imperfect sources make it difficult to determine the exact number involved, but some 250–300 persons were accused or at least suspected of witchcraft, most of them being drawn into the web of accusations before the end of 1645, of whom at least 100 were executed. This outbreak is associated with Matthew Hopkins, a Suffolk minister's son living as a petty gentleman in Essex, the so-called Witch Finder General, who, together with his associate John Stearne, rapidly established a reputation as an investigator of witchcraft. The craze was limited to eastern England, beginning in Essex, spreading rapidly into Suffolk and then Norfolk, with further trials in the areas bordering those counties. The circumstances of this great witch hunt were unique. It came towards the end of the Civil War and had its storm centre in counties which had not experienced fighting but which were of central importance, in ideological and material terms, to the parliamentarian war effort. Ideologically, the war was being seen increasingly as a battle for true religion, with parliamentarian propaganda demonising royalists. The normal controls which had inhibited extreme Protestantism in the Church of England had gone, and the eastern counties had experienced a purge of unreliable (and in many cases moderate) ministers, with Suffolk in addition undergoing officially sanctioned iconoclasm in churches which were felt to contain 'popish' adornments.

Likewise, judicial and administrative structures, geared to supporting the war effort, were stretched sufficiently to dilute that caution which the assize courts normally demonstrated in matters of witchcraft. These factors, added to the catalyst which Hopkins offered, help explain England's only large-scale witch hunt. Ironically, the long term consequences of the craze of 1645–7 was to discredit witch hunting in post- Restoration England: educated opinion was not yet ready to dispense entirely with the reality of witchcraft, but its active persecution was now associated with the low-born religious fanatics who were thought to have come to prominence in the 1640s and 1650s.

As well as the contributions already noted, Macfarlane and Thomas's works of the early 1970s were also important in highlighting the existence of 'good' witches. These were known by a variety of names. In England, the most common term was cunning (i.e. skilful or knowledgeable) man or woman, but they were also known as wise men or women or, if male, conjurers or wizards. The term 'charmer' was also frequently employed, although it has been suggested that for Scotland at least this term specifically indicated a type of folk healer. Whatever the terminology, there clearly existed a body of occult practitioners who might be called on, according to their perceived abilities, to help find stolen goods, to provide folk remedies for illness, to tell fortunes or predict marital partners, or to give advice to those who thought themselves to be bewitched.[20] Such people were clearly perceived as being useful by the bulk of the population, were unlikely to find themselves in court facing charges of witchcraft, and, indeed, were to survive in English and Scottish rural society into the twentieth century. Elite observers were very unhappy about them. English demonological writers in particular bewailed the popularity of these plebeian occult practitioners, usually arguing that they were as bad as malefic witches in that they too derived their occult powers from a demonic pact, or indeed worse than the 'hurting' witches because they led their clients to perdition by claiming to be benevolent. Thus the great English theologian William Perkins ended his 257 page tract on witchcraft by declaring that 'death therefore is the just and deserved punishment of the good witch', while the Scottish Witchcraft Act of 1563 made consulting such people a capital offence.[21] Neither Scotland nor England, however, experienced what might be termed a 'cunning folk craze'. The population were unwilling to report 'good' witches, and local judicial authorities rarely imposed capital punishments on those that did come to trial. In England, indeed, a large proportion of such village sorcerers falling foul of authority were tried in the ecclesiastical courts, which usually dismissed them following an admonition.[22]

The issue awaits more detailed research, but it seems that those who entered the historical record as cunning folk or charmers consisted of roughly equal proportions of men and women. This was not the case of those appearing before the courts on potentially capital charges of witchcraft. In Scotland, about 85 percent of those accused were women, on the Home Circuit of the assizes in England, the largest sample of trial records available for that country, around 90 percent. The reasons for this massive gender imbalance have been much debated, but remain elusive.[23] For those writing from within the women's movement around 1970, the answer was a simple one: witchcraft was one of the ways in which misogynistic and patriarchal men attacked women as a means of keeping them subjugated. Although few historians working in the field would deny the existence of misogyny, patriarchy, and the problem of gender relations in early modern society, few now accept such a simplistic explanation. One immediate objection is that witchcraft accusations were not levelled at all women: they tended to be elderly, poorer than their accusers, and were (although this point has recently been challenged) disproportionately likely to be widows. Another crucial point is, as Julian Goodare put it, that 'patriarchy was sufficiently stable not to need witch hunting', while those suggesting that it did need witch hunting are faced with the problem of determining why the witch hunts began and ended.[24] Christina Larner, whose feminist credentials were irreproachable, argued that witch hunting could not be equated with women hunting. She wrote that:

> 'The pursuit of witches was an end in itself and was directly related to the necessity of enforcing moral and theological conformity. The fact that a high proportion of those selected in this context as deviants were women was indirectly related to this central purpose'.[25]

The problem is, of course, that of establishing the exact characteristics of this 'indirect relationship'. Women, like men, were in England and Scotland, as throughout Europe, being subjected to the disciplinary pretensions of the confessional state. Why this process resulted in most areas in a disproportionate number of those accused of witchcraft being women remains contentious.

The interpretative problems are demonstrated by differing interpretations of why so many accusations against alleged female witches were levelled by other women. One interpretation of this is that the women doing the accusing were conforming to patriarchal norms: patriarchy, like any political system, to function successfully needs the co-operation, or at least the acquiescence, of those it attempts to control, while most people in any social system conform to that system's norms most of the time. Larner was among the first to follow this line, and subsequent writers have adopted a broadly similar approach. Others have gone into more detail on the interpersonal antagonisms from which the accusations arose. In particular, those involving the alleged bewitching of a child, with its mother launching the accusation, seem to locate witchcraft accusations firmly in the female sphere, with only a tenuous connection to patriarchal domination. Diane Purkiss, who has correctly stressed the need for a close reading of women's accounts of witchcraft, has suggested that witchcraft beliefs enabled women to 'negotiate the fears and anxieties of housekeeping and motherhood'.[26] Thus, those seeking to understand the connection between witchcraft and women, in Britain as elsewhere, have to steer their way through a number of competing interpretations. But one surprising point is that, unlike modern commentators, early modern writers did not find the gender issues around witchcraft in any way problematic. Epistomon, the fount of knowledge in James VI's *Daemonologie*, when asked why 'there are twentie women given to that craft, where ther is one man?', did not regard the problem as being complex:

> The reason is easie, for as that sexe is frailer then man is, so it is easier to be intrapped in these grosse snares of the Devill, as was over well proved to be true, by the serpents deceiving of Eva at the beginning, which makes him homelier with that sexe.[27]

The connection between women and witchcraft was clearly regarded as a given by early modern demonologists, something which, ironically, raises more puzzling problems than if it had been a matter for lengthy discussion.

Witch hunting in Scotland, most historians agree, was largely restricted to the Lowlands. Recent research has revealed that there were more prosecutions in the Highlands than had previously been thought, but these were largely clustered on the peripheries, leaving a core Highland zone where trials were few. This situation must have owed much to the relatively weak penetration of the Highlands by the Scottish kirk and the judicial apparatus of central government. But there is a complementary explanation, which carries considerable weight if the Highlands, the main Gaelic-speaking area of Scotland, are treated in parallel with Gaelic-speaking Ireland. In both the Scottish *Gàidheatachd* and Ireland there was a belief in witchcraft and magic, but the witch did not assume the demonic character so central to Scottish and English official witch-theory.[28] The role of the witch was taken by other spiritual beings, notably fairies. A recent commentator has identified the presence in Gaelic-speaking Scottish Highlands of

'the creatures or spirits who had a fully functioning parallel society inside hills and mounds. There is no doubt that, across the Highlands and the Western Isles, until the twentieth century, they were believed to blight human beings, especially children, and crops and livestock, in much the same manner as witches elsewhere. In particular, they were considered to be a menace to young children, both by injuring them and stealing them and leaving fairy offspring in their places'.[29]

In the mid-nineteenth century, the Irish folklorist Sir William Wilde affirmed that over much of the west of Ireland fairies were 'the great agents and prime movers of all accidents, disorders and death, in man and beast', a tendency which was most marked in the extreme western Gaelic-speaking areas.[30] The presence of these alternative agents of misfortune probably helps explain why, outside of areas dominated by English or Scots settlers, few experience witchcraft accusations. An interesting variation is provided by the Isle of Man, another Gaelic-speaking part of the British Isles where fairy beliefs were firmly rooted. Man was ruled by the English earls of Derby, and its church was incorporated into the Church of England. Two people, a mother and her son, were hanged there for witchcraft in 1617, but otherwise only two witchcraft prosecutions, both of which failed, reached the secular courts. In the Isle of Man, witchcraft records were initially screened by the Manx church courts, and investigation of their archives reveals that accusations arising from a heavily folklorised witchcraft were routinely defused at that level or ended with the supposed witch launching a defamation suit against her accuser.[31]

Then there was Wales, another linguistically and culturally separate area. Administratively, Wales had been formally integrated into the English state in 1541, one of the consequences of this process being the setting up of assize courts in the principality. The records of these survive in bulk, and they reveal little by way of witch trials, in contrast, for example, with very high levels of prosecution, frequently leading to hanging, of property offenders. Over the period when the English witch statutes were in operation, there were thirty-four trials of witches which led to eight convictions and five executions, this in a population of maybe a quarter of a million. In Wales, too, there was a traditional belief in witches, but as in Gaelic-speaking areas, these were not particularly threatening figures, and co-existed with other agents of misfortune, including fairies. During the seventeenth century, the English witch stereotype did penetrate into Wales, but it came late and was never fully internalised.[32]

Discussion of supernatural beliefs in the Celtic parts of the British Isles raises the issue of broader beliefs about witchcraft in Lowland Scotland and England. Certainly, fairy beliefs were firmly established in Lowland Scotland, and witches and fairies were sometimes conflated in accusations, possibly because James VI identified fairies as demonic beings.[33] Very rapidly, however, Scottish witchcraft accusations recognised the importance of the devil. As we have noted, the Scottish Reformation was more aggressive than the English. In 1560 the kirk's *First Book of Discipline* envisaged a new, reformed church, and a new, reformed society, that society to consist of new, reformed human beings. Witch hunting was an element in the long cultural process which obtaining these objectives entailed. Accordingly, the notion of witches as the instruments of the devil was internalised by the Scottish peasantry, with confessing witches routinely telling how they met the devil, entered into the satanic pact, and had sexual intercourse with him. Christina Larner, indeed, postulated the existence in early modern Scotland of a 'new popular demonic . . . a well rooted and well understood popular demonology'.[34] This degree of internalisation of the concept of demonic input into witchcraft was, she argued, characteristic of popular attitudes to witchcraft as the Reformed church's teachings penetrated deeper into the peasant consciousness. But the peasant consciousness was capable of retaining, far into the seventeenth century, fairly complex beliefs about witchcraft and related matters which were embedded in an earlier popular culture. In 1662 a woman called Isabel Gowdie, from Auldern in northern Scotland, was tried as a witch. In a remarkable series of confessions, she gave a heavily folklorised account of a supernatural world in which witchcraft co-existed with the operations of elves and fairies. The kirk clearly had further work to do in the remoter parts of the kingdom of Scotland.[35]

So far, the existence of a 'popular demonic' in England remains uninvestigated, although there are strong suggestions, not least on the strength of witch-trial pamphlets, that something like it existed. At the very least, demonic ideas entered English witchcraft beliefs through the notion of the witch's familiar spirit.[36] The exact nature of the familiar varied, and the origin of the belief in the familiar remains obscure. Nevertheless, familiars were of central importance to English witchcraft: one of the accused whose witchcraft was described in the first English trial pamphlet, concerning three Essex witches tried in 1566, reportedly had a familiar called Sathan, with which she entered into a pact and gave her blood in return for the ability to do harm to her enemies. In English witch lore, the familiar and the devil were frequently conflated, with confessing witches telling how the devil appeared to them in animal form, and how they entered into a pact with these strange creatures. More elusive is evidence of English belief in the witches' Sabbath. Although it was not a central feature of either official or popular belief in Scotland, witch trials there occasionally threw up accounts of the Sabbath, although these were normally folklorised versions of the phenomenon, with peasant feasting and dancing at their core, rather than the cannibalistic orgies described by some continental demonologists. In England there is less evidence even of this type, although occasional glimpses can be obtained of popular beliefs concerning witch's meetings. Perhaps the most remarkable instance came in 1673, when a woman named Anne Armstrong gave the Northumberland justices of the peace a remarkable series of depositions in which she gave an account of being ridden to a number of witches' meetings in the shape of a horse, where witches feasted, danced (sometimes in animal forms), and gave their fealty to the devil.[37]

In 1736 the British Parliament (British since the Act of Union of 1707) passed an Act which abolished the Scottish Witchcraft Act of 1563 and the English one of 1604, thus effectively decriminalising witchcraft. In both countries, prosecution and executions had been in decline for some time. In England, prosecutions had been in decline in all areas for which records survive from the Restoration of Charles II in 1660, the last execution came in 1685, and the last conviction, with the alleged witch being remanded by a sceptical judge, came in 1712. In Scotland, the mass craze of 1661–2 seems to have alerted the central judicial authorities to the dangers of uncontrolled witch hunting, and Edinburgh judges exercised greater control over witchcraft prosecutions. Trials continued, and there were incipient panics in East Lothian in 1678 and Paisley in 1697, this latter incident, with an allegedly possessed girl named Christian Shaw at its centre, resulting in seven executions. But the last execution recorded by the central authorities came in 1706, with a final witch-burning, following a trial of dubious legality, occurring at Dornoch in 1727, when Janet Horne became the last person to be executed as a witch in Britain. For England, if less certainly for Scotland, the 1736 legislation came when witch hunting had clearly lost its validity.[38]

Modern historians of witchcraft in Britain have reached no consensus about the reasons for, or indeed the nature of, the retreat from witchcraft beliefs which the 1736 Act might logically be assumed to have symbolised. One point on which they are generally agreed is that the view which has occupied mainstream thinking on this issue since the Enlightenment, that the 'Age of Reason' which supposedly pervaded Europe by the mid-eighteenth century, and which dismissed witch beliefs as irrational and superstitious, cannot be invoked to explain the decline in the belief of witchcraft in England and Scotland. The 'mechanical philosophy', associated with René Descartes and, later, with Isaac Newton, was making its impact on the intellectual life of England, and, it has recently been claimed, Scotland, but it was not sufficiently advanced to explain why there were no witch executions in England after 1685 or in Scotland, if we may discount the Dornoch case, after 1706. There were religious changes, identified in England as Latitudinarianism, which envisaged a less interventionist God and a more marginalised devil. In England, this religious tendency was firmly entrenched among the elite by 1736, but its progress had been uncertain at earlier points. In the late seventeenth century, Joseph Glanvill in England and George Erskine in Scotland had published compendia of stories aiming at proving the reality of the existence of the spirit world and of witchcraft, while even Francis Hutchinson, the clergyman and future bishop whose *An Historical Essay concerning Witchcraft* is regarded as a key sceptical text, considered the acceptance of the reality of spirits and their operations as an essential part of Christian belief. Scotland provided the one outspoken opponent of the 1736 Act, James Erskine, Lord Grange, who appears to have regarded the Act as an attack by proponents of what he regarded as the increasingly unsound Christianity practised in England on the more robust values of the Scottish kirk. Indeed, no full-scale denial of the reality of witchcraft was published in Scotland until 1815, when James Paterson's *Witchcraft unsupported by Scripture* appeared.

The judges who were apparently increasingly unwilling to convict witches were likewise unwilling to completely jettison witchcraft beliefs. Perhaps the most interesting figure here was Sir George Mackenzie, Lord Advocate of Scotland between 1677 and 1686. Mackenzie, early in his career, had been involved as a justice depute in the mass craze of 1661–2, and his experience had left him very sensitive to the dangers inherent in the lack of due legal process that could so easily affect witch trials that were not subject to strict supervision by qualified lawyers. The decline of witch hunting in Scotland owed much to his attitude, expressed clearly in his influential commentaries on the laws of Scotland. Yet he did not deny the reality of witchcraft, and in particular declared his opposition to the important sixteenth-century Dutch sceptic, Johann Weyer.[39]

The growth of judicial scepticism both north and south of the Anglo-Scottish border must have been regarded by many as suggesting that the problems of convicting witchcraft in particular cases lead to a rejection of the very possibility of witchcraft, but this was not a necessary outcome. Similarly, the brief period around 1712, following the trial of Jane Wenham, when witchcraft became a party political issue in England, with (broadly) Tories supporting witch beliefs and Whigs supporting scepticism, demonstrated how debate about witchcraft could reach heated levels unexpectedly.[40] Perhaps, in England at least, intellectual objections to witchcraft were underpinned by a cultural distancing of the educated elite away from the common people: witchcraft beliefs, certainly as evidenced in witch trials, were increasingly regarded as appropriate to the world of plebeian superstition rather than that of the refined and fashionable gentleman. Nevertheless, one exponent of fashionable taste, the writer Joseph Addison, probably encapsulated a widely held view when he declared in 1711 that 'I believe in general that there is, and has been such a thing as witchcraft, but at the same time can give no credit to any particular instance of it'.[41] Perhaps the best way of understanding the retreat from witchcraft as an intellectual possibility is not to set sceptics against believers, but rather to analyse positions based on different levels of doubt.

Throughout the British Isles, witch beliefs survived the 1736 Act.[42] On a popular level, people continued to identify other people, usually old women, as witches, and take unofficial action against them. Indeed, this phenomenon was demonstrated before the Act, when in 1705 at Pittenweem in Scotland a woman named Janet Cornfoot was brutally murdered after an attempt to prosecute her at the court had failed.[43] Similar incidents occurred in England throughout the eighteenth century, with one incident, in Hertfordshire in 1751, leading to the execution for the murder of a butcher who had orchestrated the fatal maltreatment of a supposed witch.[44] Less sinisterly, there was a continued acceptance in the powers of cunning folk and other 'good' witches, who continued to help people find stolen goods, tell fortunes, provide basic medical services, and give advice to those who thought themselves bewitched. Acceptance of the reality of witchcraft, or at least an inability to totally reject it, was also expressed by elite individuals. Perhaps most surprisingly, the eminent English jurist Sir William Blackstone, surely a paragon of Enlightenment values, thought that to deny witchcraft was 'at once flatly to contradict the revealed word of God, in various passages both of the old and the new testament; and the thing itself is a truth to which every nation in the world hath in its turn borne testimony', and adopted Addison's equivocal position.[45] Perhaps less unexpectedly John Wesley, founder of Methodism, regarded belief in witchcraft as a fundamental of the Christian faith, and deplored the way in which belief in it had been discarded, arguing (as many had done in the late seventeenth and early eighteenth centuries) that giving up witchcraft was giving up the Bible.[46]

In 1718 Francis Hutchinson, in his *Historical Essay*, noted the precarious nature of the escape from witchcraft beliefs which seemed to be in progress at that time: 'Our present freedom from these evils are no security, that such a time might not turn up in one revolution or another'.[47] Even by the early eighteenth century, this well-informed observer could not regard the end of witch hunting in Britain as a foregone conclusion.

Notes

1 James Sharpe, *Instruments of Darkness: Witchcraft in England 1550–1750* (London: Hamish Hamilton, 1996), 125.
2 There is now an extensive literature on witchcraft in early modern Scotland: key works include: Christina Larner, *Enemies of God: The Witch Hunt in Scotland* (London: Chatto and Windus, 1981); Julian Goodare, ed., *The Scottish Witch Hunt in Context* (Manchester: Manchester University Press, 2002); Julian Goodare, Lauren Martin, and Joyce Miller, eds., *Witchcraft and Belief in Early Modern Scotland* (Basingstoke: Palgrave Macmillan, 2008); Brian P. Levack, *Witch – Hunting in Scotland: Law, Politics and Religion* (Abingdon, New York: Routledge, 2008); and Lawrence Normand and Gareth Roberts, *Witchcraft in Early Modern Scotland: James VI's Demonology and the North Berwick Witches* (Exeter: University of Exeter Press, 2000).
3 The connections between the Scottish legal system and witchcraft prosecutions are discussed in Julian Goodare, "Witch Hunting and the Scottish State," in Goodare, ed., *Scottish Witch Hunt in Context*, 122–145; Levack, *Witch Hunting in Scotland*, chapter 2, "Witchcraft and the law in early modern Scotland."
4 The relevant themes are discussed in Marion Gibson, *Possession, Puritanism and Print: Darrell, Harsnett, Shakespeare and the Elizabethan Exorcism Controversy* (London: Pickering & Chatto, 2006).
5 Philip Tyler, "The Church Courts at York and Witchcraft Prosecutions, 1567–1640," *Northern History* 4 (1970): 84–109.
6 For discussions of the role of reformed religion in Scottish witch hunting, see Larner, *Enemies of God*, chapter 12, 'The Belief System (II) The Christianization of the People'; Levack, *Witch Hunting in Scotland*, 7–14.
7 Normand and Roberts, *Witchcraft in Early Modern Scotland*, 79.
8 Stuart Clark, "Protestant Demonology: Sin, Superstition and Society," in *Early Modern European Witchcraft: Centres and Peripheries*, ed. Bengt Ankarloo and Gustav Henningsen (Oxford: Oxford University Press, 1990), 46–47.
9 Sharpe, *Instruments of Darkness*, 81–88.
10 Barbara Rosen, *Witchcraft* (London: Edward Arnold, 1969); Marion Gibson, *Reading Witchcraft: Stories of Early English Witches* (London: Routledge, 1999).
11 Andrew Sneddon, *Witchcraft and Whigs: The Life of Bishop Francis Hutchinson, 1660–1739* (Manchester: Manchester University Press, 2008).
12 Alan Donald James Macfarlane, *Witchcraft in Tudor and Stuart England: a Regional and Comparative Study* (London: Routledge & Kegan Paul, 1970).
13 Keith Thomas, *Religion and the Decline of Magic: Studies in popular Beliefs in Sixteenth and Seventeenth-Century England* (London: Weidenfeld & Nicolson, 1971).
14 James Sharpe, *Witchcraft in Seventeenth-Century Yorkshire: Accusations and Counter Measures* (York: Borthwick Papers 81, 1992); Malcolm Gaskill, "Witchcraft in Early Modern Kent: Stereotypes and the Background to Accusations," in *Witchcraft in Early Modern Europe: Studies in Culture and Belief*, ed. Jonathan Barry, Marianne Hester, and Gareth Roberts (Cambridge: Cambridge University Press, 1996), 257–287.
15 These are discussed in Lauren Martin, "Scottish Witchcraft Panics Re-Examined," in *Witchcraft and Belief in Early Modern Scotland*, ed. Goodare, Martin, and Miller, 119–143; on individual panics, see: Brian Levack, "The Great Scottish Witch Hunt of 1661–1662," *Journal of*

British Studies 20 (1980): 90–108; Julian Goodare, "The Scottish Witchcraft Panic of 1597," in *The Scottish Witch Hunt in Context*, ed. Goodare, 51–72: for an excellent regional study of Scottish witch hunting, see Stuart Macdonald, *The Witches of Fife: Witch Hunting in a Scottish Shire, 1560–1710* (East Linton: Tuckwell Press, 2002).

16 Cited in Levack, *Witch Hunting in Scotland*, 87.

17 The background to the 1590–1 North Berwick trials and the composition of the *Daemononologie* receive comprehensive treatment in Normand and Roberts, *Witchcraft in Early Modern Scotland*: for broader discussions, see: Christian Larner, "James VI and I and Witchcraft," in *The Reign of James VI and I*, ed. A.G.R. Smith (London: Macmillan, 1973), 74–90; and Stuart Clark, "King James's *Daemonologie*: Witchcraft and Kingship," in *The Damned Art: Essays in the Literature of Witchcraft*, ed. Sydney Anglo (London: Routledge and Kegan Paul, 1977), 156–181.

18 For the Lancashire trials, see: Philip C. Almond, *The Lancashire Witches: A Chronicle of Sorcery and Death on Pendle Hill* (London: I.B. Taurus, 2012); Robert Poole, ed., *The Lancashire Witches: Histories and Stories* (Manchester: Manchester University Press, 2002).

19 Malcolm Gaskill, *Witchfinders: A Seventeenth-Century English Tragedy* (London: John Murray, 2005).

20 Owen Davies, *Popular Magic: Cunning-Folk in English History* (London, New York: Hambledon and London, 2003); Owen Davies, "A Comparative Perspective on Scottish Cunning-Folk and Charmers," in *Witchcraft and Belief in Early Modern Scotland*, ed. Goodare, Martin, and Miller, 185–205.

21 William Perkins, *Discourse of the Damned Art of Witchcraft, so Farre Forth as It Is Revealed in the Scriptures, and Manifest by True Experience* (Cambridge, 1608), 257, cited in James Sharpe, *Witchcraft in Early Modern England* (Harlow: Longman/Pearson Education, 2001), 102: the text of the Scottish 1563 Act is given in Normand and Roberts, *Witchcraft in Early Modern Scotland*, 89.

22 Tyler, "Church Courts at York and Witchcraft Prosecutions."

23 For differing interpretations of the connections between women and witchcraft, see: Diane Purkiss, *The Witch in History: Early Modern and Twentieth-Century Representations* (London, New York: Routledge, 1996); Marianne Hester, *Lewd Women and Wicked Witches: A Study in the Dynamics of Male Domination* (London: Routledge, 1992); James Sharpe, "Witchcraft and Women in Seventeenth-Century England: Some Northern Evidence," *Continuity and Change* 6 (1991): 179–199; Julian Goodare, "Women and the Witch Hunt in Scotland," *Social History* 23 (1998): 288–308.

24 Goodare, "Women and the Witch Hunt in Scotland," 306.

25 Larner, *Enemies of God*, 102.

26 Purkiss, *Witch in History*, 93.

27 James VI, *Daemonologie, in Forme of ane Dialogue, divided in Three Bookes* (Edinburgh, 1597), 43–44.

28 Ronald Hutton, "Witch Hunting in Celtic Societies," *Past and Present* 212 (2001): 43–71.

29 Ibid., 53.

30 Cited by Hutton, "Witch Hunting in Celtic Societies," 66.

31 James Sharpe, "Witchcraft in the Early Modern Isle of Man," *Cultural and Social History* 4 (2007): 11–28.

32 These data are taken from Richard Suggett, *A History of Magic and Witchcraft in Wales* (Stroud: The History Press, 2008).

33 Lizanne Henderson and Edward J. Cowan, *Scottish Fairy Belief: A History* (East Linton: Tuckwell Press, 2001); for the opinions of James VI and I, *Daemonologie*, 57, 73–75.

34 Larner, *Enemies of God*, 144–145.

35 Emma Wilby, *The Visions of Isabel Gowdie: Magic, Witchcraft and Dark Shamanism in Seventeenth-Century Scotland* (Brighton: Sussex Academic Press, 2010).

36 James Sharpe, "The Witch's Familiar in Elizabethan England," in *Authority and Consent in Tudor England: Essays Presented to C.S.L. Davies*, ed. G.W. Bernard and S.J. Gunn (Aldershot: Ashgate, 2002), 219–232.

37 James Sharpe, "In Search of the English Sabbat: Popular Conceptions of Witches' Meetings in Early Modern England," *Journal of Early Modern Studies* 2 (2013): 161–183.

38 Ian Bostridge, *Witchcraft and Its Transformations c. 1650 – c. 1750* (Oxford: Clarendon Press, 1997); for differing interpretations of the decline of witch hunting in Scotland, see: Levack, *Witch Hunting in Scotland*, chapter 8, "The Decline and End of Scottish Witch Hunting"; Michael Wasser, "The Mechanical World-View and the Decline of Witch-Beliefs in Scotland," in *Witchcraft and Belief in Early Modern Scotland*, ed. Goodare, Martin, and Miller, 206–226.

39 Levack, *Witch Hunting in Scotland*, 132–133, 139.

40 Bostridge, *Witchcraft and its Transformations.*

41 Cited in Sharpe, *Witchcraft in Early Modern England*, 130.

42 Owen Davies, *Witchcraft, Magic and Culture 1736–1951* (Manchester: Manchester University Press, 1999).

43 Levack, *Witch Hunting in Scotland*, 145–146.

44 Sharpe, *Instruments of Darkness*, 1–4.

45 Cited in Sharpe, *Witchcraft in Early Modern England*, 130–131.

46 Sharpe, *Instruments of Darkness*, 253.

47 Cited in Bostridge, *Witchcraft and Its Transformations*, 152.

Bibliography (selection)

Almond, Philip C., *The Lancashire Witches: A Chronicle of Sorcery and Death on Pendle Hill*. London: I.B. Taurus, 2012.

Bostridge, Ian, *Witchcraft and Its Transformations c. 1650 – c.1750*. Oxford: Clarendon Press, 2007.

Gaskill, Malcolm, *Witchfinders: A Seventeenth-Century English Tragedy*. London: John Murray, 2005.

Goodare, Julian, Lauren Martin, and Joyce Miller (eds.), *Witchcraft and Belief in Early Modern Scotland*. Basingstoke: Palgrave Macmillan, 2008.

Levack, Brian P., *Witch Hunting in Scotland: Law, Politics and Religion*. Abingdon and New York: Routledge, 2008.

Normand, Lawrence and Gareth Roberts, *Witchcraft in Early Modern Scotland: James VI's Demonology and the North Berwick Witches*. Exeter: Exeter University Press, 2000.

Poole, Robert (ed.), *The Lancashire Witches: Histories and Stories*. Manchester: Manchester University Press, 2002.

Sharpe, James, *Instruments of Darkness: Witchcraft in England 1550–1750*. London: Hamish Hamilton, 1996.

Sharpe, James, *Witchcraft in Early Modern England*. Harlow: Longman/Pearson Education, 2001.

Sharpe, James, "In Search of the English Sabbat: Popular Conceptions of Witches' Meetings in Early Modern England." *Journal of Early Modern Studies* 2 (2013): 161–183.

Suggett, Richard, *A History of Magic and Witchcraft in Wales*. Stroud: The History Press, 2008.

Wilby, Emma, *The Visions of Isabel Gowdie: Witchcraft and dark Shamanism in Seventeenth-Century Scotland*. Brighton: Sussex Academic Press, 2010.

12

WITCHCRAFT IN SCANDINAVIA

Per Sörlin

In the age of the European witch hunts, Scandinavia consisted of two major polit-ical entities: the kingdom of Denmark, or Denmark–Norway as it is often known, with its dependencies Iceland, Greenland, and the Faroe Islands; and the kingdom of Sweden, or Sweden–Finland. Norway was an independent kingdom, but in the fourteenth century had entered into a union with the Danish crown. Sweden, which then included much of what is now Finland, had expanded its territories through conquest, and also had possessions in Germany and the Baltic countries. In territo-rial terms, the two empires were very much conglomerate states, and, even though they were fairly centralized, there was still a strong element of local participation in government. In both Denmark and Sweden, the administration of justice had been brought under central control relatively early, but laymen – peasants in the country-side, townsfolk in the cities – exercised considerable influence. In terms of religion, both were again very similar, although Sweden has rightly been called one of the most confessionalized Protestant states in Europe.

Beginnings in the Middle Ages

Several of the necessary conditions for the persecution of witches were already in place in the Middle Ages.[1] There was a very long-standing belief that malicious people existed who could do harm to humans and animals by magic, and who held gatherings which they reached by flying through the air. When the Swedish historian and the last Roman Catholic titular archbishop Olaus Magnus announced in the mid-sixteenth century that witches liked to gather on the Baltic island of Blå Jungfrun (lit. blue virgin), also known as Blåkulla, the idea was anything but new; indeed, back in the thirteenth cen-tury the oldest of all Sweden's provincial laws, Äldre Västgötalagen, had set down that it was a gross insult to say that a woman had ridden on a hurdle with her hair down at dawn or the turn of the seasons. Neither was it original to think that witches were a sect ruled by the Devil, but there was no such thing as a definitive description of a sabbat or witches' Sabbath – it changed constantly, and even at the height of the witch hunts it was rare for trial testimony to include all the standard details.[2]

Medieval laws defined magic chiefly in terms of *maleficium*. True, at an early stage Norway legislated against the sort of magic that was thought to result from straightforward paganism, while the Swedish provincial laws also prohibited superstition (although later national laws omitted it altogether), yet the true scope of the persecution in the Middle Ages is impossible to determine. There are reports in various sources of witches being killed, and the option was certainly there in the legislation. In 1080, for example, Pope Gregory VII warned King Harald of Denmark against accusing women of having conjured up storms or cursing livestock. It is noticeable that the few known medieval cases concerned consorting with the Devil, diabolism, and love magic, and not what we now think of as the more traditional *maleficium*, which is still believed to have dominated the legal agenda during the Middle Ages.[3]

Patterns of witch hunting in Scandinavia

Allegations of *maleficium*, however, were to dominate the sixteenth-century witch trials, often regarded as the precursor of the wave of Scandinavian persecution that peaked in the seventeenth century. During the sixteenth century, there are glimpses of the legal practices that would pave the way for more widespread persecution – torture and ordeal by water. At the same time, more elaborate conceptions of witchcraft are also found, with witches making pacts with the Devil and participating in sabbats. Yet there were also cases that concerned more innocent superstitions.

The records of more than 400 Scandinavian witchcraft trials survive from the sixteenth century. In Denmark, there were a number of sensational trials that touched aristocratic circles and even members of the royal family. Most famous of all were the events of 1589–90, when King James VI of Scotland, who was meant to fetch home his bride from Copenhagen, was prevented from making the crossing for several weeks by a succession of fierce storms, which were believed to be the result of witchcraft. In other words, it is possible to find support for the view that the witch hunts and witchcraft legislation were both politically driven. During the seventeenth century, Scandinavian royalty continued to figure surprisingly large in the stories of witchcraft. The sources for the sixteenth century are so fragmentary, however, that they hardly permit a quantitative study of the nature and scope of the witch trials.[4]

Denmark

The witch trials in Denmark were clearly connected to the introduction of new legislative measures, even though there had been signs of increased activity in the law courts before then.[5] The majority of the known Danish witchcraft trials took place over the course of a few years, between 1617 and 1625. In 1617, in a conscious echo of the disciplinary programme of the Reformation a century earlier, King Christian IV issued a decree that included provisions against witchcraft, among them the rule that cunning people should be exiled and that those who entered into pacts with the Devil were to be burned. The decree of 1617 was later incorporated in a slightly modified form into the National Code of 1683, by which point the number of witchcraft trials in Denmark had dwindled to almost nothing.

At the same time, there were aspects to the Danish system of justice which worked against the holding of witchcraft trials. In 1547, after a series of sensational witchcraft cases, it was decreed that witches' testimony was not valid as evidence in court, and that torture was not permitted to extort a confession in order to obtain a conviction. The pattern known from so many other countries, with so-called chain trials in which people were tried on the basis of convicted witches' testimony, and then were tortured to confess and provide the names of further suspects, was thus unknown in Denmark. Torture was resorted to regularly in order to secure a confession, but only *after* conviction. Those found guilty could be asked about their accomplices, but neither the courts nor the authorities made any effort to pursue those who were then named. The result of the introduction of aggressive witchcraft legislation was not witch hunts, but rather a string of isolated witchcraft cases, sparked by accusations made by private individuals, as was called for by the strict accusatory system of the day. Another important limiting effect dated from 1576, when it became obligatory to refer all witchcraft convictions in the courts of first instance to the *landsting*, the regional high courts or appellate courts.

Few court records survive from Denmark's lower and high courts for this period. For the seventeenth century, however, the records for Jutland do survive, where a total of 494 trials were held between 1609 and 1687, more than half of them in the first eight years following the decree of 1617.[6] Up to 1650, there was a steady stream of trials, albeit at a low level after 1625. There was then a slight rise in the 1680s, which can largely be attributed to the activity of a single witch hunter, the nobleman Jörgen Arenfeldt, who terrorized a number of innocent people on his estates, but witchcraft trials ceased altogether not long after.

Almost half of those condemned to death in the lower courts had their sentences confirmed by the regional high court. In the lower courts, nine out of ten accused were sentenced to death, which one can assume did little to discourage further accusations. Denmark gives a contradictory impression, with both trial-limiting and trial-generating factors so plainly at work. Perhaps the main thing was not that the trial system was strictly accusatory, but that legal praxis was so brutal that it prompted a popular reaction. The Jutland trials were only a fraction of all the witch trials in Denmark, of course; the total number of witches executed is estimated to have been about four hundred.[7] Cunning people, who appeared before the courts in surprisingly small numbers, given that magic was anathema to the Church and the legislation of the day, were sentenced to banishment.[8] The clergy tended to hold to the older, providential tradition in their handling of malicious witchcraft, and so did little to accuse individual witches, while the populace at large, whose involvement was required if charges were to be brought, rarely lifted a finger against the cunning people in their communities, whose services they likely needed.

Danish witchcraft trials, if Jutland is anything to go by, would appear to have concerned maleficent witchcraft to the exclusion of all else. Quite apart from the restraining hand of the law, which made it much harder to bring allegations of diabolism, Denmark seems to have had little in the way of a well-developed or widely accepted notion of the sabbat, even though the idea that witches were organized into a collective was known, as is apparent from such confessions as were extorted.

The last witch to be burned in Denmark was executed in 1693. The belief in the reality of witchcraft lived on long after that, however – it even led to a lynching in 1722. The provisions against witchcraft in the 1683 National Code were formally nullified in 1866.

Norway

Apart from one case of love magic dating from 1325 in the city of Bergen, all the known witch trials in Norway fell into the period of 1540 to 1750.[9] Legal developments in the early modern era mirrored those in Denmark. Admittedly, after the decree of 1617 there was no witch hunt, but the number of witchcraft cases in the courts rose steadily from that date. Most of the trials took place between 1620 and 1665, and the total number of known individuals brought to court was some 780. Of those, more than 300 were condemned to death,[10] of which 90 per cent of the sentences that were actually carried out fell into the period between 1601 and 1670. Court proceedings were accusatorial rather than inquisitorial, yet on many occasions the individual accusers from the local farming community did not appear, and instead it was the bailiffs who had to prosecute the case.[11] In violation of the Danish decree, there were several cases where defendants were tortured before conviction rather than after. Otherwise, as in Denmark, the standards of proof were so low that it was possible to convict on the flimsiest of evidence, including unsworn statements and hearsay. Starting in the late sixteenth century, the administration of justice in Norway became increasingly decentralized, paradoxically just as a system of senior courts was introduced, with the result that local courts found themselves hearing serious criminal cases such as witchcraft for the first time. However, in the new system it was not obligatory to refer on all serious criminal cases, as was the case in Denmark and Sweden.

Broken down by region, the number of charges brought in the south-east peaked in the years following the decree of 1617. In this sense, Norway closely mirrored the Danish pattern. However, later there were widespread witch hunts in the north of the country. Of 131 individuals tried in the province of Finnmark in the far north, no fewer than 92 were executed, and major cases came in spates – as in 1620–1, 1651–3, and 1662–3 – interspersed with a number of more isolated examples. In proportion to the size of its population, Finnmark was one of the hardest hit areas in the whole of Europe. Among those accused were not only Norwegian peasants and fisherfolk, but also a number of Sami.[12] As in northern Sweden, which also saw a late wave of trials, so in Finnmark children played a role as witnesses.[13]

Witchcraft cases in Norway were considerably more varied than those in Denmark. Minor magic was more prominent, though the majority of cases that went to court still concerned maleficent witchcraft. They were also far more likely to include accounts of sabbats – elaborate accounts at that – with the special places where the witches were said to gather actually named, including Blåkulla, Domen, Dovre, and Lyderhorn. It is also worth noting that witches were said to conjure shipwrecks and drown crews, and thus were not thought the cause of only individual misfortunes.

In Norway, the last execution for witchcraft was in 1695. The later seventeenth century had seen the start of royal absolutism and the centralization and professionalization of the judicial system, which reduced the scope for local initiatives on the part of the bailiffs. The changes to the judicial system meant that trained lawyers controlled all stages of the trial process. A mere 18 cases of witchcraft are known from the eighteenth century.

Sweden

Sweden's oldest recorded witchcraft trial was held in the town of Arboga in 1471.[14] By the end of the sixteenth century, the number of cases brought before the courts seems have been on the rise. Whether this continued into the first half of the seventeenth century is unclear, however. In the 1610s, 1630s, and 1650s, there were local tendencies towards increased persecution, but the high-water mark would be reached much later, in the second half of the seventeenth century, when it overlapped with the later persecutions in Finland and northern Norway.

As in Denmark, so in Sweden there was a clear chronological coincidence between the many witchcraft trials in the latter half of the seventeenth century and new legislation. Sweden's medieval national laws, which by then were distinctly anachronistic, were supplemented in 1665 by a royal decree (reissued in 1687) that dealt explicitly with non-harmful magic and consorting with the Devil. The decree signalled the authorities' concern about witchcraft only a few years before the outbreak of the great witch hunt. Two major sets of trials ran simultaneously. In the 'Blåkulla trials' in northern Sweden (1668–1676), the main charge was that defendants had used their supernatural powers to abduct children for the sabbat. Meanwhile, at the far end of the country in the south-eastern county of Bohuslän, there was a series of witchcraft trials between 1669 and 1672. Bohuslän had only been wrested from Denmark's control in 1658, and the cases were tried according to Danish law, with several departures from standard practice strongly reminiscent of Norwegian praxis, with the regular use of ordeals by water.

There has been no attempt to establish a national chronology of those accused and executed for witchcraft in Sweden. The main events are clear enough, however, as is the number of victims. In those few years of mass persecution, some 300 people were executed. Excepting the rash of cases in Bohuslän and the Blåkulla trials, no more than 100 individuals were executed for witchcraft in the two centuries between 1550 and 1750, giving a maximum of 400 executions. However, a far greater number were sentenced to other punishments, including banishment, flogging, fines, or imprisonment on a diet of bread and water. While Denmark, in comparison, was perhaps the Scandinavian country with the greatest number of executions for witchcraft, it was the witch trials in Sweden that answered for the largest number of people accused and convicted, if only because of the great witch hunt of 1668–76 and then the prolonged tail-off in the eighteenth century.

The answer as to which was the largest witch hunt in Europe is between the Blåkulla trials and the Basque witch trails in the early seventeenth century (which also involved children) and a handful of other persecutions. The best part of a thousand adults were accused of witchcraft in the spasm that wracked northern Sweden, with several thousand children involved in the process. In the course of only one week in the parish of Torsåker in Ångermanland, 72 people were executed in 1675, in the largest mass execution for witchcraft known in Scandinavia. The great witch hunt, which started in the province of Dalarna in 1668, may well have been preceded by a popular religious revival. The stories told about the sabbat were clearly interwoven with visionary tales of heaven and hell. The witch trials then spread to most of the northern provinces, and by 1675 had reached central Sweden, including Stockholm. In addition to the regular courts, special witchcraft commissions were appointed to steer proceedings. However, the temporary delegation of central power that the witchcraft commissions represented turned out to be a serious mistake, for it meant that decisive roles in the administration of justice were left to members of lower courts. Year after year, the appointed commissioners signally failed to control the rising hysteria about witchcraft. On the contrary, the attention the commissioners drew to the situation merely increased the general sense of panic, rather than allaying it.

Although these events are deservedly famous, the usual form taken by witchcraft trials in early modern Sweden was actually very different. Most cases concerned minor offences involving non-harmful magic; often they were brought by officials of the Crown, with the clergy particularly active as accusers; and, above all, Sweden stands out for its leniency, for very few trials resulted in a death sentence. In the first half of the seventeenth century, regional high courts were established. In principle, they had to approve all death sentences, including those for witchcraft. Gradually, it became a widespread practice for all types of witchcraft cases to be referred to the high courts. And, crucially, studies of praxis in the Göta High Court shows that the appellate courts very often changed or mitigated sentences.[15]

Moreover, a great number of these trials – perhaps even the majority – took place in the eighteenth century. Of more than 500 known cases of witchcraft in southern Sweden heard in the Göta High Court between 1635 and 1779, around three-quarters date from the eighteenth century, and involved some 1,100–1,200 individuals.[16] Most of these eighteenth-century cases concerned non-harmful magic, while the importance of the other cases steadily diminished.

The broadly conservative codification of Swedish law in 1734, which retained the death penalty for witchcraft, finally saw the introduction of an explicit treatment of superstition that may have helped perpetuate public interest in witchcraft and so contributed to the numerous eighteenth-century trials. The last execution for witchcraft, ostensibly at least for breaking the laws against *maleficium*, was in 1734. King Gustav III abolished the death penalty for witchcraft in 1779, and in the same year pacts with the Devil were placed on a par with ordinary superstition.

Finland

As in Sweden, so in Finland, at least when it came to the judicial situation.[17] After a distinct drop at the turn of seventeenth century, when the country was the scene of a protracted series of wars, the number of witchcraft cases began to accelerate in the 1630s and peaked in the 1670s and 1680s. The ensuing decrease then extended into the eighteenth century. So far the literature has found nothing equivalent to Sweden's numerous eighteenth-century cases that centred on superstition, even though by mid-century it seems there were some attempts to pursue magical crimes in the courts. Considering Finland's position as a fully integrated part of the Swedish kingdom, the absence of witchcraft cases in the eighteenth century is striking. The lack of central records from Åbo High Court (now Turku) makes a close analysis of the exact circumstances in eighteenth-century Finland difficult. The total number of cases in the seventeenth and eighteenth centuries is estimated to have been about 2,000, of which 150 resulted in death sentences. Of those, approximately half are thought to have been upheld by the Åbo High Court.[18]

As in Sweden, there was a relatively large proportion of cases that were not centred on maleficent witchcraft, but on superstition. There were a very limited number of Blåkulla trials, and then only in the predominantly Swedish-speaking areas such as Österbotten and the Åland Islands. Yet Finland also differs from Sweden proper in the high proportion of men among the accused – fully two-thirds in the sixteenth century – and in the east of the country this male dominance continued, even though the number of cases was low. In terms of visibility, it was women who played a greater role when the witch trials were at their peak. Until the 1660s, the trials had concerned maleficent witchcraft, in which men were in the majority. From that point onwards, however, women assumed an ever greater role, while the scope of the allegations broadened to include a wider spectrum of witchcraft cases, such as minor magic and consorting with the devil. Allegations of the latter increased as the Blåkulla trials spread from Sweden, with accusations made against some eighty people.

Ever since the publication in 1555 of Olaus Magnus' *Historia de gentibus septentrionalibus* (*A Description of the Northern Peoples*), Finland had been thought to be home to a great many warlocks. It is tempting to associate the predominance of men among those accused of witchcraft in Finland with the shamanistic elements of its folklore. Yet apart from Sami communities, shamanism had ceased to be a living tradition back in the Middle Ages, and thus was unlikely to have played much of a role in the witch trials of later years. Of far greater significance were Finland's witch doctors or seers, who occasionally found themselves before the courts accused of witchcraft, but they do not appear to have featured often as defendants, and their activities can only be glimpsed in the surviving court records. The question of 'male dominance' has been insufficiently studied, clearly, but its uniqueness fades somewhat in a comparison with Russia, where it was usual for those accused of witchcraft to be men. Perhaps what we are looking is a belt of proto-shamanism of sorts, stretching from Iceland across northern Norway to Finland and Russia.[19]

Iceland

In Iceland, as in the other Nordic countries, there were examples of medieval witchcraft trials.[20] As early as 1343, a nun was found guilty of having entered into a pact with the Devil. It was only towards the end of the sixteenth century, however, that witchcraft trials were held in any number. Thus in 1580 a woman was convicted of having kept a milk-thieving imp. The vast majority of trials came after 1630, the year in which the 1617 decree had finally been introduced in Iceland. Like Denmark, the Devil featured rarely, and most accusations instead concerned *maleficium*. Torture was not used in Iceland. Between 1593 and 1720, there were 134 known trials which involved 186 people, of whom 166 were men. A total of 22 were condemned to death and burned, including one woman. Plainly, in Iceland witchcraft was a male crime. The term usually found in the Icelandic court records was not 'witches', but rather 'cunning people', a group that in Iceland was predominately male. This dominance may have dated back to the medieval Norwegian laws against the almost pagan rituals in which men played a prominent role. In terms of geographical distribution, cases tended to be limited to the places where Iceland's few officials and clerics were to be found, and this despite it being usual to take holy orders in Denmark—the clergy's distance from their homeland seems to have left them less inhibited about involvement in witchcraft trials.

Witch hunts in Scandinavia – some reflections

Witch hunts in northern Europe varied considerably in intensity and chronology. Broadly speaking, the persecution in Denmark and its dependencies was pursued with greater brutality. To an extent, these patterns coincided with today's national borders. A closer look, however, reveals that national differences were often in fact regional ones, which meant that the nature of the witch trials could vary at least as much within a given country.

Paradoxically, continental Denmark, with its endless *maleficium* cases, exhibited in one sense a more archaic form of persecution than the lands of the Scandinavian peninsula proper, where the crime of witchcraft acquired a much more distinct ideological colouration. The Blåkulla trials in Sweden were so widespread that they were the acknowledged focus of diabolic witchcraft. Yet their sheer scale should not obscure the fact that, at the same time, there were also other accounts of witches' gatherings circulating in Scandinavia. In Norway, there was definite notion that witches gathered to inflict *maleficium* collectively, meaning that the charges against more than one individual could be justified without having to mention the Devil and without providing detailed descriptions of the sabbat.

The role of minor magic in the long run of Scandinavian witch hunts deserves particular emphasis, because this 'harmless' brand of sorcery was in fact in ideological terms the primary target of the state's and the Church's centuries-old battle against superstition. In the eighteenth century, the persecution of magic in Sweden would gradually acquire the same character as the Inquisition in southern Europe. At the same time, the Scandinavian trials of the late medieval period should not be overlooked; spanning both diabolism and minor magic as they did, they may indicate that, instead of a medieval prologue, they were the product of very real witch hunts, the extent of which is unknown, but not so very different from subsequent events in the early modern period.[21]

One way to shed light on the regional differences would be to establish the extent to which local interests were accommodated – one need only think of the bailiffs and priests in Norway and Sweden generally or, briefly, the Swedish witchcraft commissions appointed during the great witch hunt. The hiatus between the 1617 and 1665 decrees may explain some of the differences in the Scandinavian chronology. Norway, however, and particularly Finnmark with its later trials, do not quite fit this picture. Meanwhile, in Denmark and Sweden there were distinct discrepancies between the legislation and its workings. The decree of 1617 concentrated on magic per se and not the *maleficium* that was the focus of subsequent witchcraft trials. And in Sweden, although later developments reflected the harder line on superstition, the initial response was to throw themselves into the great Blåkulla trials.

The relationship between the legislation and the witch trials emphasizes the wider state-building process then underway. Against that, it is usually said that the crises of the early modern era, like the allegations of witchcraft themselves, sprang from everyday conflicts and tensions that were local in origin. The sudden surge in the number of witch trials in Denmark thus seems to antedate the decree of 1617 coming into force, and may instead have been linked to the period of high prices that had resulted in a decline in the once lucrative cattle trade, for example. Of all the Norwegian regions, meanwhile, Finnmark was where people were exposed to the greatest extremes of climate, hardship, privation, and danger. The outbreak of witch craze in Swedish Bohuslän followed a decline in the all-important herring fisheries. With regard to the witch hunts in northern Sweden, it is known that Dalarna, where the witch hunts began, was far from the peripheral province it would later become, but rather lay on an ancient and still busy route between Sweden and Norway. New findings have also shown that the main form of agriculture in much of northern Sweden – transhumant dairy farming and cattle breeding, in which women played the dominant role – saw a significant upturn at this point, and indeed may have been first introduced only very recently, after 1550.[22] Added to that was a noticeable surplus of women because of Sweden's interminable wars. It was perhaps not a coincidence that the children who gave evidence in court referred time and again to the ostentation and flamboyance of the women who gathered at Blåkulla – signs of social inequality that seem to have touched a nerve in the more egalitarian and less feudal north of the country, with its lived culture that all but embodied the theory of limited good. At the same time, it is obvious that the capitalist elements in the rural economy were dependent on the Swedish government's expansive war economy, thus bringing the state into the picture again. And Finnmark and Bohuslän were areas where the political rivalry between Denmark and Sweden was most marked.

In the wider Nordic context, one must necessarily draw attention to the men who were accused of witchcraft, particularly in cases of minor magic and *maleficium*. For all the talk of male dominance, of course, was only really true of Iceland. In Finland, a significant number of women were caught up in the most dynamic – and late – phase of the witch hunts. A wider comparison is revealing, for in Sweden in the same period an increasing number of men, not women, were accused; paradoxically, as a result of the legislation that singled out superstition as a crime.[23]

Finally, it was Sweden's chronology that stands out. In all the Nordic countries, the witch hunts were all but over by the final years of the seventeenth century. Unlike other countries, however, in Sweden a large number of cases of minor magic continued to appear before the courts, and, while there were no more executions, they still complicate any discussion of the decriminalization of witchcraft.[24] In Sweden, the coercive state, to borrow Charles Tilly's term, worked hand in glove with the Church in its exercise of social control, and was sufficiently conservative to remain true to an ideological system long after it first emerged in the seventeenth century.

In the nineteenth century, cases of magical crime still appeared sporadically before the courts. The Blåkulla narrative took on new importance with a religious revival in Dalarna, which meant that early twentieth-century folklorists were able to interview people who claimed to have attended sabbats in their youth. In Swedish folklore, the old belief in witches lived on. The memory of actual witch hunts has been passed down in an oral tradition that still gives force to a range of familiar customs. Yet this ritualization was originally cemented in the early nineteenth century, when many people still believed that witches flew off to sabbats. This makes it difficult to argue that the whole business originated in childish pranks.[25] There is a very old, and much criticized, belief about the origins of the witches' sabbats that they were a response to an ancient fertility cult. It seems, however, that Sweden was the living proof of the British Egyptologist Margaret Murray's thesis, even though it was not the sabbat that was ritualized as much as the journey to it, the witches' ride. There is even an example from 1773 from the hundred of Lister, in Blekinge in southern Sweden, of people who were put on trial for witchcraft because they had pretended to be flying witches. At the very last, the stories of the witches' eldritch world found a basis in reality.

Notes

1 Stephen A. Mitchell, *Witchcraft and Magic in the Nordic Middle Ages* (Philadelphia: University of Pennsylvania Press, 2011).
2 Willem de Blécourt, "Sabbath Stories: Towards a new History of Witches' Assemblies," in *The Oxford Handbook of Witchcraft in Early Modern Europe and Colonial America*, ed. Brian P. Levack (Oxford: Oxford University Press, 2013), 84–100.
3 Mitchell, *Witchcraft and Magic*, 168–174.
4 Karsten Sejr Jensen, *Trolddom i Danmark 1500–1588* (Copenhagen: Noordisc Music & Text, 1988), 119; cf. Jens Christian V. Johansen, *Da Djævelen var ude: Trolddom i det 17. århundredes Danmark* (Odense: Univ. Forl., 1991), 34.
5 For the field as a whole, see Jens Christian V. Johansen, "Denmark: The Sociology of Accusations," in *Early Modern European Witchcraft: Centers and Peripheries*, ed. Bengt Ankarloo and Gustav Henningsen (Oxford: Clarendon Press, 1990), 339–365; Jens Christian V. Johansen, "Denmark," in *Encyclopedia of Witchcraft: The Western Tradition*, 4 vols., ed. Richard M. Golden (Santa Barbara: ABC-Clip, 2006), vol.1, 265–269; Bengt Ankarloo, "Witch-Trials in Northern Europe 1450–1700," in *Witchcraft and Magic in Europe: The Period of the Witch*, ed. Ankarloo and Stuart Clark (London: Athlone Press, 2002), 53–95.
6 Johansen, *Da Djævelen var ude*, 242–282 lists 676 individuals and cases.
7 Rune Blix Hagen, "Witchcraft Criminality and Witchcraft Research in the Nordic Countries," in *Oxford Handbook of Witchcraft*, ed. Brian P. Levack (Oxford: University Press, 2013), 376; cf. earlier estimates, Gustav Henningsen, "Witchcraft in Denmark," *Folklore* 93 (1982): 135.
8 For a comparative study of the Danish pattern with few cases heard, see Louise Nyholm Kallestrup, *Agents of Witchcraft in Early Modern Italy and Denmark* (Basingstoke: Palgrave Macmillan, 2015).
9 Hand Eivind Næess, "Norway: The Criminological Context," in *Early Modern European Witchcraft*, ed. Bengt Ankarloo and Gustav Henningsen (Oxford: Clarendon Press, 1990), 367–382; Hand Eivind Næess, "Norway," in *Encyclopedia of Witchcraft: The Western Tradition*, 4 vols., ed. Richard M. Golden, vol. 3, 836–839; Ankarloo, "Witch-Trials," 53–95. Several points made in these works are nuanced by Hagen, "Witchcraft Criminality," 385–391.
10 The total number of trials is estimated to have been about 1,400, with about a quarter of all defendants executed. Over the years, the figures have been revised somewhat; see Gunnar W. Knutsen, "Norwegian Witchcraft Trials: A Reassessment," *Continuity & Change* 18.2 (2003): 185–200.
11 For example, see Ragnhild Botheim, *Trolldomsprosessene i Bergenhus len 1566–1700* (Bergen: Universitetet i Bergen, 1999), 59.
12 Hagen, "Witchcraft Criminality," 385–391.
13 Liv Helene Willumsen, "Children Accused of Witchcraft in Seventeenth-Century Finnmark," *Scandinavian Journal of History* 38.1 (2013): 18–41.
14 For an overview of Swedish witch hunts *in toto*, see Per Sörlin, "Sweden," in *Encyclopedia of Witchcraft: The Western Tradition*, 4 vols., ed. Richard M. Golden, vol. 4, 1092–1096; for the seventeenth century, see Bengt Ankarloo, "Sweden: The Mass Burnings (1668–76)," in *Early Modern European Witchcraft: Centers and Peripheries*, ed. Bengt Ankarloo and Gustav Henningsen (Oxford: Clarendon Press, 1990), 285–318; Ankarloo, "Witch-Trials," 53–95.
15 Per Sörlin, *Wicked Arts: Witchcraft Trials in Southern Sweden, 1635–1754* (Leiden: Brill, 1999), 63–82.

16 Sörlin, *Wicked Arts*, 20.
17 For overviews, see Marko Nenonen, "Finland," in *Encyclopedia of Witchcraft: The Western Tradition*, 4 vols., ed. Richard M. Golden, vol. 2, 373–377; Antero Heikkinen and Timo Kervinen, "Finland: The Male Domination," in *Early Modern European Witchcraft: Centers and Peripheries*, ed. Bengt Ankarloo and Gustav Henningsen (Oxford: Clarendon Press, 1990), 319–337; Ankarloo, "Witch-Trials," 53–95; Nenonen is the only one to draw attention to the period after 1700.
18 Nenonen, "Finland," 373 and 376; Heikkinen and Kervinen, "Finland," 321, give the figures as 710 trials and 115 death sentences.
19 Rune Blix Hagen, "Witchcraft and Ethnicity: A Critical Perspective on Sami Shamanism in Seventeenth-Century Northern Norway," in *Writing Witch Hunt Histories: Challenging the Paradigm*, ed. Marko Nenonen and Raisa Maria Toivo (Leiden: Brill, 2014), 141–166; Raisa Maria Toivo, "Gender, Sex and Cultures of Trouble in Witchcraft Studies: European Historiography With Special Reference to Finland," in *Writing Witch Hunt Histories: Challenging the Paradigm,* ed. Marko Nenonen and Raisa Maria Toivo (Leiden: Brill, 2014), 87–108.
20 For overviews, see Ólína Fiordvardardottír, 'Iceland', in Golden, *Encyclopedia of Witchcraft*, ii. 533; Magnús Rafnsson, *Angurgapi: The Witch hunts in Iceland* (Hólmavik, 2003); Kirsten Hastrup, 'Iceland: Sorcerers and Paganism', in Ankarloo and Henningsen, *Early Modern European Witchcraft*, 383–401.
21 Sörlin, *Wicked Arts*, 3.
22 Jesper Larsson, *Fäbodväsendet 1550–1920: Ett centralt element i Nordsveriges jordbrukssystem* (Östersund: Jamtli-Förl., 2009), 386–388.
23 Sörlin, *Wicked Arts*, 119 f.
24 Gunnar W. Knutsen, "The End of Witch Hunts in Scandinavia," *ARV: Nordic Yearbook of Folklore* 62 (2006): 143–164.
25 Fredrik Skott, *Påskkäringar: Från trolldomstro till barnupptåg* (Gothenburg: Dialekt-, ortnamsoch folkminnesarkivet i Göteborg, 2013), passim, esp. 7–79.

Bibliography (selection)

Ankarloo, Bengt, "Witch Trials in Northern Europe 1450–1700." In *Witchcraft and Magic in Europe: The Period of the Witch Trials*, edited by Bengt Ankarloo, Stuart Clark, and William Monter, 53–96. London: Athlone Press, 2002; *Early Modern European Witchcraft*: Centers and Peripheries, edited by Bengt Ankarloo and Gustav Henningsen. Oxford: Clarendon Press, 1990, 339–365 .
Gent, Jacqueline Van, *Magic, Body and the Self in Eighteenth-Century Sweden*. Leiden: Brill, 2009.
Hagen, Rune Blix, "Witchcraft Criminality and Witchcraft Research in the Nordic Countries." In *The Oxford Handbook of Witchcraft in Early Modern Europe and Colonial America*, edited by Brian P. Levack, 375–392. Oxford: Oxford University Press, 2013.
Knutsen, Gunnar W., "Norwegian Witchcraft Trials: A Reassessment." *Continuity & Change* 18:2 (2003): 185–200.
Mitchell, Stephen A., *Witchcraft and Magic in the Nordic Middle Ages*. Philadelphia: University of Pennsylvania Press, 2011.
Nyholm Kallestrup, Louise, *Agents of Witchcraft in Early Modern Italy and Denmark*. Basingstoke: Palgrave Macmillan, 2015.
Sörlin, Per, *Wicked Arts: Witchcraft Trials in Southern Sweden, 1635–1754*. Leiden: Brill, 1999.
Toivo, Raisa Maria, *Faith and Magic in Early Modern Finland*. Basingstoke: Palgrave Macmillan, 2016.
Willumsen, Liv Helene, *The Witchcraft Trials in Finnmark, Northern Norway*. Bergen: Skald, 2010.

13

WITCH HUNTS IN EASTERN CENTRAL EUROPE

Petr Kreuz

Lands constituting the Crown of Bohemia

From the point of view of state law, the Lands of the Crown of Bohemia came into existence in the 14th century during the reign of Emperor Charles IV. The Lands of the Crown consisted of the Kingdom of Bohemia, the Markgraviate of Moravia, the Silesian principalities and the Markgraviates of Upper and Lower Lusatia. The head of state was the King of Bohemia. The Lands of the Crown of Bohemia were at the same time part of the Holy Roman Empire. Upper and Lower Lusatia ceased to be a part of the Lands of the Crown of Bohemia in 1635 and most of the Silesian principalities were separated from it in 1742. The population of the Lands of the Crown of Bohemia was mixed: Slavonic (mainly Czech) and German.

Bohemia (Kingdom of Bohemia)[1]

The former territory of Bohemia is today a constituent part of the Czech republic. From the 9th century onwards, the country was a principality, after 1198/1212 a kingdom. Early modern Bohemia was populated by Czechs with a sizeable German minority (especially in the Western frontier region).

Until the second half of the 15th century, there is no evidence for any legal proceedings against witches or sorcerers. Trials against alleged witches and sorcerers took place between the 1490s and the 1750s.[2] Bohemia witnessed the most intensive persecution in the last third of the 16th and throughout the 17th centuries.[3] Bohemia witnessed no long term or mass persecutions. In most trials for sorcery or witchcraft, there was only a single defendant.[4] The great majority of the Bohemian witch trials took place before the town courts of the royal and patrimonial towns, which constituted the basis of criminal justice in Bohemia since the second half of the 15th century.[5]

The Court of Appeal in Prague established itself in 1548. It heard appeals from all parts of the country, but in the criminal case on a large scale only since the 1680s. It had the power to confirm all the death sentences passed by all the lower courts of justice, including the town courts. The Prague Court of Appeal extended its jurisdiction into Moravia in 1700.[6]

Koldín's Town Code from 1579 was the first Czech law to define magic (sorcery/witchcraft) as a crime.[7] The 1707 Criminal Order of Emperor Joseph I. for Bohemia,

171

Moravia and *Silesia* (the so-called *Josephina*) was the first law that regulated the punishment for magic in any detail.[8]

The first known execution of a perpetrator of witchcraft (i.e. harmful magic) took place in Bohemia in 1498 in Kutná Hora (in German Kuttenberg).[9] In May of the same year, five women were executed for witchcraft in Prague.[10] The number of the witchcraft trials conducted in Bohemia increased gradually from the beginning of the 16th century onwards.[11] The execution rate began to rise in the 1540s.[12] The only major witch hunt in Bohemia took place in 1598: The nobleman Nicolaus of Bubna had 21 women burned at the stake or buried alive in a series of trials in his patrimonial town of Žamberk (Senftenberg) in East Bohemia.[13] In the series of sorcery trials conducted in the region of the Central Bohemian royal town of Nymburk in the years 1602–1617, 20 persons were investigated, with ten suffering capital sentences – among them three women.[14] The greatest child witch trial in Bohemia took place in 1644 in Prague, where 20 boys aged 8–17, mainly students of a Jesuit school, were suspected of invoking the devil.[15]

In Bohemia, magical crime was as a rule mere sorcery, i.e. malevolent magic without demonism. It was not before at the end of the 16th century that this crime acquired in some cases the character of the supercrime of cumulative witchcraft, including, besides harmful magic, contact with the devil, apostasy, the witch sabbath and membership in a sect-like secret organization. A relatively high share of such cases appears only from the middle of the 17th century onwards.[16]

The last known person to suffer capital punishment for magic in the Kingdom of Bohemia was one Jakub Trávníček, who died in 1749 in the South Bohemian patrimonial town of Milevsko (Mühlhausen).[17] In 1755, the shepherd Jakub Polák of the South Bohemian patrimonial small town of Jistebnice was sentenced to death for witchcraft. However, after the personal intervention of Empress Maria Theresa, he received a milder punishment in 1756. The witchcraft trials in Bohemia came to an end in the middle of the 1750s.[18]

The fragmentary sources suggest that about 400 persons were accused of magic in Bohemia in the late Middle Age and the early modern period; most of them suffered capital punishment.[19] However, this estimate is problematic. As we know that numerous source materials have been lost, the real number could have been more than twice as high.[20]

Moravia (Markgraviate of Moravia)[21]

The old principality of Moravia is today part of the Czech Republic. From the 10th century onwards, the country was a part of the Czech state, and from 1182 a Margraviate subject to the supremacy of the ruler of Bohemia. In the early modern period the country was ethnically predominantly Czech with a strong German minority (above all in the northern and southern border regions).

The first reliable evidence concerning a trial against malevolent magicians dates back to the middle of the fourteenth century. The trial took place in the Moravian capital Brno (Brünn). The town court ordered two women accused of sorcery to clear themselves of suspicion by swearing that they were innocent.[22] There were sporadic trials against sorcerers from the 1480s onwards.[23] The first person to suffer capital punishment was a woman who died in 1494 in the Southern Moravian town of

Uherské Hradiště (Ungarisch Hradisch).[24] The witch hunt in Moravia went on until the 1750s. From the middle of the 15th century to the end of 1720s, the basis of the court structure in Moravia were the town courts of royal towns, patrimonial towns and market towns. These courts heard the vast majority of all cases of magic which occurred in Moravia before 1648. After 1648, patrimonial courts made themselves more conspicuous in persecuting sorcery and witchcraft. As already mentioned, the Prague Court of Appeal had the power to sanction all capital trials conducted by all Moravian courts after 1700.[25]

The Northern Moravian towns treated magical offences according to the regulations of the Magdeburg law which was in force from the second half of the 13th until the 17th century. The town code of Koldín, which contains the first, more exact definition of the offense of magic (sorcery/witchcraft), was officially in force in all of Moravia only at the end of the 17th century.[26] As in Bohemia, the criminal order Emperor Joseph I (*Josephina*) issued in 1707 provided the first detailed regulations concerning magical crimes.[27]

In the years 1500–1505, Heinrich Kramer (Institoris), the author of the "Hammer of Witches" (*Malleus maleficarum*), operated in Moravia as a papal inquisitor. After his arrival in Moravia, he took up residence in the royal town of Olomouc (Olmütz), the seat of the Moravian episcopate. He lived in the Dominican St. Michael monastery. Institoris apparently remained in this monastery until his death in in Kroměříž (Kremsier) around 1505. Institoris published in two issues (1501 and 1502) two tractates directed against a group of heretics, the so-called Unitas fratrum (*jednota bratrská*).[28]

Until the middle of the 16th century, only a few witch trials took place in Moravia. The numbers began to grow in Moravia only in the 1570s.[29] Until the middle of the 17th century, we find in Moravia almost exclusively trials that focused on malevolent magic, usually with just one defendant.[30] The only known outstanding exception was a series of sorcery trials taking place in the patrimonial town of Velká Bíteš in the southwest of Moravia. Here, at least 30 women were executed for harmful magic between 1571 and 1576. Fifteen died in 1576 alone.[31] After the middle of the 17th century, there were almost no mass persecutions or long series of trials in Moravia, even though the neighbouring principality of Nysa in Silesia witnessed mass witch trials from the 1620s onwards.[32] The only, but massive, exception was the witchcraft panic in Northern Moravia between 1678 and 1696. The centre of these persecutions were the patrimonial towns of Velké Losiny (Groß Ullersdorf) and Šumperk (Mährisch Schönberg). The main witch hunter in these Northern Moravian witchcraft trials was the judge Heinrich Franz Boblig von Edelstadt (1611/1612, Zuckmantel/Zlaté Hory – 1698 Olomouc). He had studied law without obtaining a degree. It seems that Boblig had worked as a judge in the witch trials in the principality of Nysa in Silesia since the end of the 1630s. The best known victim of the witch trials in Northern Moravia was the dean of Šumperk, Christoph Alois Lautner (approximately 1622–1685), who was burned alive in September 1685 in the town of Mohelnice (Müglitz). Lautner was the only Catholic priest executed for witchcraft in the Czech/Bohemian lands. His trial lasted for five years. During the witch trials in Northern Moravia in the years 1678–1696, more than 100 people were executed, most of them women. This was the absolute high point of witch hunting in Moravia.[33]

Before 1678, the demonological concept of witchcraft had played hardly any role in Moravia.[34] The last phase of the Moravian witch hunts took place between the 1730s and the 1750s. It was accompanied by cases of alleged vampirism and vampire panics, the centre of which were the neighbouring Silesian principalities.[35]

It is still not known when Moravia passed the last death sentence for magic. Most likely, this happened sometime in the second quarter of the 18th century. The last known sorcery/witchcraft trial in Moravia took place in 1755 in Horní Město (Bergstadt) near Rýmařov (Römerstadt) in Northern Moravia: The tenant of the local mill, Thomas Manisar, was accused of having killed the director of a neighbouring manufacturing enterprise at Janovice by magic.[36]

The number of victims of the sorcery and witchcraft persecutions in Moravia may be estimated at about 300 to 400 persons, including the victims of the Northern Moravian hunts. Most trials ended with a death sentence. Given the considerable gaps in the source material – especially in the records of criminal courts – the real number of victims of the persecution in Moravia in 15th to 18th century could have been almost twice as high.[37]

Silesia (Silesian principalities)[38]

Today, Silesia belongs to Poland. Only parts of the former Upper Silesian principalities Opava (Troppau), Krnov (Jägerndorf), Těšín (Cieszyn, Teschen) and Nysa (Neisse) are in the Czech Republic. From the 14th century onwards, Silesia was a conglomerate of principalities subject directly or indirectly to the King of Bohemia (immediate and mediate principalities) and a constituent part of the Lands of the Crown of Bohemia. In 1742, the greater part of Silesia was annexed (by the so-called Breslau peace agreement) to the Kingdom of Prussia (with the exception of the principalities Těšín and parts of the principalities Opava, Krnov and Nysa). In the early modern period, Silesia was German with a Slavic minority (Czech at the frontier with Bohemia and Moravia and Polish in Upper Silesia and in the border region with the Kingdom of Poland).

Silesia was the part of the Lands of the Crown of Bohemia that suffered most from sorcery/witchcraft trials. The first known persecution in connection with the crime of magic took place in Silesia as early as 1456 in Wrocław (Breslau). Two women were condemned to drowning for using harmful spells.[39] The main part of the known persecutions before the 1550s took place in the capital of Silesia, Wrocław, as well.[40] The witch trials in Silesia ended in the 1750s.[41] The decades between the 1580s and the 1680s witnessed the most aggressive phase of witch hunting, including several mass witch hunts.[42]

The worst witch hunt in Silesia took place in three great waves in the years 1622, 1639–1641 and 1651–1652 in the Upper Silesian principality of Nysa.[43] During the last wave of these hunts, which rolled over the country from February 1651 to March 1652, more than 250 people, mostly women, were executed. Mainly responsible for the persecution was the Landeshauptmann (governor) of the principality of Nysa, Georg von Hoditz (died in 1661). The principality belonged to the bishop of Wrocław.[44] Fortunately, recent research has proven claims in the older literature to be false: It had been maintained that 23 children, including 17 very small children aged between 9 months and 6 years, were executed for witchcraft in 1651/52. We know now that all of the accused were adults.[45]

Other mass witch hunts occurred in the years 1663–1665 in the town Zielona Góra (Grünberg)[46] and in the neighbouring villages in the principality of Głogów (Glogau) in Lower Silesia.[47] This hunt led to more than 70 executions.[48] Most of the witchcraft was conducted by the town court in Zielona Góra and by the Landeshauptmann of the principality of Glogau, Franz von Barwitz (died in 1668).[49] Three waves of mass witch hunts in 1638, 1653–1654 and 1662 reached the Upper Silesian principality of Krnov (Jägerndorf), which belonged since the year 1623 to the princes of Liechtenstein. The last wave of this persecution claimed 25 victims.[50] More witch hunts, mainly ones that were only directed against individual suspects, took place in the 1650s and 1660s in two other Upper Silesian principalities: In the principality of Opava, belonging to the Liechtensteins and in the principality of Opole-Racibórz (Oppeln-Ratibor), at that time under the administration of the Crown of Poland.[51]

From the Middle Ages until the 17th century, Silesian towns mostly used Magdeburg Law. As subsidiary law sources, the *Carolina* (1532), later the Constitution of the Electorate of Saxony (1572) were in use.[52] A detailed and uniform legal regulation of the persecution of witchcraft was brought to Silesia only by the Criminal Order of Emperor Joseph I in 1707 (*Josephina*). In the regions annexed to the Kingdom of Prussia, the *Josephina* remained in force until 1794, and in the rest of the Austrian Silesia until 1770, when the Criminal Order of Empress Maria Theresa (*Theresiana*) was introduced.[53]

Responsible for the persecution of the sorcery/witchcraft in Silesia were the central courts of the principalities (under Landeshauptleute) and town courts of greater towns as well. Since 1548, the courts of the principalities and the towns and well as some other courts were *de iure* subject to the Court of Appeal in Prague. In practice the Prague Court of Appeal was only able to exercise decisive influence in some of the Silesian principalities.[54]

The late phase of the witch hunts after the end of the 17th century was in some of the Upper Silesian principalities accompanied by more numerous cases of alleged vampirism and vampire panics, which led to a *post mortem* burning of supposed witches and sorcerers as a rule after their exhumation.[55] The last execution for sorcery in Silesia took place in 1730 in Wrocław.[56] The last Silesian witch trial took place in 1757 in Wrocław as well, where a certain Paul Krottenbeck was condemned to two years in penitentiary.[57] Silesia witnessed a grand total of 444 trials for sorcery and witchcraft between 1456 and 1757. Some of the trials had more than one defendant: 593 persons suffered the death penalty, while 111 persons were sentenced to other, milder punishments or sent home.[58] Besides that, there were 264 other persons accused or investigated whose further fate is not known.[59] Most of them were probably executed, too. In these numbers are included trials against dozens of defendants which took place in the County of Kłodzko (Glatz), which never formed a part of the old Silesia. Kłodzko was regarded as a so-called outer region of the Kingdom of Bohemia. The Kingdom of Prussia annexed the county after the Peace of Breslau in 1742.[60]

Lusatia (Margraviates of Upper and Lower Lusatia)

The greater part of this region is in the southeast of today's Germany (Bundeslands Saxony and Brandenburg), the smaller part in the southwest of today's Poland. From the 14th century onwards, Lusatia was a constituent part of the Lands of the

Crown of Bohemia. Upper Lusatia (Oberlausitz) was acquired by the King of Bohemia in 1329, Lower Lusatia (Niederlausitz) in 1367. In 1635, Lusatia (in German Lausitz, in Upper Lusatian Łužica) was annexed to the Electorate of Saxony. Since the acquisition of Lusatia to its annexation to Saxony, the two Margraviates were as a rule directly subject to the Ruler of Bohemia, the chief administrator being the *Landvogt* (bailiff). In the early modern period Lusatia was an ethnically mixed, German-Slavonic region with the greater towns predominantly German, the countryside Slavic (Lusatian Serbs).

Lusatia was the region which did not witness extensive sorcery and witchcraft trials.[61] In both Margraviates, only 24 such trials took place between 1490 and 1698. Most trials happened after the cession of Lusatia to Saxony (1623/35): 24 persons were accused, among them 17 women. In eight cases the culprit suffered the death penalty, three died in prisons, five were exiled and three set free; as to the other cases, the outcome of the court proceedings is not known.[62]

Since the Middle Ages, town courts of the towns forming the so-called *Hexapolis* (Oberlausitzer Sechsstädtebund), i.e. the towns Bautzen (in Upper Lusatian Budišin), Löbau (in Upper Lusatian Lubij), Kamenz (in Upper Lusatian Kamjenc), Görlitz (in Polish Zgorzelec, in Upper Lusatian Zhorjelc), Zittau (in Upper Lusatian Žitawa) and Lauban (in Polish and Upper Lusatian Lubań), played an important role in the judicature of Upper Lusatia. Upper Lusatia was divided after the annexation by Saxony into Bautzener and Görlitzer Hauptkreis (main districts of Bautzen and Görlitz).[63] In Upper Lusatia, 14 sorcery trials took place between 1490 and 1698. The first trial took place in Görlitz. The culprit, a Niklas Weller, suffered capital punishment; he was thus the first person to be sentenced to death for malevolent magic in Upper Lusatia and all of the Lusatia.[64] The last trial in Upper Lusatia (and in the whole of Lusatia) took place in Zittau: The two female culprits died in prison in 1698 before the town court could pass a verdict.[65]

In Lower Lusatia, ten trials for sorcery and witchcraft took place between 1534 and 1667.[66] Most trials accumulated in the years 1619 and 1622 when the *Landvogt* of Lower Lusatia, one Heinrich Anshelm von Promnitz, brought successive charges against five persons. Four of them were executed and one died in prison because of the torture.[67] The first trial in Lower Lusatia took place in 1534 on the manorial estate Pförten (in Lower Lusatian Brody), whose proprietor, Ludomilla von Schönburg, widowed von Biberstein, lost her eyesight and accused a certain Kethe Sthone of causing her illness by magic.[68] The last Lower Lusatian trials took place in the years 1655–1657 at the manorial estate Dobrilugk (also Doberlug, in Lower Lusatian Dobrjolug). The 70-year-old Dorothea Hille and her husband were accused. Dorothea died in prison due to the consequences of torture, whereas her husband was finally set free because of a lack of sufficient evidence.[69]

The Lusatian towns used mainly Magdeburg Law from the Middle Ages. After the annexation to Saxony, the Constitutions of the Electorate of Saxony (1572) were in force, making the pact with the devil a capital offence.[70]

From the year 1548 until the cession to Saxony, the town courts of both Lusatian margraviates were *de iure* subject to the Court of Appeal in Prague.[71] It appears that only in one case was a Lusatian sorcery trial actually brought to the attention of the Prague court in 1564.[72] In accordance with Saxon practice, Lusatian courts requested expert opinions in witchcraft cases from the *Schöppenstuhl* (Court of Appeal) in

Leipzig, the Faculty of Law of the University of Wittenberg and the Faculty of Law of the University of Frankfurt/Oder.[73]

Slovakia (Upper Hungary)[74]

From a geographical point of view, Slovakia is identical to the territory of today's Slovak Republic, which came into existence after the division of Czechoslovakia in January 1993. It is not a traditional historical territory, but it covers notwithstanding to a great degree the territory designated as Upper Hungary in the Middle Ages and early modern age and which was in the years 1018–1918 part of the Kingdom of Hungary. In the early modern period, the territory was predominantly Slavic save for ethnically Hungarian Southern Slovakia. In some greater towns, ethnic Germans played an important role in the Middle Ages and in the early modern period.

The sorcery and witchcraft trials which took place in the territory of today's Slovakia belong to a period extending from the beginning of the 16th century to the 1750s. The persecution in Slovakia culminated in the decades roughly between 1670 and 1730.[75]

The first reliably documented sorcery/witch trial took place in 1517 in the royal town of Košice (Kaschau/Kassa) in Southeastern Slovakia. It did not end with a death sentence.[76] Until the middle of the 17th century, there were no series of trials in Slovakia. Only a few culprits suffered the death penalty.[77] These trials took place in Baňská Štiavnica (Schemnitz/Selmecbánya) in 1520 and 1581, in Komárno (Komorn/Komárom) in 1589, in Bratislava (Preßburg/Pozsony) in 1602,[78] in Bardejov (Bartfeld/Bártfa) 1629 and in Spiš (Zips/Szepes) in 1636.[79]

The courts responsible for most trials were the town and shire (*župa*) courts (the so-called *sedriae*). Ecclesiastical courts heard a relatively higher number of sorcery and witchcraft trials.[80]

The greatest number of trials in Slovakia took place in the ethnically Slavic town Krupina in Middle Slovakia (Karpfen/Korpona).[81] In the years 1662–1744, there were brought to trial at least 68 persons (mainly women), of whom at least 36 (among them one man) burned at the stake, be it alive or after being decapitated. There were series of trials in Krupina: In 1662 six persons were executed. In 1675, at least 13 persons were brought to trial, 11 of them executed. In 1716, seven were accused, six executed. In 1718, there were investigations against 16 people and one execution.[82] The last person to be executed in Krupina was a certain Dorota Koziarová, burned alive at the stake as late as 1741.[83]

A mass witch trial took place in the ethnically predominantly Hungarian royal town of Šamorín (Sommerein/Somorja) in Southern Slovakia. Twenty-one women were charged with witchcraft. Some of the verdicts are now lost, but it seems that only one of the women standing trial was executed. In November 1691, a certain Anna Maria Haczel alias Wolffin was decapitated, her body burned. Some other charged women were heavily fined: The fine was 100 florins.[84]

In the years 1716–1747, the shire court (*sedria*) in Trenčín (in Hungarian Trenczén) found at least 23 persons (among them four men) guilty of witchcraft. Most of these persons were sentenced to death and executed (as a rule burned at the stake after previous beheading).[85] At least 19 persons (two of them male) were brought to trial before the *sedria* of the shire of Turiec (in German Turz, in Hungarian Turóc) between 1674 and 1749.[86] We know of only two sorcery trials conducted in 1727 before the *sedria* of the Orava (Arwa/Árva) shire. The two female defendants did not suffer capital punishment but were sentenced to milder punishments.[87]

The shires Trenčín, Turiec and Orava lay in the northeast of Slovakia and were ethnically Slavic. The last known execution for witchcraft in the ethnically Slavic territory of Slovakia took place in 1745, when the shire court in Trenčín had a certain Dorota Kalmová from Střeženice burned at the stake.[88] The last execution for magic in Slovakia that is reliably documented was carried out in 1750 in the then ethnically predominantly Hungarian royal town of Košice.[89] The last known sorcery/witchcraft trial in the ethnically Slavic territory of Slovakia took place in the years 1748–1749 before the court of the Turiec shire against Sophia Ivanka, widow of Juraj (Georgius) Záturecký.[90] Older research literature maintained that there had been a trial in Northern Slovakia in the (ethnically mixed) royal town of Kežmarok (Käsmark/Késmárk) as late as 1777. This would have been the last witch trial in Slovakia (and consequently in the whole Kingdom of Hungary). However, the date of the trial is wrong; the case in question took place in 1717.[91]

Sorcery, witchcraft and their persecution in medieval and early modern Slovakia are still awaiting a full systematic analysis by historians. For the time being the numbers of victims of the witch hunts in Slovakia can be estimated at 200 to 300 persons. Most of them were executed. As many sources have been lost, especially those from the 16th century, the real numbers of victims might have been up to 100% higher.[92]

Poland

Poland was a principality from the second half of the 10th century on and a kingdom since 1025. In 1386, the personal union of the Kingdom of Poland with the Grand Duchy of Lithuania (including today's Lithuania and Belarus, the greater part of the existing Ukraine and a part of modern Latvia) was created. The year 1569 witnessed the birth of the Polish-Lithuanian double state (real union) which existed until the so-called division of Poland (1772–1795). The region has a predominantly Slavic population (mainly ethnic Poles).

Record of ecclesiastical courts mention cases of sorcery in the 14th and 15th centuries.[93] The earliest regulations concerning the prosecution of magic appear in Polish synodal statutes in 1279.[94] Since the 16th century, most cases of sorcery and witchcraft were dealt with by secular, mainly town, courts.[95] Until recently, the prevailing opinion was that a constitution of the Polish *Sejm* (Parliament) from the year 1543 conferred the cases in which a person charged with witchcraft should have caused material harm, malady or death to the secular, first of all town, courts.[96] This is at least misleading: The town courts in Poland had the power to prosecute witchcraft on the basis of the regulations of the medieval Magdeburg Law and the *Sachsenspiegel* (*Speculum Saxoniae*).[97]

The number of persons put to death in the sorcery/witchcraft trials in Poland was once estimated at about several thousand, indeed up to 30,000 persons.[98] The expert literature accepted for a long time the estimate of Polish historian Bohdan Baranowski (1915–1993), who wrote in 1952 that the number of victims in Poland was 15,000.[99] Later on, Baranowski reduced his estimate to several thousand persons.[100]

Since the seventies, estimates as to numbers of executed in the sorcery/witchcraft trials in the Kingdom of Polonia oscillated between several hundred and a few thousand persons.[101] Baranowski counted two types of trials as witch trials: Firstly witchcraft trials proper (i.e. cases of *maleficium*), and secondly the much more numerous law suits brought against persons who defamed others as witches.[102] More recently, two estimates were published which were based on different data. The lowest estimate (M. Ostling) is 254 trials. (This number includes the relatively few trials in the region of the so-called Red Russia/Red Ruthenia; in Latin *Russia Rubra* or *Ruthenia Rubra*, later Eastern Galicia, today the west of the Ukraine.) In these trials, charges against 509 persons were brought, more than 90% of them women. At least 248 of them were put to death. With regard to the fact that the verdict is in many cases not known, the execution rate might have approached 65%. Those who survived their trials were exiled, flogged, fined or simply sent home. Two hundred and twenty-five of these trials, with 455 defendants and 245 executions, probably took place before the town courts.[103] The higher estimate (M. Pilaszek) states there were 867 trials with 1,316 defendants and 558 executions.[104] Both estimates furnish numbers lower by one or two numeric orders than those stated by Baranowski.[105] Considering the enormous losses of archive material and the complete destruction of the archives of many towns, it isn't groundless an estimate of at about 2,000 victims of the witchcraft trials in the territory of the Kingdom of Poland during the 16th–18th century.

The first known execution for magic took place in Poland before the ecclesiastical court of Waliszewo in 1511.[106] The first execution following the verdict of a secular court was carried out only in 1544 in Poznań (Posen).[107] Only since the second half of the 16th century was the pact with the devil sporadically mentioned in Polish trials; allusions to sabbath were even rarer.[108] Witchcraft trials that mention sexual intercourse with demons appear for the first time in 1582 (Poznań)[109] and for the second time in 1613 (Kalisz);[110] but the trials did not occur more frequently until the 1640s.[111] More detailed descriptions of the witches' sabbath appear as far as the Polish trials are concerned only in the second half of the 17th century.[112]

The sorcery/witchcraft trials took place between 1511 and 1775. The overwhelming majority of trials occurred in the years 1650–1725. The witch persecutions in Poland culminated in the last quarter of the 17th century: There were 75 trials, with 151 defendants and 83 executions (estimate of M. Ostling). The persecutions continued with almost the same intensity during the first quarter of the 18th century. The persecution reached an especially high intensity in the towns of Greater Poland (*Wielkopolska*, in Latin *Polonia Maior* – west of the Kingdom of Poland) and in Lesser Poland (*Małopolska*, in Latin *Polonia Minor* – southeast of the existing Poland).[113] The local town courts had the highest execution rate.[114] A considerably smaller number of trials took place in Royal Prussia (north of actual Poland), in Mazovia (*Mazowsze* – northeast of the existing Poland) and in Red Russia, too.[115] The greatest Polish witch hunt ever took place in Greater Poland in the town of Kleczew (Lehmstädt). In this town, 47 trials took place between 1624 and 1738. One hundred and thirty-one persons were accused, of whom at least 92 were executed. The years 1682–1700 alone witnessed 41 of these executions.[116] Sixty trials occurred between the years 1675 and 1711 in the town Fordon (today a part of the town of Bydgoszcz) in Greater Poland.[117] At least a dozen witch trials were conducted in the years 1698–1722 by the court in the town Nieszawa (Nessau).[118] The court in the Greater Poland town of Łobżenica (Lobsens) sent 36 witches to the stake in the 17th century, the majority of them in the years 1675–1700.[119] In the Greater Poland town of Grodzisk (Grätz), five trials with more than one defendant took place between 1700 and 1720; at least 20 died.[120] Before the town court of Nowe nad Wisłą (in German Neuenburg in Westpreussen), 27 trials occurred during the years 1701–1719.[121] The town court of Płońsk (Plöhnen) brought charges against 44 persons, at least 26 of whom were executed between 1699 and 1713.[122] Other centres of the witch hunts were the towns Kalisz (Kalisch) (1650–1680),[123] Gniezno (Gnesen) (1670–1690)[124] and Poznań.[125] There was no significant decline in the witch hunts in Poland before 1725.[126]

Witchcraft defamations with a political motive emerged in the middle of the 16th century at the court of the Polish King Sigismud II August us (1520–1572, reigned 1548–1572). The accusations were also directed against the king's mother, Bona Sforza (1494–1557), who descended from Lombardy, and the king's second wife, Barbara Radziwiłłówna (1520–1551), who was suspected of using love magic.[127]

The Polish *Sejm* decided in 1776 on the abolition of torture and stopped the witch trials in Poland and in the whole of the Polish-Lithuanian union.[128] For a long time, the opinion prevailed that this step had been taken because of the scandal caused by the spectacular execution of 14 alleged witches, which was said to have happened in 1775 in the small town of Doruchów (about 30 kilometres south of Kalisz) in Greater Poland.[129] However, it could be demonstrated that the trial in Doruchów had taken place before 1769 and that there had been only six female defendants, all of whom might have survived their trials.[130] There was a long and difficult controversy over the alleged burning of two witches in Poznań in 1793. This case appeared in some of the older literature as the last (legal) execution for witchcraft in Europe. Polish historians rejected the case as a product of contemporary German (Prussian) propaganda.[131] The last witch trial in Poland took place apparently in 1775 in Grabów. Isolated lynching cases for witchcraft did occur in the first half of the 19th century.[132]

The first vernacular language the *Malleus maleficarum* was translated into was Polish. Stanislaw Zambonis, the secretary to the castellan of Cracow, published translation of the second part of the "Hammer" (in Polish *Młot na czarownice*) in Cracow (Kraków) in 1614.[133] In the 17th century, several works of Polish authors who sharply criticized the court proceedings in witchcraft trials appeared in Poland. In 1639, an anonymous tractate, *Czarownica powolana*, was published that was strongly influenced by Friedrich Spee's *Cautio Criminalis*.[134]

In Eastern Prussia (the so-called Prince's Brandenburg Prussia), which lay in the territory of today's Northeast Poland and existing Kaliningrad (Königsberg) territory of Russia, we find 358 witch trials which took place in the years 1534–1739 plus one more trial that dates from 1788. Charges were brought against 511 persons, most of them female. At least 164 persons (i.e. 32%) were executed, 148 women and 16 men.[135]

The witch persecutions culminated in Eastern Central Europe and Eastern Europe later than in West and South Europe and in western parts of the Holy Roman Empire: It happened as a rule in the second half of the 17th century or even in the first third of the 18th century. Only from the second half of the 17th century were the trials in Eastern Central Europe (Bohemia, Moravia, Slovakia, Poland, today's Lithuania) influenced by Western demonology to a significant degree. Mass witch hunts remained the exception.

Notes

1 General survey: Petr Kreuz, "Bohemia, Kingdom of," in *Encyclopedia of Witchcraft: The Western Tradition*, 4 vols., ed. Richard Golden (Santa Barbara: ABC-Clio, 2006), 134–135.

2 Josef Kočí, *Čarodějnické procesy. Z dějin inkvizice a čarodějnických procesů v českých zemích v 16.-18. století* (Praha: Horizont, 1973), 45–169; Bedřich Šindelář, "Konec ,honu na čarodějnice' v tereziánské době u nás," *Sborník prací filozofické fakulty brněnské univerzity*, series C 17 (1970): 99–107; Bedřich Šindelář, "Čarodějnictví a jeho pronásledování u nás do r. 1526," *Sborník prací filozofické fakulty brněnské univerzity*, series C 28 (1981): 177–206; Bedřich Šindelář, *Hon na čarodějnice. Západní a střední Evropa v 16.-17 století* (Praha: Svoboda, 1986), 170–218; Kreuz, "Bohemia, Kingdom of," 134–135; Petr Kreuz, "Der Einfluss des Rechtssystems und der Gerichtsorganisation auf Entwicklung, Dynamik und Formen der Hexenprozesse in den böhmischen Ländern," in *Hexenforschung aus den österreichischen Ländern*, ed. Heide Dienst (Münster: LIT Verlag, 2009), 231–236; Petr Kreuz, "Die späten Hexenprozesse in den böhmischen Ländern und auf dem Gebiet der heutigen Slowakei," in *Späte Hexenverfolgungen. Der Umgang der Aufklärung mit dem Irrationalen*, ed. Wolfgang Behringer, Sönke Lorenz, and Dieter R. Bauer (Bielefeld: Verlag für Regionalgeschichte, 2016), 167–203.

3 Kreuz, "Der Einfluss des Rechtssystems und der Gerichtsorganisation," 233–234; Kreuz, "Die späten Hexenprozesse," 169–170.

4 Kreuz, "Der Einfluss des Rechtssystems und der Gerichtsorganisation," 233–235; Kreuz, "Die späten Hexenprozesse," 169–172.

5 Kreuz, "Der Einfluss des Rechtssystems und der Gerichtsorganisation," 249–253.

6 Recently summarized Petr Kreuz, "Das Appellationsgericht in Prag 1548–1783. Bisherige Forschung, erhaltene Quellen und historische Entwicklung," in *In letzter Instanz. Appellation und Revision im Europa der Frühen Neuzeit (= Beiträge zur Rechtsgeschichte Österreichs*, vol. 1, ed. Leopold Auer, Eva Ortlieb, and Ellen Franke (Wien: Kommission für Rechtsgeschichte Österreichs der ÖAW, 2013), 231–250.

7 Kreuz, "Der Einfluss des Rechtssystems und der Gerichtsorganisation," 236–237.

8 Ibid., 237–239.

9 Josef Macek, *Jagellonský věk v českých zemích (1471–1526). Vol. 4 Venkovský lid. Národnostní otázka* (Praha: Academia, 1999), 77; Petr Kreuz, "Kouzelnictví a jeho pronásledování v jagellonské Praze. Příspěvek k počátkům kouzelnických a čarodějnických procesů v Čechách," *Pražský sborník historický* 40 (2012): 135.

10 Kreuz, "Kouzelnictví," 135–136.

11 Šindelář, Bedřich. "Čarodějnictví," 202–204; Macek, *Jagellonský*, 71–82; Kreuz, "Der Einfluss des Rechtssystems und der Gerichtsorganisation," 232–233; Kreuz, "Kouzelnictví," 135–143; Kreuz, "Die späten Hexenprozesse," 169–170; cf. too Josef Svátek, "Hexenprocesse in Böhmen," in *Culturhistorische Bilder aus Böhmen*, ed. Josef Svátek (Wien: Wilhelm Braumüller, 1879), 1–40.

12 Kreuz, "Der Einfluss des Rechtssystems und der Gerichtsorganisation," 232–233; Kreuz, "Die späten Hexenprozesse," 169–170.

13 Šindelář, *Hon na čarodějnice*, 247; Lambrecht, *Hexenverfolgung*, 304, 477; Kreuz, "Die späten Hexenprozesse," 170.

14 Petr Kreuz, "Čarodějnické procesy na Nymbursku na počátku 17. století," *Právněhistorické studie* 34 (1997): 127–161.

15 Kočí, *Čarodějnické procesy*, 69–81; Petr Kreuz, "'Oh Bock! Oh Teufel!' Teufelsbeschwörung auf der Prager Kleinseite im Jahre 1644," *@KIH-eSkript* 3 (2011): 50–60, www.historicum.net/themen/hexenforschung/akih-eskript/heft-3-2011/art/Oh_Bock_Oh/html/ca/05c35381f7fffa5addf 4c71827589c6e/; Petr Kreuz, "Vyvolávání ďábla v jezuitské škole na Malé Straně roku 1644. Dětský čarodějnický proces?," in *Děti ve velkoměstech od středověku až na práh industriální doby (= Documenta Pragensia 31, 2012)*, ed. Olga Fejtová, Václav Ledvinka, and Jiří Pešek (Praha: Archiv hlavního města Prahy, 2012), 371–394.

16 Kreuz, "Der Einfluss des Rechtssystems und der Gerichtsorganisation," 232–242.

17 Kreuz, "Die späten Hexenprozesse," 184–185.

18 Šindelář, "Konec," 93–96; Šindelář, *Hon na čarodějnice*, 215–216; Kreuz, "Die späten Hexenprozesse," 185–187.

19 Kreuz, "Die späten Hexenprozesse," 203.

20 Petr Kreuz, "Poznámky k problematice pramenné základny ke studiu dějin kouzelnických a čarodějnických procesů v českých zemích v pozdním středověku a raném novověku," *Folia Historica Bohemica* 25 (2010): 93–115, esp. 94–101.

21 In general: Petr Kreuz, "Moravia," in *Encyclopedia of Witchcraft. The Western Tradition*, 4 vols., ed. Richard Golden (Santa Barbara: ABC-Clio, 2006), 785–787.

22 Šindelář, "Čarodějnictví," 193–194; Šindelář, *Hon na čarodějnice*, 171.

23 Kamila Rojčíková, "Čarodějnické procesy na Moravě do roku 1648," *Časopis Matice moravské* 120 (2001): 189–190 and 202.

24 Rojčíková, "Čarodějnické," 189–190 and 202.

25 Kreuz, "Der Einfluss des Rechtssystems und der Gerichtsorganisation," 251–253.

26 Kreuz, "Moravia," 785; Kreuz, "Der Einfluss des Rechtssystems und der Gerichtsorganisation," 251–252.

27 Kreuz, "Der Einfluss des Rechtssystems und der Gerichtsorganisation," 237–239.

28 Recently summarized by Petr Kreuz, "Heinrich Kramer/Institoris and Czech Lands. With special regard to Institoris' activities in Olomouc in 1499–1505," *e-Rhizome. Journal of the Study od Religion, Culture, Society and Cognition* 2019, vol. 1: 23–59; Tamar Herzig, *Christ transformed into a Virgin woman. Lucia Brocadelli, Heinrich Institoris and the defense of the faith* (Rome: Edizioni di Storia e Letteratura, 2013), esp. 80–82; cf. too Antonín Kubíček, "Jindřich Institoris, papežský inkvizitor v Čechách a na Moravě," *Časopis katolického duchovenstva* 63 (1902): 20–26, 115–120, 222–226, 320–325, 372–378, 491–500, 521–525; Amedeo Molnár, "Protivaldenská polemika na úsvitu 16. století," *Historická Olomouc a její současné problémy* 3 (1980): 153–174; Macek, *Jagellonský věk*, 74–75; Kreuz, "Moravia," 785; Kreuz, "Die späten Hexenprozesse," 172.

29 Rojčíková, "Čarodějnické," 202–205.

30 Ibid., 205–206.

31 Antonín Verbík and Ivan Štarha, eds., *Smolná kniha velkobítešská 1556–1636* (Brno: Blok, 1973), 99–106 and 109–126; Kamila Rojčíková, "Magické praktiky velkobítešských čarodějnic," *Západní Morava* 4 (2000): 149–154; Rojčíková, "Čarodějnické," 203; Kamila Svobodová (= Rojčíková), "Magické praktiky čarodějnic na Moravě a ve Slezsku do poloviny 17. století," *Vlastivědný věstník moravský* 55 (2003): 394–402; Leona Králíková, "Čarodějnictví na Žďársku (Velký případ z roku 1571)," *Západní Morava* 22 (2018): 16–38.

32 Lambrecht, *Hexenverfolgung*, 92–204.

33 Recently summarized by František Spurný, Vojtěch Cekota, and Kouřil Miloš, *Šumperský farář a děkan Kryštof Alois Lautner, oběť čarodějnických inkvizičních procesů.* (Šumperk: Městský úřad Šumperk a římskokatolická farnost v Šumperku, 2000); cf. too Eduard Teichmann, *Rennaisance und Hexenwahn mit besonderer Berücksichtigung der Verbrennung Lautners in Müglitz* (Hohenstadt: Burschofsky, 1932); Václav Medek, "'Čarodějnický děkan' Kryštof Alois Lautner," *Severní Morava* 13 (1966): 9–18; Kočí, *Čarodějnické procesy*, 97–130; Rudolf Zuber, "K čarodějnickým procesům ve Velkých Losinách," *Severní Morava* 26 (1973): 60–66; Šindelář, *Hon na čarodějnice*, 187–211; Kreuz, "Die späten Hexenprozesse," 173–181.

34 Kočí, *Čarodějnické procesy*, 131–134; Šindelář, "Konec," 90–92; Kreuz, "Die späten Hexenprozesse," 182–183.

35 Kočí, *Čarodějnické procesy*, 151–153; Šindelář, "Konec," 92–93; Šindelář, *Hon na čarodějnice*, 214–215; Lambrecht, *Hexenverfolgung*, 383–401.

36 Šindelář, "Konec," 95–96; Šindelář, *Hon na čarodějnice*, 216; Kreuz, "Die späten Hexenprozesse," 187.

37 Kreuz, "Moravia," 785; Kreuz, "Die späten Hexenprozesse," 203.

38 In general: Ludolf Pelizaeus, "Silesia," in *Encyclopedia of Witchcraft: The Western Tradition*, 4 vols., ed. Richard Golden (Santa Barbara: ABC-Clio, 2006), 1038–1040.

39 Lambrecht, "Hexenverfolgung," 319 and 467.

40 Ibid., 318–322 and 467–474.

41 Ibid., 467–516.

42 Ibid., esp. 345–349 and 402–415.

43 Ibid., 92–204.

44 Ibid., 148–192; Bedřich Šindelář, "Příspěvek k dějinám slezských procesů s čarodějnicemi se zvláštním zřetelem k procesům frývaldovským v letech 1651–1684," *Slezský sborník* 44 (1946): 65–80; Šindelář, *Hon na čarodějnice*, 184–185 and 247–248.

45 Petr Kreuz and Zuzana Haraštová, "Nejmladší popravená evropská čarodějnice? K otázce dětských obětí ve slezských čarodějnických procesech v letech 1651–1652," *Slezský sborník* 110 (2012): 5–26; Petr Kreuz and Zuzana Haraštová, "Hexenkinder in den böhmischen Ländern und im Gebiet der heutigen Tschechischen Republik," in *Hexenkinder – Kinderbanden – Straßenkinder*, ed. Wolfgang Behringer and Claudia Opitz-Belakhal (Bielefeld: Verlag für Regionalgeschichte, 2016), 285–306.

46 Lambrecht, "Hexenverfolgung," esp. 217–245.

47 Ibid., 205–281.

48 Ibid., 217–245; Pelizaeus, "Silesia," 1039.

49 Lambrecht, "Hexenverfolgung," esp. 240–242.

50 Pelizaeus, "Silesia," 1039; Lambrecht, "Hexenverfolgung," 282–299.

51 Lambrecht, "Hexenverfolgung," 282–299 and 333–335.

52 Ibid., 32–41.

53 Ibid., 41–43.

54 Ibid., 47–55.

55 Ibid., 383–401.

56 Ibid., 515.

57 Ibid., 515.

58 Ibid., 404.

59 Ibid., 404 and 466–517.

60 Ibid., 300–316.

61 Ibid., 337–338; Manfred Wilde, *Die Zauberei- und Hexenprozesse in Kursachsen* (Köln: Böhlau, 2003), 375–381.

62 Wilde, *Kursachsen*, 375–381.

63 Ibid., 375–379.

64 Ibid., 376 and 507.

65 Ibid., 377 and 650.

66 Ibid., 379–381.

67 Ibid., 379–380, 543–544 and 595.

68 Ibid., 380 and 556.

69 Ibid., 381 and 484.

70 Ibid., 375–376.

71 Ibid., 375–377.

72 Ibid., 376–377 and 507.

73 Ibid., 381.

74 In general: Petr Kreuz, "Slovakia," in *Encyclopedia of Witchcraft. The Western Tradition*, 4 vols., ed. Richard Golden (Santa Barbara: ABC-Clio, 2006), 1051–1052.

75 Andor Komáromy, ed., *Magyarországi boszorkányperek oklevéltára* (Budapest: Magyar Tud. Akadémia, 1910); Richard Horna, "Marie Terezie a procesy s čarodějnicemi," in *Pocta k šesdesiatym narodeninám Dr. Karla Lašťovku*, ed. Erwin Hexner (Bratislava, 1936), 157–167; Ján Holák, *Beda odsúdeným. Ako sa za feudalizmu súdilo na Slovensku* (Martin: Osveta, 1974), esp. 77, 139–140 and 220–226; Gábor Klaniczay, "Hungary: The Accusations and the Universe of Popular Magic," in *Early Modern European Witchcraft. Centres and Peripheries*, ed. Bengt Ankarloo and Gustav Henningsen (Oxford: Clarendon Press, 1990), 219–255; Bedřich Šindelář, *Hon na čarodějnice. Západní a střední Evropa v 16.-17 století* (Praha: Svoboda, 1986), 211–212; József Bessenyei, ed., *Magyarországi boszorkányság forrásai II* (Budapest Balassi Kiadó, 2000); Viliam Apfel, *Čas pekelných ohňov. Procesy s bosorkami na Slovensku (1506–1766)* (Budmerice: Vydavateľstvo Rak, 2001), passim; Péter G. Tóth, ed., *Magyarországi boszorkányság forrásai IV.* (Budapest: Balassi Kiadó, 2005); Erik Štenpien, "Hlavné znaky uhorských procesov s čarodejnicami v 16.-18. storočí s osobitným zretelom na Horné Uhorsko," in *Stát a právo v období absolutismu*, ed. Karel Schelle and Ladislav Vojáček (Brno: Masarykova univerzita, 2005), 161–170; Ildikó S. Kristóf, "Witch Hunting in Early Modern Hungary," in *The Oxford Handbook of Witchcraft in Early Modern Europe and Colonial America*, ed. Brian P. Levack

(Oxford: Oxford University Press, 2013), passim; Kreuz, "Slovakia," 1051–1052; Petr Kreuz, "Die späten Hexenprozesse in den böhmischen Ländern und auf dem Gebiet der heutigen Slowakei," in *Späte Hexenverfolgungen*, ed. Wolfgang Behringer, Sönke Lorenz, and Dieter R. Bauer (Bielefeld: Verlag für Regionalgeschichte, 2016), 190–201; Tünde Lengyelová, "Procesy s bosorkami v Nitrianskej a Bratislavskej stolici v 16.-18. storočí," in *Archivum Sala. Archívna ročenka II.* (Šaľa: Štátny okresný archív, 2005), 17–18 and 24–26; Tünde Lengyelová, "Bosorky – špecifický druh zločinnosti žien v období raného novoveku," in *Kriminalita, bezpečnosť a súdnictvo v minulosti miest a obcí na Slovensku. Zborník z rovnomennej vedeckej konferencie konanej 1.-3. októbra 2003 v Lučenci*, ed. León Solokovský (Bratislava: Univerzita Komenského, 2007), 176–178; Tünde Lengyelová, *Bosorky, strigy, čarodějnice* (Bratislava: TRIO Publishing, 2013), 115–148.

76 Holák, *Beda odsúdeným*, 140–141; cf. too Apfel, *Čas pekelných ohňov*, 33; Lengyelová, *Bosorky, strigy, čarodějnice*, 48, writes about another supposed sorcery accusation in Prešov (in Hungarian Eperjes) in 1505.

77 Holák, *Beda odsúdeným*, 77–78 and 140–143; cf. Lengyelová, "Procesy," 31; Lengyelová, *Bosorky, strigy, čarodějnice*, 48.

78 Richard Horna, *Zwei Hexenprozesse in Preßburg zu Beginn des XVII. Jahrhunderts* (Bratislava [= Preßburg]: private printing, 1933); Lengyelová, "Procesy," 23–24; Lengyelová, *Bosorky, strigy, čarodějnice*, 117.

79 Holák, *Beda odsúdeným*, 77–78 and 140–143.

80 Holák, *Beda odsúdeným*, 139–140; cf. Kreuz, "Die späten Hexenprozesse," 191–192.

81 Recently summarized by Kreuz, "Die späten Hexenprozesse," 193–197; cf. too František Šujanský, "Súdy nad strigami r. 1675 a v nasl. (Zo zápisnej knihy města Krupiny)," *Slovenské pohľady* 18 (1898–1899): passim; Marie Majtánová and Milan Majtán, "Materiály o čarodejnických procesoch v Krupine z konca 17. storočia," *Slovenský národopis* 18 (1970): 137–145; Marie Majtánová and Milan Majtán, eds., *Krupinské prísne právo* (Bratislava: Tatran, 1979), passim; Milan Majtán, "Servants of the Devil in Krupina," in *The Role of Magic in the Past: Learned and Popular Magic, Popular Beliefs and Diversity of Attitudes*, ed. Blanka Széghyová (Bratislava: Pro Historia, 2005), 101–107; Lengyelová, *Bosorky, strigy, čarodějnice*, 128–131.

82 Kreuz, "Die späten Hexenprozesse," 197.

83 Ibid., 196.

84 Richard Horna, *Ein Monster-Hexenprozess in Šamorín gegen Ende des XVII. Jahrhunderts* (Bratislava [= Preßburg], private printing, 1935).

85 Recently Kreuz, "Die späten Hexenprozesse," 198–199. cf. too Emília Horváthová-Čajánková, "Liečebné praktiky čarodejníc na severozápadnom Slovensku v prvej polovici 18. storočí," *Slovenský národopis* 7 (1959): 433–445, esp. 441–443; Lengyelová, *Bosorky, strigy, čarodějnice*, 132–134.

86 Recently Kreuz, "Die späten Hexenprozesse," 199–200; cf. too Lengyelová, *Bosorky, strigy, čarodějnice*, 135–137.

87 Recently Kreuz, "Die späten Hexenprozesse," 200–201; cf. too Horváthová-Čajánková, "Liečebné praktiky," 444; Lengyelová, *Bosorky, strigy, čarodějnice*, 134.

88 Recently Kreuz, "Die späten Hexenprozesse," 199; cf. too Holák, *Beda odsúdeným*, 223; Horváthová-Čajánková, "Liečebné praktiky," 441 and 443; Lengyelová, *Bosorky, strigy, čarodějnice*, 134.

89 Wolfgang Behringer, "Letzte Hexenhinrichtungen 1700–1911," in *Späte Hexenverfolgungen*, ed. Wolfgang Behringer, Sönke Lorenz, and Dieter R. Bauer (Bielefeld: Verlag für Regionalgeschichte, 2016), 400.

90 Tóth, *Magyaroszági*, 324–326; Kreuz, "Die späten Hexenprozesse," 200.

91 Year 1777 is erroneous f. e. Lengyelová, *Bosorky, strigy, čarodějnice*, 141; Behringer, "Letzte Hexenhinrichtungen," 418.

92 Lengyelová, *Bosorky, strigy, čarodějnice*, 48–53; Kreuz, "Die späten Hexenprozesse," 203.

93 Karol Koranyi, "Czary i gusła przed sądem kościelnemi w Polsce w XV i w pierwszej polowie XVI wieku," *Lud* 26 (1927): passim; Leszek Zygner, "Kobieta-czarownica w świetle ksiag konsystornych z XV i poczatku XVI w," in *Kobieta i rodzina w średniowieczu i na progu czasów nowożytnych*, ed. Zenon Hubert Nowak and Andrzej Radzimiński (Toruń: Uniwersytet Mikołaja Kopernika, 1998), 91–101; Wanda Wyporska, "Poland," in *Encyclopedia of*

Witchcraft: The Western Tradition, 4 vols., ed. Richard Golden (Santa Barbara: ABC-Clio, 2006), 908; Joanna Adamczyk, "Czary i magia w praktyce sądów kościelnych na ziemiach polskich w późnym średniowieczu (XV-polowa XVI wieku)," in *Karolinscy pokutnicy i polskie średniowieczne czarownice. Konfrontacja doktryny chreściajańskiej z życiem spoleczenstwa średnio-wiecznego*, ed. Maria Koczerska (Warszawa, Wydawnictwo DiG, 2007), passim; Małgorzata Pilaszek, *Procesy o czary w Polsce w wiekach XV-XVIII* (Kraków, Universitas, 2008), 144–153; Michael Ostling, *Between the Devil and the Host: Imagining Witchcraft in Early Modern Poland* (Oxford: Oxford University Press, 2011), esp. 45–46.

94 Wyporska, "Poland," 908.

95 Pilaszek, *Procesy o czary*, 268–272; Tomasz Wiślicz, "Czary przed sądami wiejskimi w Polsce XVI-XVIII wieku," *Czasopismo Prawno-Historyczne* 49 (1997): passim.

96 Analysis of this constitution from 1543 esp. Michael Ostling, "Konstytucja 1543 r. i początki procesów o czary w Polsce," *Odrodzenie i Reformacja w Polsce* 49 (2011): 93–103.

97 Pilaszek, *Procesy o czary*, 185–186; Wyporska, "Poland," 908; Ostling, *Between the Devil and the Host*, 46.

98 Janusz Tazbir, "Hexenprozesse in Polen," *Archiv für Reformationsgeschichte* 71 (1980): 281.

99 Bogdan Baranowski, *Procesy czarownic v Polsce w w XVII i XVIII wieku* (Łódź: Łódzkie Towarzystwo Ludoznawcze, 1952; esp. 176 and 180; cf. Małgorzata Pilaszek, "Procesy czarownic w Polsce w XVI-XVIII w. Nowe aspekty. Uwagi na marginesie pracy B. Baranowskiego," *Odrodzenie i Reformacja w Polsce* 42 (1998): 81–87 and 96–98; Wanda Wyporska, "Baranowski, Bogdan (1915–1993)," in *Encyclopedia of Witchcraft: The Western Tradition*, 4 vols., ed. by Richard Golden (Santa Barbara: ABC-Clio, 2006), 91–92.

100 Introduction of Baranowski to Kurt Baschwitz, *Czarownice. Dzieje procesów o czary* (Warszawa, PWN, 1971); see Wyporska, "Baranowski, Bogdan," 91–92.

101 Tazbir, "Hexenprozesse in Polen," 281–282.

102 Baranowski, *Procesy czarownic*, passim.

103 Ostling, *Between the Devil and the Host*, esp. 18–20 and 86–90.

104 Pilaszek, *Procesy o czary*, 291–304.

105 Wyporska, "Poland," 908, estimates on the whole 251 trials with 511 charged (96% women).

106 Ostling, *Between the Devil and the Host*, 45–46 and 244; Wyporska, "Poland," 908.

107 Jerzy Woronczak, "Procesy o czary przed poznańskim sądem miejskim v XVI wieku," *Literatura Ludowa* 16 (1972): passim; Woronczak, Jerzy, 1972, passim; Pilaszek, *Procesy o czary*, 277; Ostling, *Between the Devil and the Host*, 244; Wyporska, "Poland," 908.

108 Wyporska, "Poland," 907.

109 Ostling, *Between the Devil and the Host*, 244.

110 Bogdan Baranowski, *Najdawniejsze procesy o czary w Kaliszu* (Lublin: Studia Etnograficzne 2, 1951), 39–55; Ostling, *Between the Devil and the Host*, 244.

111 Pilaszek, *Procesy o czary*, 312–322.

112 Ostling, *Between the Devil and the Host*, esp. 48–53, 205–208 and 214–226; Wanda Wyporska, *Witchcraft in Early Modern Poland 1500–1800* (Basingstoke: Palgrave Macmillan, 2013), 105–126; Wyporska, "Poland," 909–910.

113 Ostling, *Between the Devil and the Host*, 20–21.

114 Ostling, *Between the Devil and the Host*, 18–20; Michael Ostling, "Witchcraft in Poland. Milk and Malefice," in *The Oxford Handbook of Witchcraft in Early Modern Europe and Colonial America*, ed. Brian P. Levack (Oxford: Oxford University Press, 2013), passim; Małgorzata Pilaszek, "Witch Hunts in Poland, 16th–18th Centuries," *Acta Poloniae Historica* 86 (2002): passim; Pilaszek, *Procesy o czary*, 268, 272–276 and 509.

115 Ostling, *Between the Devil and the Host*, 18–20; Pilaszek, *Procesy o czary*, 272–274 and 509.

116 Wiślicz, "Czary," esp. 38; Tomasz Wiślicz, "The Township of Kleczew and Its Neighborhood Fighting the Devil (1624–1700)," *Acta Poloniae Historica* 89 (2004): 65–95, esp. 67; Pilaszek, *Procesy o czary*, 292–293; Ostling, *Between the Devil and the Host*, 21.

117 Pilaszek, *Procesy o czary*, 350; Ostling, *Between the Devil and the Host*, 20.

118 Pilaszek, *Procesy o czary*, 351–352; Ostling, *Between the Devil and the Host*, 20.

119 Jacek Wijaczka, "Men Standing Trial for Witchcraft and the Łobżenica Court in the Second Half of the 17th Century," *Acta Poloniae Historica* 93 (2006): 69–85, esp. 84–85; Ostling, *Between the Devil and the Host*, 20.

120 Ostling, *Between the Devil and the Host*, 20.
121 Jacek Wijaczka, "Witch and Sorcerer Hunts in the Town of Nowe, the 17th and the First Half of the 18th Century," *Acta Poloniae Historica* 98 (2008): 133; Pilaszek, *Procesy o czary*, 293; Ostling, *Between the Devil and the Host*, 21.
122 Ostling, Michael, *Between the Devil and the Host*, 21.
123 Wyporska, "Poland," 908.
124 Ibid.
125 Woronczak, "Procesy o czary," passim; Wyporska, *Witchcraft in Early Modern Poland*, 32.
126 Ostling, *Between the Devil and the Host*, 21–22.
127 Anna Brzezińska, "Accusations of Love Magic in the Renaissance Courtly Culture of the Polish-Lithuanian Commonwealth," *East Central Europe* 20–23 (1993–1996): 117–125; Wyporska, "Poland," 908.
128 Jacek Wijaczka, "Hexenprozesse in Polen im Zeitalter der Aufklärung," in *Späte Hexenverfolgungen*, ed. Wolfgang Behringer, Sönke Lorenz, and Dieter R. Bauer (Bielefeld: Verlag für Regionalgeschichte, 2016), 217.
129 Wijaczka, "Hexenprozesse in Polen im Zeitalter der Aufklärung," 218.
130 Janusz Tazbir, "Z dziejów falszerstw historycznych w Polsce w pierwszej połowie XIX wieku," *Przeglad Historyczny* 57 (1966): 590.
131 Wyporska, "Poland," 909.
132 Wijaczka, "Hexenprozesse in Polen im Zeitalter der Aufklärung," 218–221; cf. too Jacek Wijaczka, "Procesy o czary w Polsce w dobie Oświecenia. Zarys problematyki," *Klio* 7 (2005): 41–57.
133 Ostling, *Between the Devil and the Host*, 48–50; Wyporska, "Poland," 909; Wyporska, *Witchcraft in Early Modern Poland*, 122–126.
134 Ostling, *Between the Devil and the Host*, 195–237; Wyporska, *Witchcraft in Early Modern Poland*, 95–126.
135 Jacek Wijaczka, *Procesy o czary w Prusach Książęcych (Brandenburskich) w XVI-XVIII wieku* (Toruń: Wydawnictwo Universytetu Mikołaja Kopernika, 2007), esp. 297–298.

Bibliography (selection)

Adamczyk, Joanna, "Czary i magia w praktyce sądów kościelnych na ziemiach polskich w późnym średniowieczu (XV-polowa XVI wieku)." In *Karolinscy pokutnicy i polskie średniowieczne czarownice. Konfrontacja doktryny chreściajańskiej z życiem spoleczenstwa średniowiecznego*, edited by Maria Koczerska, 91–260. Warszawa: Wydawnictwo DiG, 2007.
Bessenyei, József (ed.), *Magyarországi boszórkánység forrásai II*. Budapest: Balassi Kiadó, 2000.
Klaniczay, Gábor, "Hungary: The Accusations and the Universe of Popular Magic." In *Early Modern European Witchcraft: Centres and Peripheries*, edited by Bengt Ankarloo and Gustav Henningsen, 219–255. Oxford: Clarendon Press, 1990.
Kreuz, Petr, "Der Einfluss des Rechtssystems und der Gerichtsorganisation auf Entwicklung, Dynamik und Formen der Hexenprozesse in den böhmischen Ländern." In *Hexenforschung aus den österreichischen Ländern*, edited by Heide Dienst, 231–260. Münster: LIT Verlag, 2009.
Kreuz, Petr, "Poznámky k problematice pramenné základny ke studiu dějin kouzelnických a čarodějnických procesů v českých zemích v pozdním středověku a raném novověku." *Folia Historica Bohemica* 25 (2010): 93–115.
Kreuz, Petr, "Kouzelnictví a jeho pronásledování v jagellonské Praze. Příspěvek k počátkům kouzelnických a čarodějnických procesů v Čechách." *Pražský sborník historický* 40 (2012): 131–164.
Kreuz, Petr, "Die späten Hexenprozesse in den böhmischen Ländern und auf dem Gebiet der heutigen Slowakei." In *Späte Hexenverfolgungen. Der Umgang der Aufklärung mit dem Irrationalen*, edited by Wolfgang Behringer, Sönke Lorenz, and Dieter R. Bauer, 167–203. Bielefeld: Verlag für Regionalgeschichte, 2016.
Kreuz, Petr and Zuzana Haraštová, "Hexenkinder in den böhmischen Ländern und im Gebiet der heutigen Tschechischen Republik." In *Hexenkinder – Kinderbanden – Straßenkinder*, edited by Wolfgang Behringer and Claudia Opitz-Belakhal, 285–306. Bielefeld: Verlag für Regionalgeschichte, 2016.

Kristóf, Ildikó S., "Witch Hunting in Early Modern Hungary." In *The Oxford Handbook of Witchcraft in Early Modern Europe and Colonial America*, edited by Brian P. Levack, 334–354. Oxford: Oxford University Press, 2013.

Lambrecht, Karen, *Hexenverfolgung und Zaubereiprozesse in den schlesischen Territorien*. Köln: Böhlau, 1995.

Lengyelová, Tünde, *Bosorky, strigy, čarodějnice*. Bratislava: TRIO Publishing, 2013.

Ostling, Michael, *Between the Devil and the Host: Imagining Witchcraft in Early Modern Poland*. Oxford: Oxford University Press, 2011.

Pilaszek, Małgorzata, *Procesy o czary w Polsce w wiekach XV-XVIII*. Kraków: Universitas, 2008.

Rojčíková, Kamila, "Magické praktiky velkobítešských čarodějnic." *Západní Morava* 4 (2000): 149–154.

Rojčíková, Kamila, "Čarodějnické procesy na Moravě do roku 1648." *Časopis Matice moravské* 120 (2001): 187–207.

Šujanský, František, "Súdy nad strigami r. 1675 a v nasl. (Zo zápisnej knihy města Krupiny)." *Slovenské pohľady* 18 (1898–1899): 689–692, 750–752; 19: 173–177, 243–247.

Svobodová (= Rojčíková), Kamila, "Magické praktiky čarodějnic na Moravě a ve Slezsku do poloviny 17. století." *Vlastivědný věstník moravský* 55 (2003): 394–402.

Tóth, Péter G. (ed.), *Magyarországi boszórkányság forrásai IV*. Budapest: Balassi Kiadó, 2005.

Wijaczka, Jacek, *Procesy o czary w Prusach Książęcych (Brandenburskich) w XVI-XVIII wieku*. Toruń: Wydawnictwo Universytetu Mikołaja Kopernika, 2007.

Wyporska, Wanda, *Witchcraft in Early Modern Poland 1500–1800*. Basingstoke: Palgrave Macmillan, 2013.

14

WITCH HUNTS IN EASTERN EUROPE

Petr Kreuz

Ukraine,[1] Lithuania[2] (and Belarus)

Since the Middle Ages, the Grand Duchy of Lithuania covered most of the territory of today's Ukraine. In 1386, the personal union of the Grand Duchy of Lithuania with the Kingdom of Poland occurred. In 1569, the Polish-Lithuanian double state (real union) was created, which existed until the so-called division of Poland (1772–1795). Nevertheless, the whole eastern part (the so-called Leftbank) of Ukraine was already in the years 1657–1686 annexed to the Russian Empire. The southeastern part of today's Ukraine was from the 15th until the 18th century a part of the Crimean Khanate. The southern and southwestern part of Ukraine (Black Sea region) was until the 18th century a part of the Ottoman Empire. The whole territory of today's Lithuania and Belarus and a part of existing Latvia have belonged since the Middle Ages to the territory of the Grand Duchy of Lithuania. The territory was predominantly inhabited by people of Ukrainian, Belarussian, Russian and Polish (i.e. Slavic) descent.

A relatively small number of sorcery/witchcraft trials and executions of alleged witches took place in Ukraine.[3] The first charge of witchcraft in Ukraine was brought as late as 1578 in Volhynia against Princess Maria Kurbskaia.[4] As the surviving documents are far from complete, however, it is very probable that were several sorcery/witchcraft trials in the Grand Duchy of Lithuania in the 15th and in the first half of the 16th century. A conspicuous majority of the Ukrainian witchcraft trials known up to the present time were conducted only in the 18th century.[5] The last witch trial in Ukraine took place in 1829 in the townlet of Lypovets (about 40 km to the east of the town Vinnytsia) in the western part of the Ukraine (the so-called Rightbank Ukraine). Kateryna Martynivska, a lawyer's wife, was accused of bewitching the local priest.[6]

The surviving documentation suggests that in Ukraine, 198 trials for sorcery/witchcraft took place between the 16th and the 19th centuries. In this number are included not only complaints in connection with witchcraft, but also slander suits (allegations of harmful sorcery or witchcraft). Their relation is 7:3.[7] All of these cases fall into the 17th and 18th centuries (189).[8] A total of 158 trials, more than 80% of them, took place in the palatinates (districts) of Podolia (48) and Volhynia (87) in the Rightbank Ukraine and in Ruthenian palatinate (Red Russia) (23) in the west of the existing Ukraine (later East Galicia).[9] The majority of the remaining cases occurred in the palatinate Bratslav in the Rightbank Ukraine, in the Kiev region, in Central Ukraine and in the territory of the Ukrainian Cossack (het-manate, *гетьманщина*) in the Leftbank Ukraine.[10] Charges were brought against 223 persons. Only 13 received the death penalty.[11] Other severe penalties were banishment and public flogging. In most cases, a pecuniary fine was imposed, to be paid to the court or the church. Torture was used in Ukrainian trials only sporad-ically. As Ukrainian law demanded severe penalties for witches, the relatively low number of death penalties and other severer punishments points to a conspicuous difference between legal regulation on the one hand and milder judicial practice on the other hand.[12]

The Ukrainian trials were (like the trials conducted in Russia) distinguished by a very low rate of women (10–15%).[13] It seems that this was to a considerable degree due to the character of magic practices being used and persecuted. Among the accus-ers in Ukraine, men predominated, too. In 90% of Ukrainian witchcraft cases, the defendant and the accuser were of equal social standing. Persons of high rank very rarely brought charges against people of lower standing or even against their sub-jects. There were a few episodes of persons coming from marginal social groups (beg-gars and vagabonds) or persons belonging to ethnic minorities (Roma, Jews, Turks) being accused of witchcraft.[14] The witchcraft trials in Ukraine were predominantly an urban phenomenon. Thus, most of the defendants were craftsmen and other people belonging to the urban middle classes.[15] The charges often represented the final stage of neighbourhood or other personal quarrels. Priests of the Orthodox Church and their wives were among the accused, too.[16]

As the archives of the towns of Western Ukraine are, generally speaking, in a better condition than those of the rest of the country, we have documents for a relatively high number of cases from Rightbank (West) Ukraine.[17] A great number of death sentences in the Ukrainian sorcery/witchcraft trials were passed in the 17th and 18th centuries in the palatinate of Volhynia.[18] The best known Ukrainian trial nevertheless took place in 1666 in the town Hadiach (*Гадяч*) in the Poltava region (northeast of the existing Ukraine), where six alleged witches were burned at the stake. Hadiach was at the time already a part of the Russian Empire.[19] In the 18th century, the death sentences were more common in cases that combined magic with other felonies (fraud, infanticide, sparking of an epidemic).[20]

The cases of sorcery/witchcraft in the Ukraine were dealt with by secular courts. Usually the town courts were responsible; in some cases the noblemen or castle courts were as well.[21] Only at the end of the 18th century were there several cases of superstition heard by the Kiev consistorial court.[22]

The relatively moderate, lenient and condescending attitude in the Ukraine towards the offence of magic was traditionally interpreted as influenced by the Orthodox Church, which allegedly did not create a clearly defined demonologic tradition and failed to formulate a concept of the devil's pact.[23] This explanation is obviously not satisfactory, firstly because in the works of some of the outstanding Ukrainian orthodox theologians active in the 17th century emerges a clear con-nection between the witches and sorcerers on the one hand and the devil on the other.[24] Secondly, the majority of known trials in Ukraine took place in towns that were heterogenous in terms of ethnicity and of religion. Nevertheless, the concept of the witches as a diabolical sect did not exist in Ukraine.[25] The witches' sabbath is mentioned in only one case heard in 1753 by the town court in Kremenets (*Кременець*) in the palatinate of Volhynia in the West Ukraine (about 80 km to the north of Ternopil).[26]

The town courts in the Ukraine, in Lithuania and in the territory of existing Belarus used since the Middle Ages (14th century) as a rule the Magdeburg Law, which included a statute about the prosecution of magic.[27] The oldest statute against witchcraft that was in force in the entire country came into force only in the first codification of the law of the Lithuanian state, the so-called 1st Statute of the Grand Duchy of Lithuania from the year 1529.[28] The Statute conferred the jurisdiction over the offence of magic to secular courts. Although the 1st Statute explicitly subjected the cases of witchcraft to the jurisdiction of so-called land courts and castle courts, the majority of witchcraft trials were conducted before the town and patrimonial courts. The so-called 3rd Statute of the Grand Duchy of Lithuania from 1588 (*de iure* in force until the division and destruction of the Polish-Lithuanian Union in 1795) defined witchcraft as a crime and ordered that sorcerers and witches should be burned at the stake. The burning was in practice substituted by beheading.[29]

On the base of the documentary evidence concerning the territory of existing Lithuania and completed by selected sources from several towns situated in the existing Belarus (Pinsk, Polotsk, Grodno, Slutsk), we may state that there were 97 cases of witchcraft between 1552 and 1771 and 16 cases of witchcraft/sorcery slander.[30] The majority of the sources come from the territory of the so-called Principality of Samogitia (*Žemaitija*, i.e. from Lower Lithuania, west and northwest of today´s Lithuania). In most witch trials, between one and three persons were accused. In 28 cases, the courts passed a death sentence. The executions (as a rule by burning at the stake, seldom mitigated by prior beheading) were registered in the years 1566–1726.[31] In other cases, the culprits were exiled or flogged. There were also ecclesiastical penances.[32]

The sorcery/witchcraft trials in the territory of today's Lithuania cannot be considered a mass phenomenon. According to some scholars, this was due to the late Christianization of the Grand Duchy of Lithuania which only began in the late 14th century. The first witch trial in today's Lithuania took place in 1552 before the town court of Kaunas (in Polish Kowno, in German Kauen).[33] The witchcraft trials in Lithuania reached their peak in the 1630s, shortly after the war waged by the Polish-Lithuanian Union against Russia and Sweden.[34] The last trial in today's Lithuania was conducted in 1771.[35] In 1776, a decision of the *Sejm* (Parliament) ended the witch hunts in the entire Polish-Lithuanian Union.[36]

In today's Lithuania, most victims of the witch hunts were female.[37] The men, however, represented (unlike in the Kingdom of Poland) more than one-third (39%) of the accused. In three cases, children had to stand trial (1695, 1731 and 1771).[38] The relatively low rate of women among the accused might be explained by the poor state of the work force and the more important role of women within the economy, especially since the second half of the 17th century.[39] Among the accused in the witchcraft trials in today's Lithuania were predominantly subjects of the manorial lords and people from the lowest strata of urban society. Considerably fewer cases of complaints about witchcraft were brought against noblemen or Jews.[40]

Russia[41]

The nucleus of the Russian state was the Principality of Muscowy (1276), from the 1320s until 1547 the Grand Principality of Muscowy. After shaking off the overlord-ship of the Tartarian Golden Horde in 1480, Russia was ruled by the Tsars (царь) from 1547 to 1917. From the beginning of the 17th century until 1612, large parts of Russia, including Moscow, were under occupation from the Polish-Lithuanian Union. From the mid-16th century, the Russian reign expanded eastwards into Siberia. In the 1640s, the Tsardom (царство) reached the Pacific Ocean. Eastern parts of the Ukraine (the so-called Leftbank Ukraine) were annexed by the Tsars in the 1660s. Early modern Russia was a multiethnic empire with a Slavic (mostly Russian) majority.

The persecution of witches in Russia[42] started only in the early modern period, i.e. later than in Western Europe.[43] The courts in the Grand Principality of Muscowy and in the Tsardom of Russia heard from the 16th to the 19th century almost 500 known cases of magic. The number of accused reached almost 800 persons, predominantly men.[44] Between 1601 and 1701, there were approximately 227 sorcery/witchcraft trials in Russia, in which 400 persons, mostly men, were accused.[45] In the period 1700–1740, there were 103 legal cases concerning the use of magic.[46] In the years 1741–1801, in the time from the accession to the throne of Empress Elisabeth I (1741–1761/2) until the beginning of the reign of Emperor Alexander I (1801–1825), there were 127 such cases.[47] The total number of trials taking place in Russia in the 18th century is estimated at 230–240; about 400 persons had to stand trial.[48] Sporadic cases of the prosecution of sorcery occurred in Russia until 1840. In the years 1801–1840, the Most Holy Synod dealt with nine cases.[49]

The charges in Russian trials concerned different forms of folk magic. The Russian orthodoxy rarely designed magic as satanic and did not develop an elaborate demonological theory. Demonology and idea of the pact with the devil played only a very limited role in the Russian trials. It is therefore more appropriate to characterize the magic (rather like in Ukraine) as sorcery, not so much as witchcraft.[50] As in Ukraine, the overwhelming majority of persons charged with magic were men. In the 17th and 18th centuries, approximately 80% of the defendants were men.[51]

Russian medieval chronicles mention at times that a witch or witches had been killed, but the witches only became the object of a more serious interest of the Grand Princes of Moscow at the end of the 15th century.[52] In 1467, the first wife of the Grand Prince Ivan III (1462–1505), Maria of Tver, died, allegedly due to witchcraft or poisoning. Ivan III suspected his second wife, Sophia Paleologue, of having hired witches to kill him.[53] At the beginning of the reign of Ivan IV, the Terrible (1547–1584), in June 1547, his grandmother, Anna Glinskaya, was said to have caused a devastating fire in Moscow, during which several thousand people perished, by spells. The enraged crowds did not lynch Anna, but her son and the Tsar's uncle, Prince Yuri Glinski, died.[54] Other Glinskis and the Tsar himself were also in serious danger.[55] Politically motivated accusations of magic remained an important feature of Ivan's entire reign. Similar suspicions occurred in the 17th century in the Romanov family in connection with the death of some wives and supposed brides.[56] Accusation of harmful sorcery/witchcraft as a political crime occured in Russia until the 19th century. Political witchcraft (sorcery) trials in Russia were for a long time a specific instrument in political conflicts.[57]

Russian witches usually had to face secular courts. Most cases were based on denunciations or complaints. The courts resorted to a great degree to torture (рутка, *пытка*).[58] Only about 15 % of the defendants were sentenced to death and executed.[59] Men were mostly beheaded (eventually hanged or burned), but women as a rule were burned alive.[60] Other accused were sentenced to flogging, to banishment or to internment in a monastery (for several months, for several years or for life). Long periods of penances were customary. The relatively hardest punishments for witchcraft in Russia were imposed at the end of the 17th and in the first quarter of the 18th century.[61]

The Russian Orthodox Church endeavoured for a long time without achieving any success to integrate secular institutions into its campaign against sorcery/witchcraft. Since the Middle Ages, Eastern European codifications of church law contained rules concerning the prosecution of magic, some of them secular laws and rules taken over from the Byzantine. In Russia, these collections of ecclesiastical laws were known since the second half of the 13th century as *Кормчие книги* (Kormchyje knigi). Other norms of secular and ecclesiastical law were gradually added to them.[62] Nevertheless, the emperor's courts began to hear the occasional case of magic only at the beginning of the 17th century.[63] Only in the middle of the 17th century did Emperor Aleksey I Mikhailovich (1645–1676) issue a stricter decree about the persecution of sorcery/witchcraft. In the beginning of his rule, in the year 1649, the collection of laws of the Russian state called *Соборное уложение* (Sobornoje ulozhenie) was established. It sanctioned sorcery/witchcraft.[64] All this soon led to a conspicuous increase in the numbers of trials for magic, particularly in the towns, which culminated in the mid-seventeenth century and again in the 1670s.[65]

The legal treatment of witchcraft in Russia underwent fundamental changes in the first quarter of the 18th century under the rule of Emperor Peter I the Great (1689–1725). Within the framework of his reforms of the Orthodox Church, he issued in 1721 a Spiritual Regulation (*духовный регламент*) in the spirit of the Enlightenment: The Regulation declared that witchcraft was fraud perpetrated on trusting and on superstitious persons.[66] Other laws from the reign of Peter the Great, however, took over older decrees about the prosecution of witchcraft or made them harsher. In the Military Articles (*Артикул воинский*), issued in April 1715 within the framework of the reform of the Russian army, Russian law accepted for the first time that there was a connection between witchcraft and the machinations of the devil.[67] (The main source of Peter's Articles was the Swedish Military Order introduced in the years 1621–1622 by King Gustav II Adolph, in the 1683 wording.)[68] The Articles prescribed cruel punishments for harmful sorcery and magic perpetrated in association with the devil, including imprisonment in chains, running the gauntlet and burning at the stake. It was only possible to impose public penance for sorcery, which did not cause damage and was not diabolic in nature. The above-mentioned punishments bore not only upon the magicians themselves but also upon persons who hired them.[69] The regulations of the Military Articles were in April 1720 taken over by Peter's Naval Statute (*Устав морской*), in which burning at the stake was moreover characterized as a usual punishment for magicians and perpetrators of harmful magic.[70]

An even harsher edict, which could concern not only any village healer, but his client, too, was issued in 1731 by the Empress Anna (1730–1740). This edict ordered the execution of the sorcerers as impostors and provided penalties for them as well as for those who invited such persons and took advantage of their services. After the issue of this edict came a temporary increase in the numbers of magic trials in Russia in the 1730s.[71]

Under the reign of the enlightened Empress Catherine II the Great (1762–1796), a senate decree (*указ*) from 1770 brought a fundamental change in the prosecution of magic.[72] This decree and the following legislature of Catherine the Great called sorcery a superstition and its perpetrators cheaters.[73] However, these laws did not completely deny the reality of sorcery. Russian courts continued, even if sporadically, to prosecute witchcraft into the 19th century.[74]

The last known burning at the stake for witchcraft in Russia nevertheless took place already in 1736; at that time, one Jakov Jarov was burned in Simbirsk (today Uljanovsk) as an alleged magician.[75] Given the incomplete documentation, however, it is entirely possible that there were later executions for harmful sorcery/witchcraft in Russia.

Since the 1720s, complaints about witchcraft were as a rule brought before the Most Holy Synod (*Святейший Синод*). The Most Holy Synod, created in 1721 as the highest Authority of the Russian Orthodox Church, functioned as a church court as well. It existed until 1917.[76] Being a church court, the Most Holy Synod could not use torture. Therefore, it was not allowed to interfere in cases in which the torture was already applied. Torture was only abolished in Russia in 1801 after the accession of Alexander I to the throne. Thus, the influence of the Most Holy Synod was limited.[77]

In Russia, there were no mass witch hunts like those in Western Europe. We do not find any fanatical witch hunters there. Nevertheless, the number of trials was high enough: Magic and witchcraft remained permanent objects of interest and anxiety for the Russian rulers in the early modern period.[78]

Demonology only began to influence the concept of magic in Russia at the end of the 17th century.[79] Accusations of magic perpetrated in association with the devil did not appear until the beginning of the 18th century. In that time, Russia took over within the reform framework a series of ideas and conceptions from the West, the demonological conception of witchcraft included. There were a few cases in which magic and the blasphemous abuse of Christian religious objects (crucifixes, communion wafers etc.) mingled.[80] The absence in Russia of the idea of the existence of a diabolical witches' sect with all its characteristic features conspicuously limited the number of accusations. In the greatest trials for magic in Russia, the investigations were directed against several dozens of people, but sentences were passed against at most seven or eight persons. That was the case in the trial that took place in the town of Lukh (*Лух*) (approximately 150 kilometres to the west of Nizhny Novgorod) in the years 1658–1659 (the so-called Lukh episode/*лухский эпизод*).[81] But such trials were few and far between: The accusations concerned mostly single persons. In the 18th century, we meet in Russia essentially three main types of charges and denunciations: 1. the landlord's against a servant; 2. among kindred; 3. a clergyman against another clergyman.[82]

In Russia, the alleged witches who did not fall into the category of healers quite often presented two sets of characteristic features. The first group was formed by criminals who used witchcraft in combination with robbery, theft and other crimes against property and violent felonies. That is why the law of the Grand Principality of Muscowy already classified witchcraft as a crime and used for it the name *ведовское воровство* (*vedovskoe vorovstvo*, magical criminality; literally: theft of spirits).[83] The second group consisted of so-called dishonest persons at the margin of the society and outside of the established hierarchies. The above-mentioned characteristic features were more typical of men than of women; this might have caused the specific gender structure of Russian witch trials.[84]

Heresy – real religious dissent, not imaginary Satanism – played only a marginal role in the Russian conception of the offence of magic. Magical practices were conceived as pagan rather than satanic or heretical. They differed greatly in the different regions of Russia. The Russian language created for them and their perpetrators (and partly still uses) a series of special designations with different and partly changeable connotations.[85]

Already in the time of the Grand Principality of Muscowy there appeared in some trials the so-called *klikushestvo* (*кликушество*, hysterics) as a certain form of bewitchment or possession by an evil spirit. Usually, it affected women. Cases of *klikushestvo* were more often registered only in the 18th century. Peter I began to prosecute *кликуши* (*klikushi*; hysterical, possessed women) more strictly.[86] These cases lasted throughout the 19th century until the beginning of the 20th century.[87]

In the Russian rural environment persisted belief in witches and magic healers as a part of popular beliefs and ideas until the 19th century. This seems to be one of the reasons why, even after the end of the witch trials, alleged witches were lynched (*самосуды*/samosudy) in the first half of the 19th century. There is evidence for several dozen such cases between 1861 and 1917.[88]

What was characteristic of the witch trials in Eastern Europe? The witch hunts reached the east relatively late. In Ukrainian and Russian sorcery/witchcraft trials, there was practically no place for witchcraft as defined by West European demonology. In Russia and especially in Ukraine, there were some theological treatises that discussed the relationship between magical practices and the devil, but they did not have any influence on local trials. Unlike in Western and Central Europe, in early modern Russia and Poland politically motivated accusations of magic directed against high-ranking members of the governing elites played an important role.

Notes

1 In general: Kateryna Dysa, "Ukraine, Witchcraft," in *Encyclopedia of Witchcraft: The Western Tradition*, 4 vols., ed. Richard Golden (Santa Barbara: ABC-Clio, 2006), 1139–1140; Kateryna Dysa, "Ukraine. Witchcraft Trials," in *Encyclopedia of Witchcraft: The Western Tradition*, 4 vols., ed. Richard Golden (Santa Barbara: ABC-Clio, 2006), 1140–1142.

2 In general: Parsla Petersone, "Latvia," in *Encyclopedia of Witchcraft: The Western Tradition*, 4 vols., ed. Richard Golden (Santa Barbara: ABC-Clio, 2006); Natalia Slizh, "Lithuania, Grand Duchy of," in *Encyclopedia of Witchcraft: The Western Tradition*, 4 vols., ed. Richard Golden (Santa Barbara: ABC-Clio, 2006), 658–660.

3 Kateryna Dysa, "Attitudes Towards Witches in the Multiconfessional Regions of Germany and Ukraine," in *Frontiers of Faith: Religious Exchange and the Constitution of Religious Identities*, ed. Eszter Andor and István György Tóth (Budapest: Central European Science Foundation, 2001), 285–290; Kateryna Dysa, "U tsaryny plitok. Roĺ shchodennoho spilkuvannia i reputatsiji v ukrajinśkykh sudakh pro chary XVIII st.," *Socium* 2 (2003): 185–196;

Kateryna Dysa, "Witches in the Neighbourhood: The Role of Neighbourhood Coexistence in Ukrainian Witchcraft Trials of the Seventeenth and Eighteenth Centuries," in *Mindennapi Választások. Tanulmányok Péter Katalin 70. születésnapjára*, ed. Gabriella Erdélyi and Péter Tusor (Budapest: MTA Történettudományi Intézete, 2007), 347–361; Kateryna Dysa, *Istorija z vidjmami. Sudi pro chary v ukrainskich voevodstvach Rechi Pospolitoi XVII–XVIII stolitj* (Kyjev: Kritika, 2008); Kateryna Dysa, "Orthodox Demonology and the Perception of Witchcraft in Early Modern Ukraine," in *Friars, Nobles and Burghers – Sermons, Images and Prints. Studies of Culture and Society in Early-Modern Europe. In memoriam István György Tóth*, ed. Jaroslav Miller and László Kontler (Budapest: Central European University Press, 2010), 341–360; Kateryna Dysa, *Witchcraft Trials and Beyond: Volhynia, Podolia and Ruthenia, 17–18th Centuries* (Budapest: Central European University Press, 2011). For 19th century too: Christine D. Worobec, "Witchcraft Beliefs and Practises in Prerevolutionary Russian and Ukrainian Villages," *The Russian Review* 54 (1995): 165–187.

4   Dysa, "Ukraine, Witchcraft Trials," 1141; Dysa, *Istorija z vidjmami*, 182.
5   Dysa, "Ukraine, Witchcraft Trials," 1141.
6   Ibid.; Dysa, *Istorija z vidjmami*, 11–12.
7   Dysa, *Istorija z vidjmami*, 60.
8   Ibid.
9   Ibid., 60–61.
10 Dysa, "Ukraine, Witchcraft Trials," 1141.
11 Dysa, *Istorija z vidjmami*, 64.
12 Ibid., 64–65.
13 Dysa, "Ukraine, Witchcraft Trials," 1141; Dysa, *Istorija z vidjmami*, 62–63.
14 Dysa, *Istorija z vidjmami*, 63–64.
15 Dysa, "Ukraine, Witchcraft Trials," 1141–1142.
16 Ibid.
17 Ibid., 1140.
18 Ibid., 1141.
19 Ibid.
20 Ibid.
21 Ibid.
22 Ibid.
23 Ibid.
24 Ibid; cf. too Dysa, *Istorija z vidjmami*, 79–93.
25 Dysa, "Ukraine, Witchcraft Trials," 1141.
26 Dysa, *Istorija z vidjmami*, 46.
27 Dysa, "Ukraine, Witchcraft Trials," 1141; Dysa, *Istorija z vidjmami*, 36.
28 Slizh, "Lithuania, Grand Duchy of," 658.
29 Ibid.
30 Małgorzata Pilaszek, "Litewskije procesy czarownic w XVI-XVIII w.," *Odrodzenie i Reformacja w Polsce* 46 (2002): 15.
31 Pilaszek, "Litewskije procesy czarownic," 15.
32 Ibid., 15–17.
33 Ibid., 16.
34 Ibid., 15–17.
35 Ibid., 17.
36 Ibid., 17–18.
37 Ibid., 18.
38 Ibid.
39 Ibid., 18–19.
40 Ibid., 19–20.
41 In general: Valerie A. Kivelson, "Russia," in *Encyclopedia of Witchcraft: The Western Tradition*, 4 vols., ed. Richard Golden (Santa Barbara: ABC-Clio, 2006), 980–984.
42 Cf. too William F. Ryan, *The Bathhouse at Midnight: An Historical Survey of Magic and Divination in Russia* (University Park, PA: Pennsylvania State University Press, 1999).
43 Kivelson, "Russia," 980.

44 Ibid.

45 Recently summarized by Valerie A. Kivelson, *Desperate Magic: The Moral Economy of Witchcraft in Seventeenth-Century Russia* (Ithaca and London: Cornell University Press, 2013), 29–32 and 261–272. Cf. too Russel Zguta, "Witchcraft Trials in Seventeenth Century Russia," *American Historical Review* 82 (1977): 1187–1207.

46 Alexandr V. Lavrov, *Koldovstvo i religija v Rossii, 1700–1740 gg* (Moskva: Drevlechranilishche, 2000), 353–355 and 364–365; cf. too Elena Borisovna Smiljanskaia, *Volshebniki. Bogochulniki. Jeretiki* (Moskva: Indrik, 2003), 65 – almost 200 trials in 1700–1760 involving 168 men and 36 women.

47 Tatiana Vladimirovna Mikhailova, "Koldovskie processy v Rossii. Ofitsialnaja ideologija i praktiki 'narodnoi religioznosti' (1740–1801)" (PhD diss., European University of Saint Petersburg, 2003), passim.

48 Cf. ref. 46 and 47.

49 Mikhailova, *Koldovskie processy v Rossii*, passim.

50 Kivelson, "Russia," 981–982.

51 Cf. ref. 45 and 46.

52 Kivelson, "Russia," 980.

53 Ibid.

54 Valerie A. Kivelson, "Political Sorcery in Sixteenth-Century Muscowy," in *Cultural Identity in Muscowy, 1359–1584*, ed. Ann M. Kleimola and Gail D. Lenhoff (Moscow: ITZ-Garant, 1997), 267–283.

55 Kivelson, "Political Sorcery"; Ruslan G. Skrynnikov, *Velikij gosusar Ioann Vasilievich Groznyi*, vol. 1 (Smolensk: Rusič, 1996), 136–141.

56 Kivelson, *Desperate Magic*, 11.

57 Kivelson, "Russia," 980.

58 Kivelson, *Desperate Magic*, 2.

59 Cf. ref. 45 and 46.

60 Kivelson, "Russia," 982.

61 Cf. ref. 45–47.

62 William F. Ryan, "The Witchcraft Hysteria in Early Modern Europe. Was Russia an Exception?" *The Slavonic and East European Review* 76 (1998): 56–58; Ryan, *The Bathhouse at Midnight*, 222. Cf. too Kivelson, "Russia," 980.

63 Kivelson, *Desperate Magic*, 38–39.

64 Ibid., 66 and 101.

65 Kivelson, *Desperate Magic*, 265–270.

66 Kivelson, "Russia," 981; Lavrov, Alexandr V. 2000, passim.

67 Lavrov, *Koldovstvo i religija v Rossii*, 347–349; Tatiana Vladimirovna Mikhailova, "Russkoe zakonodatelstvo v otnoshenii koldovstva. Pravovaja baza russkich koldovskich processov vtoroi poloviny XVIII veka i ee specifika," in *Антропология. Фольклористика. Лингвистика* (Saint Petersburg: European University of Saint Petersburg, 2002), 171–172; cf. too Ryan, "The Witchcraft Hysteria," 64–65.

68 Lavrov, *Koldovstvo i religija v Rossii*, 348, ref. 13; Kivelson, *Desperate Magic*, 256.

69 Lavrov, *Koldovstvo i religija v Rossii*, 347–349; Mikhailova, "Russkoe," 171–172.

70 Lavrov, *Koldovstvo i religija v Rossii*, 349; Mikhailova, "Russkoe," 172. Cf. too Valerie A. Kivelson, "Witchcraft Trials in Russia. History and Historiography," in *The Oxford Handbook of Witchcraft in Early Modern Europe and Colonial America*, ed. Brian P. Levack (Oxford: Oxford University Press, 2013), 358.

71 Lavrov, *Koldovstvo i religija v Rossii*, 362–365; Mikhailova, "Russkoe," 172–175; Elena Borisovna Smiljanskaia, "Sledstevennyje dela o „sueveriakh" v Rossii pervoi poloviny XVIII v. v svete problem istorii obshchestvennogo soznaniia," *Rossica* 1 (1996): 3.

72 Mikhailova, "Russkoe," 176–178.

73 Ibid., 178–182; cf. too Christine D. Worobec, "Decriminalizing Witchcraft in Pre-Emancipation Russia," in *Späte Hexenverfolgungen. Der Umgang der Aufklärung mit dem Irrationalen*, ed. Wolfgang Behringer, Sönke Lorenz, and Dieter R. Bauer (Bielefeld: Verlag für Regionalgeschichte, 2016), 290–297.

74 Mikhailova, "Russkoe," 182–190; cf. Worobec, "Decriminalizing Witchcraft," 296–297.

75 Lavrov, *Koldovstvo i religija v Rossii*, 365.
76 Ibid., 358–362 and 365–366; Mikhailova, *Koldovskie processy v Rossii*, passim.
77 Mikhailova, *Koldovskie processy v Rossii*, passim; cf. Worobec, "Decriminalizing Witchcraft," 296–300.
78 Kivelson, "Russia," 981; cf. too Russel Zguta, "Was There a Witch Craze in Muscovite Russia?" *Southern Folklore Quarterly* 41 (1977): 119–128; Smiljanskaia, *Volshebniki*, 30–31; Ryan, "The Witchcraft Hysteria," esp. 49–56 and 58–83.
79 Valerie A. Kivelson, "Lethal Convictions. The Power of a Satanic Paradigm in Russian and European Witch Trials," *Magic, Ritual, and Witchcraft* 6 (2011): 34–60; Kivelson, "Witchcraft Trials in Russia," 359–360.
80 Lavrov, *Koldovstvo i religija v Rossii*, 347–349; Kivelson, *Desperate Magic*, 256–257; cf. too Smiljanskaia, *Volshebniki*, esp. 119–141.
81 Kivelson, *Desperate Magic*, 152–156 and 266–267.
82 Lavrov, *Koldovstvo i religija v Rossii*, 374–375.
83 Kivelson, "Russia," 983.
84 Ibid.
85 Ibid., 981.
86 Lavrov, *Koldovstvo i religija v Rossii*, 376–393; cf. too Kivelson, "Russia," 982.
87 Christine D. Worobec, "Witchcraft Beliefs and Practises in Prerevolutionary Russian and Ukrainian Villages," *The Russian Review* 54 (1995): 165–187, esp. 168; Worobec, Christine D. 2001, passim.
88 Christine D. Worobec, *Possessed. Women, Witches, and Demons in Imperial Russia* (DeKalb: Northern Illinois University Press, 2001), passim; cf. too Kivelson, "Witchcraft Trials in Russia," 371–372.

Bibliography (selection)

Dysa, Kateryna, *Witchcraft Trials and Beyond: Volhynia, Podolia and Ruthenia, 17–18th Centuries.* Budapest: Central European University Press, 2011.

Kivelson, Valerie A., *Desperate Magic: The Moral Economy of Witchcraft in Seventeenth-Century Russia.* Ithaca, London: Cornell University Press, 2013.

Lavrov, Alexandr V., *Koldovstvo i religija v Rossii, 1700–1740 gg. (Колдовство и религия в России. 1700–1740 гг.).* Moskva: Drevlechranilishche, 2000.

Pilaszek, Małgorzata, "Litewskije procesy czarownic w XVI-XVIII w." *Odrodzenie i Reformacja w Polsce* 46 (2002): 7–35.

Ryan, William F., *The Bathhouse at Midnight: An Historical Survey of Magic and Divination in Russia.* University Park, PA: Pennsylvania State University Press, 1999.

Skrynnikov, Ruslan G., *Velikij gosusar Ioann Vasilievich Groznyi (Великий государь Иоанн Васильевич Грозный),* vol. 1. Smolensk: Rusič, 1996.

Smiljanskaia, Elena Borisovna, *Volshebniki. Bogochulniki. Jeretiki. (Волшебники. Богохульники. Еретики).* Moskva: Indrik, 2003.

Worobec, Christine D. *Possessed: Women, Witches, and Demons in Imperial Russia.* DeKalb: Northern Illinois University Press, 2001.

15

THE SALEM WITCH HUNT

Robert W. Thurston

The Salem witch hunt of 1692–93, which claimed twenty lives directly and others indirectly, has been interpreted in markedly different ways. Even as they were taking place, ordinary and prominent citizens of Massachusetts disagreed on the types of evidence that should be admitted in court and on whether any of the accused were guilty. In recent decades, several interpretations that concentrate on the background to the charge of witchcraft have dominated public consciousness, university courses, and American historical treatments. These analyses differ considerably from each other.

Yet it is crucial to emphasize the political and judicial situation in Salem at the time of the trials, which occurred a relatively short time after the English Glorious Revolution of 1688, and to focus on standards of evidence accepted during the hunt. As we shall see, various social strains and fears undoubtedly contributed to the outbreak of the panic; nonetheless, the Salem trials represented a sharp break from earlier witchcraft cases tried in New England. The Salem events were never repeated; they were unique in the number accused, 185; tried, fifty-nine; and the twenty executed; they evoked major opposition from prominent Puritans as they unfolded; and leading figures involved in the trials, including a judge and the members of one jury, soon recanted and apologized for their actions. During the Salem outbreak, fifty-three residents of the neighboring town of Andover signed a petition in favor of five accused women, citing pressure from some in the community to confess to negligence of justice/miscarriage of the law.[1] A witch hunt that might have become serious in Stamford, Connecticut Colony, in 1692 never developed momentum and ended with no executions.[2]

The Salem witch persecution had its origins in the fall of 1691, as the minister of Salem Village, Samuel Parris, began to emphasize the presence of Satan in the world and as girls in his household began to have fits. The girls would lie rigid for hours or appear to be tormented by pain. A local doctor who examined the girls found them to be "under an evil hand."[3] Soon this diagnosis became entangled with stories that a slave in Parris's household, Tituba, African by birth but brought to Massachusetts from the Caribbean, had told fortunes for several village girls. Then a helpful neighbor persuaded Tituba to bake a "witches' cake" using some of the girls' urine, which was then fed to a dog. That did not help matters. Soon other girls were also having fits, and several of the sufferers began to accuse adults in the village of causing their problems.

In late February, arrests began, at first, Tituba, and two white women. The accusations quickly led to the arrest of more adults and a 4-year-old girl, Dorcas Good, on March 23. On May 14, a new governor, William Phips, arrived in Boston from England. To try to resolve the witch problem, he appointed a special if relatively common court, of Oyer and Terminer. This phrase derived from the English affection for French legalese; the court was to hear and determine cases. Phips as well as the justices he appointed appeared to assume guilt in advance; in his directive to the new panel, he remarked that "there are many criminal offenders now in custody."[4] The governor did not supervise the new court, as he had to leave almost immediately to lead the English fight against Indians in Maine.

The first guilty verdict and hanging came in June. The last execution occurred in September. It is not clear that anyone was tortured in Salem, although John Proctor, hanged as a witch in August 1692, wrote while in prison to members of the Boston clergy that several young men had been tied "neck and heels," with their heads pulled tightly down to their feet, to get them to confess.[5] Of course, being held in a foul prison was itself an ordeal. After Dorcas Good was released in early 1693, she remained mentally disturbed for the rest of her life.

Altogether nineteen people were executed as witches, while one, Giles Cory, was pressed to death under heavy stones. He had refused to enter a plea, probably because if convicted, his property would not pass to his heirs. Therefore, the court applied the principle of *peine forte et dure*, literally strong and hard pain, in a fruitless attempt to extract a plea. Of the twenty put to death, fifteen were women. The resulting 70 percent female proportion is close to the one usually cited for European witch hunts – 75–80 percent – although there are some instances of males predominating among the accused.

Opposition to the kinds of evidence admitted in the Oyer and Terminer Court arose almost with the first execution. A group of ministers, among them the prominent writer Cotton Mather, about whom more will be said, quickly questioned the court's activities. Much had already been made of the testimony by the girls involved that the "spectre" of a defendant had attacked them. Several witnesses testified that it was the "shape" of Bridget Bishop, the first to be hanged, which pinched and tormented them, even though Bishop in the flesh was elsewhere at the time. In response to such "proof," the ministers announced on June 15 that spectral evidence or "Alterations made in the Sufferers, by a Look or Touch of the Accused" could not be considered "infallible Evidence of Guilt." Despite their dislike of such testimony, admitted in Salem and the decisive factor in a number of convictions, the ministers hedged by calling for the "speedy and vigorous prosecution of such as have rendered themselves obnoxious."[6]

Part of their reluctance to completely condemn the Oyer court's activities stemmed from the fact that belief in witches – a huge topic that cannot be discussed here – was common among white residents of Massachusetts no matter what their level of education or social standing. Another difficulty in assessing the trials was that the damage supposedly inflicted by witches extended far beyond pinching or scratching. Here the fear of witches intersected with personal tragedies. In a particularly poignant example, Ann Putnam Sr., mother of the afflicted girl Ann Jr., had just lost a six-week-old child. The mother now found an explanation for an event that had previously been unfathomable, even in seventeenth-century New England. Ann Sr. then also testified that specters of the accused were tormenting her. Livestock, apparently healthy one day and dead the next, could also be marked down as witches' victims. Given the day's knowledge of the physical world, witchcraft was a rational explanation for otherwise mysterious events. Even in societies today that embrace science in certain ways, witchcraft can be seen as quite real and dangerous.

In the Salem trials, the antics of the afflicted girls and the flimsiness of the evidence presented in court soon bothered another influential minister, Samuel Willard of Boston. He preached caution to his congregation. In late September, he defied the governor's order not to write about the trials and published, under a pseudonym, a strong critique of the proceedings. Conviction by mere suspicion, he said, was "contrary to the mind of God . . . besides, reason tells us, that the more horrid the crime is, the more cautious we ought to be in making any guilty of it." The judges did not have matters of fact "evidently done and clearly proved."[7]

In a letter to a member of the governor's council dated August 17, Cotton Mather appeared to agree, though far from completely. Spectral evidence alone is not enough to convict, he declared, but it should be used as presumptive evidence which would lead the court to investigate further. Mather suggested that the devil might impersonate good persons, perhaps even himself. He hinted at the possibility that innocent people may have been convicted; if so, they should be reprieved. But he also endorsed the judges' "great work" thus far.[8] Two days later he appeared at the Salem gallows and urged the spectators to approve the hanging of George Burroughs. Standing with a noose around his neck, Burroughs had caused a sensation by reciting the Lord's Prayer correctly, something a disciple of the devil was supposed to be unable to do. Mather nevertheless persuaded the crowd to let the execution proceed. By this time he was mired in profound contradictions about the evidence against the accused.

In October 1692, Mather published *The Wonders of the Invisible World.* Drawing on a book by the Englishman William Perkins, Mather listed a number of "presumptions" that should spark an investigation of witchcraft. These included notoriety as a witch and the death of someone following cursing by the suspect. Yet these were not "just and sufficient proofs." A confession would be enough to convict, but it had to follow "due Examination." Mather maintained that "sufficient" testimony for a guilty verdict would also be two witnesses who said they had seen a defendant make a pact with the devil; here he had arrived at the European continental standard for conviction. But he continued: proof could also be that the witch had a "familiar spirit," usually a small animal that was in fact a demon assigned by the devil for the comfort and aid of the witch. Mather says nothing about how a court could be certain that an animal was more than it appeared to be. Finally, witnesses might state that a suspect carried out an act, a "wonder," that could occur only with the help of witchcraft, for example raising a storm. "Wonder" in the lexicon of the day was opposed to miracles, which God arranged. Again, Mather does not make clear how the court was to determine that the witch had actually caused a disruption in the course of the universe. His book also ignores the question of spectral evidence.[9]

Cotton Mather's father, Increase, the most prominent minister in Massachusetts and president of Harvard College, had already begun to intervene in the whole affair, in a different direction than his son took. Cotton Mather delivered a sermon on witchcraft in early October to a group of ministers gathered in Boston especially to hear him, then quickly published a book on the subject.[10] The elder Mather followed his son's lead in one way, by asserting that the devil could appear in the shape of an innocent and pious person as well as in the form of the wicked. However, Increase pressed the point, which alone undermined much of the testimony accepted by the Oyer and Terminer Court. After all, the devil might assume the guise of an honest person and give testimony to destroy an upright resident. Noting that "the Devils have of late accused some eminent Persons," Increase Mather found that the testimony of "possessed" people should not be taken as proof of witchcraft, for then "no Person whatsoever can be in safety." What the bewitched claim has happened to other people "is not to be taken as evidence." Scripture gives not the "least Intimation" that it is proof of a diabolical connection when a possessed person falls into a fit under the glance of another individual.[11]

In stressing the position that no one could be safe from the accusation of witchcraft, and by extension that it was impossible to identify anyone as a witch, Cotton Mather had discovered the dilemma of witch finders everywhere. As H. C. Erik Midelfort wrote in his study of southwestern Germany, "witch hunters stopped because they no longer knew how to find witches."[12] It would be even better to say that others, or the community in question as a whole, stopped the witch finders; left to themselves, they seemed to have no notion of when to halt.

Increase Mather concluded that "the Evidence in this Crime ought to be as clear" as for any other capital offense. "The Oath of a distracted . . . or of a possessed Person" was not accepted in accusations of murder, theft, and so forth and therefore could not be accepted regarding witchcraft. Finally, "it were better that ten suspected witches should escape, than that one innocent Person should be Condemned."[13] This was the strong voice of skepticism not regarding the existence of witches, but about evidence that they had committed evil deeds. It was also a suggestion that innocent people had suffered.

The elder Mather was trying to allay the sense of panic about witches that had enveloped the court and much of the community. In a statement entitled "The Christian Reader" that prefaced his book, fourteen ministers added their view that "the more execrable the Crime is, the more critical care is to be used" in judging it.[14] Together, the men holding these views comprised a strong anti-persecution party in Massachusetts, which had developed in reaction to the witch hunt. In that same month of October 1692, they asked Governor Phips to halt the trials. Although he allowed another special court to convene briefly in early 1693, no more executions took place. In May, Phips pardoned and released the remaining prisoners.

For the ministers who spoke out in the fall of 1692, who were the intellectual and spiritual leaders of the Puritan community, the question of guilt or innocence turned on the kinds of evidence brought to court. In Salem, the usual standards of evidence in New England courts had been abandoned for a time, due to a strong sense that a conspiracy by evil forces against the good people was at work. Yet that sense could not have prevailed if the colony's regular political and judicial system had been in place. That feeling quickly passed, too late for the twenty dead and the dozens more who suffered grievously.

The members of one Salem jury which had found people guilty of witchcraft in 1692 reconsidered their judgments less than a year later. Using a heavily loaded phrase to begin, "We confess," the jurymen wrote,

> "that we ourselves were not capable to understand, nor able to withstand, the mysterious delusions of the powers of darkness, and prince of the air; but were, for want of knowledge in ourselves, and better information from others, prevailed with to take up with such evidence against the accused, as, on further consideration and better information, we justly fear was insufficient for the touching the lives of any."[15]

Samuel Parris met with Salem villagers in November 1694 and admitted that in 1692 he had "believed where he should have doubted." The General Court of Massachusetts ordered a day of fasting in 1697 to acknowledge the tragedy that had occurred at Salem. One of the judges of the Oyer and Terminer Court, Samuel Sewall, then gave his minister, Samuel Willard, a confession of sin in 1692. Willard read the document to his congregation in Boston as Sewall stood silently weeping by a pew. Sewall wrote of himself that "he is, upon many accounts, more concerned than any that he knows of" [. . .] "Desires to take the Blame and Shame of it," "Asking pardon of men."[16] Cotton Mather never apologized or did much more than continue to waffle about evidence used to convict witches. But in regard to witchcraft, he stayed away from direct accusations and courts.

The misuse of evidence in Salem is thrown into further perspective by the outcome of another witch scare in the area in 1692. But this affair was a matter of "escaping Salem," as Richard Godbeer put it.[17] The trouble broke out in Stamford, Connecticut, and was obviously influenced by events in Salem. A 17-year-old servant, Katherine Branch, began to have fits in April 1692 that resembled the ones afflicting girls in Salem. Following Massachusetts' practice, the Connecticut Colony's representative assembly created an Oyer and Terminer Court in June. Included on this panel were the governor and deputy governor of the colony. In September, the court set three accused women free while continuing to detain two others. Seventy-six townspeople had signed a petition attesting to the good character of one of the freed women. The two still in jail had been tested by "swimming" in June, on the folk theory that pure water would reject a witch; she would float. These two suspects had stayed on the water's surface, and so they remained in custody.

At this point, Connecticut's deputy governor, William Jones, examined the available literature on witchcraft cases and especially on tests of guilt. He found warnings that there must be "good and sufficient proofs" in any witchcraft trial. Meanwhile, Connecticut ministers announced their opinion that swimming a witch was illegal and sinful. A jury deliberating in late October found one woman guilty; her conviction was then overturned by a panel of three magistrates. No one was executed.

Thus, whatever broad patterns or attitudes troubled Puritans in the late seventeenth century, it was the particular set of circumstances in 1692 that facilitated the successful explosion of folk belief in Satan and witchcraft in one court of law. Prior to that year, witchcraft cases in New England usually involved only one or two defendants. Most accusations did not lead to a trial; those that did typically ended in acquittal, just as the Connecticut cases of 1692 did. Juries were usually reluctant to convict for witchcraft in the first place. If the initial panels returned a guilty verdict, magistrates who reviewed witch convictions on appeal often exercised their right to overturn the decision. Prior to the Salem outbreak, there were ninety-three defendants altogether in witch cases in New England; only sixteen of those were executed.[18] Even a woman who admitted to practicing witchcraft in Boston in 1652 was acquitted of the charge, only to be found guilty of infanticide and hanged.[19] No death sentences for witchcraft had been handed down in the region since 1663 except for a case in Boston in 1688, personally managed by Cotton Mather.

In short, the higher a case went in the New England judiciary before 1692, the less likely it was to result in a conviction. This pattern reflects developments regarding witchcraft cases in Western Europe; after roughly 1630, and earlier in England, the Netherlands, Spain, and Italy, among other regions, the elite ceased to accept the charge of witchcraft as a triable offense. In England, for example, after King James I personally intervened to bring a witch panic to a halt in 1616, executions for witchcraft became rare in his realm.[20] It was only during the height of the English Civil War, 1645–46, that the breakdown of the regular courts and chaos in the political system allowed a witch panic to develop in a part of Essex. Probably more than 100 people were executed, on the basis of particularly specious "evidence" collected by gentlemen with no official status. The leader of the hunt was Matthew Hopkins, who declared himself "Witchfinder General." Suspects were tried in local courts, but the assize (circuit) courts did not operate in the early stages of the pursuit.

Hopkins and his associates used methods of interrogation already in disfavor in English courts, among them sleep deprivation, starving his prisoners, and probing their bodies with needles to find a "witches' mark," a place where the devil had supposedly touched a new recruit and where the person would not feel pain. That is, Hopkins tortured his victims. When the assize justices in Norfolk heard objections to such methods, they sent a sharp inquiry to Hopkins. Apparently he never replied; in any event, the magistrates forbade most of his practices. During 1646, the hunt came to an end, and Hopkins soon died of tuberculosis.[21]

In key respects, the events in Salem of 1692–93 mimicked the story of Essex almost five decades earlier. And while Cotton Mather was no torturer, he followed Matthew Hopkins' lead in maintaining that Satan was hard at work in Massachusetts and that his minions, people who had pledged their lives and souls to him, were causing deaths as well as discernible harm to the living.

Mather was one of those European and American figures of the seventeenth century who simultaneously believed in something called science, which entailed conducting experiments and achieving verifiable results, and in the power of darkness, which could not be seen or tested but whose effects appeared to some to be quite real. In this dualism he was hardly alone, at the time or even to the present day. Mather carried out scientific experiments and collected the latest equipment for research at the same time that he argued Satan had supernatural abilities. In considering witches, Swedish cases, not the problems and the end of the Essex hunt, influenced Mather. His father, Increase, spent the years 1689–92 in London. He returned to Massachusetts as the talk of witchcraft was gaining strength. Increase and Cotton both knew of a large hunt around Mora, Sweden, in 1668–76. Cotton discussed the Swedish events with approval in his *Wonders of the Invisible World*, the book he published in Boston in October 1692. He was certain that at Mora "the Devils, by the help of Witches," had drawn "hundreds" of children into an evil plot to harm their neighbors.[22] Convictions in the hunt were based largely on testimony by children, who claimed that they had been transported to witches' Sabbaths by women. Both Mathers must have known that the Swedish trials ended with the freeing of many prisoners, after royal commissioners dispatched from Stockholm expressed skepticism about the evidence used to obtain convictions and officials in the capital finally had a chance to examine both the "proof" used at Mora and long-standing criticisms of it. Children now began to confess that they had made up their stories, and a 13-year-old boy regarded as a ringleader for others who had testified was executed.[23] But Cotton Mather did not mention that outcome to his readers.

The kinds of evidence admitted in the Salem cases, especially on specters, were disallowed in other New England cases. Nor were young girls, some not yet even teenagers, typically accepted as credible witnesses during the seventeenth century in courts based on English law. In Salem, a panic seized people and officials alike, leading them to suspend – for a fairly short time – the legal and evidentiary standards to which they had previously held. In this regard, the Salem events resemble other mass persecutions, for instance the Soviet "Great Terror" of 1936–37.[24]

One prominent interpretation of the Salem hunt argues that the Puritans of the area found it convenient to remove social deviants by labeling them "witches" and prosecuting them.[25] A second view is that the patriarchal, God- and devil-fearing Puritan society held largely negative views of women and was inclined to charge them with witchcraft when people were afflicted in mysterious ways. Females whose legal situation as widows or daughters blocked men from receiving an inheritance, or who had demonstrated their contentiousness in quarrels or court cases, were especially likely to be identified in Salem as the devil's helpers, this second argument continues.[26] A third study maintains that the major source of witchcraft charges was a long-simmering dispute between people in Salem Town, which was fast becoming a commercial port, and Salem Village, a farming community nearby. The hostility between these two different economic communities worsened as people from both were divided over a recently arrived minister, Samuel Parris,[27] who began to preach in Salem Village in late 1689. A fourth, relatively new interpretation emphasizes the emotional state of girls in Salem who had recently arrived as refugees from Maine, where particularly bloody attacks by Indians had just occurred. The Indians, "wicked cannibals" to white settlers, were linked in the Puritans' minds to the devil. Without the Indian war in Maine, this view continues, there would have been no witch crisis in Salem.[28]

In considering these analyses, it should be noted first that no direct evidence for any of them exists. No record is available, nor is there any suggestion in the surviving documents from Salem, that prominent males used the charge of witchcraft to persecute women they detested for other reasons. Indeed, nowhere in the substantial body of materials from European witch hunts has any such clear indication of a false pretext for persecution emerged. The idea that killing suspected witches had to do with state building seems equally unfounded,[29] while in various hunts it was the central authorities who brought them to an end, as happened in Sweden.

Much published work on the Salem trials has, or should have, ended in a blind alley, unable to say why there were not many more convictions for witchcraft in colonial New England. After all, Puritan attitudes toward women did not change for decades before and after 1692. Indian attacks had been much worse in the 1670s, and they continued to be a problem for whites along the frontier. Why fear of Indians would have been translated by young girls into accusations against whites in Salem must remain a puzzle. Commercial capitalism arrived slowly, and available land for inheritance continued to decrease. Nor, by the way, can the end of the hunts be attributed to the arrival of the "Scientific Revolution," itself a slow process that was well under way before 1692.

Mass persecutions discussed as events in which officials say they are pursuing one kind of enemy, but in fact have another goal in mind, rely on functional theory, whether the authors refer to it or not. The concept of "functions" is multilayered. In theory, they may be "manifest," goals readily evident in words or deeds, or they may be "latent." In the latter case, even those carrying out persecution may supposedly be unaware of the deeper or true purpose of their actions. But that idea, based originally on Freud's notion of the unconscious,[30] opens the door to pure speculation.

The theory of functionality has in any event encountered strong criticism in its home field. While introductory sociology texts still advance ideas of the 1940s and '50s on manifest and latent functions, rarely are the "concepts themselves employed in the research context." Vague and unprovable, they have not "found a home in [recent] sociological theory."[31] For some time now, sociologists have tied "function" to consequences, intended or otherwise, or to both intentions and results.[32] Studying an event's consequences is merely another way of saying the event requires analysis. Yet another problem plagues functional theory; it is unable "to cope with change," wrote the noted anthropologist Clifford Geertz.[33] Indeed, this is one of the key difficulties in trying to ascribe the Salem hunts to any strain of thought or activity not directly mentioned in the accusations: they rose and fell quickly, from the autumn of 1691 to early 1693. We are led once more to look closely at the events and immediate context of that period.

Panic about enemies within the good society, fed by ministers like Parris and Cotton Mather, erupted for a time in Salem in 1692. Disruption in the political and legal system, especially the absence of a governor as the fear spread, the lack of a charter for Massachusetts Colony in the early stages of the hunt, the attitudes and preoccupations of the new governor upon his arrival, and the lack of a steadier hand in the form of a functioning superior court, allowed the panic to result in the conviction of nineteen people, and the death of Giles Cory, for crimes they could not possibly have committed. The community recovered and, we might say, regained its bearings and its usual attitudes toward what constituted good evidence, during the fall of 1692. The whole episode lasted less than a year. Upon reflection, several leading figures in the persecutions recanted, rejected their earlier pro-persecution stances, and apologized with shame.

Considering these points, it was above all the problem of evidence during a panic, not any broader streams of thought or economic development that produced the Salem hunts. To be sure, Indian attacks in Maine, negative attitudes toward women, and other problems endemic to Massachusetts sharpened suspicion that Satan was on the scene. Yet in a more stable context, these themes would not have led to a large witch hunt, just as they had not in the past and would not in the future. Finally, the Salem events of 1692 should be seen in a European context, or more precisely as an extension of many of the worst practices of witch hunting on the European continent. Salem was an outpost of Europe, albeit one faced with particular dangers. It would be appropriate to shift the focus of thinking about the Salem hunts to questions of evidence and to regarding the persecution as an extension of witch fear across the Atlantic.

Notes

1 Elizabeth Reis, *Damned Women: Sinners and Witches in Puritan New England* (Ithaca, NY: Cornell University Press, 1997), 153.

2 Richard Godbeer, *Escaping Salem: The Other Witch Hunt of 1692* (New York: Oxford University Press, 2005).

3 Quoted in John Demos, *The Enemy Within: 2,000 Years of Witch hunting in the Western World* (New York: Viking, 2008), 159.

4 Peter Charles Hoffer, *The Salem Witchcraft Trials: A Legal History* (Lawrence, KS: University Press of Kansas, 1997), 71.

5 Chadwick Hansen, *Witchcraft at Salem* (New York: George Braziller, 1969), 133. And see Reis, *Damned Women*, 158–160.

6 "The Return of several Ministers consulted by his Excellency [Governor Phips], and the Honourable Council, upon the present Witchcrafts in *Salem* Village," Boston, June 15, 1692. Published as a postscript to Increase Mather, *Cases of Conscience Concerning Evil Spirits Personating Men; Witchcrafts, Infallible Proofs of Guilt in such as Are Accused With that Crime* (London: John Dunton, 1693). Originally Boston, 1693.

7 Samuel Willard, *Some Miscellany Observations*, cited in Hoffer, *The Salem Witchcraft Trials*, 129.

8 Hansen, *Witchcraft at Salem*, 141–143.

9 Cotton Mather, *The Wonders of the Invisible World. Being an Account of the Tryals of Several Witches Lately Executed in New-England* (London: John Russel Smith, 1862), 167–168. Originally published in Boston in 1692.

10 This was his *Cases of Conscience*.

11 Mather, *Cases of Conscience*, 283.

12 H.C. Erik Midelfort, *Witch Hunting in Southwestern Germany 1562–1684* (Stanford: Stanford University Press, 1972), 6.

13 Mather, *Cases of Conscience*, 283.

14 "The Christian Reader," in Mather, *Cases of Conscience*, 221.

15 "The Recantation of the Salem Jurors," 1693, in Alan Charles Kors and Edward Peters, eds., *Witchcraft in Europe, 400–1700: A Documentary History*, 2nd ed. (Philadelphia: University of Pennsylvania Press, 2001), 358–359.

16 Hoffer, *The Salem Witchcraft Trials*, 141, 144.

17 Godbeer, *Escaping Salem*. The following section on Connecticut is based on this book.

18 John Putnam Demos, *Entertaining Satan: Witchcraft and the Culture of Early New England* (New York: Oxford University Press, 1982), 11.

19 Elizabeth J. Kent, "Masculinity and Male Witches in Old and New England, 1593–1680," *History Workshop Journal* 60 (2005): 80.

20 George Kittredge, *Witchcraft in Old and New England* (Cambridge, MA: Harvard University Press, 1929), 322–323.

21 Christina Hole, *A Mirror of Witchcraft* (London: Chatto & Windus, 1957), 142–143, 163; and C. L'Estrange Ewen, *Witch Hunting and Witch Trials: The Indictments for Witchcraft From the Records of 1373 Assizes Held for the Home Circuit AD 1559–1736* (London: K. Paul, Trench, Trubner, 1929), 66.

22 Mather, *Wonders of the Invisible World*. Bold type was used in the book where Mather wished to emphasize similarities between the Swedish and Salem cases.

23 Bengt Ankarloo, "Sweden: The Mass Burnings," in *Early Modern European Witchcraft: Centres and Peripheries*, ed. Bengt Ankerloo and Gustav Henningsen (Oxford: Clarendon Press, 1993), 296–303.

24 I have addressed this issue in my *Life and Terror in Stalin's Russia, 1934–1941* (New Haven, CT: Yale University Press, 1996).

25 Kai T. Erikson, *Wayward Puritans: A Study in the Sociology of Deviance* (New York: John Wiley and Sons, 1966).

26 Carol F. Karlsen, *The Devil in the Shape of a Woman* (New York: W. W. Norton, 1987).

27 Paul Boyer and Stephen Nissenbaum, *Salem Possessed: The Social Origins of Witchcraft* (Cambridge, MA: Harvard University Press, 1974).

28 Mary Beth Norton, *In the Devil's Snare: The Salem Witchcraft Crisis of 1692* (New York: Alfred A. Knopf, 2002), especially 295.
29 This is the key argument in Brian P. Levack, *The Witch Hunt in Early Modern Europe*, 3rd ed. (New York: Pearson/Longman, 2006).
30 See Robert K. Merton, *Social Theory and Social Structure*, revised and enlarged ed. (Glencoe, IL: Free Press, 1957). Merton, a sociologist, began to develop functional theory in the late 1940s. He adapted the term function from biology, where it refers to "vital or organic processes" that "contribute to the maintenance of the organism." The words "vital" and "organic" suggest that a living creature, or a society, cannot live without certain processes. Immediately a problem arises in applying these ideas to witch hunts: life in Massachusetts and Western Europe proceeded without much persecution of suspected witches, or without any at all, in many places. This was so even in the periods of most intense hunting in certain areas, during the years 1580–90 and 1620–30. The waters are muddied further by attaching the adjectives "manifest" and "latent" to function, which Merton did in 1949. He adapted those modifiers "from their use in another context by Freud," although earlier thinkers had also found "latent" helpful to discuss processes "below the threshold of superficial observation." Merton declared that *manifest* functions are "consequences . . . which are intended and recognized by participants in the system." Naturally, *latent* functions are "neither intended nor recognized." That is, anyone involved somehow in enacting latent social functions does not see or think about them. So how do people trying much later to unravel the past know that function was involved in an act? Freud used "latent" when he felt he had some direct evidence of hidden intent or motivation, obtained especially through patients' dreams. Merton relied instead on what could be called commonsense observation.
31 Colin Campbell, "A Dubious Distinction: An Inquiry into the Value and Use of Merton's Concepts of Manifest and Latent Function," *American Sociological Review*, 47 (1982): 29, 30, 37; Charles J. Erasmus, "Obviating the Functions of Functionalism," *Social Forces* 45 (1967): 319; Jon Elster, "Merton's Functionalism and the Unintended Consequences of Action," in *Robert K. Merton and Contemporary Sociology*, ed. Carlo Mongardini and Simonetta Tabboni (New Brunswick, NJ: Transaction Publishers, 1998), 129. In Merton's chance to reply to critiques of his work, he spoke of "'latent' as distinct from 'manifest' *consequences*," ibid., 304; my italics.
32 Merton himself had several warnings for anyone drawing on his work. He thought that writers who endorse functionality might use his theories too quickly and fail to see more applicable "alternative modes of action." There was no need to argue that "all culture items fulfill vital functions." In other words, a social practice might not be functional at all, and it certainly might not bear latent functions within it. He added that "functional social scientists run the risk of erring in the other extreme, first, by being quick to find functional or adaptive value" in societies that are not their own – which he called "strange" or "primitive," *Social Theory*, 21, 51, 61, and 73.
33 Clifford Geertz, *The Interpretations of Cultures: Selected Essays by Clifford Geertz* (New York: Basic Books, 1973), 143.

Bibliography (selection)

Baker, Emerson, *A Storm of Witchcraft*. Oxford: Oxford University Press, 2015.
Boyer, Paul and Stephen Nissenbaum, *Salem Possessed: The Social Origins of Witchcraft*. Cambridge, MA: Harvard University Press, 1974.
Godbeer, Richard, *Escaping Salem: The Other Witch Hunt of 1692*. New York: Oxford University Press, 2005.
Norton, Mary Beth, *In the Devil's Snare: The Salem Witchcraft Crisis of 1692*. New York: Alfred A. Knopf, 2002.
Reis, Elizabeth, *Damned Women: Sinners and Witches in Puritan New England*. Ithaca, NY: Cornell University Press, 1997.

16

WITCHCRAFT AND THE EARLY MODERN MEDIA

Abaigéal Warfield

During the witchcraft prosecutions of the sixteenth and seventeenth centuries, news of witches, their crimes, confessions, and punishments made the early modern head-lines. Pamphlets and broadsheets were printed throughout Europe detailing specific cases. In this way, the early modern news media played a significant role in commu-nicating and constructing the crime of witchcraft to contemporaries. In recent years the historiography of witchcraft has become more focused on representations of witchcraft, both visual and textual. This has led to growing interest in how witchcraft was treated in early modern news media. This chapter will give an overview of some of the main historiographical developments in this emerging field of study. To date, most research has focused primarily on early modern Germany and early modern England. For this reason, these will be the geographical parameters for this overview. A number of issues will be considered: the origins of witchcraft news reports, author-ship/readership, form, content and function, the use of images, and news in trans-lation. As there is already a very useful survey of witchcraft in literature and drama, by Diane Purkiss,[1] this piece will focus purely on news media, the historiography of which has hitherto received no attention.

Historiographical context

While historians have long been aware that news reports of witches were in circu-lation at the time of the witch hunts, such reports have only become the subject of serious scholarship in the last three decades. Like images, pamphlets and broad-sides were previously used as extraneous sources in studies that focused primarily on trial manuscripts and legal sources.[2] Despite the linguistic turn of the 1990s, which saw attention shift to 'languages of witchcraft' and witnessed a closer inspection of demonological works,[3] in comparison to the erudite treatises and tracts, cheaper print media still failed to grasp the attention of scholars.

In 1984 Wolfgang Behringer began to draw attention to the role of print media by examining in detail a topical news pamphlet printed in 1590, 'The Expanded Witch-craft Report' (*Erwytterte Unholden Zeyttung*).[4] His interest in early modern news contin-ued to develop over the following two decades, and in 2009 he published 'Witchcraft and the Media' – one of the most useful overviews or introductions to the topic to date.

This looked at the use of a variety of media across various temporal and geographical boundaries, with a special focus on how news travelled. Behringer recognised that reports could be used as 'building blocks' for demonologists, an idea that was further substantiated by my own research.[5] He also argued that different media played different roles. For example, non-periodical pamphlets and broadsides tended to always promote the reality of witchcraft and rarely offered a sceptical outlook or commentary. On the other hand, monthly magazines provided authors and readers with a means to deconstruct the witch stereotype and combat superstition.[6] The nature of the medium is therefore significant, as it influenced, if not embodied, its function and message.

A number of other historians, such as Robert Walinski-Kiehl, in 2002,[7] and Harald Sipek, in 1994,[8] pointed to pamphlets as worthy sources, meriting more serious attention. The new millennium saw people begin to carry out case studies, or focus on certain aspects of printed news reports. For example, Hans Harter wrote a monograph looking at the first known witchcraft pamphlets and a broadside concerning a witch from Schiltach.[9] Ulla Krah explored the relationship between fact and fiction (a point which will be discussed further later on) in news reports, analysing a number of German broadsides.[10] Charles Zika, in 2007, highlighted the importance of images in the news and how they helped to construct an already evolving stereotype of the witch.[11]

Prior to Behringer's article in 2009, one of the most detailed discussions of witchcraft pamphlet literature was to be found in Joy Wiltenburg's work, which included a section comparing German and English witchcraft narratives.[12] This is still the only comparative analysis available, despite the growing interest in news media in Germany and England. With regards to English pamphlet literature, Marion Gibson was the first to publish in this field.[13] Her book *Reading Witchcraft* suggests ways to dissect, or in her words 'deconstruct', the narratives found in reports, in order to discern which part is legal record, and which part is fiction. She questions the verisimilitude of the reports, asking whether there is any truth to be found. While her post-modern approach is refreshing, a broader contextualisation of the reports is lacking, as is any discussion of the images. In 2007, Anna Bayman, sharing Gibson's interest in the role of fact and fiction, proposed that 'Witchcraft, located on the borders of fact and fiction, or "record and story", offers historians the opportunity to study the construction of narrative and the nature of evidence and record'.[14] She underscored the tension between commercial impulses and moralising ones and argued that the two strands of pamphlets may co-exist. Bayman hones in on reception, suggesting that perhaps reports were more entertaining than morally constructive to some audiences. Her article highlights a significant issue for historians of early modern news: not knowing how people read and understood reports.

More recently, in 2011, Carla Suhr completed a PhD on the genre of English witchcraft pamphlets, tackling them through a linguistic lens. This approach focuses more on language (not surprisingly) and less on the historical context, however, it does include an interesting analysis of the images and a useful appendix of the content of pamphlets.[15] Charlotte Rose Millar has also been working on English witchcraft pamphlets, taking a very different approach through exploring the relationship between emotion and witchcraft.[16] Her work is reflective of a broader turn to emotions in witchcraft scholarship.[17]

While Millar's work focuses on the feelings of the witches, as presented by the media, new research has begun to explore how the media shaped emotional responses to witches.[18] The role news media played in constructing fear of witchcraft in early modern Germany is the subject of my own research.[19] Unlike, Gibson and Millar, my analysis of German witchcraft news reports incorporates images and compares news reports to other contemporaneous texts, including demonological works, works of art and trial manuscripts.[20] This comparative approach uncover points of intersection between various discourses hitherto unnoticed. In order to further disentangle the web created by the 'extended mediazation'[21] of witchcraft more comparative work is needed.

Origins of witchcraft news pamphlets and broadsides

The second half of the sixteenth century saw a sharp rise in the publication of news pamphlets and reports. In early modern Germany a new genre rose to fame: *Newe Zeitungen* (new reports). These were essentially non-periodical reports[22] that were printed following notable events or happenings. They were either printed as a *Flugschrift* (a pamphlet) which were at least four pages long, or as a *Flugblatt* (a broadside), which was a single page print. While some pamphlets included a woodcut on their title page, most news broadsides included a large image depicting the contents of the report in vivid detail. Alongside witchcraft, other topics covered included reports of gruesome murders and executions, battles, monstrous births, and celestial apparitions. Publishers and printers were quick to include news of witches into reports, and in Germany, as the number of witch trials increased, so too did the number of reports. The titles of these reports were often similar, beginning with literary hooks such as 'a terrifying new report' (*ein erschreckliche Neue Zeitung*). Most of them also claimed to be 'truthful' (*warhafftig*) accounts of events that really happened.

In England, witchcraft pamphlets were part of a wider and growing pamphleteering market.[23] However, it has been argued that witchcraft pamphlets make up a distinct genre of their own, as the nature of reportage, particularly in earlier pamphlets, differed from other news pamphlets, chiefly in the way that authors utilised large parts of legal documents for the report. It is interesting to note that many of the famous or well-known pamphleteers of this period did not author witchcraft pamphlets. Bayman suggests that they did not write such reports for two main reasons: firstly, they did not think the London audience would be interested, and, secondly, following the accession of James I to the throne, they were wary of entering a discourse that King James I was clearly concerned with.[24] That said, pamphlets on witchcraft were still penned, albeit by lesser-known or anonymous authors. English witchcraft pamphlets also tended to be longer. Like the German pamphlets, there was an emphasis on the truth and trustworthiness of accounts, however, the titles' emphasis was usually focused on the 'discovery' of the witch or witches. This focus on discovery, and the corresponding discovery narrative is not a feature in the German reports. In terms of numbers of editions and prints, Suhr's research shows that there was a clear rise in publications in the latter half of the sixteenth century; such a rise is also evident for early modern German reports in this same period.

Readership and authorship

It is important to ask who the potential audience for these publications were, and also who was responsible for writing them. With regards to audience, Wiltenburg has argued that the audience for this type of literature was quite broad and could extend to people of humble status.[25] A contemporary account from Augsburg names both journeymen and students as groups who bought such reports.[26] There has been no comprehensive study of literacy in early modern Germany, but it has been estimated that the literacy rates may have been around 30 per cent for Augsburg, and similar figures have been proposed for Nuremberg and the Franconian hinterland.[27] In general it is agreed that literacy rose in this period but that in both Germany and England, levels of literacy varied sharply between the countryside and towns. David Cressy has estimated, on the basis of signatures on loyalty oaths, an overall figure of 30 per cent literacy for rural England in the 1640s.[28] However, it is important to remember that reading and writing were separate skills in this period; thus someone might have been able to read but not have been able to write. Also, it was common for people to read aloud to their families or friends. In addition, almost half of the German witchcraft news reports were written in rhyme to be sung to well-known tunes. Therefore, these news reports were far more accessible to a broader audience, both literate and illiterate: one did not have to be literate to participate in a written culture.[29]

Witchcraft broadsheets and pamphlets were produced with the intent of being sold. There is little information regarding the size of individual print runs. Travelling pedlars could pay printers to run off copies of prints. For example a travelling pedlar in the eastern Netherlands ran off 1,000 copies of a sheet with three popular songs for one guilder.[30] These shorter works provided lucrative business for printers while they were compiling more complex works in the press.[31] In the words of Andrew Pettegree: 'No publisher could make a reputation with works of this sort. But they could make money'.[32] Unfortunately, while there is often a reference to the printer and place of publication, the author is almost never named. So who were the anonymous authors of these reports? Print-shop owners and workers were possible authors, as were 'hack journalists, roving students and underemployed teachers'.[33] Churchmen, lawyers, and magistrates are also known to have penned reports about miracles, crimes and punishments.[34] In Germany some were possibly penned by *Zeitungsänger* (news-ballad singers) who would then print copies and distribute them themselves as they sang the contents from market squares or on their travels. In Germany and England reports would have been sold in book stores and markets, and in England chap-men became responsible for the distribution of pamphlets throughout the countryside.

With regards to cost, the price of news pamphlets and small tracts in Germany ranged from 3 to 6 Pfennigs in the sixteenth and seventeenth centuries, while shorter pamphlets may have been cheaper.[35] To provide some context, the daily wage of a master mason or carpenter in the early sixteenth century was about 24 Pfennigs, while a day labourer would earn about 60 Pfennigs per week.[36] In comparison, short pamphlets printed on cheap paper in England cost 3 or 4 pence, with prices rising for longer tracts. While the price of pamphlets declined as the cost of paper dropped, pamphlets continued to be affordable, but not cheap. Wiltenburg and Suhr caution that this ephemeral literature was not just targeted at and read by people of humble origin, but that intellectual or aristocratic readers were not excluded from reading these texts.[37] Indeed, many German broadsides only survived the ravages of time after being meticulously selected and collected by a reformed Swiss pastor Johann Jakob Wick (1522–1588) in Zurich.[38]

Function: between fact and fiction

What was the function of these reports? Some historians, such as Robert Walin-ski-Kiehl, have labelled them as propagandistic, believing that pamphlets played an important role in inciting audiences to action against witches.[39] Despite this claim he cautiously recognises the impossibility of ever knowing how people read them or reacted to reports. There is evidence to suggest that authorities were wary of news reports concerning witches. For example, Nuremberg, an Imperial Free City that saw very few witch prosecutions, censored a broadsheet in 1627 detailing the execution and crimes of witches in Bamberg and Würzburg.[40] Their swift act of censorship demonstrates the city council's concern about the pamphlet's potential to incite a witch panic.

However, in other cases, pamphlets were actually used by other authorities to try and authenticate and validate the prosecution of witches. For example a preacher in Sélestat in Alsace, Reinhard Lutz, printed a pamphlet following the execution of four witches in 1570 in order to set forth the reasons why their treatment had been just and in accordance with the law.[41] Lutz claimed that he wrote the tract in question so that the people of Sélestat may understand that 'a lawful sentence was pronounced'.[42] He proposed that many people, not understanding the nature of witchcraft, may have concluded or thought that one had 'dealt improperly and not lawfully with these people [the witches]'.[43] However, Lutz pointed out that the women, having entered a 'damnable, demonic and accursed covenant'[44] with the 'Evil Spirit', received their 'due punishment'.[45] Similarly, in 1666, the council printer in Augsburg, Andreas Aperger, printed a report where he quoted sections verbatim from the Council Punishment Book, taking care to point out that all of the actions taken against the witches by the authorities were according to the law.[46]

One of the biggest issues in the historiography of witchcraft news media is whether reports were meant to be taken seriously or if they were simply a form of entertainment. Baymen, writing on the Elizabethan and Jacobean witchcraft pamphlets, believes that they were both titillating and entertaining, while simultaneously moralising, with some pamphlets giving a higher priority to entertainment.[47] Gibson, similarly divided English pamphlets into 'triviall' and 'necessary' ones; however, she maintains that

> serious pamphlets can, in fact, be just as unreliable as trivial pamphlets, because they sometimes have propaganda purposes which may distort their view of witchcraft. Trivial pamphlets can be unreliable because they appear to privilege genre or style above factual reporting and produce a version of witchcraft which may be heavily influenced by the form of its narration.[48]

Wiltenburg, on the other hand, stresses that reports, especially those claiming to be 'true', were meant to be taken seriously.[49] With regards to the German news reports, it is not as easy to label the pamphlets in this manner, dividing them into two distinct categories. Certainly there are some that we know to be pure fiction, imagined up by an author, possibly for financial gain,[50] but in general, most pamphlets contain this underlying interplay between entertainment and earnestness. The pamphlets also have a religious undertone throughout. Many point to the danger of the devil. In fact, one of the most popular Biblical passages quoted in pamphlets concerning witches, alongside the well-known Exodus 22:18, 'Thou shalt not suffer a witch to live', is the less well-known, 1 Peter 5:8: 'Be sober, be vigilant; because your adversary the devil, as a roaring lion, walketh about, seeking whom he may devour'.[51] Authors forcefully remind readers to be on their guard and to be god-fearing through the stories told in the news.

With so many authors claiming that their reports were 'true', it is not surprising that this has become a point of contention in historical research. From whence did they get their facts? For English pamphlets, Gibson has shown how earlier pamphlets (pre 1590), in particular, were heavily based on, and indeed constructed from, legal sources. This is not the case in Germany. While narrative only became more popular in England after 1590, in the German pamphlets and broadsides, the stories of the witches were mostly written in narrative format. This narrative was sometimes broken to number the crimes of the witch in list format. The narrative usually began with the name and age of the witch, a description of how they met the devil before outlining the crimes that they had confessed to, ending with a description of their punishment. It is possible that authors heard this information when it was read out publicly at the witch's execution. However, by the late seventeenth century, some authors of reports stuck very close to the authoritative record as related in the Council Punishment Book.[52] The chronology here may be significant, as reports in the late seventeenth century would have been competing with periodical news reports, and hence may have strived to stick as close as possible to the official facts of the case.[53]

Aside from using trial manuscripts, German authors appear to have used a number of other sources for penning their news, such as other news reports or even demonologies. There were no copyright laws like we have today, and as a result copying and recycling of narratives was rife not only amongst authors of witch reports, but more generally in publishing. In fact, most demonologies were compiled by recycling and reusing examples and narratives from earlier demonological works. One news pamphlet, written in verse, detailing the crimes and execution of 133 witches in the County of Westphalia was reprinted multiple times. The first edition that I have found, printed in 1588, claimed that 133 witches were executed on one day in 1588. However, the same report was printed again in Jena in 1589 and then in Erfurt in 1591, followed by another print in 1596 (which claimed to be 'erstlich gedruckt zu Regenspurg').[54] Each one claimed that the witches were burnt that year; however, they were clearly a copy of the earlier pamphlet, the only thing changed was the year of the report.[55] What is more striking, however, is that some authors copied stories from demonologies and attempted to pass them off as current news.[56] In one such case an author, writing in 1581, translated an entire section concerning weather magic from Heinrich Kramer's *Malleus Maleficarm* into vernacular verse and claimed that the story related to a witch who was recently executed in the Margraviate of Baden.[57] These cases confound our understanding of reports. Was it more important for the stories to be truthful? Or was the moral of the story more important? These questions are difficult to answer, but there is a general consensus amongst historians that whether or not the stories were copied, fictionalised, imagined, or carefully noted down from legal sources, they are all valuable sources, in that they allow us to understand how the crime of witchcraft was popularly imagined.

The stories or narratives contained in the news have been deconstructed by historians. Gibson claims that there are three main witchcraft narratives evident in

English pamphlets: charity refused/denied; revenge; and motiveless malignity.[58] While some of these narratives are recognisable in the German pamphlets, especially in the 1570s and 1580s, authors very quickly began to outline the witches' crimes without going in any detail as to why the witch caused the harm. However, Gibson claims that in England the rise of narratives with motiveless malignity developed when the victims were noble or gentle and so did not want to appear to be deserving of a witch's wrath. In Germany, as the scale of the witch hunts increased detailed stories about individual witches and their specific motives became less popular. From the 1580s onwards single pamphlets were often detailing not just the crimes of one witch from one town but also the crimes and executions of multiple witches across various towns. The emphasis shifted from *why* witches caused harm to outlining what specific harm they caused. One must remember that England and the Holy Roman Empire experienced very different levels of witch persecution, and that the nature and scope of witch hunting ultimately had an impact on how the crime of witchcraft was reported. The sheer scale of witchcraft executions in German speaking lands in the second half of the sixteenth century led to the character of German witch news reports changing, as they began to offer sweeping panoramas of witch hunting rather than reporting individual cases.[59] It is interesting to note, however, that when the witch prosecutions began to decline in German speaking lands, reports once again began to focus in more detail on individual witches, what harm they caused, and why they did so.

Just as the character of the report reflected the nature of prosecution, the content and the crimes included in the reports tell us something about the contemporary, cultural and local understandings of witchcraft. The crimes reported in the German and English pamphlets are quite different. While the German pamphlets frequently allude to the witches' dance (*Hexentanz*), such references are absent from English reports (with the exception of the Lancashire 1612 pamphlet).[60] In addition, while English pamphlets often refer to witches' familiars, or spirits in the form of animals who feed on the witch through a special teat, references to familiars are most unusual in German accounts. A comparative analysis of the news reports will undoubtedly shed light on how witchcraft was imagined and constructed differently in different geographical regions and cultures.

News travels and news in translation

Just as news travels today, there were a number of witch executions that became media sensations in the early modern period. Some stories or narratives transcended geographical boundaries, and were translated into foreign languages and printed in foreign news reports, whilst others made their way into local chronicles or demonologies.

The most famous case, recognised by historians as creating a media shockwave, was the trial and story of Peter Stumpf, a werewolf witch, who was reportedly executed in a small town of Bedburg near Cologne in 1589. In the year 1589 numerous broadsides were printed in Augsburg, Nuremberg, and Cologne, detailing the case with a large woodcut depicting his crimes and unusual execution.[61] There was very little difference in the image and text in each of these single-leaf prints. There were also a number of pamphlets that included accounts of the case in Germany and abroad. Willem de Blécourt has recently tried to decipher the chronological order of these reports.[62] The story was recorded in a pamphlet printed in Antwerp in 1589 and London in 1590.[63] Interestingly, the London pamphlet contains the most elaborate and detailed report concerning Stumpf. The English author purported that it was a translation of a German ('high Duch') text that was printed in Cologne.[64] There has been no matching German pamphlet found to support this claim. This, along with the extraordinarily sensational details interwoven in the English text, has led de Blécourt to surmise that the narrative was 'an imaginative elaboration of the earlier documents'.[65] Stumpf's story became so well known it was incorporated into Martín Del Rio's *Disquisitionum magicarum* (1599/1600).[66] It was included as an example in Book Two, question 18, which asked whether magicians could transform the bodies of one species into those of another.[67] The same passage was then repeated in Maria Francesco Guazzo's work in 1608. Guazzo cited Stumpf's confession as proof that incubus and succubus devils existed in his *Compendium Maleficarum* (1626).[68] It is worthy of note, that no corresponding trial manuscript for the Stumpf case has ever been located. The trial of Stumpf, although the most well-known, was not the only report that made it into the foreign press. For example, the trial of the Pappenheimer family in Munich in 1600 was reported in an English pamphlet, printed in London in 1601.[69]

These few examples highlight the potential for news to travel, and to be transmitted from one genre, or discourse, into another, relatively fluidly. For this reason, early modern news media can offer valuable insights into the communication and transmission of ideas and narratives of witchcraft in the early modern world.

Suggestions for future research

This is still an innovative and developing area of research. While there has been much progress made, especially with regards to the treatment of witchcraft in news media in Germany and England, there has yet to be a systematic survey or investigation of news reports in other European countries. In addition, there has been little comparative work carried out, with studies tending to focus on one geographical or linguistic region. While my own work on German pamphlets and broadsides incorporated the images into the analysis, this has yet to be done for the English reports. To date, the best analysis of images of witchcraft in the early modern news is to be found in Charles Zika's *Appearance of Witchcraft*.[70] To fully understand the nature of the media, it is crucial that we explore both textual and visual elements. Finally, as Behringer pointed out in his article in 2009, there is still a broad range of other media that have yet to be mined by historians, such as periodical news reports and monthly magazines.

As we expand and enrich our approach to early modern media sources, we will simultaneously broaden our understanding of the role that media played in communicating and constructing the crime of witchcraft. Ultimately such research will help us to uncover further the cultural imaginings and meanings of witchcraft in the early modern world.

Notes

1 Diane Purkiss, "Witchcraft in Early Modern Literature," in *The Oxford Handbook of Witchcraft in Early Modern Europe and Colonial America*, ed. Brian Levack (Oxford: Oxford University Press, 2013), 122–140. See also her monograph *The Witch in History: Early Modern and Twentieth Century Representations* (London: Routledge, 1996). Lyndal Roper has also explored how the witch was imagined in visual and literary sources in her volume *The Witch in the Western Imagination* (Virginia: University of Virginia Press, 2012).

2 For example Erik Midelfort made use of pamphlets in his work *Witch Hunting in Southwestern Germany 1562–1684: The Social and Intellectual Foundations* (Stanford: Stanford University Press, 1972).

3 Some chief examples of this shift in interest can be found in Stuart Clark's *Thinking with Demons: The Idea of Witchcraft in Early Modern Europe* (Oxford: Oxford University Press, 1997), which was a momentous work seeking to more fully understand how the ideology of witchcraft was constructed and understood through language and texts. See also the edited collection of essays Stuart Clark, ed., *Languages of Witchcraft: Narrative, Ideology and Meaning in Early Modern Culture* (Basingstoke: Macmillan Press, 2001). Gerhild Scholz Williams also wrote on the nature of witchcraft discourse, investigating how popular and intellectual texts helped shaped people's understanding of the world in her *Defining Dominion: The Discourses of Magic and Witchcraft in Early Modern France and Germany* (Michigan: University of Michigan Press, 1999).

4 Wolfgang Behringer, "Hexenverfolgungen im Spiegel zeitgenössischer Publizistik. Die 'Erwytterte Unholden Zeyttung' von 1590," in *Oberbayerisches Archiv* 109 (1984): 346–354.

5 Wolfgang Behringer, "Witchcraft and the Media," in *Ideas and Cultural Margins in Early Modern Germany*, ed. Marjorie E. Plummer and Robin Barnes (Surrey: Ashgate, 2009), 217–238; Abaigéal Warfield "The Media Representation of the Crime of Witchcraft in Early Modern Germany: An Investigation of Non-Periodical News-sheets and Pamphlets, 1533–1669" (Ph.D. diss., National University of Ireland, Maynooth, 2013).

6 Behringer, "Witchcraft and the Media," 233.

7 Robert Walinski Kiehl, "Pamphlets, Propaganda and Witch Hunting in Germany c. 1560–1630," *Reformation* 6 (2002): 49–74.

8 Harald Sipek, "Newe Zeitung'-Marginalien zur Flugblatt – und Flugschriftenpublizistik," in *Hexen und Hexenverfolgung in deutschen Südwesten*, ed. Harald Siebenmorgen. 2 vols. (Ostfildern: Cantz, 1994), ii, 85–92.

9 Hans Harter, *Der Teufel von Schiltach* (Schiltach: Stadt Schiltach, 2005).

10 Ursula Maria Krah, "Fiktionalität und Faktizität in frühneuzeitlichen Kleinschriften (Einblattdrucke und Flugschriften)," in *Realität und Mythos: Hexenverfolgung und Rezeptionsgeschichte*, ed. Katrin Moeller and Burghart Schmidt (Hamburg: DOBU, 2003), 77–86.

11 Charles Zika, *The Appearance of Witchcraft: Print and Visual Culture in Sixteenth-Century Europe* (New York: Routledge, 2007). See especially chapter 7, 179–209.

12 Joy Wiltenberg, *Disorderly Women and Female Power in the Street Literature of Early Modern England and Germany* (Virginia: Virginia University Press, 1992), 238–250.

13 Marion Gibson, *Reading Witchcraft: Stories of Early English Witches* (London: Routledge, 1999); *Early Modern Witches: Witchcraft Cases in Contemporary Writing* (London: Routledge, 2000).

14 Anna Bayman, "'Large Hands, Wide Ears, and Piercing Sights': The 'Discoveries' of the Elizabethan and Jacobean Witch Pamphlets," *Literature and History* 16 (2007): 26–45.

15 Carla Suhr, *Publishing for the Masses: Early Modern English Witchcraft Pamphlets* (Helsinki: Société Néophilologique, 2011).

16 Charlotte-Rose Millar, *Witchcraft, the Devil and Emotions in Early Modern England* (London: Routledge, 2017).

17 Laura Kounine and Michael Ostling, *Emotions in the History of Witchcraft* (London: Palgrave Macmillan, 2016).

18 Abaigéal Warfield, "The Witch and the Weather: Fear of Weather Magic in German Sixteenth-Century Neue Zeitungen" forthcoming in *The Sixteenth Century Journal* 50.4 (Winter 2019).

19 Abaigéal Warfield, *Witches in the News: Constructing Fear of Witchcraft in Early Modern Germany*, forthcoming with Palgrave Macmillan.

20 Warfield, 'Witchcraft Illustrated: the Crime of Witchcraft in Early Modern German News Broadsheets' in Andrew Pettegree (ed.), *Broadsheets. Single-sheet Publishing in the first age of Print* (Leiden: Brill, 2017), 459–487.

21 Behringer coined this term in his essay "Witchcraft and the Media," 235.

22 Non-periodical reports, unlike periodical reports, were not published at regular recurring intervals.

23 Joad Raymond has done much work on the nature of pamphleteering in early modern England. See Joad Raymond, *Pamphlets and Pamphleteering in Early Modern Britain* (Cambridge: Cambridge University Press, 2006); Raymond, ed., *The Oxford History of Popular Print Culture: Volume One: Cheap Print in Britain and Ireland to 1660* (Oxford: Oxford University Press, 2011). See also Tessa Watt, *Cheap Print and Popular Piety* (Cambridge: Cambridge University Press, 1993).

24 Bayman, "Large Hands," 28–29.

25 Joy Wiltenberg, *Crime and Culture in Early Modern Germany* (Virginia: University of Virginia Press, 2013), 11.

26 Ibid.

27 Hans-Jörg Künast, *"Getruckt zu Augsburg" Buchdruck und – handel in Augsburg zwischen 1468 und 1555* (Niemayer: Tubingen, 1997), 13.

28 Wiltenburg, *Disorderly Women*, 33.

29 Helmut Graser and B. Ann Tlusty, "Layers of Literacy in a Sixteenth-Century Case of Fraud," in *Ideas and Cultural Margins in Early Modern Germany*, ed. Majorie E. Plummer and Robin Barnes (Surrey: Ashgate, 2009), 31.

30 Andrew Pettegree, *The Book in the Renaissance* (London: Yale University Press, 2010), 136.

31 Ibid., 135.

32 Ibid., 334.

33 Tom Cheesman, *The Shocking Ballad Picture Show: German Popular Literature and Cultural History* (Oxford: Berg Publishers, 1994), 48.

34 Ibid.

35 Wiltenburg, *Disorderly Women*, 35.

36 Ibid.

37 Wiltenburg, *Crime and Culture*, 11; Suhr, *Publishing for the Masses*, 21.

38 For more detail on Johann Jacob Wick and his collection see Wiltenburg, *Crime and Culture*, 106–110. Also see Franz Mauelshagen, *Wunderkammer auf Papier: die "Wickiana" zwischen Reformation und Volksglaube* (Epfendorf: Bibliotheca academica Verlag, 2011).

39 Walinski-Kiehl, "Pamphlets," 49–74.

40 Ibid.

41 Reinhard Lutz, *Warhafftige Zeittung / Von Gottlosen Hexen / Auch Ketzerischen und Teuffels Weibern / die zu Schettstadt / deß H. Römischen Reichstadt in Elsaß / auf den XXII. Herbstmonat deß 1570. Jahrs / von wegen ihrer schändtlichen Teuffelsverpflichtung rc. sindt verbrennt worden* (S.l., 1571).

42 Ibid.: '. . . deß ein billiches urtheil felle.'

43 Ibid.: '. . . vielleicht viel gedencken / auch schliessen möchten / das man vngebührlich vnd nicht rechtmessig mit diesen Personen gehandelt . . .'

44 Ibid.: '. . . schantlicher / teufflischer / vnd verfluchter verpflichtung . . .'

45 Ibid.: '. . . jhr gebürende straff'.

46 *Was die in deß heyligen Röm: Reichsstatt Augsburg etlich Wochen lang in verhafft gelegne zwo hexen / [. . .] wegen ihrer hexereyen güt vnd peinlich bekent [. . .] auf Sambstag den 18. Aprill diß 1654 Jahre hingericht worden. . . .* printed by Andreas Aperger (Augsburg, 1654).

47 Bayman, "Large Hands," 5.

48 Gibson, *Reading Witchcraft*, 119.

49 Joy Wiltenberg, "True Crime: The Origins of Modern Sensationalism," *The American Historical Review* 109.5 (2004): 1383.

50 For example, there was a report printed in 1591 by Georg Kress about 300 women who had made a pact with the devil in Julich-Berg, who could turn into wolves. There is no evidence of any such case, and it is thought that the author was trying to cash in on the popular interest in werewolves and witches following the sensational Stumpf case: *Erschröcklichen und zuvor nie erhörte newe Zeitung / welcher massen im Landt zu Gülch uber dreyhundert Weibs personen / mit dem Teuffel sich verbunden [. . .]* (Augsburg, 1591). For more see Erika Münster-Schröer, "Hexenverfolgung in Jülich-Berg und der Einfluß Johann Weyers," *Spee-Jahrbuch* 7 (2000): 59–103.

51 1 Peter 5:8 King James Bible, accessed online (London: Robert Barker, 1611). www.king-jamesbibleonline.org/1-Peter-5-8/ (accessed 20 July 2014). The German of the Luther Bible is: 'Seid nüchtern und wachet; denn euer Widersacher, der Teufel, geht umher wie ein brüllender Löwe und sucht, welchen er verschlinge' available online at Biblegateway: www.biblegateway.com/passage/?search=1+Petrus+5%2C1+Peter+5&version=LUTH1545; AMP (accessed 20 July 2014).

52 Warfield, "Media Representation," 278–294.

53 I am grateful to Wolfgang Behringer who suggested this in response to a paper I presented, 'Fact and Fiction in the Hexenzeitungen: "A terrifying truthful report . . ."', at the *Arbeitkreis interdisziplinäre Hexenforschung* conference "Hexerei in den Medien-Teil II" at Stuttgart-Hohenheim, Germany, 21 February 2014.

54 *Dreyerley Warhaffte newe zeittung. . . . Die dritte. Auß dem Landt Westuahllen/ von der Statt Ossenbruckh/ wie man auff einen Tag 133. Vnholden verbreñt hat . . . geschehen den 9. Aprilis diß 96. Jars.* (s.l., 1596). It is unclear whether the printer is referring to Regensburg in Bavaria or in Switzerland.

55 Warfield, "Media Representation," 270–271.

56 Ibid., 263–267.

57 Ibid.

58 Gibson, *Reading Witchcraft*, 87–109.

59 Behringer, "Witchcraft in the Media," 226.

60 Willem de Blécourt, "Sabbath Stories: Towards a New History of Witches' Assemblies," in *The Oxford Handbook of Witchcraft in Early Modern Europe and Colonial America* (Oxford: Oxford University Press, 2013), 97.

61 See Elmar Lorey, *Henrich der Werwolf. Eine Geschichte aus der Zeit der Hexenprozesse mit Dokumenten und Analysen* (Frankfurt am Main: Anabas Verlag, 1997): 208–212.

62 Willem de Blécourt, "Werewolf communications: on the Peter Stump case and its effects," in Rita Voltmer, ed., *Europäische Hexenforschung und Landesgeschichte – Methoden, Regionen, Vergleiche*, forthcoming.

63 Ibid.

64 Ibid.

65 Ibid.

66 Martín Del Rio's, *Disquisitionum magicarum libri sex* (Lvgdvni: J. Pillehotte, 1608).

67 Ibid.

68 For more see Warfield, "Media Representation," 74.

69 Ibid., 132. For more information on the Pappenheimer trial see Michael Kunze, *Highroad to the Stake: A Tale of Witchcraft*, trans. William E. Yulli (London: University of Chicago Press, 1987).

70 Zika, *The Appearance of Witchcraft*, 179–209.

Bibliography (selection)

Behringer, Wolfgang, "Witchcraft and the Media." In *Ideas and Cultural Margins in Early Modern Germany*, edited by Marjorie E. Plummer and Robin Barnes, 217–238. Surrey: Ashgate, 2009.

Sipek, Harald, "'Newe Zeitung'-Marginalien zur Flugblatt – und Flugschriftenpublizistik." In *Hexen und Hexenverfolgung in deutschen Südwesten*, edited by Harald Siebenmorgen, ii, 85–92, 2 vols. Ostfildern: Cantz, 1994.

Suhr, Carla, *Publishing for the Masses: Early Modern English Witchcraft Pamphlets*. Helsinki: Société Néophilologique, 2011.

Walinski Kiehl, Robert, "Pamphlets, Propaganda and Witch Hunting in Germany c. 1560–1630." *Reformation* 6 (2002): 49–74.

Warfield, Abaigéal, 'Witchcraft Illustrated: the Crime of Witchcraft in Early Modern German News Broadsheets' in Andrew Pettegree (ed.), *Broadsheets. Single-sheet Publishing in the first age of Print* (Leiden: Brill, 2017), 459–487.

Zika, Charles, *The Appearance of Witchcraft: Print and Visual Culture in Sixteenth-Century Europe*. New York: Routledge, 2007.

17

WITCHCRAFT AND GENDER

Raisa Maria Toivo

The historical study of witchcraft was one of the first fields to accept gender history as part of the mainstream. Many scholars have noted that this development has been slow, but only a few fields of history – notably the history of sexuality and the history of the family – have seen anything swifter. Of course, this does not mean that every historian of witchcraft embraces gender history, or that all witchcraft historians see gender alike. It only means that the history of witchcraft, with its vivid imagery of violence, sexuality, oppression and religion, has produced interpretations from different political and academic angles, and these differing perspectives have been forced to take each other and to take gender matters seriously. Witchcraft historians became interested in gender very early, and gender struggle has also been a part of various political interpretations of the history of witchcraft such as Mary Daly and Barbara Ehrenreich. Historians such as Marianne Hester and Lyndal Roper have pursued the issue of female oppression and feminine psychology. Lately the question on gender has revolved around men and male witches, the work of Lara Apps and Andrew Gow laying the standard starting points on the area of witchcraft theory and works such as Rolf Schulte or perhaps Johannes Dillinger on the level on social history. The purpose of this presentation, however, in not to lay out a historiography of gender and witchcraft – a job well done in other presentations – but to explore possible grounds for new generalizations and analysis on the basis of what we currently know about witches (or the accusers and witnesses), witchcraft, or witch trials in various places of early modern Europe.

Men and women accused

A look at the sex ratios among those accused of witchcraft in early modern Europe is nevertheless required before questions of gender and witchcraft can be assessed. In Europe, our understanding of the sex ratios has changed due to research on new materials and new sets of trials. According to current statistics (by Levack, Schulte, or Apps and Gow), the proportion of women accused most often varied between 60 and 80 per cent. In some places, such as the Holy Roman Empire or Habsburg Empire (including such places like the Bishopric of Basel, the County of Namur and sometimes Austrian Hungary, which did not formally belong to the Holy

Roman Empire), the County of Essex and the Wielkopolska region in Poland, the proportion of women accused was even higher. On the other hand, Iceland, Estonia, Finland, Russia and Normandy saw lower proportions of women and consequently higher proportions of men (90 per cent in Iceland, 60 per cent in Estonia, around 50 per cent in Finland and 70 per cent in Normandy).[1]

There are numerous problems with such statistics. For example, the overwhelming impact of homogenizing the widely varying conditions – such as the competing cities, bishoprics and principalities of the Holy Roman Empire – into a unified geographical entity obscures the fact that the witch hunts of neighbouring towns were often very different in terms of both intensity and sex ratios. Other problems are posed by the fact that the statistics concern uneven periods of time, varying from almost three centuries in Poland (1500–1775) and Finland (1500–1800) to just a few decades in places like Toul or Aragon. The example of Finland shows that sex ratios can change quickly over time: during the first 150-year-period, from 1500 onwards, most witches were male, although a few women appeared every now and then. However, during the most intensive period of witch trials, from 1660–1700, when new kinds of witchcraft accusations – involving the witches' Sabbath and various forms of superstitious magic – became common, women came to form the majority of the accused. During the eighteenth century, women became nearly invisible once again: 85 per cent of the accused during this period were men.[2]

Based on these statistics, it seems clear that the apparent heartlands of the witch hunts – the Holy Roman Empire, France and Scotland – were dominated by the stereotype of the female witch. The peripheries, on the other hand, especially the north-east of Europe, but also Normandy in the west, maintained a stereotype of the male witch. These concepts of centre and periphery are not necessarily geographical or cultural; rather, they are related to the intensity of the witch hunts. The proportion of men seems to be greater in the less intense and moderate hunts, such as in Iceland, with its 120 accused between 1625 and 1685, and in Estonia with under 200 accused between 1520 and 1729. The countries that blur this picture are Russia, with almost 600 accused between 1622 and 1785, and Finland, with at least 2,500 accused between 1500 and 1800. These two countries are geographically large though sparsely populated, which means that it is not easy to compare them with tightly built European cities. Russia and Finland can also be thought of as areas with low intensity witch hunts because although the trials were frequent, they were also conducted meticulously according to due procedure and the punishments were usually milder than those received further west.[3]

One can thus claim that the areas with intense witch hunts saw a greater proportion of female witches than the areas with less intensive hunts. This seems to contradict Erik Midelfort and others who claimed that male witches often appeared in the trials only after the hunt had intensified and the social characteristics of a witch had been complicated by a snowball-effect whereby the male friends and relatives of previously accused women were stained by association and chains of accusations.[4]

Nevertheless, the focus on intensive witch hunting is a crude generalization and offers a rather one-sided look at witchcraft and magic – also in terms of how gender worked in the trials. If one seeks to find out more about the gendered concepts of magic in early modern Europe, one should consider other characteristics of both the trials and the society in which they took place.

Gendered beliefs about magic

Gendered concepts of magic in Europe can be approached from two angles: from the perspective of beliefs and from the perspective of practices. In terms of beliefs, scholars have previously been rather unanimous that among the educated elites at least, and through teaching and more or less top-down cultural transmission, the female stereotype of the witch was well established. Demonologists writing on the subject are usually considered indicative: Stuart Clark concluded that due to a deep-rooted, long-standing dualism in early modern categories of thinking, witchcraft, along with inferiority, was associated with women.[5] By contrast, all good and appreciable things were associated with men. According to Clark, this was not a conscious misogyny, but rather an implicit characteristic of the early modern learned way of thinking. In what has been read by many subsequent historians as a toning down of the second wave feminists' cry of genocide by a male mainstream historian,[6] Clark's claim that prejudice was inbuilt, unintentional and unrecognized actually means that it was not the individual demonologists or witch hunters who were misogynist; rather, it was the culture and society as a whole.

Twenty-first-century scholars have amended Clark's argument: instead of a dualistic polarization of opposites, gender is now most often seen as a web of assumptions or latent qualities that could be drawn on as the situation needed. This web of assumptions was 'not so polarized as to prevent leakage across gender boundaries'.[7] A similar development has led to the argument that stereotypically feminine qualities could well be attached to individuals of both sexes: some men could be imagined to be like women, and therefore witches. According to Claudia Opitz-Belakhal, Jean Bodin regarded some educated men's greed for power and knowledge as prone to make them as vulnerable to the Devil's lure as women who were weakened by their carnal greed. Whereas Bodin associated his enemies with greed, witchcraft and femininity, he presented himself as godly, dutiful, virile and, with this combination, ultimately very masculine.[8] Other witch hunters are likely to have done the same, and as many witnesses and accusers in witch trials were women, it was obviously also possible to use witchcraft accusations to present a godly and dutiful femininity. It is also likely that witchcraft sceptics and the more cautious judges were equally able to identify their rationality and patriarchal position as masculine qualities.[9]

Gendered beliefs about magic have also been formed by various other agendas. One of these is religion. For example, Sigrid Brauner, Merry Wiesner Hanks and Rolf Schulte have claimed that Protestant ideologists – including and especially Luther – either adopted or retained for longer the stereotypical image of witches being female.[10] While this may seem a viable generalization, it is noteworthy that in the majority of the areas where most of the accused were men, the dominant religion was Protestantism.[11] The demonologists' stereotype of the female witch was not necessarily transferred into the practice of trials or the popular concepts of witchcraft. Western scholars have not yet seriously assessed the influence of the Eastern Orthodox religions and Islam on gendered concepts of witchcraft and magic, although the issue must be of significant relevance since geographically, more than a third of Europe was under the influence of these religions.

Gendered concepts of magic and the village community

Witch hunts were usually at their most intense where the idea of the witches' Sabbath took root. This Sabbath – where witches were said to congregate – was essential for chain accusations and snowballing denunciations. The majority of the accused in the Sabbath trials were women. This has been explained by the sexual nature of the Sabbath and the encounters between the witches and the Devil. Nevertheless, in Continental Europe, the concept of the witches' Sabbath grew to include men. Although it was never impossible for demonologists to conceive of female demons and devils having sex with human men, sex was not as important for the masculine experience of witchcraft. This was possibly the case because, as Lyndal Roper claims,[12] early modern understanding related sex to the subordination of the woman to the power of the man. During the witches' Sabbath, men took on other roles. In German witch hunts, Rita Voltmer and Heuser found that a wider cultural development was perhaps more important to the change than the escalation of chain accusations: the emergence of male witches was made possible by the reimagining of the witches' Sabbath in terms of the village festival; boy and male witches took on roles in the witches' Sabbath that corresponded to their roles in the village festival. This reimagining, rather than a simple escalation of accusations, was the cause of the emergence of the male witch.[13] The Sabbath has also been described as the mirror image of everyday society, which also may lead to seeing its main figures as men – similarly to everyday society.[14]

The entrance of the village festivals into the conception of the witches' Sabbath suggests that the social and cultural structures of village communities – and even households – may in other ways also be important for the gendering of the concepts of magic. In towns, the model of social organization was the hierarchical trade guild or the workshop with its established division of labour. It is therefore likely that towns-folk's ideas of the gendering of magic were also different from those in rural areas, where the agricultural farmstead organized work according to cyclical periods rather than constant hierarchies, and where physical power and ability – perhaps more than gender – were crucial in determining one's status. In the coastal fishing villages or areas where migrant labour was common, the patterns appear to have been different again.[15] One might also conjecture that close-knit village communities were likely to foster long-standing grudges and enmities between people who were bound to the locality of their villages. These people tended to be women, elderly men and boys. However, some of the areas where male witches formed the overwhelming majority – such as eastern Finland, Lapland and Iceland – were populated by semi-nomadic people. For the Sami of Lapland, the place of residence changed according to the yearly migration from winter villages to summer pastures, while in eastern Finland, slash-and-burn farmers were forced to move to new settlements every few years due to the infertility of their land. As a result of the naturally harsh living conditions and the semi-nomadic lifestyle, the mechanisms that kept social peace in these communities were different from those in settled villages. Likewise, household structures seem to be of interest, since the most intense witches' Sabbath trial areas – where women were mostly accused – seem to have been those where a nuclear family-type was dominant and people married relatively late. By contrast, in areas where male witches were prevalent, multigenerational and even sibling households were common. This is not a pattern without exception – for example, in Finland family type patterns and marriage cultures in the western mainland differed radically from those in the east of the archipelago – but it seems a potentially meaningful factor.[16]

Gender, witchcraft and daily life

A considerable part of witchcraft is related to the home and household, but this seems to have meant different things for male and female witches. According to Labouvie, in the Saar region, women were overwhelmingly more connected with *maleficium* and harmful magic connected to children, childbirth, love and death.[17] Women were naturally connected to the worlds of childbirth and death since they took care of these matters. Similarly, since women cooked food and prepared drink, they were also associated with poisoning. With their various skills and their mysterious relationship with life and death, the popular beliefs of the region traditionally connected women with the transcendent world of spirits and flying night witches, Labouvie claims. This seems a general pattern in southern parts of Germany and France, and also in Mediterranean Europe.[18] On the other hand, in north-eastern Europe, the figure in touch with the other world was the shaman or *tietäjä*, a cunning man, who could use his power for both good and evil. In these areas, men seem to have been connected with *maleficium* in at least as great a measure as women.[19] In this respect, the position of a possible druidic culture in Celtic areas would be interesting, if source material could be found.

Another explanation for the abundance of *maleficium* associated with children and childbirth is the vulnerability of children's lives in early modern society. Infant mortality was high, and sometimes only half the children born survived their first year. Even later, risks were frequent and considerable. In some German towns, new mothers represented a disproportionately large number of accusers, with their post-middle-aged help as the accused.[20] In other areas, teenage girls or young adult women accused their mothers or mother figures, such as the mistresses of the households where they were in service. This has been related to the psychological tensions between mothers and daughters in close-knit communities, where independence was delayed and disciplinary practices of bringing up children were strict and its ideals inflexible. Women who had recently given birth were also more likely to accuse an older woman in their household of witchcraft because childbirth and maternity reawakened the insecurities and tensions that they had experienced as children in their relationship with their own mothers.[21] Older women paid the price: they became the witch-figures on which these tensions were projected and vented.

Male witches were also often accused of *maleficium* against people. As was the case with women, this most often meant people in their own neighbourhood. Especially in areas where male witches were not exceptional, this *maleficium* could also involve the harm of the neighbours' and relatives' children. Although this is an ill fit for psychological explanations about the projection of motherhood-related anxieties onto an evil mother figure, it indicates the importance of fathers, which can be observed in the various kinds of source material soon after the birth, even though traditional household manuals usually give fathers a more practical role in the upbringing of older children. The father's role in children's lives was most visible when the children were old enough to be educated, guided and punished in the way that was at the time conceived rational. Masculine fatherhood was thus juxtaposed with the intimate physical and emotional care given by mothers. In rural households and in the artisanal culture of the towns, full adulthood was not achieved after reaching a set number of years; instead, it was a project gradually entered into through different rites of passage. A man was not considered a full adult until he had advanced from apprentice to master and from bachelorhood to marriage and the patriarchy of a family.[22] Fatherhood was as essential to successful masculinity as motherhood was to femininity, and this is evident even in the witchcraft trials.

Nevertheless, male witches seem to have directed their magic more often against their political opponents, such as clergymen who had come to admonish them for some misconduct or to collect their tithe. Likewise, the more powerful and dangerous witches – those accused of leading campaigns against royal families or members of nobility – seem to have been men. In these cases, the *maleficium* is described in an almost military way: male witches lead a group of other witches like troops. In Finnish trials, the illnesses sent by these witches are depicted as magical ammunition, physical bundles of concentrated ill will, like arrows or bullets. This is clearly a masculinization of witchcraft, especially as an older meaning of the Finnish word for these bundles, '*tyrä*', also refers to the testicles. Female witches could also be described as having used *tyrä*; this is congruent with the claim by Willem de Blécourt that magic could be gendered irrespective of the sex or gender of the user of magic. Nevertheless, whereas carnal lust and envy could be easily seen as feminine qualities and sources of the fuel for feminine magic, political intrigue and economic grudges were thought of as male and masculine sins.[23]

Gender and age

Historians agree that older women are generally over-represented among those accused of witchcraft in many places, even in places where male witches dominated (except perhaps in Iceland, where females accused of witchcraft were too few to allow over-representation). In scholarly explanations by Alan Macfarlane and Keith Thomas, witches were understood to be victims of the changing moral concepts of neighbourly help and charity: the local needy sought alms that the neighbours were no longer willing or able to give. The resulting moral and social tension was resolved by accusing them of witchcraft. The needy in each community were most likely to be older women who could no longer support themselves by work and were thus dependent on others.[24] This explanation has received much criticism since its publication in the early 1970s. Indeed, Macfarlane himself concluded that such a major moral change that could have explained the witch hunts in Europe (or perhaps even in England) probably never really took place.[25]

Lyndal Roper has also noted that older women were over-represented in Germany. Her explanation related this to the psychology of motherhood and an enhanced importance of fertility in early modern culture. As post-menopausal women were no longer fertile, they came to be thought of as anti-mothers: they poisoned and cursed instead of nurturing and caring. Instead of doing the God-given work of bringing children into the world, they were in league with the Devil. Old women were also seen as envious of the children, families and households that the younger women were running.[26] However, accusations aimed at older women have also been explained not by their vulnerability, but by their relative power. Post-menopausal women were often at the peak of their social power: no longer having to bear or care for children, they had time on their hands to run households in which the hard labour was performed by the younger generation. They could also concentrate on household production of butter and textiles to the extent that there was a surplus to sell, and they were often still physically quite strong.[27] It seems likely, although as yet unconfirmed, that in the areas where this kind of explanation holds true, female witches were also likely to perform the kinds of magic classified by de Blécourt and Dillinger as 'malc', such as the advancement of personal gain in dairy production or even in fishing or agriculture.

The stereotype of the witch as an old woman does not hold true equally throughout all regions of Europe, although statistical enquiry into the actual ages of the people accused is difficult in many areas. There is often a verbal description of the accused females, describing them as old, poor, filthy and lame. However, these descriptions may have been made to fit the popular notion of how a witch should appear rather than a genuinely accurate portrayal. The stereotype of the old, impoverished female witch also appears frequently in demonological writing, however, it appears more often in sceptical works, when accused witches were presented as the victims of irrationality. Women simply make a better image of weak victims. Those who sought to present witches as powerful and dangerous, agents of evil that must to be fought against, were better served by the image of a strong, rich and perhaps even politically influential male witch.[28]

Where it has been possible to connect the individuals on trial to church or tax records, many of the accused seem to have been rather average in both age and wealth, and they were often reasonably well connected, with family and friends living in the area. Indeed, the family or friends could be the source of the accusation; competitors in the community might try to attack the whole family through the female householder or – in other regions – through the husband.[29] In rural Sweden and Finland, most of the accused seem to have been landowning peasant wives or widows. In New England, it has been suggested that landownership and women's inheritance of land in the absence of a male heir made women especially likely to be accused of witchcraft.[30] It is nevertheless clear that the social stratification of witch trials varied across Europe and that this variety had an influence on the gendering of both the concepts of magic and on the rise of the suspicion and accusations of witchcraft. Currently, not enough is known about the different European regions to make a systematic analysis.

Gender, work and ownership

It is logical that gendered concepts of magic should follow the gendered concepts of the division of labour in Europe. Along with taking care of the children, the elderly and the sick, women in most European societies were responsible for the household work and for livestock. The overwhelming majority of the magic and witchcraft women were accused of related to these areas. Like motherhood, success in animal husbandry – avoiding illnesses, making fodder last until the end of the winter – and the production of household items such as butter or yarn were simultaneously important and unpredictable. Competition between women in the neighbourhood, leading to envy, greed and ill will, were thought to tempt women into witchcraft, and animosity or even simple nosiness concerning other people's households aroused suspicion.

Anthropologically influenced scholars like Diane Purkiss have also claimed that it was the woman's duty to uphold the boundaries of the household. This task was important because the boundaries around the household were symbolically linked to those between culture and nature and those around the woman's own body. Transgressing these boundaries risked contamination, and this risk was made tangible through the image of the witch.[31]

The importance of livestock and textile production in women's magic is also highlighted by the fact that in the north-eastern areas of Europe, cattle were considered to be the property of women, so much so that the individual women of the household could each own their own cows.[32] If they managed to create surplus produce, this butter, yarn or cloth could be sold for money. Nevertheless, where male witches appeared, they also performed magic related to cattle, the brewing of beer and the production of textiles. In fact, a significant number of the male witches found in Normandy were shepherd boys.

It is worthy of note that these areas of work and production were undergoing change in the early modern Europe. At the time of the witchcraft trials, the commercial production of beer and textiles was already gradually being transferred to the male domain. In north-eastern Europe, the care for cattle, however, was increasingly consigned to the female sphere of life. By the nineteenth century, it became shameful for men to enter a cowshed and authorities at times tried to prevent the hiring of male shepherds. In nineteenth-century folklore material from Finland and Karelia, cattle magic was directly connected to female genitalia: when cattle were led out to pasture, the woman who owned the cattle would straddle the gate so that when the cows walked beneath her, they were exposed to the magical power of her genitalia. This power could be used to protect one's own folk and cattle and to threaten outsiders. This magical custom is not reported in seventeenth-century trial material, nor does it seem that men strictly shunned cattle sheds (it seems that the folklore material exaggerates this), but cattle magic was already more common for women than for men. It is also striking that some of the magic performed by men for curing or preventing cattle illnesses seems very feminine in nature: it makes use of the fire in the hearth and cooking utensils, which were magical not only because they were made of metal but also perhaps because they were used to transform natural produce into cultural ones.[33]

Early modern male spheres of work related to agriculture, war, trade and travel. In north-eastern Europe, some of the magic performed by men related to ensuring a good harvest in one's own fields or driving thistles into the neighbours' plots, but not enough is known about this kind of magic in other areas of Europe. Soldiers across Europe are known to have been drawn to pacts with the Devil in order to protect themselves in battle, but although 'arrow-witches' are already mentioned in the *Malleus Maleficarum*, they were obviously more common in countries and periods affected by war.[34] Travelling men performed magic related to carriages and ships, although in coastal regions such as Norway and Scotland, this kind of witchcraft was nevertheless performed by women.[35] Swedish historian Linda Oja suggests that men seem to dominate benevolent magic whereas women dominate malevolent witchcraft on horses and horse equipment.[36] Laura Stark, a Finnish folklorist, found similar patterns in nineteenth-century eastern Finland. A horse's gear and feed were spoiled by any woman who stepped or jumped over them since they had been exposed to the power of her genitals. Only men could take care of horses and gear in a positive way.[37]

The gendered division of labour seems to have formed and changed quite gradually in early modern Europe. In many areas, work was not yet as strictly gendered as it came to be in the nineteenth century. The division of labour also varied across Europe according to the dominant forms of trade and occupation, type of agriculture and structure of the household. More comparative work is needed to understand the complexity of gendered assumptions around work and magic.

Dillinger and de Blécourt have both separately suggested that one male form of witchcraft relates to the seeking of personal profit or advancement, an idea that was shunned in communal cultures. Early modern culture was very slowly moving from an understanding of good luck and wealth as limited resources, which could only be redistributed but not increased, to a proto-capitalist understanding where production of new wealth was not only possible but also desirable. Individuals who entered this new mode of thought before the others – or who seemed more successful than 'their fair share' – could be suspected of witchcraft. According to de Blécourt, these individuals were likely to have been male merchants and artisans. Dillinger on the other hand, explains that some forms of male magic, like treasure hunting magic, were popular and relatively mildly treated in courts because they allowed their practitioners to circumvent the moral dilemma of common versus individual gain by importing wealth from outside the community. Whereas profit-seeking has previously been identified as a male sphere of magic, it could also be associated with women, especially in relation to magic with cattle and dairy production, as was the case in Finland and Mecklenburg.[38]

Gender, status and prosecuting cultures

The question of gender and ownership in witchcraft is connected to the differing legal systems in Europe. It seems that in places where the courts were dominated by elites – such as noble landlords or assizes judges or even town magistrates – as it was in many areas of Continental Europe and Britain, and where these elites used the courts to control their subordinates, the accused women were poorer and more vulnerable than if the court was a place of equals.[39] In rural Scandinavia and in parts of Britain and New England, where the landowning peasantry or small-scale burghers dominated the courts, the accused, both women and men, were also likely to come from the same social group.[40] Alison Rowlands nevertheless notes that the local magistrates may have been keen to suppress the trials in order to prevent superior or neighbouring legal authorities from gaining political power over them.[41] This does not mean that all suspected or practicing male witches were wealthy landowning peasants in these areas; it was merely the case that such people were more likely to be formally accused in court. The poor itinerant witches were dealt with informally, leaving no trace in the records.[42]

The gendering of a witch in a witch trial could assign feminine characteristics to men and masculine characteristics to women. In some areas, where the accusations were directed at the poorer members of the society, the witches on trial present a weak and vulnerable, victimized femininity. Even the men accused are thus effeminized and regarded as victims. In other areas, being accused in a court of law presumes a certain status. A position as the head of a household among the landowning peasantry or as an artisan in a town was regarded as one of the most important characteristics of success, and thus it implied a powerful masculinity. As such, the image of the witch had to portray a more successful set of gender qualities in areas where those accused in a court of law were also mostly heads of households. In these areas, the witch was never portrayed quite so much as a victim.[43] Nevertheless, the conception of the witch as a powerful masculine figure may have also influenced the image of the female witch, in turn giving it greater power and status.

The image of the female witch may have influenced regional concepts of femininity in general, and vice versa. In Scandinavia, peasant women in particular seem to have been thought of as not only capable but also responsible for organizing and doing both the household work and considerable parts of the agricultural farm work. In cases where their husbands were absent or incapable, they also took care of the various communal duties of the farmstead, such as the construction of parish buildings, the maintenance of roads, and, when required, the payment of taxes. Peasant women in Scandinavia seem to have had a gendered role that was less connected to reproduction and the household and more connected to public or communal duties and responsibilities than in the rest of the Continent and Britain. When the women in the few Finnish Sabbath trials in Ahvenanmaa (Åland) made a pact with the Devil, they did not seal their allegiance by having ritual sex – constituting a common law marriage with him – as they did in German areas studied by Lyndal Roper and others. Instead, they agreed to pay yearly taxes in butter or cash.[44]

Conclusion

When observing and interpreting witchcraft trials from the perspective of gender, one must decide whether one is examining witchcraft trials in order to learn more about early modern concepts of gender or whether one is looking at gender to find an explanation for the witchcraft trials. The former option is engaging because witchcraft trials offer rare portrayals of ordinary people's lives, often granting the people involved an opportunity to speak for themselves. Tall tales and stereotypical tropes may be put into their mouths, but they add their own personal details to their stories. This option is nevertheless also an intriguing choice because looking at gender through such monumental dramas as witchcraft trials is bound to produce a distorted picture. In investigating gender through witchcraft trials, it is evident that more work needs to be done on the gendered concepts presented by various actors involved; this includes not just the accused and the accuser or demonologists, but also the witnesses, judges, juries and bystanders. These parties should be investigated and differentiated in order to reveal the full complexity of the early modern web of assumptions concerning gender. On the other hand, the option of looking at gender to find an explanation for the witchcraft trials seems more straightforward, but there is a considerable risk of understanding gender only through its negative or weakening effect on society.

How gender is understood is also of great importance: is gender a dichotomous hierarchical power relation, as Joan Scott defines it, or is it rather a way of being and doing, as advocated by French feminism? Understanding gender in a dichotomous or binary way means that distinguishing between what male and female witches did is essential in understanding the gendering of magic and witchcraft. Understanding gender as a way of being a man or a woman may make it easier to grasp the blurring of dichotomies. If gender is not about what people are allowed to do, but about how they do it, it may be easier to understand areas where the gendering of magic seems to be contentious, for example, when considering magic related to children or personal gain. Family and household roles were equally important to men and women. These roles may have placed them in the same situations of work or representation towards the neighbours: they had to perform similar tasks and would have succeeded or failed accordingly.

Notes

1 Alfred Soman, "The Parliament of Paris and the Great Witch Hunt (1565–1640)," *Sixteenth Century Journal* 9 (1978); Alfred Soman, *Sorcellerie et justice criminelle: le parlement de Paris (16e–18e siècles)* (Aldershot: Variorum, 1992); Robin Briggs, *Witches and Neighbours: The Social and Cultural Context of European Witchcraft* (Massachusetts: Harvard University Press, 1998), 260; William Monter, "Toads And Eucharists: The Male Witches of Normandy 1564–1666," *French Historical Studies* 20 (1997); William Monter, "Witch Trials in Continental Europe," in *Witchcraft and Magic in Europe: The Period of the Witch Trials*, ed. Bengt Ankarloo and Stuart Clark (Athlone: The Athlone Press, 2002), 12–13 for considerably smaller figures. There are overviews of sex-proportions in e.g. Lara Apps and Andrew Gow, *Male Witches in Early Modern Europe* (Manchester: Manchester University Press, 2003), 45 or in Brian Levack, *The Witch Hunt in Early Modern Europe* (London: Pearson, 2006), 142 or Rolf Schulte, *Man as Witch: Male Witches in Central Europe* (Houndsmills: Palgrave, 2009), 71. As these are cited in various other introductory chapters on gender, femininity or masculinity and witchcraft, I would like to point out that the percentages for Finland and Russia are outdated. For further info see Raisa Maria Toivo, "Gender, Sex and Cultures of Trouble in Witchcraft Studies: European Historiography with Special Reference to Finland," in *Writing Witch Hunt Histories: Challenging the Paradigm*, ed. Marko Nenonen and Raisa Maria Toivo (Leiden: Brill, 2014), 90, and Marianna G. Muravyeva, "Russian Witchcraft on Trial: Historiography and Methodology for Studying Russian Witches," in *Writing Witch Hunt Histories: Challenging the Paradigm*, ed. Marko Nenonen and Raisa Maria Toivo (Leiden: Brill, 2014), 124.

2 For European information see previous reference. For details on Finland see Marko Nenonen, "Witch Trials," in *Encyclopedia of Witchcraft: The Western Tradition*, ed. Richard M. Golden, vol 2 (Santa Barbara: ABC-CLIO, 2006) and Emmi Tittonen, *'Tuomitaan taikuuden harjoittamisesta' Taikuusoikeudenkäynti 1700-luvun lopun Pohjois-Pohjanmaalla ja Kainuussa* (Jyväskylä: University of Jyväskylä, 2007), 40–41, https://jyx.jyu.fi/dspace/bitstream/ handle/ 123456789/12149/URN_NBN_fi_jyu-2007623.pdf?sequence=1 (accessed 1 February 2012). The eighteenth-century figures come from the currently unpublished PhD work of Emmi Lahti, presented in e.g. "Rakkaustaikoja, kotitalouden ja terveyden suojaamista – Naisten harjoittama taikuus Suomessa 1700-luvun jälkipuoliskolla," [love magic, household and health protection. Women's magic in Finland in the latter half of the eighteenth century] (lecture at Genealogy days in Kuopio 17.3.2012), sine page; or Emmi Lahti, "Using Sacred Spaces as a Part of Magic Rituals – Popular Beliefs Towards Cemeteries and Churchyards in 18th Century Finland" (paper presented at the 9th European Social Science History Conference, Glasgow, Scotland, UK, April 11–14, 2012), sine page.

3 Marko Nenonen, "Finland: Witch Trials," 373–377; Muravyeva, "Russian Witchcraft on Trial," 109–139.

4 H.C. Erik Midelfort, *Witch Hunting in South-West Germany, 1562–1684* (Stanford, CA: Stanford University Press, 1972).

5 Stuart Clark, *Thinking with Demons* (Oxford: Oxford University Press, 1997), 124–133.

6 Clark's work is now most often cited to his book volume in 1997, but important parts of the volume actually consists of work conducted and published as journal articles already during the 1980s and early 1990s. See e.g. Stuart Clark, "The Gendering of Witchcraft in French Demonology: Misogyny or Polarity?" in *French History* 5 (1991): 426–437.

7 Apps and Gow, *Male Witches*, 136.

8 Claudia Opitz-Belakhal, *Das Universum des Jean Bodin. Staats-Bildung, Macht un Geslecht im 16. Jahrhundert* (Frankfurt: Campus, 2006), 131–167.

9 Alison Rowlands, "Witchcraft and Gender in Early Modern Europe," in *The Oxford Handbook of Witchcraft in Early Modern Europe and Colonial America*, ed. Brian P. Levack (Oxford: Oxford University Press, 2013).

10 Sigrid Brauner, *Fearless Wives and Frightened Shrews: The Construction of the Witch in Early Modern Germany* (Massachusetts: University of Massachusetts Press, 1995); Merry Wiesner-Hanks, *Witchcraft in Early Modern Europe (Problems in European Civilization)* (Boston: Cengage Learning, 2006); Schulte, *Man as Witch*, passim.

11 See footnote 1 for the statistics.

12 Lyndal Roper, *Witch Craze: Fantasy and Terror in Baroque Germany* (London, New Haven: Yale University Press, 2004), 82–103; See also Lyndal Roper, *The Holy Household: Women and Morals in Reformation Augsburg* (Oxford: Clarendon Press, 1989).

13 Rita Voltmer, "Witch-Finders, Witch Hunter of Kings of the Sabbath? The Prominent Role of Men in the Mass Persecutions of the Rhine-Meuse Area (Sixteenth-Seventeenth Centuries)," in *Witchcraft and Masculinities in Early modern Europe*, ed. Alison Rowlands (London: Palgrave, 2009); Peter Heuser, "Die kurkölnischen Hexenprozesse des 16. und 17. Jahrhunderts in geschlechtergeschichtlicher Perspektive," in *Geschlecht, Magie und Hexenverfolgung*, ed. Ingrid Ahrendt-Schulte, Dieter R. Bauer, Sönke Lorenz, and Jürgen Michael Schmidt (Hexenforschung, Bd. 7), (Bielefeld: Verlag für Regionalgeschichte, 2002), 133–174.

14 A classic description of the Sabbath and inversion in Stuart Clark "Inversion, Misrule and the Meaning of Witchcraft," *Past and Present* 87 (1980): 98–127. Clark, however, did not make the leap to male witches. For that, see e.g. Johannes Dillinger, *Evil People: A Comparative Study of Witch Hunts in Swabian Austria and the Electorate of Trier* (Charlottesville: University of Virginia Press, 2009), 41–73, esp. 52, 55.

15 Liv Helene Willumsen, *Witches of the North. Scotland and Finnmark* (Leiden: Brill, 2013); Allyson Poska, *Women and Authority in Early Modern Spain: The Peasants of Galicia* (Oxford: Oxford University Press, 2005).

16 Cf. e.g. the generalization presented in Mary Hartman, *The Household and the Making of Society: A Subversive View of the Western Past* (Cambridge: Cambridge University Press, 2004), 1–34.

17 Eva Labouvie, "Men in Witchcraft Trials: Towards a Social Anthropology of 'Male' Understandings of Magic and Witchcraft," in *Gender in Early Modern German History*, ed. Ulinka Rublack (Cambridge: Cambridge University Press, 2002), 49. Also Robin Briggs, *Communities of Belief: Cultural and Social Tensions in Early Modern France* (Oxford: Clarendon Press, 1995), 75; Robin Briggs, *Witches and Neighbors*, 257.

18 Gunnar W. Knutsen, *Servants of Satan and Masters of Demons: The Spanish Inquisition's Trials of Superstition, Valencia and Barcelona 1478–1700* (Turnhout: Brepols, 2009), 105–106; Gustav Henningsen, "The Ladies From Outside: An Archaic Pattern of the Witches Sabbath," in *Early Modern European Witchcraft: Centers and Peripheries*, eds. Bengt Ankarloo and Gustav Henningsen (Oxford: Oxford University Press, 1990); Giovanna Fiume, "The Old Vinegar Lady, or the Judicial Modernization of the Crime of Witchcraft," in *History from Crime*, ed. Edward Muir and Guido Ruggiero (Baltimore: John Hopkins University Press, 1994); Giovanna Fiume, *La Vecchia Dell'aceto: UnProcesso Per Veneficio Nella Palermo Di Fine Settecento* (Palermo: Gelka, 1990); Maria Sofia Messana, *E Streghe Nella Sicilia Moderna (1500–1782)* (Palermo: Sellerio Editore, 2007).

19 Laura Stark, *The Magical Self: Body, Society and the Supernatural in Early Modern Rural Finland* (Helsinki: Academia Scientiarum Fennica, 2006); Raisa Maria Toivo, "Male Witches and Masculinity in Early Modern Finnish Witchcraft Trials," in *Gender in Late Medieval and Early Modern Europe*, ed. Marianna Muravyeva and Raisa Maria Toivo (London, New York: Routledge, 2013); Jari Eilola, "*Rajapinnoilla: Sallitun ja kielletyn määritteleminen 1600-luvun*

jälkipuoliskon noituus- ja taikuutapauksissa [On the Bordelines – Boundaries between the Accepted and the Forbidden in Finnish and Swedish Witchcraft and Magic Cases in the Latter Half of the Seventeenth Century.]" *Bibliotheca Historica* 81 (2003); Kirsten Hastrup, "Iceland: Sorcerers and Paganism," in *Early Modern Witchcraft, Centers and Peripheries*, ed. Bengt Ankarloo and Gustav Henningsen (Oxford: Oxford University Press, 1993), 383–401.

20 Lyndal Roper, *Oedipus and the Devil: Witchcraft, Sexuality and Religion in Early Modern Europe* (London and New York: Routledge, 1994).

21 Birgitta Lagerlöf-Génetay, *De svenska häxprocessernas utbrottsskede 1668–1671. Bakrund i Övre Dalarna. Social och ecklesiastik kontext* (Stockholm: Almqvist & Wiksell International, 1990); Evelyn Heinemann, *Hexen und Hexwenglauben – eine historisch-sozialpsychologische Studie über den europäischen Hexenwahn des 16. und 17 Jahrhunderst* (Frankfurt: Campus Press, 1986); John Demos presented the same theory earlier in John Putnam Demos, *Entertaining Satan, Witchcraft and the Culture of Early Modern New England* (Oxford: Oxford University Press, 1982) for Salem, but it has since been questioned, whether the "girls" in Salem actually were as young as they had previously been presented: see Bernard Rosenthal, *Salem Story: Reading the Witch Trials of 1692* (Cambridge: Cambridge University Press, 1993); Roper, *Oedipus and the Devil*, 228ff.; Deborah Willis, *Malevolent Nurture; Witch Hunting and Maternal Power in Early Modern England* (New York: Cornell University Press, 1995); Diane Purkis, *The Witch in History: Early Modern and Twentieth-Century Representations* (London and New York: Routledge, 1996).

22 Roper, *Oedipus and the Devil*, 146.

23 Brian P. Levack, *Witch Hunting in Scotland: Law Politics and Religion* (London and New York: Routledge, 2008), 34–35; Willem de Blecourt, "The Making of the Female Witch: Reflections on Witchcraft and Gender in the Early Modern Period," *Gender & History* 12 (2000): 187–209; Marko Nenonen, *Noituus, taikuus, ja noitavainot Ala-Satakunnan, Pohjois-Pohjanmaan ja Viipurin Karjalan maaaseudulla 1620–1700*. [Witchcraft, magic and Witch hunts in Rural Lower Satakunta, Northern Ostrobothnia and Vyborg Karelia 1620–1700] (Helsinki: Finnish Literature Society, 1992), 256–275, 223–225; Rafaël Hertzberg, *Vidskepelsen i Finland på 1600 talet. Bidrag till Finlands kulturhistoria. Akademisk afhandling.* (Helsingfors: University of Helsinki, 1889), 33.

24 Alan Macfarlane, *Witchcraft in Tudor and Stuart England* (London, New York: Routledge, 1970).

25 Alan Macfarlane, *The Origins of English Individualism: The Family, Property and Social Transition* (Oxford: Oxford University Press, 1978).

26 Roper, *Oedipus and the Devil*, 228; Diane Purkiss, *The Witch in History*, 91.

27 Paul Boyer and Stephen Nissenbaum, *Salem Possessed: The Social Origins of Witchcraft* (Cambridge, MA: Harvard University Press, 1974); Briggs, *Witches and Neighbours*, 257; Raisa Maria Toivo, *Witchcraft and Gender in Early Modern Society: Finland and the Wider European Society* (Aldershot: Ashgate, 2008).

28 Marion Gibson, *Reading Witchcraft: Stories of Early English Witches* (London, New York: Routledge, 1999).

29 Labouvie, "Men in Witchcraft Trials," 41; Eilola, *Rajapinnoilla, 202–216* Annabel Gregory, "Witchcraft, Politics and 'Good Neighbourhood' in Early Seventeenth-Century Rye," *Past and Present* 133 (1991).

30 Carol F. Karlsen, *The Devil in the Shape of a Woman. Witchcraft in Colonial New England* (New York: W.W. Norton & Co, 1987).

31 Purkiss, *The Witch in History*; Roper, *Oedipus and the Devil*, 228 and even more dramatically, Lyndal Roper, *The Witch-Craze* (London, New Haven: Yale University Press, 2004), 125–178. Another late example: Eilola, *Rajapinnoilla*, 187–232.

32 Stark, *Magical Self*. Scientiarum Fennica 1998. passim.

33 Stark, *Magical Self*, passim; Toivo, *Witchcraft and Gender*, 145; Purkiss, *The Witch in History*, 91–144.

34 Soili-Maria Olli, "The Devil's Pact: a Male Strategy," in *Beyond the Witch Trials: Witchcraft and Magic in Enlightenment Europe*, ed. Owen Davies and Willem De Blécourt (Manchester: Manchester University Press, 2004). See also Johannes Dillinger, "Unverwundbarkeit," in *Enzyklopädie der Neuzeit* 13 (Suttgart 2011): 1101–1104.

35 Willumsen, *Witches*, 242–262; Rune Hagen, "Witchcraft and Ethnicity," in *Writing Witch Hunt Histories: Challenging the Paradigm*, ed. Marko Nenonen and Raisa Maria Toivo (Leiden: Brill, 2014); Julian Goodare, ed., *Scottish Witches and Witch Hunters* (Basingstoke: Palgrave, 2013).
36 Linda Oja, "Kvinnligt, Manligt, magiskt. Genusperspektiv på folklig magi i 1600- och 1700-talets Sverige," *Kyrkohistorisk årsskrift* (1994): 43–55. Absolute numbers are small, but no women and two men in her sample seem to have magically cured horses.
37 Laura Stark-Arola, *Magic, Body and Social Order: The Construction of Gender Through Women's Private Rituals in Traditional Finland* (Helsinki: Finnish Literature Society, 1998), 203.
38 Katrin Moeller, *Das Willkur über Rech ginge. Hexenverfolkung in Mecklenburg im 16. und 17 Jahrhundert.* (Bielefeld: Bielefeld University Press, 2007), 224–231; Toivo, *Witchcraft and Gender*, 113–149.
39 For the backgrounds of the accused e.g. Levack, *The Witch Hunt*, 134–174; Roper, *Witch-Craze*, 44–66; Roper, *Oedipus and the Devil*, 146ff.
40 Nenonen, *Noituus, taikuus*, 201–220, also summarized in Nenonen, *Finland*, 373–377; Walter Rummel has also noted that in the German areas where the local groups lead the witch hunt instead of higher-ranking elites, the local groups tended to take the opportunity to attack their most powerful competitors within the group by accusing their wives. Although this did not lead to men being accused, the flip side of the coin is, of course, that the weaker ones in the community, including poorer women, were not accused as often. Walter Rummel, *Bauern, Herren Und Hexen: Studien zur Sozialgeschichte sponheimischer und kurtrierischen Hexenprozesse 1574–1664* (Göttingen: Göttingen University Press, 1991).
41 Alison Rowlands, *Witchcraft Narratives in Germany: Rothenburg, 1561–1652* (Manchester, New York: Manchester University Press, 2003).
42 Toivo, *Male Witches*, 142–144.
43 Toivo, *Gender, Sex and Cultures of Trouble*, 87–108.
44 Roper, *The Witch-Craze*, 82–103; Sari Katajala-Peltomaa and Raisa Maria Toivo, *Noitavaimo ja neitsytäiti. Naisten arki keskiajalta uuden ajan alkuun* (Jyväskylä: Atena, 2009), 209.

Bibliography (selection)

Ahrendt-Schulte, Ingrid et al. (eds.), *Geschlecht, Magie und Hexenverfolgung*, Hexenforschung, vol. 7. Bielefeld: Verlag für Regionalgeschichte, 2002.

Apps, Lara and Andrew Gow, *Male Witches in Early Modern Europe*. Manchester: Manchester University Press, 2003.

Blécourt, Willem de, "The Making of the Female Witch: Reflections on Witchcraft and Gender in the Early Modern Period." *Gender & History* 12 (2000): 187–209.

Rowlands, Alison (ed.), *Witchcraft and Masculinities in Early Modern Europe*. London: Palgrave, 2009.

Rowlands, Alison, "Witchcraft and Gender in Early Modern Europe." In *The Oxford Handbook of Witchcraft in Early Modern Europe and Colonial America*, edited by Brian P. Levack. Oxford: Oxford University Press, 2013.

Toivo, Raisa Maria Toivo, *Witchcraft and Gender in Early Modern Society: Finland and the Wider European Society*. Aldershot: Ashgate, 2008.

18

CHILD-WITCHES

Nicole J. Bettlé

From the fifteenth to the eighteenth century, ecclesiastical and secular courts, with the population's active participation, put alleged witches to trial. However, not only were adults accused of the tort of witchcraft and subsequently executed, but a considerable number of children were as well. Little of their history has been researched yet. Thus, I am presenting a series of the most important results that are based on my research of four hundred and twenty cases in Europe and New England.[1] All the literature dealing with the topic of child-witches, with all its case studies, has been listed in the bibliography to allow those keen on digging further into the matter access to this current topic of research.

Number and chronology of child-witch trials

Witchcraft researcher E. W. Monter's publication *Witchcraft in France and Switzerland* (1976) was the first to work under the supposition that child-witch trials only formed a minor part of all legal proceedings against witches and thus were actually not of major importance.[2]

However, so far research has been unable to precisely quantify this, although quite a number of documents mention a considerable amount of children in witch trials. Here are a few well-known examples: In 1705, courts and clergy in Brusio in the Swiss canton of Graubünden had to deal with an indeterminable number of catholic children suspected of witchcraft; however, only the trials of three of those children have been mentioned in detail.[3] On the other hand, in what today is known as Nidwalden, provincial governor Thomas Zelger had written a letter to the authorities in Schwyz (1631) in which he reported that witchcraft had particularly increased amongst children. Despite Zelger failing to make any attempt to supply the names of these children, it is well known that between 1626 and 1634 the courts there had convicted nine minors of witchcraft, four of whom had verifiably been executed. A short note from Fribourg in Switzerland mentions that between 1634 and 1635 several children and teenagers had fallen under suspicion for witchcraft and had subsequently been executed. In 1634 alone, it is purported, more than thirty people had been executed, with a considerable number of children among them. A year later in 1635 the number had allegedly risen to several hundred people, with about ten children and teenagers between 9 and 17 years of age being sentenced to death. In Bamberg, Germany, a pamphlet was published in 1625 claiming that quite a number of girls, aged between 7 and 10, had turned to witchcraft, and that more than twenty of them had been executed and burned at the stake.[4] Between 1683 and 1684 the district seat of Calw in Württemberg gained notoriety when over seventy boys and girls claimed that they had been seduced by the devil and that they had been flying on broomsticks, forks or animals (e.g. goats, chicken or cats).[5] Similarly, several children and teenagers had been involved in the witchcraft proceedings in the imperial city of Augsburg (1618–1730). Over half of these trials were child-witch trials.[6] Today it is proven that altogether almost fifty children and teenagers had been standing trial. Between 1723 and 1730 alone around thirty children aged between 7 and 14 years had to stand trial. The town of Würzburg (Germany) held a considerable number of child-witch trials. Soldan and Heppe published lists of so-called "burnings of witches" from between 1627 and 1629, and those lists were compiled between the seventh and the twenty-eighth burning (altogether there were forty-two burnings!).[7] Midelfort enumerates almost thirty child-witches aged between 9 and 14 years that had been executed.[8] Walinski-Kiehl counts one hundred and sixty persons executed during this time, forty-one of which were children.[9] The anonymous author of a pamphlet called *Das hexen Weßen betreffent* (1629) mentions a further four hundred people under suspicion of witchcraft that were supposed to have carried out their nefarious deeds there – among them around three hundred children and teenagers aged either 3, 4, 7, or up to 15 years of age.[10] The child-witch trials of Freising, held between 1715 and 1723, also included whole groups of children between 7 and 10 years of age.[11] In 1678 allegedly around one hundred witches and wizards had been executed in the Austrian archbishopric of Salzburg, among them many child-witches between 10 and 14 years old.[12] For this particular year the Austrian researcher Fritz Byloff lists around one hundred and eighty accused and states that around half of the witches had been younger than 20 years, including numerous children below 10 or even below 5 years old.[13] Mülleder counts ninety-five children and juveniles under 20 years of one hundred and thirty-five accused persons.[14] Eighteen of them were under 10 years old. Around 1680 approximately 70 per cent of those suspected of witchcraft and incarcerated in the dungeons of Salzburg were reported to be younger than 22 years.[15]

In 1669–70 the Swedish village of Mora had been scourged by witchcraft. In those two years alone more than seventy children had been involved in child-witch trials.[16] The Basque child-witch trials, which took place at the beginning and at the end of the sixteenth century (in Navarra), are among the earliest proceedings against children. During the peak (1610–12, 1614), when confessing witches had been promised immunity from prosecution, the Spanish inquisitor Alonso de Salazar y Frias, according to his own report, investigated 1802 people under suspicion of witchcraft, with 1384 of them being minors.[17]

At first glance, these listed cases suggest that child-witches always turned up in groups and that child witchcraft had therefore been a case of a collectively committed crime. However, my comparison of over four hundred cases instead shows that until today research has (almost) exclusively concentrated on cases in which a large number of child-witches had been involved. Individual cases, on the other hand, were either neglected or used by researchers as a prime example for their theories, but without supplying further proof in form of researched fact.[18] However, my research of the Swiss child-witch trials, with more than half of them being trials dealing with single cases, shows that, more often than not, child-witch trials were actually penal proceedings against individual children.[19] The majority of those cases shows that very often one child claiming to be either capable of witchcraft, or of being bewitched, encouraged other children to make similar claims to be child-witches. With current scientific knowledge only one thing can be stated with certainty: The amount of child-witch trials can only be estimated. However, the many short entries in available sources very clearly indicate that more children had to stand trial because of witchcraft than has thus far been thought possible.

In this regard, another claim circulating in research literature has to be mentioned, namely, that child-witch trials had been a phenomenon of a late phase or of the peak of an excessive persecution.[20] The earliest case known to us in which a child is suspected of witchcraft dates back to 1441 (Berner Simmental, Switzerland); the last child-witch trial resulting in an execution was held in 1756 (Landshut, Germany).[21] Child-trials reached their peak between 1600 and 1700. Thus, beginning, peak and end of the persecution of child-witches corresponded exactly with the persecution of adult suspects. They ran parallel to each other. Furthermore, many penal proceedings against adults indeed happened neither simultaneously nor in any one country, town or village; nor did they end in the same year. Nevertheless, the child-trials were always conducted at the same time. Here are just a few examples: In the British Isles, the period of witch trials were between the 1542 and 1712 (with the peak between the 1540s and 1640s). The last execution happened in 1684. The penal proceedings involving children, happened between 1560 and 1634 (e.g. Essex, Huntingdonshire and Lancashire). On the American continent the child-witch trials appeared at the beginning and in the middle of the wave of trials against adults (e.g. Boston 1688, Salem 1692). In the electorate of Trier and the territories of the imperial abbey St. Maximin both witch trials and child-witch trials started around the end of the sixteenth century. In Augsburg, on the other hand, the first witch trial, that was held in 1625 and ended with a burning, was actually a child-witch trial. Here both witch trials and child-witch trials actually cover the same period (1618–1730). Even the Swiss persecution of witches, that has usually been set between 1420–30 and 1782, shows parallels. Here trials involving children happened between 1441 and 1789.[22] Executions were carried out from 1571 to 1712.[23] Although further parts and regions of the country show, from a macro perspective, a simultaneous appearance of cases against both adults and children, it should also be noted that for many countries detailed information about child-witch trials is still lacking, thus making it impossible to draw clear conclusions.

Jurisdiction, offence and sentence

Since the early modern era, and under the influence of the reception of Roman law, small children (infantes) were declared as not being criminally responsible; later this was changed to being partially criminally responsible but unable to stand trial, and thus they were not subject to criminal law. Minors (impuberes) that were regarded as partially responsible from the age of 7, sometimes even 6 years, usually did not remain unpunished, but the adult penal system was only applied to a certain extent. According to sources of law, full criminal responsibility was generally set at the age of 14 years.[24] Based on this, it is assumed that child-witch trials were actually illegal criminal proceedings – but there is no proof to verify this assumption, either. Although the law usually granted offending children an exceptional position, it did not come to application in cases of children witchcraft (religious offence). Three aspects played a major role when evaluating child-witches: The belief in early sexual maturity, proof of malicious intent and the general belief in witchcraft as an exceptional crime.

As the ability to have an ejaculation or to menstruate was equated with accountability, both small children (i.e. infantes) and minors (impuberes) were deemed – in case of an offence – as having diminished responsibility and thus were also regarded as unable to give evidence. In cases of witchcraft, however, different criteria were applied when it came to the aspects of sexual maturity. Probably most important here were the views of lawyers and clergy that even children at the age of 3 or 4 years were having sexual interactions with the devil, thus allowing the onset of puberty much earlier than with other, normal children. A second aspect was proving that children were able to act with malicious intent. It was the duty of the judges at the time to pass sentence according to the Holy Scripture that saw the wickedness of mankind as one of the major reasons why evil was able to spread in the world (*Genesis* 6, 5–7). In cases involving children, proof of malicious intent was enough to lift the protection under the terms of criminal responsibility, thus declaring their exceptional position as null and void. Among the earliest texts mentioning the clause of malicious intent in writing are Canon law (according to the motto "malitia supplet aetatem") and the Italian penology ("nec correctio aliqua speranda est"). Thus in cases where the maliciousness was deemed to override considerations of age (i.e. the offence perpetrated by a minor was regarded as a serious crime, or the offence showed signs of a particularly violent nature) and there was no hope for reform of the child, then even sentencing and execution of minors was legitimate in the eyes of the law.[25] The oldest German law that includes this clause is the *Richterlich Clagspiegel* (1436). Already here it is stressed that, in case of heresy, not having reached the age of consent does not guarantee immunity from criminal prosecution.[26] In these cases even the youngest were to be sentenced according to adult law. This clause can be found in all the major legal texts of this period, including the *Wormser Reformation* (1498/99), the *Constitutio Criminalis Bambergensis* (1507, Bambergische Halsgerichtsordnung) and the *Constitutio Criminalis Carolina* (1532, Peinliche Halsgerichtsordnung Karls V.), that stayed in force until 1806. With the help of other felonies ("Malefizdelikte") it is possible to prove that in certain cases minors had been illegally executed but not in cases of child-witch trials.[27] The last important aspect that led to the execution of children according to adult law was fairly simple. To practise magic was on the one hand regarded as *crimen mixti fori*, that is, as an offence that was prosecuted by both secular and church authorities. On the other hand, witchcraft was regarded as a most serious crime in the fight against which the rule of due process could be ignored (*crimen exeptum*) and thus one of the most serious crimes according to the law at the time. The law made no exception when it came to cases of child witchery. Another fact is actually quite remarkable in this context: Although even at that time it had been decreed by law that names of minors were not allowed to be published, a notably large number of names of child-witches even below the age of 5 years are mentioned in the records. This allows us to conclude that in many cases of witchcraft involving children the clause of protection was not applied and that in cases of exceptional crimes lawyers refrained from applying this clause.

Very often child-witches were not only the defendants, but also the key witnesses for the prosecution in witch trials. The participation of minors as witnesses can be explained by the introduction of the inquisitorial system that was specifically created for the prosecution of heretics, wizards and witches. In contrast to the older accusatorial process ("Akkusationsprozess"), proceedings and evidence stood at the centre of the inquisitorial trial; this allowed groups of persons to be admitted as witnesses that had previously been excluded.[28] This meant that not only were women, accomplices, perjurers and the excommunicated admitted as witnesses, even next of kin, partners, spouses and children were admitted as well. This new definition – of who was allowed to enter the witness box and receive its legitimacy, in this case admittance of witness statements by minors both on the European mainland and on the British Isles – proved particularly devastating.[29] In particular, statements from child witnesses always had a deleterious effect for those who stood accused.

It was part of the education of children, publicly and privately, to inform them about the practises of witchcraft. Additionally, it was not unusual for children and teenagers to be present at executions – which were always preceded by the reading of the confessions. Thus, it is no surprise that even children and teenagers knew quite well about witchcraft and devilry. Special lists of questions, or so-called "Fragezettel" (notes on questions), were used during the interrogations, posing questions that, to a great extent, corresponded with contemporary demonological views; it is not surprising that there is hardly any difference between confessions of adults and those of children. On the other hand, it seems quite astonishing that adults were surprised by the extent of the children's knowledge, which meant they interpreted these extensive witness statements as proof of complicity.[30]

Altogether the elements of witchcraft mentioned most frequently by both adults and children were *maleficium* (harm to persons or animals) and attending the witches' sabbath which was usually reached by a magic flight. Many child-witches told how they had either harmed or killed humans or animals with the help of magic potions or magic powders. The act of conjuring with particular animals (e.g. mice, birds, cats, flies or toads) equally formed part of the idea of *maleficium*, thus it appears very often in children's confessions. Many of them also admitted to have participated in a witches' sabbath. Not only had they been flying there together with other witches, but equally often also with the devil himself. The pact with the devil on the other hand was a rare offence and only found in some of the sources or some of the regions. Sexual intercourse with the devil also only played an insignificant role in child-witch trials. Non-historians, on the other hand, regarded the mentioning of the illicit sex, unlike other elements of offence, as fact and as evidence that child-witches had been raped and physically abused – which is in complete contradiction to the results of serious scholarly research.[31] In Switzerland only seven out of one hundred and thirty child-witches told about sexual interaction with the devil. Although sexual offences have been mentioned in child-witch trials, these rather fall under the category of sodomy and bestiality.

In actual fact, today we hardly know what crimes – if any – these child-witches actually had committed. Reading between the lines of interrogation records and confessions you find several offences mentioned, including theft, arson, manslaughter and grievous bodily harm. Under the law at the time, all those crimes were considered to be serious crimes, punishable by death. Signs of melancholy, faint-heartedness and anxiety, believed to occur under the influence of wizardry and witchcraft, equally raised suspicions. Based on several descriptions we can also learn that many children, before they had been seduced by the devil, were known to the authorities for their naughtiness, their lack of respect, their aggressive or sluggish behaviour and for various criminal activities. According to some of the interrogation records many of those children had previously spent some time in prison.

In cases of child-witchcraft a distinction was made between witness statements and confessions of witchcraft. Whether a child under suspicion of witchcraft had observed an act of wizardry, had been bewitched by another witch, had a relation with the devil or a witch was actually irrelevant in the end because according to a demonological approach the contact with the devil alone already made the child guilty of having committed crimes against the faith. The decision as to whether a child should be regarded or treated as victim, culprit or witness was ultimately with the adults and the legal authorities. However, in each and every case – and this is quite remarkable – the decision was not immediately made, but instead it was made conditional to the further behaviour of the child. The suspicion of witchcraft was only a matter of interest as long as the child claimed to be in league with the devil. Statements by children that they had "only dreamt of witchcraft" very often turn up in interrogation records, and both judges and theologians have interpreted this as signs of the "salvation" of these children.

In the 1930s Fritz Byloff still worked under the assumption that child-witch trials had happened before the seventeenth century but that none of them had actually led to executions.[32] Actually, it is obvious that this is wrong. As mentioned at the beginning of this article, a lot more minors had been accused of witchcraft and executed than anyone thought. In Switzerland alone (i.e. the Old Swiss Confederacy) one child in three involved in a trial of witchcraft was executed. According to law the penalty for convicted witches was death by being burnt alive at the stake.[33] In case of child-witches, because of their age, the method of execution was almost always modified. The death sentence was altered equal to the adult cases in such a way that the minors were first killed by either decapitation, strangulation, drowning or hanging before burning their bodies, but sometimes their bodies were not burned at all. Other methods of mercy killings included poisoning or exsanguinations, although they were applied only rarely.[34] In the German principalities and Britain, executions were public and took place in broad daylight. However, in Switzerland the executions usually were not public, and additionally children were executed at night instead of during the day.[35]

The second-most frequent penalty for child-witches was exclusion from the community. Fearing contamination or reputational damage or simply because of ignorance, these children were isolated by having them imprisoned or deported to closed-off areas of the village (e.g. excluded from church service, kept away from fountains), or driven from their homeland. Depending on religious affiliation the courts showed different approaches and verdicts. Monter developed the theory that particularly

Catholic areas saw child-witch trials, as compared to Protestant areas.[36] This should be rephrased: In Catholic areas a lot more children were executed after being found guilty of witchcraft when compared to Protestant areas. Catholic regions are characterised by a large number of executed or tortured child-witches; in Protestants areas, on the other hand, the belief in education and salvation of a reigned, as can be seen in their preferred code of punishment. In particular, they kept child-witches as prisoners for months if not years and used them as cheap work-forces.[37] In Zurich or St. Gallen where no child-witch has been executed the authorities ordinarily deported impertinent and sluggish juvenile delinquents to the workhouses.[38] The judges of the county Lippe in turn assigned child-witches to pray and work.[39] This behaviour reflected the official line of the Protestants, especially Luther and his followers, which equated work with education.

The genesis of suspicion

The view that the concept of child-witches was a fairly new construct following in the footsteps of the persecution of witches was based on an erroneous assumption by some scholars.[40] Some demonologists, inquisitors and lawyers dealt with the idea of Satan's children (the teachings of "incubus" and "succubus") and with children possessed by demons. Those best-known today are Jean Bodin († 1596), Peter Binsfeld († 1598), Martin Anton Delrio († 1608) or Nicolas Rémy († 1612). They all were then regarded as the leading experts in the development of a devil's cult based on scientific research and witchcraft offences. And they all were strong advocates for torture and execution being applied, even to minors. However, in their judgement of child-witches, neither they nor other scholars referred to previous experts in this field; they based their prosecutions on their own experience with child-witches. As even theologians claimed that witchcraft was a novel phenomenon at the time, child witchcraft had to be a new form of danger. However, the children of the heretics were already in the focus of judgment. The belief in child-witches was consequently not without old parallels. Although the church, in all its documents, never referred to older cases of child witchcraft and always described children as victims of devils, demons or witches, according to traditional lore, it never denied the existence of children who practised witchcraft. Even at the beginning of the fifteenth century the idea of a child-witch was an integral part of the idea of witches. As already mentioned, we know of the case from 1441 in which a small child was accused of knowledge of witchcraft.

If you attempt to profile child-witches the result is quite straightforward. The majority of child-witches were between 7 and 12 years old when they attracted the attention of the people and the courts.[41] This can be proven not only with examples of the Swiss cases but also with German cases.[42] From a legal point of view this concerned "impuberes" who were to some limited extent criminally responsible, but it also concerned those children who, according to popular belief and theology, had already mastered witchcraft and who, in the eyes of educators, were easy to educate and had already recently taken their place in the work-chain.

The view of a child-witch, in its entirety, did not follow any gender stereotype, that is, accusations of witchcraft were made against boys and girls in equal measures. But looking at the confessions it is possible to see a leaning towards one or the other sex. In almost all Protestant areas (or jurisdictions) more or less as many girls were accused of witchcraft as boys; in Catholic areas the idea of child-witches was mainly applied to boys. Even in Switzerland more boys were accused of witchcraft than girls in the Catholic parts were. Moreover, the idea of witches had a rather dynamic character even where children were concerned, that is, the gender percentages were varying from interval to interval. In Augsburg, for example, a lot more girls than boys stood trial in the first half of the seventeenth and the eighteenth centuries; in the second half of the seventeenth century and in the 1720s it was predominantly boys. In the Imperial city of Rothenburg ob der Tauber a 6 year-old boy was accused first (1587), and then a girl, second. From 1627 until 1673 only girls were suspected of witchcraft, and after then and until 1709 only boys were suspected. The Swiss child-witch trials show the same trend succinctly: Before the 1650s predominantly boys were involved, and after that the cases mainly involved girls.

At first glance, child-witches do not fall into any particular social category. Affected were children with both or only one parent alive, orphans, foundlings, illegitimate children, vagabonds, pupils or students. They were children of artisans, councillors, clergy or mayors from a well-off or at least respected background, but they were equally from lower classes, or offspring of criminals, or they had relatives with a bad reputation. Some of them, while accused, either had a job or were in an apprenticeship. Witchcraft among children was a phenomenon stretching across all classes. However, amongst those children convicted of witchcraft and subsequently executed, there were none from a rich family or a well-off background. Child-witches from "respectable families" were often portrayed exclusively as victims of witches or gave evidence in witch-trials.

Both theologians and lawyers defined the term "child-witch" as a minor who had been infected/bewitched by the devil or was a descendant of someone practising witchcraft.[43] The existence of sin, demonic possession, wizardry or witchcraft in children was mainly regarded as divine punishment against the parents who had either neglected or cursed their children. The cursing of a child by its parents or by other adults is a classic motive in all descriptions of demonic possession, and it was assumed that the cursed were made susceptible to being possessed by demons. Thus, children under suspicion were first asked who had seduced them into wizardry and witchcraft. They mainly named their parents or other family members as their seducers, but also other adults and children in their immediate surroundings who had fallen under suspicion. However, the view that it was mainly members of the family that introduced their offspring to witchcraft clearly dominated. Children very often came under suspicion through one of their parents. In the majority of cases against child-witches, while they were being prosecuted, their parents or other family members had already appeared at court, having been accused of witchcraft and/or executed. The persecution of members of the same family and of their relatives over three generations was no rare occurrence, as can be proven with several cases.[44] In Appenzell, several generations of a family were persecuted for almost sixty years.[45] Even the accused child-witches of Unterwalden belonged to families, which stood under suspicion for many years.[46] Under close scrutiny, those family trials hardly exhibit the deliberate decisions by governments, authorities or clerics keen on extinguishing witchcraft. As a rule, the first accusations and complaints came from the public and from within the ranks of their own families, or sometimes from the suspects who – for whatever reason and maybe oblivious of the consequences – accused themselves. Considering the information available it would be wrong to assume that child-witch trials were only a late or fringe occurrence, or that they were a short-term phenomenon that should be researched separately from trials against adults.

Notes

1 Nicole Bettlé, "Wenn Saturn seine Kinder frisst: Kinderhexenprozesse und ihre Bedeutung als Krisenindikator," in *Freiburger Studien zur Frühen Neuzeit*, ed. Volker Reinhardt, vol. 15 (Bern: Peter Lang, 2013).
2 E. William Monter, *Witchcraft in France and Switzerland: The Borderlands During the Reformation* (London, Ithaca: Cornwell University Press, 1976), 126.
3 For the following statements about trials in Switzerland see Bettlé, "Wenn Saturn seine Kinder frisst," 178, 192ff, 209ff.
4 Wilhelm Gottlieb Soldan and Heinrich Heppe, *Geschichte der Hexenprozesse*, ed. Max Bauer, vol. 2 (München: Müller & Kiepenheuer, Hanau, 1912), 5.
5 Hartwig Weber, *Kinderhexenprozesse* (Frankfurt, Leipzig: Insel Verlag, 1991), 286. Correct figures in Johannes Dillinger, *Kinder im Hexenprozess. Magie und Kindheit in der Frühen Neuzeit* (Stuttgart: Franz Steiner Verlag, 2013), 117–123.
6 Kurt Rau, *Augsburger Kinderhexenprozesse 1625–1730* (Wien, Köln, Weimar: Böhlau Verlag, 2006), 107.
7 Soldan and Heppe, *Hexenprozesse*, 17f.
8 See also H.C. Erik Midelfort, *Witch Hunting in Southwestern Germany 1562–1684* (Stanford, CA: Stanford University Press, 1972), 283.
9 Robert S. Walinski-Kiehl, "The Devil's Children: Child Witch-trials in Early Modern Germany," *Continuity and Change* 11 (1996): 175.
10 Weber, *Kinderhexenprozesse*, 263.
11 Rainer Beck, "Das Spiel mit dem Teufel. Freisinger Kinderhexenprozesse 1715–1723," *Historische Anthropologie. Kultur – Gesellschaft* 10 (2002): 374–415.
12 Soldan and Heppe, *Hexenprozesse*, 54.
13 Fritz Byloff, *Hexenglaube und Hexenverfolgung in den österreichischen Alpenländern* (Berlin, Leipzig: Severus Verlag, 1934), 117–118.
14 Gerald Mülleder, *Zwischen Justiz und Teufel. Die Salzburger Zauberer-Jackl-Prozesse (1675–1679) und ihre Opfer* (Wien: Lit Verlag GmbH & Co. KG, 2009), 310.
15 Wolfgang Behringer, "Kinderhexenprozesse. Zur Rolle von Kindern in der Geschichte der Hexenverfolgung," *Zeitschrift für historische Forschung* 16 (1989): 39–40.
16 Soldan and Heppe, *Geschichte der Hexenprozesse*, 285.
17 Hans Sebald, *Hexenkinder. Das Märchen von der kindlichen Aufrichtigkeit* (Frankfurt: S. Fischer, 1996), 139. On the witch trials in Navarra see Pierre de Lancre: Tableau de l'inconstance des mauvais anges et démons: où il est amplement traité des sorciers et de la sorcellerie. (Paris: Aubier, 1982).
18 Dillinger arrives at the same result (Germany). Dillinger, *Kinder im Hexenprozess*.
19 Bettlé, "Wenn Saturn seine Kinder frisst," 368.
20 See Brian P. Levack, *The Witch Hunt in Early Modern Europe* (London, New York: Routledge, 1987), 130; Behringer, "Kinderhexenprozesse," 32; Sebald, *Hexenkinder*, 37; Beck, "Spiel mit dem Teufel," 375 or Rau, *Augsburger Kinderhexenprozesse*, 24.
21 Behringer, "Kinderhexenprozesse," 46. The accused was a 14-year-old orphan.
22 Bettlé, "Wenn Saturn seine Kinder frisst," 166, 259.
23 Ibid., 171, 192.
24 In fact, the age of criminal responsibility could vary and has been determined differently by various legal sources. The "Sachsenspiegel" (1220–35) or the "Constitutio Criminalis Carolina" (1532) set the age of criminal responsibility at 14 years (boys and girls). Sometimes the law made a distinction between boys (14 years) and girls (12 years). According to Old English law the age of criminal responsibility was reached at 10 years, in

Frankish and Old Icelandic law it was reached at 12 years. Adalbert Erler, ed., *Handwör-terbuch zur deutschen Rechtsgeschichte*, vol. 2 (Berlin: Erich Schmidt Verlag GmbH & Co., 1978), 719–724; Heidelberger Akademie der Wissenschaften, ed., *Deutsches Rechtswörter-buch. Wörterbuch der älteren deutschen Rechtssprache*, vol. 7 (Weimar: Verlag Hermann Böhlaus Nachfolger, 1974–1983), 809; Klaus Arnold, "Kindheit im europäischen Mittelalter," in *Zur Sozialgeschichte der Kindheit*, ed. Jochen Martin and August Nitschke (Freiburg, München: Verlag Karl Alber, cop., 1986), 6, 454.

25 Gustav Radbruch, ed., *Die Peinliche Gerichtsordnung Kaiser Karls V. von 1532 (Carolina)* (Stutt-gart: Philipp Reclam Jun., 1975), 103; Andreas Deutsch, *Der Klagspiegel und sein Autor Con-rad Hyden. Ein Rechtsbuch des 15. Jahrhunderts als Wegbereiter der Rezeption* (Köln, Weimar, Wien: Böhlau Verlag, 2004), 541–542.

26 Deutsch, *Klagspiegel*, 541.

27 See for example: Matthias Senn, ed., *Die Wickiana, Johann Jakobs Wicks Nachrichtensammlung aus dem 16. Jahrhundert. Texte und Bilder zu den Jahren 1560–1571* (Küsnacht-Zürich: Raggi, 1975), 145.

28 Soldan and Heppe, *Hexenprozesse*, 335; Erler, *Rechtsgeschichte*, vol. 2, 372.

29 Sebald, *Hexenkinder*, 89.

30 Bettlé, "Wenn Saturn seine Kinder frisst," 371.

31 Hartwig Weber, "*Von der verführten Kinder Zauberei": Hexenprozesse gegen Kinder im alten Würt-temberg* (Sigmaringen: Jan Thorbecke Verlag, 1996), 178–179; Lyndal Roper, "Evil Imag-inings and Fantasies. Child-witches and the End of the Witch Craze," *Past and Present* 167 (2000): 109.

32 Byloff, *Hexenglaube*, 88–89.

33 Erler, *Rechtsgeschichte*, vol. 5, 1619 and vol. 2, 146; Manuela Ros, "Die Malefizordnung des Standes Luzern (17. Jahrhundert)," in *Richtstätte und Wasenplatz in Emmenbrücke (16.–19. Jahrhundert). Archäologische und historische Untersuchungen zur Geschichte von Strafrechtspflege und Tierhaltung in Luzern*, ed. Jürg Manser, vol. 1 (Basel: Schweizerischer Burgenverein, cop., 1992), 243–244.

34 This information refers to Switzerland where no children had been executed by letting them bleed to death. Germany, however, applied bloodletting as a means of execution quite frequently. See also Dillinger, *Kinder im Hexenprozess*, 63.

35 Bettlé, "Wenn Saturn seine Kinder frisst," 277.

36 Monter, *Witchcraft*, 126f.

37 Meret Zürcher, *Die Behandlung jugendlicher Delinquenten im alten Zürich 1400–1798* (Winter-thur: P.G. Keller, 1960), 67–68, 71.

38 Zürcher, *Delinquenten*, 103, 149; Manfred Tschaikner, *Die Zauberei- und Hexenprozesse der Stadt St. Gallen* (Konstanz: Verlag UVK, 2003), 14.

39 Rainer Walz, "Kinder in Hexenprozessen. Die Grafschaft Lippe 1654–1663," in *Hexenver-folgung und Regionalgeschichte. Die Grafschaft Lippe im Vergleich*, ed. Gisela Wilbertz, Gerd Schwerhoff, and Jürgen Scheffler (Bielefeld: Verlag für Regionalgeschichte, 1994), 223.

40 Some researchers proceed from the assumption that the image of a witch in the body of a child took hold during the sixteenth or seventeenth centuries and was considered new. Behringer, "Kinderhexenprozesse," 32–33; Weber, *Kinderhexenprozesse*, 24; Sebald, *Hexen-kinder*, 37.

41 One of the biggest problems in the research of child-witches is the definition of the term "child". Under the term "child-witch trials" the majority of those in the field of witchcraft research included cases of adolescents and young adults who, according to the view at the time, had already come of age (onset of puberty) and were thus subject to adult law. The reasons for this are often due to the limited field of research and due to the scarcity of available sources. However, we have to work from the assumption that there is a willingness to apply the modern definition of child to older cases. Not only is this not conducive to the contemporary view of who or what a child is, it does not correspond to the historical legal criteria that the child-witch trials were subject to. According to this view all results listed here are based on cases of child-witches that were between 1 and 14 years old.

42 Bettlé, "Wenn Saturn seine Kinder frisst," 352.

43 Heidelberger Akademie der Wissenschaften, ed. *Deutsches Rechtswörterbuch. Wörterbuch der älteren deutschen Rechtssprache*, vol. 5 (Weimar: Verlag Hermann Böhlaus Nachfolger, 1953–1960), 927.

44 Guido Bader, *Die Hexenprozesse in der Schweiz* (Zürich: s.n., 1945), 85, 119, 131, 156, 161–163, 209; Mülleder, *Zwischen Justiz und Teufel*, 310; Weber, *Kinderhexenprozesse*, 286–297.

45 Emil Schiess, *Die Hexenprozesse und das Gerichtswesen im Lande Appenzell im 15.-17. Jahrhundert* (Trogen: Kübler, 1919), 108–129; Bader, *Schweiz*, 161–163.

46 Caspar Diethelm, *Die Hexenprozesse im Kanton Obwalden* (Sarnen: Ehrli, 1925), 35; Anton Odermatt, *Das Hexenwesen in Nidwalden vom Jahre 1584 bis 1684* (Ennetmoos: Staatsarchiv Nidwalden, 1870), 15, 26–27, 70–72.

Bibliograpy (selection)

Beck, Rainer, *Mäuselmacher: oder die Imagination des Bösen. Ein Hexenprozess 1715–1723*. München: C.H. Beck, 2011.

Bettlé, Nicole J., "Wenn Saturn seine Kinder frisst: Kinderhexenprozesse und ihre Bedeutung als Krisenindikator." In *Freiburger Studien zur Frühen Neuzeit*, edited by Volker Reinhardt, vol. 15. Bern: Peter Lang Verlag, 2013.

Dillinger, Johannes, *Kinder im Hexenprozess. Magie und Kindheit in der Frühen Neuzeit*. Stuttgart: Franz Steiner Verlag, 2013.

Mülleder, Gerald, *wischen Justiz und Teufel. Die Salzburger Zauberer-Jackl-Prozesse (1675–1679) und ihre Opfer*. Wien: Lit Verlag GmbH & Co. KG, 2009.

Rau, Kurt, *Augsburger Kinderhexenprozesse 1625–1730*. Wien, Köln, Weimar: Böhlau Verlag, 2006.

Roper, Lyndal, "Evil Imaginings and Fantasies'. Child-Witches and the End of the Witch Craze." *Past and Present* 167 (2000): 107–139.

Walinski-Kiehl, Robert, "The Devil's Children: Child Witch-Trials in Early Modern Germany." *Continuity and Change* 11 (1996): 171–188.

19

WITCHCRAFT IN EVERYDAY LIFE

Edward Bever

Witches, according to early modern demonologists, sold their soul to the Devil; flew at night to wild ceremonies where they worshipped him and engaged in orgies, infanticide, and cannibalism; and prepared magical potions and powders and learned spells that they used to work black magic against their neighbors back home. Not one credible example of this supposed sect has ever actually been found, but the myth of a diabolical sect of Devil-worshipping witches played a critical role in the early modern witch hunts.[1] It provided the motive to scrutinize all magical activities, caused any individual suspected of witchcraft to be treated as the tip of an iceberg, and seemed to require exceptional measures to combat: torture was used extensively to obtain detailed confessions and the names of co-conspirators.

However, the demonological myth was a necessary condition for the early modern witch hunts, but it was not sufficient. Trials seldom started with an inquisitor riding into town, picking suspects at random, and torturing them into confessing. Some did start with an inquisitor riding into town, and tortured confessions did play a vital role, but hunts seldom started with a suspect picked at random.[2] Instead, the suspect was almost always selected because somebody who knew them denounced them. Sometimes this denunciation was inspired by a fanatic outsider, but far more often it originated within the community. Once a hunt got going people were accused willy-nilly by suspects undergoing torture and neighbors caught up in mass hysteria, and the charge was sometimes hurled by religious zealots targeting deviant behavior or unscrupulous people in some mundane dispute, but initial accusations typically stemmed from long-standing suspicions that a person practiced witchcraft. Many people were suspected without actually ever being formally accused. This pool of local suspicions thus also played a critical role in the witch hunts.

Why did ordinary people in early modern Europe suspect their neighbors of witchcraft? Why were they ready to see them tortured and burned? To answer these questions, this chapter will explore what ordinary early modern people, common villagers and townsfolk, understood witchcraft to be, why they suspected certain people were witches, and how these suspicions fed into the witch hunts.

Witchcraft in the "magical universe"[3]

The demonology only played a limited role in ordinary peoples' understanding of witchcraft. Since it combined reports of local beliefs from many different places, ancient stories preserved in manuscripts, and carefully reasoned inferences, it was an alien notion everywhere, imported via broadsheets and books, word of mouth, sermons, decrees, and the higher education of local leaders. It gradually percolated into local cultures, but even when it was widely known, concern about diabolic pacts and wild orgies played far less of a role in popular concerns than *maleficium*, harmful magic.[4]

Ordinary early modern people thought that others could harm them through magic because they believed the world is populated by spirits and connected by occult (from the Latin for "hidden") forces. They imagined that the earth was the only world in the universe, the focal point of the cosmos. God in Heaven above watched to see the extent to which they obeyed His rules in order to decide whether they deserved to join him for eternity or be cast down into the fiery Hell which, they thought, lay beneath their feet. Angels and demons soared in the space between Heaven and earth, and through the same space the influence of the stars and planets radiated down into human affairs. Closer to the ground a host of spirits and monsters like elves and trolls, giants and ghosts lurked in the shadows. They inhabited specific places, appeared at specific times, and played specific roles, sometimes helping and sometimes hurting people, and sometimes simply indifferent to them. Mysterious forces governed the daily activities, yearly rhythms, and major points in the life cycles of human beings, requiring or prohibiting certain actions at specified times to achieve success and avoid misfortune.

The magical universe, or perhaps more properly the magico-religious dimension of the universe, was officially divided between the established religion, Christianity, and the diverse unsanctioned local supernatural beliefs and practices that flourished everywhere. At the beginning of the witch hunts, in Western Europe Christianity meant Catholicism. It had a complex spiritual hierarchy in which God was the ultimate, all-encompassing spirit, but he allowed autonomous spiritual entities, angels and demons, to exist. He also bestowed spiritual power on humans like the saints, the Virgin Mary, and ordained priests during mass. God could ignore the laws of nature and work miracles, but the primary focus of Christianity was not on tapping His power in this world, but on gaining salvation in the next. This was accomplished, or at least facilitated, by following His will and commandments. Few ordinary people understood all of this with the rigor of a theologian, but by the end of the Middle Ages most Europeans grasped the essence of it.

It was generally understood that in order to test people's faith, God allowed the Devil to tempt them, and the Devil and his minions therefore operated widely in the world. The Protestant Reformation in northern Europe simplified this complex spiritual system by making the active agents in worldly affairs just God and the Devil, but the Catholic and Protestant clergy agreed that one of the Devil's most powerful tools was his lordship over the other half of the magico-religious dimension of the universe: magic. Whether used for good or ill, magic was the Devil's snare because it worked through demons and therefore involved worship of a false god. Black magic blatantly manifested evil by causing harm; white magic enticed people to put their faith in the Devil instead of God.

This was the official line, but for most ordinary Christians the situation was not so clear cut. To begin with, they hoped that religion would deliver material rewards as well as salvation. Even if they understood that rituals can't make God grant material benefits – He only does this to serve His own purposes – they still prayed, worshipped, and deployed symbols in hopes of getting help from Him. The Catholic clergy actively participated in such activities, while Protestantism's rejection of all but prayer left many ordinary people unsatisfied.

On the other side of the magico-religious divide, by the early modern period magical practices were generally clothed in Christian symbolism. Healing incantations commonly called upon God or the saints for help, for example, and incorporated liturgical elements like "in the name of the Father, the Son, and the Holy Spirit."[5] So too, did magical treasure-hunting rituals. The line between religion and magic was less clear in practice than in theory.

Supernatural forces took two forms: conscious spirits and automatic occult processes. Officially, God was the ultimate source of spiritual power and the only One capable of causing truly supernatural effects, miracles. All other magic was illusory "preternatural" tricks performed by demons or the Devil based on their understanding of human nature and obscure natural processes. God might occasionally allow the Devil to accomplish truly supernatural effects, but it was ultimately His power granted for His purposes.

Ordinary people generally did not make such fine distinctions between God-given and autonomous spiritual power or supernatural and preternatural effects. They often did not worry about whether magic was produced by conscious spirits or simply manifested occult mechanical processes either. Many rituals did invoke spirits, and some magic, like astrology, involved purely occult forces, but the source of much magical power was undefined.

Of more concern to ordinary people was whether magic was helpful or harmful. Where it fit into the official theology was less important than its intent and effects, although this changed over the early modern period due to individual internalization of religious morals and collective assimilation of official values into popular culture. Some forms of magic were ambivalent, like love magic, which could be used to bring back a wayward husband or seduce an innocent virgin, and one person's righteous retribution might seem like malicious aggression to another. Nevertheless, most magic was regarded as either benign, like healing sicknesses, bringing good fortune, or foretelling the future, or malign, like fairies substituting a "changling" for a newborn baby, the heavens entering an unfavorable conjunction, or a witch casting a malevolent spell.

Magical beliefs, practices, and effects were a pervasive part of everyday life everywhere in Europe, but their specific forms varied enormously from place to place.[6] In general, though, magical beliefs included the spirits and forces that interacted with humans according to their own whims or logic, and things people could do to learn from, influence, or harness them. The spirits and forces included those governing activities in daily life that required people to do or not do certain things, like starting to sew the fields or not washing clothes on certain days; phenomena that served as omens and portents, like an owl's call portending a death; and entities like fairies and trolls that existed in on the margins of human society, interacting with people when they violated their space, encountered them by accident, or enjoyed their help or fell victim to them because of some act, failure to act, or vulnerability, like childbirth.[7]

Human magical activities included both passive and active measures that served both protective and assertive purposes. Passive and protective measures designed to ward off the undesirable influence of autonomous occult forces, spirits, and other peoples' magic were the most common. Assertive measures attempting to tap into or project magical power were employed occasionally by many people and routinely by some. Most of those who used magic assertively used it for benign purposes, but some used it malevolently, to cause harm.

Witchcraft understood most broadly was magic used by people to harm others. The means by which this harm was inflicted included both sorcery, rituals acts and utterances learned and practiced consciously, and sheer malice, one person's bile spontaneously manifested as another's bad fortune. However, it was understood that some people might uncharacteristically resort to sorcery or manifest traumatizing rage in a fit of anger, but that did not necessarily make them a witch. A witch was someone who was thought to employ witchcraft routinely. The early modern witch hunts did not occur simply because people believed in witchcraft, but because they believed some of their neighbors were witches.

Witchcraft in this world

There was in many parts of Europe belief in a "night witch," a shadowy figure barely distinguishable from the completely disembodied evil spirits that were thought to hover above the human world and swoop down to afflict people in moments of vulnerability.[8] However, far more common were ordinary "village" witches, known members of the community reputedly responsible for a series of specific harms to specific neighbors. If witchcraft was part of the magical dimension of the universe, the magical dimension of the universe was inextricably entwined with the mundane physical and social worlds, and it was in these that the animosities, rivalries, and struggles for advantage manifested in witchcraft and fears of witchcraft arose.

Conditions of life in early modern communities

Why were early modern communities home to such intense animosities that some people attempted to harm their neighbors through witchcraft and others accused their neighbors of it knowing they would be tortured and burned? To begin with the physical setting, the overwhelming majority of early modern people, roughly nine out of ten, lived in farming villages, and most of the rest lived in small towns that were not much bigger. This meant that they lived in a natural environment that took its shape and changed according to processes that humans could scarcely understand and only marginally influence. Magic, the belief that the universe is animated by implacable occult processes and filled with willful conscious entities corresponded to their immediate surroundings and experience. So too did the belief that those processes and entities were as likely to harm as to help human beings.

Furthermore, living in villages and small towns meant living in intimate and constant contact with a small circle of people: family, other household members, and neighbors. Most houses had only a few, and sometimes no, separate rooms, and most of those housed, and the beds within them often slept, several people. Consequently, most people lived in the almost constant presence of others. Even prosperous farmers, merchants, and nobles lived in close and sustained proximity to other members of their large households, which included members of their immediate and often extended families, and servants. These varied in number from one or two for a prosperous farmer to many for nobles. They generally lived in close proximity to their employers and even closer proximity to other servants.

Going out-of-doors offered at most limited relief. Towns and cities were crowded with people, and even in villages houses and out-buildings were generally closely packed. The countryside did contain vast, thinly populated stretches, but these contained predators both human and animal, so people tended to stay close to their communities. Neighbors, seen or unseen, were a constant presence. Their right, and indeed responsibility, to observe, report on, and intervene in others' behavior was enshrined in local practice and legal structures.[9]

Some people may have enjoyed some anonymity in the crowds in the major cities, and some others lived in relative isolation in scattered farmhouses and tiny hamlets, but even in the cities, neighborhoods formed relatively stable and tight-knit communities, and in tiny hamlets people lived in tight proximity to their immediate family and neighbors. A few may have lived in stark solitude, but they were a small minority. A limited number of people moved about routinely – there was some mobility in normal times as armies and merchants plied their trades and individuals moved to find employment or land – and occasional upheavals like wars uprooted entire regions, but the great majority of people were born into, lived in, and died within face-to-face communities of a few hundred people to whom they were bound over the course of their lives.

We moderns tend to romanticize this simple village and small town life, with its close personal ties, interdependent households, and communal rituals and support, but the reality was far more complex. To begin with, even villages were often divided between a small number of dominant families and a larger number of subordinate clans.[10] Villages as well as towns had formal divisions between citizens, who owned houses and land and were full members of the community, and cotters and boarders, who rented their land or quarters and hired themselves out part or full-time to their more prosperous neighbors. Agrarian communities contained additional subgroups, like herders, who formed networks that bound them more to their compatriots in other villages than to the villagers in their own communities, even while they could be strongly divided by things like what type of animal they tended. Towns were even more subdivided between various craft guilds, artisans and merchants, rich and poor, longstanding and new residents, and numerous family lineages. Within all households there were divides among and between family members and servants; close and more distant relatives; adults, children, and the aged; males and females; and step-children, step-parents, and half-siblings. Closeness was a double-edged sword: while it created a sense of comfortable familiarity and mutual support, it also bred bitter rivalries and intense hatreds.

Naturally, most people enjoyed some close friendships and many maintained amicable relations with their households and neighborhoods on the whole, but most communities were riven by factions and most people were at odds with at least a few others. Some were in conflict with most. Communal institutions actually did a remarkable job of coordinating peoples' efforts and managing their disputes, but their very success meant that angers and resentments festered.

Witchcraft and interpersonal conflict

When conflicts erupted, they could be pursued viciously. Verbal abuse, malicious gossip, physical violence, and legal action were often employed pitilessly.[11] People openly chided, chastised, insulted, harangued, threatened, and cursed each other, and fights involving hitting, kicking, wrestling, biting, scratching, and pulling hair were not uncommon. Clubs and knives were often brandished and sometimes used. People covertly slandered others, sometimes vandalized their property, occasionally injured their animals, and in some cases employed poisons, arson, and sorcery. Witchcraft and witch accusations alike were not aberrations from but extensions of neighborly conflict.

Witch-like behaviors could be blatant, but often they were ambiguous. Whether a curse was meant as harmless venting, an earnest warning, or a magical assault itself was often not clear, perhaps even to the person who hurled it. However, there was no question that physical threats could be followed by physical force, and in some cases curses were undoubtedly made with the intention that they would cause harm. Certainly, the society was rife with violence: men fought without restraint, and while women were less prone to fisticuffs on the whole, many would push, slap, and hit, and at least some used weapons, when provoked. When bodily strength or weaponry were mismatched, though, or social constraints imposed restraint, the weaker party might well have recourse to more discrete forms of attack: malicious gossip; vandalism; arson; surreptitious battery of animals or children; sorcery; or poison in gifts of food, dropped in a beer barrel, or served in a meal.[12]

At times and places surreptitious assaults were clearly suspected all out of proportion to the extent that they can reasonably be assumed to have been practiced, but there can equally be no doubt that practiced they were. Historians, have put little effort into determining how widespread such practices might have been, but the one study that has attempted to do so concluded that between 10 and 15 percent of the suspects in the Duchy of Württemberg had engaged in them.[13]

While some of these practices may have been impotent expressions of rage, others could clearly inflict serious harm. Certainly vandalism, arson, battering animals or children, and poison could cause real damage to a person's property, dependents, or self. Defamation was not a physical threat, but it could undermine a person's standing in the community, and thereby their likelihood of getting help when in need, equal treatment in communal institutions, or even the comforts of simple friendship. Overt magical acts like explicit curses, obviously intent gaze (the evil eye), symbolic gestures, and inappropriate or hostile touching could trigger psychophysical reactions, which can cause or contribute to a wide variety of ailments, from aches and pains to cardiac arrest, especially when prolonged, as would easily be the case in the emotional hothouse of a small community.[14] The hostility motivating covert magical rituals and confidence that they would take effect could also be communicated during subsequent encounters through body language, facial expression, and the implications of words, and thereby also trigger or sustain deleterious psychosomatic responses.[15]

Whether witches and sorcerers could exert a baleful influence at a distance through paranormal powers is an intriguing question, but unfortunately more than a century of scientific research on such phenomena has not yielded a scientific consensus on whether they are possible.[16] Fortunately, though, they were rarely mentioned in early modern accusations; most witchcraft involved some sort of face-to-face interaction or word-of-mouth connection.[17] So, while not every witch-like act necessarily resulted in injury, their potential to cause harms ranging from disrupted relationships through destruction of property and illness to death was real and, for the people involved, consequential.

The misfortunes ordinary early moderns saw as possible consequences of witchcraft varied widely. Certain things were almost never ascribed to witches, in particular widespread calamities like plagues and wars, and things where a mundane cause seemed obvious. The most common type of problem that was ascribed to witchcraft by far was illness, both in people and animals.[18] Other common ones were impotence in men and sterility in women, accidents, disruptions to domestic processes like churning butter and brewing beer, cows drying up, and hailstorms, and there was a miscellany of localized beliefs, like stormy weather and bad luck at fishing.[19] Some, like hailstorms and elusive fish, seem to us impervious to human influence, baring paranormal forces, but the most common ones – illness and reproductive problems, in particular, but also accidents (which stress can make more probable)[20] – can all plausibly, if not necessarily accurately in any particular case, be ascribed to physical, chemical, or psychological attack in our as well as their understanding of the world.

Early modern people recognized that these misfortunes could have ordinary causes as well, so what made them think a particular instance resulted from witchcraft? One clue was when it followed an explicit threat or curse. Other times, objects known to be implements of magic, like bundles with noxious objects or scraps of paper with written spells, were found secreted in buildings or on a suspect's person. However, it was not always clear who had done what, or why, and in most cases there was no overt evidence of witchcraft at all. Instead, it was deduced backwards when something about a malady seemed strange: a disease came on suddenly or lingered inexplicably; a healthy cow stopped giving milk suddenly; or a building burned down when the owners were sure they'd put out the fire. When a suspicious misfortune occurred, the sufferer might think of a relationship or recent interaction with someone and decide that that person was responsible. While potentially accurate, this method was notoriously unreliable, vulnerable to unwarranted conviction that a chance misfortune was intended and misattribution of responsibility when it was, and was therefore responsible, along with torture, for the fact that the great majority of suspects were innocent of any form of *maleficium* at all.

Interpersonal conflict was thus at the core of witchcraft, both actual, in the sense of rituals conducted and injuries inflicted, and suspected. All sorts of social relationships could be the context of such conflicts: an old woman denied charity; neighbors disputing a boundary between fields; one person's prosperity alongside another's poverty; two women's interested in the same man; a woman's antipathy for her step-children. The list could go on, but not indefinitely, for witchcraft was generally recognized to be the weapon of the underdog. Those with superior physical or social power were likelier to utilize them. Those in subordinate positions were drawn to occult techniques both as the most potent method available and to avoid retribution.

Consequently, in early modern Europe women, and in particular older women, but also old men, poor people, and late in the period, children were far more likely to be suspected of witchcraft, or probably to have recourse to it, than well-to-do adult men. However, what particular relationships fostered witchcraft and witchcraft suspicions varied from place to place, reflecting the specifics of the local social structure and power relations. Social structures and relations did not create witchcraft beliefs, suspicions, accusations, or activities, but they did provide the context and motivation for them.

If it is hard for us to believe that ordinary people could be so angry, violent, and hard-hearted, we have to remember, first, that we are examining a particular aspect of life in early modern Europe, not life overall. Communal customs and institutions insured that interpersonal conflicts in most places were kept under control most of the time, and most people got along with most others. Nevertheless, we have to remember also that these people lived in hard and violent times. The majority of people were smallholders with barely enough land to support themselves and their families, or not enough, and therefore forced to rely on part-time work as well. In either case, they lived at the margins of subsistence, one harvest away from starvation. Armies occasionally marauded across the countryside and brigandage was a more limited but also more regular threat. And beyond sheer survival, life for most involved a constant struggle for limited material and social resources like land, jobs, patronage, and marriage opportunities.

Furthermore, at the time of the witch hunts, times were particularly hard and getting harder. The period of intense witch hunts, roughly 1550 to 1650, corresponds closely to what has been called the "Iron Century," a period when Europe's population grew while its economy stagnated or contracted and confessional conflicts led to vicious civil discord and widespread and protracted international wars.[21] Contracting economic opportunities and bitter religious hostilities on top of the normal struggles and enmities in small agrarian communities fed rivalry, suspicion, anger, and callousness at all levels of society and set up the kind of interpersonal conflicts that led many people to fear witchcraft and some to act like witches.

Mediators between the two worlds

To the extent that there were people in early modern Europe who acted like witches, either routinely practicing sorcery or habitually behaving in ways that seemed to project a malevolent occult power, the witch was one of several roles in society that mediated between the everyday and magico-religious dimensions of the universe. Most ordinary people employed magical and religious rituals and artifacts on their own as part of their daily activities, praying to God and wearing crucifixes, reading omens and observing taboos, wearing amulets and incanting charms, but there were also several groups who specialized in interacting with the supernatural either as a service occupation or for their own purposes. Many were entirely benevolent; some were ambivalent, employing magic to help or harm depending on circumstances; a few were downright mean.

One group, the clergy, were by definition beneficent. Individual clerics might personally be corrupt or wicked, and the different confessions considered their rivals to be servants of the Devil, but Christianity itself championed benevolent spirituality.

The clergy mediated between humans and God through a combination of education and ritual. Education taught people what they should and should not do and believe to follow God's will. Rituals embodied these beliefs. The different denominations disputed the supernatural power of rituals, with Catholics considering them necessary though not sufficient to gain eternal salvation and potentially helpful in countering supernatural afflictions, while Protestants generally held them to just be aids in cultivating proper beliefs and behaviors. Almost all, however, agreed that the Eucharist involved a supernatural event, the transformation of consecrated bread and wine into Christ's flesh and blood during mass, although they could never agree on precisely what that meant.

The clergy were the only licit mediators with the magico-religious world, but most communities had illicit mediators as well. The specifics of what they were called and what they were thought to do varied enormously across Europe, but there were certain broad ranges of statuses and activities. First, they varied in status from ordinary people who occasionally helped out neighbors with an incantation or ritual they knew through part-time specialists who performed certain rituals like reciting blessings or employing magical stones for healing to full-time, full-service practitioners. Second, their compensation ranged from nothing but neighborly appreciation through voluntary gifts to set fees. Third, their most common service by far was healing, but they also helped locate lost objects, identify thieves and witches, report on the location or welfare of missing persons, teach incantations and dispense magical objects and potions to ward off evil or promote love or some other desired end, counter witchcraft, or foretell the future. Fourth, the ways they worked their magic ranged from mechanically reciting incantations and performing traditional rituals to lapsing into a trance state in which they experienced direct contact with the spirit world (with the former by far more common). Fifth, their moral orientation ranged from only working beneficial magic to occasionally performing harmful magic to featuring it.

Of course, in reality things were not so clear-cut, since a benevolent ritual like identifying the source of an illness could end up accusing a person of witchcraft, while even a malevolent person might use healing magic, divination, or protective amulets. Nevertheless, the distinction between benign and dangerous practitioners was far more important to most ordinary Europeans than the one between licit and illicit ones. The balance between the two did shift from the sixteenth to the eighteenth century, though, as the power of the state reduced the danger from malevolent practitioners while imposing penalties for patronizing benevolent ones.

What these specialists were called varied enormously, and historians have not settled on a term for them, but the closest they come is "cunning folk," an English designation in which "cunning" means "knowing."[22] However, just as "cunning" in modern usage conveys a morally dubious craftiness, cunning folk were often regarded with a degree of suspicion by their neighbors because the power to heal was often thought to be complemented by the power to harm. Indeed, the counter-magic they employed against witches and thieves often involved harming the suspect, love magic could be used to exploit someone, and divination or other magic could be used to gain an unfair advantage. Furthermore, some cunning folk worked explicitly harmful magic on their own account or for clients.[23] They were sometimes suspected of causing injuries they could then get paid to cure, and some ran veritable protection rackets, extorting tribute through implied or explicit threats of magical harm. The majority of cunning folk practiced magic benevolently, but some clearly used it in ways that were ambiguous or explicitly harmful.

When magical practitioners were thought to frequently use their arts to cause harm they came to be considered something different from a cunning person. Anthropologists call such practitioners sorcerers to differentiate them not only from beneficent magicians but also from witches, who exert a malign magical influence based on an inborn power rather than on learned magical practices.[24] This is a rather different use of the term "witch" than that of early modern demonologists, for whom it meant someone who had made a formal pact with the Devil and worshipped him in blasphemous rites. They suspected sorcerers, and even cunning folk, did these things, but thought many other people who did not openly practice magic did as well.

What ordinary early moderns understood by "witch" seems to have involved all three definitions. Almost everywhere people assumed that some people used sorcery to cause harm, and if they thought someone did it frequently they considered them to be a witch. However, in most cases they exhibited little interest in how a suspected witch caused the harm, and in some cases they described incidents in which it seemed to clearly result from a spontaneous flash of anger.[25] Finally, ordinary people became increasingly aware of the demonological definition of witchcraft over the early modern period, and increasingly mixed assumptions about the role of the Devil into their complaints. A witch was someone who seemed to frequently project a malign influence through sorcery, an innate ability, and/or by having given herself to the Devil.

Coping with witchcraft: coexistence, counter-magic, and the courts

Since witchcraft was just one of the myriad magical threats faced by early modern people, much of what they did about it overlapped with their ways of coping with the others.

The first line of defense was passive measures, things to avoid being afflicted in the first place. Many were general methods utilized against all manner of magical threats: secreting magical defenses at strategic places within buildings like under doors and windows, wearing protective talismans and amulets (including crosses and other religious paraphernalia), being cognizant of auspicious and inauspicious days and times in planning and carrying out activities, invoking the generalized protection of God or the saints through prayer and other observances, and observing local taboos and prescriptions to promote good fortune and avoid misfortune. In the case of witchcraft specifically, additional actions to keep from becoming a target included avoiding contact with reputed witches or troublesome neighbors or appeasing them with a friendly demeanor and actions, including bestowing favors and gifts.[26]

If passive methods seemed to have failed, and a person suspected that they were the target of witchcraft, the identity of the culprit might seem obvious or easily inferred. If it was unclear whether witchcraft was at work, though, or the identity of the culprit was uncertain, divination could be employed, either on a self-help basis or by calling in a cunning person. Divinatory techniques used to identify witches (as well as thieves) included scrying, staring into a reflective surface until a recognizable face appeared; the "sieve and shears," which involved balancing a sieve on the point of a pair of shears being held upright, which was expected to begin rotating when the name of the guilty party was called out in a series of possible suspects; a pendulum, which worked in a similar way; and innumerable local practices.[27]

Some of these divinatory techniques relied on essentially random events, like performing a ceremony and then noting the first person to come to visit. Others, like scrying and the "sieve and sheers" could be cynically faked, but they also could be used to "validate" hunches based on known animosity or even guilt in a way that was more culturally acceptable than a denunciation, which could be hard to substantiate and could be seen as a voluntary betrayal of communal bonds. They could also bring to the surface completely unconscious awareness of subtle expressions of latent animosity or deceptiveness. In a world without modern forensic tools and techniques, it was almost impossible to identify the perpetrator of a covert crime like theft unless she was caught in the act or with the stolen goods. Therefore techniques that exploited peoples' unconscious awareness of others' subliminal "tells" in a close-knit community offered a potentially useful, if not entirely reliable, means of identifying people who stole or committed other surreptitious misdeeds.

If witchcraft was considered confirmed and the witch identified, there were several ways that people could proceed. One was to simply utilize normal remedies to resolve the problem. If these didn't work (or, as was often the case, witchcraft was only suspected when they failed), another approach was to try to get the witch to remove the spell by appealing to her good nature, buying her off, or threatening retaliation. Retaliation could take the form of direct physical violence or some sort of counter-magic. Counter-magic might involve an entirely new spell, but often it involved turning the original spell back on the witch, either in an attempt to persuade her to terminate it, or to relieve the target while getting revenge. It could also be shifted onto something or someone else. Sometimes counter-magic was conducted without even bothering to identify the witch, since it was assumed the spell knew or was connected to whoever cast it.

As an alternative to individual action, people who thought they were the victims of witchcraft sometimes enlisted the help of their communities. One way was to bring in a specialist, a priest or a cunning person, to conduct religious or magical countermeasures. Another was to get a small party of friends or a lynch mob to attack the suspect physically. A third was to instigate formal legal proceedings. The first two were integral parts of communal life, and generally ended once the malady had been cured and/or the specific suspect had been dealt with. In the third case, though, the process left the bounds of the community and passed into the hands of the judicial authorities.

Most trials remained confined to the immediate suspect or a small group of reputed malefic witches, but with the spread of the demonology and inquisitorial trial procedures the magistrates were increasingly likely to turn the persecution of one suspect into a hunt for all the local members of the supposed diabolical conspiracy. In certain times and places communal suspicions widened into hunts through popular initiative, or the authorities empowered local "witch committees" to solicit names and bring suspects from around the countryside to trial. For the most part, though, the relationship between communal suspicions and the mass trials was more distant: communities supplied initial suspects thought guilty of *maleficium*, and the authorities tortured them into confessing to diabolism and identifying additional suspects. The role of communal suspicions decreased as the obvious candidates were implicated and the authorities still sought more names, leading increasingly to denunciations of people who were never suspected of anything by, let alone did anything to, their neighbors.

Conclusion: the impact of the witch hunts on everyday life

While the everyday witch fears and activities of villagers and townspeople fed into the early modern hunts, the hunts fed back into everyday life. The most obvious way was by throwing communities into upheaval, consigning people by the dozens or even the hundreds to torture and death. However, the campaign against the Devil's supposed worshippers encompassed small as well as mass trials since it was what motivated the governments' aggressive prosecution and harsh punishment of suspects even when trials did not metastasize.

In this sense the witch hunts constituted a single protracted witch hunt that had more widespread and longer lasting effects on everyday life. One was that by putting individuals' malice and magical practices in the framework of a cosmic struggle between God and the Devil, good and evil, they helped broaden ordinary peoples' moral horizons beyond the values and interests of their local communities.[28] Second, by repressing surreptitious forms of violence they contributed to the "civilizing process" that transformed mores and behaviors in early modern Europe. Third, by penalizing any association with magic, they contributed to the "disenchantment of the world" by discouraging its practice and patronage of its practitioners. Fourth, by punishing women in particular for involvement with magic, they curbed their role as public practitioners, at least in some places for at least for some time. Fifth, by discouraging women from exhibiting any behaviors or attitudes that might draw suspicions, they contributed to the transformation of the presumed "natural" female character from the Medieval notion that they are more violent and lustful than men to the high modern notion that they are passive and asexual.

Historians traditionally ended their accounts of the witch hunts on a note of relieved discontinuity, assuming that because they were based on a myth, their only effect was helping discredit witchcraft beliefs and thereby contributing to the decline of magic. More recently, historians have emphasized the continuation of popular magic into the modern period, but these historians, like their predecessors, have assumed that *maleficium* was as illusory as diabolism, and so focus on the persistence of witch beliefs.[29] We have seen, however, that the hunts had roots in actual behaviors and practices, and they affected as well as reflected these. Witch beliefs and fears did persist, and so, to some extent, did witch-like behaviors and practices, but the role of magic and its practitioners in everyday life after the hunts was substantially diminished. There were many causes of this change, but the witch hunts – protracted, brutal, and pervasive – played a critical part.

Notes

1 Pieter Spierrenberg, *The Broken Spell: A Cultural and Anthropological History of Preindustrial Europe* (New Brunswick: Rutgers University Press, 1991), 97–99.
2 Walter Rummel, "Popular Persecution," in *Encyclopedia of Witchcraft: The Western Tradition*, ed. Richard Golden, vol. 3, (Santa Barbara: ABC-CLIO, 2006), 917–918, 917.

3 Stephen Wilson, *The Magical Universe: Everyday Ritual and Magic in Pre-Modern Europe* (London: Hambledon, 2000).

4 Edward Bever, "*Maleficium,*" in *Encyclopedia of Witchcraft: The Western Tradition,* ed. Richard Golden, vol. 3 (Santa Barbara: ABC-CLIO, 2006), 713–716, 713–714.

5 Edward Bever, *The Realities of Witchcraft and Popular Magic in Early Modern Europe* (Basingstoke: Palgrave-Macmillan, 2008), 275, 238.

6 Wilson, *Magical,* esp. 467.

7 Ibid., 14, 54, 348.

8 Éva Pócs, *Between the Living and the Dead* (Budapest: Central European University Press, 1999), 11.

9 Bever, *Realities,* 262–266.

10 Ibid., 42–47; Spierreneurg, *Broken,* 67.

11 Bever, *Realities,* 42–47.

12 Bever, "*Maleficium,*" 714.

13 Brian Levack, *The Witch Hunt in Early Modern Europe,* 2nd ed. (London: Longman, 1995), 13; Bever, *Realities,* 56–57.

14 Edward Bever, "Witchcraft Fears and Psychosocial Factors in Disease," *The Journal of Interdisciplinary History* XXX 4 (2000): 573–590, 577–583.

15 Bever, *Realities,* 21–28.

16 Stanley Krippner and Stanley Friedman, eds., *Debating Psychic Experience: Human Potential or Human Illusion?* (Santa Barbara: ABC-CLIO, 2010).

17 Eva Labouvie, "Hexenspuk und Hexenabwehr: Volksmagie und volkstümlicher Hexenglaube," in *Hexenwahn: Magie und Imagination von 16–20 Jahrhundert,* ed. Richard van Dülmen (Frankfurt: Fischer, 1993), 83.

18 Bever, "*Maleficium,*" 714.

19 Willem de Blécourt, "Discourse and Disappearance," *Magic, Ritual, and Witchcraft* 5.1 (2010): 103–107, 105.

20 *Mind/Body Health: The Effects of Attitudes, Emotions, and Relationships,* ed. Brent Hafen (Boston: Allyn and Bacon, 1996), 6–7.

21 Henry Kamen, *The Iron Century* (New York: Praeger, 1972), 60–62.

22 Owen Davies, *Cunning-Folk* (London: Hambledon, 2003), vii–viii, 82–84; Hans de Waardt, "Cunning Folk," in *Encyclopedia of Witchcraft: The Western Tradition,* ed. Richard Golden, vol. 3 (Santa Barbara: ABC-CLIO, 2006), 237–239; although both limit the term more than here.

23 Alexandra Walsham, "Frantick Hacket: Prophesy, Sorcery, Insanity, and the Elizabethan Puritan Movement," *Historical Journal* 41.1 (1998): 27–66, 43; Peter G. Maxwell-Stuart, *Satan's Conspiracy: Magic and Witchcraft in Sixteenth Century Scotland* (East Linton: Tuckwell, 2001), 214.

24 Keith Thomas, *Religion and the Decline of Magic* (New York: Scribner's, 1971), 463.

25 Ibid., 464–465.

26 Bever, "Popular Witch Beliefs, and Magical Practices," in *Oxford Handbook of Witchcraft in Early Modern Europe and Colonial America,* ed. Brian Levack (Oxford, Oxford University Press, 2013), 50–69, 55–56.

27 Bever, *Realities,* 222–228.

28 Ibid., 76, 403–413, 429–430.

29 Blécourt, "Discourse," 103–104, 106–107; Davies, *Cunning,* 188.

Bibliography (selection)

Bever, Edward, "Witchcraft Fears and Psychosocial Factors in Disease." *The Journal of Interdisciplinary History* XXX:4 (2000): 573–590.

Bever, Edward, *The Realities of Witchcraft and Popular Magic in Early Modern Europe.* Basingstoke: Palgrave-Macmillan, 2008.

Briggs, Robin, *Witches and Neighbours.* New York: Penguin, 1996.

Burke, Peter, *Popular Culture in Early Modern Europe,* 3rd ed. Farnham: Ashgate, 2009.

Wilby, Emma, *Cunning Folk and Familiar Spirits.* Brighton: Sussex, 2009.

Wilson, Stephen, *The Magical Universe: Everyday Ritual and Magic in Pre-Modern Europe.* London: Hambledon, 2000.

20

THE INTERRELATIONSHIP OF
MAGIC AND WITCHCRAFT

Kathryn Edwards

One of the greatest challenges facing modern scholars of magic and witchcraft in Christian societies is the variable definition and emotional resonance of those terms over time and between cultures. Scholars of early modern Europe and colonial North America, the areas emphasized here, share that same problem. Frequently "magic" is used to designate specific ritual practices that direct occult forces to achieve the magician's or client's goal, and "witch" or "witchcraft" are corrupt subsets of "magician" or " magic," respectively. Yet such a distinction oversimplifies the complex relationship between pre-modern magic and witchcraft. Both magic and witchcraft overlapped in the ways in which they were discussed, conceptualized, and practiced, but aspects of both could exist without the other. Magicians and witches were believed to have distinct abilities to access natural forces, aspects of God's creation that were innately intelligible to humans. Yet the extent to which they could access preternatural powers – available to God's creations but normally beyond human understanding and capabilities – or the occult more generally varied based on the individual, circumstances, and author of the historical document discussing the case. Moreover, individual circumstances frequently determined the extent to which magic or even witchcraft was deemed corrupt, and the activities of most accused witches or magicians were not exclusively evil. This variability makes the study of magic, witchcraft, and their interrelationship in pre-modern Europe both fascinating and frustrating.

This chapter argues that conceptions and practices of magic and witchcraft were fundamentally intertwined in pre-modern Europe and the boundaries around terms such as magic, witchcraft, and sorcery reflect intellectual constructs more than common understanding and intellectual practice. To highlight the fluidity of classifying magic and witchcraft and the variations in their moral status, it begins with the most acceptable practices and concludes with those perceived as most threatening to the community and individual. Within each section, it emphasizes key questions in their interrelationship: who practiced it, what did the practice entail, what made it attractive, how was it received, and what knowledge or traditions did the practitioner draw on? Challenging outmoded assumptions that the relationship between magic and witchcraft hinges on the primitive or advanced nature of a society, this chapter argues that distinctions and similarities between magic and witchcraft in

257

early modern Europe are based as much on personal relationships and individual background than on broader social paradigms.

Historical debates over magic and witchcraft

In late medieval and early modern Europe and the European-influenced Americas, the vocabulary of magic and witchcraft was diverse and reflected ancient conceptions about the ways individuals could access and apply occult forces, that is, secret knowledge of and power from the natural world and God. Most western and central European languages distinguished between "magic/magician" and "witchcraft/ witch," and a rich classical Greek and Latin foundation supported such distinctions. Further vocabulary existed that focused on the magical practitioner's specialty. For example, in Latin individuals labeled *lamia, saga, sortilege, strix,* or *veneficia* could all fall under the category of magician/sorcerer or witch depending on who was doing the classifying.[1] In general, these terms carried negative connotations; the idea of a "white witch" is a modern development, and some variation of "cunning folk" or "wise woman," to use English terms which had vernacular equivalents in other European languages, would be used in the early modern period to distinguish people who manipulated natural forces or who accessed forces beyond the natural realm but who generally did to benefit the community. Such precise vocabulary can, however, give a false impression about how clearly magic and witchcraft were classified and distinguished. In practice, terms could be used synonymously and evolve over time. Discussions of witchcraft and magic thus drew on a diverse vocabulary that simultaneously tried to separate and meld them.

These linguistic variations benefit from and complicate modern studies of the relationship between magic and witchcraft, and they have similar effects in the pioneering works of Margaret Murray, James George Frazer, and Edwards Evan Pritchard which continue to influence modern scholarship on magic and witchcraft.[2] Both Murray and Frazier stressed the ancient roots of tensions between magic and witchcraft and saw magic as remnants of either fertility cults or prehistoric fertility religions. Witchcraft comes into play in these interpretations as a libel by Christian authorities of these ancient religious practices, a libel that developed during Christianity's expansion in medieval and early modern Europe. E. E. Evans-Pritchard brought into the discussion a more precise consideration of its key terms, founded on extensive research into non-European peoples, and argued that people living in cultures where magic is prevalent draw a distinction between magic, witchcraft, and sorcery. In these cases sorcery is a deliberate use of magical rituals to cause harm while witchcraft comes from the witch's innate power to cause harm to others, but this distinction was rarely so clear in medieval and early modern European languages.[3] All of these scholars also embedded in discussions of magic and witchcraft a distinction between magic and religion where magic channeled occult forces in nature for individual and communal benefit whereas religion supplicated a higher power for assistance.

Although each of these approaches to the relationship between magic and witchcraft, and related topics such as sorcery and religion, have proven extremely influential, they only emphasize one aspect of the relationship to the detriment of others. As such, they often fail to provide a satisfactory interpretation when applied to dissimilar cultures or types of sources or when applied to premodern historical texts.

Moreover, as recent scholars have argued, magic's practice and intellectual foundation was perceived differently depending on an individual's social class, educational level, and religious confession, to name just a few of the variables. For these reasons, some of the fundamental distinctions in these earlier interpretations, such as that between coercive magic and supplicant religion, would have been inconceivable to people in medieval and early modern Christian Europe.[4]

Scholars since the 1970s have worked to achieve a more satisfactory synthesis. Among the pioneers challenging Murray, Frazier, and Evans-Pritchard were Keith Thomas and Norman Cohn whose works, *Religion and the Decline of Magic* and *The Pursuit of the Millennium*, respectively, appeared in the early 1970s. These scholars offered new and equally influential interpretations of the relationship between magic and witchcraft alongside their broader analysis of religion and magic. For both Thomas and Cohn, magic and witchcraft were sources of power; the debate occurred over who defined each category's qualities and who wielded their power. While both authors acknowledged that belief in magic was widespread throughout premodern Europe and that local conditions influenced the acceptance of magic and accusations of witchcraft, they disagreed over the extent to which elite policy and discourse formed belief in and actions against magic and witchcraft. Despite the influence and value of such promising research, however, more recent scholarship has challenged the binary between magic and witchcraft on which these analyses were based. Contemporary research argues that definitions and perceptions of witchcraft and magic that were formed through an ongoing exchange between clergy, judicial officials, and a general population that itself experienced these qualities in a myriad of ways.[5]

The process of rejecting binaries and acknowledging the varied uses of terms related to witchcraft and magic has left many modern scholars reluctant to provide direct definitions of what constitutes magic and witchcraft for fear of imposing anachronistic classifications on categories that were pervasive in premodern Europe. This article grapples with the same challenges. Yet a general consensus for the early modern period has emerged that draws upon historical, anthropological, and philosophical analysis. It accepts that "magic," and especially "sorcery," carry in modern European languages a hint of the illegitimate or deceptive that did not necessarily exist in premodern usage, but it acknowledges that magic could also be both depending on circumstances. It eschews statements about the truth or falsity of belief in witchcraft and instead stresses that witches and witchcraft, magic and magicians were accepted components of early modern ideas and society. It focuses on the circulation of information about magic and witchcraft, the qualities that were used to judge the truth of such information, and the unconscious processes and assumptions that led to the classification of actions and signs as belonging to magic and witchcraft.[6] It accepts that such categories are by definition blurred and often actions seen as magical and beneficial by one individual might be interpreted as maleficent witchcraft by another under different conditions.

Common magic and the enchanted world

In order for magic to be practiced and, arguably, to be successful, the world had to be seen as an enchanted place in which certain humans could access forces and impulses beyond normal human experience and nature's mundane functioning.[7]

In premodern Europe the world was believed to imbued with such forces, aspects of the immanence with which creation was infused. Modern actions and attitudes that might be labeled magic or magical – and presumed to be based on ignorance or deception – were, thus, for early modern Europeans extraordinary manifestations of ordinary immanence. For laity and clergy, peasants and university scholars, magic was both the existence of these forces and the ability to access them, and it was not necessarily confined to select individuals. While a small group of intellectuals placed the analysis and practice of this magic at the heart of their ontology, for most Europeans magic was an effective tool because of a world where entities and forces beyond the human played an active and interventionist role. Witches certainly accessed such magical forces, but the application of these magical forms was not innately witchcraft. In an enchanted world, magic was one coin in a common cultural currency, and this section sketches some of the ways in which premodern Europeans accepted it and placed it alongside, but separate from, witchcraft.[8]

Secular and ecclesiastical authorities in Christian Europe shared this enchanted worldview, but simultaneously, they could challenge some of its more common assumptions and magical practices. This tension would be fundamental to their analysis and treatment of witchcraft in the sixteenth and seventeenth centuries. While some clergy, lawyers, and medical doctors were active practitioners or consumers of magic, even magic's detractors likely shared aspects of the common cultures of early modern Europe in which magic was assumed. After all, many were raised by mothers and nursemaids who told stories about humans transforming to animals; they turned to herbs such as mandrake for cures, relying on the similarities between its form and that of a man to enhance its curative properties; and they repeated preachers' condemnations about the ability of Egyptian days or singing requiem masses to speed human deaths.[9] Moreover, in Western Europe since at least the time of the Roman Republic magic had been under the purview of secular courts, and some aspects of magical practices would remain so in medieval and early modern Europe. In other words, they had likely read legal treatises about, heard law suits concerning, and testified before courts on magic. Whether cases involving magic were tried in secular or ecclesiastical courts, however, magic's very status as a potentially criminal act demonstrates that authorities accepted and, at times, feared its power. Some medieval and early modern princely courts also housed sorcerers, who had wide responsibilities ranging from divination to pursuit of the Philosopher's Stone, which could transmute lead into gold. Even those whose primary activities took place outside the university or courts, such as preachers, showed and reinforced the power and influence of this enchanted worldview in the stories they told where the dead spoke, charms repelled illness, and prayers led to the discovery of criminals. Magic was an orthodox and expected, if not common, part of everyday life; it could be dangerous, but it was not inherently corrupt.[10]

Throughout early modern European society magic could thus be an acceptable way for many kinds of people to channel extraordinary forces for human benefit. Practices involving herbs, amulets, and charms were quite common and generally regarded as legitimate, at least when used promote legal and orthodox activities. One, among many, possible examples of the integration of herbal medicine and religious practices in a way that could be labeled magical involved the steps for harvesting and preparation of leaves used to treat fever: "Before using these leaves, one is supposed to write certain Latin words on them to involve the power of the Holy Trinity, and then one is to say the Lord's Prayer and other prayers over them. . . . repeating this procedure before sunrise on three consecutive mornings."[11] The integration of writing and prayer found here echoed that found in charms, a common and orthodox magical object that could also become a tool of witchcraft. Charms often applied word magic, relying on powerful phrases from Scriptures or combinations of words and letters that were believed to be particularly potent to obtain cures for illness or to protect buildings and other shelters. They would be written onto some object – parchment, wax, stones – and placed near the person or thing that nccdcd protcction. Such practices were widespread throughout Europe and the Americas well into the seventeenth and eighteenth centuries.[12] Certain texts had specialized functions; for example, the opening of St. John's Gospel was considered powerful protection against demons. Some theologians were unhappy with such use of sacred texts; Thomas Aquinas felt that it was permitted for people to wear holy words as a sign of devotion but that it was wrong to wear them in the hopes of harnessing some supernatural power for personal benefit.[13] Despite such concern, however, the medieval and early modern Catholic Church widely produced objects that contained holy words for the benefit of its faithful. Churches were less complicit in other magical operations. For example, a common way of finding out the truth in early modern Europe and European America, in Protestant and Catholic territories like, was the sieve and the shears. In this ritual a sieve would be balanced on top of a pair of shears; usually several individuals surrounded the sieve and shears, but it was unnecessary. Once the objects were placed, the ritual could vary slightly; in some cases, one of the individuals would pose a question, and if the sieve turned, it meant that the answer was yes. In another version of the same ritual, a question could be asked about one of the people standing nearby. If the sieve turned to that person and stopped, the answer was yes regarding that person.[14]

While the sieve and the shears may seem to be innocuous, they moved participants into the realm of occult magic in a way that secular and ecclesiastical authorities mistrusted. Yet such dubious activities were also quite common, at times integrated with acceptable magical practices. In both villages and towns throughout Europe people could find specialized practitioners who provided love potions, told fortunes, and helped find lost objects, all through the use of a mixture of specially harvested herbs, religious language, and secret rituals and preparations.[15] While such magic could be relatively harmless, other practices could easily blur the line between the passable and the profane. For example, one way of assuring a beloved's devotion in early modern Venice was to put holy oil on your lips and kiss him.[16] What modern scholars might describe as sympathetic magic was also at the heart of many medical practices. Certainly sympathies and antipathies between the heavens and earth were fundamental to premodern medicine, but some medical practitioners might integrate prayer and holy objects into sympathetic practice in ways that bordered on the profane. Other practices were always considered illicit, even if their goal was essentially harmless or even beneficial. For example, one of the great fears of early modern Catholic clergy was the parishioner would take the Eucharist but not swallow it. As the actual body of Christ, the consecrated wafer contained divine power, which made it an especially effective magical object. Yet among authorities such treatment was sacrilegious because it assumed that the godhead could become a mere human tool, even if it was used for something beneficial such as an ingredient in a healing tonic.

The use of holy objects for what the clergy believed were nefarious purposes brought common magic into the realm of superstition, which carried with it significant spiritual and ecclesiastical consequences and which could readily be perceived as witchcraft.[17] For premodern European authorities superstition was not foolishness or ignorance; superstition was false belief. Someone who was superstitious could thus easily follow the path to damnation. As the improper use of holy objects or as incorrect belief, superstition could readily encompass many magical activities and transform them into something fundamentally dangerous and even heretical. For example, in 1566 Elizabeth Mortlock was publicly shamed for her integration of Catholic prayers – the Paternoster, Ave, and Creed – as part of her healing practices on behalf of those whom fairies injured. Yet her judges felt that her superstitions and application of magic were more than just ignorance. In an example of how fine the line could be between licit and illicit magical purposes and practices, she was also condemned as a witch.[18]

This connection between superstition and magic was also at the heart of many polemics during the Protestant and Catholic Reformations, polemics that would influence the early modern interpretation of witchcraft. Early Protestant reformers regularly condemned medieval Christianity as superstitious and even malicious. For these reformers, it was wrapped in inappropriate secrecy and depended on slights of hand.[19] They claimed that the clergy devised miracles to assert a supernatural, magical power over all other Christians and, in the process, corrupted the very people to whom the clergy should minister. They also condemned what they saw as a proliferation of masses used like magical tools to heal animals and people, assure plentiful crops, protect individuals on journeys, and allow the dead to be saved. The rituals surrounding and the process of transubstantiation were particularly condemned. The transformation of unleavened bread to the body of Christ and of wine to the blood of Christ appeared to many Protestant reformers to be no different than the secret conjurations of illicit magical practitioners claiming to be able to summon spirits or transmute lead to gold. As innately deceptive, transubstantiation became a false miracle – of a type demons seemed to promote. As such, some Protestant theologians were willing to argue that, at the heart of the mass, the Catholic clergy were abetting a demonically-inspired deception.

In addition to those practices and beliefs condemned as part of Reformation polemics, there had always existed a common culture of medieval and early modern magic that skirted the line of orthodoxy. Such practices often gained their problematic status because of the preconditions necessary for them to function and the involvement of supernatural entities in their production or implementation. Even relatively innocuous objects like charms could depend on secrecy, prayers, blessings, magical movements, and occult symbols, all conditions seen as potentially subversive. That such charms did not depend on clerical participation for their fabrication and efficacy made them even more suspect. Even magic used to combat witches could be dangerous if it was in the wrong hands or came from the wrong source. Chonrad Stoeckhlin, a sixteenth-century Bavarian herdsman, claimed to be able to identify witches because of powers he received from the "phantoms of the night."[20] In other words, an illicit source gave him licit powers, although Chonrad saw nothing illicit about his involvement with the phantoms. Certain Protestant confessions would go so far as to link prophylactic and demonic magic. For example, in North America Puritan clergy condemned the wearing of charms to prevent illness and misfortune as working through demonic assistance since that could be the only force so willing to attempt to undermine divine providence.[21]

The case of Matteuccia Francisci of Todi epitomizes the mixture of acceptance, suspicion, and condemnation in the common magical culture of early modern Europe. Matteuccia Francisca was brought before the courts in 1428 for magical practices, many of which had good outcomes, that she had undertaken over several years. She taught people how to cure themselves of fevers, to rid themselves of lameness, and to counteract curses. She provided the town with herbal treatments and women with contraception. Yet her activities had magical components that could readily become suspicious. For example, she gave blessed herbs to young women that they could, in turn, give to men to make them fall in love. She performed counterspells to remove spells from clients, including ones that transferred incantations onto unsuspecting passersby. As her trial progressed, Matteuccia herself provided under torture increasingly graphic statements of her activities: producing ointments that would allow her to fly, burying bones from unbaptized babies as cures for illness, and using baby fat in her magical potions. Although Matteuccia was apparently believed to be a valuable member of her community for years before her prosecution and her initial activities fell within the purviews of Europe's common magical culture, once St. Bernardino of Siena preached in her town, previously innocuous magical practices were transformed and additional magical corruption was expected. As such, the authorities determined to put her "to the question." After confessing to a litany of magical crimes and consorting with demons, Matteuccia was burned as a witch.[22]

Renaissance occultism and the treatment of magic and witchcraft

As the case of Francisci suggests, by the fifteenth century the relationship between magic and witchcraft grew closer among some intellectuals; at the same time studies in natural philosophy influenced by Jewish, Muslim, or Greco-Roman philosophical systems that did not separate magic from piety and science were gaining broader and more profound influence. Scholars often label those who analyzed or practiced such magic "occultists" to distinguish them from "magicians" and "sorcerers" who were presumed to be more duplicitous and dangerous, yet such distinctions were difficult to maintain. Occultists, by definition, studied the hidden properties and principles of nature, and they argued that only an elite few could and should be exposed to such ideas; as such, occultists could easily be perceived as a cabal trying to undermine God's natural laws. While Renaissance occultists were not necessarily involved in witchcraft, either as practitioners or prosecutors, the intellectual currents they synthesized and disseminated would influence those who tried and analyzed magic, witchcraft, and their interrelationship. The magical theories and rituals of Renaissance occultists could lead other intellectuals and authorities to question the very parameters of magic and its relationship to the demonic.[23]

Several events in the later Middle Ages would fundamentally influence the practice of magic and the understanding of the occult, and its relationship to witchcraft, in early modern Europe. The first was the increased circulation and analysis of classical Greek and Latin texts known as the Renaissance. Beginning in the four-teenth century a small community of European intellectuals argued that the writ-ings of pagan antiquity served as a better guide for contemporary life and, in some cases, morality than the scholastic tradition of the Middle Ages. Over the next several centuries these intellectuals unearthed and edited hundreds of ancient Latin and later Greek texts, disseminating those documents throughout Europe – a process to which those fleeing the Ottoman conquest of Constantinople (1453) contributed greatly. A fundamental doctrine for Renaissance humanists, some of whom would become leading occultists, was the need to go *ad fontes* (to the sources), that is, to the original authors and texts rather than translations, commentaries, and paraphrases. Linked to this principle was the conviction that only the truly learned could appreci-ate classical texts in their original language and context, so they should be the only people studying such documents. These philological and linguistic pursuits would have profound social consequences among the elite and administrative classes of fifteenth- and sixteenth-century Europe, transforming the education and definition of a learned man.

In the process of going "to the sources," Renaissance humanists could not escape magic and witchcraft. Ancient Greek and Roman writings were full of stories of witches, sorcerers, and magical spirits, and ancient Roman laws exacted harsh penalties on those convicted of practicing illicit magic. Whether they treated it in a comical or condemnatory fashion, Roman and Greek authors described a society that shared the "magical worldview" of medieval and early modern Europe. Famous fifteenth-century scholars such as Marsilio Ficino and Heinrich Cornelius Agrippa provided syntheses of such classical systems and attempted to integrate pagan perspectives on magic and witchcraft into a holistic Christian framework with varying degrees of success. The work of these scholars and other contem-poraries assured that, by the late fifteenth century, Neoplatonism and Hermeti-cism would help to shape European intellectuals' understanding of occultism and ritual magic.[24]

Both Neoplatonism and Hermeticism as understood in early modern Europe are difficult terms to define because they represent centuries of writing inspired by, not necessarily produced by, particular authors: in the case of Neoplatonism, Plato, and of Hermeticism, Hermes Trismegistus. For those interested in occult theory and magical practice, Macrobius's writings, Plato's *Timaeus*, Hermes's *Corpus hermeticum*, and dozens of other texts ascribed to these authorities complemented Christian understandings of a holistic, integrated universe that an adept could come to appre-ciate. If the budding magus appreciated natural sufficiently, he could even, in some cases, manipulate it. Drawing on ancient Egyptian magical and wisdom literature, often funneled through several layers of translation, Renaissance occultists argued for the legitimacy of certain types of ancient, pagan magic, a position that some clerical authorities, particularly those following the Augustinian tradition, found problematic at best. Opponents of this occultism also pointed to the integration into such studies of other, suspect texts, such as the *Emerald Tablets*, which described the qualities of the *prima materia*, the cornerstone of creation, and means by which it could be transmuted, thereby suggesting that God himself could be inconstant. A less threatening inconsistency that Neoplatonic magical practitioners and theorists faced was the admitted fluidity of any magic since they saw creation as mutable rather than mechanistic. As such, variable results were to be expected from any magical working, a situation that some could see as undermining the very possibility of truth.

The Renaissance impulse to go to the sources that led to the increased influence of Neoplatonic and Hermetic writings also inspired more profound and extensive examination of Jewish and Muslim occultism, although the link between such studies and accusations of witchcraft was tenuous. Major writings in both traditions had circulated in Christian Europe well before the Renaissance: the *Picatrix* provided detailed descriptions of Arabic astral magic (albeit garbled through translation from Arabic to Spanish, then to Latin) and Avicenna's alchemical texts were widely disseminated because they were presumed to be written by Aristotle. Within Europe's small Muslim community, textual magic and charms were used in similar ways as in Europe's Christian territories – passages from the Qur'an were placed in amulets as protection – and some evidence exists that, in the Iberian peninsula, Christians would see these Arabic charms as being especially effective and use them well after the association with Islam had faded.[25] In eastern Europe, Byzantine and Persian occultism had influenced each other for centuries, and the fall of the Byzantine Empire and attendant transmission of texts also increased western European knowledge of the Islamic occult tradition. The emphasis in such texts on ritual purity and asceticism, the application of natural materials to occult understanding, and even the acceptance of secondary spirits influencing the natural world could all be read in a way that complemented Christian understandings of Creation and the magical.[26] Given the circulation of texts around the Mediterranean Basin and Near East at this time, it should not then be surprising that a figure would arise in western Europe like Giovanni Pico della Mirandola whose writings were inspired by Christian sources and classical Greek and Roman texts as well the Hebrew Kabbalah and Islamic lettrism. Although his work focused on natural philosophy, the interrelationship of magic and the natural world and his willingness to turn to many non-Christian traditions in pursuit of knowledge led to suspicions that he was also a magician, suspicions that even his allies held.

As might be expected and Pico della Mirandola's case illustrates, the integration of classical, non-Christian, and Christian philosophical and spiritual systems in pursuit of a magic that reflected the most profound human understanding and appreciation of God was far from smooth. When those who pursued such learning then tried to develop magical rituals that could be applied to human needs, the relationship between magic and the occultist aspects of natural philosophy became more fraught – and more dangerous. Although these tensions could be demonstrated in many aspects of learned magic in late medieval and early modern Europe, the classification of magic into four primary categories (angelic, demonic, natural, and judicial) and the application of astral magic illustrate both the success and failure of attempts to control the understanding of magic and magic's potential to morph into corrupt witchcraft.

During the Middle Ages authors began to use the term "natural" magic as a way of distinguishing between true and false magic. Natural magic was magic done using qualities of Creation that were hidden from most, if not all, of humanity, but it was inherently pure since it drew on legitimate aspects of God's creation. It could even be argued that those who successfully practiced natural magic experienced a form of revelation; certainly they had a far more profound understanding of nature and, by implication, its Creator (God) than mere ordinary mortals. Yet it was clear that all magical practice did not have, nor was it intended to have, such pure motives. Individuals turned to fortune-tellers to learn about their future, then returned to those same magicians for aid in preventing that which had been foretold. Such attempts to control divine providence were condemned by all but a few and were classified as judicial magic. Authors on far sides of the confessional spectrum condemned such practices; both Loyola and Calvin found such activities an affront to God. Others would denounce them as witchcraft.

Astral magic was part of both natural and judicial magic; as such, its practitioners could inadvertently move from orthodoxy to unorthodoxy. Magic involving the stars was fundamental to many aspects of medieval and early modern life: herbs were picked during certain planetary conjunctions to enhance their effectiveness, medical procedures were timed to take advantage of astral influences, and astrological signs were presumed to affect the human personality. Astronomy and astrology were intertwined, and one part of the four-part *quadrivium* of the universities (the more advanced educational level) included astronomy until the late sixteenth century. Yet the extent to which astral magic was legitimate was debatable. Certainly some elites patronized astronomers for their predictive and protective skills; for example, Pope Urban VIII brought Thomasso Campanella to Rome in 1626 so that he could be the papal astrologer and magician protecting the pope from malign earthly and planetary influences, a job description that seemingly asked him to perform judicial magic.[27] While both Catholics and Protestants could share this tendency to blur magical distinctions, many evangelical communities tried to articulate a firmer division. Among such groups were Puritan theologians. They would allow that the stars could influence earthly events but saw using the stars to predict and control human activities as a challenge to divine providence.[28]

While occultists themselves were rarely accused of witchcraft, the distinctions they and their opponents made about types of magic and the increased interest in things beyond nature's ordinary parameters that Renaissance occultism reflected and spread would influence the judges and theorists involved with witch trials. Recent studies of witchcraft trials in early modern Venice, for example show a judiciary trained and focused on distinguishing between the natural and supernatural; only when all things natural were ruled out could someone be convicted for causing evil through magic. Even the medical doctors giving testimony showed great care in separating the occult from the natural, and part of their identity as physicians became their ability to render judgment only on the natural. Both doctors and judges believed in demons and the supernatural more generally, but they were increasingly aware of the complexities and, for the doctors, the dangers of classifying magical activities.[29] These professionals could see that, by the sixteenth century, natural magic could segue easily into judicial magic, leaving prosecutors and even mere observers to wonder exactly how an individual got such special knowledge and power.

Necromancy and spirits: magic becomes diabolized

As the case of Matteuccia Francisci and the writings of Renaissance occultists illustrate, the spirit world was never far from the magical world. Entities of all sorts – devils, ghosts, fairies, and more generic "spirits" – were also believed to be innately magical, whether through greater knowledge of nature (demons), experience with realms beyond those of the living (ghosts), or the ability to move between aspects of creation (various spiritual beings).[30] As such, the invocation of spirits was a key aspect of elite ritual magic and could be integrated into many more mundane magical activities. For practitioners, spirits were always unpredictable and frequently dangerous; exact adherence to magical ritual was necessary to achieve any degree of control. For authorities, spirits increased the threat of magic because they were so difficult to identify; as in the cases of men and women who claimed saintly spiritual visitations, magicians had to be able to ascertain a spirit's true identity to control the working and, if possible, to avoid charges of demonolatry or heresy. For all early modern Europeans, the invocation and participation of spirits in magic transformed the ritual into something powerful but less human and more liable to corruption. It can even be argued that the frequency, type, and number of spirits invoked played a key role in determining magic's or a magician's legitimacy.

This section outlines the ways the spirit world influenced magical practice in late medieval and early modern Europe. Beginning with ritual magic of the type a Renaissance occultist would recognize, it describes the place of necromancy in that magical tradition. From necromancy it was believed to be a small step, if even a step at all, to magic that directly involved demons. Such *magia goetia*, magic involving angels and demons, also drew from Jewish, Islamic, and Hellenic traditions, all of which, in the appropriate circumstances, could make occult practices and practitioners more suspect to Christian authorities. Although necromancers were not generally tried as members of a great demonic conspiracy – perhaps because of their scarcity and secrecy – the connection between magic and diabolism that underlay necromancy would add fuel to the fires of the early modern witch hunts and could transform some cunning-folk into witches, that is, practitioners of evil magic.

Necromancy has been commonly defined as magic done with the aid of demons, and there are good theological reasons for that definition.[31] Both Isidore of Seville (ca. 560–636) and Augustine of Hippo (354–430) repeatedly made the connection between magic and demons in their influential writings, and their definitions dominated until the twelfth century.[32] By the later Middle Ages, however, as the distinction was made between natural magic and demonic magic, the definition had grown more fluid: while necromancy as a practice remained almost always evil or at least suspect, the spirits involved in necromantic workings became more diverse, as reflected in the word itself. Necromancy is thus most exactly defined as magic with the aid of non-living beings, and such entities were believed to populate the early modern world. In their rituals necromancers could call on ghosts, angels, and other spirits as well as the more traditional demons, much like other magical practitioners could and did. The connection between necromancy and non-living, generally non-corporeal, entities may therefore have contributed to the growing fear of some traditional magical practices. The enduring link between necromancy and demons may have reinforced fears that magical practices in general, especially those involving any type of preternatural or supernatural entity were likely demonic.[33]

In the Middle Ages the traditional practitioners of necromantic magic were clergy, so much so that necromancy has been described as belonging to a "clerical underworld."[34] Several persuasive explanations have been posited for what might seem to be a paradoxical connection, such as clerical familiarity with high ritual practices and objects, clerical interest in the preternatural realm (to which demons belonged), clerical confidence, if not hubris, in the rightness of their motives and goals, and clerical engagement in academic debates of the nature of Creation. Yet studies of necromantic manuals from the fourteenth, fifteenth, and early sixteenth centuries make clear that the necromancer's motives and methods were often far from pious. Particularly common in both necromantic manuals and some of the earliest witch-craft trials was the invocation of demons, often by their individual names, in erotic magic. Detailed rites are described that allowed sorcerers to bind women to them-selves, steal women from other men, and even rape women with their full acquies-cence.[35] Clerical necromancers were also accused of working with leading nobles to overthrow rulers or obtain preferment at court.[36] The clergy's involvement in late medieval necromancy certainly did not make it more acceptable; in fact, it may have made it more abhorrent, given that it ensnared even those of superior spiritual status with a direct channel to the divinity.

Laity, too, were involved in the culture of necromancy at its most elite levels. While in both medieval and early modern Europe they could patronize necromancers, the exposure of learned laymen to non-Christian and ancient texts in the fifteenth and sixteenth centuries that contributed to the rise of Renaissance occultism also spurred laymen to study spirits' qualities, motivations, and effects on humanity. Recent schol-arship has shown that the fifteenth century saw rising production of works about demons and other spirits, although demonology is most often linked to sixteenth and seventeenth writings.[37] While these earlier texts were written primarily by clergy, laity also consumed them, judging by their influence in later witchcraft trials and demonological treatises. Early modern elites also integrated practices into magical workings that they claimed were more pious and philosophical but that observers and judges argued were necromancy, pure and simple. Such presumed knowledge of necromantic practices and their link to the demonic would plague the careers of some famous sixteenth-century natural philosophers such as John Dee and Para-celsus.[38] It would also make it easier to link other magical practices to necromancy.

The example of necromantic divination illustrates both the appeal and danger of necromantic magic. Divination had a long tradition in Europe and could be accom-plished in many ways: the interpretation of dreams, the patterns of hands, the flights of birds, or the first passage of a book that had been opened randomly. Yet each of these methods was fundamentally a way of connecting to a deeper spiritual realm. It seemed only logical that direct communication with spirits would be the clearest way to obtain information, and demons were generally presumed to be the most knowledgeable spirits that humans could potentially control. Necromantic manuals thus provide multiple spells that rely on demonic aid to envision and influence the future. In the process necromancers were guilty not just of demonolatry but of judi-cial magic – trying to overturn God's divine plan. One can see why demons might be willing partners.

Such divination was not confined to Europe's elites, however. Medieval and early modern Europe retained many practitioners of magic for whom interaction with spir-its was one tool in their belt. Whether they be called cunning folk, wise men/women, or scryers, to give just some English-language terms, the interaction of these individ-uals with spiritual entities distinguished them from and empowered them beyond ordinary human beings. Such "folk diviners" may have inherited their abilities, such as Sicily's *donas de fuera* (ladies from outside) who attracted and spoke with fairies and availed themselves of fairy knowledge because the women were believed to have "sweet blood." Others seem to have followed a sort of apprenticeship.[39] Like much of the elite divination that is more frequently tied to necromancy, common divination often had practical motivations. For example, spirits guided early modern treasure hunters to hidden caches – or at least so the hunters argued. Some hunters even saw their actions as part of a spiritual economy; they claimed that, by allowing the deceased to reveal ill-gotten gains and put them to good use, they were actually performing a meritorious deed that would benefit the spirit's soul and theirs. Not surprisingly, authorities were unconvinced.[40]

For the unsympathetic and even some practitioners, it was thus a small step from invoking and controlling spirits to pleading with demons for assistance – and even promising them assistance in return.[41] Once magic was linked with evil, and the embodiment of evil, Satan, was perceived as a willing participant in and distorter of magical practices, the preconditions were set for magic to be perceived as innately evil. In the process those who engaged in or even just studied ritual magic were linked to those who practiced magic and interacted with spirits at a baser level, the innately dangerous and deceptive witch.

Witches, demons, and *maleficia*

The escalation of witch trials and the development of panics in late medieval and early modern Europe are the products of a long redefinition of the relationship between magic, its practitioners, and the supernatural. As the previous sections have shown, magical practitioners were never morally neutral and, as helpful as they might be at times, were always seen as potentially dangerous to their community. Yet by the fifteenth century, the threat such individuals could pose more frequently seems to have outweighed the benefits they offered, and by the sixteenth and seventeenth centuries growing fears of demonic activity enhanced the danger. In linking many forms of magic to spirits and presuming that spirits were likely demonic, both clergy and laity increasingly saw occultism and magical practice as potentially evil and, therefore, as witchcraft. In the process, approximately 100,000 people would be prosecuted as witches, and over half of those individuals were executed.

In fifteenth-century Europe there appears to have been an increased obsession with demonic activity and influence in this world; this claim is conditional because it is impossible to quantify, but many specialists have noted the ways in which the devil and the evil he embodied was perceived as permeating the world and the growing number of texts trying to help Christians oppose him. Heretical groups such as the Waldensians were linked to demonic conspiracies and, thus, tried as witches. Witch trials of other individuals seen as the allies of demons occurred in Switzerland (1428–36), Dauphiné (1420–60), and the duchy of Milan (1480–1520).[42] At the same time, treatises were written describing the link between magic and demonolatry: Johannes Nider's *Formicarius* (1437–38), Nicolas Jacquier's *Scourge of Heretics* (1458), Alfonso da Spina's *Fortress of Faith against Enemies of the Christian Religion Everywhere* (1459), Petrus Marmor's *Source of Workers of Harmful Magic* (1462), and Heinrich Kramer's *Malleus Maleficarum* (1487). While none of these texts challenged the truism that *maleficia* (evil deeds) was at the heart of witchcraft, they emphasized in a new and particularly virulent way the source of inspiration to injure (demonic promptings), the ultimate beneficiary of such harm (the Devil), and the witch's place as a foot soldier in a vast demonic army. In so doing, they expanded on the demonic inspiration for divination found in medieval canon law.

Such ideas were refined and enhanced in the sixteenth century, both in Europe and in European writings about the Americas among members of all of Europe's confessions. It is well known that leading Reformers, such as Martin Luther, felt that demons harassed humanity continually, and the battles of the Reformations only contributed to a sense that the end times were near and demonic influence pervasive.[43] When judges, preachers, and theologians then argued that particular rituals were innately corrupt and corrupting, easing Satan's task, it was thus logical to link certain magic practices and practitioners to demonic and harmful magic.[44] In the Americas, Europeans from all Christian confessions relied on that logic to argue that Native Americans who retained traditional beliefs and practices, especially those who actively opposed missionaries, were willing or inadvertent tools of the Devil.[45] Those, such as Reginald Scot and Johannes Weyer, who doubted that there was such a thing as a conspiracy of witches or that witches had secret meetings with devils did not doubt that evil existed or demons were active in the world. Even as authorities became increasingly reluctant to convict individuals for witchcraft in the later seventeenth century, this impulse did not stem from disbelief in witchcraft or evil magic, but from an epistemological quandary tied to revised legal practices.[46]

Although the Reformations certainly heightened the fear of demonic activity and its consequences, and likely did so in ways that directly contributed to increased suspicion of magical activities, the growing emphasis on demonic conspiracies and human corruption found in fifteenth-century texts suggests that other factors contributed to magic becoming witchcraft. The fear of death caused by recurring plagues, the shock of "discovering" an entirely new hemisphere, the price inflation arising from the import of American silver, the sufferings caused by Europe's endemic warfare, and even the Little Ice Age have all been broached as contributing factors. Most successful, however, as a widespread cultural explanation is the idea of the limited good. Economic and social thinking in premodern Europe presumed that there were only a limited number of resources available. When population increased or a neighbor prospered, others would suffer. Early modern European societies were filled with families and individuals jockeying for limited food, land, and other goods; even if an entire community benefitted, the assumption was that somewhere, likely nearby, was another group who jealously watched those who prospered. When this attitude was added to the additional strains Europeans faced in the sixteenth and seventeenth centuries, the fears inspired by the occult powers and practice of magic could more readily overwhelm the benefits individuals and communities received. They could even transform natural magic into demonic magic.[47]

Despite this fear that the devil was increasingly effective and prevalent, when most early modern Europeans first accused someone of witchcraft it was because magical practice had caused harm, not because the devil was directly involved. Often accused witches had long histories of conflict in their communities and were known for turning to occult powers or taking extraordinary measures for vengeance. They were already seen as someone familiar with manipulating natural forces or interacting with the spirit world, although these actions could have benefitted their neighbors, too. In fact, people in the community may have turned to them for assistance for years – and turned a blind eye to the extent to which these neighbors tapped into occult forces. What transformed such individuals from powerful neighbors to dangerous and corrupt witches was their practice of *maleficia* (evil deeds). In other words, generally the magic that first brought the witch to authorities was stealing milk from a neighbor's cow, destroying crops, and causing illness, not meeting with the devil, pledging allegiance to him, or helping to bring about the end of the world. In fact, the accuser may have even taken magical steps to reverse the witch's spell or turned to the witch for counter-magic against another neighbor.[48]

Both sex and gender influenced how magic was perceived and, in certain places, the type of magic that was performed. Scholars have proven that approximately 80 percent of those prosecuted for witchcraft in early modern Europe were women, but such statistics are deceptive. The numbers varied regionally throughout Europe with men much more likely to be prosecuted in the Nordic countries whereas women dominated witch trials in the classic "heartlands" of witchcraft studies (Germany, France, Scotland, and parts of Switzerland, England, and the Basque region). Yet there are disruptions even in these patterns. For example, in Normandy close to 75 percent of those prosecuted were men.[49] When the link between sex and witchcraft is studied in the areas of the Americas colonized by Europeans in the sixteenth and seventeenth centuries, the statistics become even more complex. Not only was the recordkeeping more scattered, but indigenous religious practices were more alien and, therefore, ready to diabolize than European practices with which authorities had been familiar for centuries. Moreover, Indians frequently had male religious leaders who, as promoters of false belief and communicators with false gods according to European authorities, provided ready fodder for concepts of a satanic conspiracy bolstered by witches.

Gender influenced early modern witch trials through both the activities witches were accused of undertaking and the expectations witches defied. Violation of gender norms seems to have contributed to the virulence that transformed an individual from a more neutral magical practitioner to the innately evil witch. The educated male magician, often connected to the clergy or administration and, thereby, more associated with ritual, authority, and knowledge, was likely less disconcerting when wielding occult power than an uneducated or marginally educated local woman whose only status was communal or unofficial. In the territories where the majority of those prosecuted were women, accused witches were integrated into local society but were rarely among the loftiest members. From detailed analysis of such cases, scholars have developed psychological explanations for witchcraft accusations that range from women projecting their inability to fulfill gender expectations, such as having a baby or keeping an infant alive, to women showing inappropriate "sexual, physical, and psychological aggressiveness."[50] In territories where men dominated the prosecutions, witchcraft became a tool in commercial and political success.[51] Whether the accused was male or female, it was presumed they could and did access occult forces and, thus, had the potential to be a witch. What made them a convicted witch was their willingness to use the occult for nefarious purposes.

Although accusers stressed the evil a witch had done to them and their neighbors, often for years if not decades, and may even have noted that such activities were diabolical or involved some other entity, it was up to legal and clerical officials and authors to work out the full implications of the demonic influence on magic and to redefine the lines between legitimate occultism, superstition, and witchcraft. Such redefinition began in the fifteenth century when clerics, many of whom participated in inquisitorial courts, began writing treatises advocating for expanded jurisdiction in cases involving magic and situating magical activities in a broader epistemology and ontology. The *Formicarius* and *Malleus Maleficarum* are the most famous of these works. After a brief hiatus, the composition of such texts resumed in the middle of the sixteenth century, completing the theoretical diabolization of the figure of the witch and of secret magic. By integrating witches into a demonic conspiracy to overturn Creation, magic lost much of its moral neutrality, at least among those who could read such tomes. Some authors contributed further to the diffusion of such connections when they composed demonologies in the vernacular. Even authors who opposed the witch trials, such as Reginald Scot and Johann Weyer, disseminated ideas about witchcraft and illicit magic when they summarized their opponents' arguments. Moreover, stories from these texts could provide early modern printers with the "marvelous" or "astonishing" tales that became pamphlet bestsellers, displaying the link between witchcraft and magic to a broader audience.[52]

Yet it was in the law courts that the theories about magic, witches, and devils confronted actual experience, and as one of the leading authorities on early modern witchcraft has noted, "different jurisdictions chose to emphasize one dimension of the witch's crime to the exclusion of the other, and the judicial record reflects those differences."[53] Some judges were convinced that witches worked for the devil and, thus, their magic was diabolic, an affront to God; as such, it was the judges' duty to root out any and all suspected of being a witch. In the process objects that could be either magically neutral or have mild magical potential, such as feathers and needles, became tools of diabolic magic. Other judges were more circumspect, firmly believing in demonic activities but much less convinced that what they were hearing and seeing was actual witchcraft. Although in the sixteenth century many countries passed statutes banning the use of harmful magic, or reinforced existing statutes, in general it could be difficult to get a guilty verdict in a witchcraft trial, unless the region was experiencing a witch panic.[54] By the second half of the seventeenth century revisions in legal procedures and standards of evidence made it even more difficult to prove that magic was used to cause a misfortune or that a witch had directed the magic. What made magic illicit, or at least suspect, was evolving and distancing itself from witchcraft, at least in the eyes of some secular and ecclesiastical authorities.

Dramatic possession cases reinforced, however, the connection between illicit magic and witchcraft well into the seventeenth century. In possession a demon or group of demons took over a human body and will, although they remained unable to touch the soul. Witches were not believed to cause most possessions, but high profile cases in sixteenth- and seventeenth-century France made the link between witchcraft and possession explicit. In 1611 at Aix-en-Provence the priest Louis Gaufridy was executed as witch; in a striking reversal of the usual power dynamic between witches and demons, he was convicted for sending demons into two Ursuline nuns, whom he had also tried and failed to exorcise. Just over twenty years later, in Loudun, the priest Urban Grandier was accused of being a witch and sending demons to possess, obsess, and bewitch over twenty women in the town's Ursuline convent. He was executed for witchcraft in 1634.[55] Cases involving possessed people and witches also occurred in seventeenth-century Italy despite explicit guidelines for exorcists that "since demons could never be trusted, they must not be asked to identify witches."[56] It is likely that these cases reflected a particularly male and clerical variation of a witch's power, but the national and international circulation of texts about these cases furthered ideas about the diabolic origins of magic power and suspicions about those who wielded occult forces.

Europeans in the Americas during the sixteenth and seventeenth centuries certainly shared this fear of the connection between magic, witchcraft, and devils, and the diabolic framework for their descriptions of African and indigenous spiritual practices that were sent across the Atlantic may even have contributed to the certainty among some European intellectuals that magic in all its forms was evil. While European debates over classification highlighted the effects of education, gender, class, and a variety of factors over the interpretation of magic, in the Americas, where so many cultures interacted in such violent and dramatic ways, the attitudes towards magic, witchcraft, and the interrelationship were even more disparate and were, at times, embedded in fundamentally different worldviews. Witches or shamans were accepted in many African and Indian cultures, although they were seen as dangerous figures. The distinction between magic and religion that European missionaries in particular tried to impose was foreign to both African and Indian visions of creation. Moreover, European colonists themselves shared in the magical culture described earlier in this chapter where occult forces permeated the natural world. For these colonials, not all witches were diabolic, but they were all dangerous, wielders of an obscure and potent magic with the potential to overturn the established order. Not surprisingly, then, missionaries advocated for their repression, while colonials in the sixteenth and seventeenth centuries might support their religious leaders while also turning to African and Indian magical practitioners when more orthodox approaches had failed to solve a problem.[57] As such, they contributed to the development of a hybrid magical culture in the Americas integrating aspects of African, Indian, and Europe belief and practice.

Magic, witchcraft, and the eye of the beholder

As the colonial experience illustrates dramatically, the distinction between legitimate magic and illegitimate witchcraft was often in the eye of the beholder, although few people in early modern Europe would challenge the statement that witches were corrupt. The same magical practice, such as the preparation of a love potion, could be seen as good or evil; for the person who obtained his desired love, the magical practitioner was skilled and moral, someone who fulfilled his side of a business arrangement. Even for the person who was coerced, some could argue that the magic made accepting love easy and happy, although, not surprisingly, such magic was more often seen as the corruption of free will. The personal aspect of the interrelationship between magic and witchcraft may even have been what allowed for the continuation of what has been estimated as tens of thousands of magical practitioners at the same time that magic was being diabolized and witches subject to vicious prosecution. Magic gained its qualities, in part, through the reputation of its practitioner. If a practitioner was known as reliable and judicious, the magic was less likely to be seen as deceptive or dangerous. If cunning folk were honest, how could they or their works be in thrall to the Prince of Lies?

Notes

1 Detailed discussions of the vocabulary of magic and witchcraft in pre-modern Europe can be found in Davies, *Popular Magic*, 1–13; Fraser, "Roman Antiquity," 126–127 and 130–135; and Gareis, "Merging Magical Traditions," 41–45, in Collins, *The Cambridge History of Magic and Witchcraft*.

2 Frazer, *The Golden Bough*; Murray, *The Witch-Cult in Western Europe*; Evans-Pritchard, *Witchcraft, Oracles and Magic Among the Azande*; Purkiss, *The Witch in History*, Chapters 1 and 2, provide an engaging account of the influence of their interpretations on the modern feminist and witch movements.

3 Hutton, "Anthropological and Historical Approaches to Witchcraft," 428; Bever, "Popular Witch Beliefs," in Levack, *The Oxford Handbook of Witchcraft*, 53.

4 Kieckhefer, *Magic in the Middle Ages*, 14–16. Also see Gaskill, "The Pursuit of Reality," 1069–1088. I emphasize Christian here because, in early modern Islam, the activity or passivity of the magical practitioner contributed to the legitimacy of the magic, and passive practice was considered best: Melvin-Koushki, "Astrology, Lettrism, Geomancy" and personal communication.

5 Collins, "Introduction," 1–14, and Bailey, "Diabolic Magic," 361–392, in Collins, *Cambridge History of Magic*, 1–14; Edwards, "Popular Cultures and Witchcraft," in *Interpreting Early Modern Europe*, eds. Scott Dixon and Beat Kümin (London: Routledge, 2020), 356–387.

6 Hutton, "Anthropological and Historical Approaches to Witchcraft," 428; Davies, *Popular Magic*, 110.

7 See Sigmund Mowinckel, *Religion und Kultus* (Göttingen: Vandenhoeck and Ruprecht, 1953), who coined the term "magical wordview." Although scholars debate the modernist implications in the terms "enchanted" and "disenchanted," much current research emphasizes this binary: see Cameron, *Enchanted Europe*, the best recent synthesis of the implications of this view.

8 Several recent studies provide detailed analyses of the integration of magic into various aspects of early modern European society, but the theme is frequently noted in studies of witchcraft and folklore: see Bever, *The Realities of Witchcraft*; Bever, "Popular Witch Beliefs," 50–68; Wilson, *The Magical Universe*; Edwards, *Everyday Magic*; and Rider, "Common Magic," in *Cambridge History of Magic*, 303–331.

9 Jacobus, *Omne bonum*, British Library, MS Royal 6.E.VI, fols. 396v–397v; cf. MS Harley 275, fols. 149r–153r, as cited in Kieckhefer, *Magic*, 181.

10 See Kieckhefer, *Magic*; Zambelli, *White Magic, Black Magic*.

11 Kieckhefer, *Magic*, 3. For information regarding medicine and its relationship to witchcraft, see Elmer, "Medicine and Witchcraft," in Levack, *Oxford Handbook of Witchcraft*, 561–574.

12 Davies, *Popular Magic*, 67–73; Roper, *Charms and Charming*. They were also common in North Africa, where either Christian or Muslin prayers could be used.

13 Rider, "Common Magic," in Collins, *Cambridge Handbook of Magic*, 312.

14 For a clear description of this practice, see Godbeer, "Folk Magic in British North America," in Ibid., 463.

15 Davies, *Popular Magic*, provides a detailed discussion of English cunning folk; Dillinger, *Magical Treasure Hunting*, does so for Germany.

16 Seitz, "The Root Is Hidden and the Material Uncertain," 107. For a detailed and insightful discussion of the relationship between early modern medicine and witchcraft trials, see Seitz, *Witchcraft and Inquisition*, esp. 149–185.

17 For the debate over superstition in late medieval Europe, see Bailey, *Fearful Spirits, Reasoned Follies*; Bailey, "The Disenchantment of Magic"; Parish and Naphy, eds., *Religion and Superstition in Reformation Europe*, introduction. See the list of thirty "superstitions" from the *Indiculus superstitionum et paganiarum* (A Short List of Superstitions and Pagan Practices) of ca. 700 in Yitzhak Hen, "The Early Medieval West," in Collins, *Cambridge History of Magic*, 183–184.

18 Gaskill, *Witchcraft*, 28–29.

19 The literature on this topic is vast; the following have influenced my summary: Parish, "Magic and Priestcraft: Reformers and Reformation," in Collins, *Cambridge History of Magic*, 393–425 and *Monks, Miracles and Magic*; Waite, "Sixteenth-Century Religious Reform and the Witch Hunts," in Levack, *Oxford Handbook of Witchcraft*, 485–506.

20 Behringer, *Shaman of Oberstdorf*. Also see Ginzburg, *The Night Battles*.
21 Godbeer, "Folk Magic in British North America," in Collins, *Cambridge History of Magic*, 461–481.
22 Kieckhefer, *Magic*, 59–60; Mormando, *The Preacher's Demons*, 72–77.
23 Robert Boyle and Isaac Newton are famous as early scientists, but they were also well-known occultists, Boyle analyzing angelic communication and alchemy and Newton alchemy and numerology. For a summary of their occult interests, see Elmer, "Science and Witchcraft," in Levack, *Oxford Handbook of Witchcraft*, 548–574.
24 The classic work is Yates, *The Occult Philosophy*; for more recent analyses, see Walker, *Spiritual and Demonic Magic*; Monod, *Solomon's Secret Arts*; Kieckhefer, *Forbidden Rites*, introduction; and Copenhaver, *Magic in Western Culture*, parts II and III.
25 Kieckhefer, *Magic*, chapter 6; Saif, *The Arabic Influences*, esp. 95–143 (on Ficino and Pico della Mirandola).
26 For a clear summary of the Islamic magical tradition's influence on Western Europe, see Zadeh, "Early Islamic Thought," in Collins, *Cambridge History of Magic*, 235–267, esp. 247–258; Saif, *The Arabic Influences*.
27 Walker, *Spiritual and Demonic Magic*, 205–212.
28 Godbeer, "Folk Magic in British North America," in Collins, *Cambridge History of Magic*, 468–49.
29 Seitz, *Witchcraft and Inquisition*, esp. 73–95 and 149–195.
30 Wilby, *Cunning Folk and Familiar Spirits*, esp. 46–58.
31 Collins, "Learned Magic," in Collins, *Cambridge History of Magic*, 348–349.
32 Kieckhefer, *Magic*, 10–12, 158, and 170.
33 Bailey reaches a similar conclusion in Bailey, "Demonic Magic," in Collins, *Cambridge History of Magic*, 369.
34 Kieckhefer, *Magic*, 151–175.
35 Kieckhefer, *Forbidden Rites*, 69–95; Fanger, ed., *Conjuring Spirits*; Davies, *Grimoires*.
36 One of the most dramatic medieval examples involved Gilles de Rais, commander of the French army and companion of Joan of Arc: Heers, *Gilles de Rais*.
37 Bailey, *Fearful Spirits, Reasoned Follies*; Clark, *Thinking with Demons*; Davies, *Grimoires*; Fanger, *Conjuring Spirits*, vii–xviii.
38 Collins, "Learned Magic," in Collins, *Cambridge History of Magic*, 346; Saif, *The Arabic Influences*, 144–170.
39 The Inquisition mistrusted their claim to benevolence, and it tried a series of cases involving the *donas* in the sixteenth and seventeenth centuries: see Henningsen, "The Ladies From Outside," 191–215 and Henderson, *Witchcraft and Folk Belief*, 108 and 122; see pp. 284–285 for similar fairy magic in Scotland.
40 Dillinger, *Magical Treasure Hunting*.
41 Kieckhefer, *Magic*, 156–157, makes a similar argument but for the later Middle Ages.
42 See the discussion of Waldensian "crimes" in the *Errores Gazariorum*.
43 See Toivo, "The Witch-Craze as Holocaust," in Barry and Davies, ed., *Witchcraft Historiography*, 90–107. An influential analysis of the Devil's role in Reformation thought is Oberman, *Luther: Man between God and the Devil*.
44 Machielsen, *Martin Delrio*, esp. chapters. 9 and 11; Maxwell-Stuart, "The Contemporary Historical Debate, 1400–1750," in Barry and Davies, *Witchcraft Historiography*, 11–32, here 21.
45 Cervantes, *The Devil in the New World*. For examples, see Pérez de Ribas, *History of the Triumphs of Our Holy Faith,* chapters 35, 42, and 43.
46 Seitz, "'The Root is Hidden'"; Gaskill, "Witchcraft and Evidence," 61–63.
47 Dillinger, "The Good Magicians," in Edwards, ed., *Everyday Magic*, 120–124, gives a clear summary of this doctrine as applied to early modern European treasure-hunting. Briggs, *Witches and Neighbors*, 369–394, and Roper, *Oedipus and the Devil*, 228–251, provide clear and now classic examples of the use of psychoanalysis to interpret witch trials. Bever, *The Realities of Witchcraft*, esp. Chapter 2, integrates neuropsychology with psychoanalytical interpretations.
48 For only a few examples of these patterns, see Briggs, *The Witches of Lorraine*; Robisheaux, *The Last Witch of Langenburg*; Rowlands, *Witchcraft Narratives in Germany*; Sharpe, *The*

Bewitching of Anne Gunter, Stokes, *Demons of Urban Reform;* and Tausiet, *Urban Magic in Early Modern Spain.*

49 Apps and Gow, *Male Witches.*

50 Roper, *Oedipus and the Devil,* esp. Chapters 1 and 3; Bever, "Witchcraft, Female Aggression," 973; Hodgkin, "Gender, Mind and Boy: Feminism and Psychoanalysis," in Barry and Davies, ed., *Witchcraft Historiography,* 182–202, nicely summarizes the debates over gender's role in witchcraft.

51 Kivelson, "Male Witches and Gendered Categories," 606–631; Labouvie, "Männer im Hexenprozess," 59–67.

52 Gaskill, *Witchcraft,* 76.

53 Levack, *Oxford Handbook of Witchcraft,* 4.

54 Gaskill, "Witchcraft and Evidence," 40.

55 Ferber, *Demonic Possession and Exorcism,* 70–88; Levack, *The Devil Within,* 191–214.

56 Watt, "The Demons of Carpi," 128.

57 Godbeer, "Folk Magic in British North America," in Collins, ed., *Cambridge History of Magic,* 463; Paton, "Witchcraft, Poison," 235–264; Gareis, "Merging Magical Traditions," in Levack, ed., *Oxford Handbook of Witchcraft,* 412–428.

Bibliography (selection)

Cameron, Euan, *Enchanted Europe: Superstition, Reason, and Religion in Europe, 1250–1750.* Oxford: Oxford University Press, 2010.

Copenhaver, Brian, *Magic in Western Culture: From Antiquity to the Enlightenment.* Cambridge: Cambridge University Press, 2015.

Davies, Owen, *Popular Magic: Cunning-folk in English History.* New York: Hambledon Continuum, 2003.

Edwards, Kathryn A. (ed.), *Everyday Magic in Early Modern Europe.* Basingstoke: Ashgate, 2015.

Henderson, Lizanne, *Witchcraft and Folk Belief in the Age of Enlightenment: Scotland, 1670–1740.* London: Palgrave Macmillan, 2016.

Klaniczay, Gabor and Eva Pócs (eds.), *Communicating with the Spirits: Christian Demonology and Popular Mythology.* Budapest: Central European University Press, 2005.

Monod, Paul, *Solomon's Secret Arts: The Occult in the Age of Enlightenment.* New Haven: Yale University Press, 2013.

Roper, Jonathan, *Charms and Charming in Europe.* Basingstoke: Palgrave Macmillan, 2004.

PART 3

MODERN CONCEPTS OF WITCHES

21

CHILD EATERS AND OTHER PROBLEMS OF DEMOCRACY

Witchcraft and the American frontier

Adam Jortner

"They were detected in the act of witchcraft," declared the governor of the Nambé pueblo. "The deceased confessed they had been guilty of witchcraft and sorcery – they had eaten up the little children of the Pueblo." For their crimes, the two necromancers – Luis Romero and Antonio Tafolla – were taken north of the Nambé territory and executed by shotgun in March 1854. The nascent American territorial administration, however, did not recognize the crime of witchcraft, and soon had the witches' executioners on trial for murder. That in turn brought about the governor's testimony on the sorcerer's purported pediaphagy, and his declaration in open court that "By my order and with the consent of all the principal men of the Pueblo the two men were put to death. They were killed on my command."[1]

The deaths in Nambé were not outliers; witch executions followed the American frontier from the moment of American indepedence through the supposed "closing" of the frontier in the early twentieth century. Beginning with the Senecas in the 1790s and continuing west to the Shawnees, Chocktaws, Pueblos, Navajos, and Zunis, witch hunts spread west with the political expansion of the United States. For decades, historians hailed this expansion as the spread of democracy and liberty. Only comparatively recently have American historians come to see westward migration as an enterprise of colonialism and dispossession. It also became an enterprise of witch hunting. This essay examines the Pueblo witch hunts of 1854 as a case study that reveals the typical nature of witchcraft and witch hunts among Native Americans in the great age of American expansion, 1783–1900.

If witchcraft is (among other things) a working-out of old and new ideas of power, as Stuart Clark and other European historians have argued, then it is not surprising that it erupted in New Mexico in 1854. In just over thirty years, this rocky kingdom at the fraying edge of the Comanche, Spanish, and American empires had been ruled by Spanish colonial appointees, absentee leaders from Mexico City, a military junta, and an endless series of political appointees from a United States stumbling through a political and sectional crisis. These changes were perhaps most dramatic for the manifold Pueblo polities – the towns occupied by Native Americans speaking related languages and exercising some degree of autonomy; "Pueblo" was a Spanish misnomer which eventually took on ethnic and bureaucratic significance. The "Pueblo" lived in pueblos, but each pueblo was home to a distinct community. The Nambé

Pueblos were different from the Isleta Pueblos, for example, but all Pueblo communities received the same treatment under Spanish law. The Mexican Revolution of 1821 officially made the Pueblos citizens of Mexico, but in practice, the New Mexicans ruled themselves, and largely left the Pueblos to themselves. American occupation and annexation revoked that right, though the Pueblos were often promised self-government by territorial officials. The 1854 trial – and the subsequent verdict of "not guilty" – emerged during a critical transformation of the political and legal situation of the Pueblos of New Mexico; it was an emblematic struggle of jurisdiction and of justice.[2]

Of course, the Pueblos did not invent their witchcraft problem in order to take on the American government; Juan Ygnacia Tafolla, the governor, explained in his testimony that "We have not exercised this custom, of killing witches, since the Americans came here, because there had not been such bad doings before." One white observer thought Tafolla "simple-minded" for thinking that "the killing of two men was a matter of duty instead of a crime," but Tafolla remained steadfast in his office: "It has always been our custom to put a stop to and check bad acts."[3] Witchcraft had a long history in the American Southwest, part of an intricate pattern of supernatural beliefs that shaped the world of the Pueblos, if not their nominal American overlords. Official witchcraft accusations had been lodged in 1822 against Juan Inocencio of the Nambé pubelo, who confessed he could bring about madness by crafting a mixture of feathers, cotton, and the hair of the victim. Such ideas suggest traditional "shooting magic" of several Native American nations. Yet untangling "traditional" Pueblo beliefs about witchcraft is difficult; Malcolm Ebright and Rick Hendricks have written regarding the mass arrests for sorcery and demon possession in Abiquiu, New Mexico, from 1756–1767, that "what Spaniards called 'witchcraft' was actually resistance to priests . . . who were attempting to eradicate the native belief systems and convert the Indians to Catholicism."[4] Yet though witch troubles antedated the American occupation, Tafolla saw the issue as one of politics, not magic: "We have always governed ourselves as an independent community."[5]

The strange case of Nambé was the result of conflicting jurisdictional battles; Nambé's witchcraft trial confirmed its right to self-rule, and this legitimation in turn affected the American conquest of the Southwest. The question raised by the Nambé trials was in part the question of witchcraft and self-governance, which has received recent scholarly attention in other subfields. Outbreaks of witchcraft in postcolonial Africa and Asia – and the disastrous Manhattan Beach witchcraft panics of the 1980s – have provided sobering reminders that witch trials are not merely the province of the early modern world.[6]

American frontier historiography has little time for witchcraft, more comfortable as it is with questions of race, class, and environment. Such reticence regarding witchcraft is typical for American historiography more broadly. American history's interest in witchcraft often begins and ends with 1692; works that mention witchcraft beyond Salem routinely base their investigations in the historiography of Salem, which in turn is dominated by Keith Thomas' *Religion and the Decline of Magic*. Subsequent scholarship on that "decline" has largely gone unnoticed by Americanists. Thomas' work more or less places the end of witchcraft conveniently around the time of Salem, and therefore most Americanists have interpreted later witch outbreaks, as Karl Bell writes, as "a few anachronistic examples . . . dismissively associated with uneducated rural dwellers."[7] Most works on Salem begin with the assumption that preexisting social and economic conditions in Salem provoked the witch trials. To understand 1692, "we must take a close look at Salem Village before its moment of notoriety," according to *Salem Possessed*, the most famous entry in this school of witchcraft historiography.[8] Witchcraft accusations resolve previously established social (or economic, theological, or gender) fissures; witchcraft functions, in Mary Beth Norton's phrase, as "a replacement crime." American historians have largely assumed, as Thomas did, that the rise of elite critiques brought an end to witchcraft belief, and therefore, in Jon Butler's words, America "turned a modern corner" when Massachusetts refused to prosecute a witch in 1720.[9]

Such an outlook does not match the actual facts of the American frontier experience. As Owen Davies notes, more people were killed for witchcraft *after* 1692 than were executed during the colonial period, not by the state, but by vigilantes, mobs, and ad-hoc extralegal courts – all mainstays of frontier justice.[10] Moreover, witch trials seem to have followed the American frontier. As the inchoate line of white settlement pushed further west, witch trials and panics broke out among the Delawares (1763–64), Senecas (1799–1821), Shawnees (1806), Choctaws (1819–34), Pueblos (1854), and Navajos (1878). White communities attacked or murdered witches in Maine (1796), South Carolina (1813–14), Tennessee (1831), and western Virginia (1838), among many others.[11] Witchcraft walked along the frontier's violent path across the continent.

Indeed, considered in the light of more recent European historiography, witchcraft would seem to be connected with two very central questions of the frontier experience and historiography: jurisdictional conflict and state formation. The very concept of "nation" remained an idea more than a reality in the eighteenth century; American "nationhood" was a solution to the problem of a decentralized federal empire of Jeffersonian America. Jefferson and his allies imagined the nation as a binding material distinct from the centralized British government from which they had declared independence – but they had to create the nation first. For most of the nineteenth century, the trans-Mississippi West remained "flexible and contingent." Anne F. Hyde has explained the conflicting levels of loyalty on the American frontier and the limits to effective power those conflicts implied: "Residents of the West seemed quite ambivalent about nationality, easily claiming new citizenship" whenever required, since "no one knew which empire or nation would finally impose control." The extension of the American state across a vast swath of the continent was largely a process of negotiation and violence; the frontier was a zone where the displays of power legitimated and confirmed arrangements of rule.[12]

Stuart Clark's *Thinking with Demons* addressed similar questions regarding European demonologists: "In describing witchcraft as a social evil authors necessarily invoked a conception of the social order . . . they committed themselves to views about authority and about the general desirability of certain forms of rulership." Rulers invoked and performed such views when they successfully rid the countryside of witches; "the criminality of the witch," Clark writes, "was the product of political values and relations of power."[13] Successful elimination of witchcraft troubles could justify new or extreme political arrangements. The rise and fall of new political regimes and the establishment of legitimate authority were periennial problems in the American republic and the American frontier, 1776–1861. Witchcraft had interposed in these questions in early modern Europe, and it also did so on the nineteenth-century American frontier.[14]

Existing historiography on witchcraft among Native Americans in the eighteenth and nineteenth century has not recognized the jurisdictional aspects of witch trials. Much of the work on this subject has focused on the "prophets" – Native American leaders who advocated and preached that a formerly obscure god called the Master of Life had returned to lead Indians to a new golden age. Most prominently, these leaders included Neolin (active 1762–63), Handsome Lake (1799–1815), Tenskwatawa (1806–36). Each of these men made widespread witch accusations or adjudicated witch trials at some point in their careers. Historiography on the prophets has been dominated by Anthony Wallace's theory of revitalization – the notion that cultures under duress produced new religious leaders. These "hallucinatory" leaders manipulated religion to justify changes in the society's way of life, even as they claimed to restore traditional practices.[15] Religion acted as a cover for cultural change and renewal. Such interpretations betray a realist approach to witchcraft (and religion) – there must be some real reason for the objectively false belief in witchcraft. As such, works in this vein spend little time analyzing the content of witchcraft belief or the preferred political factors associated with controlling witchcraft. Instead, there is usually something else going on; the trials of Tenskwatawa "strengthened cultural integration" while Seneca witch trials of 1820 were a "tacit acceptance of Euro-American misogyny." As with Salem, witch trials are seen as a replacement for some other, real conflict in the community. Such interpretations favor the origins of witch trials rather than their effects. Moreover, this approach overshadows the ways witch trials or witch accusations often emerged as a point of legal conflict – between Native American legal practices (traditional or novel) and U.S. legal codes, particularly those involving self-government. Such a conflict was particularly acute in the witchcraft crisis of 1854.[16]

Archival materials from the American territorial period of New Mexico are thin, perhaps because, as Adolph Bandelier discovered in 1880, the archives had been "thrown into an outhouse."[17] From 1847–54, New Mexico had seven separate American administrations – four governors, two acting governors, and one military headman. The instability was partially bad luck – Charles Bent was assassinated, James Calhoun resigned due to illness – but also by design. The fractious politics of the Jacksonian era required new political appointments for separate presidential administrations – of which there were four in that same time span. Record-keeping suffered accordingly.

Other factors compounded administrative weakness. The Department of Indian Affairs was transferred from the War Department to the Interior Department in 1849. Security and monetary concerns hobbled the New Mexican governors as they fought the Jicarilla Apaches and the Navajo.[18] Calhoun wrote deploringly to President Fillmore that "our Treasury is empty and we are without munitions of war."[19] Calhoun's successor, William Carr Lane, warned his legislators that "We are very distant, from the States – difficult of access – and surrounded by barbarians, of doubtful faith . . . and your own people are so badly armed." Lane also inveighed against the "unreasonable jealousies and bickerings . . . between the natives of the country, and the immigrants"[20] Lane meant, of course, natives of "Castillian or Anglo-Saxon" descent, not Native American. All governors accepted the necessity of military defeat of those whom Calhoun referred to as "the wild Indians," whose "daring and impudence are equalled only by their success in their butcheries."[21]

Yet Calhoun's warning against "wild Indians" also included a reference to "our Pueblo friends," indicating that the Americans recognized the Spanish classification of Pueblo peoples as a distinct group separate from both whites and other Indians. What remained unclear was whether the Americans would acknowledge the further Mexican recognition of Pueblo citizenship outlined in the 1821 constitution.

Political rhetoric of the early 1850s suggested they would not. Calhoun told his legislature that the Pueblos were "in our midst" and "rightfully . . . without authority to mingle in our political affairs." Calhoun was particularly irritated at the Pueblos' presumed immunity from taxation, and advised the legislators "to pass an act authorizing the extension of the laws of the Territory over the Pueblo Indians," the same political stance that had allowed a host of American politicians to pursue removal policies against the Indian nations of the east.[22] Lane was even more explicit: independent pueblos represented "an *imperium in imperio*" – the terminology for a state-within-a-state, that republican rhetorical bugbear that had accompanied so many efforts to strangle autonomous political movements in the early republic.[23]

Governors talked tough, but in practice they had few options. With Comanche, Apache, and Navajo raids besieging the territory, none of New Mexico's rulers wanted to start trouble with the Pueblos. Calhoun repeatedly declined opportunities to interfere in Pueblo matters. In March 1851, he proclaimed that the Pueblo at Taos "had the exclusive right to practise their own laws and customs," up to and including the right to remove those who moved onto their lands without their consent.[24] A month later, when an Isleta delegation complained of the monetary demands of keeping their priest, he told them to revert to "such tithes and fees as they saw proper."[25] In June 1850, Calhoun wrote to all Pueblo groups that "the internal affairs of your Pueblos shall be governed by your laws and customs and by the same authorities which each Pueblo has elected."[26]

The Pueblos seem to have taken Calhoun's advice. Fragmentary evidence from early 1850s suggests the Pueblo Indians took an active role in promoting their own citizenship – which, after all, had been promised to them in the Treaty of Guadalupe Hidalgo. In 1852, the Pueblos at Santa Clara worked through the governor's office to protect their water rights. Lane constantly dealt with governors of various pueblos, adjudicating land disputes between whites and Pueblos and among Pueblos themselves. In 1854, Governor Meriwether even reported, dourly, "that in some parts of the Territory the Pueblo Indians were permitted to vote at the late election."[27]

Thus by 1854, institutional weakness and the encroachment of Apaches, Comanches, and Navajos resulted in *de facto* self-government for the Pueblos of New Mexico. In some ways, the American regime had recreated the old Spanish model of governance, with Pueblos holding a distinct place above other Indians but below citizens of European descent. Yet American preoccupations did not mean U.S. authorities were pleased with the situation. It was under this kind of tenuous self-rule that Luis Romero and Antonio Tafolla were brought before the Nambé council in March 1854 under suspicion of witchcraft.

Official court documents of the case are astonishingly brief, listing little more than the three defendants, the charge, and the verdict. They did note that "both the defendants and part of their witnesses were indians and did not speak either the Spanish or English languages," and that an interpreter was duly sworn.[28] That interpreter very likely saved the case from oblivion, since it allowed the journalist and politician W.W.H. Davis to follow the proceedings. Davis then printed a fuller account of the proceedings in the Santa Fe *Gazette*, and later wrote about the episode in his 1857 memoir. "Who would have thought," he wondered, "that the cruel scenes of Salem would have been enacted in this distant region of the world, and that too, in the middle of the nineteenth century[?]"[29]

Davis spent little time worrying about the prologue to the witch murders, but oral accounts gathered later in the century offered further details. Jean-Baptiste Salpointe, the Frenchman and future archbishop, sketched a brief account of the episode in the 1870s. Bandalier (the German ethnographer) interviewed Juan Luján and a Pueblo woman named Chino in 1888; he preferred Luján's account since Luján had been "present at least at a part of the Tragedy."[30]

These accounts describe a severe smallpox outbreak prior to the trial; many died "and the terror was great." During the outbreak, two Indians of Nambé discovered a third man, Fi-ué, drawing sigils in the dirt, whispering sounds, and fiddling with crow feathers. Chino said that the suspected witch stopped at the house of a sick man, the graveyard, and the door of church, each time performing a short ritual with crow, owl, and woodpecker feathers. "The idea came into their minds suddenly," according to Luján, "that Fi-ué was a witch." Brought before the governor of Nambé, Fi-ué confessed to witchcraft, and implicated two other men (Ca-tszi-ré and Cá-ya-mo). At some point, the three witches – after being beaten "to a Jelly" – also accused an unidentified individual in another pueblo. Both Luján and Chino agreed, however, that this final accusation was merely a ruse to throw suspicion off Juana Chávez, "the head witch." Perhaps the Nambé Indians became wise to the deception, or perhaps the suspicions surrounding Chávez were too great. She was seized and stoned to death; her corpse was disfigured and hung on a tree.

At this point, a Catholic priest named Trujillo arrived after hearing news of the trial, and pleaded for mercy towards the accused. He interviewed the witches about their practices, and – according to Luján, his companion – the men were surprisingly forthcoming about their magic. They confessed to using bones and mushrooms to transform into animals, burying bones to bring disease upon the pueblo, and throwing arrowheads into the water supply to poison it. Their objective, apparently, was to "do away with the inhabitants of the village and remain afterwards the sole owners of the land."[31] Trujillo burned their implements as satanic devices, and received a promise from the people not to act against the witches until the bishop could arrive. Then he left.

Despite this promise, the ruling council of Nambé initiated proceedings against Romero, Antonio Tafolla, and possibly another person in early March of 1854. (It seems likely that these were the Christian names of Fi-ué, Ca-tszi-ré, and Cá-ya-mo.) No one other than Father Trujillo mentioned the devil; no Nambé witnesses engaged in any Christian fantasies of a satanic sabbat. Both the testimony of Governor Tafolla and Davis' own account referred to "witchcraft and sorcery" (in the Spanish-language version of the *Gazette*, "Bruheria y maleficios"), suggesting that the crime here was evil magic. Governor Tafolla ordered the fiscal of the pueblo and three other men to execute Romero and Antonio Tafolla. The fiscal led the convicted witches to a spot "not quite a league" north of the Nambé territory, at twilight, and fatally shot them both. It is not clear what happened to the third witch; he may have escaped with the priest's assistance. With the death of the witches, the smallpox epidemic subsided.[32]

The ambiguities in the accounts are tantalizing – and frustrating. The court docket lists three executioners as defendants; Davis' account has four. Sometimes three witches are mentioned, sometimes two. The account in the *Gazette* mentions that the witches went with the executioners freely; Luján recalled that "the multitude dragged them" to the place of execution and then threw the bodies off a cliff.[33]

The ambiguity was at least in part intentional. The witnesses called to the court from Nambé engaged in a tactic of obfuscation and denial. One Nambé witnesses described Romero and Tafolla, but could not recall when he had last seen them and had never heard of the execution order. Another witness knew that they were dead, but "did not see the defendants in company with the deceased" and "don't know when the deceased were first missing." No one seemed to remember exactly where the execution had taken place, either – in the pueblo or just beyond it.[34]

That geographical inconsistency proved to be the sticking point. In the twilight of the courtroom – as "candles gave a dusky and indistinct appearance to every thing" – Judge Grafton Baker ultimately decided that since no one knew whether the execution had taken place on U.S. soil administered by the federal government or on the territory of the Nambé pueblo itself, his jurisdiction was unclear. The executioners were found not guilty, though they paid court fines.[35]

The *Gazette* proclaimed a victory for the U.S. administration. "Pueblo Indians . . . will be sensible of the fact that they cannot commit crimes without being liable to punishment." Bandalier, looking back on the trial thirty years later, thought the decision had done just the opposite; though the butchering of victims "for alleged witchcraft" was horrible, the court determined that "no interference was possible" by the American government.[36]

The Pueblos of Nambé likely took the latter lesson from the proceedings. Governor Tafolla hung his entirely testimony on the presumed independence of his little polity – and he was the only witness to answer questions about the execution directly. He noted that they followed their own laws – not exercised, of course, "since the Americans came here, because there had not been such bad doings before." He directly cited both Spanish and American precedent: "We have always governed ourselves as an independent community; and Governor Calhoun said, as we were poor and ignorant, and could not serve on juries, we might govern ourselves." Then, he quietly affirmed his own authority, even to the point of murdering witches: "I am Governor and this act was done by the command of myself and the whole of the Pueblo."[37]

The witch executioners of 1854 walked away; it appeared Nambé really was "wholly independent of the laws of the U.S. and this Territory," as the *Gazette* feared. Baker's evident confusion about the case – or at least his unwillingness to delve into the complicated and politically sensitive jurisdictional details – validated the self-rule of the Pueblo of Nambé. The independence of Nambé conceivably could have been fought over water rights, military service, or other legal questions. But it was not fought over those things; it was fought over witchcraft.[38] While the origins of the 1854 trial clearly have roots in religious and medical beliefs, its resolution had far more to do with the altered legal and political system of New Mexico under U.S. administration. By ridding his country of witches, Tafolla validated his own rule and forced the Americans to accept it, too. (Whatever white American rulers might have believed about the necessity of Enlightenment reason as a prerequisite for self-rule, they were in no position to enforce it in the midst of wars with the other tribes.) Most of the Pueblo land claims were confirmed in the next decade; self-rule at Nambé appears to have continued until the 1870s.[39]

This strange connection between witch trials and Indian self-rule has echoes elsewhere in the Native American experience. Tenskwatawa's witch hunt in Indiana in 1806 appears to have strengthened his control over his polyglot Indian communities. Among the Seneca, Handsome Lake's witch accusations in 1801 were soon followed by a meteoric rise to power, as he became "principal Sachem in all things Civil and Religious" and the Seneca ambassador to President Jefferson.[40] These trials were brutal and terrifying, and took several victims. They were also expressions of power which often resulted in the all-too-rare cases of Indian self-rule in the face of white American dispossession and military threat. Handsome Lake's condemnation of Delaware witchcraft was followed by the decampment of nearby Delawares and Handsome Lake's own ascension to power. In 1806 Indiana, Tenskwatawa identified witches *within* another Delaware tribe; the Delawares executed some of the accused and then joined Tenskwatawa's religious movement, which culminated in an independent city on the Indiana frontier (shortly thereafter destroyed by American armies at the Battle of Tippecanoe.)[41] The connection between witchcraft and self-rule is a recurrent theme on the American frontier, and it deserves further scrutiny and examination. Witches were part of the violence and power of the American frontier; the contestation over jurisdiction in the American west was also a conflict over witchcraft.

Notes

1 Santa Fe *Gazette*, 4/22/1854 (hereafter SFG).
2 Marc Simmons, "History of the Pueblos Since 1821," *Handbook of North American Indians* (New York: Smithsonian, 1979), 9: 206–223. Recent important works on the history of the Southwest in the nineteenth century include Pekka Hämäläinien, *The Comanche Empire* (New Haven: Yale University Press, 2008); Andrés Reséndez, *Changing National Identities at the Frontier: Texas and New Mexico, 1800–1850* (New York: Cambridge University Press, 2005); and Anne F. Hyde, *Empires, Nations, and Families: A New History of the North American West, 1800–1860* (Norman: University of Oklahoma Press, 2012).
3 SFG 4/22/1854.
4 *Mexican Archives of New Mexico*, "Declaration of Gaspar Ortiz," 8/21/1822, Roll 1, Frame 1294, State Records Center, Santa Fe; Malcolm Ebright and Rick Hendricks, *The Witches of Abiquiu: The Governor, the Priest, the Genízaro Indians, and the Devil* (Albuquerque: University of New Mexico Press, 2006), 5.
5 SFG 4/22/54.
6 Adam Ashforth, *Witchcraft, Violence, and Democracy in South Africa* (Chicago: University of Chicago, 2005); Wolfgang Behringer, *Witches and Witch Hunts* (Cambridge: Polity, 2004), ch. 6; on Manhattan Beach, see John Demos, *The Enemy Within: 2000 Years of Witch hunting in the Western World* (New York: Viking, 2008), 274–281.
7 Karl Bell, *The Magical Imagination* (Cambridge: Cambridge University Press, 2012), 115. American historiography routinely lists Thomas as the primary (and often the only) source on European magical beliefs. See for example Christine Heyrman, *Southern Cross* (New York: Knopf, 1997) 274 n1; Nathan Hatch, *Democratization of American Christianity* (New Haven: Yale University Press, 1989, 291 n33; Jeffrey Anderson, *Conjure in African American Society* (Baton Rouge: Louisiana State University Press) 52–55; Matthew Dennis, *Seneca Possessed* (Philadelphia: Pennsylvania University Press, 2010) 11–12, 249–250 n2; Richard

Godbeer, *Escaping Salem* (New York: Oxford University Press, 2005) 144. Fuller treatments of European historiography (and the historiography of magic) can be found in Jon Butler, *Awash in a Sea of Faith* (Cambridge: Harvard University Press, 1992) and Alison Games, *Witchcraft in Early North America* (Lanham: Rowman & Littlefield, 2010).

8   Paul Boyer and Stephen Nissenbaum, *Salem Possessed: The Social Origins of Witchcraft* (Cambridge, MA: Harvard University Press, 1974), 36.

9   Butler, *Awash*, 84.

10   Owen Davies, *America Bewitched: The Story of Witchcraft After Salem* (Oxford: Oxford University Press, 2013), 3.

11   See Davies, *America*, 107, 75, 84–85, 49–51, 44; Martha Blue, *The Witch Purge of 1878: Oral and Documentary History in the Early Navajo Reservation Years* (Tsaile, AZ: Navajo Community College Press, 1988).

12   Peter S. Onuf, *Jefferson's Empire: The Language of American Nationhood* (Charlottesville: University of Virginia Press, 2001); Hyde, *Empires*, 30, and on the Mexican War and related violence, 351–496.

13   Stuart Clark, *Thinking With Demons: The Idea of Witchcraft in Early Modern Europe* (New York: Oxford University Press, 2005), 552.

14   Related works on jurisdiction, law, politics, and witchcraft after 1736 include Andrew Sneddon, *Witchcraft and Whigs: The Life of Bishop Francis Hutchinson, 1660–1739* (New York: Manchester University Press, 2008); Brian Levack, "The Decline and End of Witchcraft Prosecutions," in *Witchcraft and Magic in Europe, Volume 5: The Eighteenth and Nineteenth Centuries*, ed. Bengt Ankarloo and Stuart Clark (Philadelphia: University of Pennsylvania Press, 1999), 1–94; Ian Bostridge, *Witchcraft and Its Transformations, c. 1650–c. 1750* (Oxford: Clarendon, 1997).

15   Wallace's theory first appeared in Anthony Wallace, "Revitalization Movements," *American Anthropologist* 58.2 (April 1956): 264–281, and received fuller treatment in Anthony Wallace, *The Death and Rebirth of the Seneca* (New York: Vintage, 1969).

16   See Clark, *Thinking*, 1–10, 49–559; Jay Miller, "The 1806 Purge Among the Indiana Delaware: Sorcery, Gender, Boundaries, and Legitimacy," *Ethnohistory* 41 (1994): 251; and Dennis, *Possessed*, 3.

17   Adolph F. Bandalier, *The Southwestern Journals of Adolph F. Bandalier*, ed. Charles H. Lange, Carroll L. Riley, and Elizabeth M. Lange (Albuquerque: University of New Mexico Press, 1975), hereafter SJAB, volume 1, 8/27/1880.

18   Meriweather Papers: Messervy, Proclamation, April 10, 1854; Message of Wulliam Carr Lane, Governor . . . to the Legislative Assembly of the Territory, at Sante Fé, Dec. 7, 1852 (Sante Fe, 1852).

19   State Department Papers, Territory of NM, Executive Journal, 3/29/1851: Calhoun to Millard Fillmore (1:16–17).

20   Message of Wulliam Carr Lane, Governor . . . to the Legislative Assembly of the Territory, at Sante Fé, Dec. 7, 1852 (Sante Fe, 1852).

21   *Message of His Excellency Hames S. Calhoun, to the First Territorial Legislature of New Mexico*, June 2, 1851.

22   State Department Territorial Papers, New Mexico, 1851–1872 (henceforth SDTP); Message of His Excellency James S. Calhoun, to the First Territorial Legislature of New Mexico, June 2, 1851.

23   *Message of William Carr Lane . . . to the Legislative Assembly of the Territory, at Sante Fé*, December 7, 1852 (Sante Fe, 1852).

24   SDTP, reel 1: 15–16; Undated Scrap, noted only as "28th" (presumably March 28, 1851 – since the record is listed as Executive Department, Santa Fe, New Mexico, March 22nd, 1851)

25   SDTP, 1:25, April 10/51.

26   University of New Mexico, Center for Southwest Research (henceforth UNMCSR), Indian Affairs Collection, Box 1, Folder 2; John Munrow and James Calhoun to the Pueblos, June 25, 1850.

27   Simmons, "History," 210; "Indian Affairs in New Mexico Under the Administration of William Carr Lane: The Journal of John Ward," *New Mexico Historical Review* 16.2 (April 1941): 206–232; SDTP, Meriwether address to the legislature, December 6, 1853.

28 Santa Fe District Court, March Term 1854, entries for March 31 and April 1, 1854. Located at the New Mexico State Records & Archives, Santa Fe.
29 SFG, 3/18/1854.
30 It seems likely that Luján's Spanish account found its way into Salpointe's papers, where it was translated as *The Indians of Arizona and New Mexico: Nineteenth Century Ethnographic Notes of Archbishop John Baptist Salpointe*, ed. Patricia Fogelman Lange, Louis A. Hieb, and Thomas J. Steele (Los Ranchos, NM: Rio Grande, 2010), 142–146. The original account from Luján and Chino can be found in UNMCSR, Catron Collection. The quotes are taken from Chino and the translation by Lange et al.
31 Salpointe, *Indians*, 144–145.
32 SFG 4/22/1854.
33 SFG 4/22/1854, Salpointe, *Indians*, 145.
34 SFG 4/22/1854.
35 *El Gringo* 329; SJAB 3:206 n1; SFG 4/22/1854.
36 SJAB 3:206 n1; SFG 4/22/1854.
37 SFG 4/22/1854.
38 Ibid.
39 Simmons, "History," 210.
40 Quoted Wallace, *Death*, 260, See also Conference with Handsome Lake, Cornplanter, and Blue Eyes; TJ Papers v. 37, p. 37.
41 Adam Jortner, *Blood From the Sky: A History of the Supernatural in the Early Republic* (Charlottesville: University of Virginia Press, 2017).

Bibliography (selection)

Blue, Martha, *The Witch Purge of 1878: Oral and Documentary History in the Early Navajo Reservation Years.* Tsaile: Navajo Community College Press, 1988.
Dennis, Matthew, *Seneca Possessed.* Philadelphia: Pennsylvania University Press, 2010.
Ebright, Malcolm and Rick Hendricks, *The Witches of Abiquiu: The Governor, the Priest, the Genízaro Indians, and the Devil.* Albuquerque: University of New Mexico Press, 2006.
Games, Alison, *Witchcraft in Early North America.* Lanham: Rowman & Littlefield, 2010.
Jortner, Adam, *Blood from the Sky: A History of the Supernatural in the Early Republic.* Charlottesville: University of Virginia Press, 2017.

22

WITCHCRAFT ACCUSATIONS IN NINETEENTH- AND TWENTIETH-CENTURY EUROPE

Owen Davies

Over the last twenty years or so there has been a slow but growing recognition that there is a history of witchcraft accusations after the end of the witch trials. From the nineteenth century onwards there were many educated European voices claiming that the belief in witchcraft was a relic of the past, and that only the peasantry and uneducated people in remote and backward areas of the countryside feared witches. There was confidence that those forces of modernity such as the expansion of education, industrialisation, urbanisation, professional policing, mechanisation, the railways, and the telegraph would eventually enlighten the darkest corners where 'superstition' was thought to linger. But over and over again across Europe the press reported with shock and revulsion some new instance of brutality against suspected witches. Clergymen wrote and published admonishing sermons about the continued abuse of those accused of bewitching in their parishes. When the folklorists of the late-nineteenth and early-twentieth centuries went collecting examples of supposedly archaic beliefs and traditions they found that belief in the existence of witches was still widespread in rural communities. Jump half a century to the 1960s and 1970s and a series of studies by ethnographers and anthropologists revealed that witchcraft accusations were still being made in France and Germany.[1] So despite two centuries of confidence that witchcraft belief was an historic stage in human progress the facts on the ground suggested otherwise.

Until fairly recently, historians did not view witchcraft accusations in modern Europe as a serious topic for study; continued manifestations of witchcraft belief were not considered significant or revealing. They were mentioned as curiosities and designated a matter for folklorists to study. In the 1980s and 1990s, however, inspired in part by the French and German ethnographic studies, some historians began to reflect more seriously on piecing together the history of witchcraft between the days of the trials and the contemporary evidence.[2] Questions began to be asked regarding how widespread witchcraft belief had been over the previous two centuries. To what extent had it declined? How reliable was the evidence collected by the early folklorists? And how should their material be interpreted by historians? Who continued to accuse people of witchcraft? And who were the accused? To what extent did the nature and pattern of nineteenth and twentieth-century witchcraft mirror the findings of early modern historians exploring the trial records? Did the European emigrants who went overseas in vast numbers continue to make witchcraft accusations in their new communities and environments? Today the history of European witchcraft in the modern era is well established yet historical studies are still relatively few. So we have some substantive work on England, Denmark, the Netherlands, Germany, Hungary, Finland, and France, but comparatively little historical research (as distinct from ethnographic work) to compare it to with regard to Spain, Scotland, Austria and Italy, for example. There is much more work to be done in all areas to better answer the questions posed here.

Historians of early modern witchcraft accusations rely on criminal records and pamphlets that provide details of witch trials. Once witchcraft was expunged from the law books of Europe these sources dry up, of course. Yet, despite the decriminalisation of witchcraft, criminal records remain an important source of information about witchcraft accusations. There are slander prosecutions, for example. Slander cases concerning witchcraft accusations occasionally occurred during the witch trials and continued to occur sporadically in some parts of Europe into the twentieth century, in German-speaking areas in particular. In June 1891, for example, a Viennese waitress named Fanny Stroble brought a slander suit against a servant girl named Maria Wirzar. The latter had accused Stroble of being a 'cannibal, witch, and night hag' who visited her at night to suck her blood, leaving her weak and emaciated. The following year Elizabeth Hörrath, of Obermichelbach, Bavaria, was imprisoned for ten days for accusing her aunt and mother of being witches. She told neighbours she had seen her mother riding on the back of a cow and that it had subsequently stopped giving milk.[3] During the late-nineteenth and early-twentieth centuries German-American immigrants also made good use of the American courts to counter witchcraft slander.[4]

As we shall see shortly, people continued to take the law into their own hands with regard to dealing with witches, and this led to what have been called 'witch trials in reverse'. These occurred when those physically abused or harassed for being suspected witches prosecuted their tormentors. Murder and manslaughter trials also took place when accused witches died from the ill-treatment meted out by their accusers. Much information about witchcraft accusations in the period can also be gleaned from the prosecution of cunning-folk. These multi-faceted practitioners of folk magic offered a wide range of services, including fortune-telling, herbal medicine, love magic, treasure hunting, thief detection, astrology, and, most importantly, protection from witchcraft, and the identification and punishment of accused witches. During the witch-trial era the laws against witchcraft forbade the practices of cunning-folk. Good magic was considered as bad as, and even worse than, the *maleficium* of accused witches. When the laws against witchcraft were repealed, the legislature continued to enable the suppression of cunning-folk and fortune-tellers. They were no longer accused of peddling Devilish if delusionary powers and leading the people astray with their blasphemous promises of magical solutions. They were now considered pestilential frauds picking the pockets of the credulous and 'superstitious'. The English Witchcraft and Conjuration Act of 1736 is a good example. It allowed for the prosecution of those that 'pretend to exercise or use any kind of Witchcraft, Sorcery, Inchantment, or Conjuration, or undertake to tell Fortunes'. The punishment was one year's imprisonment, quarterly stints in the pillory for one hour, and the payment of sureties for good behaviour. Laws against unlicensed medical practice were also employed to try and suppress cunning-folk, with the medical professions in France and Spain particularly active in pursuing magical healers.[5]

Numerous cases were heard before minor criminal courts that have not left any records, so the flourishing nineteenth-century local press, with journalists ever looking for sensational nuggets of news, often provide the only accounts of the many trials of cunning-folk and witch persecutors in the modern period.[6] The national press might then pick up such local stories or those from abroad. That does not mean the newspapers exaggerated the extent of the continued belief in witchcraft. Despite the evidence to the contrary, they usually expressed their astonishment that such things could happen in the nineteenth or twentieth centuries. As with the trial records of the early modern witch persecutions, we should always remember that cases that came to court represent only a small fraction of the witchcraft disputes that occurred in daily life across Europe.

Criminal records and newspaper reports are crucial for researching nineteenth- and twentieth-century witchcraft accusations as they enable historians to conduct record linkage. For reasons of confidentiality folklorists rarely recorded the names of the people from whom they gathered information about beliefs and customs. But prosecution records did, so we can then use censuses, parish records, maps, and other such archives to find out personal details about those involved in witchcraft disputes, how old they were, their social status, occupation, and spatial relationship to each other. A detailed study of witchcraft disputes in nineteenth-century Somerset is one of the very few studies to use this approach to the subject.[7]

The material culture of witchcraft belief is an important if little used source of information, though more attention is now being paid to it by historians. Much of this material culture concerns the protection of buildings and their inhabitants from witchcraft and harmful intruders, and also counter-magic aimed at harming suspected witches. A lot of the surviving material, often discovered during building renovations or architectural and archaeological surveys, derives from the nineteenth century.[8] Numerous so-called 'witch bottles', for example, have been found in nineteenth-century contexts in England. We know from literary sources how these were used. A bottle was filled with the urine of the bewitched, and sometimes his or her nail clippings were included. Then sharp objects such as pins, nails, and thorns were put in the bottle. The bottle was then buried or heated over a fire causing the sharp objects to get agitated. The ritual was based on the notion that there existed an imperceptible link or sympathy between witch and victim, so that the treatment of the latter's urine, whether through decay or boiling, would cause physical harm to the witch responsible. Sometimes the ritual was used to identify a witch, the excruciating pain drawing him or her to the door of the victim's house. Sometimes, particularly with the burial of bottles, it was employed to protect the home and the bewitched from an already identified witch.[9] An intriguing series of Finnish finds concern frogs sealed in miniature wooden coffins and concealed under church floors. It is clear from folklore records that they operated like witch bottles and were intended to punish specific witches.[10] Let us now examine what all these sources tell us about the nature and meaning of witchcraft accusations in European societies over the last two centuries.

Decades after the laws against witchcraft were repealed people remained unaware that the authorities no longer took any interest in the popular concerns about witches.[11] Into the mid-nineteenth century a few English people were still going to their local magistrate to request formal action be taken against suspected witches. The Bible was held up as supporting their extermination. Did it not say in the Old Testament, 'Thou shalt not suffer a witch to live?' The frustration with the lack of support with what seemed the self-evident criminality of witchery was expressed by a Somerset farmer named Hill who, in 1916, shot dead his neighbour for bewitching him. Hill told the arresting officer, 'I have a lot of worry here. He has bewitched my child and my pony. You don't believe in witchcraft, and the Government don't, but I do'.[12]

In the absence of legal support, communities occasionally took the law into their own hands. In Abergavenny, Wales, in 1827, for example, a group of men followed by a large crowd dragged a nonagenarian named Mary Nicholas for a mile to a farm where she was forced to kneel and bless a horse she was accused of bewitching. She was then stripped to the waist and thrashed with a branch of briar rose to draw her blood. The ring leaders were prosecuted for riot and common assault. At the other end of the century, in Moscow Province, Russia, in 1891, a beggar woman named Daria Vasileva was accused of witchcraft by villagers and one day two men dragged her through the street by her hair. The local policeman and several others joined them in beating her with bricks, fists, and sticks. They took her to a nearby ravine and threatened to burn her to death. She died shortly after in hospital.[13] The aim of such assaults was sometimes to wring public confessions from suspected witches or to force them to remove their spells, sometimes to bully and ostracise the accused into leaving the community permanently.

The practice of swimming witches was the most notorious expression of public justice regarding witches. In origin, swimming was a trial by water used to confirm the guilt of witches from the seventeenth century onwards. The water in a river, pool, or mill dam represented God's baptismal waters and if a suspected witch floated it was a sign of God's rejection and, therefore, a confirmation of the suspect's guilt. By the nineteenth century such swimmings were still taking place in England, the Netherlands and Germany, sometimes at the request of the person accused of witchcraft. In 1825, in the Suffolk village of Wickham Skeith, a man in his sixties named Isaac Stebbings was swum at his own asking. He was accused of bewitching a neighbour's wife. Four men were appointed to walk him into a local pond and hold him, while the local constable presided over the event to ensure it took place in an orderly fashion. Stebbings floated, and the cry went up from the gathered crowd, 'Try him again, and dip him under the water'. So he was pushed under, but continued to float. He was dragged out in a poor state. Stebbings agreed to be swum again another day with a 'control', a man his age and size to clear his reputation. This second 'scientific' swimming never took place as the local clergyman intervened.[14] Just over a decade later, hundreds flocked to see the swimming of a mother of six named Christina Ceinowa, at Hela, near Danzig, West Prussia, in August 1836. It was orchestrated by eight fishermen and a cunning-man, and Christina died from the ordeal. The administrative head of the district reported the case to the Prussian government, observing that there had been similar such popular witch hunts in recent times, and noting the 'difficulties of exterminating a madness perpetuated and continued by tradition'.[15]

Public lynchings also occurred very occasionally, with most reports of such community-sanction murders coming from Eastern Europe, Russia in particular. One such case was widely reported internationally in 1879. It concerned Agrafena Ignat-jewa, of the village of Wratschewo, Novgorod. The villagers accused her of bewitch-ing several neighbours, trapped her in her house, nailed the windows shut, and set fire to it. Sixteen people were subsequently tried for the murder. In 1932 Reuters reported that a woman in a village in eastern Slovakia had been similarly dealt with, but had been rescued at the eleventh hour by a military patrol.[16] Such collective actions against witches were very rare by the twentieth century, though. This was, in part, a consequence of increasingly sophisticated and professional policing in rural areas. We have already seen several cases in the previous century where local police-man actually participated in popular justice. There is no doubt, though, that it was increasingly unlikely for a substantive portion of a community to express solidarity with the bewitched in such a public way. Moving from a verbal accusation of witch-craft to taking physical action against the accused became an increasingly private affair.

In England it was the specific purpose of drawing blood from a witch to break his or her spell that often led to court cases. A victim from the village of Colaton Raleigh, Devon, described the experience vividly in 1860. Susannah Sullock explained to the local court:

> I was turning out my little cow in the brake, when I felt something touch me. I turned my head, and seeing the defendant [a lace-maker named Vir-ginia Hebden], said, 'How you frightened me'. She answered, 'You wanted to be frightened for what you ha' done to me'. I said, 'I have'nt a doo'd nothing to you'. And she began to scratch me over my face and hands with something sharp. I was afraid she was going to kill me. She draw'd blood both on my face and hands.[17]

Scratching was not unknown elsewhere in Europe. In July 1876 a tribunal in the Loire, France, tried farmer Jean Baron, aged 37, for assault. He believed he and his livestock were bewitched. He consulted physicians but to no avail. Some reapers in his employ suggested he draw the blood of those he suspected, a man named Ray-naud and his wife, and a girl named Jeannette Badieu. As they left church service one day he rushed at them and ran pins into their flesh. At his trial Baron denied having struck any blows against them, maintaining he had no intention other than to draw their blood. As he explained, 'I was ill every time I met them; and now that I have drawn some blood from them their sight produces no effect whatever on me, and I am perfectly cured; I have, therefore, reason to believe that they had cast on me an evil eye'. He happily submitted to his fifteen days' imprisonment. We hear the same expression of satisfaction in English cases. One prosecuted witch scratcher declared, 'I have felt better ever since I gave the scratch; it was a lucky scratch for me'.[18] With our current medical knowledge of the biochemical changes involved in creating and mitigating stress and anxiety we can better understand how the act of scratching could have had a very real cathartic impact.

In terms of one-on-one witch confrontations, in countries with widespread gun ownership we find witches being shot as well as manhandled. With the gun owner-ship laws for non-propertied citizens in England being restrictive, it is not surprising that the 1916 English witch-shooting mentioned earlier is the only British example.

In France, where gun ownership has been more pervasive historically, witch shootings were more frequent. Amongst European Americans in nineteenth- and twentieth-century America we find numerous cases of witch shootings, and an abundance of folklore about the bewitchment of guns and advice on how to unbewitch them, particularly amongst those of German and Swiss descent.[19]

As in the witch trial era, the majority of witchcraft accusations were made against women. A sample of English 'witch trials in reverse' dating from the eighteenth to the twentieth century indicated that 91 per cent of accused witches were women. An analysis of 142 such cases concerning American Europeans between 1790 and 1950 produced a similar figure of 85 per cent, with little variation over the period. In Worobec's survey of seventy-five witchcraft accusations, mostly from the late nineteenth and early twentieth-century, over 70 per cent were women, and de Blécourt's survey of newspapers in the western Netherlands, for roughly the same period, revealed 94 per cent were women.[20] Much more research is required to examine whether the same social, cultural, economic, and theological reasons were at play in the modern period as the early modern to generate this preponderance of female accused. We certainly find similar issues, environments, and situations regarding the origin of accusations in both periods. In Worobec's survey, for example, 12 per cent of the accused were poverty-stricken women, some of whom went begging, an activity that was at the heart of a number of accusations. This echoes numerous cases from the modern and early modern archives of accused female witches, often marginal and elderly, who went begging, were refused charity, and subsequently faced witchcraft accusations when misfortune struck the uncharitable householders. In terms of differences between the content of accusations in the two periods, the Devil and diabolic elements such as sabbaths, diabolic sexual relations, and familiars, are certainly less present in nineteenth- and twentieth-century witchcraft accusations. This is understandable as the prominence of such accounts in witch-trial records is principally due to the use of torture (on the continent) and the leading questions devised by the investigating authorities to confirm the existence of the satanic conspiracies that most concerned them – rather than the simple acts of *maleficium* that preoccupied most common people.

The small number of witch accusations against men usually occurred in working environments where women were largely absent, such as dealing with horses and fishing, or derived from personal rivalries. The latter would seem to lie behind a defamation suit heard in November 1893, which concerned an accusation of witchcraft made by a miner and innkeeper named Timmel against a shoemaker named Liebscher from the village of Müdisdorf, Freiburg. Timmel's chickens and cows were unproductive while Liebscher's were prolific. It was clear to Timmel that the shoemaker had a cast a spell upon his animals, thereby transferring their productivity to his.[21] Men made up the majority of cunning-folk, and some male accused witches were cunning-men. Such accusations sometimes occurred when clients consulted them about their suspected bewitchment and paid for treatment but then got worse rather than better. The suspicion then arose that certain people, the suspected witches perhaps, had employed the cunning-folk to double bewitch them. Or maybe the cunning-folk were trying to extract more money for ongoing treatment.

Digging deeper into the profile of the accused, the aforementioned nineteenth-century Somerset study of twenty-six 'witch trials in reverse' found that most of the accused were aged between fifty and seventy. Journalistic descriptions of the accused confirm that few conformed to the stereotypical 'hag-like' witch of folk tales. In other words, few accusations were made because someone *looked like* a witch. A third of them were widows and two were spinsters, suggesting that issues of female independence, marginality, and lack of patriarchal control, may have been a significant factor.

As we have seen, those accused of witchcraft had the law on their side in terms of punishing their accusers. But going to court was stressful and time consuming. In terms of slander, the accused occasionally preferred the medium of the press to broadcast their innocence and shame their accusers. When, in 1892, Victoria Seifritz was accused of bewitching the stables of the burgomaster of Schapbach, Baden, Germany, thereby causing an epidemic of hoof disease, she decided not to launch a slander suit but to take out a notice in the local newspaper stating categorically that she was not a witch.[22] In 1910 Mary Jane Dance decided to deal with the gossip about her in the Worcestershire village of Eckington by placing the following advertisement in the local newspaper:

> Whereas a certain Mary Jane Dance, wife of John Dance, of the village named, has been repeatedly slandered in common talk and gossip as a witch, together with other false and injurious accusations against her character, whereby she has suffered grievously in mind and body in the esteem and fellowship of her neighbours, any repetition of these offences will result in action being taken against the slanderer.[23]

Cunning-folk were involved at some stage in many accounts of witchcraft disputes in the period. They were employed to diagnose witchcraft, identify witches, and provide the charms and spells that could cure and prevent bewitchment. They were usually careful about naming specific people as witches, though. A common technique was to confirm the suspicions of their clients. There are numerous accounts of the tricks they played to get such information. This sometimes involved the use of stooges who sat in the waiting rooms of cunning-folk and engaged clients in conversation. The deathbed confession of a Lancashire cunning-man named Old Robinson illustrates the ruse well:

> There was a large field sloping from the house. When a person was seen coming up this field, Robinson went into a back room, where he could hear what was said in the front room. His wife asked the person to sit down, saying her husband would be in soon, and she then questioned the person about his errand. When Robinson thought he had heard sufficient, he went out at the back door, took a circuit, and came up the field; and when he came in and seemed to know everything about the matter the person was astonished.[24]

A less devious operation was to ask the client to look into some reflective surface, perform some spell, and ask the client who they saw. Sometimes the rituals they employed for identifying witches, or advised clients to carry out, led to people with absolutely no reputation for magic, harmful or otherwise, being accused and abused; they merely came calling at the wrong moment during a ritual, such as the boiling of a witch bottle. These accidental witches could be, up until this moment, long-standing friends of or good neighbours with the bewitched.

With compulsory education widespread, there was an assumption by the end of the nineteenth century that only the elderly continued to fear the power of witches.

But this was not the case. The Somerset study shows that the majority of those scratching accused witches were aged between twenty and forty. All eight male defendants were in this age group, demolishing the contemporary view that women as well as the elderly were inherently more 'superstitious' with regard to witchcraft. As to social status, most of the accused and accusers in the Somerset reverse trials were from the labouring classes. It is absolutely clear from the wider sources, though, that in Somerset, nationally, and across Europe, witchcraft accusations were made by a wider social group. As is already indicated by some of the cases mentioned earlier, farmers made up a substantial group of accusers, as well as crafts and tradespeople. It may be that the higher up the social scale the more likely that witchcraft disputes were dealt with remotely using counter-magic – in other words without directly confronting the accused, due to personal concerns over how such an assault might harm their reputations amongst their peer groups. Witchcraft accusations were not exclusive to rural areas, either. Our knowledge of witchcraft in urban areas is severely impeded by the fact that nineteenth- and early-twentieth-century folklorists largely avoided towns and cities assuming that urban industrial areas, as supposed beacons of modernity, were naturally void of 'superstitious' beliefs and practices.[25] But numerous disputes played out in small and large urban areas of Europe in the period. In March, 1893, for example, a bus driver in the town of Yeovil, Somerset, named Frederick Terrell, aged thirty-one, stood before the door of Harriett Carew, and yelled that she was an 'old witch' who bewitched his sister, and threatened to beat her brains out.[26]

There is no doubt that in Europe public witchcraft accusations were uncommon events by the mid-twentieth-century. But they continued to occur often enough to be significant for historical and ethnographic study. In post-Second World War Germany there was considerable concern about the continued belief in witchcraft and the resort to cunning-folk and magic books. In the 1950s the German Medical Information Service estimated that there were around seventy civil and criminal law suits a year concerning accusations of witchcraft.[27] From the 1920s through to the 1950s a former German schoolteacher named Johann Kruse, whose own mother had been slandered as a witch, attracted the interest of the international press for his campaign against the social and personal harm that the continued belief in witchcraft was causing. There was no such formal campaigning in neighbouring France at the time, but the courts continued to deal periodically with the results of witchcraft disputes, with sporadic shootings of accused witches occurring into the 1980s.[28] More research in other parts of Europe might reveal similar levels of legal involvement in witchcraft disputes. That said, assaults and court cases were very rare in England after the 1910s. But as the ethnographic studies of witchcraft in France and Germany show, witchcraft disputes continued to play out in dramatic fashion in private and often unspoken ways without ending in public accusations.

Notes

1 Jeanne Favret-Saada, *Les mots, la mort, les sorts. La Sorcellerie dans le bocage* (Paris: Gallimard, 1977), published in English as *Deadly Words: Witchcraft in the Bocage*, trans. Catherine Cullen (Cambridge, New York: Cambridge University Press, 1980); Inge Schöck, *Hexenglaube in der Gegenwart: empirische Untersuchungen in Südwestdeutschland* (Tübingen: Tübinger Vereinigung für Volkskunde, 1978); Hans Sebald, *Witchcraft: The Heritage of a Heresy* (New York: Elsevier, 1978).

2 See Gustav Henningsen, "Witch Persecution after the Era of the Witch Trials," *ARV* 44 (1988): 103–153; Judith Devlin, *The Superstition Mind: French Peasants and the Supernatural in the Nineteenth Century* (New Haven: Yale University Press, 1987); Willem de Blécourt, "On the Continuation of Witchcraft," in *Witchcraft in Early Modern Europe: Studies in Culture and Belief*, ed. Jonathan Barry, Marianne Hester, and Gareth Roberts (Cambridge: Cambridge University Press, 1996), 335–352; Owen Davies, *Witchcraft, Magic and Culture, 1736–1951* (Manchester: Manchester University Press, 1999); Marijke Gijswijt-Hofstra, "Witchcraft After the Witch-Trials," in *Witchcraft and Magic in Europe: The Eighteenth and Nineteenth Centuries*, ed. Marijke Gijswijt-Hofstra, Brian P. Levack, and Roy Porter (London: Athlone Press, 1999), 95–191; Willem de Blécourt, "The Witch, Her Victim, The Unwitcher and the Researcher: The Continued Existence of Traditional Witchcraft," in *Witchcraft and Magic in Europe: The Twentieth Century*, ed. Willem de Blécourt, Ronald Hutton, and Jean La Fontaine (London: Athlone Press, 1999), 141–220; Owen Davies and Willem de Blécourt, eds., *Beyond the Witch Trials: Witchcraft and Magic in Enlightenment Europe* (Manchester: Manchester University Press, 2004); Willem de Blécourt and Owen Davies, eds., *Witchcraft Continued: Popular Magic in Modern Europe* (Manchester, New York: Manchester University Press, 2004); Nils Freytag, *Aberglauben im 19. Jahrhundert. Preußen und seine Rheinprovinz zwischen Tradition und Moderne (1815–1918)* (Berlin: Dunker & Humblot, 2003); Laura Stark, *The Magical Self: Body, Society and the Supernatural in Early Modern Rural Finland* (Helsinki: Suomalainen Tiedeakatemia, 2006).

3 Edward Payson Evans, "Recent Recrudescence of Superstition," *Popular Science Monthly* 48 (1896): 77, 78.

4 Owen Davies, *America Bewitched: The Story of Witchcraft after Salem* (Oxford: Oxford University Press, 2013), 56–62.

5 For Spain see Enrique Perdiguero, "Magical Healing in Spain (1875–1936): Medical Pluralism and the Search for Hegemony," in de Blécourt and Davies, ed. *Witchcraft Continued*, 133–151.

6 Thomas Waters, "Belief in Witchcraft in Oxfordshire and Warwickshire, c. 1860–1900: The Evidence of the Newspaper Archive," *Midland History* 34 (2009): 98–116; Tom Waters, "'They Seem to Have All Died Out': Witches and Witchcraft in *Lark Rise to Candleford* and the English Countryside, c. 1830–1930," *Historical Research* 87 (2014): 134–153.

7 Owen Davies, *A People Bewitched: Witchcraft and Magic in Nineteenth-Century Somerset* (Bruton: The Author, 1999).

8 Owen Davies, "The Material Culture of Post-Medieval Domestic Magic in Europe: Evidence, Comparisons and Interpretations," in *The Materiality of Magic*, ed. Dietrich Boschung and Jan Bremmer (Paderborn: Wilhelm Fink, 2015), 379–417.

9 Brian Hoggard, "Witch Bottles: Their Contents, Contexts and Uses', and Owen Davies and Timothy Easton, 'Cunning-Folk and the Production of Magical Artefacts'," in *Physical Evidence for Ritual Acts, Sorcery and Witchcraft in Christian Britain: A Feeling for Magic*, ed. Ronald Hutton (Basingstoke: Palgrave Macmillan, 2015).

10 Sonja Hukantaival, "Frogs in Miniature Coffins from Churches in Finland Folk Magic in Christian Holy Places," *Mirator* 16 (2015): 192–220.

11 On the eighteenth-century repeals see Owen Davies, "Magic in Common and Legal Perspectives," in *The Cambridge History of Magic and Witchcraft in the West: From Antiquity to the Present*, ed. D.J. Collins (Cambridge: Cambridge University Press, 2015), 521–546.

12 Owen Davies and Simon White, "Witchcraft and the Somerset Idyll: The Depiction of Folk Belief in Walter Raymond's Novels," *Folklore* 26 (2015): 53–67.

13 Davies, *Witchcraft, Magic and Culture*, 112; Christine Worobec, "Witchcraft Beliefs and Practices in Pre-revolutionary Russian and Ukrainian Villages," *Russian Review* 54 (1995): 183–184. See also Christine Worobec, *Possessed: Women, Witches, and Demons in Imperial Russia* (DeKalb, IL: Northern Illinois University Press, 2003); Daniel C. Ryan, "Witchcraft Denunciations in Late Imperial Russia: Peasant Reactions to the *Koldun*," *Folklore: Electronic Journal of Folklore* 9 (1998): 41–50; Aldona Schiffmann, "The Witch and the Crime: The Persecution of Witches in Twentieth-Century Poland," *Arv. Scandinavian Yearbook of Folklore* 43 (1987): 147–165.

14 *Morning Chronicle*, 18 July 1825.

15 Nils Freytag, "Witchcraft, Witch Doctors and the Fight Against 'Superstition' in Nineteenth-Century Germany," in de Blécourt and Davies, ed. *Witchcraft Continued*, 29–30.
16 *London Evening Standard*, 11 November 1879; *Gloucester Citizen*, 11 January 1932.
17 *Taunton Courier*, 18 July 1860.
18 *Edinburgh Evening News*, 25 July 1876; Davies, *People Bewitched*, 125.
19 Davies, *America Bewitched*, 42–44.
20 Davies, *Witchcraft*, 193; Davies, *America Bewitched*, 68; Worobec, "Witchcraft Beliefs and Practices," 168; Willem de Blécourt, "Boiling Chickens and Burning Cats: Witchcraft in the Western Netherlands, 1850–1925," in de Blécourt and Davies, ed. *Witchcraft Continued*, 94.
21 Evans, "Recent Recrudescence," 79.
22 Ibid., 78.
23 *Nottingham Evening Post*, 20 June 1910.
24 Owen Davies, "Cunning-Folk in England and Wales During the Eighteenth and Nineteenth Centuries," *Rural History* 8 (1997): 99.
25 See, for example, Owen Davies, "Urbanization and the Decline of Witchcraft: An Examination of London," *Journal of Social History* 30 (1997): 597–617. On magic and urban culture in England in the period see Karl Bell, *The Magical Imagination: Magic and Modernity in Urban England, 1780–1914* (Cambridge: Cambridge University Press, 2012).
26 Davies, *People Bewitched*, 151–152.
27 Monica Black, "Miracles in the Shadow of the Economic Miracle: The 'Supernatural 50s' in West Germany," *Journal of Modern History* 84 (2012): 846. More generally see Joachim Friedrich Baumhauer, *Johann Kruse und der "neuzeitliche Hexenwahn": Zur Situation eines norddeutschen Aufklärers und einer Glaubensvorstellung im 20. Jahrhundert* (Neumünster: K. Wachholz, 1984).
28 Owen Davies, "Witchcraft Accusations in France 1850–1990," in de Blécourt and Davies, *Witchcraft Continued*, 107–132.

Bibliography (selection)

Bell, Karl, *The Magical Imagination: Magic and Modernity in Urban England, 1780–1914*. Cambridge: Cambridge University Press, 2012.
Blécourt, Willem de and Owen Davie (eds.), *Witchcraft Continued: Popular Magic in Modern Europe*. Manchester, New York: Manchester University Press, 2004.
Davies, Owen, *Witchcraft, Magic and Culture, 1736–1951*. Manchester: Manchester University Press, 1999.
Davies, Owen, *America Bewitched: The Story of Witchcraft After Salem*. Oxford: Oxford University Press, 2013.
Devlin, Judith, *The Superstition Mind: French Peasants and the Supernatural in the Nineteenth Century*. New Haven: Yale University Press, 1987.

23

SHIFTING FIGURES OF THE WITCH IN COLONIAL AND POSTCOLONIAL AFRICA

Peter Geschiere

Witchcraft research in context

The very term 'witch' in this title leads already to serious problems and questions in the field of African studies. After Evans-Pritchard's classical study *Witchcraft, Oracles and Magic among the Azande* (1937), anthropologists have continued to doubt the wisdom of him introducing the term 'witchcraft' to this field. And as we shall see, there were and are, indeed, serious grounds for such doubts: Western terms like witchcraft, *sorcellerie, feitiçaria* and others have distorting effects when used as translation for local notions – often they give a pejorative swing to concepts that allow for a wide array of interpretations.[1] However I can understand also the impatience of some historians with anthropologists' squeamishness about using more general concepts – this risks to make any comparison impossible.[2] So for this article I will just stick to the blatant fact that terms like 'witch' and 'witchcraft' have been appropriated so widely by Africans themselves that they have become part and parcel of everyday life. However, a caveat is necessary: such translations are 'productive' – they affect the local notions concerned but such appropriations can also give new twists to the notions that are borrowed. Historicizing the uses of these terms remains a crucial challenge, certainly in the field of African studies.[3]

When in 1971 I started my field-work among the Maka of southeast Cameroon – arriving as a political anthropologist but soon finding out that I could impossibly study politics if I was not willing to be introduced to the world of the *djambe* (witchcraft) that my informants saw as crucial to anything that was happening in daylight – I soon found out that they had, indeed, a highly historical conception of this dark force. In their mental map there were two major turning points. First of all the imposition of colonial state power – in this area first by the Germans (since 1905) and then by the French (who took over this part of Cameroon during the First World War). This meant the imposition of the 'law of the whites' who – as my informants would invariably repeat – 'do not believe in witchcraft', and therefore were in practice inclined to protect the witches! But independence (1960) brought a change (the second one) in this respect; as people in the village would add to their disparaging comments about the whites and their protection of the witches: 'But now the law is made by Africans who know that witchcraft is real'. And, indeed, soon after (by 1980) state courts in this area began to convict witches to heavy terms in jail on the basis of the testimonies of *nganga* (healers) who had 'seen' that the accused had 'gone out at night'.

Moreover, since the 1990s, a third major change swept through this area and through many other parts of the continent: the Pentecostal wave that turned the war on witchcraft into a crucial challenge. In Africa, one of the main reasons of the success of the Pentecostal message was that – in contrast to the established churches who under European influence had always denied the reality of witchcraft – it offered a cure against this supposedly omnipresent danger. Witchcraft was now equated with the devil, and the Pentecostals promised its radical eradication through their constant 'crusades'. An important element in all this was their successful use of modern media, which allowed for novel concretizations of the occult. In the Ghanaian and Nigerian video – popular all over the continent – witches play a crucial role. Showing on the screen in blatant detail what used to be largely invisible gave new impetus to people's convictions. It created a confirmation from a safe distance, without the risk of getting oneself involved in the ambiguities of witchcraft rumours (as in everyday life), and left little scope for the ambiguities of these representations.

In this brief text I will try to refer to these three moments of changes. However, it will be clear that this is impossible for the continent at large. Africa remains the continent of staggering cultural variations. Local variations are deep and dynamic; even modern influences, supposedly homogenizing, are appropriated in highly different ways. There is certainly a continuity that recurs in people's representations of occult aggression all over the continent (but elsewhere also). A 'witch' is supposed to be able to leave his or her body at night, transforming him/herself in all sorts of weird appearances, and flying off to hidden meetings with his/her companions; there they participate in orgies that in many respects transgress the normal societal values (cannibalizing one's relatives, indulging in same sex pleasures etc.); they betray people from their own group to their fellow witches from elsewhere; their victims will slowly die unless they go to a healer who, having a 'second pair of eyes', can 'see' who are behind the attack and force them to lift their spell.[4]

Another common aspect is the ease with which elements from elsewhere are integrated into local beliefs. This applies in optima forma to modern technology. Witchcraft rumours all over the continent now refer to magic planes and nightly landing strips that have to be destroyed. But borrowings can also come from neighbouring groups or from Islamic representations. Common is that these beliefs travel and mingle. Equally common is that they show a surprising capacity to relate local realities (the family, the house) to global developments. It is this linking of the local to the global – which now so deeply affects people's lives – that may explain the disturbing resilience of these notions, even (or especially) in the more modern sectors of society: the state, the school, the hospital, sports, new forms of entrepreneurship.

Yet, such general elements are interpreted in bewildering ways: people will have widely different opinions on basic questions – such as how someone can become a witch (is it a general capacity or hereditary in a specific line?); or whether witches know what they are doing or are unconscious of the harm they bring; on the role of confessions (are they necessary to neutralize the witches' power?) and so on. In view of so much variation and uncertainty, I want to start this text with a concrete example: a brief vignette from my field-work among the Maka in which the *djambe* (*sorcellerie*) came to play such a central role. From this starting point I will try to relate to historical changes and different trajectories of a more general purport.

The witch-doctor is a witch herself

A few weeks after I had settled in 'my' house in the compound of the Presbyterian *catéchiste,* (we are talking now of early 1971), I had the honour to receive the first visit – which was to become the first of many – from Madame Mendouga. This was, indeed, an honour since she was at the time the greatest *nganga* (healer) of the whole area. This meant also that she was generally considered to be an expert on the *djambe* (witchcraft), a field of study that had become a major challenge to me. It was clear that, from her side, Mendouga was interested in having a special relationship with a *ntangue* (white person). The Dutch priest who lived a few villages away had already complained to me that this woman was constantly knocking at his door. Frequently visiting white people was, for her, clearly some sort of status symbol. Most *nganga* are eager to profit from any opportunity to show how special they are. After all, their reputation has to be enhanced constantly.

Maybe this was also the reason why Mendouga spontaneously invited us – my assistant and me – to accompany her on a visit she had to make. Normally *nganga* are quite secretive about their consultations for obvious reasons – diagnosing a witch-craft case is a private thing – but she was clearly willing to make an exception for me. As she put it: 'I had bombarded her with questions about the *djambe* – so why not come and see how she tried to deal with it?' It turned out that she was on her way to visit our friend Bayard,[5] then a young man in his twenties, who had recently been quite ill. We followed her to the house of Bayard's family, where we found him in the *salon,* stretched out in an old bamboo chair, looking quite miserable. Mendouga sat down, looked at Bayard and then told his brother to call together the whole family: all his brothers, their wives, but also his old father (his mother had died already) and all the children. When they all had gathered around Bayard's chair, Mendouga started talking in a soft and apparently gentle voice. From what I could understand (and later on my assistant translated further what she had said), she tried to re-assure Bayard (he would soon be all right, he had to trust her etc.), but at the same time she was clearly threatening his relatives around him: she had "seen" already who was trying to bewitch the poor young man, and as usual the attack came from close by. However, she would know where to find the culprits and how to stop them. My assistant confirmed what I had understood: she was, indeed, menacing the people "inside" that she would attack them if they would not soon lift their spell. After half an hour, she got up to leave. A little kid was sent out and returned with a chicken for her. Before we parted, she giggled – she had a most weird way of giggling – and said "Well I warned them. The boy will soon be better." And, indeed, a few days later Bayard passed our house with his dog and his spears, on his way to go hunting in the forest, his favourite pastime.[6]

To the Maka, *djambe* – now always translated as *sorcellerie* – is a key notion that evokes a rich and dynamic imaginary. As I tried to show elsewhere,[7] it is a precari-ous undertaking to try and give a systematic summary of these *djambe* conceptions. Indeed, one can hardly speak of a system here: Maka views on witchcraft seem liable to constant change, re-interpretations and even new 'fashions'. It is precisely their open character that can explain their surprising resilience and their capacity to graft themselves upon modern processes of change. The general conceptions, sketched before, constitute a kind of core. Basic is the frightening image of the *sjoumbou*, the nightly meeting of the *mindjindjamb* (lit. "those who have the *djambe*"). Anybody can try to get a *djambe* which is supposed to live in one's belly. But only some (men as often as women) take the trouble to develop it. Those are the true *mindjindjamb*. At night, when they seem to be sleeping, their *djambe* leaves their body and flies off along the *tande idjambe* (the cobwebs of the *djambe*) to meet their fellow witches at the *sjoumbou*. There they stage horrible parties culminating in a cannibalistic banquet. What makes the *sjoumbou* especially frightening to the Maka is that it is about the eating of kin.[8] Each witch has to take his/her turn in offering a relative who is then devoured by their companions. The next day the victim will fall ill and start to fade away. Only the timely intervention of the *nganga* can save the victim. Thus, the betrayal of kin is at the very centre of the *djambe* representations. *Djambe* is so frightening because it forces people to realize that there is jealousy and aggression in the very bosom of the family.[9] To the Maka, kinship should be the main basis – not to say the only one – of trust and solidarity. *Djambe* highlights, however, that this very intimacy hides at the same time deadly dangers. This is why, as in the case of Bayard's quite innocent affliction, the first culprits always have to be sought 'inside'.

This core image of the *mindjindjamb* extraditing their own people to occult threats from the outside world (the other witches) has all sorts of elaborations. Witches are often supposed to be desperate because they have built up a 'debt' to their *sjoumbou* companions. They have to take their turn in offering a relative, but sometimes a witch can refuse to do so; then the witches will fall upon him/her. Thus, when Mekokpoam – who had a reputation of dabbling in the *djambe* – suddenly died, his brother's son told me with tears in his eyes that he had become a kind of martyr. Clearly he had refused to go on betraying his own people. Therefore the witches had fallen upon him and devoured him instead. And, as always among the witches, it will be then a sudden death: innocent people who are attacked will linger away, so that there is still time to bring them to the *nganga;* but among the witches it is a matter of win or die. Indeed, my friends talked often with some horror of the utter loneliness of a witch when he is attacked by his fellows. As a Maka proverb says 'a witch has no brother, no father, no kin'. Witchcraft is the betrayal of kinship. Thus when a witch refuses to honour his obligations and is attacked by his fellows, there is no one who will stand beside him.

The inherent link with kinship is also a core element in the story – a kind of timeless myth – that people told me to explain how djambe had come to live among men.[10] One day, Man, hunting in the forest, found *djambe* between the roots of a giant tree. *Djambe* said to him, "Give me a little meat from your booty". Man gave him some. On this day he killed many more animals. And this continued. Every day, Man gave a little meat to *djambe*, and he returned with his bag of game fuller than ever.

This made his wife suspect something. One day she followed him secretly into the forest. She saw him kneel beside a giant tree and speak to *djambe*. When he had left, she approached *djambe* herself and asked it, "Who are you?" *Djambe* answered, "Do you really want to know? Then crouch down, spread your legs, and I will show you who I am. I will make you rich too." Woman, jealous of Man's success, crouched down, spread her legs and, hop, *djambe* jumped inside into her belly. Thus, Woman brought *djambe* into the village. From this day on, *djambe* in the belly of Woman demanded meat to eat. Woman gave it all the meat Man brought back from hunting, but it was not enough. *Djambe* forced her to kill all the animals in the compound – goats, pigs and chicken – but it was still not enough. Finally she had to give it her own children, one by one. Thus, *djambe* came to live amongst men, thanks to the greed and jealousy of Woman.

This story, like any myth, allows for many readings and interpretations. There is a clear gender bias, strongly reminding of Adam and Eve. Yet most of my informants would finish the story by adding a proverb saying 'Women may have been the first to go out (that is, leave their bodies), but men were soon to follow', meaning that women may have a certain priority in the *djambe* world, but that men soon learnt their way in this domain as well.

Another implication is that *djambe* can be used in a positive way. In the story, it brings Man success as a hunter – no mean thing since this was one of the main marks of prestige in the old order. Only after Woman brought it into the village – that is, within the sphere of kinship – did *djambe* exhibit its basic instinct: the devouring of Woman's own people.

Thus, the mythical story, like the little scene described earlier of Mendougas visit', can already give some idea of the harassing ambiguities that make the *djambe* discourse – as so many other African discourses on the occult – so difficult to get out of. The idea that *djambe* powers, in spite of the menacing image of cannibalistic nocturnal meetings, can also be used in a positive sense, have all sorts of wider implications. It affects, for instance, most directly the role of the healer (*nganga*) as the main resort against witchcraft. For me it came as a surprise that all my informants would insist that, of course, Mme Mendouga had a very well developed *djambe* herself. Indeed, *nganga* are supposed to be able to heal only because they themselves are deeply involved with *djambe*; they are described as some sort of super witches – one informant even said they were *mindjindjamb* 'who had beaten all records'. Thus, they are a striking example that it is possible to canalize *djambe* in order to use it in a constructive way; but at the same time they highlight the relativity of such more positive uses of *djambe*. *Nganga* themselves will always emphasize that their 'professor', who helped them to develop their *djambe*, bound them with terrible 'interdictions' (*itsi*) to use their powers only to heal and never to kill. Yet, people are never so sure of this: the *nganga* has an extremely powerful *djambe*; this is why s/he can heal. But there is always the danger that the basic instinct of the *djambe* will break through: that is, to kill one's own kin. Indeed, many rumours about *nganga* make the link with kinship in an even more direct way. Acquiring the 'second pair of eyes' is a basic step in their initiation into *djambe*. After all, it is this 'second pair' that enables the *onkong* to 'see' what the witches are doing and to know where to find them. But people whisper that a *nganga* only received this gift from his/her *professeur* after offering a relative as a counter-gift. The *nganga* can only heal because s/he has killed; significantly, it is the betrayal of one's own kin that is crucial for one's initiation into the *djambe*.

Similar ambivalences occur in all sorts of contexts. The *lessje kande* (speakers in the council) – that is, the old men who knew how to overrule opponents in the often tempestuous deliberations in the village council – were supposed to be able to do so only because they had the *djambe idjouga* (the witchcraft of commandment). Even I had my *djambe* – *the djambe le ntangue*, the witchcraft of the white – which meant that I drove my old 2 CV Citroën without making accidents. Also the new elite (mostly public servants who had made *quick* careers through the rapid Africanization of the state apparatus after independence) were in all sorts of ways linked to the same *djambe*. People would whisper, for instance, that regularly even the *préfet*'s black Mercedes (then the new elite's status symbol) would be parked in front of Mme Mendouga's simple house. Apparently he needed her services to 'armour' him in the murderous competition among the new elites for prestigious position in the politico-administrative hierarchies. Indeed, all positions of success and power – whether traditional or modern – were and are linked to special access to in the world of the *djambe*. The basic ambivalence is, therefore, that the powers of the *djambe* can be used both for levelling and accumulating. *Djambe* is often inspired by jealousy – a dangerous weapon of the poor against the rich; but it can also serve to enhance power and success as 'armour' for the rich and the powerful.

Ambiguities and variations

There are certainly important variations in this respect, also among neighbouring societies. In anthropological parlour, the Maka and other societies in the forests of South and East Cameroon, are characterized as 'segmentary': prior to colonial conquest (around 1900) they lived in small family hamlets without any fixed position of authority at a higher level. Inside the family hamlets elders ruled over women and young men.[11] But in case of internal conflict family segments could split off and create a new village elsewhere. In those days the forest was still very much an open frontier. In neighbouring parts of present-day Cameroon, for instance among the 'Bamileke' who live in the western highlands, relations had (and have) a more hierarchical slant. Here strongly institutionalized chieftaincies, with a rich superstructure of title societies and complex court rituals, still retain great moral authority. Here the discourse on occult powers is much more compartmentalized. While among the Maka *djambe* is used as one umbrella notion, covering all sorts of manifestations of occult power people in the western highlands tend to set chiefs, healers and other dignitaries apart from the more negative sides of the occult. These authorities – just as the healers among the Maka – are certainly supposed to have their own access to such occult powers, but these are seen as different from the 'witchcraft of the night'. However, it is important to emphasize that even such conceptual distinctions remain precarious and are often contested. For instance, in the 1990s when democratization acquired full swing also in Cameroon (after decades of most authoritarian one party rule) many Bamileke chiefs had to steer a difficult course between President Biya, who desperately clung to power, and their own subjects. The latter sided massively with the opposition while President Biya used his power over the chiefs (after all, they were paid by the regime) to marshal votes for him. In those days, many people were very quick to assume that the chiefs had strayed from their sacred mandate. Rumours abounded that they were siding now with the witches, riding at night in an egoistic pursuit of riches and success.[12] It was in those days that chiefly palaces were burnt and their Pajero's (then the new status symbol) destroyed – events that would have been unthinkable in the 1980s. Apparently, the basic circularity of witchcraft discourse – powers that can heal or bring success are the same that can be used to kill and destroy – risked breaking through, even in more hierarchical settings.

Maka discourse on the *djambe*, as so many other 'witchcraft' discourses from Africa, highlights ambiguities that pose uncomfortable challenges to anyone who tries to create some order in this treacherous field – not only to authorities of state (see the next section) but also to academics. One implication is that a focus on accusations of witchcraft – almost inevitable for most historians (but in this they are often followed by many anthropologists who have more leeway to tap alternative sources) – risks leading to limitations. Of course, accusations are a tempting starting point since they are one of the few concrete manifestations of what for the rest is supposed to take place in secret and out of sight. The problem is, however, that those accusations that are openly expressed will be mostly those directed against the weak. The basic ambivalence that these occult powers can also be used by the rich and powerful risks to remain out of sight.[13]

Moreover, striking shifts in the discourses on the occult over the last decades in the wider region indicate that the balance between levelling and accumulative implications is subject to constant changes. Decolonization and the rise of a new elite through the rapid Africanization of public service (roughly since 1960) seemed to coincide with an increasing popular preoccupation with forms of witchcraft that are emphatically discussed as new: the witchcraft of 'selling' more or less replacing the one of 'eating'. In southern Cameroon people use different names for this new witchcraft: *ekong, famla, kupe, nyongou*. But the basic plot is the same: these new witches turn their victims into zombies who work on 'invisible plantations' (often located at Mt. Kupe in West Cameroon).[14] These *ekong* witches can be recognized by their ostentatious show of new forms of wealth – which apparently has been accumulated by the labour of their zombie-victims. The *ekong* panic thus seems to express people's bewilderment about the new inequalities, accompanied by ostentatious consumerism. It brings also a tilting of the balance: witchcraft becoming more explicitly associated with the rich and the powerful. Clearly, in the African context as well, witchcraft cannot be studied as a system locked into itself. The ongoing dynamics of these representations requires a constant historicizing of the notions involved and their shifting implications.

Colonial authorities confused by witchcraft's ambiguities

My informants in the early 1970's had a clear mental map of the history of witchcraft in their area. As so many African spokesmen in those days they would emphasize that the law had to change. After independence the country had inherited a white men's law. White men do not believe that witchcraft is real, so they refused to punish the witches. But now, Africans are making the law; as the representative of our *canton* (a young man with some schooling) explained it to me: 'Soon the law will be changed and then we can finally deal with the witches'.

So often this mental map of change from colonial to post-colonial did have some truth in it, but in practice developments were much more complicated – a muddling-through in which principles mixed in complex ways with trial and error. For the colonials – certainly in the early stages after 'pacification' (for Cameroon roughly since the first decade of the twentieth century) – witchcraft was not completely unreal. On the contrary, they had a clear image of the witch. For them the representative of the dark world of witchcraft was the *Medizinmann* as the missionaries of the Basler Mission – in the German period in the forefront in dealing with local beliefs – would call him. As the most concrete manifestation of the world of darkness, he was their idea of the arch-witch, and so he had to be combated at all costs: a victory over him would entail the collapse of this evil world. Note the shift of images: the 'healer' as he is called mostly in present-day literature was to the early colonials the prototype of the witch.[15] – And, indeed, until the very end of the colonial period, the main attacks of both the missionaries and the state authorities were directed against these most visible representatives of the occult.[16] In this sense there is some truth to my informants' complaints that the colonial authorities used to protect the witches – after all, as far as they did interfere with this hidden world they targeted the very persons who claimed to protect people against the witches. All over Africa the colonial period was marked by constant waves of anti-witchcraft movements: prophets and healers promising the definitive eradication of witchcraft by their medicine. And, certainly where such movements were relatively successful, the colonial authorities were highly watchful.[17]

However, underneath what was indeed the formal colonial vision – colonial rule bringing the victory of rationality over irrational and therefore unruly people – things were much more complicated. On a very concrete level, it is clear that for various regions colonial officials did realize that attacking 'witch-doctors' would be interpreted by the population as giving free reign to the witches. Karin Fields showed for British Central Africa, how circumspect and also hesitating British civil servants were in intervening in local struggles over witchcraft and anti-witchcraft. I stumbled in the Buea archives of former British Cameroon on a huge file called 'Notes on Witchcraft in Relation to Administrative Problems' (1934–1946).[18] Apparently a discussion had been started on this issue during the annual conference of all Residents of Nigeria and the Cameroons of 1933. The Chief Secretary in Lagos tried to orchestrate an ongoing discussion by continuously asking Residents to react. The file shows how conscious administrators on the spot were of being confronted by an impossible dilemma: on the one hand all too real unrest among the population about a supposed proliferation of new forms of witchcraft; on the other, the principle of the law that seemed to require interventions against 'witch-doctors' for disturbing the peace and attacking innocent persons. In many respects there is continuity here with the predicament of post-colonial officials when they do decide to intervene (see the next section).

Collateral to such colonial reconsiderations, a growing interest in local practices of healing could lead, in some instances, to a more nuanced image of 'traditional healers'. A spectacular example for Cameroon was, for instance, the much-celebrated career of Father Éric de Rosny, a Jesuit who in 1957 arrived in Douala and subsequently was authorized by the Church, to be initiated by a local expert as a *nganga*. His way of combining priesthood with a practice as healer became greatly respected in Cameroon, also after independence. It expressed again a dramatic shift in the Church's image of the witch.

More in general, the image of the colonial state as a champion of rationality – be it not a very successful one – has lately come under attack. Authors like Florence Bernault (i.p.) or Joseph Tonda (2005) emphasize most strongly that the all too easy acceptance of a basic contrast between the life worlds of the colonials and the colonized (modernity versus tradition) serves to hide deeper and often hardly conscious convergences. For Tonda, it is vital that we overcome for Africa as well the notion of 'a Great Divide' between, on the one hand, 'the work of God' (= the missionary activities), the impact of the State, the role of the world market, and, on the other *l'esprit sorcellaire* (witchcraft). All these elements were and are *converging* – and not opposed – in the production of what he calls *Le Souverain Moderne*, the Leviathan of corrupt rulers with global connections that is the pest of present day Africa. Bernault supports this overarching vision by studying in detail how colonial interventions (both ideas and practices) articulated with local views producing novel conceptions of spirits, cannibalism and evil. For my informants in the 1970s the law inherited from colonial rule remained a law of the whites and, as such, foreign to African realities. However, and this is more in line with Tonda's and Bernault's view, subsequent developments would show that this law could give rise to surprising interpretations, much more in line with local imaginaries (see the next section).

Post-colonial attempts at clarification: a judicial offensive against the witches

It was only in the 1980s that I got the news that, indeed, as my Maka friends had predicted, state courts were now willing to convict witches. They did so mostly on the evidence of local *nganga* who confirmed that they had 'seen' that the accused had 'gone out' at night. This was a complete reversal of existing jurisprudence. Still in the 1970s, *nganga* like my friend Mme Mendouga had good reason to be afraid of the authorities. She may have had powerful allies – remember what was said earlier about the *préfet's* car being parked in front of her modest house – but she was always in risk of being denounced by one of the 'witches' she had 'smelled out' for defamation. Prevailing jurisprudence would then oblige the courts to take such complaints very seriously. However, as soon as judges became rather inclined to act against people suspected of witchcraft, they came to see local healers in a different light. They needed to establish proof in one way or another. And how else could they do this than by appealing to the expertise of local witch-doctors? After all, they were the only ones who could 'see' the invisible aggression of the witches.

The first examples of state courts condemning witches we know of came from the East Province, notably from the capital Bertoua, quite close to Makaland. At the time people said it was no wonder that it was there the courts started to convict witches. Everybody knew that witchcraft was particularly rampant in the East. Even officials from elsewhere, like most of the judges, would have good reason to fear for themselves when they were affected there. The files I could study together with Cyprian Fisiy, a law specialist, then my Ph.D. student, all follow the same pattern. Witnesses from the accused's village would spell out their misdeeds. In a few cases the accused would confess, but in most cases they would severely deny.[19] However, this was not a hindrance for the judges to condemn them, since in all cases they seemed to see crucial evidence of a *guérisseur* (healer) who confirmed that he had seen how the accused 'went out at night' and had plotted together against their victims. Often it was the *guérisseur* himself who had taken the initiative. In several cases this role was played by a certain Baba Denis, who would declare that he had been asked to 'apply his scientific knowledge' in order to 'purify' a village; how certain people had refused to deliver their magical objects; how he had gone to their house and unearthed very evil *gris-gris*; and how he then had told the village chief to call the *gendarmes* to arrest the stubborn witches. For the judges such testimony was apparently so convincing that they sentenced the accused to severe punishments: up to ten years in prison and heavy fines.

A comparison with Mme Mendouga, my friend in the 1970s, shows that the changing configuration since the 1980s allowed the *nganga* to take on a new profile. Mendouga was certainly interested in the 'ways of the whites' – in those days a current expression among the villagers. She liked to frequent whites. But she preferred in general to keep a low profile. Like other *nganga* in those days she lived in quite a modest house, a bit hidden from the main road. In her daily behavior she was very much a woman from the village. *Nganga* like Baba Denis have quite a different stature: they are much more in the open, aggressively enhancing their presence and insistently offering their services to anybody who can pay.[20] For them there is little reason to keep a low profile. After all, government officials are now prepared to give them an official role in the intensification of their campaign against witchcraft. They emphasize in any way they can that they are modern figures – . they dress European style, often sport huge sunglasses; most of them returned from the city after a longer stay there and the emphasize their urban background; in the village they often build their 'hospitals' right in the center of the place, trying to attract attention with big signs; they boast of their medical knowledge, claiming to apply their 'science', and are prepared to work closely with the *gendarmes* to have unrepentant 'witches' locked up and dragged before the courts.

Meeting, for instance, Baba Denis who now lives in a village quite close to the one where I used to live was full of surprises for me. On his return from the city a few years earlier he had settled in a big house in the middle of the village – very visible at the crossing of two throughways. It was adorned by three big signs. One said *Docteur Baba Denis guérisseur*, the next one *astrologue* (astrologist – a new notion for most villagers); the third *Rosecrucien* (Rosicrucian – Cameroon's President Paul Biya is supposed to be deeply involved in this secret association). Baba received us dressed in a European costume that was somewhat shabby but included a tie.[21] He took off his big sunglasses, asking us to come into his 'consultation room' – an office-like room with a big desk, a shelf of books (some from Western medicine but also a few books on Eastern magic), and, in contrast to the formal, almost bureaucratic atmosphere, several burning candles.

Clearly Baba did not like the idea of being interviewed. So he did most of the talking himself, explaining to us how he used his 'science' to bring peace to the villages. He emphasized his important contacts in Yaoundé, mentioning that his brother still worked at the Presidency, and insisted on showing me how well he kept records on his patients, dutifully noting the dates of their visits and other details. In other aspects as well he imitated the style of a *fonctionnaire* (civil servant) with a dry, bureaucratic air. The villagers often commented that he had learned this formal style in the army, where had served for quite some time. According to some, he had been sacked because of financial irregularities, even spending some time in jail. Yet this served only to further enhance his prestige as a *nganga*, since everybody knows that the prison is the place to learn the really dangerous secrets.

Baba's ways of enhancing his credibility had other new aspects. He emphasized the scientific nature of his expertise, styling himself as a *docteur* with his books, his hospital, and his files. But even more striking was that he spoke about his patients as *les coupables* (the guilty ones). In other respects as well his approach was quite far from Mendouga's reassuring behavior. *Nganga*, like Baba, become threatening figures, working closely with the *gendarmes*, ready to hand over witches to *la Justice*. In Baba's case this was clearly related to his privileged role as one of the *nganga* who were regularly asked to testify in court. But in the 1980s many *nganga* with a lesser profile than Baba, especially younger ones, similarly became much more aggressive in their quest for potential clients. People often told me how they would be approached by a *nganga* they hardly knew who would warn them that their compound was mined with evil and assure them that he knew how to purify it – of course for a handsome fee. The *nganga* were obviously not exempt from the general trend toward increasing commercialization, and this made them all the more aggressive in their search for clients.

It is all the more striking that a *nganga* like Baba Denis, when he has to present himself before the court, invariably introduces himself as 'Baba Denis, *sorcier*'. Clearly even for a modern figure like him it is self-evident that as a healer he can only heal since he has such a well developed *djambe*. However this terminological confusion (for the judge anyone who confesses to be *sorcier* is automatically guilty, but apparently this applies not to the *sorcier-guérisseur*) is symptomatic of the state offensive stranding in the ambiguities of witchcraft. A major problem turned out to be, for instance, the inefficacy of the state's sanctions. People are beginning to wonder what good it is to lock up witches for years in prison. This will certainly not help to neutralize their dangerous power – as *nganga* used to do in the past. On the contrary, when they will come out of prison they will be even more dangerous since one learns the real secrets there.

One can wonder also what this new alliance with the state authorities implies for the the *nganga* themselves. One effect is that the *nganga* is forced to become ever more visible – and, indeed, even aspiring *nganga* who are not (yet) invited to perform in the courts seem to be eager to be out into the open. *Nganga*, like Mendouga, were working especially towards reconciliation (remember her performance at Bayard's sick bed). Someone like Baba Denis is much more of a disciplinary figure, threatening the villagers to extradite them to the feared *gendarmes*. Clearly, the image of the witch is again subjected to new and quite dramatic shifts. An open question is to what extent will these affect their role as healers?

Finally, it should be noted that all these convictions still take place under the existing law that comes straight out of the old colonial law. In contrast to what my friends said in the 1970s a change of the law was not even necessary for enabling the state to attack witchcraft as such. The judges base their sentences on art. 251:

> Whoever commits any act of witchcraft, magic or divination liable to disturb public order or tranquility or to harm another in his person, property or substance, whether by taking a reward or otherwise, shall be punished with imprisonment from two to ten years and with a fine of five thousand to one hundred thousand francs.

Under colonial rule this article seemed to be directed mainly against 'witch-doctors' (confer the mention of 'taking a reward'). It is characteristic for the fluidity of the notions involved that now the same article can be invoked for allowing judges to convict witches.

Over the last years people seem to become increasingly disappointed in the efficacy of state interventions against witchcraft. Not only that the state's sanction seem to be highly ineffective – in the East there are already several cases of convicted witches who return home after their term in jail and then are immediately the subject of other frenzied rumours – but also the inertia of the state apparatus is highly disappointing, in this respect as well. People have to wait endlessly before their case is dealt with before they are summoned to town only to find that their case is after all still not on. Moreover, over the last few decades, another countervailing force announced itself that seemed to be much more effective: Pentecostalism.

A new appearance of the witch: Pentecostalism and the diabolizing of witchcraft

For many parts of Africa – especially since the 1980s – Pentecostalism has developed into a true wave. And one of the reasons of its spectacular successes on the continent was that it promised to eradicate witchcraft. Of course Pentecostal missionaries, especially American ones, had already long been active in Africa. But the 1980s brought a sudden proliferation of Pentecostal churches, sects, and movements all over Africa. The switch in Pentecostal preaching around that time from 'asceticism to accumulation', was very important for the rapidly increasingly popularity of the Pentecostal message throughout the continent.[22] The new 'gospel of prosperity', to which most churches shifted, preached that true believers did not have to wait until the hereafter; they would get rich here and now.

Even before the switch to the prosperity gospel, Pentecostalism had brought a completely new approach for the struggle against witchcraft.[23] While the established churches – to which most Pentecostal converts belonged earlier in their lives – tended to deny the reality of witches, the Pentecostals have always taken witchcraft more seriously, equating it with the devil. Thus the struggle against witchcraft, as a major manifestation of Satan himself, became the basic theme in their version of Christianity. No wonder that in Africa the public confessions that form the climax of Pentecostal services mostly center on former escapades in witchcraft, from which the speaker was saved by a dramatic conversion. While the older churches, established by missionaries in colonial times, have difficulty in promising a cure for witchcraft (since they tend to deny its very existence), the Pentecostals offer definitive certainty that they are able not only to protect against witchcraft but also to take this evil away from anybody who does not stray from the right path (or openly repents of having strayed from it). Their cure is simple: the moment of conversion – the archetype of which is Saul/Paul's shattering experience on the road to Damascus, when God spoke to him and turned him from an unbeliever into the new church's most zealous apostle – will save the true believer from witchcraft.

Of special interest to our topic is that the Pentecostal solution for witchcraft differed not only from that of the missionary churches but also from the approach of the *nganga*. A healer like Mendouga saw it as her task to repair relations, particularly inside the family. And even a more modern *nganga* like Baba Denis, who is proud to deliver stubborn witches to the *gendarmes*, still see themselves as healers. His aim in 'purifying a village' is to neutralize the dangerous powers of the *djambe*. In contrast, the Pentecostals advocate 'a complete break with the past'.[24] In practice this means a break with the family, since it is seen as the very seat of the devil. Indeed, many authors emphasize that central to Pentecostalism in Africa is a determination to liberate the believer from the pressures of kinship.[25] Thus the new message seems to bring a decisive turn, and the solution seems to be as drastic as it is simple: the believer must leave the family behind in order to be liberated from its witchcraft-infested intimacy. Thus (s)he will enter a new intimacy, that of the global Pentecostal community, in which trust is guaranteed since it is based on faith.[26] The question is of course whether this radically new approach succeeds in puncturing the witchcraft issue in practice.

Has the Pentecostals' principled attack on the family and its intimacy, now equated with the devil, really broken open the conundrum of witchcraft as an attack that comes ´from inside the house´? The answer is far from clear yet. First of all, it seems that there are great variations in the degree to which people are admonished to keep their distance from the family. In Ghana this seems to be a major theme, even in everyday life.[27] But in Malawi, Harri Englund does not see a similar tension – on the contrary, he notes that '*mudzi*, the term for both "home" and "village." had deep moral connotations among born-again Christians no less than other residents of the township'.[28] For Congo-Brazzaville, Joseph Tonda notes Pentecostals' distrust of the family;[29] yet this does not seem to lead to a dramatic break – maybe because in this area more extensive kinship links had already been quite reduced. My Pentecostal friends in Cameroon seem to hardly see a problem in reconciling their faith with intense preoccupation with family issues – including active participation in huge funeral rituals.

Another complicating factor is the constantly contested position of the pastor, who is, of course, vital for the establishment of new forms of trust that would surpass the old predicaments. One thing that Pentecostals throughout Africa – and probably not only there – seem to have in common is that preachers are constantly scrutinized regarding whether they live up to their own preaching. Of course this raises endless rumours that they have been found wanting. As early as 1999 at Ekok, the Cameroonian border station with Nigeria, far out in the bush, I was able to buy one of these eloquent Nigerian posters showing a short strip of images: a successful Pentecostal preacher arriving in his own plane, with his Mercedes waiting for him. His driver takes the road, but he is stopped at a police checkpoint. The policemen open the boot and find it full of cranes! Clearly the reverend himself is a witch! Yet, it is all the more striking that Pentecostal movements succeed to stay, at least to a large extent, outside the vicious circles of witchcraft reasoning. As said, most anti-witchcraft movements were time and again drawn into the spirals of witchcraft suspicions – former witch hunters being sooner or later accused of being witches themselves.[30] But this is less the case for Pentecostal movements. One reason might be the Pentecostal openness for constantly new prophetic revelations, so strongly emphasized by Marshall.[31] But Marshall emphasizes at the same time that this openness blocks the possibility that Pentecostalism offers a stabilizing alternative.

Moreover, in a broader perspective the circular power of witchcraft discourse does make itself felt, also against this new opponent. All authors quoted here agree that in the end Pentcostals' radical attack on witchcraft works to confirm precisely its omnipresence. Pastors never tire to admonish their flock to remain vigilant since the devil/witchcraft is lurking everywhere – even inside the community. And the intensive use the new religious movements, especially those of a Pentecostal signature, make of the media only reinforce this sensation of an omnipresent threat. As said, especially the new video industry emerging in the 1980s in Ghana and now especially productive in Nigeria's 'Nollywood' – puts the fight against witchcraft center stage. As Meyer highlights, these video film makers are very keen on constantly improving their 'special effects' technology. Thus, many films revel in showing morbid details of nightly meetings of the witches, weird transformations and gruesome attacks – thus making the invisible visible in abundant detail. The effect is double: confirming weird suspicion but at the same time creating safe distance. One of the basic wisdoms for people in Maka villages (as elsewhere) used to be that people who saw witchcraft everywhere were like the owl (who calls the witches at night to their meetings); probably they were the first ones 'to go out' themselves. Visualizing witchcraft on the screen makes it possible to see from a safe distance – it will serve to confirm one's suspicions, without the risk of being drawn in oneself.[32]

The shifting images of the witch inspired different attacks to liberate people from this evil in colonial and post colonial Africa. The colonials – both the missionaries and the public servants – hoped to lift the spell by targeting the 'medicine men' – for them the archetype of the witch. The post-colonial authorities rather targeted persons who went out at night to join in evil conspiracies – for them the real 'witches'. The Pentecostals direct their 'crusades' against the devil who, to them, manifests himself through witches inside the family plotting to make the pious stray from the Narrow Path. What is striking is that in all these cases, such attempts at a radical eradication of witchcraft seem to be mostly counter-productive. This stands out most clearly for the Pentecostal example. Precisely the pastor's never ceasing insistence on the omnipresence of the devil and thus of witchcraft, confirms the very reality of this threat.[33] One can point to many parallel examples elsewhere. To quote a very extensively studied one, the witch hunts in early modern Europe, for that period as well it is clear that the most radical attacks seem to open an endless spiral of ever wider suspicions and accusations. Relief came rather from an increasing scepticism about certain convictions and from their expulsion from the public sphere. A recent collection *Penser la Sorcellerie en Afrique* (Fancello i.p.) makes the very valid point that at present 'counter-witchcraft' makes more victims in the continent than witchcraft itself ever could.

Eric de Rosny, whose nuanced wisdom in dealing with such urgent issues, is for me still unsurpassed, regularly quotes a proverb of the Duala, a fishing and trading group on the coast of present-day Cameroon, who gave their name to the big city of Douala: 'You have to learn to live with your witch'.[34] Maybe there is more hope for a solution of the witchcraft problem which is taking on extremely urgent forms in many parts of Africa (and again, certainly not only there) in such an attitude that suggests accommodation rather than an attempt at radical eradication.

Notes

1 Many have also emphasized that labeling local imaginaries as witchcraft has dangerous 'orientalizing' implications in African contexts, implying a basic opposition between Western rationality and African irrationality (cf. Peter Pels 1999).
2 Wolfgang Behringer, *Witches and Witch Hunts: A Global History* (Cambridge: Polity, 2004), Ronald Hutton, "Anthropological and Historical Approaches to Witchcraft: Potential for a New Collaboration?" *Historical Journal* 47 (2004): 413–434; Di Simplicio 2002.

3 Florence Bernault, "Body, Power and Sacrifice in Equatorial Africa," *Journal of African History* 47 (2006): 207–239; Andrea Ceriana Mayneri, *Sorcellerie et prophétism en Centrafrique – L'imaginaire de la dépossession en pays banda* (Paris: Karthala, 2014) for detailed studies of how the translation of local notions as witchcraft took shape and what were the implications of its subsequent generalization – a very promising direction for witchcraft studies in Africa. See also Joseph Tonda, *La guérison divine en Afrique centrale (Congo, Gabon)* (Paris: Karthala, 2002); Tonda, *Le souverain moderne: Le corps du pouvoir en Afrique centrale (Congo, Gabon)* (Paris: Karthala, 2005).

4 At first I was somewhat disappointed that the Maka imaginary resembled in so much detail the European visions of what witches do. Some borrowing can certainly not be excluded. Already at that time some *nganga* would boast of possessing books on global magic, and many of them quoted the bible. However, the recurrence of some of these basic elements (leaving one's body, transformation, flying, nightly meetings) all over the world can serve as a warning against attributing too much to borrowings from European lore.

5 No pseudonym (since the whole affair took place already more than thirty years ago, I do not think it is necessary to use any).

6 The whole story is a bit exceptional because mostly clients go and see a *nkong* in his (or her) house. But Mendouga explained to me that this was only a light case. And since she knew Bayard's family quite well and had to come to our village for other things in any case, she had accepted to come and see him at his place. However, if it would turn out that it was more serious than he would have to come to her house, because there she had her 'mirror' and all her other *miedou* (medicine).

7 Peter Geschiere, *The Modernity of Witchcraft: Politics and the Occult in Postcolonial Africa* (Charlottesville: University of Virginia Press, 1997).

8 In present-day Cameroon, the Maka have acquired a solid reputation for cannibalism. Indeed, in their stories about pre-colonial confrontations between hostile groups (and also about the conquest of the area by the Germans) cannibalism is a recurring element. However, as the elders emphasized to me, this was only possible in or after confrontations with strangers (non kin). What makes the *djambe* and the *sjoumbou* so shocking is that it is about the eating of kin (see further Geschiere, *Modernity,* 1997).

9 Eric de Rosny, trans., *Healers in the Night* (Eugene: Wipf and Stock, 2004), stresses the force of the same image for the Douala (in the coastal area of Cameroon) as the very centre of their *ewusu* representations. See also Philippe Laburthe-Tolra, *Minlaaba, historie et société traditionnelle chez les Bëti du Sud Cameroun* (Paris: Champion, 1977) on the Beti in Cameroon's Central Province. Clearly, the Maka (and other African societies) are not that exceptional in this respect. There are intriguing parallels here, for instance, with the emphasis in psychoanalysis in Western societies that primal forms of aggression come from within the family.

10 This story is certainly not special for the Maka. It is reported from several other groups from the southern forest area of Cameroon (cf. Laburthe-Tolra, *Minlaaba*, 1977; Louis Mallart-Guimera, *Ni dos, Ni Ventre* (Paris: Société d'ethnographie, 1981) on the Beti; Elizabeth Copet-Rougier, "'Le mal court': Visible and Invisible Violence in an Acephalous Society Mkako of Cameroon," in *The Anthropology of Violence*, ed. D. Riches (Oxford: Blackwell, 1986) on the Kako; Henri Koch, *Magie et chasse dans la forêt camerounaise* (Paris: Berger-Levrault, 1986) on the Badjoué).

11 Peter Greschiere, *Village Communities and the State: Changing Relations among the Maka of Southeastern Cameroon since the Colonial Conquest* (London: Kegan Paul International, 1982).

12 Miriam Goheen, *Men Own the Fields, Women Own the Crops: Gender and Power in the Cameroon Highlands* (Madison: University of Wisconsin Press, 1996).

13 This is why historical studies of processes where witchcraft accusations risk overflowing such limits, incriminating also the rich and powerful, are of particular interest. A striking example are the Trier processes of the 1580s where Jesuits used young boys as mediums who were supposed to attend witches' Sabbaths as some sort of spies. The results were dramatic since they started to accuse prominent citizens. See Johannes Dillinger, *'Evil People': A Comparative Study of Witch Hunts in Swabian Austria and the Electorate of Trier* (Charlottesville: University Press of Virginia, 2009.); Behringer, *Global*, 95–98.

14 More recently people will say that Mt. Kupe, the magical mountain about which there are so many rumours as the source of illicit wealth, is only a relay station. The zombies would no longer be put to work on the spot but rather 'sold' from there in international circuits (like the mafia) – a telling example of how witchcraft is supposed to stay in tune with an increase of scale of social relation: it seems to 'go global' now. But the special role played by the whites in rumours of *ekong* or *famla* suggests that this is nothing new. See, for instance, E. de Rosny, *Les Yeux de ma Chèvre: Sur les Pas des Maîtres de la Nuit en Pays Douala*. Paris: Pion. De Rosny reports, for instance, that when he went to a village near Douala to talk to an old chief about *ekong* he was suddenly blocked by angry young men who became very upset when they heard that a white man had come to the village to talk about zombies to the chief. Also some recurrent patterns in *ekong* stories suggest a link with old traumas about the slave trade (see de Rosny 1981; Peter Geschiere, *Witchcraft, Intimacy and Trust: Africa in Comparison*. Chicago: University of Chicago Press, 2013).

15 The shift from 'witch' to 'healer' is all the more striking since the my emphasis on the Maka notion that the healer is him/herself a witch – although corroborated by many other examples – drew severe criticism from several colleagues, to whom such an equation amounted to sacrilege (see Geschiere, *Africa*, 74–75).

16 Compare Mongo Beti 1956 and his evocative description how the main character of his novel (the priest – cf. the title *Le pauvre Christ de Bomba*) glorifies in the persecution of the Medizinmann.

17 A striking aspect, to which I will come back later, is that almost all of these anti-witchcraft movements after some time would be caught in the vicious circles of witchcraft reasoning – the witch hunters being sooner or later identified themselves as dangerous witches (see Geschiere, *The Modernity of Witchcraft: Politics and the Occult in Postcolonial Africa* (Charlottesville: University of Virginia Press, 1997, 253; 17).

18 National Archives Buea (SW Cameroon) AA 1934, 16.

19 Confessing witches have long been a challenging issue in witchcraft studies. In the African context a powerful motivation to confess might be that a confession indicates the suspect's willingness to give up his/her secret powers. Only after a confession can the *nganga* work to neutralize these powers. A witch who refuses to confess is a really dangerous one. Of course, in the Bertoua court the effect of a confession is the opposite: it is a sure way to be sent to jail. This again raises questions as to the role of the healer who is involved in obtaining such a confession: the court situation seems to block his capacity to heal (see later in the chapter).

20 Another difference is that these modern *nganga* who sport a more public profile are almost without exception men, while earlier *nganga* in the villages used to be both women and men.

21 The tie was a special sign. In the village hardly anybody wears one – only the *vende kirke* (elders of the Presbyterian Church) might put on a tie when going to church.

22 Robert Akoko, *Pentecostalism and the Economic Crisis in Cameroon* (2007)

23 Birgit Meyer, *Translating the Devil: Religion and Modernity among the Ewe in Ghana* (Edinburgh: Edinburgh University Press, 1999).

24 Birgit Meyer, "'Make a Complete Break with the Past': Memory and Postcolonial Modernity in Ghanaian Pentecostalist Discourse," *Journal of Religion in Africa* 28 (1998).

25 See Meyer, *Translating*, 1999; Rijk van Dijk, "The Soul Is the Stranger: Ghanaian Pentecostalism and the Diasporic Contestation of 'Flow' and 'Individuality,'" *Culture and Religion* 3.1 (2002): 49–67; and Marleen de Witte, "Spirit Media: Charismatics, Traditionalists, and Mediation Practices in Ghana" (PhD diss., University of Amsterdam, 2008) on Ghana R. Marshall, *Political Spiritualities: The Pentecostal Revolution in Nigeria* (Chicago: University of Chicago Press, 2009) on Nigeria Tonda, *guérison*; Tonda, *souverain* 2005 on Congo-Brazzaville; Robert Akoko, *"Ask and you shall be given": Pentecostalism and the Economic Crisis in Cameroon* (Leiden: African Studies Centre, 2007) on Cameroon. For detailed bibliographies of the by now vast literature on Pentecostalism in Africa, see Marshall, *Spiritualities,* 2009 and de Witte, *Media,* 2008.

26 Of course there are obvious parallels here with the approach of the first missionaries in Africa, who often tried to detach the first converts from their families. However, as soon as

the missions became more established, they tried to include whole families in their conversion projects. For instance, the *sixas* in South Cameroon – boarding schools at mission stations where young women were trained to become Christian housewives – indicated a determined effort to change the family from the inside (see Mongo Beti, *Le pauvre Christ de Bomba* (Paris: Robert Laffont, 1956); Vincent 1976; Guyer 1984:44). But this increasing involvement of the churches with the family made them defenceless against the creeping impact of witchcraft closely linked to this familial sphere. The Pentecostal message seems to manifest an effort to take distance once more.

27 Meyer, *Translating the Devil*; de Witte, "Spirit Media."

28 Harri Englund and J. Leach, "Ethnography and the Meta-narratives of Modernity," *Current Anthropology* 41 (2000): 235; Harri Englund, "The Village in the City, the City in the Village: Migrants in Lilongwe," *Journal of Southern African Studies* 28 (2002): 137–154.

29 Tonda, *La guérison*.

30 Geschiere, *Africa*.

31 Marshall, *Spiritualities*, 177.

32 Also the role of mostly Pentecostal pastors in exorcising 'child-witches' confirms people's suspicion of an omnipresent danger. Especially since the 1990s Kinshasa, the huge capital of the Democratic Republic of Congo, became the scene of an intensifying popular panic about children-turned-witches. More recently similar obsessions developed in Lagos and other big African cities. Parents will chase their own children out of the house because the latter would sacrifice innocent relatives for their nightly conspiracies. Such 'street-children' often confirm these rumours by boasting about their nightly escapades. Pentecostal pastors soon developed ever more dramatic therapies to exorcise Satan/witchcraft from the children. Their exact role in such panics is under debate. Filip de Boeck (2005) who was one of the first to write about this does not see the pastors as instigators of the panic (a suspicion expressed by several NGO's working with street children). On the contrary, according to de Boeck the Pentecostals' therapies would at least open the possibility that the children will be re-integrated back into their families (although many families refuse to take the child back even after it has been exorcised). But it is true that in this respect as well, the fervent activity of Pentecostal pastors and their helpers (often women and prayer groups) reinforce a vision of the omnipresence of what they seek to combat.

33 The recent diabolization of witchcraft by the Pentecostals in Africa suggests a parallel with what happened in early-modern Europe. However, there is also a striking difference that might be of special consequence for the haunting question how people will ever become less preoccupied with witchcraft. In Europe, the linking of local witchcraft rumours to the devil served to lift occult aggression out of the local sphere, making it part of a cosmic battle between God and the Devil (see, for instance, Thomas Robisheaux, *The Last Witch at Langenburg: Murder in a German Village* [New York: W.W. Norton, 2009] for a particularly telling example of how 'the last witch of Langenburg' had to reiterate her confession under torture several times until she described her evil dealings with the devil in exactly the words the judges wanted to hear; this was vital for the hold of the devil over the town to be broken). African Pentecostals' linking of witchcraft to the devil similarly seems to make it part of a cosmic battle; however, by placing the devil in the heart of the family, witchcraft is again brought back to local struggles and suspicions from which it is hard to keep one's distance (see further Geschiere 2013, *Africa*, 200).

34 De Rosny, *Afrique*, 114.

Bibliography (selection)

Ceriana Mayneri, Andrea, *Sorcellerie et prophétism en Centrafrique – L'imaginaire de la dépossession en pays banda*. Paris: Karthala, 2014.

De Rosny, Eric (trans.), *Healers in the Night*. Eugene, OR: Wipf and Stock, 2004.

Fancello, Sandra, *Penser la Sorcellerie en Afrique*. Paris: Hermann, 2015.

Fisiy, Cyprian F. and Peter Geschiere, "Judges and Witches – Or How Is the State to Deal With Witchcraft?" *Cahiers d'Études africaines* 118 (1990): 135–156.

Geschiere, Peter, *The Modernity of Witchcraft: Politics and the Occult in Postcolonial Africa.* Charlottesville: University of Virginia Press, 1997.

Geschiere, Peter, *Witchcraft, Intimacy and Trust: Africa in Comparison.* Chicago: University of Chicago Press, 2013.

Marshall, Ruth, *Political Spiritualities: The Pentecostal Revolution in Nigeria.* Chicago: University of Chicago Press, 2009.

Meyer, Birgit, *Translating the Devil: Religion and Modernity Among the Ewe in Ghana.* Edinburgh: Edinburgh University Press, 1999.

24

WICCA

Linda J. Jencson

There are many disputed histories of Wicca (also called 'Neopagan Witchcraft' or 'The Craft').[1] Narratives range from mythical claims of great antiquity promoted by the belief system itself, to scholarly endeavors to sort through evidence of a much more recent invention dating no further back than the late nineteenth century, synthesized into recognizable form in the early twentieth. Significantly, many of the scholars involved in this historical interpretation are themselves members of The Craft, a situation which has complicated issues of authenticity from the beginning of recorded references in the 1890s to what would become Wicca. This chapter attempts a synthesis of varying Wiccan practitioner, scholar, and scholar-practitioner sources on the origins of Wicca then proceeds through a description of much less obscure developments dating to the latter twentieth and twenty-first centuries.[2]

Wicca is a set of magical 'witchcraft' rituals and beliefs that practitioners characterize as being more than a mere occult practice – they see it and experience it as a genuine religious faith. This assertion can be tested through one of the most widely accepted social science definitions of religion, that of anthropologist Clifford Geertz,[3] who basically states that a religion is a system of ritual practices, justified by myth, which create powerful emotions (moods) and motivations, which inform and direct the behaviours and lifestyles of the religion's members. Wicca clearly meets these criteria in its retelling of global myths which reinterpret many gods, goddesses and lesser spirits as manifestations of Wicca's polytheistic Great Goddess, her Horned God consort, and hosts of lesser spiritual beings. It also fulfills Geertz' definition through Wicca's heavy emphasis on ritual practice as a means to evoke these deities and achieve practical (magical) results, as well as Wiccans' utilization of ritualized beliefs to justify and encourage specific (yet widely varied) sexual, gender, class, social, environmental and political behaviours in the everyday lives of participants.[4] Certain other theories of religion might reject Wicca from full qualification as a religion, most notably that of sociologist Emile Durkheim, whose definition requires the existence of a formal church and its congregation. But by his criteria, most of the small, tribal religions studied by anthropologists would fail the test. Anthropologist A. F. C. Wallace clarifies the theoretical issue by stating that there are four ways to organize a religion; they may be individualistic, shamanic (with part-time specialists serving individuals), communal (with shared rites among equals), or ecclesiastical (having fairly passive congregations led by professional religious specialists), thus demonstrating the limitations of Durkheim's definition of religion which would only fully recognize the latter as religious.[4] As will be shown, the wide variety of Wiccan encompasses all four organizational styles, while still touching upon the same over-lapping core of beliefs, myths, and ritual practices.

It should be stated explicitly that the Wiccan variety of witchcraft is not Satan worship; the Wiccan faith does not believe in the Christian worldview which posits a cosmic war between good and evil, personified by God and Satan. The primary deity of most polytheistic Wiccans is a nurturing Goddess, not a destructive male demon.[5] Yet the vernacular meaning of the term witchcraft in the English lan-guage (as well as the technical anthropological definition) is evil magic intended to harm.[6] Fear of those who do not understand, and even greater fear of those who project Christian fears of Satan-worship onto Wiccans is a major issue in the Wiccan mythical past. Throughout the twentieth and twenty-first centuries Wiccans con-tinue to identify with the victims of mediaeval and early modern witch hunts, which Wiccans describe as 'the Burning Times'.[7] Persecution, and fear of persecution both contribute to the difficulty of tracing modern Wicca's late nineteenth and early twentieth century history due to the secrecy imposed upon those who were shaping Wicca into its modern form. Although England's harshest anti-sorcery laws had been repealed by 1735, a much weaker law against fraudulent mediums still had a dampening influence on open practice of the magical arts until its repeal in the 1950s.[8] Repression still influences Wicca in the twenty-first century, as Wicca continues to be perceived all too often as unworthy of the constitutional rights granted 'real' religions.[9]

Wicca is an immanent religion, one where direct contact and interaction with the spirit world is believed possible and desirable (as opposed to worship of a distant deity in a distant heaven). It is also a set of magical practices which the faith promotes as having practical results, such as help in making one confident, healing the sick, or influencing the outcome of an endeavor such as a job search or political campaign.[10] Wicca is one of the Pagan religions (or Neopagan, a distinction emphasizing that it is modern, cosmopolitan, a living religion, as opposed to an ancient, rural, out-dated superstition of the past. Neopagan religions include revivals of ancient Greek, Norse, and Roman religions, as well as modern reinterpretations of tribal religions, borrowing from Africa, the Pacific, and Native America. They may also be composits of many religions, such as Huna, which combines deities of ancient Egypt with those of native Hawaii. Nearly all Neopagan faiths share an emphasis on the sanctity of the earth and nature, the interconnectedness of all forms of life, the place of humanity within this web of sacred interconnection. As such, Neopaganism may be defined as animistic – finding sacredness and power in all of creation, which can be tapped by human practitioners through ritual. Most are polytheistic, focusing ritual behaviour toward many deities and spirits. Congregations tend to be small, although larger festival gatherings may unite hundreds, or even thousands. All of this applies well to Wicca, which is considered to be the largest faith within the Neopagan fold.[11] In his 2011 compilation of Neopagan faiths, Graham Harvey states that Wicca is the pub-lic's most common conception of a Neopagan religion,[12] and ethnographer Loretta Orion prominently describes Wicca as 'the core of a collection of other pagan tra-ditions' on the back cover of a popular scholarly text on Wicca.[13] There are many divergent denominations or traditions of Wicca, with a variety of regional, cultural or socio-political bases.

Due to misunderstanding and fear of persecution, Neopagan religions also tend to operate in secrecy, therefore numbers of Neopagans are extremely hard to estimate.[14] Wiccan and National Public Radio reporter/broadcaster Margot Adler estimates that there may be 400,000 Neopagans (but how many of these are Wiccan?) in the United States; she also cites research by the American Religious Identification Survey that estimates 750,000 Neopgans in the United States.[15] Accurate global estimates of Wiccans are too impossible to be worth citing any attempts.

Wiccan beliefs centre around the Great Goddess and her male consort, the Horned God. The most basic Wiccan ceremony most regularly involves congregants gathering to worship in a sacred circle – often indoors, but ideally outside. Practicing groups (called 'circles', or 'covens') often fall short of, and occasionally exceed, the ideal number of 13. Sacred space around participants is created by the casting of a ritual circle of energy – usually by pointing a consecrated knife or wand while reciting appropriate invocations. Participants stand and dance within this circle. At its centre is a makeshift altar, on which is placed consecrated wine, 'god cakes', water and salt for purification, one or more candles, and other ritual paraphernalia. Spirits of the four cardinal directions are usually invoked by a member of the group facing each direction, and candles lit at the cardinal points; sometimes six directions are called upon, as sky and earth spirits may be invoked as well. Next the God and Goddess are invoked. This may be done in the form of 'drawing down the moon', a possession ritual in which the Goddess (and God) are summoned to enter and share the bodies of the High Priestess (and High Priest) or another pair of chosen celebrants. Ritual cakes and wine are passed around the circle for participants to consume in communion.[16]

Magic is then performed in a variety of ritualized ways, for example, in my own participant/observation research, objects symbolic of personality traits that worshippers wanted to outgrow were tossed into a fire. On another occasion a globe was passed from hand to hand to symbolically heal and protect the Earth. In one 'scrying' ritual – an effort to learn the otherwise unknown – we passed around a bag of Nordic rune stones, drawing one out and interpreting what it meant for each participant's near future. On yet another occasion two young children of coven members, dressed as Greek Goddesses, were initiated into the faith, blessed by affectionate laying on of hands, and allowed to participate in their first communal sharing of the wine and cakes. Such ritual actions of magic are accompanied by dancing around the circle, chanting, and musical accompaniment – usually with a variety of percussion instruments. Rhythmic repetition of the names of deities (for example: 'Isis, Astarte, Diana, Hecate, Demeter, Kali, Inana'), or even the names of participants (for example: 'Ronald is alive, magic is afoot! Mary is alive, magic is afoot!') are common chant formats. Dancing and chanting is repetitive and can be highly energetic, often resulting in emotional states of ecstasy, and varying degrees of trance. Lengthy prayers and invocations may be recited, sometimes read from handwritten 'grimoires' (personal spell books), other times taken directly from published books, including texts on the history of religions, anthropology, folklore, classical studies, and archaeology, as well as those penned by witches for witches.[17] The magical energy produced by these ritual acts is believed to be released into the world when the ritual circle is ritually broken. The groups studied by the author exited the ritual space after expression of solidarity through a friendly 'Pagan hug' before moving on to the less formal part of the festivities – a shared feast.

The mythic version of Wiccan history, which informs belief and ritual practice, states that Wicca dates back all the way to the dawn of religious sensibilities in humankind – to the Paleolithic. At this time, the myth states, a Mother Goddess, and her son/consort (a seasonal hunting deity, the Horned God) were universally worshipped by our human ancestors. Ancient images of pregnant women, such as the Venus of Willendorf, and ancient cave paintings of horned shamans in deer skins are cited as evidence.[18] It is further stated that all gods and goddesses of all religions are re-imaginings over time of these two original deities; evidence for this is perceived in the maternal nature of many goddesses, and the high frequency of horns and other animal traits appearing in images of ancient gods, such as Pan, Krishna, Woden. Horns interpreted as expressive of the Horned God even appear in mediaeval images of Moses, as well as the animals that are depicted as surrounding the newborn Christ child.[19] The evolution of monotheism is viewed as problematic in Wiccan dogma, as the monotheistic, patriarchal religions, particularly European Christianity, are remembered as hostile to the ancient worship of the Goddess and Horned God. The late mediaeval era of witch burnings are interpreted as direct assaults upon the historic traditions and practitioners of Wicca. Thus, fear of a return to 'The Burning Times' figures prominently in Wiccans' uneasy relationships with the dominant religions of today. Orion emphasizes this when she states, 'the Neopagans feel that the threat of another burning times is ever present'.[20] The Wiccan origin myth states that the faith was then driven underground, being shared and perpetuated by word of mouth and by secret, hand-copied 'books of shadows', largely within the traditions of secret witch families.[21] Around the turn of the twentieth century, through the research and writings of several anthropologists, folklorists, and practicing magician-scholar-witches (who interviewed and trained in The Craft with traditional family practitioners) the practice of Wicca was brought to public awareness. Thus began the open proselytization through mass media, and initiation of new converts to the practice that we see today.

Genuine historical evidence for the origins of the core beliefs and practices of Wicca point to the religion's coalescence far more recently than the Stone Age, antiquity, or even the mediaeval period. It is a fascinating narrative of literate scholars, well-read and articulate magician-scholar-witches with credentials in both the world of academia and witchcraft circles who used their unique positions to weave together disparate sources and form the first truly Wiccan covens – no earlier than the early to mid-twentieth century.[22] So essential to the process are reading material and scholar-practitioners that Marcello Truzzi has coined the terms 'audience cult' for those who learn a religious system through reading rather than face-to-face social contact and 'anthropologist-witch'. This latter term describes insider-practitioner-scholars who are able to articulate a religious system to the outside world, while adding their own synthesis of written and experiential sources to the body of lore available to insiders within that religion.[23]

The published texts most responsible for the rise of Wicca in the early twentieth century rise were composed by Margaret Murray and C. G. Leland. Ironically, the two researchers never acknowledged one anothers' works, which disagreed drastically on even the most basic principles. Murray had written two texts, *The Witch Cult in Western Europe* and *The God of the Witches* in which she speculated that mediaeval witchcraft beliefs were based on much more ancient folk belief in a horned, shamanic nature god, a lord of the animals dating all the way back to the Old Stone Age.[24] Leland, on the other hand, believed that mediaeval witchcraft had its origins in the worship of a goddess, Aradia, conceived of as the daughter of the Roman deities Diana and her brother/lover Apollo, also called Lucifer, 'bringer of light'.[25] Both authors stated that the ancient beliefs they studied had powerful survivals in modern European folk practices, but neither author in any way validated or acknowledged the primary deity or the theories of the other.

Murray's hypothesis was that myriad European folk beliefs and magical practices were survivals of an ancient, organized, continent-wide religion whose deity was the Horned God. She further believed this pre-classical god was a survival of an even more ancient nature deity from the Paleolithic. Her evidence includes the many and various images of horned shamans and sacred beings which she traces from Ice Age cave paintings through mediaeval and Renaissance images of devils.[26] Serious scholars today discount her excessive synthesis of unrelated imagery as symptomatic of folkloristic's early, unscientific obsession with finding 'ur-forms', the supposed single-source origin, and 'pure' original version once believed to lie behind every later custom, narrative, or folk belief. Later studies of Murray's methods and evidence can best be summed up by Eliade, who summarizes 'the countless and appalling errors that discredit Murray's reconstruction'.[27] Even most modern, well-read Wiccans – however appealing the story might be – would agree that Murray's theories far overstate the antiquity of their god.[28]

The Horned God is not the primary deity of the modern Wiccan faith, it is the Great Goddess. She is first described and associated with surviving magical folk-practices by the highly respected nineteenth century folklorist Charles Godfrey Leland. Unlike Murray whose research took place in libraries, Leland had done some actual field-work among the *strege* (folk witches) of Tuscany, as well as in England and Europe. But despite his criticism of prior scholars who 'all made books entirely out of books',[29] Leland himself relied heavily on the assistance of anonymous others to do much of his collecting – in the form of written documents allegedly penned by authentic folk witches. Such is the case for the primary material on which he based his contribution to the eventual synthesis of Wicca. It was titled *Aradia: Or the Gospel of the Witches*. The gospel which forms the basis of the book was allegedly collected for Leland by an assistant named only as Maddalena, presumably a practicing folk-witch with many elder contacts among the Tuscan *strege*, from whom she gathered hand-written stories, spell-books, and the 'witches gospel'. Leland states that Maddalena was not available for questioning about the document, it having apparently arrived by mail in 1897.[30] Thus, even in the unlikely case that *Aradia's* source material came from a genuine folk-witch author, Leland's interpretation of it, which comprises much of *Aradia's* content, are clearly his own, not those of any actual Tuscan *strege* individual, let alone any kind of traditional community.

In *Aradia*, Tuscan witchcraft of the late nineteenth century is described as the wreckage of classical Roman (and earlier Etruscan) religion, degraded through time by inaccurate transmission from generation to generation, and by the imposition of feudalism on an oppressed, yet rebellious peasantry. Murray's organized, pan-European religion of the Horned God is nowhere to be found. The primary deity is instead Aradia, a witch-goddess descended from classical Diana (no longer a virgin as she was in antiquity) and her brother Apollo (Lucifer – the Bringer of Light, no longer exclusively a god of the sun, and now his sister's lover). Aradia, the witch-goddess, is sent to earth by Diana to instruct and befriend the rebellious peasantry who 'dwelt in the mountains and forests as robbers and assassins, all to avoid slavery'.[31] Absent are the benign aspects of a nurturing mother goddess so central to most Wiccan practice today, and fully absent is the term 'Wicca'.

Despite obvious remoteness from modern Wicca, *Aradia* is the earliest known written source for important liturgical prose-poetry still common in Wiccan practice at the beginning of the twenty-first century. For example, the first several stanzas of a liturgy that evolved into the highly honored 'Charge of the Goddess', are found in *Aradia*, although Leland did not use that title for it.[32] Clearly, Leland's *Aradia* is a significant source-book for Wicca. Yet, significantly, rarely do twentieth century Wiccans focus any ritual or narrative mythic attention on the witch-goddess Aradia, although, as we shall see, Diana has become important to lesbian branches of The Craft, who in fact refer to themselves as Dianic.[33]

It would take Gerald Gardner, and the witchcraft circles around him in the mid twentieth century to unite Murray's god and Leland's goddess into a single religion.[34] Gardner was also apparently the first author to connect the term 'Wicca' to a particular style of ritual, claiming that the term derives from the Old Anglo-Saxon word for witch. It would have been pronounced 'witch-a' in Old English, but it is pronounced 'wikk-a' today. Gardner had been an insignificant overseas bureaucrat in the British Empire, having served in the Far East, prior to his return to Britain where he eventually became curator of the Museum of Witchcraft, Isle of Man. Over the course of his lifetime he traveled extensively in the Far and Middle East, and participated in the 1936 archaeological excavations at the city of Lachish. He wrote a respected book on Malaysian weaponry, and was an active member of various learnt societies, including The Royal Asiatic Society and the Folklore Society, where he presented papers in the company of such respected scholars as anthropologist Bronislaw Malinowski.[35] In an era when amateur/professional statuses were not so clearly delineated as they are today, he self-identified as both witch and anthropologist, although it has come to light that he entered scholarly society through deceptive claims to have university degrees which were entirely fictitious.[36]

In his writings, Gardner claimed to have discovered families and covens of witches, practicing a traditional form of magic, and participating in a faith of great antiquity, into which he was initiated. Yet even most of his spiritual descendants today doubt the veracity of these claims.[37] It seems far more probable that he instead synthesized Wicca from his historically verifiable initiation into secret societies practicing a particular form of Occultism – Ceremonial Magic (traditions based on Masonic and other rites with strongly Christian, mediaeval origins). Gardner most likely combined his training in Ceremonial magic, his experiences with anthropologists and archaeologists, with the highly speculative theories of Murray and Leland. For example, Gardner claimed to have learnt the words and accompanying ritual gestures of 'The Charge of the Goddess' not from reading Leland (nor from direct contact with Tuscan folk witches), but from traditional family witches in England.[38] This is an obvious untruth; even if the liturgy had existed from ancient times and been translated into different languages in antiquity from an original source, the early translators would not have made the same word choices – no two independent, historically remote translations of a poem from Italian (or any other language) into English are going to come out with such similar phrasing as 'Whenever ye have need of anything, Once in the month, and when the moon is full, Ye shall assemble . . .'[39] and 'Whenever you have need of anything, once in the month, and better it be when the moon is full, you shall assemble . . .'.[40]

Neopagan historian, and Ceremonial Magician, founder of the New Reformed Order of the Golden Dawn, Aidan Kelly believes that Gardner created 'The Charge' out of the more rudimentary material in Leland.[41] Isaac Bonewits, Neopagan historian and former Archdruid of the Redformed Druids of North America, believes that the process was one step removed. He thinks that literate folk-witches who had learnt something of witchcraft from their ancestors (people he blithely labels 'Fam-Trads'), read Leland and incorporated the material from *Aradia* into their eclectic practices, and later taught it to Gardner. In his version, Gardner may or may not have realized its literary origins. Bonewits is quoted in Adler as seeing the entire process of Wicca's emergence in the early twentieth century as dependant on academia and the publishing industry, stating,

> Somewhere between 1920 and 1925 in England a group of social scientists (probably folklorists) got together with some Golden Dawn Rosicrucians and a few Fam-Trads to produce the first modern covens in England; grabbing eclectically from any source they could find in order to try and reconstruct the shards of their Pagan past.[42]

I believe Bonewits goes too far in implying that the attempt was organized, and operated within a limited five year period, yet the fact that several folklorists and anthropologists were hot on the heals of folk practices and beliefs relating to witchcraft around the opening decades of the twentieth century, while reading in interpretations based on classical and archaeological sources, cannot be denied. Nor is it that unusual for scholar-practitioners to embellish the teachings of their folk informants or entirely make them up. Leland's Maddalena is a case in point; her existence is unverifiable, as is that of her alleged source for the witch's gospel. In another blatant example, Carlos Castaneda, the less-than-fully credentialed anthropologist whose best selling book, *The Teachings of Don Juan: A Yaqui Way of Knowledge*, contributed significantly to the spread of mysticism and the hippie counterculture, in which the author alleged to have learnt Native American Yaqui magic from a mysterious folk practitioner, don Juan. It was later proven beyond doubt that Castaneda made it up; there was no don Juan.[43]

Bonewit's own magical pedigree is an example of the scholars-as-the-actual-folk-source feedback loop. In his Druidic writings, Bonewits makes the exotic claim that he and other founding Reformed Druids of North America learnt much of their ancient practices from a mysterious spiritual teacher named John the Messenger.[44] However, it is common knowledge in Neopagan circles that modern American Druid practice emerged from a Carleton College (Minnesota) student club focused on the re-creation of ancient ritual pageantry – one that eventually lead members to begin believing in the spirits and magical forces at the heart of their ritual pageants, and led to the eventual founding of a Reformed Druid religion with thousands of adherents.[45] After I published a study on the scholar-practitioner origins of Neopaganism in Britain's *Anthropology Today*,[46] I received a letter from anthropologist John

Messenger (at that time teaching at Ohio State University), in which he explained that he had been one of the Carleton College club's advisors, had indeed taught the students what he knew of anthropological sources on ancient Druidism, and that he was fairly certain that he, in fact, was the person who had been inflated into the prophet John the Messenger in North American Druidic tradition.[47]

Gerald Gardner claimed that an important source for his own training in The Craft of Wicca, beginning around 1940, was an elderly witch named Old Dorothy.[48] Unlike Leland's elusive Maddalena, or the utterly fictitious Don Juan, Dorothy's existence has (debatably) been confirmed; it is claimed that she was Dorothy Clutterbuck-Fordham, and has been proven to have lived in New Forest, as Gardner claimed.[49] However, as in the case of the Reformed Druids' John (the) Messenger, her role may not have been exactly as reported by her famous disciple. She is elsewhere described as a respectable churchgoer, and her own surviving diaries, while they contain poetry about the glories of nature, make no mention at all of Craft participation.[50]

That Gardner was initiated into several circles of Ceremonial Magic (also called Western Mysticism) is beyond dispute. His writings constantly reference the Masonic, Cabbalistic and alchemical traditions which form the core of Ceremonial Magic.[51] Around World War Two, Gardner circulated in London occult circles centred on the Atlantis Bookstore. Those who haunted its aisles were primarily members of a variety of Ceremonial Orders, including the *Ordo Templis Orientalis* (OTO), the Order of the Silver Star, and other offshoots of the Hermetic Order of the Golden Dawn. It was there that he met a number of Ceremonial Magicians, several of whom would eventually report being initiated into Gardner's brand of witchcraft only later, through Gardner himself.[52]

Sources concur that Gardner himself was initiated into the OTO, and Gardner was an acquaintance (if not friend) of the notorious Ceremonial Magician cum Satanist, Aleister Crowley, whom he had met by 1947, perhaps earlier.[53] Although Gardner is cited as saying that Crowley was 'a bit of a joke',[54] some sources state that Gardner paid Crowley to write much of the liturgy that was to become the core of Wiccan practice.[55] Others claim that although Gardner may have gotten some Golden Dawn, Rosicrucian and other Ceremonial Magic secrets from Crowley, Crowley could not have contributed the most important aspects of Wicca, particularly the shift to significant roles for High Priestesses, and the focus on the Goddess as primary deity. The man was simply too misogynist.[56]

Another contributor to Gardner's Wicca, whose importance seems to grow as more evidence comes to light, was Doreen Valiente. As a British housewife with a Spanish husband, she experienced considerable prejudice and rejection, leading her to seek companionship in unconventional circles. She was initiated into Gardner's coven in1953, after many years' experience in Ceremonial Magic.[57] She became a prominent High Priestess, author of books on witchcraft, and founder and co-founder of many covens of her own, in both Britain and the United States. Valiente told Adler that when she joined, the rituals were disjointed – clearly being spliced together from many sources. Valiente believes, 'They were heavily influenced by Crowley and the O.T.O., but underneath there was a lot which wasn't Crowley at all, and wasn't the Golden Dawn or ceremonial magic either'.[58] Valiente concurs with Bonewits' conclusion that folklorists got together with traditional family witches in the 1920s to synthesize practices and beliefs which Gardner then encountered at the end of the 1930s. Many however believe that it was Valiente who pushed Wicca even further toward its Goddess emphasis, its 'harm none' ethics, and roles for powerful priestesses. As she told Adler near the end of her life, 'Yes, I am responsible for quite a lot of the *wording* of the present-day rituals; *but not the framework of those rituals or the ideas upon which they are based.* On that I give you my word'.[59]

Whereas Crowley's prime commandment was the amoral, 'Do what thou wilt shall be the whole of the law', Gardner's covens chose the far more ethical 'An ye harm none, do what ye will', to be the Wiccan Creed (also called Wiccan Rede), a tenet which continues to be cherished in most Wiccan circles.[60] Yet Gardner did like Crowley, emphasize sexuality as a powerful source of magic in his teachings. The 'Great Rite' aims to generate powerful emotions, hence powerful magic, through ritual sex between a coven's High Priest and Priestess. Gardner, many of his early followers who founded covens of their own, and a few Gardnerian Wiccan covens today still practice it. Most Wiccans practice it only symbolically (just as one might say that Christians practice *symbolic* ritual cannibalism by eating the Host in their most sacred rite of communion). In a dozen years of participant observation in the 1980s and 1990s, I had only witnessed the symbolic form – in which one of the sacred couple holds a chalice, into which the other plunges a phallic dagger.[61] Gardner was a 'naturist' ('nudist' to Americans) and he emphasised that the proper way to do magic was 'sky-clad', or naked.[62] Gradually most Wiccans came to do ritual dressed in colourful robes as a symbol of freedom, some covens are 'clothing-optional', and only a minority *require* nudity, often only for rare occasions, despite the continued popularity of 'The Charge of the Goddess', which strongly recommends bare witches.[63]

In 1963, a Gardnerian coven initiated Alex Sanders and his wife, Maxine. Together they would bring Wicca to America, although in modified form, dubbed the Alexandrian Tradition for its founders, who were darlings of the mass media in the 1970s. Among their innovations was the now common ritual invocation of the spirits of the four directions, as well as other classical and alchemical symbolism. Like Gradnerian covens, Alexandrians tend toward hierarchical structuring, with significant power over coven members granted to a high priestess and priest.[64] The couple's initiates rapidly splintered off, forming dozens of covens of their own. As is the norm in Wiccan circles, the splintering of covens led to splintering into new traditions. Driven by the spiritual explorations of the Sixties counterculture as impetus, formal covens, less formal circles, and new traditions erupted exponentially. It was the Alexandrian Tradition that popularized Wicca in continental Europe, beginning in the Netherlands, Belgium, and Luxemburg. Perhaps the largest of theses groups, Greencraft (an environmentally conscious version of The Craft) spread westward again into North America.[65]

Following upon the 1960s interest in alternative spirituality, Wicca was given a great boost in the 1970s, especially in the United States, by the women's movement. Its Goddess-centred practices were of natural interest to many feminists. Many of America's best-known Wiccan authors, are advocates of strong feminist traditions within The Craft; these in turn are linked with and draw inspiration from a variety of non-Wiccan, Neopagan 'Women's Mysteries' circles. Emphasis on study of goddess mythologies is encouraged, and a belief in ancient matriarchies – cultures run by nurturing, elder female leadership – is promoted in these traditions.

Feminist traditions also emphasize use of magic to promote gender equality through women's empowerment, always with the clarification that a Crowleyian dominance over others is not the goal; women's empowerment is about *self* mastery (not master/slave relations with others), and the development of agency to do one's will within the bounds of the Wiccan Creed's 'an ye harm none'.[66] However, Luhrmann's participant-observation (ethnographic) studies of Wiccan and other magical groups on both sides of the Atlantic demonstrate that the feminist interpretation of The Goddess is not a forgone conclusion; British covens are much more traditional, hence patriarchal – men still apparently dominate leadership and decision-making there.[67] My own participant-observation study in the western United States demonstrates that worship of a Goddess does not necessarily lead directly to empowerment for women. The research shows that symbols are created, interpreted, and utilized by human beings with widely diverging motives. With its strong emphasis on sexuality, Wicca can be demonstrated to be quite a convenient tool for lustful males wishing to dehumanize women into objects for male sexual gratification – through deceptive utilization of Wiccan imagery, as in 'hey, baby, wanna get worshiped?'.[68]

This should in no way detract from the contributions which feminist traditions of Wicca have made for the empowerment of women *and* non-traditional men. As Harvey states, 'feminism has affected all Pagan traditions in one way or another'.[69] Explicit Wiccan feminism began with the founding of a lesbian tradition of Wicca – Dianic. Although not all Dianic sub-traditions of covens are lesbian, all are united by emphasis on the Goddess, to the exclusion of the God (and often of men). Sexual components of ritual will either be left out or enacted between women. Zsuzsanna Budapest (who goes by the first-name initial, Z.) was a refugee of the Hungarian Uprising and its horrific repression, who settled in the United States. Sheco-founded the first Dianic coven in 1971. They called it the Susan B. Anthony Coven. Its intent from the beginning was to unite spirituality with political activism for women's empowerment, human rights, and, eventually the environment.[70]

One of Budapest's hundreds of initiates is Miriam Simos, who goes by the 'Craft name' of Starhawk. She went on to co-found several covens whith their own sub-traditions, all feminist, but many also inclusive of feminist men. One of these, The Reclaiming Tradition focuses publicly on feminist and environmentalist politics, teaching its spell craft through workshops geared toward personal empowerment and political/social change. For several decades, Reclaiming Wiccans have been organizing ritual activities at otherwise secular colleges, demonstrations, training retreats, and political occupations.[71] These rites are often a contact point between Wiccans and the general public, thus Reclaiming can be an entry point for future practitioners who may wind up in any of the other Wiccan (or Neopagan) traditions, or stay within Reclaiming itself.

With the politicization of Wicca came the impetus to organize, and the latter decades of the twentieth century have seen the proliferation of Wiccan and Neopagan newsletters, magazines, publishers, networking, and advocacy organizations. In Britain, these associations date back to the 1960s, with the publication of *The Wiccan* newsletter, later renamed *Pagan Dawn*. It focused heavily on ensuring that Article 18 of the United Nations' Universal Declaration of Human Rights be upheld for the rights of Wiccans.[72] By the 1970s there was an expanding association, the Pagan Movement of Britain and Ireland, and today several organizations, including The Pagan Federation (PF), The Sub-culture Alternatives Freedom Foundation working toward the same goals and monitoring mass media for inaccurate and disparaging depictions of Pagans. In America, similar groups including the Pagan Educational Network perform the same functions.[73]

In America (the home of the Woodstock Rock festival), a major impetus for the formation of integrative Wiccan and Neopagan networking organizations was to facilitate the production of large outdoor festivals. One such group evolved in Chicago, becoming the Midwest Pagan Association, in 1976. By 1980, they had teamed up with another organization, The Covenant of the Goddess; that year they held a Pan Pagan encampment with about 600 participants. By the mid-eighties, there were about fifty regional festivals. By 1995, Adler states that the United States had nearly 350 well-advertised, public Neopagan encampments – so many that the Covenant of the Goddess was publishing an annual listing.[74] Open to the general public, festivals attract many who come for the fun and wind up adopting the beliefs; they also spread beliefs and practices from one local group to another. As Adler says, 'festivals created a national Pagan community, a body of nationally shared chants, dances, stories, and ritual techniques'.[75] Wicca and other Neopagan practices were given an additional boost in the United States by the founding of Llewellyn, a publishing house based in Minnesota which expanded by the late 1970s from its initial focus on Gnosticism, Ceremonial Magic, New Age, astrology and general occultism into a lucrative business selling Wiccan texts as well. They also organize and sponsor festivals.[76]

The growth of Wicca has clearly relied upon the printed word from the very beginning. The age of the electronic word expanded growth opportunities for Wicca exponentially, as new 'audience cults' proliferated on the Web. Words such as 'Cyber Pagan' and 'Techno Pagan' have been coined to describe those whose initial, primary, or perhaps only contact with the wider Wiccan and Neopagan communities is through their computers. To many modern Wiccans, the work that goes into magic is similar to executing a project on a computer – it exists only as a form manipulable energy, worked upon by human will, until it becomes reality.[77] Just as paper publications and festivals can spread and unify practice, so too can the Web. By the early 2000s, the most popular Wiccan website was The Witches Voice (www.witchvox.com); it lists tens of thousands of local contacts for covens, festivals, stores, rights advocacy and other Wiccan and Neopagan organizations, as well as providing news and chatting opportunities.[78] The web has also facilitated the expansion of Wiccan charities – a function often seen as essential to governmental recognition as a legally functioning religion. Several websites have grown out of the major US festival-generating, and religious rights organization, Circle.[79]

Out of its humble beginnings (be they in the rural heaths of Britain and Tuscany, or the occult bookshops of London and San Francisco) Wicca has emerged in the early twenty-first century as a growing, rapidly splintering, yet expanding spiritual adaptation to life in the modern, urban, technological, and highly interconnected world. It provides meaning, a sense of hope, a creative outlet, systems of values, personal growth, and religious fellowship for hundreds of thousands. As such it is likely to continue to do so.

Notes

1 Although the terms are often used interchangeably, the author chooses the more specific terms 'Neopagan' and 'Neopaganism' for use throughout this essay. Out of respect for practitioners, I also make the choice of capitalizing it, as one does in the English language with the name of any faith.

2 The author's research on Wicca began as a graduate student in cultural anthropology at the University of Oregon. The study involved both mundane library research, as well as participant/observation – direct involvement and interaction with practicing Wiccans in the Northwestern United States. This included interviews, study with Wiccan teachers, and participation in rituals. My 1989 dissertation, 'Neopagan Witchcraft: Cult in Cultural Context' was passed 'With Distinction' by the University of Oregon Department of Anthropology.

3 Clifford Geertz, "Religion as a Cultural System," *Anthropological Approaches to the Study of Religion*. ASA Monographs, 3 (London: Tavistock, 1966).

4 Use of Wicca to motivate political activism is discussed in the following. Margot Adler, *Drawing Down the Moon: Witches, Druids, Goddess-Worshippers, and other Pagans in America Today*, Revised edition (Boston: Beacon Press, 1986). Zsuzsanna Budapest, *The Feminist Book of Lights and Shadows* (Venice, CA: Luna Publications, 1976). Douglas E. Cowan and David G. Bromley, *Cults and New Religions: A Brief History* (Malden, MA: Blackwell Publishing, 2008). Linda Jencson, "Neopaganism and the Great Mother Goddess: Anthropology as Midwife to a New Religion," *Anthropology Today* 5.2 (1989): 2–4; Tanya Luhrmann, *Persuasions of the Witch's Craft: Ritual Magic in Contemporary England* (Cambridge, MA: Harvard University Press, 1989). Charlene Spretnak, *The Politics of Women's Spirituality* (Garden City, NY: Anchor Press, 1982) A comparative discussion of religious definitions and social organizational types can be found in Pamela A. Morrow, *Magic, Witchcraft and Religion: A Reader in the Anthropology of Religion*, 9th ed. (New York: McGraw Hill, 2013), 1–4. Starhawk, *The Spiral Dance: A Rebirth of the Ancient Religion of the Great Goddess* (San Francisco: Harper & Row, Publishers, 1979).

5 Examples of basic texts descriptive of Wiccan belief include the following. Adler, *Drawing*; Budapest, *Feminis*, Douglas E. Cowan and David G. Bromley, *Cults and New Religions*. Linda Jencson, "Neopaganism and the Great Mother Goddess," 2–4. Tanya Luhrmann, *Persuasions of the Witch's Craft*. Charlene Sprentnak, *The Politics of Women's Spirituality*. Starhawk, *The Spiral Dance*. Pagaism's problems with Christian accusations of Satanism are concisely covered in Graham Harvey, *Contemporary Paganism: Religions of the Earth from Druids and Witches to Heathens and Ecofeminists*, 2nd ed. (Washington Square, NY: New York University Press, 2011), 211–216.

6 Lucy Mair, *Witchcraft* (New York: McGraw-Hill, 1969), 15.

7 Adler, *Drawing*, Revised ed.; Barbara Jane Davy, *Introduction to Pagan Studies* (Lanham, MD: Altamira Press, 2007). Loretta Orion, *Never Again the Burning Times: Paganism Revive* (Prospect Heights, IL: Waveland Press, 1995). Charlene Spretnak, *The Politics of Women's Spirituality*.

8 Mani Navasothy, "Anti-witchcraft Laws of England," *Witchcraft and Magic*, 2011–2015, www.witchcraftandmagic.org/html/anti-witchcraft_laws.html.

9 Michael Howard, *Modern Wicca: A History from Gerald Gardner to the Present* (Woodbury, MN: Llewellyn Publications, 2010); Starhawk, *The Spiral Dance*, 214.

10 Adler, *Drawing*. Bonewits, *Real Magic* (New York: Berkeley Publishing, 1972); Starhawk, *Dreaming the Dark: Magic, Sex and Politics* (Boston: Beacon Press, 1988).

11 Davy, *Introduction to Pagan Studies*.

12 Harvey, *Contemporary Paganism*.

13 Orion, *Never Again the Burning Times*.

14 Davy, *Introduction to Pagan Studies*; Harvey, *Contemporary Paganism*.

15 Adler, *Drawing*, Revised ed., 103–104.

16 Ibid.,

17 Jencson, "Neopaganism and the Great Mother Goddess: Anthropology as Midwife to a New Religion," *Anthropology Today* 5.2 (1989): 2–4.

18 This core belief is expressed in nearly every publication about Wicca, for some examples, refer to: Adler, *Drawing*, Revised ed.; Budapest, *The Feminist*; Gerald Gardner, *The Meaning of Witchcraft* (London: Aquarian Press, 1959).

19 Jencson, unpublished field notes collected in 1983.

20 Orion, *Never Again the Burning Times*, 225. This fear is particularly salient in the United States, where Christian extremist groups focused on the persecution of others, such as the Ku Klux Clan, anti-abortionists, and anti-gay hate groups have actively terrorized innocent citizens throughout the twentieth and into the twenty-firstt centuries.

21 Descriptions of the written spellbooks kept by Wiccans can be found in the following: Adler, *Drawing*, Revised ed.; Budapest, *Feminist*; Gardner, *Meaning*.

22 This process is outlined in: Adler, *Drawing*, Revised ed.; in Jencson, "Neopaganism and the Great Mother Goddess."

23 Marcello Truzzi, "The Occult Revival as Popular Culture: Some Random Observations on the Old and the Nouveau Witch," in *Anthropology of American Life*, ed. Joseph G. Jorgensen and Marcello Truzzi (Englewood Cliffs, NJ: Prentice Hall, 1974), 225–250; Marcello Truzzi, "Towards a Sociology of the Occult: Notes on Modern Witchcraft," in *Religious Movements in Contemporary America*, ed. Irving I. Zaretsky and Mmark P. Leone, 628–645 (Princeton, NJ: Princeton University Press, 1974).

24 Margaret Murray, *The Witch Cult in Western Europe* (Oxford: Oxford University Press, 1921); *The God of the Witches* (London: Sampson Low, Marston & Co, Ltd, 1933).

25 Charles Godfrey Leland, *Aradia, or the Gospel of the Witches* (London: David Nutt, 1899); *Memoirs* (London: William Heinemann, 1893).

26 Murray, *Witch Cult in Western Europe*, and *God of the Witches*.

27 Mircea Eliade, *Occultism, Witchcraft and Cultural Fashion* (Chicago: University of Chicago Press, 1976), 76.

28 Adler, *Drawing*, Revised and Updated ed., 477.

29 Leland, *Aradia*, vi.

30 Ibid., viii.

31 Ibid., 2.

32 Leland's untitled liturgy from *Aradia, 6–7* reads in part:

> When I shall have departed from this world,
> Whenever ye have need of anything,
> Once in the month, and when the moon is full,
> Ye shall assemble in some desert place,
> Or in a forest altogether join,
> To adore the potent spirit of your queen,
> My mother great Diana. She who fain,
> Would learn all sorcery yet has not won,
> Its deepest secrets, them my mother will
> Teach her, in truth all things are yet unknown . . .
> And as assign that ye are truly free,
> Ye shall be naked in your rites, both men
> And women also: this shall last until
> The last of your oppressors shall be dead . . .

Compare with Starhawk's prose poem, the 'Charge of the Goddess' from *The Spiral Dance*, 76, based upon Gardner's writings, which reads in part:

> Whenever you have need of anything, once in the month, and better it be when the moon is full, you shall assemble in some secret place and adore the spirit of Me who is Queen of All the Wise. You shall be free from slavery, and as a sign that you be free you shall be naked in your rites. Sing, feast, dance, make music and love . . .

33 For example, Budapest's work, *The Feminist Book of Lights and Shadows* is entirely Dianic.

34 Douglas E. Cowan and David G. Bromley, *Cults and New Religions*. Barbara Jane Davy, *Introduction to Pagan Studies*. Linda Jencson, "Neopaganism and the Great Mother Goddess."

35 Jack L. Bracelin, *Gerald Gardner: Witch* (London: Octagon Press, 1960).

36 Michael Howard, *Modern Wicca*.

37 Adler *Drawing*, 61–64.

38 Leo Martello, *Witchcraft: The Old Religion*, (Seacaucus, NJ: University Books: 1973).

39 Leland, *Aradia*, 6.

40 Starhawk, *Spiral Dance*, 76.

41 Adler, *Drawing*, Revised and updated edition, 78–80.

42 Adler, *Drawing*, Revised edition, 76.

43 Robert Marshall, "The Dark Legacy of Carlos Castaneda," *Salon*, April 4, 2007, http://salon.com/2007/04/12/castaneda/.

44 Issac Bonewits, *The Druid Chronicles (Evolved)* (Berkeley: Berkeley Drunemeton Press, 1976) and *The Druid's Progress* (New York: P. E. I. Bonewits, 1984).

45 Harvey, *Contemporary Paganism*, 18.

46 Jencson, "Neopaganism and the Great Mother Goddess."

47 John Messenger, personal communication, 1989, described in Linda Jencson, "Neopagan Witchcraft: Cult in Cultural Context" (PhD diss., University of Oregon, 1992).

48 Bracelin, *Gerald Gardner: Witch*.

49 Adler, *Drawing*, Revised and updated ed., 80.

50 Howard, *Modern Wicca*.

51 Gardner, *Witchcraft Today* and *Meaning*.

52 Bracelin, *Gerald Gardner: Witch*; Howard, *Modern Wicca*.

53 Bracelin, *Gerald Gardner: Witch*.

54 Howard, *Modern Wicca*, 70.

55 Ibid.

56 Sex and gender have been important throughout the development of Wicca, at times exhibiting polar opposites from one era or tradition to another. Crowley had a universal reputation as extremely deviant and violent in his sexuality, as well as extremely abusive to women. He described women (including his daughter) as whores. He beat women and girls, held them prisoner, and abandoned more than one in foreign counties without means of support. Many of the women under his influence died young of neglect, drug addiction, hunger, and disease including one of his abandoned daughters according to Bracelin's *Gerald Garnder: Witch*. At least one of Gardner's High Priestesses, Madeline Montalban, spoke of Crowley as a 'fraud and a pervert', Howard, *Modern Wicca*, 69. Allegedly, Crowley told Gardner that he 'had not followed the way of the witches' because he 'refused to be bossed around by any damned woman', Bracelin, *Gerald Gradner: Witch*, 158. It is highly unlikely that such a man contributed to a religion with powerful High Priestesses.

57 Howard, *Modern Wicca*, 121.

58 Adler, *Drawing*, Revised and updated ed., 81.

59 Ibid.

60 Ibid., 97. The Wiccan Rede. www.wiccanrede.dreamhost.com.

61 Jencson, "Neopagan Witchcraft: Cult in Cultural Context" (PhD diss., University of Oregon, 1992).

62 Gerald Gardner, *Witchcraft Today* and *Meaninmg*. Adler, *Drawing* Revised and updated ed., 106.

63 Davy, *Pagan Studies*, 151–152. Harvey, *Contemporary Pagamism*, 43–44.

64 Ibid., 44.

65 Adler, *Drawing*, Revised and updated ed., 119–121.

66 Some of the most influential feminist texts on Wiccan practice include: Adler, *Drawing* Revised edition, Budapest *Feminist*, Charlene Spretnak, *The Politics of Women's Spirituality*, Starhawk, *The Spiral Dance*.

67 Luhrmann, *Persuasions of the Witch's Craft*.

68 Jencson, "Misogynist Trends in Construction of Goddess and Woman," in *Spellbound: Women and Witchcraft in America*, ed. Elizabeth Reis (Wilmington, DE: Scholarly Resources, Inc, 1998), 247–267.

69 Harvey, *Contemporary Paganism*, 83.

70 Adler, *Drawing*, Revised ed., 125–130.

71 Ibid., 123–125.

72 Howard, *Modern Wicca*, 244.

73 Harvey, *Contemporary Paganism*, 215.
74 Adler, *Drawing*, Revised and updated ed., 432.
75 Ibid., 430.
76 Ibid.
77 Jencson, "Neopagan Witchcraft."
78 Howard, *Modern Wicca*.
79 (www.circlesanctuary.org; www.circlesanctuary.org/liberty/pagancharitywork.html) Adler, *Drawing*, Revised ed., 447–452.

Bibliography (selection)

Cowan, Douglas E. and David G. Bromley, *Cults and New Religions: A Brief History*. Malden, MA: Blackwell Publishing, 2008.

Davy, Barbara Jane, *Introduction to Pagan Studies*. Lanham, MD: Altamira Press, 2007.

Harvey, Graham, *Contemporary Paganism: Religions of the Earth From Druids and Witches to Heathens and Ecofeminists*, 2nd ed. Washington Square, NY: New York University Press, 2011.

Howard, Michael, *Modern Wicca: A History From Gerald Gardner to the Present*. Woodbury, MN: Llewellyn Publications, 2009.

Jencson, Linda, "Neopaganism and the Great Mother Goddess: Anthropology as Midwife to a New Religion." *Anthropology Today* 5 (1989): 2–44.

Jencson, Linda. *Neopagan Witchcraft: Cult in Cultural Context*. PhD diss., University of Oregon, 1992.

Moro, Pamela A., *Magic, Witchcraft and Religion: A Reader in the Anthropology of Religion*, 9th ed. New York: McGraw-Hill, 2013.

Sprentnak, Charlene. *The Politics of Women's Spirituality*. Garden City, NY: Anchor Press, 1982.

25

DISCIPLES OF HELL

The history of Satanism

Per Faxneld

Introduction

Satanism. The mere word conjures up all sorts of strange images: human sacrifice, sexual orgies and shadowy conspiracies. Unsurprisingly, as any scholar working on the topic will tell you, the reality of this phenomenon is more prosaic than what is commonly imagined. Certain aspects of it, which we will consider at the end of the chapter, are however almost as bizarre and startling as anything that can be imagined by paranoid Pentecostals or authors of lurid pulp horror. Between here and that point of extreme expressions, however, we first need to visit raucous English rakes, Romantic poets, anarchists, Decadents, a Danish dairy salesman, a supposed lion tamer and lover to Marilyn Monroe, a PSYOPS officer, and other colorful characters.

Defining Satanism

Before we begin our journey through the history of Satanism it is best to specify what the term will be taken to mean in the present context. Satanism is used here as a label in two ways: *sensu stricto* and *sensu lato*. The former variety refers to a system of thought in which Satan is celebrated in a prominent position. Of course, the term Satan is here interchangeable with the Devil, Lucifer and other names that have been commonly used to designate the principle of evil in a Christian context (a figure which most Satanists, however, perceive quite differently, as more or less benevolent or helpful). A "prominent position" signifies that Satan is the only or the foremost among the gods, entities or symbols revered. If this is not the case, the group or individual in question may still hold certain views that constitute a form of Satanism, but their ideology as a whole cannot be defined thus. The term "system" may designate anything from very simple constructs to highly sophisticated doctrines. This might seem a somewhat arbitrary dimension of the definition, but it is necessary in order to be able to exclude, for example, a person who lauds Lucifer in a single poem. Such an act does not make anyone a Satanist in the strict sense, any more than composing a single piece in praise of Christ would make a person a Christian.[1] Satanism *sensu lato*, on the other hand, entails celebrations of the Devil used as a discursive strategy in a fairly demarcated and restricted manner. Examples include socialists employing Lucifer as a symbol of revolution, feminists eulogizing him as an anti-patriarchal figure, and different varieties of purely literary veneration of Satan. These individuals and groups did not construct entire worldviews centered on Satan as the single most prominent symbol, even if they may have made quite prominent use of him. Hence, they are classified as representing Satanism *sensu lato*.

The polyvocality of the devil, and the "Satanists" who were not Satanists

On a popular level, Satan's identity has always been fragmented into local variations. At times, the Satan of European folklore was a beast quite different from the Satan of the Church. Naturally, there were no watertight compartments between the two, and they existed in the same cultural context – partly overlapping, partly in contradiction to one another. Thus, the figure could be simultaneously comical and frightening, for example, and function as a tool for upholding order as well as subverting it. In folklore, most entities are of a more ambivalent nature than the clear-cut good-or-evil division in official Christianity. Hence, Satan could at times be seen as a helpful spirit, whom it was possible for the peasant population to turn to for assistance.[2] A typical situation in which lowborn *women* asked the Devil for help was when they sought to avoid labor pains. God was presumably disinclined to help them with that particular problem since, according to Genesis 3:16, this suffering was meted out by him as a punishment for Eve's transgression in the Garden of Eden.[3]

The official theological stance on Satan remained constant throughout Europe even long after Luther had nailed his 95 theses on the church door in Wittenberg in 1517. The sharpest break in the traditional teachings about Satan came about with the Enlightenment, rather than the Reformation. Even though the reformers removed much in Christianity that they felt did not have a biblical foundation, most of the medieval diabology was, somewhat surprisingly, retained. The writings of Luther and other central figures clearly show how strong the time-honored teachings about the Devil remained.[4] In the generations following Luther's, an influence from the Protestant claims to a direct relationship with God made people gradually (even in Catholicism) start to see Satan increasingly as an *inner* voice tempting the individual. Ultimately, of course, the voice still issued forth from a malevolent external spiritual entity. Nevertheless, the theological psychologization of the Devil influenced portrayals of him in literature. Authors now bestowed an unprecedented psychological depth to the figure of Satan himself. This is reflected in the various versions of the Faust story from the late sixteenth century, where the Evil One often has a pensive, introspective and philosophical disposition.[5] We can also think of Milton's complex portrait of Lucifer in *Paradise Lost* (1667). Even so, Satan had certainly not been reduced to *nothing but* an inner voice or a character in cerebral fiction by this time. He was still very much viewed by most people as an active force in the world.

At an early stage in history, the Christian idea of the Devil gave rise to the notion of wicked people, Satanists, actively worshipping him. Conceptions about Satanists have been present in Western culture practically since the dawn of Christianity. Actual Satanists, in any reasonable sense of the word, have not been around for quite as long.[6] Heretical Christian sects like the Cathars and Bogomils were unjustly persecuted in the Middle Ages as Satanists, and in the early modern era supposed witches were identified as adherents of Satan and punished accordingly. However, the earliest evidence of anything that might even vaguely have resembled true Satanism concerns the disturbing circle of abortionists and poisoners that were involved with certain prominent members of Louis XIV's court in the 1670s. Some of the criminal figures that the Sun King's mistress Madame de Montespan (1640–1707) called upon to help her stay in her royal lover's favor possibly invoked demons during rituals to achieve this goal. Supposedly, this entailed "black masses" (the term is of a later date, and was not used by either the alleged perpetrators, their accusers or the officials in charge of the case) being celebrated by an apostate priest on the naked bodies of women. Possibly, it also involved the sacrifice of new-born children (but no physical evidence of this was found, we should note). On the other hand, there also seems to be a good chance that the investigating police officer, Nicholas de la Reynie, in some way skewed the testimonies to make them fit with his own deeply Catholic mindset. He was maybe in fact dealing with suspects who considered themselves Christians, and commanded demons to do their bidding by binding them in the name of the Lord and His angels. Not even this much is certain. We can be fairly confident, at least, that these were not self-professed Satanists who thought of themselves in such terms.[7]

Moving from France to England, we find the so-called Hell-Fire Club. It was established in the 1750s, and it should immediately be underscored that the melodramatic name of the club was not its self-designation. Rather, it was invented by political enemies of Sir Francis Dashwood (1708–1781), its founder. Ominous tales of demon worship in this group have circulated for centuries, but in reality it was little more than a frivolous drinking club for the upper class. At most, the occasional toast to the Devil – in utter jest – may have been said. The sporadic participation by prominent visitors like Benjamin Franklin in the drinking bouts has even so kept interest in the old rumors alive, since they are convenient additions to various conspiracy theories.[8]

Apostles of darkness: how the romantics sowed the seeds of Satanism

On closer inspection, then, none of the people mentioned earlier seem actually to have been Satanists. While *accusations* of Satanism have been rife throughout much of the Christian era, an enduring and public tradition of veritable practiced Satanism was in fact not instated until 1966, with the founding of the Church of Satan in San Francisco. Yet, there were people who nourished an intense sympathy for the Devil long before. Let us consider some of the earliest examples, which date from the late eighteenth century.

In spite of the enlightenment critique of religion, a majority of people still believed in God – and the Devil – at this time. Certain progressive poets in England therefore took it upon themselves to fight what they perceived to be naïve superstition that stood in the way of social reform. This description best suits Percy Bysshe Shelley (1792–1822), but to an extent also William Blake (1757–1827) and Lord Byron (1788–1824). What all three have in common is that they used a positive portrayal of Satan as a tool of cultural critique, and a means to break the hegemony of orthodox varieties of Christianity.[9] The starting point was the poets' admiration of the heroic individualist Satan they discerned in John Milton's portrayal of the figure in *Paradise Lost* (1667). Milton himself almost certainly had not at all intended his Lucifer to be interpreted in such a fashion, but this was no obstacle for the Romantics.[10]

Their sympathy for the Devil led to Robert Southey (1774–1843) famously describing Byron and Shelley as representatives of a "Satanic school" in poetry.[11] In spite of the heated debate inspired by the Romantic celebration of Satan, the Luciferian leanings of the radical authors in question seldom extended beyond occasional outbursts in a text or two, even if the pro-Satanic ideas they propagated hereby came to be established as a specific language of cultural protest that would be enduring.

Blake was a mystic and visionary, who (probably) based several of his startling works of visual art and cryptic prose and poetry on actual visionary experiences. In some of his creations Satan is a sort of energizing cosmic rebel, who represents an expansive force just as necessary as the limiting and conserving God. There is also a political dimension to the works, which reflects the revolutionary circles their creator moved in. Often, Blake seems inimical towards God, the great forbidder and provider of moral codes. Ultimately, however, his utopian vision centered on a union of the cosmic opposites, as alluded to in the title of his perhaps most well-known text: *The Marriage of Heaven and Hell* (1790– 1793).[12]

Byron, on the other hand, was no mystic, but an ironic provocateur. This also shows clearly in his portrayals of Satan. The perhaps most subversive of them are the long philosophical dialogues between Lucifer and Cain (in the play *Cain*, 1821). The Devil here appears as a champion of free will and independent thinking. Still, the portrait is hardly completely flattering, and many of the Dark Lord's negative traits are also retained. In certain other texts by Byron, God is held up as a sadistic tyrant. The tale of his decision to call down the great Flood upon mankind (Genesis 6–9) is retold from this angle in Byron's *Heaven and Earth* (1821). Hereby, God's opponents – Satan and fallen angels – appear as a more appealing, if not unproblematic, alternative.[13]

Shelley was far more politically radical than Byron. He propagated vegetarianism, feminism, free love and non-violence as a method of protest.[14] Furthermore, he was less ambiguous in his Satanism than his friend Byron. He would at times wrap it in several layers of allegory, but these allegories tended to be so translucent that it would have been obvious to most members of the public that they were reading a paean to Satan. A case in point is *The Revolt of Islam* (1817, also known as *Laon and Cythna*). Shelley here explains that the serpent (Satan) has been wrongly identified as the principle of evil. God, the supposedly good entity, is by contrast in fact a villain and the source of human suffering.[15] The serpent/Satan is moreover connected in this text with human rebels against earthly oppression. In the central narrative of the long poem, a woman called Cythna is the leader of a rebellion against tyranny and patriarchal religion – the latter here symbolized by Islam. Cythna defies conventional gender roles when she rides out to battle wielding a sword, and stresses that in a true revolution woman's liberation must be a key feature. Otherwise, mankind only achieves a partial freedom.[16]

The strongly negative image of Muslim culture in *The Revolt of Islam* – complete with a lustful sultan who enslaves girls in his harem – ties in with a number of islamophobic stereotypes current at the time. Islam, however, is hardly Shelley's true target. Rather, he uses it as a covert way of describing how hostile to women he felt that *Christianity* is.[17] Satan's role is similarly allegorical. The point, then, is not that Shelley wishes to celebrate Satan, even if this sublime figure appeals to him. His real goal is to undermine the power of Christianity in society. He seems to have believed this could be accomplished by deconstructing Christian myths and reversing the sympathies. Shelley's heroine Cythna speaks of attempting a disenchantment, through which mankind would become free from the religious myths constructed to keep her in check and uphold the status quo. The same vision of disenchantment was held by the poet.[18] Naturally, this meant that his glorification of Satan ought not be understood as an expression of real (inverted) religious sympathy. After all, Shelley had been expelled from Oxford University because of his pamphlet *The Necessity of Atheism* (1811). We find a similar Satanic atheist attitude a century later, in the work of the Italian Nobel Prize laureate (in 1906) Giosuè Carducci (1835–1907), who composed the poem "A Satana" (1865). In this provocative piece, the Devil symbolizes the Enlightenment, technology and human dignity – in short, all that Carducci opined that the Catholic Church stood in the way of in his country.[19]

The first Satanist? Stanislaw Przybyszewski's social darwinist diabology

Poets like Charles Baudelaire (1821–1867) and visual artists like Félicien Rops (1833–1898) emphasized Satan's connection to sensuality and carnal pleasures, making the figure an important image in some forms of resistance to Christian moralism and asceticism. Baudelaire's blasphemous 1857 poem "Les Litanies de Satan" set the standard for such transgressive Decadent outbursts, even if the poet himself, ever the repentant Catholic, never made any real commitment to being of the Devil's party.[20] The foremost portrayer of Satanism in prose fiction in late nineteenth-century Europe was Joris-Karl Huysmans (1848–1907), who claimed to base his novel *Là-bas* ("Down There", 1891) on his own experiences in Parisian circles of Devil-worshippers. This was almost certainly not true, but the claims helped make the book a bestseller. Huysmans, a troubled aesthete who longed to transcend the mercantilism and vulgarity of his era, eventually abandoned his fascination with the occult to return to the comforting arms of Mother Church.[21]

None of the Romantics and hardly any of the Decadents, then, were very consistent (symbolic) Satanists, not even *sensu lato*. The first real example of such a figure is the Polish Decadent Stanislaw Przybyszewski (1868–1927). He made Lucifer the focus of a whole system of thought that he adhered to for a long time, and he openly called himself a Satanist. A central figure in the bohemian milieu of 1890s Berlin, Przybyszewski befriended greats like Edvard Munch, Richard Dehmel and August Strindberg.[22] His own prose foreshadowed Expressionism in its focus on anguished inner states and subjective nightmarish visions of urban decay and religious doubt. Both the works of fiction and the essays that flowed from his pen expressed an explicitly Satanic worldview, where Satan became the paragon of liberty, strength and creativity. This also entailed contempt for the "herd", the weaklings who blindly obeyed God and his ministers. God, we are told in texts like *Die Synagoge des Satan* (1897), is a friend to the unfit, the cripple and the castrated. This, the Pole assures us, is not commendable, but goes to show that God wants to hinder evolution and the natural order.[23]

Evolution, to Przybyszewski's mind, was the ultimate value in the cosmos. He fancied himself part of an aristocracy of intelligence and artistic talent, far above the baseness of common men. Unsurprisingly, Przybyszewski was one of Nietzsche's first champions, even if the pessimism of Schopenhauer perhaps influenced him more.

His thinking is gloomy, and he revels in the pain of being that he deems necessary for artistic creativity. Suffering of the soul, in this sense, is good – but still a severe torment to endure.[24] This is but one of numerous semantic inversions Przybyszewski indulges in: what others call decadence or degeneration represents a new stage in the development of the human race (i.e., decadence is evolution), the deeds of evil femmes fatales are a prerequisite for our continued evolution (i.e., wicked women are "good"), Satan is a savior for the elect (i.e., Satan is to be considered "god"), and so on.[25] Even if Przybyszewski did not reject occult phenomena (preferring to describe them as fully "natural" wonders that science would be able to comprehend, but only in the future) his embrace of Satan was not really religious, but symbolic. It had no ritualistic dimension, and is best understood as an example of the Decadent philosophy of inversion at its most extreme. Many others were deeply marked by Przybyszewski's Satanic social Darwinist ideas, and for a period he was a key player in early Modernist circles.[26] His legacy is today remembered in his native Poland, and to an extent in Germany. It has also begun to attract attention from Satanists who seek the historical roots of their beliefs.

Red devils: socialist satanism in the nineteenth century

Przybyszewski's Satanism, as we have seen, diverged from the egalitarian ideals the figure was employed to embody in the writings of Romantics like Shelley. The Pole's interpretation was more or less an anomaly at the time, however. Most people who used Satan as a positive symbol primarily made him a freer of the oppressed, and an enemy of the hegemonic power structures. This is most clear in the case of socialist Satanism. Quite a few important socialists were inspired by the Romantic embrace of Lucifer. One of the most influential anarchists, Mikhail Bakunin (1814–1876), held up Satan as the archetypical rebel, and hence a role model for man, in his book *Dieu et l'état* ("God and the State", posthumously published in 1882). As in the case of Shelley and others, this should not be understood as a literal veneration of the Devil as an actually existing entity or spirit. In the same book, the staunch atheist Bakunin warns of the constant danger of slipping back into the abyss of religious superstition. Even so, his ardor is great when he enthusiastically hymns Satan as the helper of mankind. "Satan, the eternal rebel, the first freethinker and the liberator of worlds", Bakunin calls him.[27]

Other pivotal anarchist thinkers, like William Godwin (1756–1836) and Pierre-Joseph Proudhon (1809–1865), wrote in similarly glowing terms of Satan. This symbolism spread quickly among European reds, not only anarchists but also socialists of other types. For example, the turn-of-the-century Swedish social democrats were enough fond of it to start a magazine with the name *Lucifer,* where a number of inflammatory pieces of explicit socialist Satanism were published. The Church was a major enemy of socialism in Sweden (and elsewhere), and it is against this background we should understand such aggressive allegorical attacks on Christianity.[28]

It was for partly similar reasons that several feminists around this time used a pro-Satanic symbolism. In their opinion, Christianity played a pivotal role in keeping women down. Some feminists therefore chose to portray a feminized Satan as an entity on the side of women in the struggle against the patriarchal God and his male priests. Like Shelley's Cythna, they hereby hoped to destabilize the truth claims of the old myths – including their traditional implications for gender hierarchies. In particular, feminists attacked the tale of Eve's Satanically assisted transgression in Genesis 3. In their retellings of the narrative, they made a heroine of the first woman by lauding her curiosity, free thinking and courage to go against God.[29]

Mephistopheles and the magicians: the rise of esoteric Satanism

Thus far, the only Satanist we have encountered that had any ideas even approaching positive magico-religious conceptions of Satan is Przybyszewski. In the context of Western esotericism, one of the first to unequivocally praise Satan was Helena Petrovna Blavatsky (1831–1891), chief ideologist of the Theosophical Society. Founded in 1875, this organization was the most important in the realm of alternative spirituality in its time. At its height of success, it had over 200 local sections worldwide, and many of the period's central intellectuals and artists were deeply influenced by its teachings. Especially avant-garde painters like Mondrian, Kandinsky and Klee drew on Theosophy for creative inspiration and spiritual guidance. A basic notion in its cosmology is that all religions stem from the same esoteric source, but have been misinterpreted by exoteric priesthoods. The universe and man are constantly evolving, moving towards spiritual perfection. In her huge two-volume work *The Secret Doctrine* (1888), Blavatsky explains that the instigator of mankind's evolution is Lucifer. He made sure that we atethe forbidden fruit in the Garden of Eden. This made us free beings, and we escaped from God's totalitarian rule. Satan does not, however, occupy a central enough position in Blavatsky's system for it to be labeled a form of Satanism as a whole.[30]

Even more subdued were the Satanic tendencies in the writings of one of her sources of inspiration, the French occultist Éliphas Lévi (1810–1875). He had once started to study to become a priest, and retained a strong sense of loyalty to the Catholic Church in spite of all his idiosyncratic ideas and conflicts with the ecclesiastical authorities. In some of his works, Lucifer is held up as a neutral force permeating the cosmos, which can be employed for benevolent ends. Yet, he was adamant that God was ultimately the only entity one should venerate, and that Satan did not possess a true, conscious existence.[31] Neither Blavatsky nor Lévi, then, were Satanists *sensu stricto*, especially not the French magus. Notorious British magician, mountain climber and poet (and many other things) Aleister Crowley (1875–1947) is occasionally advanced as an early example of a Satanist. He courted controversy, and did admittedly enjoy designating himself the Beast 666. Satan, however, is not a conspicuous presence in his esoteric writings, which center much more on Egyptian mythology.[32]

The first person to actually build an entire esoteric system, albeit a rather miniscule one, around Satan was the obscure Danish occultist Ben Kadosh (Carl William Hansen, 1872–1936). In 1906, he published a Luciferian pamphlet presenting a bizarre mixture of Masonic mythology, odds and ends from conspiracy theories, and various other strands of high and low esoterica. Claiming to be in direct contact with the Powers of Darkness, Kadosh urged those with similar leanings to get in touch with him at his home address. His Satanic circle, if it was even realized in the manner he intended, was as tiny as the volume of his writings. We know that he attracted at least a handful of acolytes, but exactly what they were up to is less well-documented.

Kadosh himself, who made his living as a dairy salesman, was mostly occupied with obtaining a staggering amount of Masonic degrees and patents, and his (for the period) uniquely Satano-centric system did not spread in the grand fashion he had envisioned. He remained a somewhat tragic local oddball, who became famous only indirectly through portraits of him in several well-regarded novels by different Danish authors.[33]

The German 1920s' esoteric order Fraternitas Saturni was considerably more populous than Kadosh's circle. It viewed Satan as an initiator and conducted Luciferian masses, but whether these features were sufficiently pronounced to merit a designation of the entire group as Satanic is not self-evident.[34] The "Satanic" temple (this was a term she herself used) briefly operated by Maria de Naglowska in 1930s Paris presents similar problems. Its aim was an integration of Satan and God, and ultimately God seems to have been more important to Naglowska.[35] Naglowska's importance lies in her being the first to hold rituals open to the public, which were called Satanic by the congregation itself.

None of these groups and individuals founded lasting Satanic traditions. Fraternitas Saturni still exists, but seems to have toned down the Satanic content almost entirely. This applies even more to the Theosophical Society. A small Luciferian organization in Scandinavia today draws on Kadosh's ideas, but this is a revival rather than a direct continuation.[36] To summarize the history of Satanism thus far, it probably did not exist as a religious practice or coherent philosophical system any earlier than around the year 1900, when figures like Przybyszewski and Kadosh pioneered such ideas. But as a more or less fixed and distinct strategy for cultural critique – a colorful form of drastic counter-discourse organized around Satan as the root metaphor, and utilized by socialists, radical individualists, feminists and others – it has been around for at least twice as long.

The dark side of the age of aquarius: counter-culture and the Church of Satan

After World War II, there was a brief hiatus in Satanist activity. The motif was no longer fashionable in literature, and many of the old esoteric orders had disbanded. The occult was not, to use the lingo of the time, "hip" any more. But this would soon change. In 1968, the Rolling Stones sang of "Sympathy for the Devil", and one of the biggest hits in cinemas was Roman Polanski's adaptation of Ira Levin's 1967 novel *Rosemary's Baby*. This tale ends with a gathering of Satanists proclaiming it is "the year one", the dawn of a new Satanic era. It must certainly have seemed that way to many people. 1969 saw the release of the ominous (but hardly pro-Satanic) eponymous debut album by Black Sabbath. More obscure bands like Black Widow and Coven also unleashed albums (in 1970 and 1969, respectively) with lyrics about diabolical rites and glamorous witches. All this was part of a shadowy underbelly of the hippie movement and the nascent new age milieu.[37]

The allure such themes apparently held for many was what made an editor at Avon Books (a division of the Hearst Corporation) suggest to a locally semi-famous eccentric in San Francisco, one Anton Szandor LaVey (1937–1997, born Howard Stanton Levy), that he write a Satanic Bible. The editor felt sure such a book would earn a significant sum of money. LaVey certainly had some sort of qualifications for this. He was well-read in esoteric matters. And more importantly: since the 1960s, he had regularly held lectures on the occult to a select group of (paying) participants, including anthropologist (and later neo-shaman) Michael Harner and several established horror writers. From the lectures and discussions in this informal group grew something vaguely resembling a philosophical system, which used Satan as a metaphor of certain desirable characteristics. Literal belief in Satan as a spirit did not feature. LaVey himself later described his ideology as "secular Satanism". In 1966, LaVey shaved his head and grew a beard and moustache in the style of Ming the Merciless (of Flash Gordon fame). Together with his partner Diane Hegarty he produced a series of small mimeographed sheets presenting his Satanic philosophy, as he had settled on designating it.[38] 1967 was an eventful year for the would-be Satanic leader, as he conducted a Satanic wedding ceremony, a baptism (of his daughter Zeena) and a funeral (a member of the group who had died). Even if these spectacular attention-seeking rituals (to which the press was invited) bestowed a limited but global fame to LaVey, the Church of Satan (CoS), as it was now called, remained a local phenomenon at this point.[39]

When approached by the editor at Avon, LaVey – again with some help from Diane – cobbled together a provocative and entertaining delineation of his atheist Satanic philosophy. Doing this, they borrowed quite freely (some would say plagiarized) from nineteenth-century social Darwinist Ragnar Redbeard, and also drew on the fiercely pro-capitalist philosophy of Ayn Rand. As can be discerned from this, LaVey's Satanism propagated social stratification, elitism and individualism. In a way, this was not very far removed from generally held American values – a fact the Satanic high priest was keen to emphasize. His teaching, however, also had a strongly epicurean orientation, with LaVey underscoring that we should take what pleasure we can here and now, since no Heaven (or Hell) awaits us in an afterlife. This aspect was certainly less in synch with mainstream Americanism, at least the forms of it that were socially acceptable to profess. In reality, the pleasure-oriented mindset was hardly that much of an aberration.[40] Combining it with the allure of the occult certainly struck a chord with quite a few people, and the Church of Satan started growing rapidly. It is open to speculation how many of the members were truly dedicated to LaVey's tenets. Some probably merely felt it would be a chic thing to be able to brandish the fiery-red membership card at cocktail parties, as a sign of transgressive coolness. A number of local so-called "grottos" were now set up, and the Church soon had members all over the world. Eventually, this form of organization proved difficult to administrate, and it was abandoned in favor of a more loose structure.[41]

Part of LaVey's genius was his skill when it came to generating publicity and reinventing himself. According to the official biography, LaVey grew up with a gypsy grandmother telling him tales of vampires and demons. As an adolescent, he travelled with an uncle to allies-occupied Europe, and attended a private screening of footage documenting secret occult rituals of the Nazi elite. He later worked at carnivals and strip joints as an organist, and travelled with a circus as lion tamer. During this period, he had a relationship with then-unknown Marilyn Monroe. Working the carnival circuit, LaVey provided the background music for both striptease shows on Saturdays and Evangelical services on Sundays. He would then see the same men that had lusted after the naked women the night before sit in the pews the day after asking forgiveness for their sins. This made him draw the conclusion that Christianity functioned as a hypocritical suppression of our true desires. Other jobs included police photographer and oboist with the Ballet Orchestra of San Francisco. He also studied criminology at college, and later acted as occult advisor to Polanski during the filming of *Rosemary's Baby*. In the scene where Rosemary is raped by Satan, LaVey played the fiend, wearing a rubber suit. Perhaps unsurprisingly, critical examinations of these stories have fairly conclusively proved them all to be inventions. This is somewhat beside the point, though, as "fake it till you make it" and a carny hustler mentality is very much part of the CoS ethos. LaVey *was* spectacular in a sense, because he could make people believe he was. He evidently had enough charisma to attract celebrities like Jayne Mansfield and Sammy Davies Jr. to his church.[42]

In many respects, LaVey stands in the tradition of Decadent dandies like Baudelaire and Rops, who were also masters of self-mythologization. His celebration of the eccentric, the unique and the darkly erotic fits quite well with such predecessors. A major difference, however, is that LaVey is, as he was once described "a junkyard philosopher".[43] That is, his aesthetic is partly far removed from the high art avantgarde snobbism of the European Decadents, as it valorizes elements of American pop culture, especially "forgotten" and "camp" artifacts.[44] His writing style reflects this double nature, mixing bombastic condemnations of God, worthy of a Parisian absinthe-sipping Decadent, with slang-filled street-smart paeans to dirty knickers and carny showmanship. Unlike many earlier Satanists, LaVey has a sense of humor and often uses jokes to make his point.

While LaVey was more or less an atheist, he still believed in the efficacy of magic.[45] This can be understood in terms of psychological self-help, or in accordance with more classical conceptions of sorcery.[46] Perhaps half-jokingly, LaVey enjoyed telling the story of how his acolyte Jayne Mansfield was decapitated in a car crash after he had accidentally clipped off her head in a photo while cutting articles from a newspaper.[47]

Where does Satan come into all this, then? To LaVey, Satan is a symbol of the natural urges in man that have been suppressed by the collectivist "slave morality" of Christianity (to speak with Nietzsche). Satan also represents the individual him- or herself, and symbolically worshipping Satan thus equals self-adoration.[48] There are additional ambiguous phrasings in *The Satanic Bible* about the Devil as a dark force in nature, but as a whole LaVey's Satanism is quite firmly atheist.[49] In a sense, the Church of Satan can be considered fellow travelers with the international humanist movement. So, the question remains. *Why Satan?* An important reason why the Devil is chosen as the symbol of LaVey's church is, as he explains, that this is the central figure of opposition to Christian morality. Besides, being shocking and scary are obviously useful for promotional purposes. Moreover, we need "ceremony and ritual, fantasy and enchantment".[50] Hence, Satanism.

In the desert of Set: Satanism in the shadow of the pyramids, and diabolical pluralism

Not all members of the Church of Satan were fully content with this worldly form of Satanism. Some longed for a more "spiritual", theistic alternative. Perhaps because of this, and perhaps due to LaVey's decision to start selling initiatory degrees in the Church, a group of members, led by the top official Michael Aquino (1946–), broke off in 1975 and started an organization of their own: the Temple of Set (ToS). Aquino, unlike LaVey, has a colorful background that is actually true. He is a former green beret, served as a PSYOPS officer in Vietnam, and later alternated between a successful academic career in political science and working for the military in various capacities. After his break with LaVey, Aquino purportedly channeled *The Book of Coming Forth by Night*, straight from Satan himself. Here, the Prince of Darkness declares that he no longer wishes to be called Satan, but prefers the name of his earliest manifestation among humans, the Egyptian god Set.[51]

From this text grew the Egypto-centric theistic system of the Temple of Set. The ultimate goal in this order is self-deification in a literal sense, where one can live on after the death of the physical body and attain miraculous powers. Set is seen as a benevolent "older brother" who can aid in this process, and whom the Setian sorcerer (or sorceress) can communicate with directly. The Temple of Set as such has seldom had more than a few hundred members at a given time, but this new form of Satanism became influential in a much wider esoteric milieu.[52] It is sometimes claimed that the Temple of Set should no longer be defined as Satanists, due to their strong Egyptian focus and distancing from the term Satanism.[53] Yet, they still employ the inverted pentagram as their main symbol, and Set remains firmly identified with the Devil. It therefore seems fairly reasonable to count them as Satanists, albeit with certain caveats.

Anton LaVey left school in his teens. Michael Aquino and several of his cohorts hold Ph.D.'s.[54] This is naturally reflected in their respective teachings. The CoS constructs itself as a sort of "Devil's carnival", while the ToS prefers to think of itself as a continuation of Plato's academy. This can be seen very clearly when one compares their respective websites. The CoS site displays cartoonish devils in garish colors, alongside buxom demon women. The ToS site features images of Greek temples, and voluminous texts filled with footnotes and scholarly references.[55]

In the wake of the Temple of Set there followed other theistic Satanists. Today, there exists a quite dynamic set of such groups, especially in the United States. Among the more prominent figures we find for example Venus Satanas, well-known for her YouTube broadcasts, and Diane Vera. The latter emphasizes Satan as an egalitarian freedom fighter, much like Romantics and socialists did in the nineteenth century.[56] Venus Satanas and Diane Vera share a pluralistic vision of the Satanic milieu, where atheist and theistic Satanists should respectfully acknowledge one another as branches of the same tree (this also fits well with the pluralism of accepting multiple princes of darkness, as the ToS does). The CoS, on the other hand, is severe in its condemnations of anything existing outside their own fold as "heretical" pseudo-Satanism.[57]

In the 1980s, musicians from the noise and industrial scenes were attracted to the CoS. Figures like Boyd Rice and Nikolas Schreck goaded the establishment by combining Nazi symbols with Satanism in their avant-garde projects. In this context, it was not always clear where to draw the line between irony, iconoclasm taken to its extreme and actual fascist sympathies of some bizarre variety.[58] The High Priest himself kept a fairly low profile, but emerged to mass media prominence again in the 1990s. Due partly to the rise of the black metal scene (see the next section), Satanism was experiencing a new peak at this time. After LaVey's death in 1997, his partner (and mother of his only son) Blanche Barton took over the role as leader. In 2001, she handed this responsibility over to Peter H. Gilmore, whose period in office has seen a particular emphasis on LaVey's atheist ideas.[59] This may have something to do with a wish to more clearly demarcate the boundaries towards the theistic Satanists that are – as mentioned – becoming a more vocal group with the help of the internet.

The ToS has had a succession of leaders through the years, with Aquino returning as high priest a couple of times but mostly leaving this responsibility to others. This has led to the ToS being far less intimately bound up with a personality cult than what is the case in the CoS, where there is a strong tendency among members to mimic LaVey's personal aesthetics and appearance. This might seem paradoxical given the CoS focus on individualism, but on the other hand the group could also be seen as simply a club for individualists that share certain quite specific tastes and preferences.

Violent worship: Satanic crime, terrorism and rock concerts as rituals

The major Satanic organizations have a zero-tolerance attitude towards criminality, and the Church of Satan has even made a point of regularly cooperating with police and authorities. Most organized Satanists are accordingly law-abiding individuals, who may have an idiosyncratic aesthetic taste and a penchant for provocation but can hardly be deemed dangerous. Yet there are also exceptions to this rule, on the extreme outer fringes of the milieu. In the UK, the media have reported quite extensively on one David Myatt, who has held prominent positions in Satanic, neo-Nazi and Muslim jihadist circles. Ever since the 1960s he has been one of the leading intellectuals among British national socialists. He was allegedly the mentor of notorious Combat 18 nail bomber David Copeland, whose 1999 bombing campaign resulted in three deaths and numerous serious injuries. Myatt himself had by now converted to Islam, and became somewhat influential among radical Muslims. For example, he spoke in extremist mosques and wrote an essay defending suicide bombings, which was displayed on Hamas' website for several years. It has been suggested that his Nazism and militant Islamism are both only tools in a (literally) Satanic scheme, which aims to bring down the current order. Danish scholar Jacob Senholt has convincingly demonstrated that Myatt – though he himself denies it – is the man behind the Order of the Nine Angles (ONA), a sinister theistic Satanist group with roots that may stretch as far back as the 1960s. Hiding behind a plethora of different identities, Myatt has been the chief ideologue of this secretive order all along. Using extreme political groups to further the apocalyptic goals of the order is fully congruent with tactics suggested in various ONA documents. There have probably never been more than a handful of members in the ONA, but, as Senholt points out, this is no reason not to be wary of extremists of this type, since they may have an unexpectedly great and dangerous indirect impact.[60]

An enthusiasm for all types of extremism links the ONA with the subculture and musical genre known as black metal. In its initial stages, the genre was all about spectacle and image. However, as the 1990s began, a small clique of musicians in Scandinavia decided they wanted to practice what their predecessors had only sung about. Black metal, they laid down, should be about actually worshipping death, darkness and the Devil, not just play-acting. Borrowing a line from Milton's Satan, we can say that these individuals cried out "Evil, be thou my good".[61] What the psychological mechanisms behind such a decision were, we can only speculate about. The radicalization of this subculture soon had tangibly tragic consequences. A great number of churches were burned down by Satanists and affiliated figures in Norway, Sweden and Finland. Even worse, at least three murders were committed by young men belonging to this milieu. One could question whether these deeds were direct results of the ideologies propounded in the black metal scene. The perpetrators may have been anti-social or pathological individuals who were drawn to black metal because it reflected their own already twisted mental state, rather than well-adjusted persons being warped by the influence of an extreme music subculture. Similar questions can be asked about Jihadist terrorists or racist terrorists like Anders Behring Breivik as well. Yet, it would seem quite probable that even if some of the Satanic church burners and murderers were dysfunctional to begin with, the influence of black metal's celebration of misanthropy, violence and extremism would have made things worse and may have pushed some of them over the edge. To a degree, there are here parallels to the processes of radicalization that have been delineated by scholars of violent Islamist extremism.[62] It would furthermore be fair to describe church burnings as acts of terrorism, as they were ideologically motivated acts of destruction aimed at symbolic targets representing an opposing creed. The rationale may not always have been carefully thought-through, but that surely equally applies to many other acts that are commonly labeled terrorism.

Alongside these dark deeds, black metal was, and remains, an artistically interesting and often quite innovative genre. Today, there are many thousands (sic!) of artists producing such music across the world.[63] Some bands have won prestigious music awards, and the more commercially oriented artists sell huge amounts of records. At present, black metal straddles the fence between mainstream semi-acceptance (at least in Scandinavia, the major newspapers regularly feature appreciative reviews of such records and concerts) and anti-social Satanic activism. This is often an uneasy balancing act, as the musicians struggle to maintain underground credibility by appearing truly dangerous and simultaneously want to avoid being marginalized from various lucrative contexts.[64] Some, of course, care little for making money (believe it or not) and retain a hardline theistic Satanist worldview. Classic 1990s black metal Satanism views the Devil as an evil entity existing outside of man, who the Satanist bows down to. Spreading misery and suffering pleases Satan, and black metal is to be a tool in this endeavor. Rock concerts, according to this view, are rituals celebrating Satan.[65] Here, the more "orthodox" Satanic musicians and fans are close to the paranoid fantasies of Evangelicals concerning the dangers of rock music. Indeed, Christian conspiracy theories (alongside horror fiction) may have been a source of inspiration in the first place for the guitar-wielding worshippers of darkness.

Much, if not most, black metal Satanism is quite primitive (often intentionally so) and is hardly built on serious theological (diabological) reflection. During the 2000s, this has partly changed, and a more intellectual strain of bands has emerged. In the mid-1990s, on the other hand, this was not the case, and some figures in Sweden's scene were frustrated by it. They were thus party to the formation of an extreme order, which combined black metal's unflinching devotion to the sinister with more classic esoteric practices. The name of this group was the Misanthropic Lucifer Order, later the Temple of the Black Light (TotBL). It would be incorrect to reduce the TotBL to a by-product of the black metal scene, but many of its members at first came from this background. In terms of cosmology, the TotBL are a neo-Gnostic group, and they perceive themselves as struggling against an oppressive demiurge that has imprisoned them (the "fireborn" divine spirits) in flesh and an illusory physical world. The leading members of the order committed a murder in 1997, for which they were subsequently jailed. One of them was a successful musician, who resumed his artistic career after being released from prison in 2004. In 2006, he committed ritual suicide.[66] The TotBL remains active and publishes texts that have had a considerable impact in the international theistic Satanic milieu. Their radical brand of Satanism is something of an anomaly and should – along with the teachings of the ONA – be understood as the furthermost extreme in an already controversial and antinomian religious current.

Notes

1 I first advanced this more narrow definition in Per Faxneld, *Mörkrets apostlar: Satanism i äldre tid* (Sundbyberg: Ouroboros, 2006), xiv–xv. For more on the discussion concerning defintions of Satanism, see e.g., Jesper Aa. Petersen, "Introduction: Embracing Satan," in *Contemporary Religious Satanism: A Critical Anthology*, ed. Jesper Aa. Petersen (Burlington, VT: Ashgate, 2009), 7–10; Ruben van Luijk, *Satan Rehabilitated? A Study into Satanism During the Nineteenth Century* (PhD diss., Tilburg University, 2013), 7–12; Mikael Häll, "It is Better to Believe in the Devil: Conceptions of Satanists and Sympathies for the Devil in Early Modern Sweden," in *The Devil's Party: Satanism in Modernity*, ed. Per Faxneld and Jesper Aa. Petersen (Oxford: Oxford University Press, 2012), 23–26.

2 Ulrika Wolf-Knuts, *Människan och djävulen: En studie kring form, motiv och funktion i folklig tradition* (Åbo: Åbo Akademis Förlag, 1991), 286–287; Jan Wall, "Wilt tu nu falla nedh och tilbedhia migh: Folkets tro och kyrkans lära om djävulen," in *Djävulen: Seminarium den 13 november 1990*, ed. Ulrika Wolf-Knuts (Åbo: Folkloristiska institutionen, 1992), 32.

3 On this, see Per Faxneld, *Satanic Feminism: Lucifer as the Liberator of Woman* (Stockholm: Molin & Sorgenfrei, 2014), 100–101. For some intriguing early-modern Swedish examples of folk magic that appears to almost have crossed the border into Satanism *sensu stricto*, see Häll, "It is Better to Believe in the Devil," 29–39.

4 Jeffrey Burton Russell, *Mephistopheles: the Devil in the Modern World* (Ithaca: Cornell University Press, 1986), 26, 30, 53–54.

5 Darren Oldridge, *The Devil: A Very Short Introduction* (Oxford: Oxford University Press, 2012), 35.

6 For a fairly complete survey of Satanism – and ideas about Satanism – prior to 1966, see Faxneld, *Mörkrets apostlar*. A benchmark-setting recent study of nineteenth-century (literary) Satanism and conspiracy theories concerning Devil worship is van Luijk, *Satan rehabilitated?*, which partly overlaps with Faxneld, *Satanic Feminism*. The two most important older studies of the topic are Joachim Schmidt, *Satanismus: Mythos und Wirklichkeit* (Marburg: Diagonal Verlag, 1992) and Massimo Introvigne, *Enquête sur le satanisme* (Paris: Éditions Dervy, 1994/1997). For an exhaustive overview of research on contemporary religious Satanism, see Jesper Aa. Petersen, "Between Darwin and the Devil: Modern Satanism as Discourse, Milieu, and Self" (PhD diss,, Norwegian University of Science and Technology, 2011), 23–32.

7 van Luijk, *Satan Rehabilitated?*, 58–69. For full accounts of the case, see Lynn Wood Mollenauer, *Strange Revelations: Magic, Poison, and Sacrilege in Louis XIV's France* (University Park, PA: Penn State University Press, 2007); Anne Somerset, *The Affair of the Poisons: Murder, Infanticide and Satanism at the Court of Louis XIV* (London: Weidenfeld & Nicholson, 2003).

8 Evelyn Lord, *The Hell-fire Clubs: Sex, Satanism and Secret Societies* (New Haven: Yale University Press, 2008). See also Eric Towers, *Dashwood: The Man and the Myth* (s.l.: Crucible, 1986).

9 The best study of this topic is Peter A. Schock, *Romantic Satanism: Myth and the Historical Moment in Blake, Shelley and Byron* (Houndsmills, Basingstoke: Palgrave Macmillan, 2003).

10 However, for a well-argued problematisation of such a straightforwardly orthodox reading of Milton, see Neil Forsyth, *The Satanic Epic* (Princeton, NJ: Princeton University Press, 2003).

11 Faxneld, *Satanic Feminism*, 131.

12 On Blake's Satanism, see Peter L. Thorslev Jr., "The Romantic Mind Is Its Own Place," *Comparative Literature* 15 (1963): 250–268; Hannes Vatter, *The Devil in English Literature* (Bern: A Francke AG Verlag, 1978). On its political dimensions, consult Schock, *Romantic Satanism*.

13 Lord Byron, *The Complete Poetical Works*, Vol. VI (Oxford: Clarendon Press, 1991), 235–243, 259–275, 346–381.

14 On Shelley's radicalism, see Michael Henry Scrivener, *Radical Shelley: The Philosophical Anarchism and Utopian Thought of Percy Bysshe Shelley* (Princeton, NJ: Princeton University Press, 1982).

15 Percy Bysshe Shelley, *The Revolt of Islam*, canto I, stanza Xxxvii, lines 361–378, in *The Poetical Works of Percy Bysshe Shelley* (London: Oxford University Press, 1908), 46–47.

16 Shelley, *Revolt of Islam*, canto II, stanza 43, line 1045, in *The Poetical Works*, 63.

17 The Middle-Eastern setting is also used to conceal the parallels to the French revolution (much-admired by Shelley) that would otherwise have been too provocative for English readers.

18 Shelley, *The Poetical Works*, 32 (Shelley's preface).

19 Giosuè Carducci, *Poesie di Giosuè Carducci* (Bologna: Nicola Zanichelli, 1927), 377–385.

20 The perhaps most insightful study of this theme in Baudelaire's poetry is Pierre Emmanuel, *Baudelaire: The Paradox of Redemptive Satanism* (Alabama: University of Alabama Press, 1970).

21 One of the best studies of Huysmans's involvement with Satanism remains Baldick, *The Life of J.-K. Huysmans* (Oxford: Clarendon Press, 1955), 137–171. See also Faxneld, *Satanic Feminism*, 366–369; van Luijk, *Satan Rehabilitated*, 174–187.

22 For a biography of Przybyszewski, see George Klim, *Stanislaw Przybyszewski: Leben, Werk und Weltanschauung im Rahmen der deutschen Literatur der Jahrhundertwende* (Paderborn: Igel Verlag, 1992).

23 Per Faxneld, "Witches, Anarchism and Evolutionism: Stanislaw Przybyszewski's fin-de-siècle Satanism and the Demonic Feminine," in *The Devil's Party*, ed. Faxneld and Petersen, 55, 58–60.

24 Ibid., 57, 60.

25 Faxneld, "Witches, Anarchism and Evolutionism," 64–65, 67.

26 Ibid., 61–63.

27 Per Faxneld, "The Devil Is Red: Socialist Satanism in Nineteenth-Century Europe," *Numen: International Review for the History of Religions* 60 (2013): 537–539.

28 Ibid., 530–531, 535–537, 539–551.

29 For a comprehensive treatment of this, see Faxneld, *Satanic Feminism*.

30 An excellent short overview of the history of Theosophy is Bruce F. Campbell, *Ancient Wisdom Revived: A History of the Theosophical Movement* (Berkley: University of California Press, 1980). On Satan's role in this movement, see Per Faxneld, "Blavatsky the Satanist: Luciferianism in Theosophy, and Its Feminist Implications," *Temenos: Nordic Journal of Comparative Religion* 48 (2012): 203–230.

31 Faxneld, *Satanic Feminism*, 84–86, 172–173. On Lévi and Satan, cf. the exhaustive and balanced discussion in van Luijk, *Satan Rehabilitated?*, 148–167.

32 A useful biography of Crowley is Richard Kaczynski, *Perdurabo: The Life of Aleister Crowley* (Tempe: New Falcon Publications, 2002). On Crowley and Satanism, see Asbjørn Dyrendal, "Satan and the Beast: The Influence of Aleister Crowley on Modern Satanism," in *Aleister Crowley and Western Esotericism: An Anthology of Critical Studies*, ed. Henrik Bogdan and Martin P. Starr (Oxford: Oxford University Press, 2012).

33 The only scholarly studies of Kadosh so far are Per Faxneld, "The Strange Case of Ben Kadosh: A Luciferian Pamphlet From 1906, and Its Current Renaissance," *Aries: Journal for the Study of Western Esotericism* 11 (2011); Per Faxneld, "In Communication With the Powers of Darkness: Satanism in Turn-of-the-Century Denmark, and Its Use as a Legitimating

Device in Present-Day Esotericism," in *Occultism in a Global Perspective*, ed. Henrik Bogdan and Gordan Djurdjevic (Durham: Acumen, 2013).

34 Faxneld, *Mörkrets apostlar*, 177–188. In this book I argue that the early Fraternitas Saturni should be labelled Satanists, but having read more of their material from the 1920s and 1930s I am no longer quite so sure about this. A fine recent discussion of their teachings can be found in Hans Thomas Hakl, "The Magical Order of the Fraternitas Saturni," in *Occultism in a Global Perspective*, ed. Henrik Bogdan and Gordan Djurdjevic (Durham: Acumen, 2013).

35 Hans Thomas Hakl, "The Theory and Practive of Sexual Magic, Exemplified by Four Magical Groups in the Early Twentieth Century," in *Hidden Intercourse: Eros and Sexuality in the History of Western Esotericism*, ed. Wouter J. Hanegraaff and Jeffrey J. Kripal (Leiden: Brill, 2008), 465–474; Faxneld, *Mörkrets apostlar*, 189–194.

36 Faxneld, "The Strange Case of Ben Kadosh". On Satanism and the construction of tradition, see also Per Faxneld, "Secret Lineages and *De Facto* Satanists: Anton LaVey's Use of Esoteric Tradition," in *Contemporary Esotericism*, ed. Egil Asprem and Kennet Granholm (London: Equinox, 2013).

37 On the dark side of the 1960s, see Gavin Baddeley, *Lucifer Rising* (London: Plexus, 1999), 43–66.

38 Hugh B. Urban, *Magia Sexualis: Sex, Magic and Liberation in Modern Western Esotericism* (Berkeley: University of California Press, 2006), 203; Michael Aquino, *The Church of Satan*, 6th ed. (San Francisco: Self-published, 2009), 24–28; Blanche Barton, *The Secret Life of A Satanist: The Authorized Biography of Anton LaVey* (Los Angeles: Feral House, 1990/1992), 71; Blanche Barton, *The Church of Satan* (New York: Hell's Kitchen Productions, 1990), 42–44 (LaVey quote on p. 123).

39 Stephen Flowers, *Lords of the Left-Hand Path: A History of Spiritual Dissent* (Smithville: Rûna-Raven Press, 1997), 177–178; Barton, *The Church of Satan*, 11–21.

40 Mattias Gardell, *Gods of the Blood: The Pagan Revival and White Separatism* (Durham: Duke University Press, 2003), 289; Aquino, *The Church of Satan*, 52–55.

41 Flowers, *Lords of the Left-Hand Path*, 178–179.

42 Lawrence Wright, "Sympathy for the Devil: It's Not Easy Being Evil in a World That's Gone to Hell," *Rolling Stone*, September 5, 1991, 63–64, 66–68, 105–106; Flowers, *Lords of the Left-Hand Path*, 175–176. On LaVey and *Rosemary's Baby*, see Aquino, *The Church of Satan*, 36–37.

43 Walt Harrington, "Anton LaVey: America's Satanic Master of Devils, Magic, Music and Madness," *The Washington Post Magazine*, February 23, 1986; Flowers, *Lords of the Left-Hand Path*, 175.

44 See e.g. Barton, *The Secret Life of A Satanist*, 149–150, 153–154.

45 LaVey was an atheist at least in the sense that he did not believe in a personal God, who cares about humanity. If there is such a thing as God, LaVey explains, it is better to conceive of this power as a balancing factor in nature, an impersonal force permeating the cosmos. Anton LaVey, *The Satanic Bible* (New York: Avon Books, 1969), 40.

46 Ibid., 110; Barton, *The Secret Life of A Satanist*, 95–96, 98.

47 Barton, *The Church of Satan*, 23.

48 LaVey, *The Satanic Bible*, 96.

49 Ibid., 62.

50 Ibid., 53.

51 Gardell, *Gods of the Blood*, 290–291, 389.

52 Kennet Granholm, "The Left-Hand Path and Post-Satanism: The Temple of Set and the Evolution of Satanism," in *The Devil's Party: Satanism in Modernity*, ed. Per Faxneld and Jesper Aa. Petersen (Oxford: Oxford University Press, 2013), 217–223.

53 Ibid., 223–225.

54 Barton, *The Secret Life of A Satanist*, 55.

55 www.churchofsatan.com; www.xeper.org

56 On these figures, see Per Faxneld, "Intuitive, Receptive, Dark: Negotiations of Femininity in the Contemporary Satanic and Left-Hand Path Milieu," *International Journal for the Study of New Religions* 4.2 (2013): 214–217.

57 On this, see Jesper Aa. Petersen, "Satanists and Nuts: The Role of Schism in Modern Satanism," in *Sacred Schism: How Religions Divide*, ed. James R. Lewis and Sarah Lewis (Cambridge: Cambridge University Press, 2009).

58 On this type of Satanic avantgarde art, see Jesper Aa. Petersen, "Modern Satanism: Dark Doctrines and Black Flames," in *Controversial New Religions*, ed. James R. Lewis and Jesper Aa. Petersen (Oxford: Oxford University Press, 2005), 428–429; Jesper Aa. Petersen, "Smite Him Hip and Thigh: Satanism, Violence and Transgression," in *Violence in New Religious Movements*, ed. James R. Lewis (Oxford: Oxford University Press, 2011); Gardell, *Gods of the Blood*, 296–304.

59 www.churchofsatan.com/cos-ever-forward.php

60 Jacob C. Senholt, "Secret Identities in the Sinister Tradition: Political Esotericism and the Convergence of Radical Islam, Satanism, and National Socialism in the Order of the Nine Angles," in *The Devil's Party: Satanism in Modernity*, ed. Per Faxneld and Jesper Aa. Petersen (Oxford: Oxford University Press, 2013); Gardell, *Gods of the Blood*, 292–294.

61 Milton. For full accounts of the genesis of the black metal scene, see Michael Moynihan and Didrik Søderlind, *Lords of Chaos: The Bloody Rise of the Satanic Metal Underground* (Venice, CA: Feral House, 1998); Ika Johannesson and Jon Jefferson Klingberg, *Blod, eld, död: En svensk metalhistoria* (Stockholm: Alfabeta, 2011). Both are journalistic books, but are nevertheless the best sources for descriptive background information. The many interviews with key players make these works quite invaluable to scholars.

62 On radicalization, see e.g., Donatella della Porta and Heinz-Gerhard Haupt, "Patterns of Radicalization in Political Activism," *Social Science History* 36 (2012).

63 To grasp the vast scope of the genre, consult www.metal-archives.org.

64 This has been an issue that musicans have had to negotiate from the start of the scene in the early 1990s. On this, see Keith Kahn-Harris, *Extreme Metal: Music and Culture on the Edge* (Oxford: Berg, 2007).

65 Kennet Granholm, "Ritual Black Metal: Popular Music as Occult Mediation and Practice," *Correspondences: Online Journal for the Study of Western Esotericism* 1.1, http://correspondencesjournal.files.wordpress.com/2013/09/11302_20537158_granholm.pdf (accessed 3 September 2014).

66 Benjamin Hedge Olson, "At the Threshold of the Inverted Womb: Anti-Cosmic Satanism and Radical Freedom," *International Journal for the Study of New religions* 4.2 (2013): 231–249; Johannesson and Klingberg, *Blod, eld, död*, 191–223.

Bibliography (selection)

Faxneld, Per, *Satanic Feminism: Lucifer as the Liberator of Woman*. Stockholm: Molin & Sorgenfrei, 2014.

Faxneld, Per and Jesper Aa. Petersen (eds.), *The Devil's Party: Satanism in Modernity*. Oxford: Oxford University Press, 2012.

Flowers, Stephen, *Lords of the Left-Hand Path: A History of Spiritual Dissent*. Smithville: Rûna-Raven Press, 1997.

Introvigne, Massimo, *Enquête sur le satanisme*. Paris: Éditions Dervy, 1997.

Petersen, Jesper Aa. (ed.), *Contemporary Religious Satanism: A Critical Anthology*. Burlington, VT: Ashgate, 2009.

PART 4

WITCHES AND THE ARTS

26

WITCHCRAFT AND EARLY
MODERN ART (1450–1550)

Sigrid Schade

Introduction

During the last thirty years the new interest in and the re-discovery of the figure of the "witch" by historical, gender, religious, economic, legal and media studies, art history and studies in popular culture has also led to a re-discovery of a flood of pictorial images. Witches and witchcraft had become a prominent theme not only in theological, humanistic, juridical and medical treatises, historical chronicles as well as in moralizing literature of the time but also in pictorial representations – being produced and circulated often as part of the print publications or distributed independently. What can be called in retrospect the "imaginary of witchcraft" produced a dangerous reality for those being accused of it. One of the questions rising within the research on these representations is whether or not, (and how) they have been involved in and contributed to the discourses and the circulation of concepts of demonic magic and the witches as a sect, which finally supplied the arguments for legal and institutionalised prosecutions of "witches" and the execution of about 50,000 persons – not all but the majority of them being women.[1] Among these representations we find miniatures in manuscripts, drawings, woodcuts and etchings, news sheets and last but not least paintings. Some of the representations are anonymous some of them can be attributed to masters and artists or their workshops, some of them have been received as major contributions of those artists whose works are considered to be paradigmatic for the history of art between 1500 and 1600.[2]

Remarkable is the historical coincidence of the media revolution of print-making, the first historical "mass-medium" enabling reproductions in a quality, speed and geographical reach unexperienced before with the rise of the modern concept of the (male) "artist" as a "godlike" creator and inventor at the end of the Middle Ages. The transformation of the social status of artists distinguished them from former craftsmanship, a concept linked to notions of authorship, authenticity and "free" individual imagination, still dominant ideas in traditional art history up to today.[3] Yet – transdisciplinary analyses of the images in central Europe show that the imaginations depicted represent less individual but rather popular beliefs and that "inventions" of the artists were embedded in theological and humanist discourses spreading around in diverse sources and practices.[4] The set of qualifications making a witch 'a witch' had been synthesised and standardised by demonologists from the beginning of the fifteenth century onwards. Research on the variety and mix of tropes and elements of witchcraft concepts in different images considers the choices of sources, relates them to specific interests and situates them within local and historical cultural frames. Important questions are to whom the images had been addressed, who the patrons might have been and in which social groups the images circulated.

While many of the representations reflect demonic magic the witches were supposed to be able to practice with the help of the devil (malefic sorcery) – for the demonologists the main evidence for their sinfulness – the concepts of the witch and witchcraft deeply rooted in (Christian) phantasies on "female" seductiveness began at the time to become overtly eroticised not only by the narratives but also by the formal organisation and painterly techniques of the art works. Sexuality practiced outside of marriage was considered a sin from the Christian theological perspective, and lust one of the seven sins. The representations of women as witches allude to diverse imaginations about perverse sexual practices with demons or the devil, and about the powers or qualities reflected in behavior and gesture as well as in the depiction of erotic naked bodies, allowing for a new kind of voyeurism and adding to the attractiveness of the pictorial image. The so called female nude became a genre in itself as one of the central painterly "quotations" from Antiquity in the Renaissance period. The artists of early modern Europe inscribed the familiar set of motives into the theme of the erotic witch, they thus contributed to the iconology of the erotic female nude which became a dominant element in European art history and visual culture up to today.[5] Though the motive of seduction and the endangering of male reason which had already been a part of the witches' myths, artworks of the Renaissance shifted the concept of witchcraft clearly from combined sinfulness and demonic magic (the so called malefic sorcery, the *Maleficium*) to the visual attractiveness of the female nude as the body of a witch – a bewitching body – reflected in drawings, woodcuts and paintings.

The fascination of these images for viewers even nowadays has to do with a historical continuation of phantasies of "female" sexuality which is a gender-specific attribution of seductive powers to women – by no means an exclusive qualification of the figure of the witch – and with the continuity of voyeuristic structures within painting and other visual media. The frame for the reception of their erotic content has become different now when sexualised images are omnipresent even in public spaces and social media and "free" sexuality is celebrated as one of the markers with which western societies are identified. So it is of no surprise that publications on the topic of witches usually are heavily illustrated; even more so if they appeal to a broader public. Recycling and circulation of the images add to the attractiveness also of coffee table books, exhibition catalogues and of the position of the historical expert him or herself – an effect which should be reflected also by the researcher. The *use* of the pictorial images within diverse strategies of showing can be observed within the historical sources themselves as well as in the perspectives of research and of publishing the material. The term "illustration" hints at one of the problems of their use in historical compendia: very often they are neither analysed in detail nor related to historical sources but are considered to illustrate the sources or, even worse, to "document reality".

The following article focusses on examples of witchcraft and early modern art from 1450 to 1550 in the heartland of the persecutions. It will acknowledge that artworks don't speak for "themselves". The perspective of the analysis is always dependent on the concepts with which one proceeds and this perspective is even responsible for the choice of objects included in or excluded from the corpus of analysis. Historians for example have tended to concentrate on representations accompanying theological, philosophical and humanist treatises, while traditional art history focussed on the art-works of acknowledged artists as being related exclusively to other artworks. In order to close the gap and take into account that the subject is embedded in a wider field of cultural practices the researcher is drawn to the transdisciplinary approaches of studies in visual culture while observing interrelations between the cultural artefacts and sources. This includes approaches provided by social art history, i.e. concepts focussing on the function of convention within the processes of transfer, transla-tion and reading of images through histories and societies. To this complex belong iconological, iconographical as well as semiological approaches, and the concept of a repertoire of images that processes a "cultural memory".[6] The circulation of images and the building of a repertoire of images are powerful processes in which the (art) historian always participates.

Imagination and construction of witches as a heretical sect and the Sabbath

Probably one of the earliest depictions of women as witches riding and/or flying on a besom in the fifteenthcentury is the illumination at the margin of a folio in Mar-tin le Franc's manuscript "Le champion des dames" from 1451 composed at around 1440–1441. **(Figure 26.1)**. Martin le Franc, living some time in Arras in the north of France around 1435, then secretary of the duke of Savoy, Amadeus (the anti-pope Felix V), and provost of the chapter of Lausanne and participant at the reform Council of Basle 1431–1449, provides one of the first literary descriptions of the witches' Sabbath as a manifestation of a sect-like counter-church perverting Chris-tian rites in the tradition of heretics. At the same time duke Amadeus encouraged his advocates to cooperate with Franciscan and Dominican inquisitors in establish-ing proceedings against heretics, Jews, sorcerers, witches and magicians. The pros-ecution and executions of persons as witches spread then from Savoy to western Switzerland.[7]

Witches' persecutions in the Wallis between 1420 and 1430 were already reported as early as 1430 for example by the Lucerne chronicler Hans Fründ,[8] and one of the first compilations of experiences from witch trials and witches' persecutions in the cantons of Bern, Wallis and Vaud was published by the Basle council theologian Johannes Nider in his treatise "Formicarius" 1437, repeatedly quoted in the most influential book written against witches, the "Malleus Maleficarum" of Heinrich Kramer, (Institutoris) first published in 1486. Martin Le Franc is one of the first who attributes the "Sabbath" or "Synagogue" especially to women, both terms referring to Jewish religious rituals – in a description of heresy of course no accident. In his allegorical poem narrating stories of courageous women like Jeanne d' Arc, Martin le Franc transforms an assumed sect of heretics (the Vaudois, Waldensians), into an assumed sect of witches.[9] In the illumination the women are depicted as "normal" women in usual traditional rural garbs comparable to illustrations of the time, rid-ing on brooms being the only "unusual" element. The flying witch riding on sticks,

Figure 26.1 Ms Fr 12476 fol.105v Two witches from "Le Champion des Dames" by Martin le Franc (1410–61) 1451 (vellum) (b/w photo), French School, (fifteenth century)/Bibliotheque Nationale, Paris, France/Bridgeman Images

brooms or animals became an integral element of representations of the Sabbath – an assembly of devil worshipping and practising perverse sexuality as in the miniatures illuminating the three French manuscripts of the influential Cologne theologian Johannes Tinctoris' "Traité du crime de vauderie" published around 1460,[10] when the trials against Waldensian heretics in Arras were still ongoing pursued by the Inquisitor of Arras, Pierre Broussart.[11] All three illuminations show "Waldensians worshipping the devil and kissing the anus of the devil as gout". The depiction by the French illuminator Philippe de Mazerolles living and working at the time in Bruges shows one female and eleven male Waldensian in a group around the goat holding lighted candles, some of them praying, one of the men kneeling and approaching the anus with his head.[12] The scene is situated in a nocturnal land-scape outside the city-walls seen in the background. Five more men and women are shown still flying to the assembly through the sky, two women on brooms, one on an animal, one man and one woman with courtly headdress being carried through the air by demons or devils. Beside the fact that the "obscene kiss" is depicted the illumination is not an erotic image. It shows the women and men in their normal urban or – in one case courtly – garbs. Beside the flying heretics in the sky and the demons there is no sign that the scene should not be "real", it does not differ from other illuminations in chronicles from the same illuminator in the Parisian manuscript style of the time. The illuminations seem to underline the aim of the treatise which was to convince its readers of the reality of the events described as Waldensian heresy.

The theme of the witches' Sabbath – at least in the combination of all elements – disappears then for the next hundred years from witchcraft imagery. The cultural historian Charles Zika proposes the interpretation that this might be a possible effect of the victory of the appellants in the Arras trials in 1491, declaring the descriptions of the Sabbath as illusionary.[13] Yet more detailed research on this phenomenon is necessary, since the topic did not disappear from the demonol-ogists' propaganda and publications. Illuminated manuscripts, even if circulated in several copies, did not have the same width of audience as printed publications and woodcuts which became successful in distributing codes of witchcraft in the second half of the fifteenth and in the sixteenth century in different contexts and geographical areas. We are left with some interesting questions: why, when and how the Sabbath – with its ensemble of motives – became (again) an interesting subject for chroniclers and painters from the end of the sixteenth century onwards, dominantly in the northern parts of the Holy Roman Empire of German Nation, in Flanders and the Netherlands?

Evil practices of witches: malefic sorcery

At the end of the fifteenth century the most influential theological treatise against witches, the *Malleus Maleficarum* (Hammer of the witches) of the Dominican inquis-itor Heinrich Kramer (Institoris) was published and reprinted between in 1485 until 1669 in thirty editions.[14] A manual of demonological popular witch beliefs and descriptions of witchcraft quoted from theological and other sources, it concen-trated on the sins and the malefic sorcery of the dominantly female witches – the pact with the devil being the precondition. The treatise shows that witches and their crimes existed and challenges the civil authorities and civil lawyers to prosecute the witches as criminals. The publication *De laniis et phitonicis mulieribus* (*On Female Witches and Seers*)[15] of the Constance doctor of laws Ulrich Molitor, one of the first reactions to "The Hammer of the witches", reflects this strategy and opposes it within a conversation between three participants on the possible reality of the crimes of witches.[16] It discusses the questions whether the witches are able to cook up hail-storms, to lame men with arrows (or to make men impotent), to transform them-selves and others into animal shapes, to ride on anointed forks or animals through the sky, whether they practice intercourse with the devil and – last not least – whether they would be able to recognise each other as witches. The last question suggests that the sect of the witches uses secret signs and languages, assuming that in everyday life they usually would not look different from other people. This is a question which in fact illustrators and painters had to ask themselves too when representing witches: how can they be made recognisable to the viewer? Which signs does the viewer need to understand the images?

Whereas Molitor's treatise admits the reality of the devil as source for all evil it negates the effectivity of evil practices of witches. Yet, the illustrations added to the chapters of the treatise show malefic sorcery as being practiced by the witches themselves, not by the devil.[17] The series of six woodcuts appeared in variations and copies in more than twenty illustrated editions of the bestseller between 1490 and 1510 in more than nine German cities.[18] The single crimes as depicted in the illustration were by then common belief, their mode of representation had become common knowledge. Among the motives quoted most frequently are the ride of the witches on sticks or animals and the group of witches cooking hailstorms by throwing snakes and cocks into the boiling cauldron above a fire **(Figure 26.2)**.

The Swabian artists Hans Schäuffelein, an apprentice to Albrecht Dürer's workshop in Nuremberg between 1503 and 1507, clearly addresses viewers familiar with the single elements of the composite woodcut he produced for a treatise on civil law "Der neü Layenspiegel" ("The Laymen's Guide") written by the city secretary Ulrich Tengler and published as a revised version by Tengler's son Christoph, a professor of canon law, in 1511[19] **(Figure 26.3)**. Surrounding a central circle within a landscape on which a magician invokes demons the witches' crimes are depicted: on the left side a witch cooking a hailstorm; a witch sending an arrow to the crippled man in the right corner below (alluding to the witches' crime of laming a man); on the right side a witch stealing milk from a tree trunk. Above her we see a witch embracing the devil and on the left of that scene a man dealing with a chandler while being indoctrinated by a devil on his shoulders. Two witches with forked sticks ride on goats through the sky. Below the magician's circle on the left side we see two lawyers, perhaps Ulrich Tengler and his son, discussing and watching the legal punishment of the witches and sorcerers: their execution by fire.[20] Though this woodcut shows the scenes simultaneously and compiles them like a dictionary it organises them at the same time within an illusionary, almost unified pictorial space which is interrupted only by the circle of the magician. The landscape is supposed to portray a "real" space, the women and men do not show specific bodily qualifications or garbs, they are recognisable as witches and sorcerers only by what they do as something happening in "reality". The woodcut illustrates an added chapter in the revised version of the treatise, definitely integrating witchcraft and sorcery into a manual about the punishment of civil crimes. Legal punishment of crimes can be demanded only if these are considered to be effective and real – not imaginary.

Schäuffelein's woodcut among others is proof that Renaissance artists were familiar with recent publications on witchcraft and theological, humanistic and juridical debates on black, demonic and white, spiritual magic, that they were often familiar with the authors and that they cooperated with editors and printers, that they

Figure 26.2 Two witches cooking up a hailstorm, illustration of malefic sorcery in Ulrich Molitor,
"Von den bosen weibern, die man nennet die hexen" (De laniis et phitonicis
mulieribus), Ulm, Johann Zainer 1490/91. INTERFOTO / Alamy Stock Photo.

Figure 26.3 Hans Schäuffelein, Crimes of malefic sorcery, woodcut, in Ulrich Tengler "Der neü Layenspiegel", ed. b. Christoph Tengler, Augsburg 1511. Wikimedia: https://commons.wikimedia.org/wiki/File:Sorcery_and_witch_craze.jpg

delivered the illustrations which made the books attractive and marketable. For the pictorial language of his woodcut, Hans Schäuffelein did not refer to the woodcuts as those in the diverse editions of Molitor's treatise alone but recycled representation of witches he knew from his master Albrecht Dürer and his colleague Hans Baldung Grien, working at Dürer's workshop at the same time. These two German artists were the main agents contributing to the transformation of the figure of the witch in the sixteenth century.

Albrecht Dürer takes part in the transformation of the social status of artists at around 1500 and in the transformations of social and theological perspectives.[21] An apprentice to Michael Wolgemut (beginning 1486) he might have participated in producing some of the illustrations for the "Nuremberg Chronicle" published in 1493 by his godfather Anton Koberger, the most successful publisher in Germany of his time. Dürer established his own workshop in Nuremberg 1497 after having traveled to the Netherlands and Italy and before traveling there again. He became familiar with protagonists of the Italian Renaissance. Jacopo de' Barbari triggered Dürer's interest in the rediscovery of antique techniques in perspective, proportion and anatomy leading him to take on his own research. Dürer corresponded with humanists and reformers such as Willibald Pirckheimer, Philipp Melanchthon, Agrippa of Nettesheim and Erasmus of Rotterdam on humanist and reformers' concepts; he sympathised with the reformation. He was not only interested in fusing figures of classical mythology (Medea, Circe, Aphrodite and others) with associations of the Northern European figures of the witch and the vices but also in the form of the classical nude which he used 1497 for the engraving known as the "The four witches", four female nudes in classical positions building a group within a central perspective interior watched by a devilish monster.[22] The influential engraving "Witch riding backwards on a Capricorn/goat" 1501 (**Figure 26.4**) has been interpreted as picture puzzle synthesising humanist astrological concepts with the witches' ride familiar to him, the Furious Horde (a ride of restless dead and demons) and representations of the vice of lust and sexual disorder.[23]

The witch riding backwards on a Capricorn with the tail of a fish or serpent, together with the winged putti, build a sort of circle inscribed into the space of the engraving which is split up into a sky and earth spheres separated through a small line of the sea as horizon. The circle signifies the cycle of the periods of a year represented in the Zodiac. Belief in astrology – at the center of humanist philosophy of Ficino and others considered as "spiritual" magic – sees the celestial bodies dominating and influencing micro- and macrocosms for a specific period of the year; a heritage of classical antiquity. Witches are the planet Satan's "children", as well as criminals, Jews, the poor, miners and others. The pictorial image can be read as allegory of "the world turned upside down" at the time of the winter solstice. For this interpretation it provides a number of signs: the backward ride, the somersaults of the putti, the hair of the witch flying in contrary direction against the possible wind and Dürer's monogram turned around. The witch's body shows formal elements of classical nudes and the signs of representations of the vice of lust. She holds one corn of the goat/Capricorn with one hand, with the other she keeps a distaff between her legs – allusion to sexual autonomy – her hair is flying wildly and she obviously has something to do with the hailstorm in the left upper corner. The depiction of such a witch in the context of an astrological concept stages the power of the witch as an inversion of the "normal" social order similar to carnival rituals. This inversion underlines the order which is considered to be "normal", it does not last – the end of the reign of women is foreseeable. Humanist defenders of spiritual magic claimed that astrological magic contrasted to sinful

Figure 26.4 Witch riding backwards on a goat, c.1505 (Burin engraving), Dürer or Duerer, Albrecht
(1471–1528)/Private Collection/Photo © Luisa Ricciarini/Bridgeman Images

demonic magic which had to be accepted by Christian theology since the planets and their movements were created by God, therefore also their influence on life on earth. With the permission of God, the humanist magician practices white magic in order to react to the imagined influences of the planets.

Dürer's allegory of the world "turned upside down" was addressed to circles of humanists and friends who were familiar with the astrological allusions. In combination with the more popular figure of the riding witch, the engraving seems to suggest that even witches' crimes and power have a place in God's universe; the Lutheran version being that God allows the devil do his work to a specific point for enabling the distinction between sinners from not sinners. It does not seem likely that Dürer doubts the reality of the devil and the witches – neither did the humanists nor the reformers. They all were involved in a complex discussion on magic, declaring that one of the witches to be demonical for distinguishing their own beliefs and practices as part of the theological order.

The eroticisation of the witches in the imagery of Hans Baldung Grien

The Swabian artist Hans Baldung stemming from a family of scholars, younger than Dürer – his nickname Green (greenhorn) deriving from the times he worked at the latter's workshop – focussed on representations showing groups of mostly attractive naked young women contrasted often with an old hag as witches sitting around a cauldron.[24] He deliberately exploited the voyeuristic aspects of such images and alludes to diverse erotic imaginations accompanying the witches' mythology. Group scenes of witches promise indirect access to the initiated who can be watched from "outside" without danger. Those scenes of female nudes became extremely fashionable at the beginning of the sixteenth century starting with Dürer's "Four witches". Baldung Grien after having been an apprentice in Strasbourg went to Dürer's workshop in 1503 which he directed while Dürer was traveling. In 1510, the year Baldung got married and founded his own workshop in Strasbourg, a city known for its tolerance at the beginning of the Reformation, he produced the most influential woodcut of his series of witch scenes (**Figure 26.5**), most of them drawings produced between 1514 and 1515 while he was working on the altar piece for the Freiburg cathedral, and one an oil painting in 1523. During his lifetime he became one of the most successful artists and an acknowledged citizen of Strasbourg. Baldung was familiar with publications such as the "Hammer of the witches", recent discussions on witchcraft and of course with the tradition of its depiction. At the time he installed himself in Strasbourg, Johann Geiler of Kaysersberg, a popular preacher, had held sermons 1509 in the cathedral discussing the different aspects of witchcraft. The sermons were published under the title "Die Emeis" ("The Ants") by the Franciscan author Johann Pauli. The printed edition was enriched with illustrations, some – or at least one of them – coming from Baldung's workshop, an illustration linking the scene of witches to the topos of the "reign of women over men" (Weibermacht).[25]

The woodcut "Witches preparing for the Sabbath" of 1510 shows a group of three witches in a forest surrounding, sitting and kneeling around a boiling cauldron, the

Figure 26.5 Hans Baldung Grien, Group of witches preparing for the ride to the Sabbath, chiaroscuro woodcut 1510 (Schade, Schadenzauber, Abb. 18, S. 54) INTERFOTO / Alamy Stock Photo

latter and one of the witches situated within a magical triangle of cooking forks. The witch riding backwards on a goat above the scene in the nocturnal sky is the youngest and about to join the fogs and clouds streaming from the cauldron; she is a quotation of Dürer's "Witch riding backwards". Almost hidden by the main group of witches and the vapours from the cauldron, parts of another goat and another witch become visible. The most agitated old witch in the middle of the group raises her arms holding a cloth and a platter with animal parts. The diverse objects lying around the witches hint at sacrificial practices, the cooking of hailstorms without natural means (no fire) and of flying ointment used for rubbing forks or themselves before flying. The cat sitting back to back to the witch on the right side seems to be a transformed witch herself. The cauldron seems to be linked to the myth of Pandora's Box, since the evil evaporates while the same witch opens the cover only slightly.[26] The sausages collected on the fork on the left side refer to the popular wording of the time meaning male genitals, signifying to those familiar with the moralising literature and demonology the crime of "impotentia ex *maleficium*" (impotence by sorcery). The image has been exercised within a refined new technique, a chiaroscuro woodcut for which several woodblocks are necessary, a technique which had been invented by the Augsburg artist Hans Burgkmair the Elder. It allows for dramatic effects of light and dark zones, for the plasticity of the female bodies adding to them a painterly dimension and creating the illusion of natural bodies in a real environment.

Whereas this image is more than filled with attributes recognisable from the iconography of the witch, Baldung's most astonishing chiaroscuro drawing of "Three witches" of 1514 lacks them with almost only one exception completely (**Figure 26.6**). It is a pen drawing on a tinted paper heightened with white. The eroticisation of the theme is evident: the viewer is confronted with a group of two young witches and one old, presenting their bodies and their genitals without shame, one shows her backside spreading her legs, the other one covers her genitals with her right hand (which can be interpreted also more actively). It should be noted here that art historical description as the one just given often fails to name the agency correctly: it is not the witches but indeed Baldung who presents the bodies. Beside the steaming pot held up high by one of the witches – a reference to Venus also – and the flying hair there is no other sign identifying the women as witches. To those familiar with the tradition of their depiction in fact more signs are no longer necessary. The bodies build a kind of dynamic pyramid over the wooden plate with the artists' monogram helping each other to scrub them with flying ointment. The witch stepping on top of the back of the one crouched on hands and legs seems just about to leave through the sky. The gaze upside down through her legs to the viewer makes the women crouching on her legs the most provocative since she addresses the viewer directly. Baldung confronts the viewer with his desire to see while seducing him and letting him know that he is observed at the same time. But who is the viewer? The drawing shows also an inscription "DER COR CAPEN EIN GUT JAR". If it translates how it was first proposed, that it can be read as a new years' wish dedicated to a cleric (*Chorkappe* in German), the drawing then ironically alludes to the debates around the problem of the concubines of the clerics (*Mönchshuren* in German) who at the time did not obey to the order of celibacy, giving reason to polemics between the reformers and the traditional church, and

Figure 26.6 Hans Baldung Grien, Three witches (New years' greetings), pen drawing on tinted
paper, heightened with white, 1514, Wien Albertina, (Schade, Schadenzauber,
Abb. 51, S. 112) Art Heritage / Alamy Stock Photo

leading to Luther's proposal that clerics should also be married to one woman alone.[27] The image addresses voyeuristic impulses, plays with the desires expected from a male viewer and was shown in private circles as well as the later oil painting "Two weather witches" of 1523. Baldung's representations of witches had been widely copied by his contemporaries and his naturalising and illusionist depiction of women's bodies have been quoted throughout the further tradition of witchcraft imagery.

Illusion or reality: the furious horde and witches in Lucas Cranach's allegories of Melancholy

The "wild hunt" or "furious horde" (or the wild cavalcade, das Wütische Heer in German) had been a folkloristic element which was quoted in most of the treatises dealing with witchcraft, so in the "Hammer of the witches" or in Geiler of Kaysersberg's sermons. The latter describes the furious horde as revenants having been killed through executions condemned to restless strife through the night. Paracelus links the furious horde to the witches. For him it is an assembly of witches and demons altogether.[28]

While the furious horde had already been integrated in representations of witches as early as in Albrecht Altdorfers' drawing "Departure to the Sabbath" in 1506 the motive was taken up, shifted and framed within the representation of Melancholy in four paintings by Lucas Cranach the Elder between 1528 and 1533. I will concentrate on the one version now in the Museum Unterlinden in Colmar of 1532 (**Figure 26.7**). Cranach, court painter to the Electors of Saxony in Wittenberg from 1505 and embracing the Protestant Reformation becoming a close friend of Martin Luther, referred in his allegories of melancholy to Dürer's engraving "Melencolia I" of 1514, an image having caused abundant scholarly interpretation in art history, mostly analysed as an optimistic humanist re-interpretation of the temperament as a precondition even for genial creativity.[29] In Cranach's versions the main figure, the winged personification of melancholy and the putti refer to Dürer's engraving, also the sphere, the sleeping dog, chisel and compass depicted in three of them. Yet, in Cranach's paintings the personification of melancholy – a temperament attributed to the "children" of Saturn and part of the astrological concept of the influences of the celestial bodies on the humours – is situated in an interior with a large wall opening towards a landscape outside with a city and castle in the background leads the view to a large dark cloud in which the furious horde is depicted. In the painting of 1532 the participants of the furious ride are four naked women, clearly associated with the figure of the witch, three old and one young, riding on a boar, a horned cow and a dragon. The only man in the clothes of a German nobleman of the time rides on a Capricorn and seems to participate not on free will but pushed by the old women with a fork and pulled forward by the woman on the dragon. One of the most interesting elements in this painting is the putto swinging between the two levels of "reality" within an anyway illusionary frame. It links the personification of melancholy to the devilish fantasies ascribed to the temperament not only by astrological concepts but also by the Lutheran theology. The devil's insinuations were considered to be real and melancholy a sinful vice one has to fight.

Figure 26.7 Lucas Cranach the Elder, *Melancholy,* oil on panel 1532, Museum Unterlinden, Colmar Peter Horree / Alamy Stock Photo

The appearances of the witch and of witchcraft – a proof of the artist's virtuosity

Throughout the theological, demonological and humanist treatises one of the main questions addressed is, what exactly can be taken as "real" and what exactly as fantasy, whether the agency of the devil or the agency of the witches, the crimes of the witches, their ability of flying to Sabbath assemblies and/or perverse sexual practices and rituals being performed at those occasions. The different answers lead to different consequences. The power ascribed to women as witches mirror the power of the inquisitor, the exorcist or the legal persecutor ascribes to himself. All the descriptions of sinful excesses show that they empower themselves by narrating or depicting the forbidden scenes.

The artist at the time of early modern art is a new agent on the scene. The examples of Dürer, Baldung, Cranach and others show that the topic of the witch was discovered as means of establishing a new kind of identity[30] and demonstrating virtuosity in a field, where competitiveness leads to a new understanding of their task: who will be the best magician? Isn't it the artist who is the master of delusion and illusion? While contributing to the discourses around the powers of witchcraft the artist not only adds to their attractiveness but also vice versa exploits the lustful projections of the debated crimes and seducing powers for his own purpose, claiming the power of these for his own profession and status, one of the heritages of early modern art.

Notes

1 Johannes Dillinger, *Hexen und Magie*(Frankfurt: Campus Verlag, 2018), 87–90.
2 See Sigrid Schade, *Schadenzauber und die Magie des Körpers: Hexenbilder der frühen Neuzeit* (Worms: Werner, 1983); Richard van Dülmen, ed., *Hexenwelten. Magie und Imagination* (Frankfurt a. M.: Fischer Taschenbuch-Verlag, 1987), 170–218 and 391–415; Jane P. Davison *Hexen in der nordeuropäischen Kunst*, 1470–1750 (Freren: Luca Verlag, 1988); Margaret Sullivan, "The Witches of Dürer and Hans Baldung Grien," *Renaissance Quarterly* 53 (2000): 332–401; Linda C. Hults, *The Witch as Muse: Art, Gender and Power in Early Modern Europe* (Philadelphia: University of Pennsylvenia Press, 2005); Charles Zika, *Exorcising Our Demons: Magic, Witchcraft and Visual Culture in Early Modern Europe* (Leiden, Boston: Brill, 2003); Charles Zika, *The Appearance of Witchcraft: Print and Visual Culture in SixteenthCentury Europe* (London, New York: Routledge, 2007); Hexen, *Mythos und Wirklichkeit*, catalogue of the exhibition, ed. Historical Museum of the Pfalz (Munich: Edition Minerva Herrmann Farnung GmbH, 2009); Martine Ostorero, *La chasse aux sorcières dans le pays de Vaud (XVe-XVIIe siècles)*, with contributions by Kathrin Utz Tremp and Renilde Vervoort, exhibition catalogue (Fondation du Château de Chillon, 2011).
3 Sigrid Schade, and Silke Wenk, "Strategien des 'Zu-Sehen-Gebens': Geschlechterpositionen in Kunst und Kunstgeschichte," in *Genus. Geschlechterforschung und Gender Studies in den Kultur- und Sozialwissenschaften*, ed. H. Bussmann and R. Hof (Stuttgart: Kroener, 2005), 144–184.
4 Zika, The Appearance; Sigrid Schade, "Kunsthexen – Hexenkünste. Hexen in der bildenden Kunst vom 16. bis 20. Jahrhundert," in *Hexenwelten. Magie und Imagination*, ed. R. v. Dülmen (Frankfurt a. M.: Fischer Taschenbuch-Verlag, 1987), 170–218 and 391–415.
5 Lynda Nead, *The Female Nude: Art, Obscenity and Sexuality* (London, New York: Routledge, 1992).
6 For methodological reflections see Sigrid Schade, "Religion, Beliefs and Medial Layering of Communication: Perspectives from Studies in Visual Culture and Artistic Productions," *Journal for Religion, Film and Media* 1 (2015): 75–88.

7 Rita Voltmer, "Von dämonischen Zauberern und teufelsanbetenden Ketzern: Die Erfindung des Hexereidelikts und die ersten Verfolgungen," in *Hexen. Mythos und Wirklichkeit*, ed. Historisches Museum der Pfalz (Speyer: Edition Minerva, 2009), 22–35, here 28, 29.

8 Martine Ostorero, "Elaboration et diffusion e l'imaginaire du 'sabbat des sorcières'", in: La chasse aux sorcières, 18–26, here 22.

9 Martine Ostorero, *La chasse aux sorcières dans le pays de Vaud (XVe-XVIIe siècles)*, with contributions by Kathrin Utz Tremp and Renilde Vervoort, exhibition catalogue, Fondation du Château de Chillon, 2011, pp. 18–26.

10 Renilde Vervoort, "Les representations artistiques du sabbat (XVe-XVIIe siècles)." In: Ostorero, 79–89, here 81 ff, ill. 19, the other two illuminations see 2 and 80.

11 For further historical details see Charles Zika, *The Appearance*, 61–63.

12 Ibid., 63.

13 Ibid., 67.

14 Introduction to Heinrich Kramer (Institoris), Der Hexenhammer. Malleus Maleficarum. Kommentierte Neuübersetzung, edited and introduced by G. Jerouschek and W. Behringer, (München: Deutscher Taschenbuch Verlag 2003, 10th revised edition, 2013), 11.

15 German title: "Tractatus von den bosen Weibern, die man nennet die hexen".

16 Ulrich Molitor himself, archduke Sigismund of Austria and the major of Constance, Konrad Schatz, see Sigrid Schade, *Schadenzauber*, 25–32.

17 Schade, *Schadenzauber* 25–32; Zika, *The Appearance*, 17–20.

18 Ibid., 17.

19 Schade, *Schadenzauber*, 31–34; Zika, *The Appearance*, 36.

20 Schade, *Schadenzauber*, 32.

21 For the following paragraph see the bibliography in Konrad Hoffmann, "Dürer's Melencolia," in *Kunst als Bedeutungsträger: Gedenkschrift für Günter Bandmann*, ed. W. Busch (Berlin: Gebr. Mann, 1978), 251–277; JaneCampbell Hutchison, *Albrecht Dürer: A Biography* (New Jersey: Princeton University Press, 1990); Kurth Wilhelm, ed., *The Complete Woodcuts of Albrecht Durer* (Dover Publications, 2000).

22 Zika, *The Appearance*, 87–87, 88.

23 Maxime Préaud, "La sorcière de noël," in L'ésoterisme d'Albrecht Dürer, 1, (Hamsa 7, 1977), 47–50; Schade, *Schadenzauber*, 73–76; Hults, *The Witch*, 73–75; Zika, *The Appearance*, 27ff.

24 For the following paragraph see Schade, *Schadenzauber*, 42–62, 80–118; *Hults, The Witch*, 75–103; Zika, *The Appearance*, 11–17, 82–87.

25 Schade, *Schadenzauber*, 107–112; see also Birgit Franke and Sigrid Schade, "Weiberregiment, Weibermacht, Weiberlisten," in: Lexikon der Kunst, ed. H. Olbrich et al. Vol. 2, (Leipzig, 1994), 739–740.

26 Schade etc.

27 Schade, *Schadenzauber*, 112–118.

28 Ibid., 62–67, Zika, *The Appearance*, 99–124.

29 For a general overwiev see Erwin Panofsky et al*., Saturn and Melancholy: Studies in the History of Natural Philosophy, Religion, and Art* (London: Basic Books, 1964).

30 Hults, *The Witch*.

Bibliography (selection)

Davidson, Jane P., *Hexen in der nordeuropäischen Kunst, 1470–1750*. Freren: Luca Verlag, 1988.

Hults, Linda C., *The Witch as Muse: Art, Gender and Power in Early Modern Europe*. Philadelphia: University of Pennsylvania Press, 2005.

Ostorero, Martine, *La chasse aux sorcières dans le pays de Vaud (XVe-XVIIe siècles)*, Veytaux: Fondation du Château de Chillon, 2011.

Schade, Sigrid, *Schadenzauber und die Magie des Körpers: Hexenbilder der frühen Neuzeit*. Worms: Werner, 1983.

Schade, Sigrid, "Kunsthexen – Hexenkünste. Hexen in der bildenden Kunst vom 16. bis 20. Jahrhundert." In *Hexenwelten. Magie und Imagination*, edited by Richard van Dülmen, 170–218 and 391–415. Frankfurt a. M.: Fischer Taschenbuch-Verlag, 1987.

Sullivan, Margaret, "The Witches of Dürer and Hans Baldung Grien." *Renaissance Quarterly* 53 (2000): 332–401.

Zika, Charles, *Exorcising Our Demons: Magic, Witchcraft and Visual Culture in Early Modern Europe.* Leiden: BRILL, 2003.

Zika, Charles, *The Appearance of Witchcraft: Print and Visual Culture in Sixteenth Century Europe.* London, New York: Routledge, 2007.

27

THE WITCH FIGURE IN NINETEENTH-
AND TWENTIETH-CENTURY
LITERATURE

Justyna Szachowicz-Sempruch

The early nineteenth century's portrayals of witches are under the spell of European Romanticism with the spectacular revival of spirituality, medieval inspiration and imagery of the powerful, unencumbered nature. Art and poetry (e.g. by Rosamund Marriot Watson, Sir Walter Scott, Mary Coleridge, Edgar Alan Poe or William Butler Yeats) is filled with images of twilight, horror, occult and various ecstatic enactments of altered states of consciousness and transgression. The witch figure is both, a femme fatale and a muse: the dark 'other' of the poet, the symbol of a spellbinding nature, and the embodiment of the suppressed, pagan soul, such as Scott's *The Lady of the Lake* (1910). Shaped by these new aesthetic categories, literature elevates the figure from the dark ages of Christian persecution towards a new form of emotional intensity, a new form of desire to confront and experience the unknown aspects of humanity. Literary texts part from heavy, moral obligations to speak in the name of society or that of an institution be it the church or the monarchy. The limited iconography of malevolent witches (recorded mostly in fairy tales, particularly by Brothers Grimm) and powerless victims of witch hunts, promulgated by seventeenth-century witch hunters and eighteenth-century rationalist philosophers, is in the nineteenth-century literature replaced by mysterious temptresses, wise-women, fairy god-mothers, sorceresses, mythical immortals and enchantresses, shaping the conscious and subconscious witch imagery of the times. Generally, institutions condemning witchcraft had significantly diminished in influence across the nineteenth century when the majority of (educated) people no longer believed in the existence of witchcraft.[1] Consequently, the witch figure becomes far more metaphorical, increasingly symbolizing areas of social dissonance and transgressive behaviour of women and men who rebel against the society. Bigamists, homosexuals, criminals, tricksters, prostitutes, madmen, and vampires appear in the nineteenth-century literature as boundary crossers, suspended between gender, class, sexuality and various other socio-economic areas of belonging. They offer an alternative discourse on human nature and initiate important processes in the cultural interrogation of existing representations of women and men.

Bodily and mental spontaneity of the witch-woman, characteristic especially of the nineteenth-century women's literature, unsettles Victorian readers by pointing to the repressed desire to reach beyond rational behaviour. Women writers begin to interrogate the concept of a 'perfect lady/mother', the guardian of 'domestic bliss', depicting heroines who question the confines of culture, society and home, who return to nature or join the supernatural. A spectacular example of such literary exploration is Catherine Earnshaw, a passionate, nature-bound woman-temptress in Emily Brontë's *Wuthering Heights* (1847). Catherine is introduced to the reader after her death, through a discovery of her diary describing the all-consuming, almost demonic love between her and Heathcliff, a foundling adopted by Catherine's father. Suspended between the worlds of what is proper and improper for a young lady, she is not only wanting but cannot truly exist without both dimensions. The evocative descriptions of the wild and lonely moorland emphasize Catherine's unencumbered passions that juxtapose her final decision to surrender to culture, a choice with fatal consequences. It is the male hero, Heathcliff, humiliated by Catherine's family and wrongly believing that Catherine has rejected him, that returns years later as a witch-like figure of subversion. Behind his noble posture of a wealthy gentleman, there hides a monstrous, revengeful soul that can only be comforted by post-mortal reunification with his beloved.

The nineteenth-century witch figures also embrace the exotic (colonial), the unfamiliar, and the distant, occurring mostly as marginal, underdeveloped characters harnessing readers' imagination. Bertha Mason, a peripheral figure of Creole heritage in Charlotte Brontë's *Jane Eyre* (1847), is portrayed as violently insane, first wife of Edward Rochester, kept by him in the attic of their gloomy mansion. Rochester, persuaded by his father to marry Bertha, but also initially entranced by her wealth and beauty, explains that he was not warned against the insanity present in her family for generations. Upon their arrival to England, Bertha's mental health deteriorates, while years of confinement destroy her physical attractiveness. She becomes a frightening, culturally unacceptable creature, standing in the way of Rochester marrying Jane, his (mature) love. Once confronted with Jane, Bertha appears as a vampire-like primordial destroyer of life, the monstrous feminine,[2] a witch-figure who eventually dies in the flames of fire.

The theme of the unfamiliar and the monstrous is most famously explored in *Frankenstein; or, The Modern Prometheus* (1818), a novel by Mary Shelley. Depicting a scientist, Victor Frankenstein, who creates a monstrous man, the story tackles a dilemma of human desires, choices and responsibility for the other. Facilitated by the growth of liberal individualism, the novel focuses on the tragic rejection of the creature by Frankenstein himself. Abandoned, it becomes a (symbolic) outcast from society but, in fact, it embodies innocence, good-naturedness and faith. The rejection leads into deeper, philosophical inquiries about the complexity of the nineteenth century social transformations, resulting in the increasing diversification of the witch imagery towards the monstrous, gothic and inhuman.

Gothic literature, with Bram Stoker's *Dracula* (1897) as one of its most popular representations, begins, in fact, much earlier in the century with John Polidori's *The Vampyre* (1819), a novella, which made an immense impact on contemporary sensibilities, and multiplied in numerous editions and adaptations. *Carmilla*, one of such Gothic narratives, by Joseph Sheridan Le Fanu, published in 1871, and thus predating Dracula, narrates the story of a young woman's susceptibility to a female vampire. Carmilla, the title character, appears as a prototype of a lesbian (vampire-witch) in the form of a beautiful, nocturnal temptress who crosses the forbidden border towards illicit acts of sexuality. Her exclusively female victims succumb to perverse temptations, as Carmilla resurrects from her coffin, teases, transforms and passes through walls of her mansion. Her calculative mind rejects emotional involvement, suggesting a cultural collapse of female warmth and attachment, the very symbols of domesticity inscribed within heterosexual and class ideology.

Throughout the nineteenth century, the witch-like characters are increasingly delineated as women dissatisfied with their cultural roles and obligations, who, often through diaries, manifest various desires to abandon their unhappy lives and make their own independent decisions. Anne Brontë's novel *The Tenant of Wildfell Hall* (1848) portrays a young widow who mysteriously arrives with her son at an abandoned Elizabethan mansion. She lives there in seclusion under the assumed name of Helen Graham but soon becomes a victim of gossip. Gilbert Markham, a farmer who refuses to participate in this local slander, discovers Helen's diary, in which she identifies herself as a married woman and describes her husband's physical and moral decline and cruelty, which she has decided to leave behind. Lucy Snowe, Charlotte Brontë's other strikingly modern heroine in *Villette* (1853), flees from her miserable past in England to begin a new life as a teacher at a French boarding school. Her independence, soon challenged by her male encounters, is underscored by profound loneliness and a realization that in the society there are no men with whom she can live and remain free.

In a similar vein, Hester Prynne, the protagonist in *The Scarlet Letter* (1850), Nathaniel Hawthorne's novel depicting the seventeenth-century Puritan Boston, conceives a daughter through an adulterous affair, and attempts to begin a new life based on dignity and independence. Despite the penalty, (she is forced to wear a scarlet 'A' on her dress, symbolizing adultery, and to stand daily on the scaffold, exposed to public humiliation), Hester refuses to name the father of her child, even under severe pressure from the church and her long-lost but re-appearing husband. Following her release from prison, Hester settles (with her unruly daughter, Pearl) in a cottage at the edge of town, earning a living with her needlework. Reverend Dimmesdale, tormented by his guilty conscience of being Pearl's father, eventually falls in severe illness, admits his guilt and dies in Hester's arms. Hester returns to her cottage, resumes wearing the scarlet letter, and offers solace to women in similar positions. Upon her death, she is buried near Dimmesdale; their graves share a tombstone with an engraved scarlet "A", a romantic symbol of freedom and transgression from societal constrains.

Over the century, readers become increasingly attracted to the theme of human madness as a suspension between the good (reasonable and culturally proper) and the evil (insane and the tabooed). Split personality, a theme explored directly in connection with these anxieties, appears in Robert L. Stevenson 1886's novella *The Strange Case of Dr Jekyll and Mr Hyde.* Dr Jekyll, the protagonist, is a respectable scientist and a diabolical magician, who suffers from a dissociative identity disorder. Suspended in desperate attempts to control the switches of his personality, he lives in(as) two identities excluding each other on the levels of class and morality, and eventually succumbs to the abyss of Mr Hyde, his dark state of consciousness. Still, fascination with madness is particularly interwoven with the imagery of female villains.

In *Lady Audley's Secret* (1862), Elisabeth Braddon's novel based on real-life events, the source of madness derives directly from within the domestic sphere. The seemingly immaculate Lady Audley turns out to have been a violent criminal, bigamist and a cold-blooded mother who abandons her child in the name of financial luxury. It is the increasingly urban, anonymous city surroundings that allow Lady Audley to falsify her identity and destroy various hints to her past. In such rebellious circumstances, her upward mobility suggests a serious threat to the nineteenth century paradigm of class, a threat, which expands the meanings of insanity towards a conscious manipulation and an escape from distress. Moreover, anxieties about Lady Audley's unstable identity are mirrored throughout the novel in other characters and relationships. Homosexuality, questions about the upper and lower classes, proper and improper love are constantly explored in various conversations. The figure of the 'witch' amounts here to the negative otherness of a woman as an 'abysmal sex',[3] an association spectacularly accomplished in the enigmatic figure of Lydia Gwilt, a flame-haired temptress, bigamist, laudanum addict and husband-poisoner, the heroine of Wilkie Collins' mystery novel, *Armadale* (1866).

In the late nineteenth and the first half of the twentieth century, literature, influenced by fundamental socio-political transformations is no longer preoccupied with romantic human transgression. The witch imagery moves away from the sublime, increasingly addressing the social and economic concerns, and relying on fact-based portrayals of contemporary life. Naturalism, Marxism and Modernism alike, focus on the villains' bodies, which are to be medicated, hospitalized, and, if necessary, made extinct. Evoking both medical and sexual implications, the vampire, the criminal and the homosexual are now posited as tropes for cultural incompatibility and deviance, which, "if excessive, will be vomited into protected spaces – hospitals, asylums, prisons".[4] There, the witch, especially the witch-woman, is 'veiled', hidden and kept under restraint. Such attitudes toward women's mental health is illustrated in 'The Yellow Wallpaper' (1892), a short story by Charlotte Perkins Gilman, regarded as a significant early feminist work and exploring the nineteenth century sociological projection of 'woman' as deficient and biologically inferior, conceived to assist and support a masculine 'consciousness to itself'.[5] The narrative is in form of journal entries written by Jane, imprisoned by her husband (a physician) in the upstairs bedroom of a house rented for the summer. Confined, controlled and forbidden to write, Jane is supposed to recuperate from what he diagnoses as a temporary nervous breakdown – a slight hysteria. This should be seen as a reference to Freud's famous studies of his female patients, 1926 and the parallel between the hysterical woman and the witch or demonica in Charcot's work. In a rebellious gesture, which evokes association with Catherine Earnshaw's destiny, Jane slips into insanity, asserting a type of freedom in her entrapment in marriage. Another early feminist protagonist, Edna Pontellier, in Kate Chopin's novel, *The Awakening* (1899), goes a step further and, by ending her own life, turns her emotional despair into a cultural refusal of marital confines. The novel, most probably influenced by Leo Tolstoy's *Anna Karenina* (by then translated into English), is set in New Orleans, and centres on Edna's struggle to reconcile her controversial views on femininity and motherhood with the prevailing social attitudes of the turn-of-the-century American South. It is one of the earliest American novels opening doors for women's emancipatory twentieth century writing, with the central figure of a witch as a symbol of female liberty, feminine power and subversion to patriarchal order.

Indeed, post-World War I literature brings such works by women authors as Colette's *Claudine* series (1900–1922), Virginia Woolf's *A Room of One's Own* (1929), and finally, Simone de Beauvouir's *The Second Sex* (1949), each following a different agenda towards women's emancipation. Following the controversial publication of Colette's *Chéri* (1920), various figures of women-artists and women-philosophers, courtesans, lesbians and unmarried women appear in literature as heroines who reject the confinement of women to the mysterious and secondary human 'other', voiceless muses, dutiful daughters and proper lady-mothers. It is yet, in the post-World War II literature, under profound influences of postmodern, poststructural, postcolonial and feminist philosophies, that the witch imagery unfolds as an unquestionable, political symbol of female liberation. From the 1960s onwards, we witness the birth of various cults of pagan goddesses, such as the White Goddess and Wicca that cherish male and female powers, subdued by patriarchal religions.[6] Drawing on these, predominantly re-imagined, meanings and practices of witchcraft, popular literature (such as Terry Pratchett's *Discworld* and Anne Bishop's fantasy novels) portrays and re-invents witches as essentially positive, magical characters, good-natured and powerful sorceresses.

Following the proliferation of witch characters across literature beyond popular productions, we can distinguish several literary trends, which clearly complicate the mass-oriented, one-dimensional approaches. Arthur Miller's *The Crucible* (1953) takes on a political approach to the history of witchcraft. A re-telling of the Salem witch trials, it is a dramatized allegory of McCarthyism with its persistent, hysterical persecution of Communist thinkers. The central theme explored is the empowerment of previously marginalized female inhabitants of Salem. The orphan girl Abigail, having few options in her life (servantry, marriage, prostitution), aligns herself with God's will and gains power over the courtroom as her narrative of accusations becomes unassailable. Tituba, the black servant, knowledgeable of witchcraft practices, and whose status is lower than that of anyone else, similarly manages to deflect blame by accusing others. The entire witch trial thrives on accusations, the only way that witches can be identified, and confessions, which provide the proof of justice (on which the court proceedings operate). Proctor, a male hero and a counterpart to Abigail, attempts to break this cycle of madness with a confession of his own (he admits to the affair with Abigail), however this confession is trumped by the accusation of witchcraft against him as well as his wife. Proctor's courageous decision to die rather than confess to a sin that he did not commit, finally breaks the vicious circle. The court collapses, undone by the refusal of its victims to participate in the hysterical reproduction of falsehood.

John Updike's novel *The Witches of Eastwick* (1984) represents another literary direction: a satire, written by a male author, and targeting contemporary female-male relationship pressures. Portraying family issues and anxieties with respect to societal power, or the lack of it, across genders, the story is set in the fictional town of Eastwick in the late 1960s, and follows three women-witches Alexandra Spofford, Jane Smart, and Sukie Rougemont, who acquired their magical powers after leaving, or being left by their husbands. Unfortunately, their female coven becomes upset by the arrival of a demonic character, Darryl Van Horne, who seduces each of them separately and makes them play with their powers in ways that contradict their initial visions of independence. The three women soon share Darryl in a foursome at his extravagant mansion until he unexpectedly marries their much younger friend, Jenny. This marks the end of the witches' admiration and tolerance for Darryl. They now resolve to have revenge by making Jenny die from cancer, an act, which they soon regret having realized that it was Darryl who betrayed them all. After Jenny's death, Darryl disappears with her brother, Chris, who appears to have been his actual lover and true object of sexual desire. Although Updike's novel introduces some interesting pro-feminist concepts of female power, it is underscored by satirical approach that, in fact, ridicules the craft in the hands of (emotional) women. Feminist critique rendered the book misogynistic, that is, reinforcing homoerotic foundation of male cultural dominance as well as the patriarchal conceptions of women who take care of their children, but require a man for personal growth. Indeed, the novel ends with witches going separate ways, as each summons her ideal man and leaves.

In a way, the radical feminism in the late 1960s and onwards represents the opposite literary envisioning of the witch. Drawing on the historically documented medieval and early modern European witch-craze, the witch-woman becomes in these narratives a victim of phallogocentric hegemonies.[7] This identity construction derives from mythologized sources invented (and invention is one of the key words here) at the point when the second wave feminist movement 'began to turn away from rights-centred public-sphere issues towards crime-centred, private-sphere issues'.[8]

> Sexuality was to be identified as the site of women's oppression in the sense that property was for Marx the site of class oppression. Rape, sexual violence, pornography, wife-battering and (eventually) child sexual abuse became the central signifiers of patriarchy, replacing signifiers such as legal asymmetries and pay differentials.[9]

Women writers from this period focus on rediscovering women's history silenced by the previous centuries, revise stories about marginalized, witch-like characters from the literary past, and assign them new cultural significations. Jean Rhys in *Wide Sargasso Sea* (1966), for example, accounts for Bertha's marginality in her (unwritten) story in *Jane Eyre*. In Rhys' novel, Bertha appears as Antoinette Cosway and is portrayed from the time of her youth in the Caribbean towards her unhappy relocation to England. Brontë's witch-like madwoman in the attic is thus re-imagined. In a similar vein, an array of female mythological figures, such as Innana, Kali-Ma, Pandora, Lilith, Eve or Jezebel are re-discovered as carriers of specifically female empowerment, subdued by male epistemology.[10] These are so-called *herstorical* (in contrast to historical) narratives, understood as a resistance to a phallogocentric 'woman', with all her incompleteness, deficiency, and envy.[11]

Sara Maitland's re-writing of the figure of Cassandra in *Women Fly When Men Aren't Watching* (1988) is a powerful example of such a narrative reconstruction of history in form of a fantasized biography of Cassandra. Maitland's figure is a maybe not a witch but a female magician, a prophetic madwoman unable to recognize herself as an autonomous consciously speaking (and remembering) subject. Alluding to Ovid's account in the *Metamorphoses*, Maitland describes Cassandra's initial fascination with Apollo, but emphasizes her lack of experience in sexual matters and the ease with which Apollo has seduced her. Maitland's narrative focuses on Cassandra's refusal to submit her body to Apollo's sexual force that is incompatible and incommensurable with her desire. Her pain originates in the encounter with phallic desire, with an eroticism so different from her own that it violates rather than excites her senses. As a punishment for her insubordination, Cassandra remains frozen in non-speech, in non-structure, and subsequently infused with a distorted form of language and memory: 'She has a knowing that [Agamemnon] will not . . . that he will wait . . . that he will . . . she does not know the word for what it is she fears, for what it is she knows he will not do. Then the next minute it is gone, it is all gone.'[12]

Especially in the early second wave of feminist writing, the 'witch' becomes the *other woman*, the one who is not only possible, but actually is needed and desired: 'a woman who does not yet exist, but whose advent could shake the foundations of patriarchy'.[13] Within this radical paradigm, Mary Daly's *Gyn/ecology* (1978) and Andrea Dworkin's *Women-Hating* (1974) focus their critical interest on the witch as a signifier for physically abused and culturally neglected 'woman'. Similarly, Barbara Walker draws on the hag's metamorphosis from the wise-woman into the witch that transforms her medieval cauldron 'from a sacred symbol of regeneration into a vessel of poisons'.[14] According to Daly, the hag is a female *eccentric*, in reference to the Greek *ek* (out of) and *kentrum* (centre of a circle),[15] who deviates from established patterns and defines gynocentric cultural boundaries.[16] The witch-crone, Daly's most prominent 'archetype' of female powers, becomes a guardian of birth-giving as well as of virginity and homosexuality unstained by patriarchal semen. Daly's rewriting of *hagiography* as *Hag-ography* modulates the *hag*, making her the very embodiment of feminist sisterhood.[17] Dworkin 'uses both the image of the demonised witch-step-mother of fairy tales and the figure of the persecuted witch-victim of the Burning Times as figures for the suffering woman-victim of pornography and rape'.[18] Her narratives are manifestos of female powerlessness and, simultaneously, they celebrate the survivor-figure who lives to tell the tale. In fact, radical feminists equate themselves with witches in order to ensure 'that anyone who disagrees with [them] can be cast as an inquisitor'.[19] Despite a detailed analysis of the torture inflicted on witches, Daly and Dworkin are reluctant to provide (historical) references or to describe particular cases of witch trials. According to Purkiss, 'male historians never tire of observing that radical feminist histories of witchcraft use almost no early modern texts as a source for views about witchcraft except the *Malleus Maleficarum*'.[20]

Hélène Cixous, widely translated into Anglo-Saxon context, also refers to this understanding of the witch in 'The Laugh of the Medusa' (1975): the woman 'in her inevitable struggle against conventional man', the 'universal woman subject who must bring women to their senses and to their meaning in history'.[21] This 'universal subject' performs 'a sort of tetralogy, tackling the problem of the four elements: water, air, fire, earth, applied to philosophers nearer our time', and simultaneously, it interrogates the philosophical tradition.[22] Because it operates on a basis of assumed identity politics, *herstory* emerges as a form of feminist mythology,[23] and constitutes a challenging alternative to the established male-centred master-story about witches.[24] This phase of intellectual rebellion and separatism belongs to 'a crucial period in the experience of women who had always played subordinate roles as dutiful academic daughters, research assistants, second readers, and faculty wives'.[25] In *The Newly Born Woman* (1986), Cixous's and Clément's witches replicate the traces of subversive symbols (the evil eye, menstrual pollution and the castrating mother) as well as feminine symbols of transcendence (the virginal mother/goddess). The woman as a hysteric figure, the witch-woman as a creature which manifests a 'distinctively female bonding' of mind and body,

> the inescapable female connection between creation and procreation. . . .
> And the sorceress – the witch, the wise woman, destroyer and preserver of
> culture – is she not the midwife, the intermediary between life and death,

the go-between whose occult yet necessary labours deliver souls and bodies across frightening boundaries?[26]

It is in her 'orgasmic freedom' that Cixous's witch figure personifies the assimilated abjection of the witch's body, her ambiguity of form, and her re-enactment of the absence of patriarchal culture that cannot be conceptualized in the historical language of 'the symbolic'. The self-touching 'witch' 'lives with her body in the past', the past referred to by Cixous as a spectacle of forgotten roles: the *ambiguous*, the *subversive* and the *conservative*.[27] She is *subversive*, 'because the symptoms – the attacks – revolt and shake up the public' (the phallic gaze of the others to whom they are exhibited). She is *conservative*, 'because every sorceress ends up being destroyed, and nothing is registered of her but mythical traces'. Her *ambiguity* is 'expressed in an escape that marks the histories of sorceress and hysteric with the suspense of ellipses'.[28]

Such radical assimilations of the witch figure into various cultural, linguistic and geographical contexts involve also Black women writers, who revive their own cultural traditions across layers of history that leads to the emotional re-discovery of the witch hunting that is presented as an incontestable archaeological proof of universal female oppression. Toni Morrison's *Paradise* (1998) and Alice Walker's *In Search of Our Mothers' Gardens* (1983) are abundant with references to witches that seem to fall into this category of emotional 'digging'. As explained by Lissie, one of Walker's protagonists in *The Temple of My Familiar* (1990), the

> first witches to die at the stake were the daughters of the Moors. . . . It was they (or, rather, we) who thought the Christian religion that flourished in Spain would let the Goddess of Africa 'pass' into the modern world as 'the Black Madonna'. After all, this was how the gods and goddesses moved from era to era before, though Islam, our official religion for quite a long time by now, would have nothing to do with this notion; instead, whole families in Africa who worshipped the goddess were routinely killed, sold into slavery, or converted to Islam at the point of the sword. Yes . . . I was one of those 'pagan' heretics they burned at the stake.[29]

Such emotional proofs explain, perhaps, why 'the radical feminist history of witches often appears to offer a static, finished vision of the witch',[30] one that reflects the feminist desire for an irrefutable reference that could be considered ultimate and eternal.

Victimization of the female body as a site of patriarchal oppression is also evoked in Monique Wittig's *Les Guérillères* (1985), Sally Gearhart's *Wanderground* (1985), Elana Nachman's *Riverfinger Women* and Bertha Harris' *Lover*, all presenting communities of strong, witch-like women rebelling against patriarchy and drawing on the myths of Amazons and other pre-historical matriarchies. These are predominantly eco-feminist and lesbian manifestos about witch-Amazons, the rebel-warriors riding bare-breasted under a brilliant helm of crescent horns that appear at the point in history

> when there was one rape too many . . . the earth finally said 'no'. There was no storm, no earthquake, no tidal wave or volcanic eruption, no specific moment to mark its happening. It only became apparent that it happened, and that it happened everywhere.[31]

Although the identifications with the Amazon as a figure of female autonomy and creativity were 'both too radical and too narrow for a broadly based critical movement',[32] such acute and legitimate refusals to cooperate with the phallocentric culture enabled a turning point in feminist imagery of witches.

Angela Carter's witch- and vampire-like characters in her short story collection *Burning Your Boats* (1996) belong to the most extraordinary examples of the literary shift that started in the late 1980s. Her witches are usually depicted as apocalyptic, castrated creatures, producing death instead of life. Often, their barren wombs (alluding to their suspended reproductive function) associate with the tomb and the denigration of female autonomy in culture. These prototypes are no longer of a female but of an apocalyptic, abysmal sex, infinitively poised between the woman and the monster. As with all other cultural attributes of the non-conforming female body, the witches are defined in terms of hysterical sexuality. A reader of Foucault, Carter argues that this sexuality is never expressed in a vacuum,[33] but is bound to the 'metaphysics' of politics and gender. She formulates her interpretation of power structures and places them in the context of partly abused and partly romanticized female body. Her aim is to demystify the hysterical locations of both female and male sexuality by disrupting the prohibitions placed on the body, a strategy deriving from the conviction that 'where there is a desire, the power relation is already present'.[34]

Under the influence of poststructuralist thought, the 'witch' figure has undergone many transformations and increasingly begun to convey the diasporic status of sexuality, especially sexually incompatible with the dominant discourse. The late twentieth century writers' interest in the history of sexuality, especially the history of madness, violence and hysteria, attest to these new cultural horizons. Mapping the intellectual territory of nineteenth century Canada, Margaret Atwood's *Alias Grace* (1996) reclaims the documented but enigmatic story of Grace Marks, who was convicted in 1843 of murdering her employer and his housekeeper, and was subsequently held in the Lunatic Asylum in Toronto and the Kingston Penitentiary. The controversial conviction sparked much debate about whether Marks was actually instrumental in the murder, or merely an unwitting accessory. A number of theories were offered as to Marks' psychic state: that she acted as if she suffered from mental illness in order to be placed in an asylum, that she had multiple personality disorder, or that she was possessed by the consciousness of her deceased friend Mary Whitney. Atwood chooses to explore the 19th century conception of 'female difference' intertwining neurological aspects of possession and hysteria with fragments of biblical imagery, superstitions, and demonology. Grace's madness is brought into immediate association with her culturally restricted and exploited body, subjected not only to science and law, but also to the private fantasies of the doctors and judges. The novel depicts the nineteenth century (women's) body, designed to be domesticated, 'caged in wire crinolines . . . so that they cannot get out and go rubbing up against the gentlemen's trousers',[35] just as they are destined to become pregnant in order to preserve their cultural entrapment. In this oppressively phallocentric structure of knowledge, Grace's mental condition seems to be deriving from her connection with the distorted mother of mankind, Eve, who was seduced by the snake and infused with disobedience. Focusing on Grace's absence of mind (God, Law) in the moments of her 'hysterical' attacks, Atwood inscribes madness as 'mysteria', a 'Western nineteenth-century view, which linked hysteria to a specific version of femininity as itself a "mystery"'.[36]

Also, Susan Fletcher's *The Highlands Witch* (2010) represents a more contemporary portrayal of the witch figure in a historical romance, written in an epistolary form. Playing on the traces of the witch-woman suggested by the – in historical terms highly problematic – work by Ehrenreich and English, the novel is a poetic narrative about Corrag, a child-bodied witch-herbalist with amazing healing powers. The novel recounts a historical event, the Massacre of Glencoe, which took place in Scotland, 1692, when families of the MacDonald clan (that refused to pledge allegiance to the Protestant king William), was brutally murdered by soldiers who had enjoyed their hospitality. Corrag, condemned for her involvement with the clan, is imprisoned, accused of witchcraft and sentenced to death by burning. As she awaits her death, Charles Leslie, an Irish Jacobite, seeking any evidence against the king, pays Corrag a visit, and day by day, becomes increasingly enchanted by her amazing storytelling talent, as she unfolds her life story filled with love, tenderness and hope towards life. While a true and rare friendship develops between the two, eventually Corrag's tantalizing story makes Leslie question his own socio-political beliefs and leads to his courageous act of rescuing her from the prison.

These historical representations of the 'witch' mark a turning point in philosophical understandings of marginalized bodies in the social structure. Most recent literary imagery of the witch, under the impact of postcolonial and transnational thought, suggests that social alienation, and exclusion from the mainstream politics and culture, is subject to multiple conditions, such as gender, sexual orientation, class, origin, race, accent, and religion. Over the last three decades, and most recently, at the turn of the twenty-first century, new significant diversifications across race, class, and political systems have taken place. Along with these diversifications, the 'witch' continues to represent new forms of heresy, stigma, and cultural provisionality within the framework of socio-political relations. Radically neither a word nor a concept, but rather a condition of possibility and move, the 'witch' as a subject is continuously departing from Western logocentric models, and continuously 'becoming' in its cultural incommensurability. As an overlapping cultural trait (of language, system, or geography), a moment of crossing, or transgressing culture, the experience is charged with tension, instilling constant changes in the subject value. This topography of the 'witch', radical in its persistent desire to transcend hostilities of the dominant structure, still interferes with the very structure, and transforms its foundations.

Notes

1 Andrew Sanders, *A Deed Without a Name: The Witch in Society and History* (Oxford: Berg, 1995); Susan Elsley, "Images of the Witch in Nineteenth-Century Culture" (Ph.D. diss., University of Chester, 2012).

2 Barbara Creed, *The Monstrous-Feminine: Film, Feminism, Psychoanalysis* (London: Routledge, 1993).

3 Tina Pippin, *Apocalyptic Bodies: The Biblical End of the World in Text and Image* (London: Routledge, 1999).

4 Hélène Cixous and Catherine Clément, eds., *The Newly Born Woman*, trans. Betsy Wing (Minneapolis: University of Minnesota Press, 1986), 6.

5 Shoshana Felman, "Women and Madness: The Critical Fallacy," in *The Feminist Reader: Essays in Gender and the Politics of Literary Criticism*, ed. Catherine Belsey and Jane Moore, 2nd ed. (London: Macmillan, 1997), 133–153.

6 Carol P. Christ, *Rebirth of the Goddess: Finding Meaning in Feminist Spirituality* (New York: Addison-Wesley, 1997); Pamela S. Anderson, *A Feminist Philosophy of Religion: The Rationality and Myths of Religious Belief* (Oxford UK and Cambridge, MA: Blackwell, 1998).

7 Justyna Sempruch, *Fantasies of Gender and the Witch in Feminist Theory and Literature* (West Lafayette: Purdue University Press, 2008).

8 Diane Purkiss, *The Witch in History: Early Modern and Twentieth-Century Representations* (London: Routledge, 1996), 15.

9 Ibid., 15.

10 Esther de Boer, *Mary Magdalene: Beyond the Myth* (Harrisburg, PA: Trinity Press International, 1997); Tikva Frymer-Kensky, *In the Wake of the Goddesses: Women, Culture and the Biblical Transformation of Pagan Myth* (New York: Fawcett Columbine, 1993); Susan Haskins, *Mary Magdalen: Myth and Metaphor* (London: HarperCollins, 1993); Jo Milgrom, "Some Second Thoughts about Adam's First Wife," in *Genesis 1–3 in the History of Exegesis: Intrigue in the Garden*, ed. G.A. Robbins (Lewiston, NY: Edwin Mellen Press, 1988); Barbara B. Koltuv, *The Book of Lilith* (York Beach: Nicolas-Hays, 1986).

11 Sempruch, *Fantasies*.

12 Sara Maitland, *Women Fly When Men Aren't Watching* (London: Virago, 1993), 55.

13 Margaret Whitford, *Luce Irigaray* (London: Routledge, 1991), 29.

14 Barbara Walker, *The Crone: Woman of Age, Wisdom and Ritual* (San Francisco: HarperCollins, 1985), 122.

15 Mary Daly, *Gyn/Ecology* (Boston: Beacon, 1978), 186.

16 Walker, *Crone*, 122.

17 Justyna Sempruch. "The Sacred May Not be the Same as the Religious: Angela Carter's 'Impressions: The Wrightsman Magdalene' and 'Black Venus'," *Women: A Cultural Review* 16.1 (2005): 73–92.

18 Purkiss, *The Witch*, 15.

19 Ibid., 16.

20 Ibid., 11.

21 Hélène Cixous, "The Laugh of the Medusa," in *Feminisms: An Analogy of Literary Theory and Criticism*, ed. Robyn Warhol-Down and Diane Price Herndl, trans. Keith and Paula Cohen (New Brunswick, NJ: Rutgers University Press, 1989), 347.

22 Luce Irigaray, "The Bodily Encounter with the Mother," in *The Irigaray Reader*, ed. Margaret Whitford (Oxford: Blackwell, 2000), 35.

23 Joanne Russ, "What Can a Heroine Do? Or Why Women Can't Write," in *Images of Women in Fiction: Feminist Perspectives*, ed. Susan Koppelman Cornillon (Bowling Green, OH: Bowling Green University Popular Press, 1973).

24 Sempruch, *Fantasies*.

25 Elaine Showalter, "A Criticism on Our Own: Autonomy and Assimilation in Afro-American and Feminist Literary Theory," in *Feminisms: An Analogy of Literary Theory and Criticism*, ed. Robyn R. Warhol-Down and Diane Price Herndl (New Brunswick, NJ: Rutgers University Press, 1997), 213–233.

26 Cixous and Clément, *Newly Born*, 8.

27 Ibid., 12.

28 Ibid., 15.

29 Alice Walker, *The Temple of My Familiar* (London: Penguin Books, 1990), 222.

30 Purkiss, *The Witch*, 10.

31 Sally M. Gearhart, *Wanderground: Stories of the Hill Women* (Boston: Alyson Publications, 1984), 171.

32 Showalter, "Criticism," 225.

33 Angela Carter, *The Sadeian Woman and the Ideology of Pornography* (London: Pantheon Books, 1979), 11.

34 Michel Foucault, *The History of Sexuality*, trans. Robert Hurley (New York: Vintage, 1990), 83.

35 Margaret Atwood, *Alias Grace* (Toronto: McClelland & Stewart, 1996), 33.

36 Juliet Mitchell, *Mad Men and Medusas: Reclaiming Hysteria and the Effects of Sibling Relations on the Human Conditions* (London: Penguin, 2000), 112.

Bibliography (selection)

Creed, Barbara, *The Monstrous-Feminine: Film, Feminism, Psychoanalysis*. London: Routledge, 1993.

Sanders, Andrew, *A Deed Without a Name: The Witch in Society and History*. Oxford: Berg, 1995.

Sempruch, Justyna, "The Sacred May Not Be the Same as the Religious: Angela Carter's 'Impressions: The Wrightsman Magdalene' and 'Black Venus'." *Women: A Cultural Review* 16 (2005): 73–92.

Sempruch, Justyna, *Fantasies of Gender and the Witch in Feminist Theory and Literature*. West Lafayette: Purdue University Press, 2008.

Purkiss, Diane, *The Witch in History: Early Modern and Twentieth-Century Representations*. London: Routledge, 1996.

28

WHERE HAVE ALL THE WITCHES GONE? THE DISAPPEARING WITCH AND CHILDREN'S LITERATURE

John Stephens

Witches have had some presence in children's literature since the nineteenth century, when their provenance was primarily retellings of certain Grimms' fairy tales (*Hansel and Gretel, Rapunzel, Jorinde and Joringel*), George Dasent's *Popular Tales from the Norse* (1859), and various folktales in which sundry female characters with supernatural origins or magic-working abilities, such as minor goddesses or ill-disposed fairies, are bundled together within the category of the witch. Such representations are reshaped in L. Frank Baum's *The Wonderful Wizard of Oz* (1900), which Marion Gibson considers a turning-point in the history of American witchcraft because it includes both 'good' and 'wicked witches.[1] In England, they peak with C. S. Lewis's *The Lion, the Witch and the Wardrobe* (1950),[2] which encapsulates how the constant in an otherwise semantically fuzzy area is a female disposition to evil. Vagueness in children's literature as to what characterises a witch has thus been endemic from the outset and, apart from a brief period during which the literature directly addressed the question, persists up to the present time.

The hey-day of the witch in children's literature proved to be surprisingly short, extending from around 1980 to 2000, and during this time witch stories probably only reached a large international audience through the 'witches' sub-set of Terry Pratchett's crossover teen/adult novels in the 'discworld' series – that is, from *Equal Rites* (1987) to *Carpe Jugulum* (1998). With some notable exceptions, the literature has subsequently included few witches at its 'high culture' end, which appears to have happened for several reasons: the dominance of the 'Harry Potter' (*HP*) series (1997–2007), in which the representation of witches has become a literary convention and has lost most of its earlier complexity and its social function; a widespread cultural shift reflected in children's and young adult literature whereby concerns with feminism and cultural tradition have diminished; the discrediting of the unhistorical feminist mythology of 'the burning times'; and the flourishing interest in the adaptation of fairy tales which employ a cognitive map for fairies which occupies much the same imaginative space as the schematic map for witches. This tendency to conflate fairies and witches is quite old, however, and Susan Jennifer Elsley has identified its presence as early as 1859.[3] A further contributing factor has perhaps been the expansion of gothic fiction for young readers, whereby monsters such as vampires that inhabit the border territories between life and death and between aberrant and normative subjectivities have pushed witches to the narrative periphery. A good example of how such displacement occurs is Neil Gaiman's gothic novel *The Graveyard Book* (2008). The ghost of a witch, Liza Hempstock, is introduced in Chapter 4, and is the focus of Bod's almost fatal encounter with the outside world, but subsequently appears only sporadically, as she has no further role to play. She is thus a minor character in comparison with Bod's guardian and mentor, the vampire Silas. Liza in fact embodies a schematic figure from what Diane Purkiss terms 'radical feminist histories of witches'[4] that arose in the 1970s and which characterised witches as victims of patriarchal ideology – as Liza describes her own death by torture and consignment to oblivion, 'drowned and burnded and buried here without as much as a stone to mark the spot' (100).[5]

The movement of witches to the periphery of narrative had occurred already in the 1990s – Philip Pullman's *His Dark Materials* series presents a prominent example – and the only major examples of a witch as main protagonist and focaliser in twenty-first century children's fiction have been Pratchett's inventive, highly-regarded 'Tiffany Aching' series (2003–2015), which he built around adaptations of British and Scottish folklore, and Carolyn MacCullough's *Once a Witch* (2009) and its sequels. In addition to their innate appeal, the five Tiffany Aching books may prove to be historically important because they sustain the core scripts and schemas which underpinned representations of witches as they were formulated in the 1970s and further developed subsequently. While Pratchett's books sell prolifically and have been translated into numerous languages, their audience is nevertheless smaller than that reached by the 'Harry Potter' series, and the 'Tiffany Aching' books have received very little critical or media attention (principally Baker and Gruner), in sharp contrast to the scholarly treadmill that was generated by the *HP* series.

Children's literature is highly responsive to shifts in social ideology, and the women's movement of the 1970s produced one of the most significant twentieth-century paradigm shifts in the literature. It began to incorporate feminist and quasi-feminist stances and to represent women and girls shaped by 'second wave' feminist concerns – primarily in terms of equality of representation in numbers and functions – and hence the new conception of the witch as a subject who resisted patriarchal efforts to victimize her because of her skills, strength and independence offered an attractive schema. Since the first transformations of the witch in feminist mythology in the 1970s, and her subsequent deployment as a significant figure in children's literature, characters identified as witches have been found in most literary forms, ranging from picture books through to young adult fiction. As Robin Briggs observed in 1996, 'Witches are everywhere in modern children's literature. Sometimes they retain their old character, representing evil in its most virulent form, but more often they have become either harmless tricksters or repositories of ancient wisdom'.[6] The witches thus described can be classified according to three distinct schemas: the ancient crone (variously embodiment of evil or harmless comic figure), the malevolent sorceress witch, and the wise woman who is a healer and midwife. In each case, the witch is assigned to the category of 'people who in some sense or other are not full members of the community'.[7] The identification of witches as strangers, outsiders and nonconformists is also virtually absolute in children's literature. This otherness is commonly a catalyst for story events, but it also has a significant thematic function in that it constitutes a site from which the excluding community can be evaluated and judged. The witch's apparently eccentric behaviour both marks her as an object of suspicion and defines the host community as narrow-minded, petty and malicious. This is the representation reproduced in *The Graveyard Book*.

Texts pivoting around witch-figures are inevitably intertextual, existing in a dialogic relationship with history, historiographic discourses, scholarly research and popular culture, religious belief, and classic literary works (especially fairy tales and Shakespeare's *Macbeth*). Whether implicitly or explicitly, books for young readers engage with how these discourses have figured and regulated the shape and boundaries of cultural formations: the nature of belief; the antithesis of scientific positivism and myth; the delineation of subaltern groups at the margins of sociality; the role of the feminine in patriarchal societies; and so on.

Witches, then, are commonly depicted as people finding their own way outside the boundaries of mainstream society, and their representation is a way of looking at the relationships between past and present and the nature of cultural paradigm shifts. In many late twentieth-century children's books the witch-figure had undergone rehabilitation, though this was not universally so, and with the substantial dismantling of the 1970s witch mythology by 1996 (most influentially in the works of the cultural historians Briggs and Purkiss), the status of the witch in children's literature changed from a quasi-historical feminist icon to a literary convention. From whatever cause, the shift is already evident in *Harry Potter and the Philosopher's Stone*, in which social centre and periphery are transposed and mainstream society is identified as that of witches and wizards. The principal witch character, Hermione, is marginalized not because she is a witch but because she is pervasively represented as a girlie swot, or, as Christine Schoefer puts it, 'a smart goody-goody who annoys the boys by constantly reminding them of school rules'. The somewhat febrile debate about gender representation sparked by Schoefer's online article focused on untheorized content analysis of Hermione's interpellation within a recognisable late twentieth/early twenty-first century society.[8] No attempt was made to explore how the representation of her subjectivity might – or might not – relate to witch schemas. Instead, discussion turned to 'capable young woman' schemas in the period of text production.

The witch in the *HP* series falls within a popular culture version of postfeminism more recently formulated by Stephanie Genz as a blending of feminism and femininity: 'a more flexible and open-ended model of agency that is doubly coded in political terms and entwines backlash and innovation, complicity and critique'.[9] In contrast, the rehabilitation of the witch in late twentieth-century children's fiction was grounded in second-wave feminist analysis, which, in drawing attention to the discourses and power structures which are dominant in a given society, enabled a revaluation of the nature of female 'others', of women who choose or endeavour to lead lives outside the gendering frame of establishment discourses. In other words, it creates the possibility of validating what hegemonic patriarchy has rendered marginal. Purkiss points to the connection of ahistorical feminist accounts of witch persecutions with 'contemporary questions of authority, authenticity and public politics', and the rhetorical function of pseudo-histories 'not as a reconstruction of the past, but an account of the way things *always* are'.[10] However, the evocation of the suffering female body characteristic of this rhetoric makes only rare appearances in children's literature. The extended representation of the motif in Donna Jo Napoli's *The Magic Circle* (1993) is thus unusual, although its concomitant affirmation of traditional feminine roles and domestic space is not. Fiction for children has, rather, one of two foci, depending on a novel's temporal setting. First, fictions set in the past may attempt to invert historical representations by depicting a witch-figure from a sympathetic perspective. Thus Monica Furlong's *Wise Child* (1987) is narrated by a young girl who, having been left without any adults to take care of her, is given a loving home by Juniper, the local 'witch,' and quickly becomes embroiled in the difference between actuality and representation. The other children, the village adults, and especially the village priest place Juniper in the subject position of the traditional evil witch. Wise Child, who as narrator embodies the novel's most authoritative perspective, soon learns that Juniper is the most upright and meritorious member of the community. Second, fictions set in the present, such as Theresa Tomlinson's *Summer Witches* (1989), are apt to deal with the theme of escaping from the limiting and confining structures of the past in the process of forming a contemporary female subjectivity.

The construction of witch schemas in the 1970s was also shaped by a second cultural factor temporally parallel with second-wave feminism. This factor was a bundle of ideas which derived its represented witch-schema and its somewhat New Age grounding philosophy from several streams. The representation of witches in contemporary, twenty-first century teen and cross-over novels – for example, Carolyn MacCullough's *Once a Witch* (2009) – reproduces this schema. An important catalyst has been a myth derived from elements of Margaret Murray's theory about witches as devotees of an ancient pre-Christian fertility religion. While the 'Murrayite' hypothesis has been generally discredited since its enunciation in 1921,[11] it has also been enormously influential and appears to inform many of the modern representations of witches. As Jacqueline Simpson points out, because Murray was given the opportunity to present her theory in the 1929 *Encyclopedia Brittanica*, where it remained as an apparent fact until 1969, her views were accessible 'to journalists, film-makers, popular novelists and thriller writers, who adopted them enthusiastically' (89). As Simpson concludes, 'by now [i.e. 1994] they are so entrenched in popular culture that they will probably never be uprooted'. The subsequent appropriations of Murray's theory offer a telling example of how people construct alternative pseudo-histories in order to challenge familiar representations in history. Subsequently wrapped in with this image is that of the midwife-healer, which, as Purkiss points out,[12] originated as recently as 1973 in Barbara Ehrenreich and Deirdre English's *Witches, Midwives and Nurses*. An attractive effect of such an alternative history is that it inverts the conventional, Enlightenment, probably masculine, privileging of history over myth. The entry for 'Witchcraft' in Barbara Walker's *The Woman's Encyclopedia of Myths and Secrets* is a convenient symptomatic example of how history, anecdote and fancy become inextricably imbricated.[13]

For contemporary fictional representations of witchcraft, however, discriminations between fact and fancy are less important than the pervasiveness of the pseudo-history as an enabling myth. Other, often related, recent influences shaping the modern witch-schema are neo-paganism, goddess-worship, eco-feminism, and the late twentieth-century mania for Celtic traditions. All of this yields up a bundle of ideas centred on a quasi-pantheistic conception of the cosmos as an ordered and coherent universe in which all parts are interrelated but from which most human beings are alienated. This bundle of ideas is used to interrogate or reject Western historical traditions and cultural metanarratives of various kinds, ranging from the ethics of individualism to the social codes which regulate sexual practice and its meanings. It is often an effective mode of analogical thinking, but can also slip into discourses that are little more than sentimental essentialism. A crucial function of the modern witch-schema is that it is used to fill a gap opened up by the other strand of this second cultural factor, a pervasive unease with or anxiety about (post-)modernity.

To recognize that reality is socially constructed, along with the conceptual categories used to order and reproduce it – history, science, reason, self, subject, sex, sanity – is to destabilize the ground of children's literature. It is no accident that Kenneth Lillington's *An Ash-blonde Witch* (1989), for example, problematizes all of those conceptual categories just listed, or that other books reaffirm from various perspectives the existence of immanent, as opposed to transcendent, good and evil prior to the social construction of experience. Within the surface-without-depth, fragmented culture of post-Christian postmodernism, witches can be used to evoke an important function: to offer visions of wholeness, and to reassert certain values either present in or ascribed to the past, and to suggest that those values are recuperable in our mundane modern world. Witches such as Juniper, the two very different witches depicted in *An Ash-blonde Witch*, or the Northern witches in Philip Pullman's *His Dark Materials* (see especially *The Subtle Knife* (1997), Chapter 2) are positioned on the outside of both patriarchal institutional religion and patriarchal secular society, and they either practice or move toward new versions of spirituality. What such a witch stands for is a neo-humanistic protest against postmodernism's denial of ethical values and a resistance to late twentieth-century human indifference. As a figure (self-)excluded from patriarchal, 'old humanist' society and belief, the witch embodies the inverted hierarchical oppositions of modernity, but invests them with ethical and aesthetic value. Thus she sees others as fellow human beings rather than strangers, and privileges the other over the self, the object over the subject, society over the individual, myth over history, emotion over reason, intuition over knowledge, female knowledge over male knowledge, nature over culture, and immanence over transcendence. In her embodiment of these emphases, and her conversion of them into social praxis, she makes her world both meaningful and a better place.

One of the problems implicitly attributed to late modernity is that it separates people from their cultural history and alienates them from their own selves. In this context the witch-figure can be used as a counterweight to a cultural paradigm shift, which seems to be the basis for Tomlinson's *Summer Witches*, an overtly simplified rethinking of the traditional idea of witch as crone and its cultural transmission, presented through a story about the evolution of young female friendship and subjectivities. It is a story about two girls – Sarah and Susanna – who are thrown together and negotiate friendship as they convert an old air-raid shelter into their own special place, inadvertently replicating what two female neighbours had done there during World War Two. The girls have identified one of these women – Miss Lily – as a witch because she is speech- and hearing-impaired, and have used her perceived otherness as a basis for a misconstruction in terms of the witch of fairy-tale imagination, especially in *Hansel and Gretel* and *Rapunzel*. The novel does not merely falsify and expel the girls' misconstruction, as happens elsewhere, as, for example, in Helen Griffiths' *The Mysterious Appearance of Agnes* (1975), a historical novel which debunks ideas about witchcraft as mere unreasoned prejudice and suspicion of otherness. Rather, *Summer Witches* replaces the crone stereotype with the 'wise woman' schema. This happens quite overtly toward the end of the book, when Chapter 11 is entirely given over to a conversation about constructions of 'witchiness.' The positive image offered here is that of the conventional 'green' witch, the woman in touch with the natural world and its cycles and with her own instinctual responses. In the following chapters the girls apply their new knowledge, first by deconstructing the life-size representation of a crone-witch found in a local history museum, and second by using their own newly discovered witchiness to help Lily overcome the trauma of her wartime memories. The novel thus builds in a double recuperation of the past – of the near past of the mid-twentieth century and of the deeper past of cultural misogyny and subaltern womanhood, presenting now an image of witches as conservers of nature and tradition, healers, and agents of renewal.

Summer Witches explores the idea of the witch by contrasting two schemas familiar from the historiographical discourses about witches, encapsulated here by 'Horrid, ugly old things who ate children and rode broomsticks' and 'wise women . . . [who] grew herbs and made medicines that often worked well'.[14] These are the schemas which tend to dominate representations in children's books, though by the 1970s the crone-schema of an old woman wearing the conventional uniform of black clothing, pointed hat, and boots, and travelling by broomstick, or 'borrowing' the bodies of animals, was falling out of serious use. It was being dismantled in three ways: by being rendered comic (as in, for example, the picture books of Mahy and Williams, and of Nichols and Pienkowski), by being dismissed as a stereotype, and by becoming supplanted as versions of the Murrayite wise witch emerging within children's literature. The crone-schema did not entirely disappear, however, but has persisted in retellings of more intransigent stories, especially of *Hansel and Gretel.* Shelley Duvall's melodramatic *Faerie Tale Theatre* retelling (1982) depicts the crone-witch in her aged ugliness – literally, warts and all. Resistance to this representation appears in Pratchett's *The Wee Free Men* (2003), when Tiffany logically dismantles an adaptation of the tale and concludes that, in accordance with the ideology of folktale, an old woman was persecuted and left to die because 'she just looked like a witch in a story'.[15] The series often returns to this stereotype, assumedly because, in his comprehensive grasp of the power of story, Pratchett strives to dismantle unexamined cultural labels. Such a need is illustrated in that even a retelling by an adapter as astute as Neil Gaiman (*Hansel and Gretel* 2014) reproduces the schema by concealing the evil crone within a person who appears to be 'not an ogre or a monster, but a kindly-faced old woman, leaning on a stick, who peered about her short-sightedly with dim eyes',[16] but who quickly reverts to the expected role once she has captured the children.

In opposition to the wise witch is the third witch-schema, that of the sorceress-witch; fascinating, young, beautiful, but malevolent, the sorceress-witch expresses the dark, wild and subversive elements of female desire, female pain, and female nature more generally. As far as I know, no work of children's fiction situates such a character as primary protagonist, although she does appear in *The Craft* (1996), a popular film for late adolescent audiences and upward, marketed as 'a hip, sexy, supernatural thriller.' This film links witchcraft and femininity gone wrong and, not very subtly, reaffirms the wisdom of official society's control over the lives and bodies of young women, of reconstituting the subversive as subaltern. Otherness here constitutes a threat, and is where the sorceress-witch schema most closely overlaps with the wicked fairy figure of, for example, *Sleeping Beauty* and *Snow White* adaptations. Robin

McKinley's *Spindle's End* (2000), an adaptation of *Sleeping Beauty*, only describes the malevolent Pernicia obliquely – she is tall and dressed in 'black and grey streaked with purple and magenta and cerise, and a necklace of black stones',[17] but the control of dark magic is almost irresistible. It may be that the popularity of the title character of Disney's *Maleficent* (2014) will further obliterate the witch from children's fiction. The film's dismantling of the misogyny normally associated with the depiction of the sorceress-witch may not be subtle, but has a greater potential to erase the schema than to recuperate it.

A text generally identifies its witch-figure as such, most usually by the suspicious, prejudiced and hostile attitudes of other characters toward her, and this enables exploration both of the nature of otherness and of the functions of historical patriarchy in deploying ideas about witchcraft to induce female conformity and docility. The wise-witch schema is therefore always an intertextual representation and often overtly presented as a contrast with or even deconstruction of the crone- and sorceress-witch schemas, so that the three possibilities are brought into dialogic relationships with one another and into relationships with historiography. Because witches have been constructed, historically, as possessing an evil disposition that sets them apart from common humanity, narratives about good witches will seek to recuperate the idea of the witch. Furlong thus defines her witch as 'someone who loves all the creatures of the world . . . the animals, birds, plants, trees and people and who cannot bear to do any of them any harm. It is someone who believes that they are all linked together and that therefore everything can be used to heal the pain and suffering of the world. It is someone who does not hate anybody and is not frightened of anyone or anything'.[18] As a character type, and in intertextual contrast with the received notions attached to her less savoury sisters, the wise witch conforms to a bundle of conventional schematic attributes. Further, the three principal components of the wise-witch schema as deployed in children's fiction – her place in the community, her personal appearance, and her spiritual beliefs – function as social critique.

In appearance, the wise witch is apt to be young, healthy and handsome. Her overall wholesomeness contrasts both with the extreme ugliness of the crone and with the 'bewitching' beauty of the sorceress-witch. She is nevertheless usually comely enough to be an object of desire, envy, or slander. Moreover, she tends to be sexually active in a community with a patriarchal social structure, and this contributes to community representations of her as 'witch' and 'evil'. As Mair puts it, 'A witch . . . is a person who does not control the impulses that good members of society must keep in check'.[19] When, in *An Ash-blonde Witch*, the crone-witch Dorcas wants to eliminate the beautiful newcomer, Sophie, her method is to promulgate an insinuation attributing to Sophie the perverted, insatiable, and destructive sexuality of the sorceress-witch. Because Sophie is no such thing, and is the novel's principal focalizing character, the effect of such attributions is to interrogate the cultural formations which shape and regulate sexual practices, whether in the past or the present.

The wise witch is most set apart from the local community by her spiritual beliefs. She does not conform with, or subscribe to, the beliefs of whatever contemporary, hegemonic religion prevails (usually a form of Christianity), but either has an ecumenical view of religion, or is a pantheist, a polytheist, or a Goddess-worshiper. This makes her an inevitable object of suspicion, and sometimes a target for pulpit-oratory, and in *Wise Child*, for example, where such attacks are presented as unjustified, the effect is to separate spiritual experience and insight from organized religion. Juniper's ecumenical adherence to a broad-based spiritual immanence challenges other characters, and readers, to think about the nature of spiritual experience and the bases for religious pronouncements about such issues as gender. More polemically, the witches in Pullman's *His Dark Materials* not only worship gods and goddesses linked with nature and the earth, but are overtly critical of 'the church', which strives 'to suppress and control every natural impulse. And when it can't control them it cuts them out. . . . That is what the church does, and every church is the same, control, destroy, obliterate every good feeling'.[20] The opposition to mainstream Christianity in Pullman's work is widely acknowledged, but the significance here is that part of his critique is grounded in late twentieth-century witch lore.

The witch in children's and young adult literature remains an outsider outside society, but with the power to change society. This formulation underpins the two most notable contemporary witch narratives, Pratchett's 'Tiffany Aching' series and Margo Lanagan's young adult novel *Sea Hearts* (2012). Offering contrasting visions, both reach back into the twentieth century witch schemas to rethink the power of the witch as a force in women's lives. Where the *HP* witches are narratively subordinated to dynamic male characters and perform magic which is mechanical and formulaic, Pratchett's Tiffany Aching walks in spaces between worlds and drives back supernatural forces that persist across ages to find embodiment in Tiffany's present. She saves everydayness and articulates its inherent value by preserving the boundaries between her world and the myriad worlds that lie contiguous with it, but also by performing everydayness – tending to the ill and the dying, birthing sheep, and embodying the essence of the land whose witch she is. *Sea Hearts* is an adaptation of the selkie legend, but turns on the power of its witch, Misskaella, to summon selkie women out of their seal bodies. That power constitutes her malice, since these displaced and captured women represent women without agency, afflicted with depression and grief for the subjectivity they have lost. They replicate the most abject female condition imagined within second-wave feminism, and thus Misskaella's actions dismantle the quest for agency and female independence pursued by the late twentieth-century wise witch. While enriching herself by supplying selkies to the men, Misskaella exacts a terrible revenge for the outsider status thrust upon her because of her innate power and physical unattractiveness. The novel's narrative form is unique amongst witch stories: from the opening line – 'The old witch is there' – she is positioned at the centre of events, both because of her role in the story and of the strategy of organizing the narrative as seven discrete sections narrated by six characters, but she occupies the centre as an influence or idea rather than an actor. The narrators are mostly unreliable, either because they are self-interested or lack information readers have gained or inferred from other narrators, but Misskaela and her actions always shadows their thoughts. The effect is to block reader empathy with the witch until the final pages, which disclose – only to readers – the witch's anguish over the loss of the three sons she had borne to a selkie, but which she had to give back to the sea because they were unable to survive in human form. The witch's apprentice, Trudle, describes the package containing the carefully preserved baby clothes Misskaella had instructed should be buried with her, but her inability to know the significance of what she holds focuses reader attention on that gap and produces a strong empathic response. The novel thus closes with an intriguing experiment with reader positioning which delivers an exploration of the subjectivity of a witch unsurpassed in YA fiction.

Sea Hearts has the potential to prompt readers to revaluate the history of witch representations in children's and YA fiction. The wise witch performs as a liberating force and agent of change, but is sometimes required to overcome expulsion by 'official society'. Misskaella, however, is only positioned as focalizer of events in the second section of the novel, which she narrates as a pre-school child, and is subsequently depicted as others perceive her, so the important effect of narrative point of view becomes foregrounded in an unprecedented way. The crone, as I observed earlier, is commonly rendered as a comic non-conformist figure with subversive potential, notably in the novels of Pratchett,[21] and in picture-books and junior fiction, whereas Lanagan reinvests the crone with darkness and danger. Where official society most forcibly reasserts traditional hegemonic structures and values, especially gendered behaviours, is in the depiction of the sorceress-witch. When positioned as a supplementary participant, she tends to represent femininity gone wrong, choosing to evade the hegemony of patriarchy by exercising her power in a dangerous and destructive manner. For example, in Donna Jo Napoli's experimental rewriting of the Rapunzel story, *Zel* (1996), the stepmother-witch traded her soul to the devil in return for the power to ensnare Rapunzel's parents and gain possession of their child. To escape her contract and redeem herself, she must lose her power by yielding her claim to the prince's, and so is instrumental in returning the young lovers to the hegemony of a romantic outcome under patriarchy, where Zel exemplifies 'good' femininity. In contrast, *Sea Hearts* subverts patriarchy in two ways: first, through the witch's actions which ensure that happiness will be impossible, and then through the development of moral insight in the selkies' sons, who recognize their mothers' pain and secretly enable their flight back to the sea. Lanagan's novel interrogates how effectively the three witch-schemas deployed in texts for young audiences challenge patriarchal society and empower women and girls. The witch may subvert contemporary social attitudes and practices, but, finally, how transformative is her impact?

Notes

1   Marion Gibson, *Witchcraft Myths in American Culture* (New York: Routledge, 2007), 139–140.
2   The best-known American witch story for young readers remains Elizabeth George Speare's historical novel *The Witch of Blackbird Pond* (Boston: Houghton Mifflin Harcourt Publishing Company, 1958), which draws on the New England witch persecution of the Seventeenth Century.
3   Susan Jennifer Elsley, "Images of the Witch in Nineteenth Century Culture" (PhD diss., University of Liverpool, 2012), 16.
4   Diane Purkiss, *The Witch in History* (London: Routledge, 1996), 10.
5   Neil Gaiman, *The Graveyard Book* (London: Bloomsbury, 2008), 100.
6   Robin Briggs, *Witches and Neighbours: The Social and Cultural Context of European Witchcraft* (London: HarperCollins, 1996), 5.
7   Lucy Mair, *Witchcraft* (London: World University Library, 1973), 46.
8   See for example: Sarah Zettel, "Hermione Granger and the Charge of Sexism," in *Mapping the World of the Sorcerer's Apprentice: An Unauthorized Exploration of the Harry Potter Series*, ed. Mercedes Lackey (Dallas, TX: BenBella Books, Inc., 2005), 96–97.
9   Stéphanie Genz, *Postfemininities in Popular Culture* (Basingstoke: Palgrave Macmillan, 2009), 92.
10 Purkiss, *The Witch in History*, 10–11.

11 See especially: Mair, *Witchcraft*, 226–231; Norman Cohn, *Europe's Inner Demons* (St Albans, Herts.: Paladin, 1976), 107–120; Carlo Ginzburg, *Ecstasies: Deciphering the Witches' Sabbath* (New York: Pantheon Books, 1991), 8–9; Purkiss, *The Witch in History*, 62–63.
12 Purkiss, *The Witch in History*, 19–20.
13 Barbra G. Walker, *The Woman's Encyclopedia of Myths and Secrets* (Cambridge: Harper and Row, 1983), 1081–1091.
14 Theresa Tomlinson, *Summer Witches* (London: Julia MacRae Books, 1989), 69.
15 Terry Pratchett, *The Wee Free Men* (London: Doubleday, 2003), 50.
16 Neil Gaiman, *Hansel and Gretel* (New York: Toon Graphics, 2014), 32.
17 Robin McKinley, *Spindle's End* (New York: G.P. Putnam's Sons, 2000), 40.
18 Monica Furlong, *Wise Child* (London: Victor Gollancz, 1987), 240.
19 Mair, *Witchcraft*, 38.
20 Phillip Pullman, *The Subtle Knife: His Dark Materials* (London: Scholastic Children's Books, 1997), 52.
21 Stephens, John. "Not Unadjacent to a Play about a Scottish King: Terry Pratchett Retells *Macbeth*," *Papers: Explorations into Children's Literature* 7 (1997): 29–37.

Bibliography (selection)

Baker, Deirdre F., "What We Found on Our Journey Through Fantasy Land." *Children's Literature in Education* 37 (2006): 237–251.
Genz, Stéphanie, *Postfemininities in Popular Culture*. Basingstoke: Palgrave Macmillan, 2009.
Gibson, Marion, *Witchcraft Myths in American Culture*. New York: Routledge, 2007.
Gruner, Elisabeth Rose, "Teach the Children: Education and Knowledge in Recent Children's Fantasy." *Children's Literature* 37 (2009): 216–235.
Gruner, Elisabeth Rose, "Wrestling With Religion: Pullman, Pratchett, and the Uses of Story." *Children's Literature Association Quarterly* 36 (2011): 276–295.
Stephens, John, "Not Unadjacent to a Play About a Scottish King: Terry Pratchett Retells *Macbeth*." *Papers: Explorations into Children's Literature* 7 (1997): 29–37.
Stephens, John, "Witch-figures in Recent Children's Fiction: The Subaltern and the Subversive." In *The Past in the Present*, edited by Ann Lawson Lucas, 195–202. Westport, CT: Praeger, 2003.
Walker, Barbara G., *The Woman's Encyclopedia of Myths and Secrets*. Cambridge: Harper and Row, 1983.
Zettel, Sarah, "Hermione Granger and the Charge of Sexism." In *Mapping the World of the Sorcerer's Apprentice: An Unauthorized Exploration of the Harry Potter Series*, edited by Mercedes Lackey, 83–101. Dallas, TX: BenBella Books, Inc., 2005.

29

WITCHCRAFT IN FILM

David Nash

A chapter on witchcraft in film, one that appears in a book primarily about the history of the phenomenon clearly has a different purpose than the numerous treatments of witchcraft that appear in film studies and popular culture volumes. Thus, this chapter will consider several of the central themes thrown up by numerous depictions of witchcraft in film and will focus upon these in specific examples. Perhaps one overarching theme that cultural historians should most be interested in is how depictions of witchcraft in film have been a communicative and exploratory device. That is, they should be regarded as methods by which the public at large learn aspects of otherwise specialist or academic knowledge. As such, they have a crucial role in shaping popular perception of the particular phenomena depicted. This chapter displays illustrations of witchcraft practice, vivid re-creations of what particular periods of historiography have established as fact and interpretation and, lastly, a variety of themes which seek to place witchcraft in a wider historical and cultural context. As such, these have lasting influence upon popular perceptions of witchcraft and the occult. Indeed we might consider how far some of these depictions have become cultural archetypes in themselves, further influencing cultural products and outputs about this particular subject.

One of the first themes we notice in witchcraft films is the theme of knowledge. This has many different dimensions and modes, and witchcraft films regularly unpack this idea in various directions. Knowledge can be portrayed as the conscious and studious acquisition of ideas and concepts generally considered alien to conventional and normal life. This knowledge can be secret and hidden and only uncovered after considerable effort or scholarship, or surrendering of self and power. Once such knowledge is acquired it can be used for good or for evil. This propensity sometimes appears as a warning to those who have a disposition to mistakenly involve themselves in what is so often referred to as 'the black arts'. Excursions into these arts, and the knowledge surrounding them, can be portrayed variously as obsessive scholarly interest, the folly of youth or as a pursuit liable to be undertaken by the decadent or the bored. Knowledge, and the power it conveys, is also frequently the battleground between good and evil. At various moments in witchcraft films the superior nature of knowledge, or its application by skilled practitioners can appear to have evil triumph over good or vice versa. The interface between ideas of knowledge and power also reminds us that there is a tension between different witchcraft films that portray the phenomenon as a fully fledged system, as opposed to the more random acquisition of occult powers, or the intention to acquire these. Elsewhere, there are places where the fanatical application of knowledge makes the whole concept of knowledge itself acquire a sceptical and dangerous ambivalence. Knowledge can likewise become a source of related problems for protagonists within such films. Curiosity and the acquisition of knowledge can lead individuals into situations and circumstances that are dangerous and very frequently unforgiving. This preoccupation with power might make us think of Foucauldian analysis and its perspectives on historical change in the West. However the fit is less than exact. Whilst power seems to drive these plots and their resolution to a considerable degree, it is modernity that is generally seen as the innocent party. Witchcraft films so often show premodern authority as a type of driven and righteous specialist knowledge, one wielded by the professionals of the period (of both sides) against the more innocent subjectivity of individuals. Far from being a problematic labyrinth of control and enslavement, modernity is often portrayed in witchcraft films as the simplistically innocent counterpart to the agenda-driven darkness of the early modern period and its practices.

Related to the issue of knowledge is the issue of power, and often in these films knowledge is power – quite literally. Elsewhere power is used to convert, dazzle, liberate, mislead and oppress in a variety of ways. Several early modern period pieces in particular focus upon the misuse of power, largely by those engaged in the pursuit of witch hunting. Very frequently this graphically creates the sustained portrayal of gendered oppression. This oppression takes many guises, from the application of the law through subjugation of the will and even to acts of what we might term sexual terrorism. As such this visual playing out of the misuse of power has assisted in the cultural acceptance of the gender dimension of witchcraft as occasion for persecution. Authority to control errant behaviour, sexuality and identity is very often portrayed as male which has served to culturally underpin many gender explanations of witchcraft and its history. Likewise, attempts to see the oppressive destruction of independently minded women, merely pursuing activities that liberate them or that recapture older knowledge, produce studies in inequality of gender power and its distribution.

One further dimension of this is the appearance of anticlerical themes in some witchcraft films (or those about possession such as Ken Russell's *The Devils*) which also emphasise elements of single-mindedness, something which sometimes shades over into oppressive fanaticism that, almost always, results in the systematic abuse of power. Equally, it is often significant how the dissolution of power, broadly defined, is generally the conclusion of such films. Thus, the witchcraft film is broadly speaking a simple Manichaean universe and the action turns around the restoration of good over evil, albeit with some notable exceptions. A further theme, we might even call part of an anti-Foucauldian central trinity, is the action of knowledge and power upon the individual will. Very frequently there is action or circumstances which lead protagonists to either surrender their will, or have it twisted and shaped by circumstances, the action of others or their perception of the supernatural occult world and its nature.

Another singularly common factor in most witchcraft films is the ambivalent nature of time, chronology and historical context. Although some films are simply early modern period pieces that re-enact actual or skilfully invented and plausible stories, others use time and history as essential motifs that drive narrative or dramatic action. Several turn on the idea of an ancient curse which self-consciously brings the past into the present. Within such plots witchcraft, and the knowledge surrounding it, are portrayed as dramatically out of kilter with modernity. This juxtaposition is frequently used to problematise the supposedly secure nature of modernity, but it is also used to induce fear about aspects of our past selves reaching out to unsettle us from the mists of time.

A further aspect of this reaching out from the mists of time is emphasised by the regular invocation of geographical remoteness as an important signifier within witchcraft films. This serves to distance such beliefs from the rational and modern world, whilst allowing for, perhaps celebrating even, the ability of the past to envelop characters from the present who stray off course in various ways. The sense of stumbling into the persistent nature of anachronistic practices and beliefs – if one is foolish enough to stumble off the beaten track – is also a method of destabilising modernity and emphasising its very fragility, as its writ does not run as far as audiences hope or are led to fear.

One film which perhaps straddles the world of academic study and active entertainment is also arguably one of the first in the canon of twentieth-century witchcraft films. Benjamin Christensen's 1922 *Häxan* is probably the one most responsible for providing audiences with a self-conscious education about witchcraft and its history. This film engaged closely with the *Malleus* and consciously reflected several of its beliefs, whilst carefully critiquing them. The film blends scholarly exposition with dramatic reconstruction of plausible events. Throughout, the film is modernist in tone, ascribing witchcraft beliefs to a failure of primitive man to have adequate tools with which to comprehend the universe. The film's first section is an unashamed history lesson with sequences which move towards an analysis of witchcraft and the witch hunt which was academically prevalent until the end of the 1960s. *Häxan* suggested that these phenomena were the products of species of extreme and deranged thoughts and behaviour – as befitted a film which expounded its own close engagement with the *Malleus*. Thus, both witches and witch hunters were victims of their historical context that identified this as an unfortunate episode which would be recast by Trevor Roper as the 'Witch craze'.[1]

Further sections of the film outline crucial aspects of the 'making of a witch' which again must have had a profound influence on twentieth-century visualisation of the witch as an archetype. She is shown at work creating potions in her kitchen and then the action moves to the detailed portrayal of a witch trial. This takes the viewer through accusation of bewitchment and then the arrest and torture of the witch. During the course of the latter a description of attendance at the sabbat emerges, and under torture the witch implicates others, allowing the film to depict the consequences of a witch hunt and the dynamics which drove this. A later section strongly suggests witchcraft beliefs, and the indulgence of them by practitioners and opponents, were likely the product of hysterical reactions. The cause of such hysteria was likely to be forms of repression of the mind, which again was an approach which took its place in the arsenal of pre 1960s explanations – but would re-emerge in the work of Norman Cohn in *Europe's Inner Demons*.

Examination of post *Häxan* films with a more obvious intent to entertain should begin with the 1960 film *City of the Dead* (John Moxey), which tells of the perils of researching the witchcraft of the past. The central character is killed by Devil worshippers after travelling to a sleepy New England town in search of insights into the history of witchcraft.[2] This is a film which sought to give American audiences a taste of their own indigenous witchcraft history. As with many of our films the rational pitched against the irrational with both belief in witchcraft and scepticism which describes it as 'mumbo-jumbo' both plainly evident within the first reel. The inhabitants of the 'City of the Dead' are still surviving undead from the seventeenth century – a period when one of their number was executed for the crime of witchcraft. This yokes together two long-running traditions in filmmaking about the occult. Firstly, that it comes down to us from a remote past, more often than not systematically and deliberately unaltered. Likewise, this village is remote and is, literally, untouched by the twentieth century. It can also only be reached by a significant and dangerous detour re-emphasising for American audiences stepping off the main thoroughfare or highway is most times fraught with difficulty and danger. This narrative became so central to American horror that it informed everything from *Psycho* right through to the *Texas Chainsaw Massacre*. The ending has a strong motif which engulfs the coven members when they are touched by the shadow of a crucifix.

Success and power within the academy have even been the subject of witchcraft's flirtation with dialogues of power. In Sidney Hayer's 1962 film *Night of the Eagle* Peter Wyngarde's university career is nurtured and promoted by the spells and charms cast by his wife, in conflict with the spells cast by other wives in the faculty. When Wyngarde's sceptical nature destroys these his own academic career falls apart, leaving the film as an interesting discourse upon fate and superstition.[3]

Later mid-1960s films explore these themes in a number of ways. Piers Haggard's 1970 film *Blood on Satan's Claw* contains some interesting new varieties of witchcraft, whilst also critiquing and rendering ambivalent some elements of the sixties counter-culture. In the film the youths of an early modern rural English village become entranced and follow a 'personification' of evil that leaves its mark upon them as the so called 'Devil's skin'. This leads to the exploration of their own burgeoning erotic power which similarly stands as a challenging motif, ranged against the world of adults that this manifestation of evil wishes them to throw aside. Although relatively low budget (and quite hammy) there are moments of menace, even if the ultimate confrontation with evil is something of a disappointment. Nonetheless, there remain interesting things to note about this film. The action is deliberately and self-consciously set in the post Restoration period distancing itself from the 1640s – the central authority character offers a Jacobite toast in one scene. This idea is further developed by the suggestion that superstition and beliefs about witchcraft are a thing confined firmly to the past, even if it is recent. This sceptical line is firmly reinforced by the central authoritative character's forthright declaration of its obsolescence. Nonetheless, when strange events occur he is forced to change his views. The youth of the village begin to spectacularly maltreat individuals echoing 1960s experiments in 'theatre of cruelty'. However, all is not lost since the beliefs of the village are contrasted with more sophisticated urban knowledge and practices. The central authoritative character declares he must leave the village, taking with him the one piece of evident print culture that seeks to explain the happenings in the village. His destination is the town where he hints he will consult with other learned authorities. His return is heralded with hope and confidence that the knowledge he brings with him from the town will enable him to combat the evil in the rural locality.

However, there are no incantations, no erudite discussions of demonology that we might expect from Hammer's finest. Instead the choice of weapon he has sought from his consultations is in fact (disappointingly) an over large sword which slays the personification of evil – making for a considerably dull and anti-climactic finish.

Witchfinder General (Michael Reeves, 1968) is not so much a film addressing the act of witchcraft, but rather a consideration of the consequences and possible motivations for witch hunting. The most important evident narrative within this film is of the breakdown of order, and this is stated in one of the film's early scenes. The Civil War and its impact upon judicial systems is another important theme and elements of this persist in the pursuit of the film's villains into the very final scene. These villains are real historical individuals in the shape of the witchfinder general Matthew Hopkins (in this instance played by a, for once, not overly camp Vincent Price) and John Stearne. The latter, interestingly, is portrayed as a plebeian rogue bent on moneymaking and debauchery. Price's Hopkins is slightly ambivalent and the film can almost not make up its mind about this. In several scenes the Hopkins character appears cynically intent upon moneymaking and the illicit exercise of power, the latter especially geared towards the seduction of vulnerable women. Nonetheless, within other crucial scenes Hopkins declares himself to be quasi genuine in his desire to rid the Suffolk locality of witches. However, the film does involve some nods to historical accuracy with a real enough depiction of walking a suspect and of swimming a witch. *Witchfinder General* also gave audiences their own visual encounter with pricking for the witches' mark and the ducking stool. Likewise, the accusations involving individuals consorting with their familiars does lean on evidence from the Hopkins witch hunt of the 1640s.

However, it is also worth noting how this film has distinct parallels with the later (1976) Clint Eastwood epic *The Outlaw Josie Wales*. Both depict the consequences of lawlessness emanating from the breakdown of order as a result of civil war. The heroes of both films, Josie Wales and Cornet Marshall, are away fighting when forces that embody predatory disorder violate the virtue of their womenfolk. Whilst the Wild West was normally portrayed as terrorised by guns and routine violence, this British 'Western' incorporates witchcraft accusations as an analogous motif. Given such lawlessness the issue of revenge and exacting revenge on such figures drives the plot in some interesting ways. *Witchfinder General* has been considered a flawed masterpiece, but critics also note the amorality (for this particular genre) of the films ending and the dizzying array of violence contained within. Alan Bennett was notably appalled by the violence in *Witchfinder General* which provoked a comment from Reeves that the viewer should rightly be appalled by the violence in the film, rather than be led into accepting it through a casual or comic book treatment.[4] As such, the film is also part of a wider dialogue that saw gender relations as under strain around issues associated with witchcraft, and how they are both a simultaneous challenge to authority and an attempt to assert newer kinds of this. In particular the construction of patriarchal society – which some gender historians of witchcraft have demonstrated – finds expression in films like *Witchfinder General*. Beyond its witchcraft subject matter it contains strongly demarcated and gendered spaces for the characters, and is seen to deal with what Peter Hutchings has described as the 'maintenance of a male authority that is largely dependent on female submission in the face of an increased female resistance to this submissive role'.[5]

Gordon Hessler's (1970) *Cry of the Banshee* again featured Vincent Price as a witch hunting authority figure placed under a curse by a witch named Oona. Although generally dismissed as inferior to *Witchfinder General* this piece is intriguing as a study of an individual psychologically dealing with the real-life consequences of a witches curse, and the desperate attempts he makes to retain rational explanations of the world in the face of misfortune.[6] The apparently enduring nature of witches' curses is also a theme that ignites terror and death in Norman J. Warren's *Terror* (1978). Again another entry in this plot line borrowed from cinema appeared in 1973's *Spell of Evil*, an episode in ATV's *Thriller* series directed by John Sichel from a story by *The Avenger's* writer Brian Clemens. In this the reincarnation of a witch comes to torment a widower from several hundred years previously to fulfil a curse. Such themes and treatments, once again, brought the ancient into the late twentieth-century living room of both protagonists and audiences.[7]

The coven in witchcraft films also became a later focus of controlled and predatory menace. Polanski's *Rosemary's Baby* is perhaps the ultimate in the objectification of women as receptacle of good and evil as well as a sacrifice. Mia Farrow becomes powerless as a result of enforced domesticity as much as her unlucky circumstance to be merely the vessel containing the child of Satan: 'most chillingly of all is the implied notion that she is merely fulfilling her destiny. She was built for such work.'[8] *Satan's Slave* (Norman J. Warren, 1979) revisits the theme of a contemporary coven conspiring to plot evil and harm against innocent characters in the name of a past legacy of witch belief – in this case reincarnation.[9] Tipping over into the genre of pornography was 1970's *Virgin Witch* (directed by Ray Austin) which played on the zeitgeist idea of aspiring young women lured by offers of modelling contracts, only to be ensnared by a lesbian coven. Though there is considerable voyeuristic content and soft-core porn, the twist in this feature is that one such woman defeats and supplants the coven's leader.[10] Nonetheless, this was not a serious examination of female power and its struggles and was perhaps a culmination of a filmmaking trend which associated witchcraft with the aspirations of the male libido. This drew upon fantasy narratives of availability and licentiousness provided by filmmakers provoked by the gradual relaxation censorship regimes.

Although not directly about witchcraft, Hammer's adaptation of Dennis Wheatley's *The Devil Rides Out* (released as *The Devil's Bride* in the United States), was classily done for the period (1968) by the renowned Terence Fisher. This likewise contains elements that address popular understanding of many of the phenomena associated with witchcraft. Curses, the ability to command demons, supernatural power over humans and nature as well as necromancy, satanic worship and allusions to the power of the coven all appear in this work. The film also is quite forthright in its depiction of the Devil himself, exploring this at length in the opening title sequence and credits – complete with horns and red glowing eyes.

Although this is something of a classical fairy tale, with a slightly implausible happy ending, it is part of constructing an obviously Manichean universe where the forces of good regularly stumble across pernicious evil that is liable to corrupt the innocent. As such, the film rather dips into Wheatley's Duc de Richelieu series of books with only a sketchy concept of this central character (played by Christopher Lee) and the context he springs from. As a result quite how he has such a developed level of arcane knowledge is never properly explored or explained. The witchcraft systems adopted and used against each other by the hero de Richelieu and the villain Mocata (modeled on Aleister Crowley) are a blend of Egyptian and Judeo-Christian motifs by which spirits and the wills of individuals are secured and commanded. Nonetheless, to update and enrich this knowledge, as in other films mentioned, De Richelieu disappears to the British Library to acquire further wisdom that he can use to combat and outflank the presence and activities of evil. Thus, this act of stumbling upon instances of witchcraft and satanic belief in every corner of the world makes De Richelieu appear to the audience as though he is a latter day inquisitor or witchfinder – only this time portrayed as driven by the very purest of motives. As such, this does display a sense of orthodox rational power systems lapsing and fading when the occult and matters of witchcraft swing into view. *The Devil Rides Out* is sometimes seen as a struggle between father/authority figures who both lay claim to superior skills and knowledge that the rest of the cast must acknowledge and obey, particularly the young and impressionable. Yet equally it is the female characters of three generations who, through their own independent agency, conspire to bring about the demise of the villain Mocata.[11]

Other elements in the film cleverly associate the appearance of witchcraft within modernity with the imminent danger it somehow carries into the twentieth century. Debates over modernisation, and its juxtaposition with witchcraft as a forgotten past that gets revived, had earlier been rehearsed in the opening scenes of the 1964 Hammer production *Witchcraft* (directed by Don Sharp).[12] In *The Devil Rides Out* the Devil's horns on display in the titles are cleverly juxtaposed in the first scenes with an aircraft and an airport, alongside the very important motif of the motor car which, from this first scene, conveys characters away from specific situations. The motor car itself also plays an ambivalent role throughout the film, since it provides a means of transport for both good and evil and a means of rapid escape for both – styling itself as the broomstick of modernity. Likewise, it enables good to pursue evil alongside the opportunity for evil to influence how the motor car itself is driven by individuals through the use of interventionist mesmeric powers. The power of the motor car is further emphasised in one memorable scene in which the coven arrive for the meeting at the sabbat in a procession of opulent luxury cars, rather than broomsticks. At this same meeting it is the latent power of the motor car and its accessories that enables the Duc de Richelieu to physically attack the embodiment of the Devil (billed by the Duc as the horrifying Goat of Mendes), within the midst of his followers in the context of a convened sabbat. The car's headlights answers the Duc's desperate imploring request 'oh if only there was some light'. Likewise, other period features are turned to invoke other disturbing cultural resonances. Some of the central characters enticed into the orbit of devil worship are flappers – apparently emblematic of the damned 'between the wars' generation. Regular motifs of opulence, wealth and clandestine retreats at unnamed manor houses also evoke disturbing elements of country house fascism – however this adds another series of interesting dimensions to the discussion of evil and its discourses within the film.

These discourses and their wider resonances boil down to seeing good and evil as two opposing 'systems' which again invites identification with the historical period. The leading characters personifying good (Christopher Lee as the Duc de Richelieu) and evil (Charles Gray as the sinister Mocata) are each given narratives of how each 'system' works and has its place in the universe. In particular the resolution of this film emphasises that equilibria, in all its senses, must be restored.

In one scene Lee with his companion Rex (Leon Greene) confronts his suspicions about his friend's son Simon (Patrick Mower) and his involvement in something infinitely more sinister than an 'astronomical society'. When the tell-tale signs of Devil worship are discovered and ridiculed by the sceptic Greene the following exchange occurs:

De Richelieu (Lee):   Do you believe in evil?

Rex (Greene):   As an Idea

De Richelieu: Do you believe in the power of Darkness?

Rex: As a superstition

De Richelieu: Now there you are wrong! The power of Darkness is more than just a superstition. It is a living force which can be tapped at any given moment of the night.

Later a similar discussion from the opposite perspective occurs from the arch magus Mocata (echoing Crowley) as he tries to control the mind of one of the central characters:

Mocata: I do not propose to discuss with you the rights and wrongs of practicing the magic art, I will confine myself to saying I am a practitioner of some experience. . . . In magic there is neither good nor evil it is merely a science. The science of causing change to occur by means of one's will. The sinister reputation attaching to it is entirely groundless and is based on superstition rather than objective observation. The power of the will is something people do not understand, attributing to it mysterious qualities it does not possess.

Throughout, the idea is that the occult exists as a series of tools that can be utilised for good and evil and that are merely parts of an interlocking and intricate system. These are merely at the mercy of knowledge used by the virtuous or the corrupt and evil. As such the link here with modernity comes full circle and is completed.

Robert Hardy's 1974 *The Wicker Man* shows a clash between conflicting systems, but this is rather played out in the sensibilities of the protagonists, rather than a straight battle between good and evil.[13]

The Wicker Man has been a touchstone of modern Western society's popular knowledge of Wicca and, as such, has been the source of many semi-myths. As historians we should regularly bear in mind how the mass of the population learns its view of specialist and arcane knowledge. *The Wicker Man*, through its cult status and fairly literate script (by Anthony Shaffer) put into the mainstream the idea of human sacrifice, connectedness with nature and an opulently permissive approach to sexuality and sexual licence.

Last of all it provoked, once again, a deeply enduring suspicion of geographically remote communities, and the apparent limits of civilisation (another theme evident in the earlier *The Witches*) that can be seen as cultural constants that appear in subsequent generations of filmmaking. Forgotten and primitive rural society is a threat to civilisation that appears in cinematic and televisual works as diverse as *American Werewolf in London* and *League of Gentlemen*. One of the writers of the latter, Mark Gatiss, labelled *The Wicker Man*, *Witchfinder General* and *Blood on Satan's Claw* as films of a sub-genre he called 'Folk Horror'. Summerisle in *The Wicker Man* is again off the map and the central protagonist, Sergeant Howie, has to move from a place of modernity, where he is in control, to one alien and untouched by it where he is not.[14] Elements of the central character's attachment to evangelical Christianity and its morals are sharply contrasted with the licence and permissiveness of the Summerisle community's Wiccan paganism. As such the plot unfolds so the latter's ultimate morality and behaviour is questioned, effectively showing the same note of caution and censure against elements of the counter-culture we saw on display in *Blood on Satan's Claw.*

Perhaps the new millennium's most obvious way of acquainting mass audiences with witchcraft, sorcery and its associated ideas has been the series of *Harry Potter* films. In many respects these represent something of a departure from previous representations, yet equally some aspects are similar – particularly in the obvious re-creation of a Manichaean universe. Nonetheless, it is the differences that are particularly striking. The first most striking difference is that the world which magic inhabits in *Harry Potter* is hidden from the rest of humanity – indeed regular instances of magic impinging upon the world are punished as transgressions. The world of magic within *Harry Potter* films is immensely organised, regulated and eventually overly bureaucratic. The suggestion is that a hidden world can really exist with its own quirky and amusing practices (Quiddich, Platform Nine and Three Quarters, the Ministry of Magic, secret societies, brotherhoods and fellowships, magical recipes and ingredients). Witches and wizards are born with powers and thus there is arguably no choice but to accept a career in magic. This is very different from some of the other earlier films discussed which portray witchcraft and Devil worship as a conscious lapse from the straight and narrow, more often than not as a result of a tragic flaw within the individual personality – or as a foolhardy pursuit of arcane knowledge.

In *Harry Potter* the skills of witches and wizards are developed through education – in large part the essence of the early *Harry Potter* books and films was an identification with adolescent schooling as a method of seeking the audience's empathy. Magic within this schooling environment, is divided into disciplines which pull together a considerable and multicultural range of magical subjects and practices. Many of these skills are focused on in turn and it is made quite plain that witches are supposed to be 'all rounders'. Magical creatures and practices are brought together from a vast range of anthropological and ethnographic data from throughout the world. Likewise, those enrolled on courses at Hogwarts School of Witchcraft and Wizardry are self-consciously reflective of the multicultural twenty-first-century world. Indeed this attempt to present an international fellowship of shared cultural values is one that might well have pleased Sir James Fraser and, most pertinently of all for historians of witchcraft studies, Margaret Murray. The films also have a slightly problematic relationship with modernity. Magic is used to enable individuals to undertake mundane tasks by persuading anachronistic inanimate objects do their bidding in the manner of modern household appliances; thus brooms and mops operate cleaning functions of their own volition whilst magical Routemaster buses invisibly career around. Likewise, lifts disguised as antiquated red London telephone boxes convey individuals from ground level to the darkest recesses of the Ministry of Magic. There are also elements of classical 'retrochic' in evidence, such as the individual-carriaged steam train and the flying car appearing as a 1960s Ford Anglia. Although this time-warp post-war Englishness was clearly intended to appeal to the American market, it does also create a further element of nostalgic remoteness for pretty well every audience.

The stories conveyed in the films reflect some very classic adolescent rite-of-passage themes and metaphors that echo much teenage fantasy writing stretching back to *Lord of the Rings* and beyond. Interestingly, to reinforce this aspect so much about the portrayal of both good and evil within the *Harry Potter* films is very closely related to the idea of the development of the self. This is arguably extended by the fact that there is no conception of the Devil within this world. Both good and evil spring from the individual and are a consequence of the individual's character or circumstances of his or her own singular personal development. This particular aspect is made plain in portrayals of the development of the central evil character Voldemort. This individual begins life as someone whose disturbed attitude and ambition is what leads him astray. He is not part of evil's opposition to good that has been in existence since time immemorial. Voldemort learns to pervert and twist many of the established symbols, rituals and tools of conventional magic to bring them into the service of his evil wishes. Intriguingly, when the plot resolves itself at the end of the last film it is through a simple trial of strength. There is no inherent reason why the forces of good should triumph over the forces of evil. Perhaps it is this potential for amorality that has led the *Harry Potter* series of films to fall foul of species of American evangelicalism.

Thus, witchcraft and its appearance in films as we have noted continues to discuss and sometimes problematise a number of recurrent themes. The golden age of their appearance in front of audiences – perhaps between 1950 and 1980 – potentially linked up with the struggles for identity of numerous groups seeking greater recognition of their individuality within post-war society. Witchcraft films generally have some motifs of illegitimate control which are often juxtaposed with counter-cultural tendencies. These offer alternatives based on an assertion of youth, gender or some identity that can be considered a breakaway from the norm of a given social context. In the new millennium perhaps the witchcraft film's dissolution into a fable of, and for children, which adults may wish to peek at, reflects a re-creation of the original power of Grimm's fairytales. Perhaps it also suggests that the powerful mix of gender and countercultural challenges to religious and social norms are no longer as powerful an artistic inspiration as they once were. Moreover, perhaps twenty-first-century society is now more terrified by the real in the shape of bullets and bombs which, like spells and potions once were, are now seen in spectacular, incongruous, and therefore ultimately terrifying, contexts.

Notes

1 Hugh Trevor Roper, *The European Witch Craze of the Sixteenth and Seventeenth Centuries* (London: Harper and Row, 1967).

2 Gary A. Smith, *Uneasy Dreams: The Golden Age of British Horror Films, 1956–76* (London: McFarland and Company, 2000), 50.

3 Ibid., 166.

4 Peter Hutchings, *Hammer and Beyond: The British Horror Film* (Manchester: Manchester University Press, Manchester, 1993), 137.

5 Ibid., 144–151.

6 Harvey Fenton and David Flint, eds., *Ten Years of Terror* (Guildford: Fab Press, 2001), 24–26.

7 Ibid., 302 & 324.

8 David J. Hogan, *Dark Romance: Sex and Death in the Horror Film* (London: Equation, 1986), 80.

9 Smith, *Uneasy Dreams*, 190.

10 Ibid., 232.

11 Hutchings, *Hammer and Beyond*, 152–155.
12 Ibid., 130.
13 Hogan, *Dark Romance*, 84.
14 Tony Magistrale, *Abject Terrors: Surveying the Modern and Postmodern Horror Film* (New York: Peter Lang, 2005), 175–176.

Bibliography (selection)

Fenton, Harvey and David Flint (eds.), *Ten Years of Terror*. Guildford: Fab Press, 2001.
Hogan, David, *Dark Romance: Sex and Death in the Horror Film*. London: Equation, 1986.
Hutchings, Peter, *Hammer and Beyond: The British Horror Film*. Manchester: Manchester University Press, 1993.
Magistrale, Tony, *Abject Terrors: Surveying the Modern and Postmodern Horror Film*. New York: Peter Lang, 2005.
Smith, Gary A., *Uneasy Dreams: The Golden Age of British Horror Films, 1956–76*. London: McFarland and Company, 2000.

INDEX

Note: Numbers in bold indicate a table. Numbers in italics indicate a figure.

abortionists 334; anti- 329
Acts of Andrew 32
Acts of Matthew 1 32
Acts of Paul 24
Acts of the Apostles 32
Acts of Thecla 34
Acts of Thomas 33
Adeimantos 6
Addison, James 156
Africa 273, 318, 377; anti-witchcraft in 306; Pentecostalism in 310–312; postcolonial 280, 299–312; *see also* Cameroon; Ghana; Nigeria
Against Aristogeito (Theoris) 10
Agamemnon 22, 375
Agrippa 15
Agrippa, Heinrich Cornelius 264, 359
Ahab (King) 22
Äldre Västgötalagen 160
Alias Grace (Atwood) 378
"Alphabet of Ben Sira" 23
Altdorfer, Albrecht 365
Amadeus II 85
Amadeus VIII (Duke) 62, 66, 68, 353
amatorium 3, 14; *see also* potions
amulet 19, 21, 23, 25, 33; maker 42; protective 252, 253
Anna Karenina (Tolstoy) 373
Aphrodite 359
Apocalypse of Abraham 23
Apollo 32, 321, 322, 375
Apollonius of Tyana 3, 30
Apuleius 3, 12–13, 34, 42
Aquinas, Thomas 51, 52, 70, 71
Aquino, Michael 342
Aradia (goddess) 321–322
Aradia (Leland) 321–323; *see also* Wicca
Armadale (Collins) 373
Armstrong, Anne 154

Arras 67, 114, 117, 353–355
Artapanos 21
Artemis 32
Ash-blonde Witch, An (Lillington) 388
Asmodaeus/Ashmedai 22, 23
Assyria 22
Astarte 319
astrology 246, 290, 327, 359; in antiquity 15; and astronomy 266; and early Christianity 34; and demons 50, 51, 54; and the Enoch tradition 26; and the Jewish tradition 32
atelestoi ("without being complete") 5, 16
Athenagoras 30
Athens 6, 34; fourth-century 10–12; *see also* Greece
atheos 3
Atwood, Margaret 378
Audollent, Auguste 4, 5
Augustan Edict of 11AD 15–16
Augustine of Hippo 26, 33, 34, 41, 47, 50, 70
Augustus 15
Awakening, The (Chopin) 373
Azazel 23, 24

Baal Zebub 23; Beelzebub 24
Baal Zebul 23
Baba Denis 307–310
Babylon 20, 22, 34
Bakunin, Mikhail 337
Baldung Grien, Hans ("Baldung") 358, 361, *362*, 363, *364*, 365, 367
Bandelier, Adolph 282
Baranowski, Bohdan 178, 179
Barton, Blanche 342–343
Baudelaire, Charles 336, 341
Baum, Frank L. 382
Bayman, Anna 209, 210
Beast 666 338
Beauvoir, Simone de 374

Behringer, Wolfgang 85, 208–209, 215
Belarus 178, 188, 190
Beliar, Belial 23
Bell, Karl 280–281
ben Dosa, Chinina (Hanina) 21, 28, 31
ben Perachja, Joshua 31
Bent, Charles 282
Bernault, Florence 306, 307
Bible (Christian) 157, 292, 313; demonology in 19; King James 51; New Testament 19, 23, 31, 39, 138; Old Testament 20–22
Bible (Hebrew) 20, 22, 28
Bible (Satanic) 339, 341
"binding magic" 4, 8, 334; "ritual" 6
binding spells see spells
Binsfeld, Peter 95, 115, 119, 239
Biya, Paul 308
black magic 244
Black Mass 136, 334, 339
black metal music 342–345
Black Widow (musical group) 339
Blackstone, William (Sir) 156
Blake, William 334
Blavatsky, Helena Petrovna 338
Blécourt, Willem de 114, 215, 224, 225, 227
Blutebuch 131
Bodin, Jean 121, 127, 221, 239
Bogomils 333
Boguet, Henri 131
Bohemia 171–176, 180
Bon, Philippe le 67
Bonewits, Isaac 323, 324
Borromeo, Carlo 84
Braddon, Elisabeth 372
Briggs, Robin 383
Brontë, Anne 372
Brontë, Charlotte 371, 375
Brontë, Emily 371
Brothers Grimm 370, 382, 401
Broussart, Pierre 354
Brown, Peter 36
Budapest, Zsuzsanna ("Z") 326
Burchard of Worms 50
Burning Your Boats (Carter) 378
Busch, Peter 30
Butler, Jon 281
Byron, George Gordon (Lord) 334–335

Calhoun, James 282, 283, 285
Cameroon 299, 304–306, 308, 311–312; Maka 299–305, 307, 312
Canidia 8, 9
cannibal, cannibalism 32, 46, 307; accusations of 290; banquet 302; Indians 204; meetings 303; symbolic ritual 325; witches 62–64, 66, 136, 154, 244

Canon episcopi 138
canon law 52, 53, 99, 138, 236, 356; medieval 270; and scholastic demonology 49–51, 90
Carducci, Giosuè 336
Carmilla (Le Fanu) 371–372
carmina (incantation) 4
Caro Baroja, Julio 134
Carter, Angela 378
Cassandra 375
Cassius Dio 15
Castaneda, Carlos 323
Cathars, Catharism 138, 333
Catholic Church 50, 82, 83, 88, 96, 121; attitudes towards magic 90; diminished role of 127; priests executed for witchcraft 98; and witch hunts 99; witch trials 119; see also Christianity
Catholic Reform 132
Catholic Reformation 262
Cautio Criminalis (Spee) 95, 180
Celtic peoples 35, 154, 223, 385; see also Druids
Charles II 155
Chérie (Collette) 374
child eaters 279–286; see also cannibalism
child-witches 233; boys 170, 240; girls 240; trials 233–236
Chopin, Kate 373
Church of England 146, 147, 150, 153
Church of Satan (CoS) 343; see also Satan
Christianity 20; and demonology 22; earliest 19–20; emperors 15; cvangclical 266, 340, 344, 400, 401; magic in 29–35; pre-14, 20; and sexuality, abhorrence of 19
Cicero 13, 14
Circe 7, 359
City of God (Augustine) 25, 47
City of the Dead (film) 394–395
Cixous, Hélène 376
Clark, Stuart 146, 221, 279, 281
Claudius 15
Clément, Catherine 376
Cohn, Norman 259, 394
Coleridge, Mary 370
Collette 374
Collins, Wilkie 373
colonialism: Africa 280, 299–312; New England 204, 281; North America 257, 273
Combat 18 343
Constitutio Criminalis Bambergensis 236
Constitutio Criminalis Carolina 236
Copeland, David 343
Cornfoot, Janet 156
Corpus hermeticum 264
Corrector sive medicus 50
Cory, Giles 199, 205

council of Ancyra 49
Council of Basel 62, 65, 66, 67
Council of Brabant 118
Council of Elvira 27
Council of Flanders 118
Council of Trent 90, 121, 139
courtesans 7–9, 87, 374
Coven (musical group) 339
covens 319, 322–326; Dianic 326; in England 323, 326; Gardnerian 325; lesbian 397; in literature 374; Susan B. Anthony 326; Wiccan 320
Covenant of the Goddess, The 327
Craft, The (film) 387
Cranach the Elder, Lucas 365, *366*, 367
crime 74, 194, 200, 211; against Christianity 50, 60; of heresy 82; magical 52, 55, 68, 100, 165, 173–174, 263; of *lèse-majesté* 69; maleficent 61, 67; execution for 10, 11; pacts 101; political 191; Satanic 343; by sorcerers 73, *358*; of sorcery 114; superstition as 168
Crimea 188
crone 383, 386, 390
crone-witch 376, 387, 388
Crowley, Aleister 324–326, 330, 338
Crucible, The (Miller) 374
crucifix 193, 251, 395
crucifixion 14, 39
Cry of the Banshee (Hessler) 397
curses 297

Daemonolatriae (Rémy) 132
daimon: Christian theory of 37; Gospel portrayal of 38; possession by 37, 42; *see also* demons
Daly, Mary 219, 376
Dasent, George 382
Dashwood, Francis (Sir) 334
Davies, Owen 281
Davis, W.W.H. 284, 285
death penalty 12–13, 82, 85, 126, 128, 131–132, 145, 165
Decadents 332, 336, 341
defigens (practitioner) 4
defixio ("holding down in place") 4–6
defixiones (binding spells) 4, 13–15
defixiones (leaden curse tablets) 26, 32
defixus (victim) 4
Dehmel, Richard 336
Deianeira 7
Delrio, Martin Anton 121, 239
Demeter 5, 319
demons 36–42; and the devil 22; pact with 20
demonology 19; Christian 22, 24; and Dead Sea Scrolls 28; and folk belief 109;

fifteenth-century 114; fourteenth-century 52–54; ignoring 101; and James VI 149; Le Franc on 67; the Middle Ages 24, 46–56; popular 154; in Russia 191, 193; scholastic 49–51, 74; secular law and 54–56; sixteenth-century 268; and society **94**, 94–98; theology and 50; treatises on 61, 69–70, 73; Western 180; and witchcraft 118–121, 245, 254, 363
Demosthenes 10–12
Denmark 160; *see also* witch trials
devil 23, 203, 266, 270–273, 332, 341–344; associating with 192–193; belief in 24; casting out 55; children and 234, 236–239; consorting with 164, 166; conspiring with 120; and the Enlightenment 336; evil and 269; God and 245–246, 334; Ignatius and 38; images of 321; impersonation by 201; invoking 172; -fearing 204; Jesus and 29; magic and 61, 71, 194; metamorphosis of 67; minions of 39; names for 25; pact with 20, 46, 81, 86, 96, 116, 149, 165, 178–179, 189, 191, 200; Pentecostals and 311–312; power of 41, 73, 131–132; reality of 72; red 337; servants of 251; soldiers and 226; sympathy for 335, 339; witch and 47, 62, 63, 70, 74, 118, 154–155, 160, 222, 244, 253; witchcraft and 49, 300, 310; women and 64, 221–222, 224, 228; worship of 65–66, 87, 127, 135–139, 255; *see also* Satan
Devils, The (Russell) 393
diabolism 161
Diabolos 24, 25
Diana (goddess) 49, 138, 319, 321–322
Dickie, Matthew W. 7
Dido (Queen) 12
Dillinger, Johannes 219, 225, 227
Dirae Teiorum 10, 11
Directorium inquisitorum (Eymerich) 53
divination 15, 20, 26, 31–34; astrological 47; condemnation of 49–50; demonic 270; necromantic 21, 64, 268; paganism and 24; sorcerers and 260; techniques 253–254; and witches 53
djambe (witchcraft) 299–305, 309–310
Druid 32, 323
Druidism, Druidic 223, 323–324
Dürer, Albrecht 356, 358, 359, *360*, 361, 363, 365, 367
Durkheim, Emile 317, 318
Duvall, Shelley 387
Dworkin, Andrea 376

Edelstadt, Heinrich Franz Boblig 173
Egypt 40, 318, 338

Ehrenreich, Barbara 219, 379, 385
Eleazar 27
Eliade, Mircea 321
Emerald Tablets 264
English, Deirdre 379, 385
English Witchcraft and Conjuration Act of 1736 290
epagōge (sending a ghost) 6
Ephesia Grammata 31
Ephesians 33, 34, 38
Ephesus 31
episcopate 135, 139, 173
Episcopi 49, 50, 54, 73
epōidai (incantation) 4
Erasmus of Rotterdam 359
Erichtho (witch) 9–10
Errores gazariorum 62, 64, 65, 66
Erskine, James 155
esprit sorcellaire, l' 207
Estonia 220
Eucharist 33, 37, 38, 46, 56, 130, 252; reversed 136
Eunomos 10–12
Euripides 7
Evangelicals *see* Christianity
Evans-Pritchard, Edward Evan 258, 259, 299
Eve (biblical) 338, 376, 378
Expressionism 336
Eymerich, Nicolas 53, 54, 68

fairy tales 32, 33, 370, 376, 382, 384, 386
Faraone, Christopher A. 4, 8
Felix V 62, 66, 353
Fillmore, Millard 282
Flagellum hereticorum fascinariorum (Jacquier) 70–73
Flagellum maleficorum (Mamoris) 70–73
Fletcher, Susan 379
Folia (witch) 8, 9
Formicarius (Nider) 62–64, 269, 272
Fortress of Faith (Spina) 269
fortune telling 10, 120, 156, 198, 261, 266, 290
Foucault, Michel 378, 393
Franc, Martin le 62, 66–67, 353, *354*
Francisca, Matteucia 263, 266
Frankenstein (Shelley) 371
Franklin, Benjamin 334
Fraser, Kyle 42
Frazer, James George 21, 258
Fründ, Hans 62, 63, 95, 353
Furlong, Monica 385, 388

Gaiman, Neil 383, 387
Gardner, Gerald 324–325
Gaufridy, Louis 272

Gearhart, Sally 377
Geertz, Clifford 205, 317
gender: in the ancient world 3, 7; magic and 221–222, 326; roles 8, 9, 335; sex and 317; and status 227–228; witches and 86, 127, 130, 151–152, 194, 240, 351; witchcraft and 219–229; and work 225–227
Genz, Stephanie 384
Ghana 300, 311, 312
ghosts 6, 9, 245, 266, 267, 383
Gibson, Marion 209, 212, 213, 214, 382
Gilmore, Peter H. 343
Girbelli, Thomas 66
Glanvill, George 155
Gnosticism 19, 33, 327; neo- 345
God 22, 24–28, 70, 155; abandoning 63; child of 41; crimes against 68; and the Devil 315, 318; divine plan 268; and early modern worldview 245–246, 251–255; -given 224; High 38; of Israel 21; Kingdom of 30; and magic 272; nature and natural law 258, 264, 266; and Puritanism 204; renunciation of 137; Salem trials and 200; treason against 138; and witches 292; word of 156; *see also* Yahweh
Godbeer, Richard 202
goddess (pagan) 49, 317, 374; Diana 67, 81, 322; Great Goddess 319, 324–326; mythologies 324; *see also* Wicca
goddess-worship 385
godliness 146, 148, 149, 221
gods 9, 15, 21, 317; and demons 36, 39, 41; disbeliever in 3; chthonic 5; "forcing the" 32; language of 31; and magic 47; Native American 282; pagan 23; will of the 6; wrath of the 11–12; *see also* Horned God
Godwin, William 337
goēteia (sorcery) 4
Golden Dawn: Hermetic Order of 323, 324; New Reformed Order 323
Graf, Fritz 5
Grandier, Urban 272
Gratian 50
Great Basque Witch Panic 128
Greece: magic and the law 10–12; witches in 3–16
Gregory VII (Pope) 161
graveyard 5, 284; grave-robbing 9, 135; violating 48
Graveyard Book, The (Gaiman) 383–384
Griffiths, Helen 386
Grillando, Paolo 121
Grimm Brothers *see* Brothers Grimm
grimoire 28, 319
Gui, Bernard 53
Guichard of Troyes 55

Gustav III (King) 165
Gyn/ecology (Daly) 376

Habsburg 101; Empire 219; Spanish 113, 131; territories 103
hag 376; monstrous 9
Hag-ography (Daly) 376
Harald, King of Denmark 161
Harner, Michael 340
Harris, Bertha 377
Harry Potter series 382–384, 400–401
Harvey, Graham 318, 326
Hecate 5, 319
Hegarty, Diane 340
Helios 29
Hell-Fire Club 334
Henri IV 128
Heracles 7
herbalist 42; and witch 110, 379
herbs 53, 263; invisibility achieved using 63; magic and 261, 263, 266, 290; medicinal 50, 90, 260
Heraclitus 6
heresy, heretics 37, 39, 54, 56, 63, 194; children of 239; Christian sects 333; Christian vs. 41; magic as 127, 139, 194; prosecution of 237; Protestant 83, 115; superstition as 262; teachers 24; on trial 82; witches as 72; *see also* Cathars; Waldensians
Hermes 5, 29, 264
Hermēs Katokhos 5
Hermes Trismegistus 264
Hermeticism 264–265, 324
Hessler, Gordon 397
Hester, Marianne 219
Hexapolis 176
Hexentanz 214
hexen Weßen betreffent, Das 234
"Hexenausschüsse" 115
Hexerei 46
Hilkijah, Abba 28
Hincmar of Reims 50
His Dark Materials (Pullman) 383, 386, 389
Historical Essay Concerning Witchcraft (Hutchinson) 155, 156, 157
Holy Roman Empire 67, 84, 99, 101, 131; Bohemia as part of 171; of the German Nation 109; persecutions of witches 180, 214, 219, 220
Homer 7
homosexuality 370, 373, 376
Honi the Circle-drawer 28
Horace 7
Horned God 319, 320, 321, 322
Huna 318

Hutchings, Peter 396
Hutchinson, Francis 155, 156, 157
hysteria: mass 244; in Scandinavia 165; in Spain 129; witchcraft 105, 373, 374, 394
hysteric 194, 376, 377, 378

Iceland 166, 168, 220, 222, 224
Ignatius 34, 38, 39, 42
Ignatjewa, Agrafena 293
Inana 319
India, magical practices of 273
Innocent IV 55
Inquisition (Spanish) 81–87, 90, 119, 128–129
inquisitions 62, 66, 68, 69
Isidore of Seville 47, 267
Islam 221, 265, 267, 300; culture 335; militant 343, 344; modern 274
Iulian Apostata 34
Ivan III, Grand Prince of Russia 191
Ivan IV, the Terrible 191

James I of England 149, 203, 210
James VI of Scotland 148, 161
Jacquier, Nicolas 70–73, 269
Jeanne d'Arc (Joan of Arc) 125, 130, 353
Jeanne of Burgundy 56
Jefferson, Thomas 281, 286
Jesus 19, 27, 39–40, 120; and demons 37, 38; exorcisms performed by 24, 29, 38; historical 28; and magic 34; and miracles 30–31
Joan of Arc *see* Jeanne d'Arc
John Chrysostom (Saint) 33, 34
John XXII (Pope) 52, 53, 56
Johnston, Sarah 5
Josephus 24, 27, 28, 30
Judaism: ancient 19–35; Rabbinic 22, 23, 25, 28, 29
Justin II 41 (emperor)
Justin 30, 34
Justin Martyr 39
Juvenal 7–8

Kadosh, Ben 338–339
Kali 319
katadesis or *katadesmos* ("binding down") 4
katadesis (binding ritual) 6
Kelly, Aidan 323
Kieckhefer, Richard 67, 89
klikushestvo 194
Krah, Ursula (Ulla) 209
Kramer, Heinrich 69, 74, 95, 131, 213, 269, 353; as papal inquisitor 173; witch hunt conducted by 97
Krottenbeck, Paul 175

Lanagan, Margo 289, 390
Lancre, Pierre de 126, 128
Lane, William Carr 282
Larner, Christina 152
LaVey, Anton Szandor 339–343
Lea, Henry Charles 134
Le Fanu, Joseph Sheridan 371
Leland, Charles Godfrey 320–324
lesbianism 322, 326, 371, 374, 377, 397
Lévy, Eliphas 338
Levin, Ira 339
Lewis, C.S. 382
Lex Cornelia 14–15
Lilith 22, 23, 375
Lillington, Kenneth 386
Lion, the Witch, and the Wardrobe, The (Lewis) 382
Lithuania 178, 180, 188; *see also* witch trial
Loos, Cornelius 120
Lord of the Rings (Tolkien) 411
Louis X 56
Louis XIV 125, 131, 334
Lucan 9
Lucian 7, 33
Lucifer 25, 321, 322, 332–339
Lucifer (magazine) 337
Luhrmann, T. M. 326
Luther, Martin 221, 239, 270, 333, 361, 365
lynching of witches 129, 132, 180, 191, 194; in Denmark 162; in Eastern Europe 292; in France 126; unofficial 131
lynch mob 254

Macbeth (play) (Shakespeare) 384
MacCullough, Carolyn 383, 385
Mackenzie, George (Sir) 156
Macrobius 264
Maddalena 321–324; *see also* Leland, George Godfrey
Magdeburg Law 173, 175, 176, 178, 190
magic: Arabic 265; astral 51, 92, 265, 266; binding 4; erotic 6, 8, 9, 268; gendered beliefs and concepts 221–223; harmful 3, 26; love 7, 53, 88; medieval 262, 263; natural 266; *orazioni* 88; *philia* 8; spiritual 361
magical papyri 4–5, 8, 21, 30, 32
magic and the law: Bohemia 171–172; Greece 10–12; Lusatia 175–177; Moravia 172–173; Poland 178–180; Rome 12–16; Silesia 173–174; Slovakia 177–178
Magic Circle, The (Napoli) 384
Magnus, Olaus 160
magos, magoi 3, 6, 12, 19, 26, 34
Maitland, Sara 375
malediction 13

Maleficent (film) 388
malefici, maleficium 15, 48, 51, 53, 160, 179
Malleus Maleficarum 269, 272, 353, 355–358, 365, 376, 394
Mamoris, Pierre 70–73
Maria of Tver 191
Marmor, Petrus 269
Marx, Karl 375
Massacre of Glencoe 378
Master of Life 282
Mather, Cotton 199–205
Mather, Increase 200–201
Mazerolles, Philippe de 354
Medizinmann 305
McKinley, Robin 388–389
Medea 7
melancholy 62; allegories of 365, *366*; signs of 238
Melanchthon, Philipp 359
Mendouga, Madame 301, 303–304, 307–311
Ménendez Pelayo, Marcelino 141
Mephistopheles 338–339
Meroe 9
Metamorphoses (Ovid) 375
Methodism 156
Mexican Revolution of 1821 280
Millar, Charlotte Rose 209
Miller, Arthur 374
Milton, John 333, 334, 343
Misanthropic Lucifer Order 344
misogyny 151, 221, 282, 324; critique of 375; cultural 387
Mog Ruith 32
Molitor, Ulrich 95, 355–358
Monballyu, Jos 114, 118, 121
Monter, E. William 233, 238
Moravia 171–175, 180
Morrison, Toni 377
Mowinckel, Sigmund 22
Munch, Edvard 336
Murray, Margaret 168, 258–259, 385, 400; 'Murrayite' hypothesis 385, 387; studies by 320–321
Muslim *see* Islam
Myatt, David 343
Mysterious Appearance of Agnes (Griffiths) 386

Nachman, Elana 377
Naglowska, Maria de 339
Nambé 279–286
Napoli, Donna Jo 384
Native Americans 270, 279, 281–286, 323; attempts to convert 280; in New England 199, 204–205
Nazi symbols and propaganda 99, 340, 342, 343

necromancy 9, 88, 136, 279, 297; clerical 52; divination 21; rites and rituals 8, 54, 56; and spirits 266–269

Neopagan *see* pagan; witchcraft

netherworld 5

Newly Born Woman, The (Cixous and Clément) 376

nganga (healers) 300–303, 306–308, 310, 313

Nider, Jean (Johan, Johannes) 62–64, 95, 269

Nietzsche, Friedrich 336, 341

Nigeria 300, 306, 311; 'Nollywood' 312

Nuremberg Chronicle 359

occult 27, 245, 300; in Africa 303–306; in Britain 151; in films 392, 393, 395, 398, 399; forces of the 247, 257, 258, 273; in literature 370; and magic 261; power of 251; and the supernatural 247; symbols 262; techniques of 250; Wicca as 317

occultism, occultists 263–273, 327, 337, 338, 341; and Ceremonial Magic 322

Odysseus 7

Odyssey, 7, 21

Ogden, Daniel 7, 9

Old Dorothy 324

Old Testament *see* Bible

Once a Witch (MacCullough) 385

On the Sacred Disease 6

Order of the Nine Angels (ONA) 343

Origen 23, 25, 26, 30, 33, 34, 39

Orion, Loretta 318, 320

Ostorero, Martine 90

Ovid 375

pagan 21, 22; antiquity 264; beliefs 37; deities 23, 29, 81; 'hug' 320; invocations 28; literature 19, 31; monotheism 36; neopagan 317, 323; religion 25, 318, 319; rites 49; texts 27

paganism 20, 24, 36, 161; and feminism 326

Pagan Movement of Britain and Ireland 327

Palestine 25, 28

pantheism 44, 385, 388

Paracelus 365

Paradise Lost (Milton) 333–334

Parlement of Paris 101, 125–127, 131

Parlement of Toulouse 130

Parris, Samuel 198, 202, 204, 205

Pastor Hermae 33

Paterson, James 155

Paul (the Apostle) 23, 24, 30–32, 37, 40, 138

Penser la sorcellerie en Afrique 312

Pentecostalism, Pentecostals 300, 310–312, 332

persecution of witches 27, 32, 101, 214, 291; in Bohemia 171; of child-witches 235, 239; Christian 39, 370; in Denmark 161, 166; in Eastern Central Europe 180; in England 146, 151; of families 240, 254; fear of 318–319; in Germany 101–108; in Holland 116; in Italy 83; in France 66, 73, 125–132; in the Middle Ages 160; in Moravia 173–174; in Northern Netherlands 116; in Poland 179; in Russia 191–192; in Scandinavia 161; in Silesia 175; in Slovakia 177–178; in Swabia 97; in Sweden 164, 167; in Switzerland 94, 235; in the United States 198; in the Wallis 353; witch-hunt understood as 81; *see also* Salem witch trials; Vauderie d'Arras

Persephone 5

Peter (Saint) 31, 32

Peter I the Great 192, 194

pharmaka 3; *pharmakeia* 4

Philip IV (King) 55, 56, 139

Philip V 56

Philip VI 56

Philochoros 10–11

philtron 3

Picatrix 265

Pico della Mirandola, Giovanni 265

Plato 5, 6, 11, 12, 36, 38; academy 342; Neoplatonism 264, 265

Plutarch 7, 10, 42

Poe, Edgar Alan 370

poison 7, 25, 47, 68, 378; lethal 3; making 32; village witches and 51

poisoners 334, 373

poisoning 56, 249; death by 191; accidental 11; mercy killings by 238; murder by 11, 12, 14; sorcery and 114; witches and 136; women and 223, 224

Poland 194, 220, 337; Crown of 175; Kingdom of 188, 190; Silesia and 174; *see also* magic and the law; witch trials

Polanski, Roman 339, 341, 397

Polidori, John 371

potions 10, 12, 401; creating 394; evil 63; love 3, 7–9, 11, 261, 273; magic 237, 244, 252, 263; maleficent 61, 65; minglers 120; "zombification" 32

Practica inquisitionis (Gui) 53

Pratchett, Terry 374, 382–383, 389, 390

Prayer of Jacob 25

Protestant Reformation 83, 90, 128, 245, 246, 262, 365

Proudhon, Pierre-Joseph 337

Prussia 109, 180, 292; Kingdom of 174–175; Royal 179

Przybyszewski, Stanislaw 336–339

Pueblos Indians 279–286
Pullman, Philip 383, 386, 389
Purkiss, Diane 152, 208, 226, 383

Qumram texts 23, 27, 32
Qur'an 265

Radziwiłłówna, Barbara 180
Rand, Ayn 340
Reading Witchcraft (Gibson) 209
Redbeard, Ragnar 340
Red Russia/Red Ruthenia (*Russia Rubra* or
    Ruthenia Rubra) 179, 188
Religion and the Decline of Magic (Thomas)
    280
Rémy, Nicolas 121, 131, 239
Renaissance 263–267
Resheph 23
Revolt of Islam, The 335
Reynie, Nicolas de la 334
Rhys, Jean 375
Rice, Boyd 341
Romanticism 334–337, 342, 370
Rome: executions in 82; Imperial 7, 16; and
    magic 12–16; witches in 3–16
Romero, Luis 279, 283–285
Roper, Lyndal 216, 219, 222, 224, 228
Roper, Trevor 394
Rops, Félicien 336, 341
Rosemary's Baby (film) 339, 341, 397
Rosicrucian 308, 323, 324
Rosny, Éric de 306, 312
Russell, Jeffrey 46
Russell, Ken 393
Russia 166, 188–194, 220, 292

Sabbath; *see* witches' Sabbath
Sadeian Woman, The (Carter) 378
Salazar y Frias, Alonso (Inquisitor) 128–129,
    134–135, 234
Salem Possessed 281
Salem witch hunt 198–205, 280–282, 374
Samuel (prophet) 21
Satan 25, 339; agents of 150; children of 239,
    359; Church of 339–341; denial of the
    existence of 120; early Church concepts of
    38, 39; and evil 269; and demons 37; folk
    belief in 202; Milton's 333, 343; Romantic
    celebration of 335, 337; in Salem 205;
    servants of 54; supernatural abilities
    of 203; as symbol of resistance 336; as
    tempter 24; witchcraft as manifestation
    of 310; and women 49; in the world 198;
    worship of 318
Satanic: crime 343–345; "school" 335;
    worship 397

Satanic Bible 339, 341
'Satanic school' in poetry 335
Satanism 34, 191, 324, 342; black metal 344;
    conspiracy 271, 294; defining 332–333;
    esoteric 338–339; history of 332; imaginary
    194; and Nazi symbols 342; sabbat 284;
    "secular" 240; socialist 337–338
Satanists 333–334, 338; theistic 342
Saul (King) 21
Saul/Paul (Saint) 310; *see also* Paul
Schäuffelein, Hans 356–358, *358*
Schreck, Nikolas 342
Sea Hearts (Lanagan) 389
Secret Doctrine, The (Blavatsky) 338
Sejm 178, 180, 190
Senholt, Jacob 343
Set (Egyptian god) 341–343
Scot, Reginald 272
Scotland 149, 150, 379; folklore 383; legal
    system 148; Presbyterians 145; Reformation
    146; witch hunting in 153, 154
Scott, Joan 228
Scott, Walter (Sir) 370
Scottish Witchcraft Act of 1563 151, 155
Scourge of Heretics (Jacquier) 269
Second Sex, The (Beauvoir) 374
seer 6, 10, 12, 166, 355
Servius 12
sex: with demons 46, 47, 96, 179; with the
    devil 61, 154, 294; orgies 64–66, 332;
    pacts consummated through 47; and the
    Sabbath 222
sexuality 4, 325, 378–379; abuse 375;
    asexuality 255; deviant 62; female 19,
    352; homosexuality 370, 373, 376; illicit
    372; impotence 50, 54, 69; inappropriate
    271; lust and 359; marriage and 23, 54;
    and oppression 219; perverse 354, 367;
    social codes of 386; and violence 330, 375;
    virginity 376; witchcraft and 388
sexual violence 375
Sforza, Bona 180
shaman, shamanism 166, 223, 273, 317;
    horned 320, 321; neo- 340
Shelley, Mary 371
Shelley, Percy Bysshe 335–337
Sibylline Oracles 25, 32
Sigismund II Augustus 180
Silesia 171–175
Simaetha 6, 8
Simon Magus 30–32
Sixtus V 84
Smith, Morton 30
slaves, slavery 10, 27, 32, 48, 198, 322, 329;
    master/slave relations 326; sold into 377
Socrates 8, 11, 12, 39

Soman, Alfred 126
sorcerers, male 19, 87
sorcery 4, 22, 247, 249; in children's
    literature 400; classical concepts of 341; as
    demonic 33, 65, 68, 72; and demonology
    114; and the devil 352; as evil 33, 67,
    355–358; harmful magic as 46; 'harmless'
    167; heretics and 69; impotence by 363;
    Jesus suspected of 34; in Jewish literature
    32; and the law 69, 318; malefic 355–358,
    357, 358; *sortilegium* 50; trials for 84, 88,
    171–179, 188–194; witch and 253; and
    witchcraft 49, 135–136, 257–259, 279;
    see also Malleus Maleficarum
Source of Workers of Harmful Magic (Marmor)
    269
Spee, Friedrich 94, 95, 180
spells 24, 25–31; "binding" 4, 6; books
    321; counter spells 363; and the devil
    138; erotic 8; evil 64, 70, 71; harmful
    21, 84, 174; killing 65; simple 51; verbal
    53; women and 136; written 250; *see also
    defixiones*
Spina, Alfonso da 269
spirits 49, 153, 247, 317–319, 323;
    communication with 268; dangerous 22;
    of the dead 21; demonic/demons as 70,
    269; evil 23, 26, 28, 52; magical 264, 267;
    necromancy and 266–269; pagan 47;
    reality of 155; summoning 262; and the
    supernatural 246; "unclean" 24; witches'
    familiars as 214; world of 223, 245
Stadera, Bernardina 88
Stoker, Bram 371
strege 321
Strindberg, August 336
Stoppani, Giovan Pietro 84
Stumpf, Peter 214
Suhr, Carla 209, 210, 211
Summa theologiae (Aquinas) 51
Summer Witches (Tomlinson) 385
Synagoge des Satan, Die 336
synagogue 67, 71, 353; "of the devil" 72
Synoptic Gospel 38

tablets: curse 4, 6, 8, 26, 32; laminae 33;
    wax 5
taboo 23, 25, 251, 253, 372
Tacitus 15, 29, 31
Tafolla, Antonio 279, 283–285
Tafolla, Juan Ygnacia 280
talisman 33, 253
Talmud 22, 23, 25, 26, 27, 29, 30; Babylonian
    20, 25
*Teachings of Don Juan: A Yaqui Way of
    Knowledge* 323

Temple of Set 342
Temple of the Black Light (TotBL)
    344–345
Tenskwatawa 282, 286
terrorism 343–344; sexual 393
Tertullian 26, 30, 31, 34, 39
Thekla (Thecla) *see* Acts of Thecla
Theodosian Code of 438 47
Theodote 8
Theoris 10–12
Theosophical Society 338, 339
Thinking with Demons (Clark) 281
Thomas, Keith 259, 280
Thomasius 95
Tibullus 6
Tinctoris, Johannes 354
Tituba 198–199, 374
Tobit, book of 23
Tolstoy, Leo 373
Tomlinson, Theresa 385
Tonda, Joseph 306, 307, 311
Torquemada, Juan 74
Torrentius, Laevinus 119, 120
torture 70, 128, 163, 247, 250, 394; abolition
    of 180; analysis of 376; Catholicism and
    239; of child-witches 239; confession
    under 129, 139, 162, 234, 254, 263, 294;
    death by 176, 383; inquest and 56; killed
    by 84; 'normal' 109; Oberrat and 107;
    permission to 126; revival of 55; in Russia
    192, 193; in Salem 199, 203; sessions 121;
    sixteenth-century 161; unauthorized 146;
    in the Ukraine 189; use of 95, 100–103,
    118; witch hunts and 255
Trachiniae 7
Tractatus contra invocatores demonum (*Treatise
    Against Demon Invokers*) (Vinet) 70
Traité du crime de vauderie (Tinctoris) 353
Twelve Tables 12–14
tyrä 224

uenena 3, 13, 14
ueneficium 4, 15
Ukraine 178–179, 188–191, 194
Underworld 5
Updike, John 374–375
Urban VIII (Pope) 266

Valiente, Doreen 324–325
vampire 174, 340, 373, 377, 382–383
vampire-witch 67, 89, 371
Vampyre, The (Polidori) 371
Vauderie d'Arras 66, 73, 126
Vauderie de Lyon 66
Vaudeyre de Lyonois en Bref 62, 64, 66
Vebus (Roman goddess) 25, 363

Venus of Willendorf 320
Venus Satanas 342
Vera, Diane 342
vices 33, 359, 365
Vinet, Jean 70–73
Virgil 12
Virgin Witch (film) 397
Visconti, Girolamo 74

Waldenses, Waldensianism 65, 65, 73, 114, 269, 353–355
Walinski-Kieh, Robert 209, 212, 234
Walker, Alice 377
Walker, Barbara 385
Wallace, Anthony 282
Wallace, A.F.C. 317
Warren, Norman J. 397
Wars of Religion 132
wax 261; figurines 5; tablets 5
Wenham, Jane 156
werewolf witch 214
Wesley, John 156
Weyer, Johann 272
Wicca 317; and Aradia 322; craft of 324; Creed 325, 326; growth of 327; history of 320
Wiccan, The 326
Wicker Man, The (film) 399
Wide Sargasso Sea (Rhys) 375
William of Auvergne 51
Wiltenburg, Joy 209, 210, 211, 212
Wise Child (Furlong) 385, 388
witch-Amazon 377
witch-bishop 102, 121

Witchcraft in France and Switzerland (Monter) 233
Witchcraft, Oracles and Magic among the Azande (Evans-Pritchard) 299
Witchcraft Unsupported by Scripture (Paterson) 155
witch doctor 166, 301–304, 307, 309
Witches of Eastwick (Updike) 374
witches' Sabbath 20, 46, 47, 50, 61–67, 70, 160; child witches at 237; representations of 353–355, *354*, 361, *362*; and witch hunts 222
Witches, The (film) 399
Witchfinder General (film) 397, 399
witch of Endor 21
Wittig, Monique 377
wizard 87, 88, 90, 98, 234, 384; in England 151; Jesus as 30; prosecution of 237
Woman's Encyclopedia of Myths and Secrets, The (Walker) 385
Women Fly When Men Aren't Watching (Maitland) 375
Wonders of the Invisible World, The (Mather) 200
Wormser Reformation 236

Xenophon 8

Yahweh 21, 22, 24
Yaqui magic 323
Yeats, William Butler 370

Zambonis, Stanislaw 179
Zauberei 46
Zika, Charles 209, 215, 355

Printed in Great Britain
by Amazon

17480997R00240